SECRET SOLDIERS

June 14 63

D1487776

Also by Peter Harclerode

SECRET
SOLDIERS

SPECIAL FORCES IN THE WAR
AGAINST TERRORISM

PETER HARCLERODE

CASSELL&CO

Cassell Military Paperbacks

Cassell & Co
Wellington House, 125 Strand
London WC2R OBB

Copyright © Peter Harclerode 2000

All rights reserved. No part of this book may
be reproduced or transmitted in any form or by any
means electronic or mechanical including photo-
copying recording or any information storage
and retrieval system without permission in
writing from the Publisher.

First published 2000
Reprinted 2001
This Cassell Military Paperbacks edition 2001

British Library Cataloguing-in-Publication Data
A catalogue record for this book is available from
the British Library

ISBN 0-304-36379-0

Distributed in the USA by
Sterling Publishing Co Inc
387 Park Avenue South
New York
NY 10016-8810

Printed and bound in Great Britain by
Cox & Wyman Ltd., Reading, Berks.

For Annie

CONTENTS

PREFACE

International terrorism reared its head during the late 1960s when Palestinian organisations adopted tactics of terror in an attempt to force the West to take heed of their long-running struggle against Israel. In the 1970s European ultra left-wing groups, some of whom adopted the Palestinian cause, also resorted to violence as a means of attempting to achieve their objectives. Meanwhile, conflict had erupted in Northern Ireland and would continue for the next thirty years. The early 1980s saw the emergence of Islamic extremists who, heeding the call of the ayatollahs of Iran, during the next twenty years spread their gospels of terror and violence throughout the globe, their principal targets being the 'Great Satan' of the United States and its allies. The 1990s saw the advent of narco-terrorism, with terrorist organisations using the proceeds from dealing in narcotics to finance their operations. Organisations such as the Popular Front for the Liberation of Palestine, Black September, the Provisional IRA, Ulster Volunteer Force, Action Directe, the Red Army Faction, Japanese Red Army, Shining Path, FARC, ETA, HAMAS, Hizbollah, the GIA, Osama bin Laden's al-Qaida and the Japanese cult Aum Shinrikyo are just some of those who have attempted to achieve their respective aims through the use of violence and terror over the last thirty years.

Some readers will be unfamiliar with those dark days when the word 'hijack' first became part of the everyday vocabulary. It is for this reason, therefore, that the first three chapters of this book are devoted to an outline chronological history of international terrorism during the last three decades of the 20th century, covering major terrorist organisations and events.

The early 1970s saw governments throughout the world taking countermeasures during the rest of that decade and into the 1980s, among them the formation of military, para-military and police counter-terrorist units. This book gives an account of the leading role played by such forces, as well as details of how they are organised, trained and equipped, while also providing accounts of operations in Britain, France, Italy, South America, the Middle East, Africa and South-East Asia.

Despite the unceasing war waged against it, terrorism is still a threat. This was graphically illustrated early in the new millennium when the Spanish group ETA resumed its campaign of terror in its continuing efforts to establish an independent Basque homeland. More recently, members of the Greek organisation November 17 murdered the British military attaché in Athens as he drove to his office at the embassy. In Italy, there are apparent signs of revival of elements of the Red Brigades while in Colombia, the terrorist group FARC still exercises control over a large area of the country. In Northern Ireland, meanwhile, the peace brought about by the Good Friday Agreement is proving to be a fragile one with the province and British mainland still experiencing bomb attacks perpetrated by both republican and loyalist terrorist groups.

A number of people were kind enough to provide assistance during the research for this book. Among them were: Neville Brown of the Press Department at the Foreign & Commonwealth Office; Liam Clarke of the *Sunday Times* in Belfast; Alison Clayton, Editor of *Jane's Intelligence Review*; author and Far East specialist, Kenneth Conboy; Major 'D', a former officer in the Israeli Defence Forces; Mark Daly, Editor of *International Defence Review*; journalist, author and Middle East specialist Adel Darwish; author Barry Davies; Nicholas Davies – author of *Ten-Thirty-Three – The Inside Story of Britain's Secret Killing Machine in Northern Ireland*; journalist Chris Dobson, himself an author of a number of books on terrorism; Polizeihophmeister Hans Jurgen Goldmann of the Bundesgrenzschutz Command West Press Office; Glenn Goodman, editor of *Armed Forces Journal International*; George Grimes of the Public Affairs office at Headquarters US Army Special Operations Command; Steven Guest, press officer at the city hall in Barcelona; Dr. Rohan Gunaratna of the Centre for the

Study of Terrorism & Political Violence at the University of St. Andrews; Janet Hancock, research analyst at the Foreign & Commonwealth Office; Toby Harnden, *Daily Telegraph* bureau chief in Washington and author of *Bandit Country – The IRA & South Armagh*; translator and interpreter Barry Harrison; author and authority on small arms Ian Hogg; Lt M.J. Ijzermans of the Royal Netherlands Marine Corps; Polizeiobberat Olaf Linder of Grenzschutzgruppe-9; Mrs. Fadia Mashua, press officer at the Jordanian embassy; journalist Alastair McQueen; Dr. Martin Melaugh of the CAIN Project at the University of Ulster at Magee; John Parker, author of *Death of a Hero – Captain Robert Nairac GC and the undercover war in Northern Ireland*; Mr Juan Tirado, Counsellor at the Peruvian Embassy, and his assistant Miss Giovanna Salini; webmaster Tracy White; and Mark Wilson, Librarian at *The Belfast Telegraph*.

To them all I express my sincerest thanks.

I am also most grateful to author James Rennie and his publishers, Century, for permission to quote a passage from his book *The Operators – On the Street with 14 Company*.

Finally, I should like to thank my commissioning editor at Cassell Military, Barry Holmes, for his enduring patience over what has proved to be an ever-expanding project, and David Gibbons and Meredith MacArdle at DAG Publications for putting everything together.

Peter Harclerode
July 2000

1

THE TERROR INTERNATIONAL

At 7.23 p.m. on the bank holiday evening of Monday 5 May 1980, television viewers throughout the United Kingdom were startled when the normal evening diet of light entertainment and soap opera was dramatically interrupted without warning as BBC and ITV broadcasters switched to live coverage of an extraordinary scene: figures in black appearing on the roof of the Iranian embassy in Princes Gate, London, which had been the scene of a siege for the past six days. As viewers gaped at their screens, two further figures appeared stealthily on a balcony at the front of the building and placed what appeared to be a short ladder against a window. It was in fact an explosive charge and seconds later it detonated with a deafening roar. As it did so, the figures on the roof abseiled down the rear of the building, disappearing inside to the accompaniment of deafening explosions of stun grenades which were swiftly followed from inside by the faint rattle of submachine-guns.

To the majority of the public and media the identity of these black-clad figures was a mystery, but within a few hours the television and radio networks were trumpeting the success of a counter-terrorist operation carried out by men of the British Army's 22nd Special Air Service Regiment (22 SAS). During the following weeks every available detail about the operation was seized upon and published in newspapers, magazines and eventually books. While the existence of the SAS may have been common knowledge to the public, that of the counter-terrorist capability of 22 SAS had been kept at the lowest possible profile since its establishment some eight years previously.

Events leading to the regiment's adoption of the counter-terrorist role had begun some twelve years previously with the start of a major campaign of terror by the Popular Front for the Liberation of Palestine (PFLP) which staged a series of hijackings and bombings commencing in 1968. In the summer of that year, an El-Al

Boeing 707 airliner en route to Tel Aviv from Rome was hijacked to Algiers where the passengers and crew were held hostage for two months. On 26 December another El-Al 707, with fifty-one passengers and crew aboard, was attacked by two terrorists, armed with a submachine-gun and incendiary grenades, as it took off from Athens; one passenger was killed and a stewardess badly injured as she attempted to jump from the aircraft which had caught fire. The two terrorists responsible, later identified as Mahmoud Muhammad and Maher Suleiman, were arrested by Greek police and subsequently tried and convicted of a number of offences, including murder. In March 1969 they were sentenced to lengthy terms of imprisonment.

In February 1969, another El-Al Boeing 707 was attacked by a machine-gun while preparing for take-off at Zurich; one terrorist was killed and three others were arrested by an Israeli skymarshal. On 29 August of that year a group of PFLP terrorists, led by a known female Palestinian terrorist named Leila Khaled, hijacked a Trans World Airlines (TWA) aircraft flying from Rome to Tel Aviv and forced the pilot to fly to the Syrian capital of Damascus. All 213 passengers were released with the exception of two Israelis who were held hostage, subsequently being exchanged for two Syrian pilots being held prisoner by Israel. The aircraft was later blown up.

The PFLP was also responsible for the mid-air destruction on 21 February 1970 of a Swissair aircraft en route to the Israeli capital of Tel Aviv, resulting in the deaths of forty-seven people. A bomb had been placed in a parcel posted airmail to Tel Aviv, the terrorists' intention being that it should go aboard an El-Al flight and explode at a pre-determined altitude, but by an error on the part of the Swiss postal service, it was included in a consignment loaded aboard the Swissair aircraft.

These outrages were followed on 6 September 1970 by the simultaneous hijackings of four aircraft by the PFLP. The first was an El-Al Boeing 707 flying from Tel Aviv to New York via Amsterdam. The original plan had been that five terrorists, again led by Leila Khaled, should carry out the hijack, joining the aircraft at Amsterdam, but three of them were prevented from boarding after Dutch security officials became suspicious. Khaled, however, accompanied by a Nicaraguan accomplice named Patrick Arguello, succeeded in doing so and ten minutes after take-off from Amsterdam they hijacked the aircraft. Khaled stood in the aisle of the passenger cabin holding two grenades while Arguello, armed with a .22 calibre pistol, made his way towards the flight deck. Unfortunately for the pair, Israeli skymarshals were aboard the aircraft. One, dressed as a steward, shot and fatally wounded Arguello but not before the latter had shot him three times in the stomach. Another tackled Khaled as she entered the first-class cabin, tying her up with string and a male passenger's tie.

The captain of the aircraft had meanwhile transmitted a Mayday message and requested permission to divert to London Heathrow which was the nearest airport. On landing, the aircraft was met by police who, having persuaded the reluctant El-Al crew to hand over the two terrorists, arrested them both. Arguello died shortly afterwards and Khaled, who was charged with illegal entry into the United Kingdom, was taken to a police station where she was locked up.

Meanwhile a TWA Boeing 707, carrying 145 passengers from Frankfurt to New York, was hijacked as it crossed the coast of France. The crew were forced to fly to the Middle East where the aircraft landed at Dawson's Field, a disused wartime airfield in the sandy wastes of the Jordanian desert. There it was subsequently joined by a Swissair DC-8 which had been flying from Zurich to New York with 140 passengers aboard.

The fourth aircraft to be hijacked was a Pan American (Pan Am) Boeing 747. The three terrorists who took control of it were none other than those who had failed to take part in Khaled and Arguello's unsuccessful attempt. Their intention was to force the crew to fly the aircraft to Dawson's Field to join the other two aircraft already there. However, they were unable to do so and instead instructed the pilot to fly to Beirut. On the following day the aircraft, having been refuelled, flew on to Cairo. Having disembarked all the passengers and crew, the terrorists destroyed it with explosives.

At Dawson's Field, meanwhile, more than 300 hostages waited in the sweltering heat aboard the two aircraft parked on the airfield which by then had been surrounded by troops of the Jordanian Army flown in by helicopter. The situation for the hostages was made all the worse by the knowledge that the terrorists had laid explosive charges in both aircraft and were threatening to blow them up unless Leila Khaled and six other Palestinians, serving prison sentences in Switzerland and Germany for terrorist offences, were released. Those in Switzerland were the three arrested after the unsuccessful hijack attempt on the El-Al Boeing 707 at Zurich in February 1969.

Three days later the two aircraft at Dawson's Field were joined by another, a British Overseas Airways Corporation (BOAC) VC-10. Carrying 115 passengers, including twenty-five children, and en route from Bahrain to Beirut, it had been hijacked over the Persian Gulf by the PFLP in order to increase pressure on the British government to free Leila Khaled. After refuelling at Beirut, it flew to Dawson's Field where the passengers and crew joined the rest of the hostages, bringing the total number to 425.

In London there was intense deliberation on the part of Prime Minister Edward Heath's government which had only recently been elected to power. Seeking to find a way out of the dilemma caused by the political and humanitarian considerations of the situation, his legal advisers concluded that Leila Khaled had not committed a crime within British jurisdiction because the hijack had taken place outside British airspace and thus the grounds for her continued imprisonment and prosecution were unsafe.

To reinforce their demands the terrorists disembarked all the passengers and crews from the Swissair DC-8 and TWA Boeing 707 which were promptly blown up in full view of the world's media whose television cameras recorded the event from afar. Frantic discussions between US, British, Israeli, Swiss and West German authorities were meanwhile being held in Washington.

The subsequent blowing up of the BOAC VC-10, reinforced by a threat that the British hostages would be shot, brought capitulation from the British government which joined the Swiss in agreeing to the terrorists' demands. Leila Khaled was placed aboard a Royal Air Force aircraft which flew to Switzerland and Germany, collecting her six fellow terrorists before flying them all to Beirut.

The shock-waves from the explosions at Dawson's Field spread far beyond the fringes of the Jordanian desert, reverberating throughout the West, which had hitherto ignored the warning signals emanating from the Middle East, and forcing it to realise that it was facing a major threat.

The causes of the PFLP's acts of terror have their roots in the early part of the 20th century and the duplicity of Britain during the latter part of the First World War when it sought to enlist the support of the Arabs in the war against Turkey while at the same time attempting to satisfy Zionist aspirations for a homeland for Jews in Palestine. During negotiations, the British gave the impression that independence would be granted to much of the Arab world, thus persuading the Arabs to side with them against Turkey and preventing them from declaring a *jihad* or holy war. In 1916, however, the newly elected government of David Lloyd George, which included a number of Zionist sympathisers in the Cabinet, came to power. The Foreign Secretary was Arthur James Balfour who on 2 November 1917 wrote a letter to Lord Rothschild which made clear that the British government favoured the establishment of a Jewish homeland in Palestine. The timing of the letter was significant; five weeks later British forces under General Edmund Allenby captured Jerusalem and ended 401 years of Turkish rule. The British no longer needed the support of the Arabs and thus felt free to renege on their promises to them.

The period between the First and Second World Wars saw Britain, which ruled Palestine under a League of Nations mandate, carrying out a precarious political balancing act. During the early 1920s, immigration by Jews was temporarily halted in an effort to placate the Arab population who refused to accept the idea of a Jewish homeland being forced upon it. This proved unsuccessful and the situation was worsened in the early 1930s by rising Arab nationalism and an increasing number of Jews arriving in Palestine as refugees from Hitler's Germany. Arab protests were suppressed by the British who did little to check the flood of refugees arriving in the country. From 1933 to 1936, 166,000 Jewish immigrants were admitted into Palestine, while an unknown number also entered the country illegally. By 1936, Jews formed a third of the population and it was in that year, when the Jews were found to be importing a large consignment of arms, that Arab resentment finally boiled over.

The period from 1936 to 1939 saw the Arab Revolt in which Arabs attacked the Jews and increasingly the British, the latter meanwhile fruitlessly seeking a solution to the problem. In 1938, with war in Europe looming, the British, who once again needed to enlist Arab support throughout the Middle East, decided to declare Palestine an independent state which would come into existence after ten years, with the Arab population remaining in the majority. This was rejected by the Palestinian leader, Amin El-Husseini, the Grand Mufti of Jerusalem, but the British ignored his objections. Jewish opposition to the plan was also brushed aside and shortly afterwards it was announced that the number of Jewish immigrants would be limited to 75,000 during the next five years, which would restrict the Jewish population to one-third of the country's total.

Ten years later, however, the reality was very different. In 1947 Britain, weakened and bankrupt after six years of war against Nazi Germany, handed over responsibility for Palestine to the United Nations (UN). By now British forces, attempting to keep order between Jew and Arab, were under frequent attack from Jewish terrorist groups such as the Stern Gang and the Irgun. Meanwhile, large numbers of Jewish refugees were entering the country illegally.

In the meantime the UN had been attempting to find a solution and on 29 November 1947 a plan was adopted in which Palestine would be partitioned: a Jewish state would be formed from the parts of the country already occupied by Jews, the remainder becoming part of neighbouring Jordan under its king, Abdullah. The UN turned to Britain for help in implementing the decision, but the latter refused to do so on the grounds that Arab approval had not been forthcoming for the plan. On 14 May 1948, Britain withdrew its forces from Palestine and the country slid into chaos.

On that same day, the state of Israel was proclaimed in Palestine. On the following day Egypt, Jordan, Iraq, Syria and the Lebanon attacked. The Jews, however, had a well-organised and well-armed 60,000 strong army of seven brigades in the form of the *Haganah*, many of whose members had served in the British Army during the war against Hitler. The fighting continued until January 1949 during which the Israelis inflicted a resounding defeat on the combined Arab armies. Jordan's British-trained and led Arab Legion, numbering 4,500 and by far the most professional and capable force in the Middle East, had moved into the areas of Palestine allocated by the UN for the Palestinians but took no part in the war, having been forbidden to do so by the British.

During the first seven months of the war, the Israelis had expelled the Palestinians from their homes and lands and they were forced to seek refuge in other Arab countries. In 1947 the Arab population of Palestine had numbered 1,157,000 but by 1949 only 200,000 remained in those parts of Palestine that had become the State of Israel. The Jews, who had previously owned a mere 12 per cent of this land, now owned 70 per cent, of which 80 per cent had been forcibly appropriated.

Nearly twenty years later, in 1967, the situation was made even worse for the Palestinians by the defeat of the Arab nations in the Six Day War when Israel occupied the West Bank of Jordan and the Gaza Strip. Some 400,000 Palestinians became refugees in their own homeland, eking out a miserable existence. The poverty and squalor of the refugee camps became a fertile breeding ground for bitterness and hatred of Israel, leading ultimately to the formation of various Palestinian resistance groups which, supported by Syria, established their own training camps and eventually began to carry out attacks against Israel.

In 1964, the Arab Summit Conference established the Palestine Liberation Organisation (PLO) as the entity responsible for furthering the Palestinian cause and achieving the ultimate objective of the recovery of Palestine as the homeland for all Palestinians. Ten years later the PLO achieved recognition by the United Nations, being granted observer status.

Effectively, the PLO acted as an umbrella organisation for the majority of Palestinian organisations, some more radical than others. The largest of these was Al-Fatah, led by Yasser Arafat, who was also chairman of the PLO, and Salah Khalaf, who was also known by his alias of Abu Iyad. Formed in the early 1960s, it numbered some 7,000 and possessed a military wing called Assifa (The Storm). Its aim was the destruction of Israel and the restoration of Palestine to the Palestinians.

Of equal importance, from the point of view of international terrorism, was the Popular Front for the Liberation of Palestine (PFLP) which was formed in 1967 by Dr. George Habash. Its principal aim was not only the destruction of Israel but also the establishment of a Marxist–Leninist revolution throughout the Middle East and ultimately worldwide. This led it to establish contact with other organisations of similar sympathies throughout the rest of the world, ultimately providing sanctuaries, training and material support for terrorist groups from a number of countries while making use of them to carry out operations on its behalf.

Contact was also established with the Soviet Union which subsequently became a major supplier of arms. The first consignment was supplied in 1970 by Department V of the KGB and comprised fifty MG-ZI machine-guns, fifty M-16 assault rifles, five Sterling silenced submachine-guns, fifty pistols (of which ten were fitted with silencers), twenty Soviet-manufactured mines (of which five were a radio-controlled type) and 76,000 rounds of ammunition. The consignment was transported aboard a Soviet Navy intelligence-gathering vessel, the *Kursograf*, from Vladivostok to the Gulf of Aden where it was transferred to a PFLP vessel.

Like Al-Fatah, the PFLP came under the umbrella of the PLO. While George Habash was its political figurehead, however, the organisation's chief of terror was Wadi Haddad, a close friend of

Habash and his chief of staff. The first major outrage perpetrated by Haddad took place in March 1968 when PFLP terrorists mined a road leading from Tel Aviv to the Negev desert. Tragically, a bus carrying a party of Israeli schoolchildren hit one of the mines which resulted in two of the children being killed and twenty-eight injured. The Israelis mounted a retaliatory operation against a Fatah base in the East Bank village of Karameh and a major battle ensued in which the Jordanian Army came to the guerrillas' aid, attacking the Israelis in the rear and forcing them to withdraw.

The PLO, neglecting to mention the principal role played by the Jordanians, claimed the credit for a great victory over Israel and was acclaimed by the rest of the Arab world. The immediate result was that the Palestinian groups were seen as standard-bearers for the cause of Arab liberation from Israel and their ranks were swelled as Arabs worldwide travelled to Jordan to join the organisation. Inevitably this caused problems for the tiny kingdom and King Hussein himself as it soon became evident that the Palestinians ultimately sought his downfall in order to take over his country as a first step towards reclaiming their own. Increasingly self-confident, the Palestinians moved out of the refugee camps into Jordan's capital Amman, much to the displeasure of the Jordanians who resented the swaggering, cocky and heavily armed guerrillas who set up their own roadblocks, stole from shops and established their own courts which dispensed a particular brand of rough justice.

The aftermath of the 1970 hijackings of the four airliners and their subsequent destruction, however, provoked a backlash in Jordan against the Palestinians. Until then, beset with domestic problems and with his army severely weakened by heavy losses during the Six Day War three years previously, King Hussein had been unable to take action against the heavily armed Palestinians. Now, however, his patience snapped and on 17 September he unleashed his recently re-equipped Bedouin troops whose armour surged into the refugee camps, slaughtering hundreds of Palestinians and forcing thousands to flee for their lives to Syria and the Lebanon. By the end of that month, the guerrillas had been expelled from Jordan.

It was at this juncture that a new organisation appeared, calling itself 'Black September' to commemorate those who had died in the fighting. It was a name that would become notorious in the annals of international terrorism. Comprising radicals from Fatah, the new organisation wasted little time in bringing itself to the attention of the world. On 28 November 1971, four of its members murdered the Jordanian prime minister, Wasfi al-Tal, in the lobby of the Sheraton Hotel in Cairo during a visit by the latter to Egypt. His murder was in direct retaliation for Jordan's actions against the Palestinians two months earlier.

In the early hours of 5 September 1972, during the Olympic Games being held in Munich that year, eight Black September terrorists occupied a building containing living quarters occupied by the Israeli athletes. Shooting two of them, wrestler Moshe Weinberger and weightlifter Yossef Romano, they took eleven others hostage. Negotiations with the terrorists took place the following day, during which they made a number of demands which included the release of 200 Palestinians being held prisoner by Israel. The latter refused to accede but the West German authorities did agree to the demand for safe passage to Egypt for the terrorists and their hostages, and helicopters were provided to fly them to a military airfield at Fürstenfeldbruck.

The Germans, however, had laid a trap. Lying in wait at the airfield were armed police who opened fire as the terrorists and hostages disembarked from the helicopters. Two of the terrorists were killed and three wounded. The others, dragging their hostages with them, re-embarked on the helicopters and, as police in armoured vehicles tried to intercept them, turned their guns on the hostages. A few seconds later both helicopters exploded, killing all on board. All the hostages, five terrorists and one police officer were killed. The remaining three terrorists survived and were arrested.

On 2 March 1973, Black September struck again when it murdered the American Ambassador to Sudan, Mr. Cleo Noel, and his deputy, George Curtis Moore, in the capital Khartoum. Also killed was a Belgian diplomat, M. Guy Eid.

In June 1974, the PLO produced a ten-point plan proposing that it should establish at the earliest opportunity a Palestinian authority on territory freed from occupation by Israel. This was a major compromise on the organisation's previous hard-line position which had hitherto called for the destruction of Israel and the establishment of a Palestinian state. While the plan was widely accepted among Palestinians, certain factions rejected any idea of a political settlement with Israel and formed a loosely knit coalition calling itself the Front Rejecting Capitulationist Solutions – more popularly known as the Rejection Front – under the leadership of George Habash. Among those organisations forming it were the PFLP, the Popular Front for the Liberation of Palestine–General Command (PFLP–GC), the Arab Liberation Front (ALF), the Democratic Front for the Liberation of Palestine (DFLP), and the Palestinian Popular Struggle Front (PPSF).

A particularly hard-line group which always advocated military, rather than political action, the PFLP–GC was headed by Ahmed Jibril, a former Syrian army officer and Marxist–Leninist revolutionary known for his close connections to the Soviet Union and the KGB. Formed in October 1968 from a breakaway faction of PFLP and supported by Syria and Libya, it engaged in cross-border raids into Israel which in May 1970 included an attack on an Israeli school bus near the border with Lebanon. In 1977 a faction within the PFLP–GC, unhappy with Syrian influence within the organisation, broke away to form the Palestine Liberation Front (PLF). Initially led by Talaat Yaqub and numbering some 250 in total, it joined the Rejection Front and was thereafter supported by Iraq, being based in the Lebanon from where it carried out raids into Israel.

The Arab Liberation Front (ALF) was formed in 1969 by Iraq to counter the influence of Syria which supported Al-Sa'iqa (The Thunderbolt), an organisation formed in 1968 from members of a Palestinian unit within the Syrian army. Numbering some 500 members, ALF was closely integrated with the Iraqi Ba'ath Party which funded it. Based in the Lebanon, it also participated in raids into Israel.

Initially known as the Popular Democratic Front for the Liberation of Palestine, the DFLP was formed in 1969 from Marxist–Leninists from the PFLP and the Movement of Arab Nationalists (MAN). Led by Nayef Hawatmeh, a Christian-born Jordanian and orthodox Communist of long-standing, it numbered some 1,000 members and was supported by South Yemen, which provided it with a base, and by the Soviet Union and China. The DFLP was ideologically opposed to terrorism outside Israel and the 'occupied territories' and thus confined itself to attacks within those areas. On 15 May 1974, it was responsible for a massacre carried out at a school at Ma'alot during which twenty-two Israeli children were killed.

The PPSF was an offshoot of the Palestinian Liberation Army (PLA) which had been established as the armed forces of the PLO, numbering some 4,500 and being trained and equipped as a conventional force in Egypt. In 1968, it was formed from some 200 members of the PLA's commando units. Led by Bahjat Abu Garbiyya, it subsequently joined the Rejection Front and thereafter received support from Iraq.

Although not part of the Rejection Front, the most hard-line and violent organisation was that of Abu Nidal. A co-founder with Yasser Arafat of Al-Fatah in the early 1960s, Abu Nidal (whose real name is Sabri al-Banna) had by 1973 become disenchanted with Arafat's attempts to dissociate the PLO from terrorism, as well as his readiness to recognise the existence of Israel and his advocacy of a Palestinian mini-state alongside it. This switch to a moderate approach infuriated Abu Nidal and during that year he established in Baghdad a break-away faction called Fatah – The Revolutionary Council. In 1974 he sent a group to Damascus to assassinate Arafat but the attempt failed and the latter sentenced Abu Nidal to death *in absentia*.

During the next four years, Abu Nidal's organisation carried out a number of operations against the PLO, despatching assassins to kill its representatives based in a number of countries including the United Kingdom, France, Portugal and Kuwait. In October 1974 they tried unsuccessfully to assassinate Mahmud Abbas (alias Abu Mazin) who was a close associate of Arafat's. In 1976 Abu Nidal formed a new movement called Black June which had the backing of the Iraqis and its headquarters in Baghdad. In January 1978 Sa'id Hammami, the PLO representative in London who was well known for his moderate views, was shot dead by a member of Black June. In June Ali Yassin, the PLO representative in Kuwait, was murdered and two months later, in August, Izz al-Din Qalaq, the PLO representative in Paris, was also killed. During the same month, four members of the PLO office in Istanbul died and Yusif Abu Hantash, the PLO representative in Pakistan, narrowly escaped being assassinated by Black June gunmen. On 25 July 1979 Zuhair Mohsin, leader of the Syrian-controlled Saiqa terrorist group, was shot dead outside his apartment in Cannes, on the French Riviera, by Black June terrorists acting on behalf of the Iraqi intelligence service which was involved in an on-going war with its Syrian counterpart. These murders were followed by a truce between Abu Nidal and the PLO, and Black June thereafter maintained a low profile until, as covered in Chapter 2, it became active again in the early 1980s.

In the United States and Europe, meanwhile, student unrest in the late 1960s had become a phenomenon which spread throughout both continents. It found focus in the anti-Vietnam War movements and manifested itself primarily in protest demonstrations with most of the groups involved employing peaceful methods in the form of sit-ins, strikes and demonstrations. Other less patient factions considered such methods to be inadequate and advocated more forceful means.

In April 1967, West Berlin was the scene of major anti-Vietnam War demonstrations held in protest against the visit of US Vice President Hubert Humphrey. Two months later, further demonstrations took place in protest against the visit of the Shah and Empress of Iran. In both instances there were clashes between students and the police who reacted violently.

In May 1968, major riots took place in Paris with large numbers of students, whose leading lights were Daniel Cohn-Bendit, Jacques Sauvageot and Alain Geismar, openly confronting the police on the streets of the city. In London on 27 October of the same year, Grosvenor Square was the scene of a major battle between rioting students and the police during an anti-Vietnam War demonstration.

In May 1970, Kent State University in Ohio was the scene of a major anti-Vietnam War protest against the US invasion of Cambodia; four students were shot dead, and ten wounded, when troops of the Ohio National Guard opened fire without warning. This resulted in disorder and riots at other universities throughout the US.

It was in West Germany, however, that European elements of the international protest movement first graduated to violence and ultimately to terrorism. The death of a student, Benno Ohnesorg, during the June 1967 demonstrations against the visit of the Shah of Iran, had almost immediately led to a hardening of attitudes among the leaders of the Marxist groups leading the protest movement in the country, some of whom would also play a leading role in organising the riots in Paris in May of the following year.

Among these, student revolutionaries such as Rudi Dutschke, Fritz Teufel, Dieter Kunzelmann, Bommi Baumann and Rainer Langhans preached a gospel advocating the abolition of the exercise of power over people by others. This struck a chord among a small group of young middle-class intellectuals – individuals who believed the Marcusian theory that violence could be justified for oppressed minorities. They were to play prominent roles in international terrorism during the next ten years of what would truly be the first of three decades of terror.

The leaders of this group were Andreas Baader, the son of a historian, and Ulrike Meinhof, a university lecturer at the Free University of West Berlin and daughter of a museum director. Other members included Baader's girlfriend, Gudrun Ensslin, Jan-Carl Raspe and a couple named Thorwald and Astrid Proll, all of whom had studied at the Free University, and a girl named Ingrid Schubert who was the daughter of a rich businessman.

The philosophy of the group was one of violence with the aim of provoking the West German authorities into retaliation and thus laying themselves open to charges of repression. Andreas Baader was no stranger to this ploy; in 1968 he and Gudrun Ensslin had planted an incendiary device in a department store in Frankfurt with the help of two young accomplices, Horst Söhnlein and Thorwald Proll. Little damage was caused and all four were arrested shortly afterwards, subsequently being imprisoned.

In June of the following year, however, Baader and his three companions had been released pending an appeal in November. When this failed, all but Horst Söhnlein went underground and escaped to Switzerland via France. Three months later Baader returned to West Germany but at the beginning of April 1970 was arrested in Berlin and incarcerated in Tegel Prison in Berlin.

Ulrike Meinhof, who in 1968 was a well-known figure throughout Europe in what was known as the 'New Left' movement, had first encountered Baader while working as a columnist for the left-wing magazine *Konkret*, whose publisher editor, Klaus Rohl, she had married in 1961. It was later discovered that she and her husband were both closet Communists and that *Konkret* had been financed by the Soviets to the tune of a million or so deutschmarks in an attempt to use the magazine to influence public opinion in West Germany.

Meinhof had covered the story of Baader and Ensslin's raid on the Frankfurt department store in her column in *Konkret*, describing it as 'progressive' on the grounds that it boldly broke the law. Shortly afterwards, however, she left her husband and the magazine, attacking the latter and its editorial policies. Taking her young twin daughters with her, she moved to West Berlin where she obtained her post as a lecturer at the Free University. It was at this time that she joined the group which would subsequently bear her name. Another recruit was a left-wing lawyer by the name of Horst Mahler who had defended Andreas Baader in court.

In May 1970, Meinhof and the other members of the group mounted a carefully planned operation to free Baader from prison. The latter was permitted visitors among whom were Horst Mahler, Meinhof and a woman named Dr. Gretel Weitermeyer who, it was later established, was none other than Gudrun Ensslin. He was also allowed to continue his sociology studies which included visits to libraries in West Berlin as part of the pretext of writing a book called *Organisation of Young People on the Fringes of Society*, which was in fact part of a plot to spring him from prison. Assisting him in his research was none other than Meinhof.

It was on one such visit, on 14 May, that he was taken to the Institute for Social Questions in the Berlin suburb of Dahlem. Already in the library, awaiting his arrival, were Meinhof and two young women ostensibly carrying out research on juvenile criminals, but who were in fact members of his group – Ingrid Schubert and Irene Goergens.

Not long after Baader's arrival a hooded gunman with a pistol, accompanied by a masked Gudrun Ensslin, forced his way into the library and shot the librarian, Georg Linke, who retreated to his office and with two of his staff escaped via a window. Schubert and Goergens meanwhile had produced pistols and were engaged in a gun battle with Baader's two guards, while also lobbing tear-gas grenades into the library as Baader, closely followed by Ulrike Meinhof, jumped from a window and ran to a waiting car with Astrid Proll at the wheel. Seconds later they were joined by Ensslin, Schubert, Goergens and the masked man (later thought to be one Peter Homann) who had lost his pistol in a struggle with Baader's guards.

In the ensuing pandemonium, Baader and his accomplices made good their escape. Shortly afterwards the Baader–Meinhof Gang, as it initially became known, hit the newspaper headlines again when it robbed a bank to provide itself with much-needed funds. During the following month of June, its principal members, including Baader and Meinhof, departed for the Middle East to undergo training as terrorists. They arrived at the Syrian capital of Damascus from where they made their way to Jordan via Lebanon. There they were accommodated in an Al-Fatah training camp where they were viewed with mixed feelings by their Palestinian instructors. Their penchant for drugs, sex and nude sunbathing did nothing to endear them to their Muslim hosts who considered such behaviour deeply offensive. They were eventually expelled and in August returned to West Berlin. By now, however, they had established valuable contacts with members of other terrorist groups from a number of countries world-wide.

They also succeeded in attracting considerable numbers to their cause within West Germany, finding fertile ground for recruitment principally among bored young middle-class Germans seeking a cause to provide an outlet for their desire for protest. Those who were sufficiently hard-line in their beliefs were given training in guerrilla warfare while others committed themselves to provide funds, vehicles and other forms of support. It has been estimated that the number of sympathisers actively supporting the group at one point numbered between 1,200 and 1,600. Among them were some seventy radical left-wing lawyers who, like Horst Mahler, would provide legal services, including defence in court, when required.

In September, twelve of the gang's members carried out three bank robberies simultaneously in West Berlin, stealing a total of DM 220,000. These were followed by other robberies and soon the group was being accused of concentrating on amassing funds rather than carrying out 'revolutionary actions'. The gangsters attempted to justify their actions on the grounds that bank robberies were logistically correct and were acts of dispossession by the proletariat. At this juncture, the group began calling itself the 'Red Army Faction', a title adopted to imply that it was part of a world-wide revolutionary movement.

During the first week of October, however, the group suffered a setback when five of its members, Ingrid Schubert, Horst Mahler Monika Berberich, Brigitte Asdonk and Irene Goergens, were arrested in Berlin. In November Astrid Proll and Manfred Gashof narrowly escaped capture in Frankfurt, the latter drawing a gun and opening fire on police. On 6 May 1971, Proll was captured in Hamburg. Two months later Mahler, Goergens and Schubert went on trial for their parts in the springing of Baader.

On 22 October 1971 three members of the group, Margrit Schiller, Irmgard Möller and Gerhard Müller, were involved in a gun battle with police in Hamburg. During the exchange of fire a police officer was hit four times, subsequently dying on his way to hospital. Thus murder was added to the crimes of robbery, arson and grievous bodily harm for which the members of the group were wanted already.

In May 1972 the Red Army Faction began a series of bomb attacks on US military targets in West Germany. The first was at the headquarters of the US Army's V Corps at Frankfurt and resulted in the death of one officer and the wounding of thirteen other personnel. Two weeks later another attack took place at a US Army headquarters at Heidelberg, killing three and wounding eight. Other bomb attacks were subsequently mounted on the police headquarters in Augsburg and the State Criminal Investigation Office in Munich, and on the offices of the Axel Springer publishing organisation in Hamburg where several bombs were planted, thirteen people being badly injured in the explosions.

The West German authorities initially faced major problems in tracking down the active element of the Red Army Faction, which by now was estimated to number some 100 supported by large numbers of sympathisers. The group possessed an arsenal of weapons which had been supplied from abroad together with training and other materiel support, including radio communications equipment. It was also well equipped with false identity papers and a network of safe houses.

The West German law enforcement and security agencies, until then labouring under restrictions imposed by liberal-minded, post-war federal and state governments, were eventually permitted to put in hand effective countermeasures. The Bundeskriminalamt (Federal Criminal Bureau) was increased in strength and a new counter-terrorist agency was established in the capital of Bonn to co-ordinate operations. In addition, as described in Chapter 4, a new counter-terrorist unit, Grenzschutzgruppe–9 (GSG–9), was formed by the Bundesgrenzschutz, the federal border guard service. Moreover, special legislation was drafted and made law, including the granting of immunity from prosecution to criminals or terrorists prepared to turn state evidence and testify against their former accomplices

These measures proved effective and brought swift results. At the beginning of May 1972, police in Frankfurt were tipped off that a garage was being used for the manufacture of bombs. In the early hours of 1 June, three men, Andreas Baader, Holger Meins and Jan-Carl Raspe, were seen arriving at the garage in a car. Baader and Meins entered the building while Raspe stayed outside. As the police closed in, they were spotted by the latter who opened fire and ran off, being caught shortly afterwards in the garden of a nearby house. Baader and Mains took refuge in the garage as the police blocked the doors with a vehicle and fired CS gas rounds through glass panels in the rear of the building. The siege of the garage lasted two hours until 7.45 a.m., when an armoured vehicle was driven into the garage doors and more CS gas rounds were fired into the building. Shortly afterwards, Baader was shot in the leg and Meins surrendered.

Two weeks later, on 15 June, Ulrike Meinhof was arrested in Hanover, her whereabouts having been reported to the police by a schoolteacher, Fritz Rodewald, in whose house she was sheltering. Although left-wing in his sympathies, Rodewald had decided to turn Meinhof in because he was concerned that the Red Army Faction's operations could lead to circumstances in which the movement might be exploited by extreme right-wing organisations. Not long after Meinhof's capture, Gudrun Ensslin was also arrested in Hamburg after one of two 9mm pistols, with which she was armed at the time, was spotted by a passer-by. Although she offered resistance, she was unable to reach her weapons when apprehended by the police shortly afterwards.

On 9 November 1974, almost two and a half years after his capture with Baader, Holger Meins died after a two-months long hunger strike. Next day the Red Army Faction took its revenge when a splinter group, the 2nd June Movement, shot dead the President of the Berlin Supreme Court, Gunther von Drenkmann, at his home in Charlottenburg. The murder was counter-productive because it provoked public outrage and sabotaged the terrorists' efforts to portray Holger Meins as a 'martyr of the revolution'.

Such was the threat posed by the Red Army Faction that a special prison was built, at vast expense to the state of Baden–Württemberg, to hold the captured members of the group's hierarchy. Situated at Stammheim, on the northern edge of the city of Stuttgart, it was guarded by 600 armed police and featured highly sophisticated security systems. Also constructed as part of the prison complex was a court in which the terrorists would be tried. It would be almost three years, however, before Baader and his companions would stand trial.

The trial of Baader, Meinhof, Ensslin and a fourth member of the group who had also been captured, Jan-Carl Raspe, was initially delayed by their continual hunger strikes and by various legal complexities. Eventually, however, it commenced in May 1975. The four, who were represented by an army of lawyers, refused to answer any of the charges and it would be January of the following year before any of them would appear in the dock. Despite the secure conditions in which they were held, Baader and Meinhof took full advantage of German prison regulations, their lawyers and visitors being briefed to communicate with their supporters outside and pass instructions to them. They also spent their time writing political manifestos, propaganda and escape plans; eventual searches of their cells uncovered these and other documentation.

The arrests of the leaders of the Red Army Faction did not result in the end of the group or its operations. Splinter groups were subsequently formed, among them the 2nd of June Movement so-called to commemorate the death of Benno Ohnesorg during the June 1967 demonstrations against the visit to Berlin of the Shah of Iran. Led by Ralf Reinders and numbering some fifty hard-core members, supported by an estimated 2,000 sympathisers, this group continued the Red Army Faction's policy of violence but, instead of bombings and bank raids, concentrated on kidnappings of prominent West German individuals.

In February 1975 it kidnapped Peter Lorenz, the chairman of the Christian Democratic Union in Berlin. In return for his release, the terrorists demanded that of six principal members of the Red Army Faction who had also been arrested by then and were languishing in prison: the left-wing lawyer Horst Mahler; Verena Becker, serving six years for bomb attacks and armed robbery; Ingrid Siepmann, serving twelve years; Rolf Heissler, sentenced to eight years for armed robbery; and Gabrielle Kröcher-Tiedemann, who before long would achieve notoriety through her involvement in two major terrorist outrages described later in this chapter.

One of the six, Horst Mahler, declined to be included and chose to stay in prison, stating that he wished to remain loyal to the revolution. However, in the light of his apparent volte-face twenty-four years later in 1999, when he declared his support for right-wing politics, it is more likely that he was already in the process of shedding his left-wing beliefs and possibly feared that this might bring retribution from his erstwhile accomplices. The remaining five were taken to Frankfurt airport and flown to Aden, the capital of South Yemen, where they were given political asylum.

Two months later, the Red Army Faction struck again. On 24 April 1975 six members of a splinter group, calling itself the Holger Meins Commando and armed with submachine-guns and grenades, hijacked the West German embassy in the Swedish capital of Stockholm and took the Ambassador and his twelve staff hostage. Shortly afterwards, as the Swedish police threw a cordon around the building, a female hostage was released, bringing with her a document which demanded the release of the twenty-six members of the Red Army Faction held in West German prisons.

While the West German government pondered the ultimatum, which threatened the destruction of the embassy if it were not met, the terrorists decided to reinforce it by killing the military attaché, Lieutenant Colonel Baron Andreas von Mirbach, and the economic counsellor, Herr Heinz Hillegaart. This did not have the desired effect because Chancellor Helmut Schmidt's government refused to give in to the terrorists' demands. This was followed by the release of three more female hostages bearing a document stating that the terrorists had withdrawn their ultimatum.

That night, at just before midnight, explosions were heard inside the embassy building and soon the building was ablaze. It transpired that the terrorists had been attempting to blow it up but had bungled it. The remaining hostages succeeded in escaping to safety, as did four of the terrorists who were arrested. They were subsequently identified as: Hanna-Elise Krabe, Karl-Heinz Dellwo, Lutz Taufer, and Bernd Maria Rössner. The other two terrorists had sustained fatal injuries: Ulrich Wessel died two hours later from wounds sustained from a hand grenade which he had dropped out of fright when the charges exploded in an adjoining room; Siegfried Hausener, whose faulty wiring of the explosives had caused the premature detonation, died ten days later. It transpired that all six were members of an extremist group called the Socialist Patients' Collective (SPK), an organisation formed from former patients of a Dr. Wolfgang Huber, of the Heidelberg University Psychiatric-Neurological Clinic, who believed that violence played a major role in curing mental illness.

Just over a year later, the Red Army Faction was shaken by the suicide of Ulrike Meinhof. At 7.30 a.m. on Sunday 9 May 1976, she was found hanging from the window of her cell by a rope fashioned from a towel torn into strips. She left no letter, so the reason why she killed herself is not known.

By now the West German authorities were making matters difficult for the Red Army Faction. Federal and state governments were increasing the crackdown and some members of the group made their way to other countries. In France they carried out attacks against West German government offices and commercial concerns, including the consulate in Nice and the offices of Mercedes–Benz in Paris. Responsibility was claimed under various *noms de guerre* including 'Holger Meins Brigade', 'Ulrike Meinhof Commando' and 'Baader Solidarity Group', but these attacks were all the work of the Red Army Faction.

West Germany was not the only country in Europe to be suffering from the scourge of terrorism. In Britain a group of eleven students who had taken part in the protest demonstrations in London in 1968, decided in 1970 to follow the example of the Red Army Faction. Calling themselves the Angry Brigade, during the following year they planted twenty-five small bombs in London, including two at the residence of the Home Secretary and others at those of the Attorney-General and the Commissioner of the Metropolitan Police. Others were planted at a Territorial Army barracks, a department store in Kensington, the Albert Hall and a police computer centre. Some members of the group were arrested in August 1971 and during the following year three of its principals were sentenced to ten years' imprisonment. Thereafter the Angry Brigade's activities ceased.

The principal terrorist threat in the United Kingdom, however, was from the Irish Republican Army (IRA) which had been formed in 1916. During and after the Second World War it had remained dormant, but in 1956 it had carried out a series of raids on military armouries in the mainland and Northern Ireland.

Countermeasures by the authorities in the Irish Republic and Northern Ireland, which had led to the imprisonment of several principal members of the organisation, had hampered the IRA's operations. In 1962, realising that it had failed to enlist the support of the Catholic population on both sides of the border, it set about the task of re-establishing itself. A large number of new recruits were trained in camps situated within the Irish Republic. At the same time, it was laying down a long-term strategy for the expulsion of the British from Northern Ireland and the attainment of its ultimate goal, a united republic of Ireland under socialist rule.

In 1968, the first of a wave of protests took place against the inequality and discrimination suffered by Catholics in Northern Ireland. Spearheaded by the Northern Ireland Civil Rights Association (NICRA), it manifested itself in a series of peaceful protest marches, the first of which took place at Dungannon in August of that year and passed off without incident. In October, however, further peaceful marches were broken up with force by the Royal Ulster Constabulary (RUC).

In January 1969, a civil rights march from Belfast to Londonderry was obstructed at Burntollet by Protestants who stoned the marchers while the RUC looked on and made no attempt to stop the ensuing violence. The general security situation throughout the province worsened, this being illustrated by the blowing up of a water pipeline at the Silent Valley reservoir and of an electricity pylon at Annabow, Kilmore. Three days later a water main in the area of Clady, in County Antrim, was also damaged. The result was that troops from the garrisons in the province were deployed to guard sixteen keypoints which included key installations and government buildings.

Violence in Northern Ireland worsened with the arrival of the Orangemen's marching season. On 12 July, there was violence in Belfast, Londonderry and elsewhere. Behind such scenes lurked the IRA which, allying itself with activists in political organisations such as Young Socialist Alliance and People's Democracy, sought to destabilise the province by engineering confrontations between the Catholics and the authorities. Its short-term plan was to gain recognition and support within the province and overseas, notably in the United States, as the protector of the Catholic minority against Unionist and British oppression.

In August violence throughout the province worsened and on the 14th the British government agreed to a request from the Unionist government at Stormont, the Northern Irish parliament, to provide troops to act in support of the RUC. At 5.15 p.m. on the same day, troops of the 1st Battalion The Prince of Wales's Own Regiment of Yorkshire were deployed into the Bogside area of Londonderry while others of the 2nd Battalion The Queen's Regiment were deployed to areas in Belfast where they were subsequently joined by the 3rd Battalion The Light Infantry.

This was the start of what would become, at the time of writing, a 30-year-long counter-terrorist and internal security campaign between the British Army and the RUC on one side and not only the IRA but also other nationalist and loyalist groups on the other. An account of it within the context of this book appears in Chapters

5 and 14, but overviews of principal events during the thirty years, concerning the various terrorist groups in Northern Ireland and the Irish Republic within the framework of international terrorism during the period 1969–99, are given here and in Chapters 2 and 3.

The first two years of the conflict in Northern Ireland saw its restriction to the province itself. 1969 saw the splitting of the IRA as a result of dissension between two factions with irreconcilable differences: the Official IRA and the Provisional IRA. The Officials' leadership comprised an extreme Trotskyist faction led by the organisation's chief-of-staff Cathal Goulding, and the president of the Republican Party or Sinn Fein, Thomas MacGiolla. In 1962 this body had rejected the re-unification of Northern Ireland with the Irish Republic, declaring that its avowed aim was the establishment of a Marxist republic governing the whole of Ireland. It saw the incorporation of the industrialised North as essential and believed that the only way that this could be achieved was by attracting both Catholic and Protestant working-class support against 'capitalist exploitation of the masses' in the province, thus avoiding and condemning the use of violence in both Protestant and Catholic working-class areas.

The more militant Provisionals, led by hard-liners such as Martin McGuinness, Gerry Adams, Seamus Twomey, Sean McStiofain and Ivor Bell, were less sophisticated than their 'Official' counterparts, of whom they were suspicious and whose Marxist leaders they distrusted. They took the more traditional IRA stance, advocating the use of violence as the primary method of achieving their aim of driving the British out and establishing a united Ireland. In December 1969 they broke away from the IRA and on 10 January 1970 formed their own 'Provisional Committee', subsequently being dubbed the 'Provisional IRA'.

The Officials, however, were fully prepared to use violence against those representing the British and Northern Irish authorities, as was illustrated by the murder on 12 December 1971 of a Northern Ireland senator, Jack Barnhill, and the attempted murder in early 1972 of the Northern Irish Home Affairs Minister, John

Taylor. They also had no qualms about carrying out punishments and 'executions' on those Catholics whom they believed to have betrayed the nationalist cause by serving in the British security forces. On 8 December 1971 an Official IRA gunman had shot dead Sean Russell, a 30-year-old Catholic part-time member of the Ulster Defence Regiment (UDR), a force formed to replace the Protestant-recruited Ulster Special Constabulary, better known as the 'B-Specials', which was disbanded in 1969. The murder was carried out in front of the victim's five children, his eldest daughter aged 10 being wounded in the leg.

On 22 February 1972, three weeks after the riots of 'Bloody Sunday' in the Bogside area of Londonderry on 30 January, during which thirteen demonstrators were shot dead, the Official IRA carried the war to the mainland by carrying out a retaliatory bomb attack on the officers' mess of 16th Parachute Brigade in Aldershot, Hampshire. In fact, the results of this bombing could not have been more counter-productive for the Officials: those who died were a Catholic padre, five women and a gardener.

During 1972, the Official IRA began to receive support for its operations from the Soviet Union. In the latter half of that year it received the first of a number of consignments of arms delivered by Department 8 (formerly Department V) of Directorate S of the KGB. Two machine-guns, seventy assault rifles, ten Walther pistols and more than 40,000 rounds of ammunition, were delivered by a Soviet intelligence-gathering vessel to the Stanton Sandbank, an area some fifty-six miles off the coast of Northern Ireland, where they were lowered on to the sandbank, their location being marked with a buoy. A few hours later, the consignment was retrieved by a trawler under the supervision of Seamus Costello, a known hard-liner.

On 8 March 1973, an eleven-man active service unit (ASU) planted four bombs at various locations in London. Two were put in cars outside the Old Bailey and at the Central Army Recruiting Office in Whitehall; both exploded, killing one person and injuring approximately 265. Two more were found outside New Scotland

Yard and the offices of the British Forces Broadcasting Service in Westminster and were defused. The police and the Security Service were already hot on the tails of those responsible. Four hours before the two bombs exploded, ten people were arrested at London Heathrow airport on board an aircraft as it was about to take off for Ireland. On 14 November 1973, nine of them were found guilty of involvement in the bombings: Gerard Kelly, William McLarnon, Robert Walsh, Martin Brady, Paul Holmes, William Armstrong, Hugh Feeney, Marion Price and Dolours Price. All received sentences of life imprisonment with the exception of William McLarnon who was sentenced to fifteen years.

On 18 August, the Provisionals launched a fire and letter bomb campaign in London, Birmingham and Manchester. This lasted six weeks during which a total of thirty people were injured by forty bombs; a large number of other devices were discovered and defused. The end of 1973 saw retaliation by the Provisionals for the imprisonment of those responsible for the Old Bailey and Whitehall bombings in March. On 18 December, two car bombs and a parcel bomb exploded in London, injuring sixty people.

The beginning of 1974 brought further bomb attacks, with five separate incidents occurring in two days during January: three bombs exploded at Madame Tussauds, the annual Boat Show at Earl's Court and in Chelsea respectively. Two others were found and defused in Ealing, west London, and outside the Kensington, west London, home of the Army's Adjutant-General, Major General Sir Cecil Blacker.

On 3 February, the Provisionals struck again when they placed a 50-pound bomb aboard a coach travelling on the M62 motorway with soldiers and their families aboard; nine soldiers, a woman and her two children were killed. Nine days later, on 12 February, a bomb exploded in Buckinghamshire and injured ten people. Shortly afterwards, the Provisionals established a number of ASUs in the Birmingham area. Each comprised a cell of four or five members who were reinforced by others from Ireland or recruited locally from local Irish communities as and when required.

During July, an ASU was also established in London. Initially it comprised a hard core of three men: Martin O'Connell, who arrived in August, and Eddie Butler and Harry Duggan who joined him in October. They were subsequently joined by two others: Hugh O'Doherty, Brendan O'Dowd and an Irish-American named Liam Quinn. All lived in north London, Martin O'Connell and Harry Duggan in Stoke Newington and the others in Crouch End.

A total of fourteen bombs were planted by this ASU whose targets in 1974 included Heathrow Airport, Westminster Hall, the National Defence College and the Tower of London where a bomb killed a woman and injured forty-one children. It also attacked targets outside London: on 5 October, a bomb exploded in the Horse and Groom pub in Guildford, Surrey, killing four off-duty soldiers (two of them women) and a civilian, and injuring fifty-seven others; thirty-five minutes later a second bomb exploded nearby in the Seven Stars, injuring only eight people as the pub was being cleared because of the first explosion. A month later, on 7 November, a bomb was thrown through a window of the King's Arms pub in Woolwich, killing an off-duty soldier and a barman and injuring twenty-eight people in the bar.

The Provisionals were also active in the Birmingham area. In November they attempted to attack a telephone exchange in Coventry but the bomb exploded prematurely, killing the bomber, James McDade. Nineteen bombs were planted throughout the city area and on 21 November two exploded in crowded pubs, killing twenty-one people and injuring 182. As a consequence the government enacted immediate legislation in the form of the Prevention of Terrorism Act.

The London ASU continued its operations into 1975, but on 26 February a man was spotted by three police officers in plain clothes, acting suspiciously before entering an apartment in Fairholme Road in the Hammersmith area of west London. He was stopped and questioned when he came out of the building, but he broke away and ran off. A passing off-duty police officer, Constable Stephen Tibble, joined the chase on his motor-cycle and caught up with the man. Cornered, the latter produced a pistol and shot the officer twice in the chest at point-blank range, inflicting two mortal wounds from which he died two hours later in hospital. A massive police hunt was launched, during which a search of the apartment in Fairholme Road revealed fingerprints and uncovered a cache of weapons, explosives and other bomb-making equipment, as well as a list of potential targets.

The killer made good his escape, but forensic examination of the house and ensuing investigations pointed to the Irish-American member of the London ASU, Liam Quinn. Further investigations revealed that there was a strong possibility that Quinn had returned to the Irish Republic immediately after the murder of the police officer. Shortly afterwards, however, he was arrested by the Irish authorities and was subsequently tried for being a member of the IRA and imprisoned for nine months. Released in January 1976, he returned to the United States in 1979 and in 1981 was arrested in San Francisco by the FBI on a warrant issued as the result of a request for extradition by the British government. In 1986, after five years of legal wrangling, Quinn was extradited to England. He was subsequently tried and convicted of the murder of Constable Tibble, being sentenced to life imprisonment on 16 February 1988.

Despite this setback, the London ASU had continued operations. On 27 August 1975, a bomb exploded in the Caterham Arms pub in Caterham, Surrey, injuring thirty-three people. Nine days later, on 5 September, a bomb attack was carried out on the Hilton Hotel in Park Lane, London, killing two people and injuring sixty-three. This was followed by attacks on three restaurants in the city. Two days later a bomb was found in Church Street, in the Kensington area of west London. A bomb-disposal expert, Captain Roger Goad, was in the process of attempting to disarm the bomb when it exploded, killing him instantly. According to a statement made later by one of the members of the ASU, the specific aim of the operation had been to kill a member of a bomb-disposal team and the device had been fitted with an anti-tamper switch.

On 29 September, a bomb exploded in Oxford Street in central London, injuring seven people. Ten days later, on 9 October, another exploded at Green Park underground station, killing one person and injuring twenty. Two weeks later, on 23 October, the ASU placed a bomb beneath the car of a Conservative member of parliament, Sir Hugh Fraser. It exploded prematurely and killed Fraser's neighbour, Professor Gordon Hamilton-Fairlie, an eminent expert on cancer, who was walking past the vehicle.

In November, a bomb fitted with a timer was discovered beneath a car parked outside the house of former Prime Minister Edward Heath in Belgravia. This too had an anti-tamper device, but it was defused by a police bomb-disposal expert, Major Geoffrey Biddle. On 27 November Harry Duggan shot dead the publisher Ross McWhirter who had earlier offered a £50,000 reward for the capture of those responsible for the ASU's attacks. Duggan made his escape in a car belonging to Mrs McWhirter, driven by his accomplice, Hugh O'Doherty.

This reign of terror came to an end on the night of 6 December 1975 when all four members of the ASU took part in an attack on Scott's Restaurant in Mayfair, central London, spraying it with gunfire; three weeks earlier they had attacked it with a bomb. While fleeing the scene they encountered a police patrol car which set off in pursuit. After a lengthy chase the four men were cornered in Balcombe Street, north-west London. Taking refuge in a nearby building, they forced their way into an apartment and took hostage the owners, a middle-aged couple named John and Sheila Matthews. Having sealed off the area and surrounded the building, the police played a waiting game, negotiating with the four terrorists but making it perfectly clear that there was no way they would be allowed to go free. Eventually, on the morning of the eighth day of the siege, while listening to an evening news bulletin over the radio, the terrorists heard that the SAS were on the scene and that the police were preparing to hand over to them for an assault on the apartment. They surrendered soon afterwards.

The four members of the ASU, subsequently more familiarly known as the 'Balcombe Street Gang', were tried and convicted of a total of eight murders, two charges of manslaughter and a total of fifty bombings and shootings in London and the south-east of England during 1974 and 1975. In February 1977 Martin O'Connell, Eddie Butler, Harry Duggan and Hugh O'Doherty were sentenced to forty-seven terms of life imprisonment. As mentioned earlier, the fifth member of the ASU, Liam Quinn, was extradited from the United States in 1986 and two years later was sentenced to life imprisonment.

Two months before the arrest of the Balcombe Street Gang, the Provisional IRA had kidnapped Dr. Tiede Herrema, the managing director of a subsidiary of the Dutch commercial group Akzo. He was seized in Limerick, in the Irish Republic, on 3 October 1975 by an ASU led by an individual named Eddie Gallagher, which had during the previous year attacked the RUC station at Strabane by dropping two milk churns filled with explosives on it from a hijacked helicopter; the attack failed because the explosives failed to detonate. Gallagher had been arrested later in the year, but four days later was free again after blasting his way out of Portlaoise Prison with explosives that had been smuggled in. On 21 October, the Gardaí Síochana (Police, lit. Guardians of the Peace) ran Gallagher and his gang to earth at a house at Monasterevin in County Kildare. On 7 November, after a siege lasting seventeen days, they surrendered and Dr. Herrema was released unharmed.

Meanwhile, the mid-1970s saw the Provisionals continuing their campaign of violence in Northern Ireland, including attacks against Protestant civilians. Loyalist death squads retaliated, killing Catholics. At the same time, renewed feuding broke out between the Official IRA and the Provisionals, ten republicans dying in a number of internecine killings.

This period saw the emergence of a breakaway faction of the Official IRA. Comprising some of the Officials' most violent members, the organisation was formed as the Irish Republican Socialist Party (IRSP) on 8 December 1974. Also created that day was a military wing of the IRSP, called the Irish National Liberation Army (INLA). A radical group, it was led by Seamus Costello, the hard-liner who had become disenchanted with the Official IRA and its policies after the split with the Provisionals in 1970. Its aim was the expulsion of the British from Northern Ireland and the establishment of a revolutionary socialist government throughout the thirty-two counties of Ireland.

The INLA soon incurred the wrath of the Official IRA when it helped itself to weapons from some of the latter's arm caches, and a feud soon developed between the two organisations. On 20 February 1975 a member of the INLA was killed by the Officials. The INLA was quick to respond by shooting dead Sean Fox, the Officials' quartermaster in Belfast. More deaths followed as the two organisations indulged in tit-for-tat killings which included, on 28 April, that of the commander of the Officials in Belfast, Liam McMillen, which effectively ended the feud. Thereafter, Costello turned to overseas sources for supplies of arms, among them the PLO and other terrorist groups in the Middle East. During 1976 small consignments of weapons were smuggled from France in cars which travelled to Ireland by road and ferry. These were followed by a larger consignment which was being driven from Turkey into Greece by two members of the INLA, Seamus Ruddy and Phelim Lally, when it was seized at the border.

In addition to feuding with the Officials, the INLA carried out operations against the security forces in Northern Ireland, frequently using the cover names 'People's Republican Army' and 'Catholic Reaction Force', but in 1977 it suffered a setback when Costello was killed by an Official IRA gunman who was himself later murdered by the INLA in retaliation.

Meanwhile the Provisional IRA continued its campaign of violence against not only the security forces in Northern Ireland but also the British establishment itself. On 21 July 1976, it struck a major blow when it murdered the British Ambassador to Ireland, Sir Christopher Ewart-Biggs, who had taken up his appointment only twelve days before. Accompanied by two civil servants, Brian Cubbon and Judith Cook, he had just left his residence at Sandyford, in County Dublin, when a remote-controlled 200-pound culvert bomb exploded under his armoured limousine which was travelling in a four-vehicle convoy. The Ambassador and Judith Cook were killed, while Brian Cubbon and the driver were badly injured. In the aftermath of the explosion, two terrorists were seen running to a car nearby.

During the following year, the Provisionals continued their bombing campaign in Northern Ireland and resumed their attacks on London which continued during 1978. On 27 August 1979 they struck a devastating double blow against the United Kingdom in Donegal Bay off Mullaghmore in County Sligo, on the north-west coast of the Irish Republic. Terrorists exploded a radio-controlled 50-pound bomb concealed under the deck of the boat carrying Earl Mountbatten of Burma and members of his family who were spending their summer holiday in Ireland. Earl Mountbatten, his 14-year-old grandson, Nicholas Knatchbull, the Dowager Baroness of Brabourne and a 15-year-old local boy, Paul Maxwell, died in the blast and other members of the earl's family were severely injured.

The reported reason for the murder of Mountbatten was the Provisional IRA's implacable opposition to a proposal for a federated Ireland, known as the Fitzgerald Plan, which had found favour with both political parties in the Irish Republic, moderate Protestant and Catholic elements in Northern Ireland, the British government and the Irish-American establishment in the United States. The Provisionals rejected the Fitzgerald Plan out of hand and their position was summed up by their spokesman, Ruairi O'Bradaigh, who declared that not only did the Provisional IRA not want a confederation between the north and the south of Ireland, nor an independent Ulster, but it wanted to replace the existing establishments in both the Irish Republic and Northern Ireland with a democratic socialist republic.

North of the border, on the day of Earl Mountbatten's murder, troops of the 2nd Battalion The Parachute Regiment and the 1st Battalion The Queen's Own Highlanders were caught in a double explosive ambush near the village of Warrenpoint, on the northern shore of Carlingford Lough, in which eighteen men were killed and several badly injured.

It was not only the Provisional IRA that made the headlines during 1979. On 30 March the INLA murdered Airey Neave, the Tory opposition member of parliament and close friend of Margaret Thatcher whose Conservative government was subsequently elected to power later that year. Neave was targeted because of his outspoken criticism of terrorism and his publicised suggestions for dealing with it. The INLA, which was keen to make its name within the Irish republican movement as an effective force, selected him in the knowledge that his murder would prove popular with republican hard-liners and thus enhance the organisation's reputation.

A four-man INLA cell was given the task of assassinating Neave. After some weeks of keeping him under surveillance and recording his movements, the terrorists gained access to his car and attached an explosive charge fitted with a mercury tilt-switch and a timing mechanism set to arm the device while the vehicle was in the car park under the House of Commons at Westminster. The bomb exploded as Neave drove up the ramp of the car park. He lost both legs in the blast and died half an hour later in hospital.

The following year, however, saw the deaths of three prominent members of the INLA. On 26 June 1980 Miriam Daly, a university lecturer and political strategist for the IRSP/INLA, was found murdered in the hall of her home. Indications were that she had been killed by a professional hit-man: she had been bound and gagged and shot four times with a 9mm pistol muffled by a cushion. Despite extensive police investigations, no one was ever charged with her murder, but there was strong suspicion that the Ulster Defence Association (UDA), a Protestant group covered later in this chapter, was responsible for her death. On 15 October Ronnie Bunting, who had succeeded Sean Costello as leader of the INLA, was shot dead in his home in the Andersonstown area of Belfast by two masked gunmen who also shot and wounded his wife. Also killed was Noel Lyttle who had replaced Miriam Daly as the organisation's political strategist and who had been visiting Bunting to discuss plans. Like the Daly murder, the killing of Bunting and Lyttle bore the hallmarks of professional assassins who have never been brought to book for their crime.

By the end of the 1970s, the Provisional IRA had become a highly sophisticated terrorist organisation, financed largely by sympathetic Irish-Americans in the United States or by armed robbery within Northern Ireland. It also received support from Libya during the early and mid-1970s. A consignment of Libyan-supplied arms, aboard the Cypriot-registered vessel *Claudia*, was intercepted by patrol vessels of the Irish Naval Service on 28 March 1973. The vessel, whose captain was a known and convicted West German arms smuggler named Gunther Leinhauser, had been kept under surveillance throughout its voyage by submarines of the Royal Navy and by Royal Air Force maritime reconnaissance aircraft. When boarded, the vessel was found to be carrying six senior members of the Provisional IRA led by Joe Cahill, a former commander of the Provisionals in Belfast, and a consignment of arms comprising 250 Kalashnikov AK-47 assault rifles, 100 anti-tank mines and 500 hand-grenades. When subsequently questioned, Leinhauser stated that he had been furnished with a list of arms requirements by the Provisionals and had negotiated the purchasing of them with Cahill in the Libyan capital of Tripoli.

One of the principal suppliers of arms to the IRA was George Harrison, an Irish-American who joined the organisation in 1931 at the age of sixteen. Emigrating from Ireland to the United States during the 1930s and serving in the US Army during the Second World War, he later became active in the trade unions movement and several Irish-American organisations. During the 1950s Harrison, who lived with his family in Brooklyn, New York, became one of the founder-members of an IRA arms supply organisation in the United States. Several consignments of weapons, notably a number of M-1 Garand .30-06 rifles, M-1 .30 carbines, Thompson .45 submachine-guns, two Browning M-2 .50 heavy machine-guns and bazooka anti-tank rocket-launchers, were shipped from Brooklyn docks to Ireland. In 1960 the Irish poet Brendan Behan assisted in the shipment of one of these consignments which included pistols, revolvers, Thompson submachine-guns and a quantity of ammunition.

During the 1960s, following the termination of the IRA's campaign against the British at the end of February 1962, Harrison was inactive. In early 1969, however, following the outbreak of the troubles in Northern Ireland, he was approached by the IRA and soon afterwards shipped a consignment of some seventy weapons, comprising M-1 carbines, M-3 .45 submachine-guns, pistols, revolvers and 60,000 rounds of ammunition, which arrived in the province in the summer of that year. In 1970 Harrison reactivated his old arms supply organisation of the 1950s and by early 1971 was shipping consignments of AR-15 5.56mm rifles, the so-called 'sporting' semi-automatic-only version of the M-16 which was by then in service with the US armed forces; the latter part of that year, however, saw Harrison acquire the first of a number of M-16s.

Harrison's principal supplier was George De Meo, a Corsican arms dealer and owner of a gunshop just outside Brooklyn. De Meo reportedly obtained considerable quantities of weapons via the military, sourced from US Army and US Marine Corps (USMC) bases in North Carolina. Troops sold weapons and ammunition to local dealers who supplied them to De Meo. Harrison would ultimately deliver the weapons to predetermined delivery points from where they were collected and shipped across the Atlantic to Ireland.

In 1976, a US National Guard armoury at Danvers, near Boston, Massachusetts, was raided and its contents stolen by a gang reported to be members of the Mafia. Shortly afterwards, Harrison was approached and offered a quantity of M-16 rifles and seven M-60 7.62mm general-purpose machine-guns (GPMGs). He purchased the entire consignment and in July six of the M-60s were among the weapons shipped to Ireland. They made their début during the following year when they were used in a number of attacks on the security forces.

In 1979 Harrison assembled one of the largest of his consignments which comprised more than 150 weapons and 60,000 rounds of ammunition. Included were two more M-60 GPMGs, fourteen M-16 rifles and a large number of Ruger Mini-14 5.56mm rifles. The source of the M-60s and M-16s was the USMC base at Fort Lejeune in North Carolina. In September, the consignment was shipped by sea from New York, arriving in Dublin in late October. The US, British and Irish authorities were aware of the quantities of arms reaching Ireland from America and were maintaining surveillance on those suspected of being involved. A trans-Atlantic telephone call from Dublin confirming shipment of the weapons was monitored and when the vessel carrying the consignment docked in Dublin, the Gardai Siochana were waiting. The ship was kept under close observation for several days, but the Provisional IRA had somehow learned that its arms supply operation had been compromised. No one arrived to collect the arms and spirit them away and eventually the vessel was raided and the arms confiscated.

Examination of the weapons and investigations led to George De Meo and eventually to his sources of supply at military bases in North Carolina, including Fort Lejeune. It was subsequently estimated that a staggering 10,000,000 rounds of ammunition had been pilfered from the USMC base of which 1,000,000 had found their way to the Provisional IRA via Harrison, the remainder disappearing elsewhere in the United States. De Meo was arrested, tried, convicted of smuggling arms to the Provisional IRA and sentenced to ten years' imprisonment. In 1981, however, he negotiated a reduced prison sentence in return for co-operating with the Federal Bureau of Investigation (FBI) in setting up an operation to entrap Harrison.

In May 1981 Harrison was arrested after purchasing a consignment of weapons, including fourteen M-16 rifles, a 20mm cannon and a flame-thrower, from an FBI agent posing as an arms dealer. Four other individuals were also arrested, among them Michael Flannery, one of the founders of the Irish Northern Aid Committee, better known as NORAID, which had been providing funds for the nationalist cause in Northern Ireland since its formation in 1970. Harrison and his accomplices were tried in late 1982, but all were acquitted on the grounds that there had been possible involvement by US government agencies: during the trial it had been successfully alleged by the defence that George De Meo had connections with the Central Intelligence Agency (CIA) and that the latter must have been aware of his and Harrison's activities. The demise of Harrison's arms supply network was a major blow for the Provisional IRA which thereafter experienced difficulty in obtaining weapons from the United States, although it would continue in its efforts to do so.

Republican terrorist organisations were not the only ones active in Northern Ireland during the 1970s. Loyalist factions also made their presence felt, among them the Ulster Volunteer Force (UVF) which was formed in 1966 by Gusty Spence. They began attacks on Catholics in March, and in April declared war on the IRA. After the arrest of Spence in June, however, the UVF fell into disarray, but two years later saw the organisation, by now led by Kenneth Gibson, carrying out five bomb attacks against water and electricity installations supplying Belfast. During the late 1960s, the UVF numbered some 500 in strength and financed its operations through protection rackets. In 1972, the organisation saw a brief revival after the release on parole of Spence. In 1974 it was responsible for the murders of sixteen Catholics in retaliation for the murders of a judge and a magistrate by the Provisional IRA. It was in July 1975, however, that the UVF gained wider notoriety when a gang from its 'Mid-Ulster Battalion' were involved in the murder of three members of a well-known Northern Irish pop group, the Miami Showband. Several of the terrorists were subsequently identified as being part-time members of the UDR.

In 1969 the Shankill Defence Association (SDA) was formed by John McKeague, who became its chairman, and Fred Proctor. In August of that year the SDA took part in rioting at Unity Flats, a Catholic residential area near the Shankill Road in Belfast, which resulted in seventy policemen and some 200 civilians being injured. In September it was also involved in confrontations with the Army and in October once again in unrest in the Unity Flats neighbourhood. It has been claimed that it was partly in response to the terror tactics used by the SDA against Catholics in Belfast during this period that the Provisional IRA was formed. Subsequently, however, the SDA was riven by internal factions which eventually led to the break-up of the organisation.

The principal loyalist organisation was the UDA which was formed in 1971 as an umbrella organisation for various Protestant defence groups in Belfast. Its activities were overseen by a council of thirteen members whose chairman was Harding Smith. During the period until October 1972 when a truce was called, it conducted operations against the security forces in Northern Ireland as well as against the IRA. Thereafter it concentrated on the latter, carrying out bomb attacks across the border into the Irish Republic. By January 1973 membership of the organisation had reached 60,000 and throughout the 1970s it featured prominently as the most important of the loyalist organisations.

An offshoot of UDA was the Ulster Freedom Fighters (UFF), which was formed in 1973 from a number of militants. The UFF carried out a number of attacks against the IRA throughout the 1970s and was also involved in inter-factional feuding with elements of the UVF.

The Red Hand Commandos was another group established in 1972 by former members of the UDA. Led by John McKeague, the former leader of the Shankill Defence Association, who was later expelled from the UDA, it was a small violent organisation whose activities were considered to be more criminally, rather than politically, motivated and it received little if any support from the Protestant community. In 1982, McKeague was shot dead by gunmen of the INLA.

Great Britain and Germany were not alone in fighting a war against indigenous terrorist groups. Italy, which played host to both left- and right-wing terrorist groups, suffered from one of the highest levels of political terrorism. During the 1970s a total of 11,780 terrorist attacks took place in the country. The situation was not helped by the chaotic state of Italian politics at the time, the average duration of a government in power being six months, and the fact that provincial governments paid little heed to the central government in Rome. In addition, corruption was endemic and the country's principal organised crime bodies, the Sicilian Mafia, the rival Neapolitan Camorra and New Camorra, and the Calabrian 'Ndrangheta, maintained massive influence at all levels of society.

From 1965 onwards, there were a number of right-wing terrorist groups in Italy. These underwent a continual process of splitting, reforming, merging and reforming and eventually were reduced to about six in number: Armed Revolutionary Nuclei; Black Order; Mussolini Action Squads; New Order; Revolutionary Action Movement; Revolutionary Fascist Nuclei. The left-wing groups in Italy numbered six in total: Red Brigades; Front Line; Armed Proletarian Nuclei; October XXII Circle; Partisan Action Groups; Permanent Struggle; Workers Vanguard. In the context of international terrorism, however, only two of these were of any significance: Front Line and the Red Brigades.

Front Line first made an appearance in November 1976 when it carried out an attack on the Fiat company. With an estimated strength of several hundred active members, organised in independent cells located in the cities of Milan, Florence and Naples, the group had no central leadership, its operations being carried out under the direction of the more prominent members. Its targets were the State, commercial organisations and supporters of the Christian Democrat Party. By December 1978 Front Line had carried out twenty-five acts of terrorism. In January 1979 it assassinated the Milan Assistant Attorney-General, Emilio Alessandrini, who was in the process of assembling a database of information on Italian terrorist groups. Later in the year, fifteen members of the group attacked the School of Industrial Management in Turin, holding hostage the staff and students and shooting ten of them in the legs. The end of the year, however, saw 131 of its members either arrested or identified and a further 164 arrested and convicted during the following three years, among them two prominent individuals: Suzanna Ronconi and Maurice Bignami.

The Red Brigades were formed in 1970 from a number of far-left groups that had become frustrated by what they saw as the Italian Communist Party's (PCI) lack of revolutionary zeal and its readiness to take part in 'bourgeois' democratic processes. Furthermore, they saw a threat from right-wing groups which were already indulging in acts of terrorism: in December of the previous year, an unidentified group had been responsible for planting a bomb in a bank in the Piazza Fontana in Milan, killing seventeen people and injuring eighty-eight.

The Red Brigades' hard core was drawn from a number of different elements. These included: a group of students from the sociology department at Trento University, led by Renato Curcio and his wife, Maria Cagol; a number of young Communists from Reggio Emilia, led by Alberto Franceschini, who had been expelled from the PCI for their extreme views; and some groups working in factories in Milan.

During the first three years or so of their existence, the organisation indulged in kidnaps of factory managers as part of a campaign to force companies to provide better terms and conditions for workers, thereby endearing themselves to factory hands and establishing a large army of sympathisers. In April 1974, however, it first attracted attention with its kidnap of a public prosecutor, Mario Sossi, releasing him after thirty-five days in captivity. On 17 June, in retaliation for a right-wing terrorist attack on 28 May on an anti-fascist rally in Brescia, in which eight people were killed and 102 wounded, it attacked the headquarters of a right-wing political party, the MSI, killing two party workers.

The Red Brigades were organised in 'columns', each with its own area of responsibility. These were located in Milan, Turin, Genoa, Rome, Naples, the region of Veneto and, for a while, the island of Sardinia. Within the columns were specialists responsible for different aspects such as intelligence, weapons, logistics, forgery of documents, accommodation and vehicles. At the peak of their existence the Red Brigades' columns were estimated to comprise some fifty full-time paid 'regulars', responsible for carrying out the kidnaps and murders. These were headed by a 'strategic directorate' which delegated to an executive committee. The actual 'brigades' were formed by some 450 unpaid, part-time 'irregulars' who were responsible for organising 'direct action' on the streets or in fertile areas such as factories or universities. The use of the word 'brigade' is misleading; each normally comprised a cell of only four to five activists.

In September 1974, however, Renato Curcio and Alberto Franceschini were arrested at a meeting to which they had been lured by an agent of the special Carabinieri counter-terrorist unit, which had been formed in the aftermath of the Sossi kidnap. During the following month the Red Brigades suffered a further blow when another of its leaders, Roberto Ognibene, was also arrested. By the end of the year, nine founder members of the organisation were in prison.

February of the following year saw Curcio free again, after being sprung from prison by his wife, Maria Cagol, who had visited him with a pistol concealed in a bag of laundry. In June 1975, Cagol and a number of others were surrounded by Carabinieri in a villa in which they were holding a victim, the millionaire Villarino Gancia. Their attempt to shoot their way out failed and Cagol was killed in the attempt. In January of the following year, Curcio was arrested again and spent the next twenty-three years in prison, being released in 1999.

The loss of their leaders did not deter the Red Brigades from continuing their campaign of terror. Now headed by Mario Moretti, a surviving founder member, they proceeded to assassinate public prosecutor Francesco Coco in June 1976, and in January 1977 kidnapped millionaire ship-owner Pietro Costa, releasing him in early April for a ransom of 1.5 billion lire. During the next twelve months they carried out the murders of four prominent people: on 28 April 1977, the president of the Turin Lawyers Association; on 16 November 1977, the deputy editor of the newspaper *La Stampa*; on 14 February 1978, a senior judge; and on 10 March 1978, a senior officer of the Carabinieri.

It was in March 1978, however, that the Red Brigades carried out the operation which would gain them world-wide notoriety. On the morning of 16 March the Rome column, reinforced by members of the Milan and Turin columns and led by Mario Moretti himself, kidnapped the former prime minister and Christian Democratic Party leader, Aldo Moro, as he drove through the streets of Rome with an escort of police bodyguards. The convoy of two cars was ambushed in a narrow street and all three of his bodyguards and the two drivers were killed in a hail of fire from automatic weapons. Moro himself was spirited away and for the next fifty-five days was held captive in an apartment, in the Via Montalcini in south-west Rome, belonging to a founder member of the Red Brigades, Prospero Gallinari.

In return for Moro's release, the terrorists demanded the release of Renato Curcio and twelve other members of the group who were due to stand trial on 21 March. Despite intense political debate over the affair, the Italian government refused to accede to the terrorists' demands. Meanwhile the Carabinieri and police mounted a drag-net operation throughout the city but to no avail. On 9 May, as the result of a telephone call, Aldo Moro's body was found in the boot of a car.

January 1979 saw a split occur between the leadership and dissidents within the rank and file of the Red Brigades as the result of the murder of Guido Rossa, a Communist shop steward, who had been accused of informing on the organisation. The dissidents, led by Valerio Morucci and Adriana Faranda, accused the leadership of being out of touch with the working class, maintaining that only proletarian unrest could be the basis for revolutionary action. They also accused them of being Stalinist and authoritarian, and of using the murder of Aldo Moro as an assault on Italian society rather than as a way of highlighting the desperation of the proletariat seeking to bring attention to its cause. Despite such internal problems, the Red Brigades continued to wage a campaign of disruption and would continue to be a thorn in the side of the Italian establishment during the next two years.

Elsewhere in Europe, political violence was also on the rise. In Spain, the terrorists of Euskadi Ta Askatasuna (ETA) (Freedom for the Basque Homeland) had been making headlines through a continual campaign of terror since 1968.

ETA was a separatist-nationalist group formed in 1959 with the aim of gaining independence for the Basque homeland in northern Spain which comprises four provinces: Guipuzcoa, Vizcaya, Alava and Navarra. Initially it had employed peaceful methods in pursuit of its cause, but faced with total intransigence on the part of the government in Madrid, had soon switched to armed struggle. In 1964, members of ETA underwent training in guerrilla warfare in Cuba, Uruguay and Argentina. Four years later a number of them were to be found in training camps in Algeria where they rubbed shoulders with fellow terrorists from Palestine, Ireland, Italy and West Germany.

Five years later, in 1973, ETA came to world attention when it assassinated the Spanish prime minister, Admiral Luis Carrero Blanco, in Madrid with a bomb. During the following year, the organisation split into two factions: the militant ETA–M, which advocated a purely armed struggle to achieve independence, and the more moderate ETA–PM which espoused a political approach combined with a certain amount of armed activity.

The death of General Franco on 20 November 1975, and the subsequent peaceful transition of Spain from a fascist regime to a democratically governed country with a constitutional monarchy by 1977, did not see any let-up by ETA–M. In early 1976, a total of 143 members of the organisation travelled to Algeria where they underwent three months' training in guerrilla warfare and terrorist skills at a police academy at Souma, near Algiers, instruction being provided by Algerian and Cuban instructors. Contact had previously been established with the Provisional IRA in 1972, and in 1977 members of ETA attended the Provisionals' annual convention in Dublin; later that year Ruairi O'Bradaigh, the President of the Provisional wing of Sinn Fein, paid a visit to the Basque country.

ETA–M's prime targets were the Spanish security forces, including the Army, National Police, Civil Guards and the Basque

Autonomous Police. Of the 239 killings during the period of three years following the transition of the country to democratic rule, some 60 per cent of the victims were members of the security forces. The group also targeted the Spanish economy, exacting 'revolutionary taxes' under threat of kidnap, death or sabotage from owners of businesses as a way of financing its operations. It carried out a number of kidnaps, releasing its victims in exchange for large ransoms, and bank robberies. It also exploded bombs in coastal resorts, attacking the tourist industry which is Spain's largest source of foreign currency.

The leaders of ETA–M were meanwhile safely ensconced in the Basque region of France from where, much to the fury of the Spanish authorities, the French government declined to extradite them. France also served as a sanctuary for ETA–M activists who carried out attacks in Spain and then fled back across the border to safety. This led in the late 1970s to right-wing Spanish groups, reportedly with the support of the Spanish police, pursuing members of ETA–M into France and murdering them.

During the 1970s, ETA–M established links with other terrorist organisations in Europe, including the Red Army Faction, Revolutionary Cells, Provisional IRA, Red Brigades and Front Line. In October 1978 a number of ETA–M's members attended a terrorist 'summit' in Yugoslavia which was also attended by the PFLP and members of Latin-American groups.

Following the Spanish transition to democracy in 1976, the response of the Spanish government to ETA–M's campaign of violence had been to legalise ETA's political party and devolved a considerable amount of power to a Basque autonomous regional government. A national referendum in 1979 produced a 67 per cent turn-out of which 88 per cent voted in favour of devolution. This was achieved despite a boycott by more than half of the population in the Basque region on the orders of ETA–M. The government also took measures in strengthening its hand against ETA–M and terrorism in general, passing new legislation and forming a National Police anti-terrorist unit.

Meanwhile, other terrorist organisations had emerged in Spain after the death of Franco. Foremost among these was the First of October Anti-Fascist Resistance Group, better known by its Spanish acronym of GRAPO, a Marxist–Leninist group which acted as the military wing of the Reconstituted Spanish Communist Party (PCE–R). During 1976, GRAPO made its presence felt when it murdered four police officers and carried out bombings on the French Lycée and the US Cultural Institute in Madrid, as well as airline offices in Barcelona. It also carried out raids on banks in Madrid, Barcelona and Valencia to fund its operations, and acquired weapons by raiding military armouries in Madrid, Seville and Santiago de Compostela. In December, it kidnapped the president of the Council of State in Madrid and the following month abducted the president of Spain's highest military tribunal. Both were freed unharmed after swift action on the part of the police.

During the next three years, despite arrests of a large number of its members during 1977 and the identification of a number of its safe houses during the following year, GRAPO assassinated a further thirty policemen, the director-general of the prison service, a supreme court judge and a number of senior army officers. In April 1979 one of GRAPO's leaders, Juan Carlos Delgado de Codex, was killed by police and in November another, José María Sánchez, was arrested. Two years later the head of GRAPO, Cerdán Calixto, was killed by police in Barcelona, a similar fate being suffered in December 1982 by his successor, Juan Martin Luna.

In South-East Asia, meanwhile, the 1970s witnessed the appearance of one of the most violent organisations in the history of international terrorism: the Sekigun – better known in the West as the Japanese Red Army (JRA). Formed in 1969 with world revolution as its cause, it was a radical left-wing organisation comprising militant Japanese students who had seen in the student riots in Paris in 1968 a blueprint for the means to bring about world revolution. They believed that their own greater determination, combined with the prevailing social and political circumstances in Japan at that time, would enable them to achieve their objective.

On 21 October 1969 the JRA, under its leader Takaya Shiomi, took to the streets for the first time in an attempt at a show of strength. This failed thanks to the efficiency of the Japanese police whose riot squads made quick work of dispersing the demonstrators. Such was Shiomi's displeasure at the pathetic performance of his force that he expelled a number of its members, saying they could only achieve reformation and redemption in his eyes if they carried out a series of bomb attacks as part of a protest campaign at the forthcoming visit of Japan's prime minister to the United States. A series of rather half-hearted attacks on the police ensued, in which a number of petrol bombs were thrown. Despite the fact that they achieved little, Shiomi re-admitted the expelled members to his organisation.

At the end of March 1970, the JRA carried out its first major operation when a group of nine, armed with pistols and explosives, hijacked a Boeing 727 airliner carrying 131 passengers to the city of Itazuke in western Japan. There the aircraft refuelled before taking off, under the orders of the hijackers, for the North Korean capital of Pyongyang. On arrival, the passengers were released and the terrorists were granted political asylum. This outrage brought the JRA to the attention of the PFLP and in particular George Habash who shortly afterwards travelled to Pyongyang to meet the nine hijackers. Thereafter representatives of PFLP travelled to Japan to establish contact with the JRA leadership and before long members of the organisation were making their way to camps in Lebanon where they underwent training in guerrilla warfare.

During the next two years, the JRA perpetrated a number of robberies and kidnappings within Japan. In January 1972, nine of its members joined forces with another radical group called Keihin Amp Kyoto to form a new organisation, Rengo Sekigun or United Red Army (URA). It was a series of actions by the URA, including a series of bank raids and robberies from gun shops, that finally goaded the Japanese authorities into a crackdown on terrorist activities within the country.

In February of that year the Japanese police tracked down five armed members of the URA to the holiday resort of Karuizawa, located in a range of mountains eighty miles north-west of Tokyo. The gang, led by a man named Tsuneo Mori and a woman named Hiroko Nagata, took refuge in a chalet, taking a woman hostage. A siege developed with more than 1,200 police surrounding the building in the bitter cold of a Japanese winter. Various methods were sought to persuade the terrorists to surrender, but to no avail. The police brought up searchlights and subjected the five and their hostage to a constant barrage of noise transmitted through powerful loudspeakers, but without success.

Eventually, in full view of the Japanese media, whose television cameras were recording every stage of the proceedings, the police assaulted the building, using a large crane to knock holes in the roof and walls through which freezing water was sprayed from powerful hoses. This was followed by copious quantities of tear-gas grenades before assault squads stormed the building. The terrorists fought back, killing two police officers, and eventually the police withdrew, deciding to attack again later under cover of darkness. This they proceeded to do and the terrorists, by now hiding with their hostage in a bedroom on the top floor, surrendered without further resistance.

During subsequent interrogation of the five, the police learned of the brutal regime imposed on members of the URA. This led them to the Japanese Alps and the mountains in the area of Maebashi where fourteen graves were found on wooded slopes, containing victims of URA kangaroo courts who had been sentenced to death. Post-mortems revealed that the occupants had been tied up, tortured, and left to freeze to death. Four of them were women, one of whom was pregnant – a crime for which she had been executed. Other instances of death sentences handed down by the URA included one man being stabbed to death by his younger brothers and a woman being bound and gagged before being placed under the floorboards of a hut, inhabited by the other members of her group, where she died a painful and lingering death. The crackdown on the URA resulted in its destruction as an effective revolutionary force in Japan. Thereafter it supplied volunteers for training for the JRA which by now was working hand-in-glove with the PFLP in the Lebanese capital of Beirut.

By this time the JRA was headed, unusually for a male-dominated society such as Japan, by a woman named Fusako Shigenobu. A founder member of the movement, she was a ruthless fanatic. Originally employed as a nurse in PFLP camps, she had soon graduated up the ladder of the JRA hierarchy until she had been appointed head of the organisation's political committee. Her responsibilities included the planning of operations which were carried out by bodies known as the Military, Organisation and Logistics Committees. Operating under the name of 'Shamira', given to her by her Arab colleagues, Shigenobu worked alongside George Habash and was known to be a close friend of Leila Khaled's.

Europe, the Middle East and Asia were not the only continents in which terrorism spawned during the 1960s and 1970s. In Canada, in 1963, a French–Canadian separatist group called the Front for the Liberation of Quebec (FLQ) was formed by a splinter group from another organisation, the Réseau de Résistance. Initially, it mounted bomb attacks against government targets, English-speaking commercial organisations and those with connections to the United States. A number of arrests were made, among them the three leaders of the FLQ: Gabriel Hudon, Georges Schoeters and Raymond Villeneuve. In the wake of these, a small FLQ splinter group calling itself the Quebec Liberation Army (ALQ) and led by Hudon's younger brother, carried out a series of bank robberies. The members of this group were also arrested and another group took their place, the Revolutionary Army of Quebec. The leader of this group, François Schirm, and four others were jailed for murder in 1965.

During the mid-1960s, the FLQ established links with left-wing extremists in America and resumed its campaign of violence in 1966. This was followed by a number of arrests and there were no further attacks until 1968 when bombs exploded in Montreal and Ottawa. In 1970 the FLQ reached the peak of its activity and during

October of that year kidnapped the British trade commissioner, James Cross, and the Canadian minister of labour, Pierre Laporte, demanding the release of François Schirm and four others. The Canadian authorities arrested 250 suspects and the FLQ retaliated by murdering Laporte. Cross was released in exchange for safe passage to Cuba for the four kidnappers identified as Paul and Jacques Rose, Francis Simard and Bernard Lortie. Thereafter the FLQ became inactive and has remained so.

In the United States, the 1960s saw the formation of a number of groups of extremists together with the advent of political violence connected with black civil rights and the Vietnam War. The period following the assassination in 1963 of President John F. Kennedy witnessed an increase in mass protests and racial violence which began in the south and during the mid-1960s spread to cities throughout the country, eventually culminating in 1967 in periods of massive disorder. The 1960s also saw the formation of organisations which represented the left in North American universities, championing the causes of anti-Vietnam war groups, blacks and other ethnic groups, homosexuals, feminists and any other faction which felt itself to be at a disadvantage. Among these was a left-wing faction called the Students for a Democratic Society (SDS) which was involved in direct action against the US authorities. In 1969, however, SDS splintered into various factions including the October League, Revolutionary Union and New American Movement. These in turn produced other groups which included the Venceremos Brigades, which was an extreme left-wing faction based in California, the Red Guerrilla Family and the New Year's Gang.

One of those spawned from SDS was the Weathermen, a group formed by Bernardine Dohrn and Mark Rudd with the aim of promoting revolution throughout the United States by means of armed struggle. During that year Dohrn and Rudd visited Cuba together with members of the Venceremos Brigades. Attacks were subsequently mounted against government targets and in July 1970 Dohrn, Rudd and another member of the group, William Ayres, were charged *in absentia* with conspiring to carry out a series of bombings. On 29 January 1975, a bomb attack was carried out on a US State Department building which caused damage but no casualties; the Weather Underground, as it was now called, claimed responsibility. In 1977, Rudd surrendered to the US authorities and three years later Bernardine Dorhn and William Ayres were located and arrested in Manhattan.

Prominent among the organisations formed by blacks was the Black Panther Party (BPP) which was founded in 1966 by Huey Newton and Bobby Seale. During the following year it made the headlines when twenty-six armed Black Panthers invaded the state legislature in California to read out a political communiqué. In 1969 twenty-one members of the organisation were arrested in New York and charged with conspiracy to carry out a series of bomb attacks. In June of that year, a major armed confrontation between police and Black Panthers took place in Sacramento, thirteen police officers being wounded. Similar gun battles took place in other cities, including Chicago and Los Angeles. By the early 1970s, however, several of the BPP's leaders had either gone underground, fled abroad or had been imprisoned, and from 1972 onwards the organisation became increasingly inactive.

One of the groups most active during the 1970s was the New World Liberation Front (NWLF), formed in 1973. Although small in number, no more than some twenty members in all, the NWLF was responsible for sixteen bomb attacks in California during 1974. Its targets were large commercial concerns such as the Union Oil Company and the Pacific Gas and Electric Company, both of which suffered damage to their installations by NWLF bomb attacks which continued during the late 1970s.

Another group which enjoyed a period of brief notoriety was the Symbionese Liberation Army (SLA) which was formed in 1973 by a black named Donald DeFreeze. Like the NWLF it numbered only some twenty members who were mostly white and from wealthy backgrounds. In November of that year, members of the SLA murdered a black school head teacher, but two months later those responsible were arrested when police located the group's headquarters. In February 1974, the SLA made headlines when it kidnapped Patricia Hearst, heiress to the Hearst newspaper empire, who was brainwashed to the extent that she subsequently took part in a bank raid in San Francisco. In May, however, the SLA hideout was located and in the gun battle that followed, six members of the group died. Two others were arrested and subsequently received life sentences; Patricia Hearst was sentenced to seven years' imprisonment.

In 1974 the Armed Forces of National Liberation (FALN), a separatist group calling for the independence of the island of Puerto Rico, drew attention to itself when it carried out a bomb attack on a bar in New York, killing four people and injuring fifty-four others. This was followed by further attacks, a total of fifty being perpetrated during 1976, some involving the use of incendiary devices in the city's department stores during the summer. The FALN also turned its attention to major companies and in 1978 attacked banks and stores in Puerto Rico. By the end of 1979 it had carried out a total of 100 bombings. The early 1980s saw it also attacking US military installations on the island.

Further south, in Central and South America, meanwhile, the 1960s had witnessed a number of Marxist-Leninist inspired insurgencies in several countries, taking place predominantly in rural areas. Despite the support of Cuba, those in Argentina, Bolivia, Brazil, Colombia, the Dominican Republic, Ecuador, Guatemala, Paraguay, Peru and Venezuela proved to be failures, some ending in the deaths of principal guerrilla leaders such as Ché Guevara. These abortive campaigns were followed in South America by a second wave of revolutionary violence which took place primarily in towns and cities; those masterminding it in fundamentally wealthy countries, such as Argentina and Uruguay, took advantage of the social, political and economic hardships suffered by the underclasses to drum up support for their aims.

In Argentina some ten terrorist groups were formed during the late 1960s and 1970s. Of these, however, only two could be considered to be of any significance. The largest and best known were the Montoneros who first hit the headlines when on 29 May 1970 they kidnapped former President Pedro Aramburu whom they executed after subjecting him to a 'people's trial'. During the early 1970s they penetrated the Peronist movement and supported the cause of the exiled dictator Juan Peron. Following his return to power in October 1973, however, Peron broke with the Montoneros in May of the following year, two months before his death.

The Montoneros resumed their campaign of violence and two months later, on 15 July 1974, assassinated former Foreign Minister Arturo Mor Roig. In September they kidnapped two brothers named Born for whom a $60 million ransom was paid. On 1 November they murdered the federal police chief and his wife and three months later, on 26 February 1975, kidnapped the US consul, John Egan. That same month, however, saw the Argentinian military assume control of counter-terrorist operations and in December Roberto Quieto, who with Mario Firmenich headed the Montoneros, was arrested. In 1976 the deaths of 1,600 members of the organisation were followed by a further 500 in the first half of 1977. The remainder went into exile that year, with Firmenich and the rest of the leadership fleeing to Italy where they established their base, financed by funds provided by the ransoms from previous kidnap operations.

Unlike the Montoneros, the People's Revolutionary Army (ERP), the military wing of the Argentine Trotskyist Workers' Revolutionary Party, was an army. Commanded by a general staff, it was organised on a regional basis in battalions, companies and platoons. It became of significance in 1972 and soon made its reputation as being one of the most notorious of the guerrilla organisations in Latin America. On 10 April, ERP terrorists carried out two murders: that of the head of Fiat in Argentina, Dr. Oberdan Sallustro, and of General Juan Carlos Sánchez. On 30 April, Rear Admiral Hermes Quijada was assassinated by an ERP gunman, and in May an unsuccessful attempt was made to kidnap an executive of the Ford Motor Company who later died of his wounds. In

December, the oil company Esso paid a ransom of $12 million for one of its managers kidnapped previously.

In February 1973, thirty ERP guerrillas held off a force of troops while raiding an armoury at Cordoba, and in January of the following year seventy guerrillas attacked a garrison at Azul with the intention of taking prisoner a number of senior army officers. A similar attack in August at Catamarca, however, resulted in the guerrillas being routed: nineteen were killed, fifty captured and the remainder scattered. On 23 December 1975, ERP mounted its largest assault when 150 guerrillas attacked a barracks and armoury at Monte Chingolo, diversionary attacks being launched simultaneously against a number of police stations. The following year, however, saw two of ERP's leaders arrested and the organisation suffering heavy casualties, with many of its members fleeing abroad. By 1977 the eight members of the organisation's leadership were in exile in Europe.

In Brazil, the late 1960s saw the birth in February 1968 of a group called National Liberation Action (ALN), formed from a Brazilian Communist Party splinter group under Carlos Marighella. It first came to prominence eighteen months later in September 1969 when, in collaboration with another group, the Revolutionary Movement of 8 October (MR–8), it kidnapped the US Ambassador, Charles Burke Eldbrick, who was freed in return for the release by the government of fifteen prisoners who were flown to Cuba. In November 1969, Carlos Marighella was killed in an ambush by police in São Paulo.

Another prominent Brazilian terrorist group was the Revolutionary Popular Vanguard (VPR) which in October 1968 assassinated a US Navy officer, Captain Chandler, in São Paulo during a series of bombings and attacks on Brazilian and US targets. In March 1969 it kidnapped the Japanese Consul in São Paulo, releasing him in exchange for five prisoners being held in Brazilian jails. During the following month, it tried to abduct the US Consul who was wounded during the attempt. In June the group kidnapped the West German Ambassador in a joint operation with the ALN; he was later freed in exchange for the release of forty prisoners. In September 1969, however, the VPR's leader, Carlos Lamarca, was killed. Despite this, in December 1970 the VPR kidnapped the Swiss Ambassador who was later freed in exchange for the release of seventy prisoners. By now it numbered only some fifty members and the improving economic climate in Brazil, coupled with a crackdown by the security forces following the kidnapping of Ambassador Eldbrick, saw the demise of Brazilian left-wing groups whose leaders were all in prison by the end of 1971.

In Colombia, two major terrorist groups were formed in the latter half of the 1960s. The Fuerzas Armadas Revolucionarias Colombias (FARC) was formed in 1966, but achieved little during the initial years of its existence, partly because of US support for Colombian government counter-insurgency operations. The situation changed in 1977 when FARC started to collaborate with the Army of National Liberation (ELN) and expanded its scope of operations. During the late 1970s, it also began to specialise in kidnappings, demanding large ransoms in return for the release of their hostages and earning Colombia, in particular its capital Bogotá, the sobriquet of the 'kidnap capital of the world'. Initially numbering only some 200, FARC eventually grew to number several thousand well-armed guerrillas, dominating large areas of the country.

The other principal Colombian group was the Movimiento 19 Abril (M-19) formed in 1973 by Carlos Toledo Plata and a former member of FARC, Jaime Bateman. Both had been members of the National Popular Alliance (ANAPO) political party but left after its poor performance in elections in April 1970, switching to armed struggle to further their political ambitions and forming M–19. The group's initial forays into terrorism consisted of kidnapping and bank robberies, but these achieved little. The group had little trouble in recruiting, however, and eventually comprised some 10,000 well-armed guerrillas. Its terrorist network commenced operations in 1976, two years later beginning attacks against government and commercial targets, the latter including US oil companies operating in Colombia. These were highlighted by the kidnappings of the Nicaraguan Ambassador and a member of Texaco Petroleum who died when police attacked the terrorists' hideout on 4 January 1979.

In El Salvador, the late 1970s saw the Farabundo Marti Popular Forces of Liberation (FPL) as the most active of the guerrilla groups in the country. During 1978 and throughout 1979, the FPL carried out a number of assassinations and bomb attacks, some against US interests in the country. In November 1979, the group murdered the South African Ambassador as a sign of its solidarity with the black movements there.

The FPL collaborated with another group, the People's Revolutionary Army (ERP), which had been formed in 1971 and made its first appearance with a series of bomb attacks on government and commercial targets during 1973. In 1975, the ERP expanded the scope of its terrorist operations, attacking small towns and police posts. In 1978 it mounted forty bomb attacks in the capitals of El Salvador's six states and carried out a number of assassinations.

In Guatemala, ten separate terrorist groups were active during the 1960s and 1970s. Prominent among these were the Rebel Armed Forces (FAR) which during the 1960s concentrated on guerrilla operations in rural areas. Then a government counter-insurgency campaign, supported by elements of the US Army Special Forces, during 1967 forced the FAR to switch to urban operations after it had suffered heavy casualties. In August 1968, it ambushed the US Ambassador, John Gordon Mein, with the purpose of kidnapping him but he was killed during the attempt. In March 1970, they kidnapped the US Labour Attaché and a few days later murdered the West German Ambassador. By now government countermeasures were taking their toll of the FAR which until 1975 indulged in only sporadic operations. By the summer of 1978, however, it had recovered its strength and by 1979 was operating once more in Guatemala's cities.

In Mexico, some nine groups appeared during the 1970s, but all were short-lived. The most violent and ruthless was the 23rd September Communist League which began its activities in 1974.

Among its principal targets were members of the Mexican security forces; from June to August 1975, it killed some twenty-two policemen. The group collaborated closely with another group, the People's Armed Revolutionary Forces (FRAP), with whom it carried out on 14 September 1977 eighteen bomb attacks on banks and government buildings in Mexico City, Oaxaca and Guadalajara.

The early 1970s saw the beginnings of a guerrilla warfare campaign in Nicaragua waged by the Sandanista National Liberation Front (FSLN), established in 1958 by Carlos Fonseca Amador, against the right-wing dictatorship of Anastasio Somoza Debayle whose family had ruled the country since 1934. In December 1974 the organisation attracted world attention when it carried out a raid in Managua and kidnapped a large number of members of high-ranking Nicaraguans attending a function, these subsequently being released for a ransom of $1 million.

Despite this success the FSLN, or 'Sandanistas' as they were popularly known, suffered a series of setbacks during the next two years, losing three of their leaders in clashes with the security forces. In 1977 the FSLN split into three factions. One, led by Tomás Borge Martinez and supported by Cuba, favoured continuation of operations in rural areas. The second, led by Jaime Wheelock, Luis Carrión Cruz and Carlos Nuñez Tellez, followed the strategy of rural guerrilla and urban terrorist operations. The third, led by Daniel and Humberto Ortega Saavedra and Tirado López, opted for military attacks on towns and cities.

In 1978 a major offensive was launched by the FLSN but it proved unsuccessful. Heavy fighting took place and it is estimated that as many as 5,000 people were killed and some 16,000 wounded. In 1979, despite this setback, the FSLN succeeded in toppling the Somoza regime and in July formed a government under Daniel Ortega and Moisés Hassan Morales.

In Uruguay the left-wing National Liberation Movement (MLN), better known as the 'Tupamaros' (taking their name from that of the Peruvian Indian leader Tupac Amaru who was executed by the Spaniards in 1782), held sway as the country's only guerrilla and terrorist organisation. Formed in the early 1960s by Raúl Sendic, the MLN began operations in 1963, robbing banks and attacking government and diplomatic targets, the latter being notably American and Brazilian. Throughout the rest of the decade, the MLN went from strength to strength, continuing its campaign of bombings and assassinations of members of the security forces. In July 1970 it kidnapped a US Agency for International Development (AID) officer, Dan Mitrione, demanding the release of 150 MLN members who were in prison. Mitrione was murdered in August following the capture of the MLN leadership.

In 1971, the MLN made the headlines world-wide when it kidnapped the British Ambassador, Geoffrey Jackson, who was held hostage for eight months before being released. In 1972, it began an assassination campaign aimed at the individuals it claimed were behind the operations of right-wing death squads in Peru. In May of that year, however, it suffered a major setback when the Peruvian security forces uncovered full details of its organisation, recruitment system, *modus operandi*, 200 safe houses and hideouts, two fully equipped laboratories and a hospital. This resulted in the arrest of 2,600 people and the deaths of forty-two, and was followed by the capture of two of the MLN's principal leaders, Raúl Sendic and Amílcar Manera Lluveras, a blow from which the organisation never fully recovered.

Meanwhile, in Venezuela, 1961 saw the formation of the Armed Forces of National Liberation (FALN) from a small nucleus of activists from the Movement of the Revolutionary Left and the Venezuelan Communist Party (PCV), reinforced two years later by a number of Army officers who deserted from the government forces. Initial targets were mainly US interests, attacks being launched in 1962 in retaliation for American pressure on Cuba during the missile crisis in October. During August 1963, the deputy head of the US military mission in Venezuela, Colonel James Chenault, was kidnapped in Caracas but was subsequently released unharmed. Shortly afterwards, the FALN lost the support of the PCV for its armed struggle in the wake of a major defeat for the latter in the presidential and congressional elections and an offer from the new government for PCV activities to be legalised if it renounced terrorism.

Thereafter, led by Douglas Bravo and Elías Manuit Camero, the FALN turned to guerrilla warfare in rural areas. Support was provided by Cuba until 1969 when it was cut off as a result of pressure from the Soviet Union which wished to establish diplomatic and trade relations with the Venezuelan government. This was a major blow to the FALN which by 1972 was a spent force.

The latter part of the 1970s saw another group, the Red Flag, active in Venezuela. Led by Carlos Betancourt and Gabriel Puerta, who were arrested and imprisoned in 1973 but escaped in 1975, it financed its activities by kidnapping politicians and wealthy businessmen for whose release large ransoms were demanded and paid. Terrorist activity was mainly directed against Venezuelan government security forces and continued until 1978 when it subsided, partly as a result of the recapture of Betancourt.

Support for left-wing terrorist groups in Latin America came primarily from the Communist state of Cuba under its dictator Fidel Castro. In January 1966, the Cuban government and Communist Party held a gathering heralded as the 'First Conference of Solidarity of the Peoples of Africa, Asia and Latin America', but better known subsequently as the 'Tricontinental Conference'. This was attended by 513 delegates representing eighty-three groups from countries including: the Dominican Republic, Guatemala, Peru, Venezuela, Colombia, Panama, South Africa, South-West Africa, Zaire, Rhodesia, Angola, Mozambique, Cyprus, North Yemen, South Yemen, Palestine, Cambodia, Laos and South Korea. Also in attendance were representatives of the Soviet Union which was intending to exert its malign influence through the Communist Parties in each country concerned.

The avowed aims of the conference were wrapped in verbose and convoluted declarations, but in effect its purpose was the co-ordination of international terrorism. Ten months later a network of camps was established in Cuba to train terrorists from Europe, Asia, Africa and the Americas. During the 1960s–70s some 1,500 guerrillas passed through these camps each year, being trained by Russian and Cuban instructors in national groups of approximately twenty men for security purposes, with courses in guerrilla warfare and sabotage lasting up to six months. Promising candidates also received training as intelligence agents and the best of them were subsequently despatched to Moscow and to the Patrice Lumumba University where they underwent indoctrination and further training.

Among the trainee guerrillas sent to Cuba were Palestinians of the PFLP who first appeared in Cuba in 1966 and continued to arrive in large numbers throughout the rest of the decade and the ensuing 1970s. In December 1973, Cuba sent the first of a large number of instructors to South Yemen where they appeared in training camps belonging to Wadi Haddad and the DFLP under Nayef Hawatmeh. Thereafter, Cuban instructors made their appearance in training camps established elsewhere in the Middle East and North Africa, notably Lebanon, Algeria and Libya, and farther south in countries such as Angola and Mozambique.

As outlined earlier, by the end of the 1960s the PFLP had established close relations with left-wing terrorist groups world-wide. In May 1972, a terrorist summit was held in a Palestinian refugee camp at Baddawi in Lebanon. It was attended by the Red Army Faction, represented by Andreas Baader, together with Fusako Shigenobu of the Japanese Red Army and Abu Iyad of Black September who was accompanied by Fuad Shemali, another of the group's senior members. Among others who attended were representatives of the Provisional IRA (PIRA), the Liberation Front in Iran, Turkey's People's Liberation Army and a number of Central and South American terrorist groups. The outcome of this summit was the formation of an international network of terrorist groups which had agreed to collaborate.

At the end of May came the first of the outrages to be perpetrated by the new terror collective. Three months earlier, on 29 February, a 24-year-old member of the JRA, Kozo Okamoto, left Japan and flew via Paris to Beirut under the alias of Daisuke

Namba. There he had met two other Japanese, Takeshi Ukudaira and Yasuiki Yashuda, who were using the aliases of Jiro Sugisaki and Ken Torio respectively. All three subsequently underwent guerrilla warfare training by the PFLP at a camp at Baalbek, the curriculum including the use of automatic weapons and grenades.

On 23 May the three men left Beirut and flew to Paris from where they travelled to Frankfurt. Two days later they travelled by train to Rome where on 30 May they met Fusako Shigenobu herself who issued them with forged passports, three Czech VZ58 7.62mm assault rifles and fragmentation grenades. She also briefed them on their forthcoming task which was a joint PFLP/JRA operation.

On the night of 30 May, Okamoto, Ukudaira and Yashuda flew on an Air France flight from Rome to Lod Airport at Tel Aviv. When the conveyor belt delivered their suitcases they retrieved their weapons and opened fire indiscriminately into the crowds of travellers around them, while throwing their grenades with deadly effect. Twenty-five people were killed and seventy-two were wounded in the massacre. Ironically, Ukudaira and Yashuda also died: one accidentally shot by one of his accomplices and the other killed by one of his own grenades. Kozo Okamoto survived and was captured by Israeli security forces; under interrogation, he provided full details of the JRA/PFLP operation. He was tried and sentenced to life imprisonment.

The massacre brought universal condemnation and opprobrium on the Palestinians and their cause once details of the connection became known. It also caused a split within the PFLP. George Habash, who believed firmly that terrorist action should be restricted to military targets, and only Israeli ones outside Israel itself, was violently opposed to Wadi Haddad's policy of indiscriminate acts of terrorism against civilian targets and roundly condemned it, dissociating the PFLP from any acts of international terrorism. This resulted in a bitter and very public disagreement between the two men and Haddad stormed out. Immediately afterwards, he announced that he and his followers had formed a new organisation, the Popular Front for the Liberation of Palestine – Special Operations Group (PFLP–SOG).

In December 1972, the PFLP–SOG carried out the first of a number of efforts to obtain the release of Kozo Okamoto. A group of Black September terrorists occupied the Israeli embassy in Bangkok and demanded his release together with that of thirty-five other prisoners languishing in Israeli prisons. Eventually, however, they settled for a safe passage out of Thailand.

During the following year, the PFLP–SOG and JRA jointly took the stage again. On 20 July 1973 one of the latter's members, Osamu Maruoka, who was reported to be the husband of Fusako Shigenobu, boarded a Tokyo-bound Boeing 747 of Japan Airlines at Amsterdam. Also on the flight were four accomplices: three Arabs and a South American woman, travelling under the name of Peralta, who was the leader of the group. Her identity has never been definitely established, but she was later identified by one source as a Christian Iraqi woman named Katie George Thomas.

The hijack was precipitated by accident when Peralta accidentally dropped a grenade while drinking champagne in the first-class cabin. It exploded, killing her and wounding a member of the cabin crew. The other terrorists immediately sprang into action, but having taken over the aircraft and ordered the pilot to fly south, were unsure what to do next as Peralta had been the only one briefed as to the group's intended destination.

The 747 flew over Germany, Switzerland and Italy, heading for Lebanon. At Beirut, however, it was refused permission to land and an attempt to land at Basra was unsuccessful because the runways were inadequate. Finally, it was permitted to land at Dubai where it remained for three days, its occupants suffering from the heat inside the cabins. The wounded steward was disembarked, as was Peralta's body though this was subsequently returned to the aircraft at the demand of the terrorists.

Having been refuelled, the aircraft took off and once again the terrorists sought sanctuary, but none was forthcoming. Requests for permission to land were refused by Bahrain, Abu Dhabi and Saudi

Arabia, and a further request to Beirut also met with a refusal. Syria permitted refuelling at Damascus, but it was not until Libya eventually agreed on the grounds of 'humanitarian reasons' that the aircraft's aimless wandering around the skies came to an end. No sooner had the passengers and crew disembarked in haste via the emergency exits than the terrorists set the fuses on the explosive charges they had planted around the aircraft and shortly afterwards the 747 exploded in a ball of flame.

The hijackers were initially welcomed with open arms by the Libyans who claimed that the hijack had been carried out by Japanese, Palestinians and Ecuadorians, the latter obviously being a reference to the mysterious Peralta. However, this statement met with a denial from the PLO. This was followed by a swift change in tune by the Libyans who announced in effect that the hijackers were criminals and would be tried under Islamic Law for armed robbery. Western observers found this development strange when bearing in mind the known involvement of Colonel Muammar Gadaffi's regime with terrorist organisations and considering the normal punishment for robbery under Islamic Law which is the severing of the offender's right hand. The fate of the three Arab hijackers is unknown, but Osamu Maruoka served a year in a Libyan prison before being released and allowed to make his way back to the fold of the JRA.

January 1974 also saw the PFLP–SOG and JRA in action together again when on the 31st two of their number, Haruo Wako and Yoshiaki Yamada, accompanied by two members of PFLP, blew up an oil storage tank at a refinery in Singapore. Although subsequently cornered by Singaporean security forces, they succeeded in escaping and hijacking a ferry in which they sailed out into international waters, with five hostages, from where they demanded an aircraft and safe passage from Singapore.

Six days later the PFLP–SOG mounted a rescue mission when a group of five terrorists stormed the Japanese embassy in Kuwait, taking the Ambassador and twenty-eight others hostage. They subsequently demanded that the Singaporean authorities fly the five terrorists and five hostages on the ferry to Kuwait; in return for this, the Ambassador and the other hostages in the embassy would be released. Capitulation on the part of Singapore was swift and shortly afterwards a Japan Airlines aircraft flew the five terrorists to Kuwait where it collected the five Palestinians before flying all ten terrorists to sanctuary in South Yemen.

Perhaps the best examples of operations of the Terror International, however, are those which were carried out or masterminded by the Venezuelan terrorist Ilich Ramírez Sánchez, more often than not referred to by his *nom de guerre* of 'Carlos'.

Ramírez was the eldest son of a Venezuelan millionaire revolutionary lawyer named José Altagracia Ramírez Navas who fervently espoused the Communist cause and inspired the strongest possible Communist zeal in his offspring. From a very early age, he was indoctrinated with extreme Marxist ideology and cut his teeth as a revolutionary while engaging in urban guerrilla operations conducted by the various Venezuelan groups opposed to the dictatorship of President Raul Leoni.

In 1966, having finished his studies at the Fermin Toro Lycée in Caracas, a known hotbed of radicalism, Ramírez reportedly travelled abroad to complete his education. It has previously been alleged that he eventually made his way to Cuba where he underwent training at Camp Mantanzas, near Havana, in the skills of political indoctrination, subversion, sabotage and guerrilla warfare. However, there has never been any official confirmation of Ilich's presence in Cuba during this period. Indeed, in his book *Jackal – The Secret Wars of Carlos the Jackal*, author John Follain states that Ramírez denied undergoing training in Cuba; he also maintains that such reports emanated originally from the United States' Central Intelligence Agency (CIA) which had no evidence of such.

In August 1966, Ramírez arrived in London where he lived with his mother and three brothers while continuing his education at a college in Kensington. In early 1968, accompanied by his father, who had arrived from Venezuela during the latter part of the previous year, and one of his brothers, Lenin, he travelled to Paris with the aim of securing a place at the Sorbonne. This plan, however, was frustrated by the student riots which took place in May, causing turmoil throughout Paris.

Later that year, Ramírez and Lenin appeared in Moscow at the Patrice Lumumba University in Moscow where they spent the next year undergoing training and indoctrination. By all accounts they also enjoyed the high life which they could easily afford courtesy of a generous allowance from their father. Ramírez acquired a name for wild behaviour, including drinking to excess and womanising, and apparently had to be rebuked on more than one occasion.

In March 1969, he was involved in a demonstration outside the Libyan embassy in Moscow by Libyan students protesting at the new government of Colonel Muammar Gadaffi, who had just taken over the country in a *coup d'état*. During the demonstration, Ramírez was arrested for throwing a bottle of ink, aimed at the embassy but flung wide of the mark, through the window of an adjoining house. During the following months his already poor academic performance deteriorated even further and in 1970 the university authorities, their patience exhausted, expelled him and his brother.

In July of that year Ramírez travelled to Beirut where he made contact with the PFLP. Having been accepted, he was given the *nom de guerre* of 'Carlos'. From there he went to the Jordanian capital of Amman and a training camp in the hills north of the city where he joined other recruits to the Palestinian cause. There he underwent training in weapons, explosives and political indoctrination. Thereafter he was sent to another camp for further specialist training. In September he took part in the fighting against the Jordanians, sufficiently impressing Wadi Haddad that the latter admitted him fully to the ranks of the PFLP. Before the end of the year, however, he was ordered to travel to Beirut where he underwent further training under Haddad himself.

In February 1971, on the orders of George Habash, Ramírez returned to London where he studied at the University of London and the Central London Polytechnic, while once again enjoying life to the full. His high living was financed not only by the continuing generous allowance from his father, but also by funds from an account opened for him by a member of the PFLP, a Lebanese named Fouad Awad, who used the Ecuadorian *nom de guerre* of Antonio Dagues-Bouvier.

During this period, Ramírez took his orders from an Algerian named Mohamed Boudia, Wadi Haddad's chief operative in Europe, who was based in Paris. One of his primary tasks was to identify potential targets for assassination or kidnapping and he gradually drew up a list of names and addresses of some 500 individuals connected to the worlds of politics, business and the arts. Among the better known of these were Prime Minister Edward Heath, business tycoons Edward Sieff and Lord Sainsbury, publisher Lord Weidenfeld, film directors Richard Attenborough and Sam Wanamaker, and singer Vera Lynn.

In December 1971, Ramírez narrowly escaped arrest when the Metropolitan Police Special Branch visited and searched his mother's flat, having previously raided the house of a friend after the discovery of an arms cache elsewhere. Ramírez and his mother were present, but neither were taken in for questioning, although he was kept under surveillance for a few days afterwards.

From the latter half of 1972 to the summer of 1973, he taught Spanish at a secretarial college in London's Mayfair district. During this period, he met a Colombian woman, 37-year-old lawyer Maria Nydia Romero de Tobon, who was a member of the Colombian Communist Party. He quickly established a close relationship with her and subsequently recruited her to his cause, using her to help him establish a network of safe houses in London and to store false passports and money for him.

It was the death in June 1973 of Mohamed Boudia, at the hands of an Israeli Mossad 'Wrath of God' assassination team, that brought an end to Ramírez's *dolce vita* in London. Until now he had been kept in reserve by his terrorist masters until such time as his skills could be put to good use. Now he was activated as the PLO's principal assassin, operating under the orders of Boudia's replacement, a 32-year-old Lebanese named Michel Moukharbel. Having lived in France since the 1960s, the latter acted as a quartermaster for Black September in Europe, maintaining a stock of weapons, explosives and false passports.

It was at this juncture that a major event occurred which would have far-reaching consequences as far as Ramírez himself was concerned. On 6 October, the fast of Yom Kippur (Day of Atonement), Egypt and Syria attacked Israel which was caught completely by surprise. Israeli forces were driven back beyond the ceasefire lines of the Six Day War of 1967, but during the following eighteen days of fighting they regrouped and counter-attacked on the Egyptian front, crossing the Suez Canal and establishing a bridgehead on its west bank. In the north, meanwhile, they drove a wedge into Syria. Any further Israeli advances, however, were forestalled by the intervention of Russia and the United States acting in concert with the United Nations to halt the conflict.

In the meantime, Ramírez had moved to Paris where he and Moukharbel established a safe house in a villa in the town of Villiers-sur-Marne, south of Paris, where they stored weapons and radio communications equipment. The villa was also the headquarters of a group of the Turkish People's Liberation Army which was to prove its undoing. French police, acting on a tip-off from the Israelis, stopped a car on the French border with Italy and questioned its occupants who confessed to having delivered a consignment of explosives from Bulgaria. The villa was raided and Ramírez's cache of weapons and equipment was discovered. Ramírez and Moukharbel fled France and returned to London where they received orders from the PFLP to begin operations as part of a campaign to disrupt American initiatives for a peace settlement in the aftermath of the Yom Kippur War.

On 30 December 1973, Ramírez carried out the first of the many terrorist attacks which later would be attributed to him. Just before 7.00 p.m. he called at the home of Edward 'Teddy' Sieff, the chairman of Marks & Spencer and a leading figure in the Zionist establishment. Entering the house at pistol-point, he forced the butler, who had answered the door, to lead him to Sieff who was at that moment in the bathroom. Ramírez shot Sieff in the face, but the latter was saved from almost certain death by his teeth which deflected the bullet. Fortunately for him, Ramírez fled without ascertaining that he had succeeded in killing his victim. Next day, the PFLP claimed responsibility for the murder attempt.

On 24 January 1974, a man threw a shoe box containing a bomb into a branch of the Israeli Hapoalim Bank in the Cheapside area of the City of London. It bounced off a door and only the detonator exploded without activating the charge itself, but a window was shattered and a secretary was injured by fragments. A witness gave a description of the bomber which matched that of Ramírez exactly. Once again, the PFLP claimed responsibility for the attack and forensic analysis identified the explosive as a type previously used by the group

Despite the police hunt for the perpetrator of these two crimes, Ramírez remained in London, living with a young Spanish Basque girl, Maria Angeles Otaola Baranca, in a flat in Hereford Road, Bayswater. He travelled to Europe, using aliases of various nationalities for which he had forged passports. When not in use, these and other documents were kept for him by his Colombian girlfriend, Maria Nydia Romero de Tobon, who also kept false documents and money for Moukharbel and Fouad Awad.

In June 1974, Ramírez returned to Paris where he lived in a small apartment in the Rue Toullier, in a student quarter on the Left Bank, belonging to another of his numerous girlfriends, a Venezuelan student named Nancy Sánchez. The area was ideal for him as it enabled him to come and go unnoticed and without anyone asking any awkward questions. He also had the use of other apartments, each belonging to a woman with whom he had established a relationship. In August he carried out bomb attacks on the offices of three newspapers: the Jewish *L'Arche* and the right-wing *L'Aurore* and *Minute*, both of which supported the Israelis. Responsibility was claimed by the Mohamed Boudia Commando. A car bomb attack on the Maison de Radio-France broadcasting station failed when the charge failed to explode because of a faulty timer. At the same time, he and Moukharbel were planning a major operation, namely an attack on the French embassy in The Hague, Holland, to be carried out by members of the JRA.

On 13 September three Japanese terrorists, Jun Nishikawa, Junzo Ukudaira (younger brother of Takeshi Ukudaira, who had taken part in the attack at Lod Airport on 30 May 1972) and Haruo Wako, attacked the embassy, wounding two Dutch police officers who happened to appear on the scene and taking hostage the Ambassador, Count Jacques Senard, and ten of his staff. Their demands were for one million dollars in cash, the release of Yoshiaki Yamada (one of the JRA terrorists who, with Wako, had taken part in the JRA operation in Singapore nine months earlier, but who had subsequently been arrested on his arrival in France later in the year on Fusako Shigenobu's abortive fund-raising operation) and an aircraft and safe passage to the Middle East.

Two days later, on 15 September, while negotiations between the terrorists and the Dutch government continued, Ramírez carried out an attack in the Paris district of St-Germain des Prés, hurling an American M-26 fragmentation grenade into a crowded store, which killed two people and wounded thirty-four. The weapon was subsequently identified as one of seventy-five stolen by the Red Army Faction from a US Army base at Niesau, West Germany, in June 1972. Two days later the terrorists' demands were met although the sum of a million dollars was reduced to $300,000 and that was confiscated by the Syrians on the group's arrival at Damascus after a tour of the Middle East during which all other airports were closed to them. Shortly afterwards, Ramírez carried out the murder of the military attaché at the Uruguay embassy in Paris, Colonel Ramon Trabal, who had previously been employed on counterterrorist duties against the Tupamaro guerrillas in Uruguay.

The beginning of 1975 saw no let-up in Ramírez's operations. On 13 January he and an accomplice, a West German named Johannes Weinrich, opened fire with a Soviet-manufactured RPG-7 anti-tank rocket launcher on an El-Al Boeing 707, carrying 136 passengers bound for New York, as it taxied on to the runway at Paris's Orly airport. They missed with their first rocket, hitting instead a Yugoslav Airlines DC-9. A second rocket also missed, impacting on a nearby building. Ramírez and Weinrich then fled, dropping a Russian pistol on the ground and later abandoning their car which was found in a nearby suburb with the rocket launcher on the back seat.

Six days later Ramírez tried again at Orly, this time in the company of three Palestinians. However, a police officer observed the group preparing its rocket-launcher on a terrace of the airport buildings overlooking one of the runways. He opened fire with his submachine-gun and Ramírez and his accomplices fled, one of them hurling a grenade at pursuing police. Another of them pointed the rocket-launcher at an El-Al aircraft, carrying 222 passengers, which was 400 metres away and beginning to taxi towards the runway, but then panicked and ran after his accomplices.

Ramírez slipped away unnoticed, but the three Palestinians took refuge in the airport lavatories, taking ten people hostage. Seventeen hours of negotiations between French government officials and the terrorists followed before the latter were allowed to leave on an Air France flight to Baghdad after releasing their hostages. Later a Russian pistol and grenades were found in two abandoned hire cars. Further investigations by the French police identified the man who had hired the vehicles as Johannes Weinrich, known to them and the German authorities as a German left-wing lawyer and anarchist, living in Frankfurt, with connections to the Red Army Faction. Two months later, Weinrich was arrested in Frankfurt; after eight months in prison, he jumped bail and disappeared.

In March 1975, two members of the JRA were arrested in Stockholm while photographing and carrying out surveillance on the building which accommodates the embassies of a number of countries including Austria and the Lebanon. The men, Jun Nishikawa (who had taken part in the raid, masterminded by Ramírez, on the French embassy in The Hague) and Kazuo Tohira, were deported to Japan where, under questioning by police, they revealed details of JRA fund-raising plans. One involved the kidnapping and ransoming of Japanese businessmen in Europe, the other an attack on a Lebanese embassy in Scandinavia with hostages being taken and a ransom being demanded for their release.

Fusako Shigenobu was determined to obtain the release of the two men and in August five members of the JRA attacked the US consulate and the Swedish embassy in Kuala Lumpur, Malaysia, taking fifty hostages, including the American Consul, Robert Stebbins, and the Swedish chargé d'affaires, Fredrik Bergenstrahle. Shigenobu demanded the release from Japanese jails of seven members of the JRA and an aircraft and safe passage to Libya. The Japanese government agreed to these demands but two of the seven refused to go. The remaining five were flown to Kuala Lumpur where they were joined by the five terrorists who, after releasing their hostages, were permitted to fly to Tripoli.

In France, meanwhile, the French security service, the Direction de la Surveillance du Territoire (DST), and police were hot on the trail of the terrorists who had carried out the bombings in Paris and the two abortive attacks at Orly. Although they had managed to trace the origins of the vehicles and weapons used, they had no clues as to the identities of those responsible. In early June, however, reportedly as the result of tip-offs by the French intelligence service, the Service de Documentation et du Contre Espionnage (SDECE), and the CIA, Moukharbel was arrested by the Lebanese authorities at Beirut airport, but was released after questioning. On returning to France he was permitted to enter the country, but was kept under surveillance by the DST as he made his way to an apartment where he was later joined by Ramírez and Wilfried Böse, a member of the Red Army Faction and friend of Johannes Weinrich, Ramírez's accomplice at Orly.

On 7 June, Michel Moukharbel was arrested in Beirut while boarding a flight to Paris. A search of his briefcase revealed false passports, a large sum of money and documents which appeared to be plans for terrorist operations. Under interrogation, meanwhile, he revealed his connection with the PFLP. This information was passed to the chief of the SDECE station at the French embassy.

Unfortunately, however, security in the Lebanese police was somewhat lacking and news of Moukharbel's arrest also found its way to the ears of the PFLP and subsequently Ramírez.

On 13 June Moukharbel was released and flew to Paris where he met Ramírez at the Rue Toullier apartment of the latter's girlfriend, Nancy Sánchez. On 20 June, Moukharbel travelled to London, but was refused entry by the British authorities who had been warned by their French opposite numbers. On returning to France, he was arrested by the DST and under questioning admitted to knowing Ramírez but maintained that he was no one of any importance. After five days of interrogation, however, he broke down and also divulged the address of the latter's apartment. On the evening of 27 June three officers of the DST's international anti-terrorist squad, including its head, Chief Commissioner Jean Herranz, accompanied by Moukharbel, arrived at the apartment in the Rue Toullier. On being confronted by the DST officers and Moukharbel, Ramírez drew a 9mm pistol and shot all four, killing Moukharbel and the two junior DST officers, and wounding Chief Commissioner Herranz – it later transpired that the DST officers had been unarmed, having foolishly decided not to take their pistols with them.

Ramírez succeeded in escaping from France, travelling south to Lyons and then to the port of Marseilles, despite the dragnet that was mounted to apprehend him. The consequent publicity resulted in his being identified in London as Ilich Ramírez Sánchez and led to the discovery in a bedsitter in Bayswater of a cache of pistols, grenades, explosives and an Iranian passport. Further investigations led to his Colombian lawyer girlfriend and banker, Maria Nydia Romero de Tobon, who was found in possession of forged passports belonging to him.

In France, meanwhile, further investigations by the DST and police tracked down other girlfriends of Ramírez's and the apartments which he had used as safe houses. A search of one in the Rue Amélie uncovered a large cache of arms, explosives, forging equipment, false passports, target lists and plans of buildings bombed during the previous year. They also uncovered connections between Ramírez and agents of the Cuban DGI in France, which led to the expulsion of three diplomats from the Cuban embassy in Paris. Such was the media coverage that within a very short time Europe became too hot for Ramírez who was meanwhile making his way by boat to sanctuary in Algeria. However, it would not be long before he made his next appearance.

On the morning of Sunday 21 December 1975, a group of five men and a woman entered the headquarters of the Organisation of Petroleum Exporting Countries (OPEC) in the centre of the Austrian capital of Vienna. The group was led by none other than Ramírez. Two of his accomplices were Hans-Joachim Klein and Gabriele Kröcher-Tiedemann, members of a West German terrorist group called Revolutionaire Zellen (Revolutionary Cells). Known popularly as RZ, the group was an offshoot of the Red Army Faction formed in 1973 by one of its members, Wilfried Böse. The other three were a Lebanese, a Palestinian and a Yemeni identified only by their *noms de guerre* of Khalid, Yussef and Joseph.

On reaching the first floor, all six produced machine-pistols and entered the reception area firing wildly. Klein put the telephone switchboard out of action with shots from a handgun, but not before the very brave female receptionist had succeeded in telephoning the police and raising the alarm. Two Austrian police officers in the reception area attempted to resist, but one was shot dead by Kröcher-Tiedemann while the other was pushed into a nearby office as the terrorists ran towards the conference room where the OPEC oil ministers were gathered. Seconds later, an Iraqi security guard attached to Iraq's OPEC delegation tackled Kröcher-Tiedemann, but was shot dead by her. Shortly afterwards a member of the Libyan delegation attempted to wrest Ramírez's machine-pistol from him but was killed by the latter who drew a pistol.

Meanwhile, the surviving Austrian police officer had also succeeded in using a telephone, from the office into which he had been pushed by Ramírez, to call the Vienna police headquarters. Minutes later a squad of eight armed police arrived at the OPEC building, by which time the terrorists had rounded up all eleven oil ministers and fifty-one staff. After coming under the terrorists' fire from the windows of the building, three officers gained the stairs and reached the first floor, but were driven back after a firefight in which one terrorist, Hans-Joachim Klein, was hit in the stomach and a police officer was wounded in the buttocks. Shortly afterwards, one of the female hostages and the wounded police officer were permitted to leave the building, taking with them a document listing the terrorists' demands. These included the broadcasting by Austrian radio of a political communiqué drafted by Ramírez and an aircraft and safe passage for his group and their hostages to the Middle East.

Ramírez and his gang had taken sixty-two hostages, including the oil ministers of all the OPEC member countries. Negotiations between the terrorists and the Austrian authorities ensued, being conducted through the night by the Iraqi chargé d'affaires in Vienna, Riyadh al-Azzawi, who acted as the intermediary. Food was sent into the building and Hans-Joachim Klein was taken to Vienna's hospital for treatment for his bullet wound which was serious. The Austrian government quickly caved in to Ramírez's demands. The latter's communiqué, a verbose document full of demands and threats, was broadcast and an Austrian Airlines DC–9 was made ready at Vienna's airport.

Early in the morning of Monday 22 December the terrorists, including Klein who had been returned to them after medical treatment, and their hostages were taken to the airport in a bus with curtains drawn over its windows. There they boarded the DC–9 which took off just after 9 o'clock; it was only when the aircraft was airborne that Ramírez revealed that the destination was to be Algiers.

Two and a half hours later the aircraft landed at Algiers where it was met by the Foreign Minister, Abdel Aziz Bouteflika. The wounded Hans-Joachim Klein was immediately carried off the aircraft and taken away in an ambulance. During the next five hours Ramírez negotiated with the Algerians, demanding an aircraft that would fly his gang and their hostages to their ultimate destination, the South Yemen capital of Aden. The Algerians refused, stating that they had no such aircraft available. Ramírez was thus forced to change his plans and decided to fly to the Libyan capital of Tripoli instead. Meanwhile the hostages remained on the aircraft, awaiting their fate. Eventually, all but fifteen hostages were released; among those who remained were the Saudi Arabian and Iranian oil ministers, Sheikh Ahmed Zaki Yamani and Dr. Jamshid Amouzegar.

At 5 p.m. local time, the aircraft took off again and flew to Tripoli where it circled the airport while Ramírez radioed a demand that the Libyan prime minister, Major Abdul Jalloud, should meet him at the airport to conduct negotiations. Having landed at just after 7 p.m., Ramírez received a cool reception from the Libyans, Jalloud keeping him waiting for an hour and a half before boarding the aircraft to talk with him. Negotiations were conducted throughout the night on behalf of Ramírez by Khalid, his second-in-command, who went into the airport control tower with the Libyan and Algerian oil ministers, with the Austrian Ambassador to Libya acting as intermediary between Khalid and the Libyans. The terrorists' demands were simple: they wanted a large ransom from Saudi Arabia and Iran in return for the lives of Sheikh Yamani and Dr. Amouzegar.

At midnight on 22 December, King Khaled of Saudi Arabia telephoned the Shah of Iran. An hour later a banker in Zurich received a telephone call and orders to transfer a large sum of money to a bank in Aden, into the account of the PFLP–SOG. The amount was never revealed, but subsequent reports from intelligence and other sources put it at between twenty and fifty million dollars.

News of the payment of the ransom was relayed to Ramírez in the early hours of 23 December, one of the conditions of the ransom being that the remaining hostages would be released in Algiers once Wadi Haddad had received the money in Aden. As a gesture of goodwill, he released a further seven hostages, including the Libyan and Algerian oil ministers.

Shortly afterwards, the DC–9 took off once more and headed for Algiers where it arrived just before 4 a.m. There Ramírez and his gang awaited confirmation from Wadi Haddad that the ransom money had been received before disembarking with their hostages from the aircraft. While waiting in the airport VIP lounge, however, Khalid approached Sheikh Yamani and Dr. Amouzegar who were in conversation with the Algerian Foreign Minister, Abdel Aziz Bouteflika. As he did so, an Algerian security guard blocked his way and Bouteflika, realising that Khalid was distraught and posed a threat to the two oil ministers, handed him a drink at which point Algerian security guards surrounded Khalid and relieved him of a pistol. He subsequently admitted that he had intended to kill Yamani and Amouzegar.

Having handed the hostages over to the Algerian authorities, Ramírez and his accomplices were driven off in a convoy of three cars. The OPEC saga was over, but it was not the last that the world would hear of Ramírez.

Accounts differ as to who conceived the plan for the OPEC raid. Some point the finger at Ramírez himself, stating that he approached Wadi Haddad with the idea in the autumn of 1975. Others claim that it was the latter who had long wished to punish Saudi Arabia and other Arab states whom he saw as having betrayed the Palestinians and their fight against the Zionists. The plan had originally called for an airborne whistle-stop tour, by Ramírez and his gang together with their hostages, of the capitals of the Middle Eastern OPEC member-countries except Saudi Arabia and Iran. On arrival, each oil minister would either be released or executed, depending on the willingness of his government to pay a ransom. Sheikh Zaki Yamani and Dr. Jamshid Amouzegar, however, were to be executed.

In the event, however, the inability of the Algerians and the Libyans to supply an aircraft prevented Ramírez from carrying out his tour and thus forced a change of plan which resulted in the oil ministers being released. Despite the payment of a large ransom for Yamani and Amouzegar, Wadi Haddad was not pleased at the outcome of the operation and it would not be long before Ramírez would feel his severe displeasure. While the plan may have been Haddad's, others were reputedly involved behind the scenes of the OPEC raid. Colonel Gadaffi of Libya has been named frequently as being one of those who allegedly sponsored the operation and the finger of suspicion has also been pointed at Saddam Hussein of Iraq.

Such had been the scale of terrorism in Europe and the countermeasures adopted by Western governments, as covered in Chapter 4, that by 1976 Wadi Haddad's PFLP–SOG was finding it increasingly dangerous for its terrorists to operate there. In West Germany his allies of the Red Army Faction, although still a potent threat, had been largely dispersed into splinter groups and their leaders imprisoned. The JRA had seen its strength reduced to some thirty trained terrorists, and his own chief assassin, Ilich Ramírez Sánchez, was now wanted throughout the Western hemisphere. Furthermore, the civil war in the Lebanon had forced Haddad to move his headquarters from Beirut to Aden, in South Yemen. He was thus forced to look for fresh areas in which to operate and Africa offered opportunities.

In an attempt to strike a major blow against Israel and show that he and the PFLP–SOG were still a force to be reckoned with, Wadi Haddad mounted a major hijacking operation with the help of Ramírez who assisted in the planning and recruitment of the personnel who would carry it out. The operation comprised the hijacking on 27 June 1976 of an Air France A-300B Airbus, Flight 139, en route from Tel Aviv to Paris via Athens. The aircraft was carrying 256 passengers, eighty-three of them Israelis, and twelve crew who found themselves being abducted to Uganda where they were incarcerated in a disused terminal building at Entebbe surrounded by Ugandan troops. The terrorists who led the hijacking were two members of the Red Army Faction, Wilfried Böse and Brigitte Kuhlmann, assisted by two senior members of Wadi Haddad's organisation: Fayez Abdul-Rahim Jaber and Jayel Naji al-Arjam. At Entebbe, they were joined by a group of six more terrorists which increased their strength to ten.

During the ensuing seven days, the terrorists demanded US $5 million in cash and the release of fifty-three terrorists imprisoned in jails in Israel, West Germany, France, Switzerland and Kenya, threatening to kill all the hostages if their demands were not met.

Those listed in West Germany were members of the Red Army Faction or its affiliated splinter group, the 2nd June Movement: Jan-Carl Raspe, Fritz Teufel, Ralf Reinders, Inge Viett, Ingrid Schubert and Werner Hoppe. Meanwhile all the Israelis and other nationals of Jewish origin were segregated from the rest of the passengers who were released and flown to Paris. The Israeli government was considering the courses open to it and by Thursday 1 July had decided to negotiate with the terrorists.

In the meantime, however, the Israeli Defence Forces (IDF) had produced a plan for a hostage rescue operation. By Friday 2 July, having observed a dress rehearsal of the operation, the Chief of Staff of the IDF was convinced that it could succeed and advised the Israeli prime minister, Yitzhak Rabin, and his cabinet that there was a viable military option. On the afternoon of Saturday 3 July, the rescue force took off from Israel and shortly afterwards the Israeli cabinet voted to allow the operation, code-named 'Thunderball', to proceed.

On Sunday 4 July, the rescue force landed at Entebbe and succeeded in rescuing the hostages, but suffered the loss of its commander and three hostages, all of whom were killed. A detailed account of the hijacking and the subsequent rescue operation appears in Chapter 6.

Three days later in West Germany, satisfaction at the Israeli victory over terrorism was marred by the escape from prison of four members of the Red Army Faction. On 7 July, Inge Viett and three other female terrorists overpowered their guards, using guns smuggled into their cells previously, escaped from West Berlin's Lehrterstrasse prison and within forty-eight hours had left Europe. Viett had been arrested in West Berlin in September 1975, together with Ralf Reinders and Juliane Plambeck, another member of the 2nd June Movement. All three had been imprisoned for their part in the kidnapping of Christian Democratic Union chairman Peter Lorenz in February 1975 and the murder of West Berlin Supreme Court president Gunther von Drenkmann. Viett had also been found guilty of involvement in a number of bank robberies.

The following year, 1977, also saw a number of major operations carried out by the Red Army Faction. In January, the group carried out an attack on a US military base at Giessen. The significance of this particular operation was that the base accommodated the US Army's principal nuclear munitions depot in Europe containing large quantities of 8-inch nuclear artillery shells and warheads for Lance short-range battlefield missiles. On the night of 4 January a bomb was planted on a large aviation fuel tank located near the perimeter of the base. Fortunately the tank contained only some 20,000 gallons as opposed to its maximum capacity of 100,000 and the explosive charge was placed above the level of the fuel, blowing a hole in the tank but without igniting the fuel or causing any spillage. Seconds later another charge, placed on the ground below the tank and designed to ignite the fuel spilling out of the ruptured tank, also exploded without achieving the required result.

The attack was intended to act as a diversion for a main attack aimed at the nuclear ammunition storage bunkers. Shortly after the bomb exploded, twelve terrorists, who had cut their way through the outer fence of concertina barbed wire, were spotted attempting to cut through the next obstacle confronting them, a chain link perimeter fence. The infantry platoon guarding the bunkers sounded the alarm and opened fire and a major firefight ensued with the terrorists returning the fire. The battle lasted ten minutes, by which time German police had arrived and joined battle with the terrorists who withdrew and made good their escape into the woods nearby. At the same time, a reinforcement company of infantry in armoured personnel carriers also arrived on the scene.

The presence of the nuclear munitions at Giessen was a closely guarded secret and details of the attempted attack on the bunkers were suppressed, subsequent press reports merely stating that terrorists had attacked a fuel tank with explosives. The full details of the story were only made public in 1997 by journalists Andrew and Leslie Cockburn in their book *One Point Safe*. Both the nuclear shells and the missile warheads were in fact stored in containers fitted with special security and disable-on-command devices to prevent their being stolen in an operable state. Nevertheless, this was a serious attempt by the Red Army Faction to lay its hands on nuclear devices.

On 7 April, Dr. Siegfried Buback, West Germany's chief federal prosecutor, was shot dead in Karlsruhe. Almost four months later Jürgen Pronto, the chairman of the Dresdner Bank, was murdered by a group which included his own god-daughter, Susanne Albrecht. In both cases, the murders were the work of elements of the Red Army Faction.

The group's next target was Hanns Martin Schleyer, president of both the Federation of German Employers and the Confederation of German Industry. Schleyer was a major target for the Red Army Faction, being a staunch Christian Democrat, honorary consul for Brazil (a country ruled at that time by a right-wing regime) and a former officer of the SS. The West German authorities had graded him as a high-level risk and he had been given three police bodyguards.

At 5.28 p.m. on 5 September, Schleyer was being driven in a two-car convoy along the Vincenz-Statzstrasse in the Cologne suburb of Braunsfeld when the Red Army Faction struck. A Mercedes saloon swerved in front of his car and stopped diagonally across the road. At the same time, a child's pram was pushed into the road, forcing Schleyer's driver to swerve towards the Mercedes and bring his vehicle to a halt. The escort car was unable to stop and cannoned into the rear of Schleyer's vehicle. At that point, five terrorists opened fire with submachine-guns, killing Schleyer's driver. Two of the bodyguards succeeded in returning the fire, but all three were shot dead almost immediately afterwards. Schleyer was dragged out of his car at gunpoint and hauled into a Volkswagen minibus nearby. Three minutes after the ambush began, the terrorists sped away with their victim.

Nothing was heard from the terrorists, but that evening the minibus was discovered in a basement garage in Wiener Weg. In it police found a document demanding that the government desist from any search for Schleyer. It was signed 'Commando Siegfried Hausner R.A.F.' That night the apartment of a known member of the Red Army Faction, Frederike Krabbe, was raided by the police, but the bird had flown.

At 3 p.m. on 6 September a letter was delivered to the residence of the Dean of the Protestant church in Wiesbaden. Addressed to the West German federal government, it demanded the release from prison of eleven members of the Red Army Faction: Andreas Baader, Gudrun Ensslin, Jan-Carl Raspe, Verena Becker, Werner Hoppe, Karl Heinz Dellwo, Hanna-Elise Krabbe, Bernd Maria Rössner, Ingrid Schubert, Irmgard Möller and Günter Sonnenberg. The document also demanded aircraft and safe passages out of West Germany to their individual countries of choice, plus $100,000 cash to be given to each of them.

While West German intelligence and law enforcement units were bringing all their resources to bear in the hunt for Hanns Martin Schleyer and his kidnappers, Chancellor Helmut Schmidt's federal government played for time in negotiations with the terrorists over their demands. The twelve prisoners had been invited to state their preferred destinations on being released. The government despatched an envoy, the Minister of State in the Chancellor's office, Hans-Jürgen Wischnewski, on a tour of the specified countries as part of its efforts to spin out negotiations – in all but one he met firm refusals. Meanwhile the terrorists communicated through a series of documents and videotapes, featuring Schleyer who acted as a mouthpiece for his kidnappers.

The negotiations dragged on for five and a half weeks until mid-October. At that point, the Red Army Faction and its allies of the PFLP decided to put further pressure on the West German government and on 13 October Lufthansa Flight LH 181 was hijacked by four PFLP–SOG terrorists. The full story of the hijacking of Flight LH 181 and the events which followed is told fully in Chapter 7. Suffice to say here that after five days it ended with the rescue of all the hostages and crew, and the deaths of three of the terrorists, the fourth being captured.

News of the rescue reached Germany in the early hours of 18 October where it was broadcast on radio at 12.38 a.m. At Stammheim jail in Stuttgart, housing four captured members of the Red Army Faction, the internal radio broadcast system had been switched off at 11.30 p.m. on the previous evening, but many prisoners possessed portable radios which they held to their cell windows so others could also hear. The news of the failure of the PFLP to secure the release of the Red Army Faction terrorists spread like wildfire through the jail.

At just after 7.41 a.m., on the seventh floor, which housed the special section accommodating the four members of the Red Army Faction, the guards arrived to serve breakfast. As they opened the door of Cell 716, they discovered Jan-Carl Raspe lying on his bed with a bullet wound in his head. He had shot himself with a 9mm pistol which apparently he had concealed in his cell. The guards immediately checked the other Red Army Faction prisoners: Andreas Baader was lying dead on the floor of his cell, a 7.65mm pistol on the floor beside him; Gudrun Ensslin was also dead, hanging by a length of electrical cord from her cell window; Irmgard Möller was lying on her bed with stab wounds to her chest but still alive. Raspe was rushed to Stuttgart's Katharine Hospital but died at 9.40 a.m.; Möller was taken to the city's Robert Bosch Hospital where she underwent emergency surgery and survived.

Inevitably there were allegations that the four had been murdered by the West German authorities and repercussions by the Red Army Faction were not long in coming. On 19 October the Paris newspaper *Libération* received a communiqué from Hanns Martin Schleyer's kidnappers, stating that he had been killed and giving details of where his body could be found: in a green Audi 100 parked in the Rue Charles Péguy in Mulhouse. The vehicle was located that afternoon but it was not until three hours later that French police opened the vehicle's boot and found Schleyer's body; he had been shot through the head. The German authorities immediately launched a manhunt throughout Europe for the kidnappers whom they believed to be responsible: Susanne Albrecht, Christian Klar, Jorg Lang, Willy Peter Stoll, Elisabeth von Dyck, Silke Maier Witt, Adelheid Schulz, Sigrid Sternebeck, Angelika Speitel, Frederike Krabbe, Juliane Plambeck, Inge Viett, Brigitte Mohnhaupt, Rolf Heissler, Rolf Clemens Wagner and Christoph Michael Wackernagel.

Despite the suicides of its leaders, the Red Army Faction still posed a serious threat. In France two German warehouses, a Mercedes-Benz dealer's premises in Limoges, the offices of a German paper company in Toulouse and a German-owned factory in Versailles were all burned down. In Italy there were some twenty bomb attacks on German businesses throughout the country, and in Greece two police officers were wounded in a gun battle with four terrorists attempting to carry out a bomb attack on a German-owned electronics factory near Athens.

During the next twelve months, however, the organisation suffered some setbacks. On 17 November Ingrid Schubert committed suicide in her prison cell in Munich, this being followed by a further wave of demonstrations and terrorist actions in Europe. On 20 December 1977 Gabriele Kröcher-Tiedemann and Christian Möller were arrested by the Swiss police near Basle after wounding two Swiss customs officers on the Franco–Swiss border, one of whom died of his wounds shortly afterwards. In July of the following year, they were sentenced to fifteen years' imprisonment for murder; on the day following the end of their trial in Berne, a bomb attack was carried out on the courthouse.

On 20 August 1978, Astrid Proll was arrested in London and extradited to West Germany. In September, Angelika Speitel and Michael Knoll were wounded in a gun battle with police in a forest near Darmstadt which left one police officer dead. During the same month, Willy Peter Stoll was killed in a gun battle with police in a restaurant in Düsseldorf.

In early 1979, Elisabeth von Dyck was shot dead by police in Nuremberg. In June Rolf Heissler, one of those wanted in connection with the Schleyer kidnapping, was arrested in a restaurant in Frankfurt. On 29 June, Rolf Clemens Wagner and Werner Lotze failed in their attempt to kill the Supreme Allied Commander Europe, General Alexander Haig, with a bomb as he travelled to his headquarters in Belgium.

Despite these setbacks, however, the Red Army Faction remained active and regrouped under the leadership of Christian Klar as the 1970s drew to a close. As shown in the following chapter, it would be another twelve years before the organisation could no longer be considered a serious threat.

2

THE WAR CONTINUES

The end of the 1970s saw further developments in international terrorism with increased terrorist activity in Europe. One of the foremost groups which emerged at that time was Action Directe, a French revolutionary group formed in May 1979 under Jean-Marc Rouillan, a former student in Toulouse which had in the early 1970s been the scene of protests against the rule of the fascist dictator of Spain, General Francisco Franco. Rouillan had taken part in demonstrations and other forms of protest in Spain, as well as in France, and in 1974 had joined the Groupes d'Action Révolutionnaire Internationalistes (GARI), a clandestine radical group. He had subsequently been arrested that year, being freed in 1977. In July 1978 he was arrested again, spending a further six months in prison. During the following year he formed Action Directe with five others: Nathalie Menigon, Régis Schleicher, Frédéric Oriach, Mohand Hamami and Laouari Ben Shellal, the latter two being French-Algerian. Two other individuals, based in Lyon, who would become prominent members of the group were André Olivier and Max Frerot, the latter being an explosives expert.

The group first made its presence felt that year with machine-gun attacks on government buildings, the headquarters of the Police Nationale and the offices of large corporations, the latter including those with Zionist connections. During the following year it carried out a further twenty-one attacks, mainly in the areas of Paris and Toulouse, including one with a rocket-launcher on the offices of the Ministry of Transport. 1980 also saw the arrest in Paris on 13 September of Rouillan and Menigon who were lured into a trap by police using a Lebanese informer, Gabriel Chahine, who was subsequently murdered by an Action Directe gunman for his treachery.

Rouillan and Menigon were tried and convicted but did not remain in prison for long. In 1981, the newly elected President

François Mitterand, announced an amnesty for all convicted terrorists as part of a truce he was seeking with Corsican separatists. Rouillan, Menigon and twenty-five other members of Action Directe were all pardoned and released. The truce was short-lived, however, and Rouillan and Menigon soon disappeared underground again.

In 1982, in the wake of the Israeli invasion of Lebanon, Action Directe took up the Palestinian cause. It acquired recruits from the Arab quarters of the 18th and 20th arrondissements of Paris, and from groups of Turkish workers, a large number of whom were illegal immigrants. In April, a group of close associates of Action Directe, the Factions Armées Révolutionnaires Libanaises (FARL), attacked a building in Paris housing a delegation of the Israeli defence ministry and later in the same month murdered Ya'acov Bar-Simontov, a second secretary at the Israeli embassy. This was followed by two further attacks by the FARL: a parcel bomb delivered to the commercial attaché at the US embassy exploded, killing two police officers; and a bomb planted in the car of an Israeli diplomat injured others. In January of the previous year, the FARL had assassinated Lieutenant Colonel Charles Ray, an assistant attaché at the US embassy, and had made an unsuccessful attempt on the life of the chargé d'affaires, Christian Addison Chapman.

The summer of 1982 saw Action Directe carrying out a machine-gun attack in Paris on a restaurant in the city's Jewish quarter, resulting in the deaths of six people, and three bombings, also directed at Jewish targets. It also launched a series of attacks against American targets in France, coinciding with the attendance of President Ronald Reagan at a world summit conference at Versailles. This resulted in the French government declaring on 18 August 1982 that Action Directe was a prohibited organisation. In 1983, the group became involved with two Italian groups, Front Line and the Communisti Organisti per la Liberazione del Proletariat (COLP), in raising funds for their respective causes. In Paris on 31 May of that year a member of Front Line, Ciro Rizzato, shot dead two police officers when they stopped his car in the Avenue Trudaine and asked to see his papers and those of his companion in the vehicle. A chase through the streets of the city ensued, ending with Rizzato being shot dead by the police and his accomplice escaping and avoiding capture.

On 25 January 1984, a bomb attack was carried out on the Châtillon offices of a major French company, Aérospatiale. Four days later, another took place at the factory of Panhard–Levasseur in Paris. Shortly afterwards, however, Jean-Marc Rouillan and Nathalie Menigon were forced to flee to Belgium where they sought sanctuary with the Cellules Communistes Combattantes (CCC), a small group led by Pierre Carrette, a former member of Action Directe who had fled to Belgium in 1981.

Later in the year, as the result of a European terrorist summit held at Lisbon in June, an alliance of European groups was formed. Largely Marxist-orientated, it was opposed to NATO, the United States, international agencies, government organisations, and large commercial companies. The principal elements in this alliance were Action Directe, the CCC and the Red Army Faction, with occasional involvement of Dutch, Spanish, Italian and Portuguese groups. In October 1984 the CCC carried out an attack on the firm of Litton Data Systems in Belgium. During the following eighteen months, it was responsible for more than twenty bombings and murders in Belgium, all of them aimed at NATO targets or at companies that had dealings with the organisation's armed forces.

Meanwhile, Action Directe carried out a wave of ten bomb attacks in France, all aimed at targets connected with NATO, the United States or the French defence industry. On 23 August, a car containing twenty-four kilograms of high explosive was positioned outside the Paris offices of the Western European Union. Telephone warnings were given, but were ignored by the police; fortunately the bomb failed to explode. In the meantime, the vehicle had been towed to a car pound where it remained for four days before it was eventually searched.

In West Germany meanwhile, the Red Army Faction had also been active. On 31 August 1981, it planted a car bomb at the Ramstein headquarters of the US Air Force in Europe, injuring twenty people. Two weeks later, on 15 September 1981, it carried out an unsuccessful assassination attempt at Heidelberg on General Frederick J. Kroesen, the commander of US Forces in Europe. In this attack the terrorists used a Soviet RPG-7, but fortunately for Kroesen his limousine was armoured and he escaped death or injury.

Further attacks were carried out on US bases in Germany until October 1982 when a Red Army Faction arms cache was discovered as a result of signs of digging and unusual activity noticed by people picking mushrooms in woods in the area of Gravenbuch, near Frankfurt. Alerted by the police, the headquarters of the Bundeskriminalamt passed the matter to Grenzschutzgruppe–9 (GSG–9), the counter-terrorist unit of the West German federal border guard, which positioned a five-man team to carry out surveillance on the cache. Six days later two members of Red Army Faction, Brigitte Mohnhaupt and Adelheid Schulz, approached the cache and were arrested by the GSG-9 team.

In addition to weapons, ammunition and explosives, the cache yielded a considerable amount of documentation including boxes of forged military passes and vehicle registration documents, reports on surveillance of US bases and on the movement of potential targets, including West German politicians. Most importantly, however, were maps giving details of the locations of other caches. These led to the arrest five days later of Christian Klar, the Red Army Faction leader, who surrendered without resistance while recovering money from a cache.

Two years later, on 11 December 1984, six bombs were planted on sections of a secret NATO oil pipeline at Verviers near Brussels. This attack heralded the start of a combined new anti-NATO bombing campaign by the Red Army Faction, the CCC and Action Directe.

On 7 January 1985, Red Army Faction terrorists broke into an explosives store at a cement factory in the town of Geisingen in Baden–Württemberg, and stole quantities of fuses and detonators. The group subsequently put these items to use in bomb attacks carried out jointly with Action Directe and the CCC against American military targets in West Germany. On 1 February, two members of the organisation, later identified as Bernhard Lotze and Barbara Meyer, tricked their way into the Munich home of Ernst Zimmermann, president of the West German Aerospace and Armaments Association, who was subsequently shot dead by Lotze.

On 15 June of that year, an attack was mounted on the base of the American Forces Network at Pomcus, responsibility subsequently being claimed by the 'AD-RAF-CCC alliance'. Four days later, a bomb exploded in a left-luggage locker at Frankfurt airport, killing three people. On 22 June a letter bomb exploded at the offices of Bayer Pharmaceuticals in Brussels. On 7 August another attack was carried out at the US Air Force base at Rhein-Main, near the city of Frankfurt, where a car bomb killed two Americans and injured more than twenty, responsibility being claimed by Action Directe and the Red Army Faction.

On 8 August, the organisation carried out a car bomb attack on the US Air Force base at Rheinmain, killing two Americans: a soldier and one female civilian. This was the seventh attack that year by the Red Army Faction on US and NATO bases in West Germany. During 1986 it struck twice again when on 9 July it murdered a German industrialist, Dr. Karlheinz Beckurts, and on 10 October when it shot dead a senior Foreign Ministry official, Gerold von Baumnühl, bringing the total number of murders carried out by the group during 1985 and 1986 to six.

Two years later, in September 1988, the Red Army Faction emerged once again in an unsuccessful attempt to murder a senior official in the Ministry of Finance, Hans Tietmeyer. On 30 November 1989, it hit newspaper headlines again when it used a remote-controlled bomb to murder the chief executive of the Deutsche Bank, Alfred Herrhausen, outside his home in Bad Homburg.

Meanwhile, the 1980s also saw increased activity on the part of another West German terrorist group. As mentioned in Chapter 1, the Revolutionary Cells (RZ) had been formed in 1973 by Wilfried Böse as an offshoot of the Red Army Faction, but broke away in the early 1980s. By then the group had reached a strength of some 300 hard-core activists organised in independent cells of five or six and supported by some 2,000 active sympathisers. RZ had close links with another organisation, solely comprising female terrorists, called Rote Zora (Red Zora), the latter first coming to public attention in 1981 when on 11 May it assassinated the finance minister of the state of Hessen, Hans-Herbert Karry.

RZ tended to concentrate on targets within NATO and the West German defence industry, and on commercial organisations which it considered to have 'imperialist' connections, for example those dealing with countries such as South Africa and Israel. Among its targets were a chemical plant in Cologne and a branch of the Deutsche bank in Düsseldorf. In 1984, it attacked the offices of coal merchants in Hamburg and the industrial area of the Ruhr, apparently in support of the striking miners in Great Britain and in retribution for the export of coal from West Germany to the United Kingdom.

RZ's campaign peaked during the period 1985 to 1986 when it worked in close co-operation with the Red Army Faction and another group called Autonomous Groups (AG). RZ itself carried out a total of 200 attacks in 1985, some unsuccessful, and in 1986 was involved in a further 464 of which 90 per cent were carried out by AG. Of these, more than half were attacks on banks, plants and companies within the defence industry, the rest being directed at transport, energy and communications installations.

While terrorist attacks continued in Germany and Belgium, France was suffering from a major escalation in terrorist violence. On the evening of 25 January Inspector-General René Audran, Director of International Affairs at the Ministry of Defence and a leading figure in the French military establishment and defence industry, was shot and killed by a gunman outside his home. Responsibility was claimed by Action Directe, but the French authorities suspected a Red Army Faction connection, not least because a similar attack had been carried out in Germany: Audran's counterpart in West Germany, the industrialist Ernst Zimmermann, had also been murdered at his home in almost identical circumstances.

During this period, Action Directe also carried out a number of bomb attacks in protest against French economic connections with

South Africa and the allocation of radio air time to the ultra right-wing National Front. On 27 April 1985, it exploded a car bomb outside the Paris headquarters of the International Monetary Fund. The explosion blew out every window in the building and a large number in those nearby. On the following day, however, police and customs officers at the Gare du Nord in Paris arrested an Action Directe courier, a Turk named Muzaffer Kacar, who was found to be in possession of sixteen kilograms of high explosive and four detonators, as well as a number of false Belgian driving licences and identity cards. Examination of the explosives traced them to a quantity which had been stolen in a raid on a store at a quarry at Ecaussines, some thirty-five kilometres from Brussels, on the night of 2 June 1984.

A Spanish dimension to evidence that the European military-industrial complexes and defence industries had been targeted by the region's terrorist groups came three months later, on 29 July 1985, when Rear Admiral Fausto Escrigas Estrada, the Director-General of Defence Policy at the Spanish Ministry of Defence, was killed when his car was ambushed en route to his office in Madrid. One of the gunmen was subsequently identified as a member of ETA–M.

Early 1986 finally saw progress on the part of the French authorities in taking effective action against Action Directe. On 28 March André Olivier, the leader of the group's Lyon element, was arrested. On 21 February 1987 Marc Rouillan and Nathalie Menigon were captured with two other members, and on 27 November Max Frerot was also apprehended. By that time a large number of members of Action Directe were in custody and in February 1988 thirty of them were tried and given sentences of up to thirteen years' imprisonment. Rouillan, Menigon and two others were tried in January of the following year for the murder on 17 November 1986 of Georges Besse, the president of Renault; they were found guilty and sentenced to life imprisonment. On 29 June, Max Frerot and one other were tried and found guilty of two murders, both receiving life sentences. At the same time, a number of other members of Action Directe were also tried: two received sentences of eighteen to twenty years; fourteen others received shorter, suspended sentences for lesser offences.

The early 1980s also saw the re-appearance of Ilich Ramírez Sánchez, alias Carlos, of whom little had been heard after his kidnapping of the OPEC oil ministers in December 1975. In mid-February 1976 Ramírez, Gabriele Kröcher-Tiedemann and Hans-Joachim Klein had flown to the South Yemeni capital of Aden where they were confronted by Wadi Haddad. The latter had been displeased at the outcome of the OPEC operation and, despite his attempts to deflect criticism of himself on to his two accomplices, Ramírez was heavily censured by Haddad who subsequently expelled him from the PFLP–SOG, much to the former's fury.

It was at this juncture that Ramírez decided to form his own terrorist group. A few weeks later, accompanied by Klein, he left Aden and paid a visit to Beirut before making his way to Yugoslavia where the pair spent three weeks. By now, however, Western intelligence services had picked up his trail and the Yugoslavs, at the request of the West German government which demanded his extradition, arrested him and Klein. Four days later, however, they were released and deported, being placed on a flight to Syria. On arrival at Damascus, however, the two men were refused permission to enter the country and their flight was forced to fly on to Iraq. After several weeks in Baghdad, Ramírez made his way back to South Yemen while Klein travelled to Italy where he lay low in the Alps. During the next few months, Ramírez set about forming his own organisation. He first travelled to South America and then returned to the Middle East in December 1977, arriving in Iraq where he established links with the Iraqi intelligence service, the Mukhabarat.

In March of the following year, Wadi Haddad died of leukaemia – some reports state in Aden, others in East Berlin. Six months earlier, as described in Chapter 7, another of his major operations, the hijacking of a Lufthansa Boeing 737, had failed when troops of GSG-9, assisted by two members of 22 SAS, stormed the aircraft at Mogadishu airport in Somalia, rescuing the eighty-six passengers and four of the crew being held hostage, the pilot of the aircraft having been murdered earlier by the terrorists. The hijack had been intended as revenge for Haddad's defeat at the hands of the Israelis at Entebbe; in the event, it proved to be his swansong.

After Haddad's death, the PFLP–SOG fragmented, but leadership of the core element, comprising some fifty members, was taken over by Salim Abu Salem (alias Abu Mohammed) who renamed the group Popular Front for the Liberation of Palestine – Special Command (PFLP–SC). Salim retained Haddad's links with European terrorist groups, including those with the Armenian Secret Army for the Liberation of Armenia (ASALA), a terrorist group which is covered later in this chapter.

Another breakaway faction of the PFLP–SOG became the 15 May Organisation under Muhammad al-Umari, better known as Abu Ibrahim, and moved to Baghdad where it based itself until 1984 when it disbanded, its members being absorbed into Fatah's Special Operations Group. During the early to mid-1980s, it was responsible for bomb attacks on a hotel in London in 1980, and on El-Al offices in Istanbul and Rome during 1981. In August 1982 the group failed in an attempt to bomb a Pan Am aircraft in Rio de Janeiro, but succeeded in an attack on another flying from Tokyo to Honolulu, killing one person.

Haddad's death made matters easier for Ramírez who lost little time in recruiting a number of experienced terrorists whose loyalties hitherto had primarily been with Haddad. Within a relatively short period he had assembled a group which comprised extremists of various nationalities as well as a number from the West German group RZ. His right-hand man was Johannes Weinrich, who had been one of his accomplices in the January 1975 attack on the El-Al airliner at Orly airport.

In January 1979 Ramírez, who by now was being hunted actively by Western intelligence services, appeared in East Berlin where he made contact via Johannes Weinrich with Section 22, the counter-terrorism department of the Stasi (Ministry of State Security). He also travelled to the Hungarian capital of Budapest where he established a number of safe houses and a base for himself and his wife,

Magdalena Kopp, a member of RZ whom he had married in January in Beirut before travelling to East Germany. His frequent journeys also took him to other countries in the Eastern Bloc, including Czechoslovakia which provided training facilities for his organisation.

Colonel Muammar Gadaffi of Libya was another who availed himself of Ramírez's services to liquidate opponents in exchange for providing him with funds and *matériel*. In 1979, Ramírez visited Tripoli where he was welcomed by Gadaffi personally. Arms, explosives and other equipment were thereafter supplied in liberal quantities by the Libyans in return for his assistance in tracking down and eliminating exiled opponents of Gadaffi's regime. Ramírez and his lieutenants soon became disenchanted with Libyan inefficiency, however, and relations between him and Sayed Gaddafadem, the head of the Green Brigade assassination teams, soured after Ramírez criticised him to his face. Matters came to a head in September 1981 and it was at this point that Ramírez and the Libyans parted company.

By now, however, Ramírez had established good relations with Syria and the regime of President Hafez al-Assad which had provided arms, training and other facilities since 1979. The Syrians also supplied him and his wife with diplomatic passports in the names of Michel Khouri and Maryam Touma respectively. All this was achieved through the good offices of a Syrian intelligence officer, Ali Al Issawe (alias Abu Hakam), who was a key member of Ramírez's organisation and who was his link with President Assad's brother, Rifaat al-Assad, who headed the Syrian Army's special forces.

The Syrians, however, demanded a price for their support, namely assistance in dealing with dissident groups in exile, among them the Paris-based National Front for the Liberation of Syria and its allies of the Moslem Brotherhood operating from West Germany. In 1982, Ramírez was tasked with organising operations against both these groups which in January of that year attempted to overthrow Assad's government with an uprising by the Moslem Brotherhood in the town of Hama which was crushed with a great deal of bloodshed by the Syrian army. In addition to eight assassination teams sent from Syria, Ramírez also used elements of his own European organisation and other terrorist groups to hunt down opponents of Assad's regime.

During this period, his organisation was also providing services to those regimes in the Eastern Bloc and the Middle East which supported it. Among those who made use of it was the Romanian dictator, Nicolae Ceausescu. He commissioned Ramírez to assassinate five leading Romanian dissidents who had defected to the West, among them the former deputy head of Romania's intelligence service. In the event, only two attacks were carried out, using parcel bombs, and both failed. Another operation on behalf of Ceausescu proved more successful. On the evening of 21 February 1981 a building in Munich, housing a CIA-funded radio station called Radio Free Europe, was badly damaged by a car bomb. Ramírez reportedly received $400,000 for this operation.

In the meantime, Ramírez maintained close links with a number of other groups within Europe, among them the Basque separatist group ETA and the West German RZ. He also established contact with an organisation of extremists in Switzerland and in January 1982 undertook an operation on their behalf. On 18 January, at Creys-Malville in central France, five RPG-7 rocket-propelled grenades were fired at the Super-Phénix nuclear reactor which was under construction. Although the outer shell was hit, its thick concrete casing was unaffected and the attack thus failed.

On 16 February, two members of his organisation were arrested in Paris after being spotted behaving suspiciously in an underground car park. One was a Swiss named Bruno Bréguet; his companion was none other than Ramírez's wife, Magdalena Kopp. When approached, Bréguet had drawn a 9mm pistol and attempted to escape, but was arrested by police when his weapon jammed. A search of the couple's car revealed explosives, timing devices, fragmentation grenades and another pistol. Under questioning, neither Bréguet nor Kopp would divulge any information other than to say that they belonged to the 'International Revolutionary Organisation'.

It later transpired that they had travelled from Budapest to Paris with the intention of carrying out a bomb attack on the offices of the magazine *Al Watan al Arabi* (The Arab Nation) which had published an interview with Ramírez three years earlier. This was the second time that Bréguet had been arrested. In April 1970, he had been apprehended in Israel while attempting to smuggle explosives into the country on behalf of a Palestinian group. Tried and convicted, he had been sentenced to fifteen years, but had been released in 1977.

On 26 February, ten days after the arrest of Bréguet and Kopp, the French embassy in The Hague received a letter from Ramírez in which he demanded their release within thirty days and threatened reprisals if this were not forthcoming. The French authorities did not comply and it was not long before he carried out his promise. On 15 March a bomb exploded in a French cultural centre in Beirut, injuring five people. Two weeks later, on 29 March, another exploded on the Paris–Toulouse express, killing five people and injuring thirty. On 15 April in Beirut, an officer of the French intelligence service, the Direction Générale de la Sécurité Extérieure (DGSE) (formerly the SDECE – renamed in 1981), and his wife were murdered in their apartment by a gunman belonging to Ramírez's organisation. On 21 April, a car bomb exploded outside the French embassy in Vienna, killing a policeman.

On the morning of 22 April, a car bomb exploded outside the offices of *Al Watan al Arabi* in the Rue Marbeuf in Paris, killing one person and injuring seventy others. At the very same moment, the trial of Bréguet and Kopp at the Palais de Justice on the Isle de la Cité was just beginning. These attacks were intended to pressurise the authorities into releasing Bréguet and Kopp, but both were sentenced to five years' imprisonment. Ramírez nevertheless persevered and continued to attack French targets: the first, a rocket attack on the French consulate in Beirut, was launched shortly after the Rue Marbeuf bombing, followed by another in May when a car bomb exploded inside the French embassy compound in Beirut, killing eleven and injuring twenty-seven.

They continued into 1983 with, on 25 August, a bomb attack on the Maison de France cultural centre in West Berlin in which one person died and twenty-two others were injured.

Four months later, on 31 December 1983, two more bombs exploded: one on the Paris–Marseilles high-speed TGV express, killing three people and injuring twelve; the other at Marseilles' Saint Charles railway station, killing two and injuring thirty-four others. When claiming responsibility for these two attacks in the name of the Organisation of Arab Armed Struggle, Ramírez claimed that they were in retaliation for a raid on training camps in East Lebanon carried out in November by French aircraft.

By this time, Ramírez's campaign of terror had become a cause of some embarrassment to those Eastern Bloc countries providing him with support. Furthermore, his presence had become an obstacle to the improvement of relations between East and West and the sorely needed economic advantages they would bring. In the summer of 1984 the US government exerted pressure on the five East European countries identified as 'sponsoring' Ramírez – East Germany, Hungary, Czechoslovakia, Romania and Bulgaria – to cease their support for him forthwith. By September of that year, it was being made plain to him that he was no longer welcome and by April 1985 he had returned to South Yemen.

Before long, he surfaced in Syria where President Hafez al-Assad had agreed to provide him with a new base. By now, however, his influence was declining and his organisation, having suffered a number of defections from its ranks, was beginning to disintegrate. From 1988 onwards, the Syrians made little use of him and he spent the rest of the decade in a virtual state of retirement, living in Damascus with his wife, Magdalena Kopp, who had joined him there in 1985 after being released early by the French.

During the 1980s, Ramírez was not the only terrorist to cause problems for France which had been plagued by the activities of a number of separatist groups. Foremost among these were the Breton Armée Républicaine Bretonne (ARB) – the military wing of the Front de Libération de la Bretagne (FLB); the Corsican Front de la Libération Nationale de la Corse (FLNC); and the French Basque Iparretarrak.

The first to announce its presence was the FLB which exploded a few bombs outside government buildings during the period 1966 to 1968. In 1969 about sixty of its members were arrested and a quantity of explosives seized. A number were charged and received sentences of imprisonment, but were released a few months later under amnesty. In 1971, however, the FLB resumed its bombings which continued into 1972. That year saw a split in the organisation and thereafter the more militant elements grouped themselves within its military wing, the ARB.

The mid-1970s saw the arrests of four of ARB's leaders, Yann Fouéré, Yann Puillandre, a doctor named Gourves and a priest, Father Le Breton. All were subsequently released in 1976. The group was at the peak of its activities during the late 1970s, numbering some 100 in strength. It confined itself to bomb attacks, its targets being television and radio installations as well as police stations and courts. In 1978, two of its members planted a bomb in a wing of the Palace of Versailles, both subsequently being arrested and receiving sentences of fifteen years. This attack, however, proved counter-productive as the ARB lost a considerable amount of public sympathy. By the beginning of the 1980s most of the organisation's members had been arrested and thereafter its activities were minimal.

The FLNC was formed in May 1976 under the leadership of Jean Paul Roesch. It commenced its operations in Corsica and on the French mainland in 1976, attacking banks, tourist areas and holiday homes belonging to French mainlanders. One such attack was on the Château de Fornali while a formal dinner was in progress; under the eyes of the local press, who had been invited to watch, the terrorists led the dinner guests to safety at gunpoint before the building was destroyed with explosives.

In January 1978, the FLNC attacked the French Air Force base at Solenzara on Corsica. It subsequently released a communiqué announcing its support for the PLO and its opposition to French military operations in Chad and the Western Sahara. During that year it mounted a total of 379 bomb attacks aginst targets on the island. In 1979 it took the war to the French mainland, carrying out 329 bomb attacks. Among its targets in Paris were banks, the Ministry of Finance and the Palais de Justice. Despite the arrests of a number of its members who were subsequently sentenced to terms of imprisonment, the organisation increased its activities. During 1980, 463 bomb attacks were carried out and a number of hostages were kidnapped although there was no loss of life. In April 1981 a truce was called and negotiations commenced with the newly elected socialist government of François Mitterand. During 1982, however, the bomb attacks on Corsica and the mainland were resumed by a splinter group which also resorted to coercion to raise funds. At the same time, it began to establish links with other terrorist groups in Europe.

In March 1986 the FLNC made clear its hostility towards the tourist trade on Corsica, which it had previously condemned as undermining Corsican culture, when it exploded a bomb in a holiday village on the outskirts of the island's capital, Ajaccio. On 28 and 29 March on the French mainland, a further thirteen bombs blow up banks, public buildings and airline offices in Marseilles, Nice and Aix-en-Provence. On 1 May, a holiday village at Cargese on Corsica was attacked by fifteen masked members of the FLNC. The camp staff and thirty tourists were tied up by the terrorists who left after planting a bomb which later exploded while the owner of the village was unwisely attempting to defuse it, killing him and a policeman and injuring three others. These were the first fatalities in the FLNC's ten-year bombing campaign.

Like the FLNC, the French Basque group Iparretarrak first resorted to violence in 1976 when it carried out three bomb attacks. During the next four years a small number of similar attacks were carried out. In 1981 twelve bombs exploded, six of them in Bayonne. During the following year the group changed its tactics and on 19 March carried out an ambush on a police patrol at St-Etienne-de-Baïgorry, during which two men were killed.

Over the border in Spain, meanwhile, the 1980s saw a gradual stepping-up of violence by ETA as it attempted to increase pressure on the government in Madrid. This commenced in February 1980 with the firing of an anti-tank rocket at the Prime Minster's residence in Madrid. In January of the following year, one of the richest men in Spain was kidnapped and held for fifty-eight days before being released after payment of a ransom of $3.29 million.

January 1982 saw another kidnapping, that of a leading industrialist who was held for a month before being released after payment of a $1.3 million ransom. In October, ETA began to employ more violent methods when it planted approximately two dozen bombs in several banks in the Basque region. This was followed on 4 November 1982 with the murder of a senior Army officer, Lieutenant General Victor Lago, the commander of the Brunete Armoured Division. Four months later, in February 1983, a bomb was planted in a Bilbao bank, killing three people and injuring nine. The bank had apparently refused to agree to a demand for payment of 'revolutionary taxes'.

In April 1984 a retired Army officer was murdered in Pamplona. His killers' getaway car was later found, but exploded while being examined, killing two policemen. On 29 November another senior Army officer, Lieutenant General Guillermo Lacaci, was shot dead by ETA gunmen in Madrid while walking home with his wife after attending Mass; he was the sixth Spanish general to be murdered since 1978.

As mentioned earlier, in July 1985 another senior officer, Rear Admiral Fausto Escrigas Estrada, the Director-General of Defence Policy at the Ministry of Defence, was shot dead and his chauffeur seriously wounded as he was being driven through Madrid. On 6 February of the following year, Vice Admiral Cristobal Colon was murdered in a gun and grenade attack on his car in Madrid. He was the fifty-fourth senior officer to be killed since the murder of Admiral Luis Carrero Blanco, the Franco regime's prime minister, in December 1973.

The month of July saw a series of bombings by ETA in Madrid, each resulting in a number of killed and injured, and an attack on the Ministry of Defence in which a dozen anti-tank rockets were fired at the ministry's buildings by remote control, wounding two officers. After the attack, the vehicle in which the launcher had been concealed exploded, injuring a further ten people. In October the governor of Guipuzcoa Province, General Garido, and his family were murdered by ETA terrorists who placed an explosive charge on the roof of their car as they were being driven through the streets of San Sebastian. December featured the kidnapping of a businessman who was held for sixty days before payment of a $1.5 million ransom.

In 1987, ETA increased the level of violence even further. In January in Zargoza, it carried out a car bomb attack on a military bus, killing two soldiers and injuring forty. During January and February, it launched a series of bomb and arson attacks against French interests in Mondragon, Bilbao and Lasarte in protest against France's deportation of Basque terrorists to Spain. March saw a number of attacks directed against Spanish Army personnel, the first being a machine-gun attack in Vitoria in which an officer was seriously wounded. This was followed by an ambush on an Army officer in Pamplona who was also wounded.

The months of March and April also featured a number of bomb attacks. The first was in Barcelona, at the entrance to its port, one Civil Guardsman being killed and fifteen civilians injured. This was followed by arson and bomb attacks on French property in the city, as well as in Ordizia and Pamplona. On 1 April a bomb exploded near the Civil Guard barracks in Barcelona, killing one person and injuring seven.

ETA continued its relentless bombing campaign throughout the summer of 1987. In May, three car bomb attacks were carried out near the Madrid headquarters of the Navy, Air Force and Civil Guard, one person being killed and nine injured. June saw a number of similar attacks: in San Sebastian a car bomb blew up two police vehicles, injuring six policemen, while another blew up a garage under a supermarket in Barcelona, killing twenty-one people and injuring thirty two.

The second half of 1987 saw further attacks against the Spanish security forces. In July, ETA carried out a grenade attack in San Sebastian on the offices of the military governor, injuring six people. Shortly afterwards, two attacks were launched against the Civil Guard: the first a bomb attack in Onate on a patrol car, killing two guardsmen and wounding two others, and the second a bomb attack on a Civil Guard building, injuring twenty people and causing serious damage. In August, an attack was carried out with rocket-propelled grenades on a Civil Guard barracks at Zarauz, wounding six guardsmen. This was followed by a car bomb attack in Vitoria on a National Police vehicle, killing two policemen and wounding one. In September, a car bomb exploded in San Sebastian as two National Police vehicles were passing, killing one policeman and injuring six passers-by. In December, a car bomb exploded outside a Civil Guard apartment block, killing eleven people and injuring forty as well as causing extensive damage.

In Italy, meanwhile, the Red Brigades had remained active since the murders of Aldo Moro and Guido Rossa, although suffering losses through the arrests of several members in September 1979. On 19 February 1980 the organisation suffered a major blow when a leading member, Patrizio Peci, was arrested and subsequently turned state's evidence. This led to the arrest of a further eighty-five members of the Red Brigades and the establishment of the 'pentiti' informer system developed by the chief of the Carabinieri's anti-terrorist command, General Dalla Chiesa. On 29 April the head of Front Line, Roberto Sandalo, was also arrested and shortly afterwards became an informer. By the end of 1979, some 360 members of Red Brigades had either been arrested, indicted or imprisoned.

In December of that year, however, the Rome column of the Red Brigades struck back with the kidnapping of Judge Giovanni D'Urso. Led by Giovanni Senzani, a former criminologist who had worked for the Ministry of Justice, it demanded first the closure of the prison on the island of Asinara and secondly the broadcasting by the Italian media within forty-eight hours of a number of documents drafted by a body called the 'Action Committees of Prisoners

Accused of Terrorism' whose members were incarcerated in high-security prisons at Trani and Palmi. Non-compliance would result in the death of D'Urso.

The Italian government gave in to the terrorists' demands: orders to close the prison on Asinara were issued on 24 December, the radio station belonging to the Parliamentary Radical Party broadcast the contents of the documents, and D'Urso's 14-year-old daughter appeared on television on 11 January 1981 to read an extract from them. Four days later, D'Urso was released. Three months later, in April, Mario Moretti was arrested and Senzani took over the leadership of the Red Brigades which he had long coveted.

On the evening of 27 April Ciro Cirillo, a principal member of Italy's Christian Democrat party, was kidnapped as he arrived with an armed escort at his home in Naples where he was responsible for the reconstruction of the area in the city devastated by an earthquake in November of the previous year. As he stepped from his car, another vehicle pulled up and terrorists shot dead his chauffeur and bodyguard. Cirillo was seized and driven away at high speed; he had been kidnapped by the Naples column of the Red Brigades.

The group's demands, designed to enhance support for the under-privileged in Naples, were for further funds for the reconstruction programme, increased payments to victims of the earthquake and unemployment benefit for those rendered redundant by its effects. In addition, it demanded a ransom of an undisclosed amount for Cirillo.

Negotiations took place between the Red Brigades and the Italian government, but these soon foundered. The Christian Democrats meanwhile had turned to Raffaele Cutolo, the head of Naples' own Mafia, the Camorra. Discussions took place, attended not only by senior members of the Party, but also by officers of the Italian military intelligence service. Cutolo's price for his help was the cutting back of police operations against the Camorra, a reduction in his sentence and a psychiatric test which would show that he was mentally irresponsible for his actions; the latter was designed to ensure his transfer to a hospital from which he had escaped in 1979, using explosives to blast his way to freedom. A final demand was that Camorra-owned construction companies would be awarded contracts as part of the post-earthquake reconstruction programme.

All of Cutolo's demands were met. The Camorra leader also agreed to negotiate the ransom for Cirillo's release. It was subsequently announced publicly that the agreed amount was US $1 million. In fact the amount was $2 million, paid by the Christian Democrats, of which $1 million was pocketed by Cutolo and the Camorra. It later transpired that, in return for this commission, the latter had agreed to carry out the assassinations of certain people designated by the Red Brigades. On 24 July 1981, Ciro Cirillo was released unharmed and was found that evening in a block of apartments, abandoned after the earthquake, in the area of Poggioreale on the outskirts of Naples.

Carabinieri counter-terrorist operations against the Red Brigades continued to score successes and the autumn of 1981 saw most of the Milan column arrested. In December, however, the terrorists struck once again when they kidnapped the Deputy Chief of Staff for Logistics and Administration at the NATO area headquarters in Verona, an American brigadier general named James Dozier. His kidnappers remained silent until 27 December before releasing a communiqué accompanied by a photograph of him. Meanwhile the Italian authorities had mounted a massive manhunt, rounding up large numbers of suspects in the process.

On 25 January 1982, as a result of continued monitoring of Red Brigade radio transmissions and a tip-off from a terrorist informer, attention narrowed to an apartment block in Padua. Electronic surveillance was concentrated on a second-floor apartment and three days later an assault was mounted on it by ten members of an élite counter-terrorist unit who captured two terrorists and released Brigadier General Dozier unharmed. The full story of the operation to rescue him is told in Chapter 9.

The successful rescue of Dozier and the capture of his kidnappers, some of whom turned state's evidence, was another body blow to the Red Brigades which splintered into four separate groups.

These continued to pose a threat and during the mid-1980s the Italian authorities, noticing a sharp increase in terrorist violence, suspected that the remnant of the organisation had regrouped and retrained. Their suspicions were well-founded; in February 1984 the Red Brigades claimed responsibility for the murder of Leamon Hunt, the director of the multi-national peacekeeping force in Sinai. On 22 February 1986 Antonio da Empoli, economic adviser to the Prime Minister, Bettino Craxi, was wounded in an assassination attempt by a group of Red Brigades terrorists that included a woman who was killed by Empoli's armed driver.

In 1987 100 members of one group were arrested in Italy, France and Spain, but by the end of the 1980s the Red Brigades, although reduced greatly in number, were still active. On 2 September 1989, five of their number were arrested in Paris. They were found to be in possession of weapons and plans for the assassination of a senior official of the Italian foreign ministry, to be carried out in co-operation with Red Army Faction. Other documents found on them provided evidence of links between the Red Brigades and Abu Nidal's organisation; this information led to the arrest in Rome on the following day of a suspected female Red Brigades terrorist, Caterina Calia, who was found in the company of Khalid Thamer, a suspected member of Black June.

Italy was also the scene of the aftermath of a major terrorist outrage perpetrated by a Palestinian group in 1985. On the morning of 7 October, four members of the Palestine Liberation Front (PLF), one of the smaller groups operating under the aegis of the PLO, hijacked the 23,000-ton Italian cruise liner *Achille Lauro* in the Mediterranean. The full story of the hijacking, and the abortive rescue operation which ensued, is told in Chapter 9.

Elsewhere in Europe the 1980s also saw the reappearance of Abu Nidal's organisation. On 22 April 1980 in the Yugoslav capital of Belgrade, it unsuccessfully attempted to assassinate Salah Khalaf (alias Abu Iyad), the PLO head of intelligence, who had once been a close friend of Abu Nidal himself. Five weeks later, on 1 June, the PLO's representative in Brussels, a leading moderate named Na'im

Khudr, was shot dead by an Abu Nidal gunman named Adnan al-Rashidi. On 27 July Abu Nidal's men in Belgium struck again when they threw two grenades into a group of Jewish schoolchildren in Antwerp, killing one and wounding twenty-one others.

The following year again saw Abu Nidal much in evidence as his organisation continued to target prominent individuals within the PLO and Fatah in Europe. On 27 July in Warsaw an attempt was made to murder Abu Dawud, the prominent commander of Fatah's guerrilla forces, who was in the city to conduct talks with the Polish authorities. As he sat in his hotel, two gunmen approached him and fired four times, hitting him in the hand, jaw and body. One of the gunmen was arrested by the Polish police, but was released after payment to the latter of $200,000 by a Polish company owned by Abu Nidal.

Two months later, on 29 August, two Abu Nidal gunmen stormed a synagogue in Vienna, killing two Jews and wounding nineteen more. Both were arrested and one was identified as Adnan al-Rashidi who three months earlier had gunned down Na'im Khudr in the streets of Brussels. Abu Nidal's campaign of violence against Fatah and the PLO continued when on 8 October Sulaiman al-Shurafa (alias Abu Tariq), the Fatah representative in Libya, narrowly escaped being shot in Malta by a member of Black June who killed someone else in error.

The following year, 1982, saw yet more activity on the part of Abu Nidal's hit teams in Europe when on 3 June in London three members of Black June gunned down Shlomo Argov, the Israeli Ambassador to Great Britain. The gunman himself, Navoft Rosan, was shot and wounded by armed police at the scene of the shooting which took place on the steps of the Dorchester Hotel in Park Lane; the others, Marwan al-Banna (Abu Nidal's nephew and leader of the team) and Hussein Said, escaped but were later arrested by police in south London. All three were subsequently tried and convicted, Rosan receiving a sentence of thirty years and his accomplices thirty-five years each.

On 10 April 1983 Dr. Issam Sartawi, a leading moderate member of the PLO, was murdered in Albufeira, Portugal, while attending the Socialist International Congress. He had repeatedly accused Abu Nidal of being an agent of Mossad, the Israeli intelligence service, and there were strong suspicions afterwards of Israeli involvement in his death. At the time, however, it was reported that his murder was in revenge for his involvement in the arrest of two of Abu Nidal's gunmen in Vienna and the assistance he provided to the Austrian police during their subsequent interrogation.

During 1984, Abu Nidal once again turned his attention to Britain. On 28 March Kenneth Whitty, the cultural affairs counsellor at the British embassy in Athens, was gunned down while driving to his office. Responsibility was claimed in Beirut by the Revolutionary Organisation of Socialist Muslims, an Abu Nidal front. Whitty's murder was in revenge for the imprisonment of the three-man hit team who had attempted to murder Shlomo Argov in London in June of the previous year. On 27 November Percy Norris, the British deputy high-commissioner in Bombay was also shot dead. Two days later a bomb exploded in the British Airways office in Beirut. The Revolutionary Organisation of Socialist Muslims claimed responsibility for both these attacks.

The year 1985 saw the first allegations of the involvement of Libya's Colonel Muammar Gadaffi with Abu Nidal who by now, having also been in the pay of Iraq and Syria, appeared to be acting as a mercenary rather than serving the Palestinian cause. His paymasters in Tripoli were already strongly suspected of deep involvement in international terrorism, this being the principal reason for the deportation a year later, on 25 April 1986, of twenty-two Libyans from the United Kingdom.

On 10 March 1984, a number of bombs had exploded in London at establishments frequented by opponents of Gadaffi's regime. On 17 April, during a demonstration by Libyan dissidents outside the 'Libyan People's Bureau', a gunman inside the building had opened fire with a submachine-gun, killing Woman Police Constable Yvonne Fletcher. On 8 July, a Libyan businessman was found murdered in a flat in Bickenhall Street, London. He had been due to stand trial for his involvement for the bombings of anti-Gadaffi dissident meetings; it was subsequently reported that he had been killed by the Libyan intelligence service to ensure his silence.

On 23 November 1985, Egyptair Flight 648, en route to Cairo from Athens, was hijacked by four Black June terrorists. An Egyptian skymarshal shot dead one of the hijackers, but was himself killed in an ensuing mid-air gun battle. The aircraft was subsequently forced to fly to Luqa, on the island of Malta, where six passengers were killed by the terrorists. Next day, troops of the counter-terrorist unit of the Egyptian Army's special forces stormed the aircraft which caught fire, either from the terrorists' grenades or from the explosive charges used by the assaulting troops to blow in the doors. Fifty-seven passengers died in the operation which is covered further in Chapter 4.

In the aftermath of the disaster, President Mubarak of Egypt accused Libya of involvement with Abu Nidal in carrying it out. It was later reported that this was the case, the hijack being one of two anti-Egyptian operations carried out on Libya's behalf, the other being an attempt to attack the US embassy in Cairo with a truck bomb in May of that year. It was subsequently revealed that members of the Libyan People's Bureau in Athens used their diplomatic passports to gain access to the transit lounge at the airport where they handed over weapons to the four terrorists who carried them aboard the aircraft. The original plan had been for the aircraft to fly to Libya, but at the last minute permission to land at Tripoli was denied by the Libyan government and the gunmen were ordered to fly to Malta.

A further example of Libyan involvement with Abu Nidal was the major operation mounted by the latter at the end of 1985. On 27 December, simultaneous attacks were carried out at airports at Rome and Vienna. At 8.15 a.m. at Leonardo da Vinci airport, four gunmen threw grenades and opened fire with submachine-guns on passengers queueing at the El-Al and TWA check-in desks in a crowded terminal, killing fifteen people and wounding more than seventy. Most of those who died were Israelis and Americans, but Greeks, Mexicans and Arabs were also among those who were killed. Italian and Israeli security guards killed three of the terror-ists and captured the fourth, later named as Mohammed Sharam.

Meanwhile a similar attack was mounted in a passenger terminal at Schwecat airport at Vienna. Three Abu Nidal gunmen threw grenades and opened fire on passengers queueing at the El-Al check-in desk, killing two and wounding forty-five. The three terrorists then shot their way out of the building, commandeered a car and sped away with Austrian police in hot pursuit. Road-blocks were set up, however, and eventually the terrorists were trapped six miles from the airport. During the ensuing gun battle one of them, Mongi bin Abdullah Saadoui, was killed and the other two, Abdul Aziz Merzough and Ben Ahmed Chaoval, were captured.

The original plan had called for Frankfurt airport also to be attacked with the assistance of Ahmed Jibril's PFLP–GC, but Abu Nidal had changed his mind. All seven terrorists involved in these two attacks were young Palestinians, one aged nineteen, who had been recruited from refugee camps by Abu Nidal and then sent for training in camps in the Bekaa Valley of the Lebanon. Heavily drugged with amphetamines prior to the attack, they had been briefed that the passengers standing at the check-in desks at Rome and Vienna would be members of the Israeli Air Force returning home, in civilian clothes, after a training exercise.

It later transpired that the Libyan intelligence service had partici-pated in the planning of the operation and had supplied the weapons; among those Libyan intelligence officers allegedly involved were Sayyid Qaddaf al-Damm, Salih al-Druqi and Abdallah Hijazi. They had collaborated closely with Dr. Ghassan al-Ali, head of Abu Nidal's Intelligence Directorate's Committee for Special Missions. Further-more, it was subsequently discovered that the Tunisian passports which the terrorists were carrying had been confiscated from Tunisian workers expelled from Libya earlier in the year.

On 17 April 1986, El-Al security staff at London's Heathrow airport found a bomb, comprising 1.5 kilograms of Semtex high-explosive and an initiation mechanism, concealed in the hand baggage of an Irishwoman named Ann Murphy who was travelling to

Tel Aviv. Arrested and questioned, she revealed that the bag in which the explosive was concealed had been given to her by her fiancé, a Jordanian named Nezar Narwas Mansur Hindawi, whom she was due to meet in Israel where they would be married. The bomb, which had been primed by Hindawi while accompanying Murphy to the airport, was timed to explode once her flight was airborne.

On the following day, Hindawi surrendered himself to the police in London, having been persuaded to do so by his brother who was anxious that the Syrians might kill him to ensure his silence. Under questioning, he revealed that Syria was behind the plot to blow up the El-Al aircraft. The plan had been hatched by senior officers of Syrian Air Force intelligence, among them its chief, General Muhammad Al-Khuly, and members of Abu Nidal's organisation. The bomb had been manufactured by the latter's technical committee and sent via the Syrian diplomatic bag to London where it had been collected by Hindawi from an employee of Syrian Arab Airlines in London. In Damascus he had received training in Damascus in the handling of the bomb from a senior Syrian officer, Colonel Haitham Sa'id, who had shown him how to prime it. Sa'id had also briefed him on the operation and furnished him with a Syrian passport under a false identity.

The information supplied by Hindawi subsequently led to the expulsion of three Syrian diplomats from London and to the arrest of his own brother in connection with the bombing of a discotheque in West Berlin on 5 April in which an American soldier and a Turkish woman had been killed, an outrage for which Libya had been accused of being responsible. Hindawi was tried at the Old Bailey in October, found guilty and imprisoned for forty-five years.

The Syrians by now had increasing suspicions that Abu Nidal's organisation had been penetrated by the Israeli intelligence service, Mossad. They also believed that the latter had had a hand in the Hindawi affair which they saw as having been set up to provide Israel with an excuse to carry out a retaliatory strike against Syria. Furthermore, they had not known beforehand of the hijacking of the Egyptair airliner in November 1985 or the subsequent attacks on the

Rome and Vienna airports. Relations were thus strained between Abu Nidal and his hosts and worsened as his campaign of violence continued, inevitably bringing further opprobrium on the latter.

On 3 August 1986, acting on the Libyans' behalf, Abu Nidal carried out a rocket and mortar attack on the British air base at Akrotiri, in Cyprus, following Colonel Gadaffi's call for the Cypriot government to close down all British bases on the island. The Libyans supplied the boat which landed the terrorists and evacuated them after the attack. The terrorists were led by an experienced Abu Nidal guerrilla, Hani Sammur, and the operation was directed from the Lebanon by Abd al-Rahman Isa, at that time head of Abu Nidal's intelligence directorate. One member of the team, named Hisham Sa'id, was arrested, but the remainder escaped.

On 5 September 1986, four Abu Nidal terrorists hijacked a Pan Am Boeing 747, carrying 358 passengers from Bombay to New York, after it landed to refuel at Karachi airport in Pakistan. Armed with assault rifles, they soon afterwards killed a passenger and tipped his body on to the tarmac below. The flight crew, meanwhile, managed to escape from the aircraft, effectively immobilising it, and before long troops surrounded it at a distance. Negotiations were conducted between the hijackers and the Pakistani authorities, during which the former made a series of demands, including the release of three terrorists imprisoned in Cyprus for the murder during the previous year of three Israelis. After several hours, however, the aircraft's generator ran out of fuel, plunging the aircraft interior into darkness. This caused panic among the terrorists who opened fire on the passengers, killing nineteen. A stewardess meanwhile bravely succeeded in opening the emergency exits and deploying the escape chutes but was shot dead immediately afterwards. As panic-stricken passengers poured out, they met troops who stormed the aircraft, arresting the four terrorists, one of whom was wounded.

The operation had been planned by Samih Muhammad Khudr, a senior member of Abu Nidal's organisation, and the motive was apparently revenge on behalf of Colonel Gadaffi for the American bombing of Libya in April of that year. Based in Lebanon, Khudr was in Karachi at the time of the hijack, but escaped capture. His assistant, Muhammad Harb Al-Turk, was not so fortunate, being arrested by Pakistani police. The terrorists had been trained in the Bekaa Valley, by Abu Nidal's Intelligence Directorate, after which they were flown to Syria from where they subsequently departed on their mission.

On the day following the Karachi hijack, Abu Nidal terrorists carried out an attack on the Neve Shalom synagogue in Istanbul, killing twenty-one worshippers and wounding scores more. The terrorists were subsequently trapped by Turkish police and committed suicide using hand-grenades.

The summer of 1986 had seen Abu Nidal begin to move his head-quarters from Syria, having become *persona non grata* with the regime of President Hafez al-Assad as a result of the Hindawi bomb plot and the hijacking of the Pan Am 747 at Karachi. The move was completed by 31 March 1987 and during the rest of that year there were reports of members of his organisation being seen as far afield as Brazil, Colombia, Peru, Venezuela, Costa Rica and even the United States. It was also suspected as being involved in terrorist attacks on US targets in Europe although, once again, it was never established whether Abu Nidal himself was directing the operations or merely allowing his men to be used as mercenaries by others.

In 1988 his organisation was again active. On 11 May, it exploded a car bomb in the Greek Cypriot capital of Nicosia and fifteen people were injured, some fatally. Four days later, in the Sudanese capital of Khartoum, five terrorists attacked the Sudan Club, frequented by British and Commonwealth expatriates, and the Greek-owned Akropole Hotel. Five Britons, including two small children, and two Sudanese, one a general, were killed and seventeen wounded in these attacks.

Two months later, on 11 July, five terrorists attacked the Greek ferry *City of Poros* with submachine-guns and grenades, killing nine people and wounding eighty. In Athens on that same day, Samih Muhammad Khudr, head of Abu Nidal's Intelligence Directorate's Foreign Intelligence Committee, died when a bomb, concealed in his car, exploded as he drove to the port of Piraeus. It later transpired that he had been the mastermind behind the *City of Poros* operation and was due to hand the vehicle over to his men for it to be loaded on to the ferry. Unknown to him, however, one of his men, on the orders of Abu Nidal himself, had primed the bomb to explode after fifteen minutes when Khudr would be driving the car. Various reasons were mooted for Abu Nidal's assassination of Khudr: one was that Khudr had disagreed with the *City of Poros* operation, arguing that it would serve no purpose and questioning the reasoning behind it; another that he had become too powerful within the organisation.

Abu Nidal claimed that the three attacks in Cyprus, Sudan and Greece were conducted on behalf of the Palestinian cause, but in fact they inflicted great damage on it. Cyprus, which had hitherto been sympathetic to Palestinians, retaliated by expelling some and increasing immigration controls. The Sudanese, who had until then supported the Palestinian struggle, were infuriated and arrested all five terrorists, subsequently trying them and sentencing them to death. In Greece the government of Andreas Papandreou, which had until then showed sympathy to the Arab cause, was highly embarrassed and its eventual demise was expedited by the attack on the *City of Poros*.

Samih Muhammad Khudr was only one of a large number of Abu Nidal's followers to be executed by their leader. Others had suffered a similar fate during the 1970s but it was during the period from November 1987 to the end of 1988 that Abu Nidal carried out a major purge throughout his organisation's ranks of those he suspected were questioning his motives and methods. Approximately 600 were killed, 171 of them in a single night in southern Lebanon in November 1987. Machine-gunned *en masse*, their bodies were bulldozed into a large trench and buried; some of them still alive as they were interred. Among these were some of Abu Nidal's most senior officers and members of his central committee. In Libya 165 were executed and buried in a mass grave, the majority being young Palestinians who had been under the impression that they had been sent to Libya to fight in Chad alongside

Libyan troops. For some obscure reason, Abu Nidal's twisted mind conceived the idea that they had been plotting against him.

These purges inevitably led to defections from his organisation as details of the mass killings in Lebanon and Libya filtered out. Large numbers disappeared from its ranks as they sought refuge with other Palestinian organisations or fled to Syria, Jordan, Tunisia, the Gulf states or Europe. One of the most senior to break ranks was Atif Abu Bakr, the head of Abu Nidal's Political Department. Initially he remained in the Libyan capital of Tripoli, under the protection of Ahmed Jibril's PFLP–GC, but in August 1989 he fled to Algiers and made his way to Tunis a few days later. There he was joined in late October by Abd al-Rahman Isa, Abu Nidal's former chief of intelligence.

Shortly afterwards, the two men established an alternative organisation called the Emergency Leadership. Financed and equipped by Fatah, they soon found former members of Abu Nidal's organisation flocking to join them and it was not long before open warfare was being waged between the two organisations. This resulted in a major engagement in June 1990 in which Abu Nidal's forces were defeated and another in September near Sidon, in the Lebanon, when he lost a further eighty killed and 250 wounded, together with the loss of one of his headquarters.

During the 1980s Abu Nidal maintained that he had established close connections with other terrorist organisations, but in reality these were little more than nodding acquaintanceships. One group with which he did establish an alliance, however, was the Armenian Secret Army for the Liberation of Armenia (ASALA) which modelled itself on the more extreme of the Palestinian groups from which it received support. Formed in 1975 by Gourgen Yanikian as a left-wing pro-Soviet organisation, its long-term aim was the establishment of an independent Armenian republic. At the same time, it sought revenge for the deaths of approximately 1.5 million Armenians killed by the Turks during the period 1915 to 1916.

From 1977 to 1982 ASALA terrorists underwent training in PFLP training camps in southern Lebanon. After the Israeli invasion of Lebanon and the expulsion of the Palestinians from the south of the country in 1982, ASALA was forced to seek alternative support and this was afforded by Abu Nidal who provided the Armenians with funds and the use of his camps in the Bekaa Valley.

Active in Western Europe, the Middle East and North America, ASALA concentrated on attacking Turkish diplomats. Two members of the organisation were arrested by the Swiss in 1980 for travelling with false passports and the organisation responded in late 1980 and early 1981 by bombing Swiss targets in London, Paris, Rome, Milan, Berne, Los Angeles and Beirut. The Swiss authorities capitulated, releasing the two men without further ado. During 1981 ASALA carried out more attacks than any other terrorist organisation, conducting a total of forty in some eleven countries. These included the hijacking of the Turkish consulate in Paris, and the murders of Turkish diplomats in France, Switzerland and Denmark.

In September 1982, two members of ASALA carried out an attack at Ankara airport, killing ten people and wounding eighty. One of the terrorists was captured and revealed under interrogation that the weapons used in the attack had been supplied by Abu Nidal. During the following year, on 15 July 1983, ASALA terrorists carried out a bomb attack at Orly airport, Paris, in which eight people died and sixty were injured. During the hunt for the perpetrators, the leader of the ASALA team, Varoujan Garbidjan, was arrested, tried and sentenced to a lengthy term of imprisonment.

Another organisation which was active in Turkey throughout the 1980s was the Kurdistan Workers' Party, better known by its initials PKK, which was formed by its leader, Abdullah Ocalan, at the end of November 1978. A Marxist–Leninist organisation, its principal aim was the liberation of the Kurdish people and the establishment of an independent homeland in south-eastern Turkey. Driven underground, the PKK's leaders left Turkey just prior to the military coup of 12 September 1980 and made their way to the Lebanon and the Bekaa Valley. They were followed by Kurdish militants who later underwent training in guerrilla warfare, some of them subsequently fighting alongside their Palestinian counterparts during the Israeli invasion of the Lebanon in 1982.

In 1982, the first PKK guerrillas returned to Turkey and began operations in 1984, concentrating their attacks on villages of Kurdish tribes loyal to the government in Ankara, and in particular on the para-military forces established to protect them. In 1985, the PKK established a separate arm, the Kurdistan Popular Liberation Army (ARGK), to recruit religious non-Marxist Kurdish elements. By 1987, the PKK's sympathisers were numbered in their thousands and the ARGK comprised a large army of full-time guerrillas. During 1988 and 1989, the organisation continued its campaign of terror which resulted in the killings of several hundreds of people in the region despite the best efforts of Turkish security forces to prevent them. By the end of the 1980s, however, it had become apparent to the PKK that as a Marxist–Leninist, and thus atheist, organisation it was not attracting support from a population in which Islam played an important role. In 1989 Abdullah Ocalan changed tack, establishing links with Iran and incorporating promotion of Islam in PKK propaganda and political material. At the same time, the PKK switched from conducting its campaign of terror against the civilian population to targeting the Turkish security forces.

In Greece, the 1980s saw activity on the part of the Revolutionary Organisation 17 November, a small radical left-wing group formed in 1975 and named after the November 1973 student uprising in Greece in protest against the military regime in power. Among its aims were the removal of Greece from NATO and the ending of the US military presence in the country. It first came to prominence shortly after it had been formed when on 23 December 1975 one of its members shot dead CIA station chief, Richard Welch, in Athens after he had been named by an American magazine *Counterspy*. Within a relatively short period of time, it established a reputation as one of the most proficient and violent groups in Europe. At the beginning of 1979, it assassinated a senior Greek police officer and in November shot dead a US Navy officer,

Captain George Tsantes, and his driver. In April of the following year a US Army NCO narrowly escaped death when two gunmen on a motorcycle opened fire on him in his car; despite taking evasive action, he was wounded.

In February 1985 the group shot dead a Greek newspaper editor, Nikos Momferatos, claiming in a subsequently published communiqué that he had been a CIA agent. Three years later, in June 1988, members of the group exploded a remote-controlled car bomb, killing the US defence attaché, Captain William Nordeen, just after he left his house in Athens. Thereafter, the group widened the scope of its attacks to include other foreign concerns in Greece, including those of European multi-national companies.

Another group which targeted US personnel in Greece during the late 1970s and 1980s was the Revolutionary Popular Struggle (ELA). Like November 17, with whom it was believed to have links, it was a radical left-wing group formed from opposition to the military junta ruling Greece at the time. In November 1975, it carried out a firebomb attack on the US Air Force commissariat in Athens and two years later, in October 1977, planted a bomb at a USAF NCO's club in Glyfada. In January of the following year it mounted bomb attacks on the offices of the US Information Agency and American Express in Athens.

The early 1980s saw further bomb attacks against US targets. In April 1982, it planted a bomb outside the residence of the US Ambassador. Two months later, four bombs exploded in Athens in protest against the visit of the Supreme Allied Commander Europe, General Bernard Rogers. In March 1986 a similar protest was made against a visit by the US Secretary of State, George Schultz, when a bomb exploded at the Hellenic–American Union in Athens. Eighteen months later, the USAF commissariat in Athens was once again the target of an ELA bomb. During the following month, however, the group suffered its first setback when three of its members were involved in a gun battle with Greek police, two being arrested and one wounded. Despite this, however, the bombings continued throughout the 1980s.

In Latin America, meanwhile, the beginning of the 1980s found Colombia still suffering a high level of terrorism. In February 1980, members of the M–19 group led by Rosemberg Pabón Pabón invaded the Dominican embassy in Bogotá during a reception and held fifteen diplomats captive while demanding the release of a number of their compatriots. The siege lasted sixty-one days, only ending after a ransom was paid; the terrorists' demand for the release of a number of their compatriots was turned down.

Like many Latin-American terrorist groups, M–19 had established links with drugs traffickers who were happy to pay the terrorists a percentage of their profits in return for the latter's protecting them and their assets from government security forces. In 1984 Carlos Toledo Plata, one of the founders of the group, was assassinated by a gunman later discovered to be in the employ of a police 'death squad' with links to the traffickers. It later transpired that disagreement within M–19 over its involvement with drugs trafficking may have been the reason behind Toledo's murder, although it has never been confirmed. A faction led by a member of the group's five-man council, Ivan Marino Ospina, had advocated support for the traffickers' threat to murder five members of the US community in Colombia for every trafficker extradited to the United States. This view, however, did not find favour with the rest of the group and Marino was expelled; he was killed in the following year after a gun battle with troops who cornered him in the town of Cali.

By late 1985 M–19 had suffered a number of reverses, including the arrest of a number of its leaders. Moreover, it had lost much of its political credibility and had been outmanoeuvred by the government of President Belisario Betancur and its relatively liberal policies. In November, the group hit back by staging a major operation which hit the headlines world-wide. Fifty heavily armed terrorists stormed the Palace of Justice in Bogotá, taking control of the building and holding hostage a large number of people including twelve judges among whom was the President of the Supreme Court, Dr. Alfonso Reyes Echandia. The government refused to negotiate with the terrorists who responded by killing all the judges and tossing Dr. Reyes' body out into the street. On the following day, the Army attacked the building and a major battle took place in which all the terrorists were killed, some of them detonating explosives worn round their waists. Tragically, the building caught fire and some fifty hostages also died. The operation proved counter-productive for M–19 which lost even more support throughout the country.

M–19 collaborated closely with another group, the National Liberation Army (ELN), with which it had announced a joint guerrilla front in May 1979. During the 1980s, however, the ELN was not particularly active and left much of the field to the largest of Colombia's major terrorist organisations, the Revolutionary Armed Forces of Colombia (FARC). In 1977, the two groups had come to an informal agreement that FARC would concentrate its efforts on the rural areas, leaving the ELN a free hand in the cities and towns. In practice, however, the ELN did not stick strictly to the agreement and on occasions conducted operations outside urban areas. Like the ELN, FARC had come to rely heavily on funds generated from kidnapping to fund the expansion of its organisation. Foreign employees of large corporations were favoured targets, as was the oil industry infrastructure with pipelines and installations frequently being attacked and blown up. In 1988 alone, fifty attacks were mounted by the ELN against the 500-mile-long Cano–Limon pipeline as part of its campaign to force the government to nationalise the Colombian oil industry. Both groups also turned their attention to the coca and opium growers in Colombia, extorting money in return for protection of crops against government efforts to destroy them. FARC went further, establishing links with the drugs-trafficking cartels from whom it extorted a percentage of profits in return for protection against government counter-narcotics operations.

In Peru, meanwhile, the 1980s witnessed the arrival of a Maoist organisation called Sendero Luminoso (Shining Path) which soon established a reputation as the most violent and ruthless terrorist group in Latin America. It had originally been formed in 1970 from a Peruvian Communist Party splinter group called the Revolutionary Student Front for the Shining Path of Mariátegui whose leader was Abimael Guzmán Reynoso, a professor at the University of Huamanga in Ayacucho who used the alias Comrade Gonzalo. Its membership initially comprised young intellectuals from Peru's universities who subsequently sought support from among the country's Indians who were won over by Shining Path's emulation of the principles and tactics of two famous Peruvian Indian rebel leaders of bygone days, Tupac Amaru and Juan Santos Atahualpa. This appealed greatly to the Indians, many of whom had long nursed deep-seated grievances against white people whom they viewed as having robbed them of land, wealth and influence.

In May 1980, the Sendero Luminoso began a campaign of terror and violence in the rural areas, mainly in the districts of Ayacucho and Lima. By the end of the year more than 240 attacks had taken place, with government establishments in particular being bombed. During the following year the number increased to a rate of forty per month and the terrorists expanded their scope of operations to include raids on banks and attacks on police stations. In February 1982, an attack was mounted on the prison at Ayacucho and 300 prisoners were released by the terrorists. Thereafter, the organisation also turned its attention to foreign companies and organisations as part of its efforts to rid Peru of foreign influences. It carried out a number of assassinations and kidnappings, demanding large ransoms for the lives of its hostages to whom it showed no mercy if its demands were not met.

The second half of the 1980s found Sendero Luminoso collaborating with another group, the Tupac Amaru Revolutionary Movement (MRTA). Named after the famous 18th-century Indian rebel leader, Tupac Amaru, this radical left-wing organisation was formed in 1984 with the aim of ridding Peru of imperialism and establishing a Marxist regime. Numbering some 500 members, the MRTA commenced operations in 1986, initially operating in the northern areas of San Martin, Loreto and Uyacali but thereafter spreading out to Cajamarca, Jaen, the Huallaga Valley, La Libertad, Lambayaque and Amazonas. It carried out a large number of bombings, ambushes, assassinations and kidnappings. During February 1987, it seized a number of radio stations in Lima and broadcast an anti-government communiqué. In 1989, however, the organisation suffered a setback when its leader, Victor Polay, was arrested and imprisoned. This did not deter it from its aims, however, and by the end of the decade it was becoming increasingly active in the rural areas of Peru.

In Britain, the 1980s saw the conflict in Northern Ireland continuing unabated. During the six-month period from October 1981 to March 1982, the level of violence in the province was high, with an increase in sectarian killings following the end of the hunger strike during which Bobby Sands, the terrorist and hunger striker who had won the by-election for Fermanagh and South Tyrone, died on 5 May 1981. During the hunger strike, which ended on 3 October, the Provisionals committed sixty-four murders, twenty of their victims being members of the security forces. Following this, there were indications that they intended to carry out a series of assassinations and bombings with the aim of provoking a Protestant backlash. A further series of murders were committed during the autumn, resulting in reprisals by extremist Protestant groups, including the Ulster Freedom Fighters, who murdered several Catholics in response.

During October and November 1981, the Provisionals carried out five bomb attacks on the British mainland. The first was on 10 October when a remote-controlled bomb was detonated near Chelsea Barracks in London. Its target was a bus carrying members of the 1st Battalion Irish Guards returning from public duties at the Tower of London. Two civilians were killed and forty others, including twenty guardsmen, were injured in the blast.

A week later, on 17 October, the Commandant General Royal Marines, Lieutenant General Sir Steuart Pringle, was seriously injured when a bomb in his car blew up outside his home in south

London, the general losing a leg in the blast. On 26 October a Metropolitan Police bomb-disposal expert, Kenneth Howarth, died while attempting to disarm an explosive device in a restaurant in London's Oxford Street. Other devices were discovered and disarmed in two department stores in Oxford Street on the same day.

On 13 November, a bomb attack was carried out on the south London flat belonging to the Attorney General, Sir Michael Havers, seriously damaging it. Ten days later, on 23 November, a booby-trapped toy pistol exploded at Woolwich Barracks in southeast London, injuring two Army wives.

The following year saw the Provisionals continue their bombings on the mainland. On 20 July 1982, a nail bomb exploded as the Queen's Life Guard of the Household Cavalry was riding along the South Carriageway of Hyde Park on its way to the daily guard mounting ceremony at Horse Guards. Four soldiers, two policemen and seven horses were killed and seven civilians injured in the blast. A few hours later, a bomb exploded beneath the Regent's Park bandstand on which the band of the 1st Battalion The Royal Green Jackets was playing. Six bandsmen were killed and a seventh died of his injuries two weeks later; the remainder of the band and four civilians were injured.

The sectarian violence in Northern Ireland continued. On 22 October 1982 the UVF kidnapped a Roman Catholic, Joseph Donegan, and beat him to death in retaliation for the kidnapping of a part-time NCO of the UDR, Sergeant Thomas Cochrane, whose body was found on 29 October. The Provisionals retaliated on 16 November by shooting Lennie Murphy, reportedly the head of the UVF, who later died in hospital. Also murdered during that month was Robert Bradford, a leading Ulster Unionist and member of parliament for Belfast South.

The first half of 1983 passed without any major incident in Northern Ireland or the mainland. In the Irish Republic, however, the IRA made the headlines again in February when a group kidnapped Shergar, the Derby winner owned by a syndicate led by the Aga Khan, from the Ballymoney Stud at the

Curragh. A ransom demand having been refused, the horse is presumed to have been destroyed.

Other kidnappings by the Provisional IRA also took place in the Irish Republic later that year. In June a father and daughter were abducted from their holiday home in County Mayo but were later released without harm. In August an attempt to kidnap Canadian multi-millionaire Galen Weston, from his home in County Wicklow, ended in a gun battle between five Provisionals and members of the Gardai Siochana's Special Branch who arrested them.

On 22 September, a major event occurred when thirty-eight republican prisoners, armed with pistols and knives, staged a major breakout from the Maze Prison. Fierce fighting took place between prison warders and the escaping prisoners who attempted to drive out of the prison in a hijacked truck but found their route blocked. One warder was killed and six were wounded, while one prisoner was shot. The rest of the prisoners escaped on foot over the neighbouring fields, subsequently hijacking cars or hiding in houses and farm buildings. Several were recaptured but the remainder succeeded in escaping and returning to the Provisional IRA.

On 26 October, on the British mainland, a cache of explosives was discovered on an estate at Pangbourne, in Berkshire. This was reported immediately to the police who placed the cache under surveillance. Shortly afterwards a Provisional IRA quartermaster, Natalino Vella, and two members of an ASU, Thomas Quigley and Paul Kavanagh, travelled from London to Berkshire to inspect the cache where they were promptly arrested by the police. Four years later all three were tried and convicted: Vella was sentenced to fifteen years for firearms offences while Quigley and Kavanagh both received sentences of thirty-five years for their part in the bombings in London in October and November 1981.

Meanwhile, the Metropolitan Police Special Branch had members of another Provisional IRA ASU under close surveillance. This led them to another cache which was found in Salcey Forest, in Northamptonshire. The members of the ASU were later arrested, tried and convicted of conspiracy to cause explosions.

In December, terrorist violence returned to London once again. On 13 December a bomb was discovered in an abandoned holdall in Phillimore Gardens, West London, by an alert member of the public; it was subsequently destroyed with a controlled explosion by bomb-disposal experts. Four days later, on 17 December, the Provisional IRA carried out a bomb attack on the Harrods department store which was crowded with Christmas shoppers. Two police officers and three civilians were killed, with ninety-one injured of whom thirteen were police officers. The attack was a public relations disaster for the organisation which was forced to claim that the bombing had not been authorised by its Army Council.

In December 1983 a British industrialist named Don Tidey was kidnapped by the Provisional IRA at Ballinamore, in County Leitrim in the Irish Republic, and held in an underground bunker by his captors. The Irish security forces succeeded in locating the terrorists and their victim, and units of the Gardai Siochana and the Irish Army approached the area where Tidey was being held. The terrorists opened fire and a battle ensued during which a policeman and soldier were killed. Although assurances had been given that no ransom would be paid for Tidey, it subsequently emerged that the sum of £2 million was paid to the Provisionals for his release.

Early 1984 saw a marked increase in terrorist activity in Northern Ireland. On 6 March the Assistant Governor of the Maze Prison, William McConnel, was shot dead outside his home in East Belfast. Two days later a part-time soldier of the UDR was murdered near Moira and a number of shooting incidents took place during the following five days. On 8 March, terrorists opened fire with an RPG-7 rocket-launcher on troops travelling in an armoured vehicle along Belfast's Springfield Road.

On 14 March the UFF carried out an unsuccessful attempt to murder Sinn Fein MP Gerry Adams and four of his associates travelling through Belfast's city centre. All but one of the men was hit; Adams himself was hit three times but miraculously survived. As explained in Chapter 14, although he did not know it at the time, the Army had a hand in his survival.

September 1984 saw a major blow struck against the Provisional IRA when the authorities in the Irish Republic intercepted a large shipment of weapons destined for it. On 29 September, the trawler *Marita Ann* was apprehended by the Irish Naval Service patrol vessels *Emer* and *Aisling* off the coast of County Kerry. She was found to contain a large consignment of weapons and explosives from the United States.

As recounted by John Loftus and Emily McIntyre in their book *Valhalla's Wake*, the consignment had been assembled by Joseph Murray, the Provisional IRA's senior representative in Boston, Massachusetts. Unknown to his superiors in Dublin, Murray was also a senior member of the Mafia, involved in narcotics, counterfeiting and the fencing of stolen goods. He had been provided with a list of weapons required by the Provisionals who were planning a major armed confrontation with the security forces in Northern Ireland that autumn. He was assisted in his task by three other Provisionals: John Patrick 'Sean' Crawley, a former member of the US Marine Corps who had lived in the Irish Republic since 1979; John McIntyre, a former US Army electronic communications and intelligence specialist; and Patrick Nee, a former US Marine who had seen service in Vietnam.

Between them, Murray, Crawley, McIntyre and Nee procured seven tons of weapons, ammunition and explosives. The weapons included: a Browning .50 calibre heavy machine-gun, forty-eight M-16 rifles, which had been stolen by the Mafia from an Ohio National Guard armoury; twenty-three Colt AR-15 5.56mm rifles; thirteen Heckler & Koch 7.62mm calibre assault rifles; six Ruger Mini-14 5.56mm calibre semi-automatic rifles; an M-1 .30 calibre carbine; eight submachine-guns; nine assorted rifles, six shotguns and fifty-one handguns either purchased locally or stolen in the Boston area; and large quantities of ammunition of various calibres purchased from dealers throughout the United States.

Most ominous of all, however, were three Redeye shoulder-fired surface-to-air missiles, purchased from an arms dealer in Newark, Ohio, which the Provisionals intended to use against British Army and Royal Air Force (RAF) helicopters. Other items in the consignment included: Korean fragmentation grenades; high-explosives; Swedish-manufactured electronic weapon sights; eleven sets of body armour; image intensifier night sights; telescopic sights; other miscellaneous military equipment; a large number of military training manuals; and a quantity of electronic surveillance, counter-surveillance and communications security equipment.

Murray and McIntyre had also acquired a 75-foot trawler, the *Kristen Lee*, and hired an experienced captain, Robert Anderson, to sail her to a rendezvous off the Porcupine Bank, 120 miles off the coast of County Kerry in the south of the Irish Republic. Anderson knew the *Kristen Lee* well; he had been her previous owner until January 1981 when he had been caught by the US Customs illegally fishing for swordfish. The vessel had been confiscated and in July 1984 had been put up for sale at auction by the US authorities, at which point she had been bought by John McIntyre using one of Murray's companies as a front. Subsequently renamed *Valhalla*, she was refitted for her trans-Atlantic voyage.

On 14 September the *Valhalla* left Gloucester Harbour, on the north-east Atlantic coast of the United States, ostensibly seeking swordfish off Newfoundland. Unlike other vessels departing for the fishing grounds that day, however, her fish pens were already full.

On 20 September Joseph Murray and Patrick Nee, accompanied by Murray's pregnant wife, Nee's girlfriend and another couple, flew to Dublin. The plan was that Murray would board the *Marita Ann*, a small wooden trawler captained by Michael Browne, a member of a well-known Kerry fishing family, and rendezvous off the Porcupine Bank where the arms would be transferred from the *Valhalla*. He would be accompanied by Martin Ferris, the Provisional IRA's commander for the south-west of Ireland. Nee meanwhile would wait at the landing point with trucks to transport the arms to a secret location where they would be cached. He and Crawley, who would transfer from the *Valhalla* to the *Marita Ann* and land with the arms, would then drive to a safe house. The two men would thereafter be responsible for training a group of Provisionals in the skills of guerrilla warfare at a secret training camp which they would help to establish in one of the Irish Republic's counties bordering Northern Ireland. On 24 September, however, Murray and his wife suddenly returned to the United States, stating that complications had arisen with the latter's pregnancy. Nee, meanwhile, was ordered to proceed with his part of the operation as planned.

On the morning of the following day, the *Marita Ann* sailed from the port of Fenit and three days later, despite engine trouble, rendezvoused with the *Valhalla* in the late afternoon of 27 September. Conditions were bad and a storm was rising, but despite a heavy sea the arms had all been successfully transferred by dawn of the following day. At this juncture, however, an RAF Nimrod maritime reconnaissance aircraft suddenly appeared and flew low over the two vessels. One of the Provisionals aboard the *Marita Ann* reportedly attempted to shoot the aircraft down with one of the Redeyes, but the Nimrod successfully evaded the missile and flew out of range. Shortly afterwards, the vessel set sail for the intended landing point on the Kerry coast and its rendezvous with Patrick Nee and the transport which would spirit away the arms.

Unknown to all concerned, however, Britain's Secret Intelligence Service (SIS) had already learned of the arms shipment and had informed the Irish authorities. On 24 September, a party of armed Gardai Siochana embarked in the patrol vessels *Emer* and *Aisling* which set sail from the Irish Naval Service base at Cork Harbour, heading for Skellig Rocks off Ballinskelligs Bay where they lay in wait for the *Marita Ann*. Meanwhile the RAF Nimrod tracked the trawler during its passage from Fenit to the rendezvous with the *Valhalla*, monitoring radio transmissions between the two vessels and photographing them as dawn broke. Thereafter the aircraft continued to track the *Marita Ann*, giving details of her progress as she approached Irish territorial waters.

At just after midnight on 28/29 September, the *Emer* intercepted *Marita Ann* which ignored commands to heave-to until four warning shots were fired across her bows. By now she was less than two miles from the coast. Shortly afterwards a boarding-party from

Emer boarded the trawler and a search soon uncovered the consignment of arms. Ferris, Crawley and the crew of three were arrested, all except Michael Browne being transferred to the two patrol vessels.

News of the interception broke on Irish radio on the morning of 29 September. Within hours Patrick Nee, his girlfriend and the couple accompanying them, had caught a ferry to England from where they travelled to France by train and ferry. On 2 October they flew from Paris to Boston.

The *Valhalla* meanwhile, despite damage caused by the increasingly bad weather during the initial stage of her return voyage, had succeeded in reaching Boston Harbour which she entered on the evening of 13 October. Her crew, together with two Provisionals who were on the run from the British and Irish authorities and who had transferred from the *Marita Ann*, dispersed swiftly.

That evening, however, John McIntyre was arrested and questioned by US Customs, but was released thirty-six hours later after convincing his interrogators that he had no connection with any gun-running for the IRA and that he could help them intercept a major drugs shipment being planned by Joseph Murray. A few days he was rearrested, together with Robert Anderson, but both were released a few hours later after McIntyre had reassured Customs agents that he was still working for them.

On 30 November, however, John McIntyre disappeared and was never seen again. It was later claimed that he had been killed as part of a British disinformation operation to protect the identity of an SIS 'mole', operating at high level in the Provisional IRA, who had been the source of the information about the arms shipment. It was also rumoured that a two-man SIS team had tracked him down and that he had subsequently been killed by two members of the SAS.

This was, however, disproved sixteen years later in early 2000, during investigations into an allegedly corrupt FBI agent and his involvement with the leader of the South Boston Mafia leader, James 'Whitey' Bulger, for whom Joseph Murray worked. Bulger had allegedly financed the entire *Valhalla* operation and the major drugs shipment mentioned by McIntyre when being questioned by the US Customs. News of the latter's willingness to talk allegedly reached him via a source within the FBI's organised crime unit in Boston and it is believed that he and an associate, Stephen 'The Rifleman' Flemmi, murdered McIntyre along with two others, a minor criminal named Arthur 'Bucky' Barrett and Deborah Hussey, the daughter of Flemmi's girlfriend. McIntyre was killed to ensure his silence, Barrett for his share of a $1.5 million robbery and Hussey because she knew too much about Bulger's and Flemmi's activities. In early 2000 a member of Bulger's gang arrested by police led investigators to a highway embankment in the area of Boston where the remains of three bodies were found, including those of John McIntyre. By that time Bulger had long since vanished, having disappeared in 1995. At the time of writing he is still on the run as one of the United States' ten most wanted criminals.

In the aftermath of the interception of the *Marita Ann* and the arrests, the Provisional IRA assumed that a 'mole' had compromised the operation and launched an internal investigation, later claiming that it had identified and executed the individual responsible. It was correct in its assumption but it appears the wrong man may have suffered retribution as the terrorist-turned-informer Sean O'Callaghan later claimed that he had been responsible for passing information about the operation to the British.

On 16 April 1986 Joseph Murray, Patrick Nee and Robert Anderson were arrested by the US authorities and charged with conspiracy and illegal arms trafficking. Three years later, on 21 May 1987, Murray was convicted of drugs smuggling and illegal export of arms, receiving a sentence of ten years' imprisonment. Nee and Anderson were also convicted and sentenced to four years each. Meanwhile in the Irish Republic, Martin Ferris and Sean Crawley had both been convicted and sentenced to ten years' imprisonment.

Two weeks before the interception of the *Marita Ann*, the Provisional IRA had mounted its most spectacular attack on the British mainland. On 15 September Patrick Magee, one of the Provisionals' most experienced bomb makers, who had been a member of a group which had planted a total of sixteen bombs in London and other cities during 1978, booked himself under a false identity into the Grand Hotel in Brighton where the Prime Minister, Mrs Margaret Thatcher, and members of her Cabinet would be staying during the annual week-long Conservative Party conference in October. During the next three days he planted a bomb, comprising between twenty and thirty pounds of explosive, behind the panelling in the bathroom of his sixth-floor room. The timer was set to detonate the charge at 2.54 a.m. on Friday 12 October.

The bomb exploded at the appointed hour, destroying much of the hotel. Five people died and a number were injured while Mrs Thatcher herself narrowly escaped death as she had only minutes earlier used a bathroom which took the full force of the blast. Magee, who had been imprisoned during the early 1970s and whose details were thus on police files, was soon identified by his fingerprints. He was kept under surveillance by the police and security services who had been alerted to his involvement in another operation which later transpired to be the planting during July of four bombs in London and a further twelve at hotels in seaside resorts. One was subsequently discovered in a room in the Rubens Hotel in London. Nine months later, on 22 June 1985, the police raided an apartment in Glasgow where they arrested Magee and four other members of the ASU of which he was a member. A cache of 140 pounds of explosives and a quantity of electronic timing devices, was also found in the apartment. In June 1986, Magee was convicted and sentenced to thirty-five years' imprisonment, the other members of the ASU also receiving heavy sentences.

Meanwhile violence in Northern Ireland, which had been at a relatively low level during the summer of 1984, had started to escalate again. On 19 October a soldier was shot dead and another wounded by the Provisional IRA in an ambush in Turf Lodge in south-west Belfast. On 28 October another ambush of an Army patrol took place in Londonderry, and on the following day a joint Army/Royal Ulster Constabulary patrol engaged two gunmen in Armagh.

There were heavy losses on both sides in 1984. The Provisional IRA suffered serious losses with twelve of its men dying in terrorist attacks or being executed as suspected informers. During an eighteen-day period in December, a further five Provisionals died while carrying out missions against the security forces. The Army meanwhile had experienced its worst year for deaths since 1981, losing nine soldiers, and the UDR and the RUC lost a total of nineteen men and women.

One of the more notorious terrorists apprehended that year was the INLA's Chief of Staff, Dominic 'Mad Dog' McGlinchey, who was arrested in the Irish Republic by the Gardai Siochana on 17 March and extradited to Northern Ireland next day. A search of the house in which he was arrested revealed fourteen weapons and 600 rounds of ammunition. By McGlinchey's own admission (later retracted) during a newspaper interview, he had been involved in a total of thirty murders and 200 bombings. He was subsequently tried and convicted of the murder of the mother of an RUC officer, being sentenced on Christmas Eve to life imprisonment. In October of the following year, however, his conviction was quashed by the Belfast Appeal Court and on 12 October 1985 McGlinchey was handed over to the authorities in the Irish Republic where in March 1986 he was tried on firearms charges and sentenced to ten years' imprisonment.

McGlinchey had previously been a member of the Provisional IRA and during the 1970s had served two terms of imprisonment in Northern Ireland and the Irish Republic respectively, being released by the latter in February 1982. He had quarrelled with the Provisionals' leadership while in prison and so joined the INLA as Operations Officer for the area of South Derry. Six months later he assumed the leadership of the organisation as Chief of Staff and set about re-organising and building it up. Cells were established in South Armagh, South Down, Louth, Tyrone, Donegal and elsewhere. Internal feuding, which had hitherto plagued the organisation, was stamped out ruthlessly.

By the end of 1982 the INLA had claimed responsibility for the murders of twenty members of the security forces. One such attack took place on 6 December 1982 when a bomb was placed in the Droppin' Well discotheque at Ballykelly, County Londonderry, killing seventeen people, including eleven soldiers of the 1st Battalion The Cheshire Regiment, and injuring sixty others.

Under McGlinchey's tutelage, the INLA had also turned its attention to raising funds. During 1982 it carried out a number of robberies in the Irish Republic and Northern Ireland, two in County Cork alone netting more than £300,000. On 20 November 1983 an attack was carried out on the Mountain Lodge Pentecostal Gospel Hall at Darkley, in South Armagh, by a group calling itself the 'Catholic Reaction Force'. A gunman opened fire on the congregation of sixty people with a semi-automatic weapon, killing three and wounding seven. Forensic ballistics later identified the weapon as having been used in previous INLA operations.

The pattern of violence in Northern Ireland continued into 1985. At the beginning of February the driver of a school bus, who was also a part-time soldier in the UDR, was murdered by the Provisional IRA; both his brothers, also in the UDR, had already suffered the same fate and he himself had survived a previous attempt in October 1980.

On 23 February an Army patrol encountered three armed terrorists and opened fire, killing all three who were subsequently identified as Charles Breslin, Michael Devine and his brother, David Devine. The terrorists were heavily armed, with an FN FAL 7.62mm self-loading rifle (SLR), an FN FNC 5.56mm SLR, a Ruger Mini-14 5.56mm rifle, two grenades and two rifle-grenade projectors.

A few weeks later, the Provisionals carried out an attack on the RUC police station at Newry, on the borders of Counties Down and Armagh. A salvo of mortar bombs, launched from a battery of home-made mortar tubes mounted on a flat-bed lorry positioned 200 metres away in a car park in a neighbouring street, hit the station. One bomb exploded in the canteen, killing nine police officers, two of them women, and injuring eight others and twenty-five civilians.

On 27 March a joint RUC/Army patrol passing the Divis Flats in the Lower Falls area of West Belfast was attacked with a remote-controlled bomb. One soldier of the 1st Battalion The King's Own Royal Border Regiment was killed in the blast. Two days later in Rathfriland, a reserve constable in the RUC was shot dead by two Provisional IRA gunmen.

The Provisionals meanwhile had turned their attention once more to the mainland, and were planning to carry out a major operation involving a number of bomb attacks in twelve seaside resorts. The police and the Security Service were, however, at a high state of vigilance and the plot was thwarted at the end of June.

They suffered a further setback on 26 January 1986 when security forces in the Irish Republic found three arms caches: two in County Sligo and one in County Roscommon. Their contents included crates marked 'Libyan Armed Forces', some of which contained Yugoslav-manufactured ammunition.

That year saw the Provisionals increasing their use of improvised explosive devices, targeting the security forces and commercial businesses in the province. On 3 May two of their members, Seamus McElwaine and Kevin Lynch, were killed and wounded respectively in an Army ambush while they were planting an 800-pound bomb. McElwaine had been serving a life sentence when he took part in the mass breakout from the Maze Prison on 25 September 1983. Both men were armed with AR-15 rifles which forensic ballistic analysis revealed had been used in February to murder an off-duty policeman and a barman.

On 7 August, the Provisionals announced that they were increasing their list of targets to include civilian contractors carrying out work on military and government installations. This not only had an adverse effect on the Catholic population, many of whom were employed on such work, but also resulted in retaliation from the Ulster Volunteer Force which announced that it would target Catholics working for Protestant companies.

The period 1985 to 1987 saw the Provisional IRA receive four large consignments of arms supplied by Libya which replaced Irish–American factions in the United States as principal arms suppliers to the organisation after a crackdown by the US authorities.

The murder of Woman Police Constable Yvonne Fletcher in April 1984, the subsequent expulsion of twenty-two Libyan diplomats and British support and assistance for the American bombing of Tripoli had led to an all-time low in relations between the British and Colonel Muammar Gadaffi's regime.

The first consignment, comprising ten tons of small arms and anti-tank rockets, was delivered in August 1985. Two months later this was followed by a quantity of machine-guns. In July 1986 fourteen tons of weapons were delivered, followed in September by eighty tons of Semtex explosive. In November 1987 the trawler *Eksund* was inter-cepted by the French authorities off the coast of France. It was found to be carrying 150 tons of weapons and explosives comprising ten Russian 12.7mm heavy machine-guns, twenty *Strela* SAM-7 shoulder-fired surface-to-air missiles and two tons of Semtex.

In Northern Ireland 1987 proved to be a year of great violence. In January, the INLA was once again rent by the long-running feud between its two factions when the leader of one, Gerald 'Dr. Death' Steenson, murdered the leader of the other, John 'Big Man' O'Reilly, at a hotel in Drogheda. This led to a spate of killings, including that of Steenson, until a truce was called. One of the victims of these killings was the wife of Dominic McGlinchey who was in Portlaoise Prison, in the Irish Republic, at the time.

In February the Provisional IRA stepped up the level of its activ-ities, mounting a number of attacks against the RUC and the Army, with the same pattern continuing throughout March and April. On 25 April Lord Justice Gibson, the second most senior judge in Northern Ireland, and his wife, lost their lives at Killen in County Armagh while returning from holiday to their home at Dumbo in County Down. Crossing the border from the Irish Republic, they had just left their Gardai Siochana escort prior to meeting one provided by the RUC when a 500-pound mine exploded, killing both of them and destroying their car. Lord Gibson, who was the fifth member of the Northern Ireland judiciary to be killed by the IRA, had been a marked man since he had acquitted three RUC officers of the murder of a man named Eugene Toman who had on

11 November 1982 been shot dead at an RUC roadblock together with two others, Sean Burns and Gervaise McKerr. Much controversy had surrounded the shooting, particularly as all three men had been unarmed, and Lord Gibson had added fuel to it by praising the three officers for bringing all three men to 'the final court of justice'. His remarks had caused uproar by giving the impression that there was in existence a judicially approved policy of 'shoot to kill'. Thereafter, he was on the Provisionals' hit list.

In May, the Provisional IRA suffered a setback when it lost eight of its men in an ambush laid by 22 SAS at Loughgall, a detailed account of which appears in Chapter 14. On the mainland in August, three Provisionals were apprehended near the home of the Secretary of State for Northern Ireland, Tom King. They were found to be in possession of a list of addresses and registration numbers of cars belonging to King and a number of others who were potential targets. Refusing to make any statements, they were subsequently tried and convicted of conspiracy to murder, each receiving a sentence of twenty-five years' imprisonment.

The Provisionals continued their attacks against the security forces, not only in Northern Ireland but also in Europe where a number of their ASUs were based in West Germany, Holland and Belgium. In March 1987 they carried out a car bomb attack on the headquarters of the British Army of the Rhine at Rheindahlen, in West Germany. Thirty people were injured in the blast which was the first of some twenty attacks in West Germany and Holland against British service personnel over the next three years. Such attacks, particularly in the case of one in which two Australian tourists were shot dead after being mistaken for off-duty soldiers, proved to be counter-productive for the Provisionals. They resulted in bad publicity for them and proved to be costly in terms of resources and personnel, a dozen or so of the latter being arrested by the authorities in the countries concerned.

As 1987 drew to a close, the Provisional IRA committed one of the most horrific acts it has perpetrated during the last thirty years of conflict in Northern Ireland. On 11 November, a bomb exploded without warning in the St. Michael's Reading Rooms in Belmore Street in Enniskillen, County Fermanagh, as people gathered outside the building prior to the annual Remembrance Day service at the town's war memorial. Eleven were killed, among them six pensioners and a nurse, and sixty-one injured. The adverse political fallout from this inexcusable atrocity was such that the Provisional IRA disbanded its West Fermanagh unit which had carried out the bombing.

The following year, 1988, got off to a promising start for the security forces with the interception of a UDA arms haul in two cars stopped at an RUC vehicle checkpoint in Portadown, yielding sixty-one Czech-manufactured 58P assault rifles, thirty Browning pistols, 150 Soviet-manufactured hand-grenades and more than 11,000 rounds of ammunition. Meanwhile in the Irish Republic, the Gardai Siochana located a major Provisional IRA arms cache on a beach in County Donegal.

Thereafter, however, the level of violence escalated to an extent that 1988 proved to be worst year for Army casualties and has been unequalled since. During March alone, there were seventeen bomb attacks and twenty shooting incidents. That same month was also marked elsewhere by the killing of three Provisional IRA terrorists in Gibraltar by troops of 22 SAS, an account of which appears in Chapter 14.

The summer of 1988 saw the Provisionals active again in Europe. On 1 May, they mounted two simultaneous attacks against British servicemen stationed in West Germany. The first took place at the town of Roermond, near the border with Holland, when three NCOs of the RAF in a car came under attack from gunmen with automatic weapons. One was killed and the other two were wounded in the attack. Fifteen minutes later, two more RAF NCOs were killed and a third was seriously injured thirty miles away at Nieuw Bergen when a bomb planted under their car exploded as they got into the vehicle after leaving a nearby discotheque.

The following month, however, saw the arrest in Belgium of Patrick Ryan, allegedly a Provisional 'godfather' and suspected of being a quartermaster for Europe-based ASUs, at the home of a known IRA sympathiser where a quantity of bomb-making equipment and manuals was seized together with a large sum of money. The British authorities immediately applied for Ryan's extradition, but the Belgian government, fearful of repercussions, deported him instead to the Irish Republic, where he eventually escaped prosecution.

On 15 June, at Lisburn in Northern Ireland six off-duty soldiers taking part in a charity half-marathon, died when a bomb exploded under their van. During the period July to September, nineteen soldiers were killed in attacks by the Provisionals. On 1 August, a Provisional IRA bomb exploded in an accommodation block at the Royal Engineers Postal Communications and Courier Depot at Mill Hill in north London, killing an NCO and injuring nine other soldiers. On 20 August, eight soldiers of the 1st Battalion The Light Infantry were killed and nineteen injured when a culvert bomb was detonated under the bus in which they were travelling.

Further attacks were mounted against servicemen in Europe. In July, nine soldiers were injured after a bomb exploded at a British Army barracks at Duisberg in West Germany. On 12 August, a warrant officer in the Royal Regiment of Wales was shot dead by two Provisional IRA gunmen at the port of Ostend in Belgium while travelling home on leave. During the same month a bomb exploded at a base in Düsseldorf, wounding three members of the Royal Engineers.

During 1989, the Provisionals continued their bombing campaigns on the British mainland and in Germany. On 20 February three bombs exploded at Tern Hill Barracks, in Shropshire, the base of the 2nd Battalion The Parachute Regiment, the only casualty being a soldier who suffered a minor injury to his face. During the summer further attacks were carried out against British troops and their families serving in West Germany. On 2 July, a corporal in the Royal Tank Regiment was killed and his wife and two children injured when a bomb attached beneath his car exploded outside his rented house in Kaiserallee, a suburb of Hanover. On 7 September at Dortmund, the German wife of a British staff sergeant was killed in her car near the British Army base at Unna-Messen near Dortmund; she was shot at point-blank range with an AK-47 assault rifle by four Provisionals who later claimed that they had mistaken her for her husband. In October, an RAF corporal and his 6-month-old baby daughter were shot dead at a petrol station in Wildenrath.

On 22 September, ten bandsmen of the Royal Marines School of Music, at Deal on the coast of Kent, were killed when a bomb exploded in a rest room in the barracks; an eleventh died of his wounds a year later. In November, a car bomb exploded under a soldier's car outside his quarters in the garrison town of Colchester in Essex, blowing off his legs and seriously injuring his wife.

In Northern Ireland, meanwhile, attacks on the security forces continued. On 18 November, three members of 3rd Battalion The Parachute Regiment died and a fourth was seriously injured when a 900-pound landmine was detonated as their two-vehicle patrol was travelling along the Drumlough road north of Mayobridge. On 13 December, two members of the 1st Battalion The King's Own Scottish Borderers were killed during a Provisional IRA attack on a vehicle checkpoint at Derryard in County Fermanagh. A large number of terrorists, later estimated at some two dozen, took part in the attack which began when a truck halted at the checkpoint. As the soldiers approached the vehicle, terrorists opened fire from inside the back of it, shooting one of them dead. Immediately afterwards, the terrorists drove a van through the perimeter of the checkpoint and detonated a bomb inside it, killing an NCO, before making their escape in the truck towards the border.

A further international dimension to the conflict in Northern Ireland had been revealed earlier in the year when on 21 April three loyalists and a South African diplomat were arrested in Paris in the company of British-based arms dealers. It transpired that they were negotiating the purchase of weapons in exchange for missile components stolen from the factory of Shorts Missile Systems in Belfast.

In fact, there had been a connection between South Africa and the loyalist movement since a visit to Belfast in 1985 of an individual named Dick Wright. Originally from Portadown, he had emigrated to South Africa where he was employed by the state-owned arms corporation, Armscor. The South Africans were keen to acquire details of a surface-to-air missile being developed by Shorts and had given the task of obtaining them to Wright who possessed useful contacts within the loyalist movement. Among them was his nephew Alan Wright, a senior member of Ulster Resistance, a group which the latter had founded with the Reverend Ian Paisley and Peter Robinson, leader of the Democratic Unionist Party (DUP).

During his visit, Dick Wright visited a senior member of the UDA living in East Belfast and offered to supply the organisation with arms. While the minimum order value was £250,000, the South Africans would be happy to accept missile components or plans in lieu of cash. The UDA gave lengthy consideration to his offer and in October 1986 despatched one of its members, Brian Nelson, who was living and working in Germany, to investigate the matter further. At that time, it had just undergone a radical restructuring, reducing its numbers to a hard core of some 200 members organised into cells of up to eight men whose identities were only known to themselves. In addition, the organisation was intending to increase and upgrade the stocks of weapons held by its military wings, the UVF and UFF, which consisted of a small number of handguns, machine-pistols and submachine-guns.

The principal reason for the UDA's programme of reorganisation and seeking of arms was the signing in November 1985 of the Anglo-Irish Agreement by Britain and the Irish Republic, an accord which for the first time gave the latter a say in the governing of Northern Ireland. Under its terms, the Irish government established a secretariat in the province with a brief to monitor the day-to-day running of the province. In addition, the British undertook to address the question of Catholic minority grievances over lack of impartiality in administration of justice within the province. The quid pro quo was that the Irish Republic recognised the existence of Northern Ireland, its legitimacy being based on the wish by the majority of the province's population to remain part of the United Kingdom. Needless to say, loyalists were infuriated that the Republic had been permitted a role in the governing of the province, and were convinced that the British government had sold them out. Opposition to the accord manifested itself in the form of a general strike and violent protests by loyalists who launched a long-running campaign against it.

The UDA meanwhile realised there was a very real possibility that it could be called upon to defend the loyalist communities in the province, not only against the Provisional IRA but also against the security forces in the event of the latter cracking down on loyalist paramilitary organisations. It was well aware, however, that the UVF and UFF were ill-equipped to do so and for that reason commenced looking for sources of arms and explosives to purchase with the considerable funds at its disposal. The organisation had renewed contact with right-wing groups in Italy, Spain, Portugal, Turkey and the United States but had been unsuccessful in finding reliable suppliers. South Africa and Armscor thus represented the only possible source of supply.

Brian Nelson spent three weeks in Johannesburg during which he arranged the purchase of £150,000 worth of weapons which comprised 200 AK-47 assault rifles, 90 Browning pistols, approximately 500 RGD-5 fragmentation grenades, twelve RPG-7 rocket-propelled grenade launchers and 30,000 rounds of 7.62mm and 9mm ammunition. Funds for payment for the weapons were raised at a stroke in June 1987 by a raid on the Northern bank in Portadown which netted £300,000.

The weapons left South Africa at the end of December 1987 when they were despatched by Joseph Fawzi, a Lebanese employed by an American arms dealer acting on behalf of Armscor. During January 1988, the entire consignment was landed at a location on the coast of County Down and, having been divided into three lots apportioned to the UVF, UFF and Ulster Resistance respectively, thereafter disappeared into well concealed arms caches.

The three loyalists arrested by French police in Paris on 21 April 1989, along with South African diplomat Daniel Storm, were members of Ulster Resistance: Samuel Quinn, Noel Lyttle and James King. Quinn was a senior NCO in a Territorial Army (TA) air defence unit based in Northern Ireland, while Noel Lyttle was a civil servant and former member of the UDR, as well as being a close associate of the Reverend Ian Paisley and DUP leader Peter Robinson. The British-based arms dealer was a South African-born, naturalised American named Douglas Bernhardt who ran a company named Field Arms situated in the London district of Mayfair. It transpired that the three loyalists were offering the South Africans, who had already made a down-payment of £50,000, plans, components and a dummy Blowpipe missile stolen from Quinn's TA unit's base at Newtownards. Quinn, Lyttle and King were released on bail by the French and it is believed that no action was taken against Bernhardt by the British authorities. Shortly afterwards, the latter expelled three South African diplomats based at the embassy in London for their involvement in the affair.

In other parts of the world, the 1980s also featured a number of other terrorist organisations who made their presence known from the beginning of the decade onwards.

On 10 March 1980 a synagogue in the Rue Copernic, Paris, was the target of a bomb attack; one of a series carried out by the PFLP–SC formed by Salim Abu Salem after the death of Wadi Haddad in March 1978. On 30 April 1980 in London, six Arab terrorists hijacked the Iranian Embassy in London and took twenty-six hostages. A full account of the subsequent siege of the embassy, and the rescue operation which ended it, is given in Chapter 8.

Three months later, on 31 July 1980, the Norfolk Hotel in the Kenyan capital of Nairobi was blown up by Salim Abu Salem's PFLP–SC, apparently in revenge for Kenya's role in helping the Israelis mount their rescue operation at Entebbe. Two days later, on 2 August 1980, a bomb attack was carried out at Bologna railway station by a right-wing fascist group calling itself the Armed Revolutionary

Nuclei. Eighty-four people died and 186 were injured in the blast. In October 1980, the PFLP–SC again bombed the synagogue in the Rue Copernic, in Paris, killing four people.

During the following year, on 13 May 1981, an assassination attempt was made on the life of Pope John Paul II by Mehmet Ali Agca, a former member of a Turkish group called the Grey Wolves, the unofficial armed wing of the National Movement Party founded during the 1960s, but banned after the military coup in Turkey on 12 September 1980. Allegations were made by the CIA that the Bulgarian intelligence service, acting on behalf of the KGB, was behind the attempt, but this was never proved; in later years other evidence came to light which pointed to the increased likelihood that right-wing elements in Turkey were responsible.

On 18 January 1982 Lieutenant Colonel Charles Ray, the assistant military attaché at the US embassy in Paris, was murdered in the Passy district of Paris by members of FARL, the Christian Lebanese group formed in 1980 to strike at American and Israeli targets. On 3 April 1982, the group struck again when it murdered Ya'acov Bar-Simontov, the second secretary at the Israeli embassy, who was killed by a female terrorist in his apartment.

On 31 October 1984 the prime minister of India, Indira Gandhi, was assassinated by two of her personal bodyguards who were members of an extremist group seeking revenge for the Indian Army's assault on the Golden Temple of Amritsar five months earlier.

In January 1985 the Forças Populares do 25 Abril, commonly known as FP–25, a left-wing Portuguese group formed in 1980, carried out a number of attacks on NATO targets in Portugal, including one with a mortar on warships in Lisbon harbour. Other targets included the US embassy and NATO headquarters in Lisbon, other military installations, vehicles belonging to German military personnel based in the town of Beja, industrialists, banks and members of the police. Seventy-three suspected members of FP–25 were subsequently arrested, including Lieutenant Colonel Otelo Saraiva de Carvalho, a national hero and leader of the 1974 revolution by the Portuguese armed forces which overthrew the previous long-established right-wing dictatorship. A former member of FP–25, José Rosa Barradas, who had turned state's evidence, was shot in the summer of 1985 just prior to the start of the trial of those indicted for terrorist offences.

Terrorists also struck in various other parts of the world during 1985. In Belgium, April saw a bomb attack on the headquarters of the North Atlantic Assembly in Brussels by a hitherto unknown group, calling itself the Revolutionary Front for Proletarian Action, which also claimed responsibility for the bombing on 21 April of the AEG–Telefunken offices in the city.

On 23 June a bomb on an Air India Boeing 747, en route from Toronto to London, blew up over the Irish Sea, killing all 329 people on board. At the same time, another exploded in a suitcase being unloaded from a Canadair flight for transhipment to an Air India flight to Tokyo, killing two baggage handlers. Sikh extremists were suspected of being responsible for both bombings as further reprisals for the attack on the Golden Temple at Amritsar during the previous year. On 25 September a team of three terrorists, comprising two Arabs and an Englishman named Ian Davison, of the PLO's Force 17, murdered three Israelis on board their yacht in Larnaca harbour, Cyprus. All three were arrested, tried and sentenced to life imprisonment. Israel retaliated by bombing the PLO headquarters on 1 October.

On 2 April 1986 a bomb exploded aboard a TWA Boeing 727 as it approached Athens airport from Rome. The aircraft landed safely, but an 18-month-old baby died after being sucked out of a hole in the fuselage. A woman named May Mansur, the widow of a Syrian Socialist National Party terrorist, was named as the alleged bomber. On 17 September, FARL carried out a series of bomb attacks in Paris, culminating in the bombing of a crowded department store in which five people were killed and sixty-one injured. The purpose of the campaign was to force the French authorities to free the group's leader, Georges Abdallah.

In November 1987, a bomb exploded aboard a Korean Air Lines aircraft en route from Baghdad to Seoul, killing all 115 passengers and crew. It was subsequently determined that two agents of the North Korean intelligence service were responsible.

Just over a year later, on 21 December 1988, a Boeing 747, Pan Am Flight 103, en route from London Heathrow to New York, blew up over the Scottish town of Lockerbie, killing 259 people aboard the aircraft and eleven on the ground. Subsequent investigations pointed to the bomb having been concealed in a Toshihiba 'Bombeat' radio/tape recorder in baggage loaded aboard the aircraft at Frankfurt and consigned to New York via London.

Two months beforehand, fifteen members of a cell of the PFLP–GC, the organisation led by Ahmad Jibril, had been arrested by police in Frankfurt and Düsseldorf. A search of a car belonging to one of them, Hafez Dalkamoni, revealed three Toshiba 'Bombeat' radio/tape recorders, each with a bomb concealed inside, and barometric fuses of the type used in the bomb on Flight 103. Under questioning, members of this group alleged that another of those arrested, Marwan Khreesat, had assembled five such bombs, each containing eleven pounds of Semtex high-explosive; the same amount estimated by investigators to have been in the Pan Am 103 bomb.

Further investigations uncovered links between the PFLP–GC and Iran, while also linking the latter with Islamic fundamentalists living in the large Turkish *gastarbeiter* (guest worker) community in Germany. Suspicion grew that a Turkish member of the labour force at Frankfurt airport might have inserted the bomb into baggage being loaded aboard the aircraft. An alleged motive for Iran was retaliation against the United States for the accidental shooting down earlier in the year, on 4 July, of an Iranian Airbus by the battleship USS *Vincennes* in the Gulf. A US intelligence report alleged that Iran's Interior Minister, Ali-Akbar Mohteshemi, had paid $10 million to Ahmed Jibril to blow up an American airliner. Subsequent investigations would further point the finger of suspicion at Libya. Two members of its intelligence service, Abdel Basset al-Megrahi and Lamen Fhimah, were named and indicted by a US grand jury for the murder of the 270 people aboard the aircraft, ultimately being brought to trial in the Netherlands in 1999.

The 1980s was the decade which saw the appearance of a large number of Islamic fundamentalist groups, some of which had been formed in the late 1970s. After the Iranian Islamic revolution of 1979, many of these groups received support from the regime of Ayatollah Ruhollah Khomeini. The nerve centre for such support came from the Taleghani Centre, an inconspicuous but heavily guarded four-storey building in Tehran. Islamic fundamentalist groups, each with its own leadership and military element, from a number of countries including the Gulf states, Iraq, Saudi Arabia, North Africa, the Lebanon and the Philippines, were based in the building under the auspices of the Council for the Islamic Revolution headed by Ayatollah Hussein Ali Montazeri, and its advisers included members of the Syrian and Libyan intelligence services.

Among those organisations formed in the late 1970s was Al-Gama'at al-Islamiya (The Islamic Group), an Egyptian group whose spiritual leader was Sheikh Omar Abdel-Rahman, and whose aim was, and still is, the overthrow of the Egyptian government and its replacement by an Islamic state. With a strength of several thousand, it engaged in attacks against the Egyptian security forces, members of the Coptic Christian community and opponents of Islamic fundamentalism within Egypt. Also active in Egypt since the late 1970s was the Al Takfir Wal Higra led by Abbud al-Zumar, and the Vanguards of Conquest headed by Dr. Ayman al-Zawahiri. Like Al-Gama'at al-Islamiya, the aim of these two groups was the imposition of Islamic rule on Egypt.

Also active from the late 1970s onwards was the Palestinian Islamic Organisation (PIO) which was formed from militant Palestinians in the Gaza Strip. With its largest faction based in Syria, this group's areas of operations were Israel and the occupied territories, as well as Jordan and Lebanon. Its aim was the establishment of an Islamic Palestinian state and the destruction of Israel through holy war.

One group which concentrated its attacks on targets within the United States, the 'Great Satan', was Jamaat ul-Fuqra. An Islamic sect which uses violence as a means to 'purify Islam', it was formed in the early 1980s by a Pakistani cleric named Shaykh Mubarik Ali Gilani, last known to be based in Pakistan. Cells were established in the United States, their members buying remote areas of land in which they lived communally and isolated from Western society. During the 1980s attacks, including assassinations and firebombings, were carried out on targets throughout the Unites States on those perceived to be 'enemies of Islam', including Muslims.

One of the most notorious and significant of all the Islamic extremist groups established during the 1980s was Hizbollah, a radical Shi'ite group formed in 1983 in the Lebanon and enjoying the logistical and operational support of Iran. As described in further detail in Chapter 10, on 18 April 1983 it carried out a car bomb attack on the US Embassy in Beirut. Sixty-three people, including nine senior CIA Lebanon-based agents, died in the blast, and hundreds were injured.

Seven months later, on 23 October 1983, Hizbollah struck again when a suicide bomber drove a truck loaded with explosives through the perimeter defences of the headquarters of the US Marine Corps' 24th Marine Amphibious Unit, the US element of the multi-national peacekeeping force in the Lebanon at the time, and detonated his bomb. A similar attack was carried out almost simultaneously on the headquarters of the French contingent of the peacekeeping force located in the city itself. In these two attacks 241 Marines and US Navy personnel and fifty-eight French paratroops died. The following month of November saw yet another suicide bomb attack by Hizbollah, on an Israeli military government building in Sidon, which killed sixty-seven people.

The largest of the Shi'ite groups in the Middle East was Al Dawa al-Islamiya (the Islamic Call) which was based in Tehran. On 12 December 1983, it gained further prominence by carrying out a number of bomb attacks in the Emirate of Kuwait. The first took place at the US embassy when a truck carrying forty-five cylinders of gas wrapped in plastic explosive careered through the compound gates and crashed into the annex to the embassy. The massive explosion demolished the three-storey building and caused considerable damage throughout the surrounding area. Five people died in the blast and scores were injured. The toll would have been greater but for the fact that only a quarter of the explosives and gas cylinders had exploded.

Another attack took place at the French embassy, where the Ambassador narrowly missed being crushed by a large chandelier which, dislodged from its fastenings, crashed down on to his desk. Meanwhile, car bombs exploded at Kuwait's international airport, the control centre of the Emirate's electricity supply company and the living accommodation of Americans working for the Raytheon Corporation which was at that time installing missile systems for the Kuwaiti armed forces. The largest bomb, however, was reserved for the Emirate's principal oil refinery at Shuaiba. A truck carrying 200 gas cylinders and explosives was parked inside the refinery and duly blew up. Once again, some of the gas cylinders failed to explode and total destruction of the refinery was avoided.

Those responsible for the bombings comprised a group of eighteen members of Al Dawa and three members of Hizbollah. A thumb belonging to the suicide bomber of the US embassy enabled the Kuwaiti authorities to identify him and twenty-one suspects were arrested. All were tried, and four others were tried *in absentia*. Six, including three still at large, received death sentences while eighteen were imprisoned.

On 31 July 1984 an Air France Boeing 737, en route from Frankfurt to Paris, was hijacked by members of Islamic Jihad and forced to fly to Tehran. There the terrorists demanded the release of terrorists imprisoned by the French for the attempted murder of Shapour Bakhtiar, a leading opponent of the regime of Ayatollah Khomeini. Two hostages were killed, but the terrorists' demands were not met. Subsequently there were suspicions that the Iranian government had colluded with the terrorists.

Seven weeks later Hizbollah struck again at the Americans. On 20 September, a suicide bomber drove a truck loaded with explosives into the compound of the US embassy annex in Beirut. However, as described further in Chapter 10, the terrorists' plot was foiled by the bodyguard of the British Ambassador, who was visiting his US counterpart. He shot and killed the terrorist driving the vehicle which swerved off-course before exploding. Fourteen died and dozens were injured in the blast.

On 3 December, a group of Islamic Jihad terrorists hijacked a Kuwaiti airliner en route from Dubai to Karachi and forced it to fly to Tehran where they demanded the release of the Al Dawa and Hizbollah terrorists imprisoned in Kuwait for the bombings carried out in December 1983. Two hostages, Americans working for the US Agency for International Development (AID), were killed by the hijackers before they surrendered six days later. Once again, the Iranian government was suspected of collusion with the terrorists.

Just over six months later, Islamic Jihad hijacked another airliner, this time a TWA aircraft, Flight 847, flying from Athens to Rome. The hijacking subsequently escalated into a major crisis with the aircraft flying to and fro between Beirut and Algiers as the terrorists once again demanded the release of those imprisoned in Kuwait. The full story of the hijacking of TWA Flight 847 and the ensuing events is told in Chapter 12.

The end of the 1980s saw yet another attack on aircraft by Islamic Jihad. In August 1989, a bomb aboard a French airliner exploded over Chad, killing 171 people. Islamic Jihad claimed responsibility.

Another group which came to prominence during the late 1980s was HAMAS, which was founded by Imam Sheikh Ahmad Ibrahim Yassin who subsequently became its spiritual leader. Formed in the Gaza Strip in late 1987, within a few months its influence equalled that of the PLO and thanks to the Intifada, the mass revolt by Palestinians, which began to spread throughout the occupied territories that year, it found fertile ground among young and militant Palestinian males who had become disillusioned with the PLO which they regarded as having lost its cutting edge.

In southern Asia, 1983 had seen the start of the long-running guerrilla war between the Sri Lankan government and the Liberation Tigers of Tamil Eelam (LTTE). Led by Velupillai Prabhakaran and seeking the establishment of an independent Tamil state in the north and east of the island, the LTTE from the very start of its campaign employed a combination of an insurgency campaign and terrorist tactics, the latter including assassinations and bombings, and it soon gained a reputation for ruthlessness. In addition, the organisation established a network among the 450,000 Tamils who had fled to the southern Indian state of Tamil Nadu and to more than fifty countries throughout the world after a series of ethnic riots which had started during the 1970s and culminated in the most severe of them in 1983.

Tamil insurgency had begun during the early 1970s in the northeast region of Sri Lanka, being marked by a series of bombings. A number of different organisations were spawned during this period, the LTTE being formed in 1974, initially as the Tamil New Tigers, with links to political organisations such as the Tamil United Liberation Front (TULF), the Eelam Revolutionary Organisers (EROS) and the Tamil Liberation Front (TLF).

From 1977 onwards, the LTTE established an international network in countries where there were Tamil communities, including Great Britain which became the organisation's principal base in Europe. By the 1980s its tentacles reached throughout the Middle East and North Africa where an LTTE presence was established in countries which included Iraq, Iran, Syria, the Lebanon, Algeria, Morocco and the Yemen. In some instances, links were established with other separatist movements and terrorist organisations although the LTTE exercised caution in doing so to avoid attracting the attention of foreign security and intelligence agencies.

In Tamil Nadu 1982 saw the establishment of LTTE training camps, although military assistance from the Indian government did not commence until August 1983 when Prime Minister Indira Gandhi decided to support the Tamil separatists. The task of providing it was given to the Third Agency of India's national intelligence service, the Research and Analysis Wing (RAW), which by mid-1987 was providing funds, arms and training for more than 20,000 Tamil insurgents in thirty-two camps. Initially, most of the training was provided at camps in Uttar Pradesh, specialist training being given by Indian Army instructors attached to the RAW. Highly secret training was conducted at Chakrata, north of Dehra Dun, where similar instruction had been given previously to guerrillas from Pakistan, Bangladesh and Tibet.

From 1983 onwards, the LTTE set up a highly sophisticated arms procurement system from sources throughout the world. It also established commercial companies in countries such as Singapore, Malaysia, Burma, Bangladesh, Cyprus and elsewhere, while investing its funds, raised from Tamil communities world-wide, through its offices in thirty-eight countries, on the stock-markets in London and New York. In 1985 the organisation, which had hitherto leased vessels, established its own fleet of ships to carry arms and equipment from India to its forces in Sri Lanka. Two were subsequently lost: one, carrying two and a half tons of arms, ran aground in Greece; the other, loaded with weapons supplied by a Singapore-based Australian arms dealer, was seized by the authorities in Madras. In late 1987, the organisation established a base in the town of Twante, in Burma's Irrawaddy delta, for use as a trans-shipment point. In October of that year an LTTE vessel was observed entering the port of Rangoon to load a cargo of arms which was subsequently unloaded off the area of Mullaitivu in the north-east of Sri Lanka. At the same time, however, the organisation continued to maintain a shipment base at Phuket, on the coast of Thailand. Another facility used to good effect by the LTTE was an island in the Andaman Sea, off the coast of Malaysia, where combat swimmers were trained in the techniques of underwater demolition by Norwegian mercenaries; they were subsequently formed into special underwater operations units known as 'Sujolan' which became part of the Sea Tigers, the LTTE's naval wing.

During this period the government, headed by President Junius Richard Jayewardene, also faced a resurgence of Sinhalese militancy on the part of the Janatha Vimukti Peramuna (JVP), led by a Moscow-trained Sinhalese Marxist named Rohana Wijeweera. At the same time there was growing anti-Tamil sentiment in many parts of the country and riots took place in Colombo and elsewhere with Sinhalese mobs attacking Tamils and their properties, resulting in the latter fleeing to the north-east region and to Tamil Nadu. Increasing concern in India led to initiatives on the part of the government of Prime Minister Rajiv Gandhi who had succeeded his mother, Indira, after her assassination in October 1984. In 1985, he ordered the termination of all RAW assistance to the LTTE and on 29 July 1987 India and Sri Lanka signed the Indo–Sri Lanka Accord under which the Tamils were offered an autonomous integrated province in the north-east of a united Sri Lanka. The agreement also provided for Indian peacekeeping troops to enforce its terms. Despite this, however, the LTTE's main logistical support bases initially remained in Tamil Nadu, but some elements were subsequently moved to cities such as Mysore, Bangalore and Bombay after Indian law enforcement agencies in the state started to take a close interest in the organisation's activities.

By 4 August 1987, an Indian Peace Keeping Force (IPKF) of 10,000 troops had been deployed in Sri Lanka, initially comprising a division under the command of Lieutenant General A. S. Kalkat. Under the terms of the Indo–Sri Lanka Accord, the presence of the Sri Lankan Army would be restricted to areas occupied by Sinhalese communities. The IPKF's arrival, however, caused considerable resentment among the Sri Lankan Army and the relationship between the two forces was not an altogether happy one.

On 5 August, under the terms of the accord, the LTTE surrendered the majority of its weapons during a ceremony at Pallali military air base and a presidential proclamation was published declaring an amnesty for all LTTE detainees. Relations between the IPKF, the local Tamil population and the LTTE were initially good and all went well for a few weeks. However, the situation changed dramatically during the first week of October when the Sri Lankan government ordered twelve members of the LTTE, being held in custody by the IPKF at Pallali, to be handed over to the Sri Lankan Army and flown to Colombo for interrogation. Hitherto, it had agreed to an LTTE request that they should remain at Pallali. On 5 October, when the organisation discovered that the prisoners were due to be handed over on the following day, cyanide capsules were smuggled into the air base and the twelve men committed suicide.

That same day, the LTTE resumed operations against the Sri Lankan security forces, killing eight policemen and murdering eight members of the Sri Lanka Army who had been held captive since May. At the same time it launched attacks on Army bases at Point Pedro and Thondamannar. Next day the military base at Jaffna was also attacked, as was a cement factory at Kankesanthurai where the two senior managers were shot dead. In the village of Sagarpura, twenty-five Sinhalese villagers were murdered.

On 9 October, the IPKF abandoned its peacekeeping role and commenced operations against the LTTE. Two days later, large-scale operations to clear the terrorists from the Jaffna Peninsula were mounted and a fortnight later the area was under IPKF control, the LTTE having been forced to retreat into the jungles of Vavuniya. There the terrorists regrouped and established new bases, sallying forth to engage in hit-and-run operations against the IPKF and to extort 'taxes' from the inhabitants of local towns and villages.

Because of its increased mandate, the IPKF's strength was raised to just under 55,000 men. It conducted a classic counter-insurgency campaign, employing cordon-and-searches, ambushes and raids on suspected terrorist hide-outs, keeping the LTTE confined to the jungles and inflicting heavy casualties on the terrorists when armed confrontations took place. A large number of the terrorists' middle-ranking commanders were killed, as were a few members of the organisation's leadership. The IPKF, however, suffered heavy casualties during its deployment in Sri Lanka. Having originally been deployed as a peacekeeping force, it was not equipped with artillery, armour and adequate radio communications equipment and these proved to be serious deficiencies.

The situation changed dramatically on 19 December 1988 when Ranasinghe Premadasa was elected president, replacing Junius Richard Jayewardene who had retired. Premadasa had always been opposed to the Indo–Sri Lanka Accord and to the presence of the IPKF. Shortly after coming to power, he established contact with the LTTE while demanding the withdrawal of Indian troops by 29 July 1989. In the meantime, he began negotiations with the terrorists who insisted on withdrawal of the IPKF as one of their preconditions for calling a truce and holding discussions with the government concerning a political solution. These negotiations inevitably undermined the Indo–Sri Lanka Accord and the positions of the IPKF and the Indian government which eventually agreed to a phased withdrawal by 31 December 1989.

Meanwhile, the LTTE continued its attacks in the north-east of the country which was administered by a governing body called the North East Provincial Government (NEPG), the chief minister of which was at loggerheads with the national government. The terrorists had proposed to Premadasa that the NEPG be dissolved and the entire north-east of Sri Lanka be handed over to the LTTE following the withdrawal of the IPKF. On 5 November 1989, in the district of Amparai, a major assault was launched on two bases belonging to the Citizens Volunteer Force, a provincial local defence militia, resulting in thirty deaths. Meanwhile, large quantities of arms and ammunition were clandestinely handed over to the LTTE by members of the Sri Lankan Army acting on the orders of President Premadasa who was actively seeking to undermine the IPKF.

The phased withdrawal of Indian troops commenced when two brigades withdrew between April and June 1989. Other elements followed during the ensuing months and on 24 March 1990 the last of the IPKF left Sri Lanka. Three months later, however, the truce between the government and the LTTE came to an end. The latter was by now well armed with large quantities of weapons either handed over to it by the Sri Lankan Army during the truce, captured from local defence militia equipped by the IPKF, or acquired from abroad. The terrorists recommenced their campaign of violence by attacking police stations and Army bases, and within a short period of time had gained control of a large part of the north-east of Sri Lanka.

3

THE THIRD DECADE OF TERROR

The beginning of the 1990s saw no let-up in the litany of terrorism. In Northern Ireland, the Provisional IRA had decided to take the war once again to the British mainland and to Europe, where it targeted British servicemen.

On 27 May 1990 in The Netherlands, Provisional gunmen shot dead two Australian lawyers, Nick Spanos and Stephen Melrose, at Roermond in the mistaken belief that they were off-duty British soldiers. The two men, accompanied by Spanos' girlfriend and Melrose's wife, had been on holiday and were returning to London, where they both worked. En route to Calais, they stopped at Roermond for a meal and afterwards were preparing to resume their journey when a hooded gunman opened fire with an automatic weapon, killing both men. The killings caused outrage in Australia where support among elements sympathetic to the Provisional IRA's cause was damaged.

A few days later, on 6 June, the Provisionals planted a bomb on the roof of the barracks of the Honourable Artillery Company, a Territo rial Army unit based in the City of London. It subsequently exploded, injuring seventeen people attending a birthday party in the building. During the same month, a bomb was found in a rucksack near a building at RAF Stanmore Park, in north-west London. The area was evacuated before the device exploded without causing any casualties. Towards the end of the month, on 25 June, the Carlton Club, situated in London's West End district of Mayfair and a haunt of Conservative Party politicians, was also the scene of a bomb attack.

A few weeks later, the Provisionals struck again. On 20 July, a bomb exploded in the London Stock Exchange, causing massive damage. Ten days later, on 30 July, a bomb exploded under the car of Ian Gow, a former Conservative minister and a close confidant of the Prime Minister, Margaret Thatcher, outside his home at Hankham in

Sussex. A supporter of the Unionist cause, Gow had frequently stated his opposition to the Anglo–Irish Agreement. While the Provisionals claimed that he had been killed because of his role in British policy in Northern Ireland, it was felt by some that, as with Airey Neave, he was killed possibly because of his close relationship with the prime minister who was the terrorists' principal target.

The latter part of 1990 saw the Provisional IRA resorting to the use of 'human bombs'. On 24 October three Catholic men, whom the Provisionals claimed had been informers for the security forces, were forcibly tied into the driving seats of their cars which had been loaded with explosives. They were then ordered to drive to three checkpoints at Coshquin, near Londonderry; Killeen near Newry; and Omagh in County Tyrone. At Coshquin the bomb exploded, killing five soldiers as well as the driver, and a soldier died at Killeen. The third bomb failed to explode. This particularly barbaric tactic caused widespread revulsion and outrage, and a loyalist group, the Protestant Action Force, shot dead a Catholic taxi driver in Moy, County Tyrone, in retaliation.

Early in the following year, the Provisionals once again took the war to the heart of the British political establishment. On 7 February 1991 they carried out a mortar attack on 10 Downing Street. Three bombs, each carrying twenty pounds of an explosive mixture of ammonium nitrate and nitrobenzene, were launched from a battery of three home-made 6-inch mortars concealed in a Ford Transit van parked opposite the Ministry of Defence in Whitehall. At the time, Prime Minister John Major and his cabinet were in session, discussing the Gulf War; all took cover under the Cabinet Room table as the bombs landed in the garden. No one was injured and the terrorists escaped; shortly after the bombs were fired, the van exploded in a ball of flame.

On 18 February, the Provisionals carried out another two attacks, this time on the general public. A bomb exploded at Victoria Station, during the early morning rush-hour, killing one person and injuring thirty-eight; shortly afterwards, another smaller device exploded at Paddington station, causing no casualties and only minor damage.

The following year, 1992, saw killings continuing to be perpetrated in Northern Ireland by both the Provisional IRA and loyalists. On 17 January, a culvert bomb exploded as a van, carrying fourteen Protestant workers, crossed the Treebane cross-roads; eight of them died and the other six were injured in the blast. The men had been returning home from an Army base at Lisanelly where they had been working for a local construction company. Retaliation came on 5 February, two UFF gunmen shooting dead five Catholics, one of them a 15-year old boy, in a betting shop in Ormeau Road, Belfast.

Later in the year, the Provisional IRA launched an attack on one of the government agencies principally involved in the war against terrorism in Northern Ireland. During September, a massive bomb weighing 3,000 pounds exploded outside the perimeter fence of the Northern Ireland Forensic Science Laboratory situated just outside Belfast, demolishing the building completely. Within a fortnight, however, the laboratory had been relocated to temporary premises and was handling priority cases; six months later it was fully operational at a new location to the north of Belfast. This was not the first attack on the laboratory since the start of the troubles in 1969: it was bombed in 1970, while located in the city centre, and three years later terrorists raided it and seized weapons and ammunition. In 1975 it was damaged by a bomb and a year later was the target of an arson attack which caused considerable damage.

Meanwhile, the Provisionals had been continuing their campaign of terror on the mainland. On 10 April, at 9.25 p.m., a huge bomb exploded outside the Baltic Exchange in the City of London, killing three people and injuring ninety-one, and causing massive damage to the tune of £350 millions. It later transpired that the device, made from a fertiliser-based mixture packed in plastic sacks bound with detonating cord used as a booster charge, had been manufactured by the Provisionals' South Armagh Brigade. Shipped to England, it was loaded into a van bought by two Irishmen on the morning of 10 April. Later that day it was driven into the City of London, parked in St. Mary Axe and the timer was set.

On 7 October, a bomb exploded in central London in the area of the Centre Point Tower, but no casualties were incurred. On the evening of 8 October, two smaller devices exploded, one of them at the London Dungeon Museum near London Bridge, injuring one person slightly. On the following day, two similar devices exploded in a residential area of north London without causing any damage. On the morning of 10 October a bomb exploded outside the high-security police station at Paddington Green. Two days later, another exploded in the Sussex Arms pub in the Covent Garden area of London; five people were injured in the blast, one man later dying in hospital. On 21 October three more bombs exploded, one of them on a railway bridge which injured three people and damaged a train.

On the night of 13 November, another attack saw the Provisional IRA using different tactics. A group of terrorists hired a taxi in north London and, having placed a bomb in the boot of the vehicle, forced the driver to drive to Whitehall where they abandoned the vehicle near Downing Street. The bomb exploded shortly after-wards, causing only minor damage and no casualties. Two days later, on the night of Sunday 15 November, security guards at the Canary Wharf development in east London encountered two armed men who ran off after threatening them with a gun. Police called to the scene shortly afterwards found a van containing a large bomb; some time later they discovered an abandoned car two miles away which was suspected of being the men's getaway vehicle.

December 1992 saw the launch of a Christmas bombing campaign by the Provisionals who targeted Oxford Street, other shopping centres and tube stations. These attacks on London continued into 1993, following a similar pattern: on 3 February, bombs exploded at South Kensington tube station and Kent House main line station. On 27 February, a bomb exploded in Camden High Street.

On 26 February, a bomb attack was carried out on a gas works at Warrington in Cheshire, causing considerable damage. A month later the Provisionals struck again in Warrington, on this occasion with more devastating results. On 20 March bombs exploded in rubbish bins in a shopping centre, killing a 3-year-old boy, Jonathan

Ball, and injuring fifty-six people. A second boy, 12-year-old Tim Parry, died later in hospital.

The following month saw the return of the bombers to London. On 24 April, a truck bomb exploded in the Bishopsgate area of the City, killing a newspaper photographer and injuring forty-four people. The bomb was a huge one, containing 2,200 pounds of a fertiliser-based explosive, and caused damage estimated at £500 million. The National Westminster Tower, one of the tallest buildings in Europe, was severely damaged by the blast. That same day, however, saw two other attacks foiled. Two taxis were hijacked and bombs placed inside them, their drivers being ordered to drive to New Scotland Yard and Downing Street respectively. The two drivers, however, abandoned their vehicles in King's Cross and Finsbury Park and contacted the police. Both taxis exploded shortly afterwards without causing any casualties.

The autumn of 1993 saw the Provisionals mounting a further bombing campaign in London, this time in the area around Highgate, Finchley, Archway and Hornsey. On 2 October, ten bombs exploded causing injuries and damage; two others failed to explode. Two men, Gerard Mackin and Derek Doherty, were later arrested, tried and imprisoned for these bombings.

In Northern Ireland, meanwhile, sectarian killings continued. On 23 October, the Provisionals bombed a shop in Belfast's Shankill Road, killing ten people. A week later, seven Catholics were shot dead in a bar, in Greysteel, by Protestant terrorists in retaliation for the Shankill bombing.

The beginning of 1994 saw further bombings in Belfast, but shortly afterwards the Provisional IRA announced a ceasefire. However, it was soon broken. On 9 March, the Provisionals fired four home-made mortar bombs at Heathrow Airport which fortunately caused no casualties. Next day, four more bombs were fired at the aircraft parking area at Terminal Four, but none exploded. On 13 March, a third mortar attack was carried out, but no casualties or damage were caused; two bombs were later found. All three attacks had been carried out from a range of 400 yards.

In Northern Ireland the summer of 1994 saw considerable activity on the part of loyalist terrorists who carried out a number of attacks on Catholics. One of these took place on the night of 20 June when two UVF gunmen opened fire on a crowd of customers watching a World Cup football match in the Heights Bar in the predominantly Catholic village of Loughinisland near Downpatrick. Six men died and five were seriously wounded in the shooting. The gunmen fled, abandoning their car a short distance away; police later found one of the weapons, a Czech-manufactured assault rifle, hidden near south Belfast.

On 31 August 1994, the Provisional IRA announced a further ceasefire after another series of loyalist attacks had resulted in the deaths of a number of Provisionals. This held for seventeen months and nine days until 9 February 1996 when a massive bomb exploded at South Quay in east London's Docklands area, killing two people, newsagent Inam Bashir and his assistant John Jefferies, and injuring scores of others. Only one hour's warning had been given by the Provisionals, so the police had little time to clear the area completely before the bomb exploded, causing £150 million worth of damage.

Other bombings took place in London during the following few weeks. On 15 February, a five-pound Semtex bomb was left in a telephone box in Charing Cross Road. At 10.38 p.m. on Sunday the 18th, Edward O'Brien, a member of the Provisional IRA ASU carrying out the bombings in London, was killed when the bomb he was carrying exploded prematurely while he was travelling on a Number 171 bus passing along the Aldwych in central London. The explosion destroyed the vehicle, killing O'Brien who was standing at the foot of the stairs carrying the bomb in a bag, and injuring eight other passengers, six of them seriously. A Walther 9mm pistol, bearing O'Brien's fingerprints, was found among the debris of the bus and a search of his flat in Lewisham and further investigations revealed that he had been responsible for the planting of the bomb in the telephone box in Charing Cross Road three days earlier.

On 9 March, a small bomb exploded in Old Brompton Road, causing only minor damage and no injuries. A month later, on 17

April, another exploded in a vacant house in The Boltons, in the Earl's Court area, but caused no casualties. On 24 April, the Provisionals attempted unsuccessfully to blow up Hammersmith Bridge, which crosses the Thames in south-west London, with two bombs each containing a total of thirty pounds of Semtex. While the detonators went off, the main charges fortunately failed to explode. Two days later, the Provisionals admitted responsibility for the attack.

The Provisional IRA's next attack took place farther north, in Manchester. On 15 June, the city's local television station received a warning of a bomb which had been planted in the area of the Arndale Centre, Manchester's principal shopping precinct. The bomb, comprising one and a half tons of fertiliser-based explosive mixture, was in a truck parked less than 100 yards from the Centre. The vehicle was found at approximately 9 a.m. and the area had been cordoned off and partially evacuated by 10 a.m.. The device exploded thirty minutes later, the blast waves being funnelled through nearby sidestreets and thus affecting buildings up to a quarter of a mile away which were not in the direct line of fire of the explosion. More than 100 people suffered injuries and massive damage, totalling £150 million, was caused to the Arndale Centre, a nearby branch of Marks & Spencer and the city's historic Royal Exchange Theatre.

Two weeks later, the Provisionals struck even further afield from London. On 29 June, they carried out a mortar attack on a British Army base at Osnabruck, in Germany. No casualties were caused and the bombs missed their target, a petroleum storage area.

In Northern Ireland, just after midnight on Saturday 13 July, a 1,250-pound bomb, packed in a vehicle stolen two weeks previously in Dublin, exploded in a massive blast outside the Killyhevlin Hotel in Enniskillen. A warning had been given beforehand and 250 people, most of them guests attending a wedding reception, were evacuated before the device exploded. Nevertheless, seventeen were injured and the hotel suffered massive damage while thirty vehicles in its car park nearby were totally destroyed. Although the Provisional IRA denied responsibility, intelligence sources were reported as stating that a republican group, possibly a splinter group of the

Republican Sinn Fein, a minor political faction which split from the official Sinn Fein movement in the mid-1980s, were the culprits.

July saw the Provisionals suffer the first of two setbacks to their plans for a major bombing campaign, later thought to have been aimed at electricity installations and other public utilities in London and the south-east of England. On 15 July, the Metropolitan Police raided a number of houses in Tooting and Peckham and arrested seven men. Two more people, a man and a woman, were subsequently arrested in Birmingham. Two months later, on 23 September, armed police raided the Glenthorne Road Hotel in the Hammersmith area of west London. One man, Diarmuid O'Neill, was shot dead and two other people were arrested. Two more men were arrested at two houses in the Fulham area, one of which had been bought for cash two weeks after the Provisional IRA had declared its ceasefire at the end of August 1994. A fifth man, a British Airways engineer, was arrested at 4.30 a.m. on the following day as he completed a shift at Gatwick Airport. These raids by the police were the culmination of a three-month-long surveillance operation.

A further raid was carried out on the Abacus Self-Storage Depot on the Cranford Way industrial estate at Hornsey Vale in north London. There police found an arms cache comprising three AK-47 assault rifles, two pistols, ten tons of improvised explosives, two pounds of Semtex, detonating cord, detonators, timers, two booby-trap bombs fitted with magnets for use on cars, and other bomb-making equipment. The depot had been rented four months previously to a group of men who had also parked two trucks which were obviously intended to transport two huge bombs to their targets somewhere in London.

The end of September saw a return to bombings in Northern Ireland. On 29 September, a car containing a 250-pound bomb was found abandoned in Belfast; a Provisional splinter group, the Continuity IRA, subsequently admitted responsibility. On 7 October, the Provisionals scored a considerable success in the first attack carried out by them against the security forces in Northern

Ireland since the end of the ceasefire declared on 31 August 1994. Two car bombs, containing an estimated total of 800 pounds of home-made explosives, were smuggled into the car park of the headquarters of the British Army in Northern Ireland at Thiepval Barracks in Lisburn, south of Belfast. Thirty-one people were injured by the explosions and an Army warrant officer died four days later in hospital.

Violence in Northern Ireland continued up to the end of 1996. On 20 December, two Provisional gunmen attempted to murder a Democratic Unionist councillor, Nigel Dodds, in the Royal Victoria Hospital in Belfast; they failed, but shot and wounded the police officer guarding him. This attack was followed by a series of bomb, mortar and rocket attacks on security forces in the province that continued daily into January of the following year. Meanwhile, loyalist terrorists retaliated with car bomb attacks against nationalists.

On 1 January 1997 two bombs, with a total estimated weight of 500 pounds, were planted in the grounds of Belfast Castle, but both were defused. No responsibility was admitted by any organisation. On 5 January, a 250-pound bomb was found near Cullyhanna in County Armagh and was also defused. Five days later a rocket attack was carried out by the Provisional IRA on the Royal Courts of Justice in Belfast, injuring a police officer.

Throughout the rest of the month, the Provisionals also carried out a number of attacks on the RUC. On 7 January a bomb was thrown at a mobile patrol of two RUC armoured Land Rovers in the Shantallow area of Londonderry and four days later an unmanned police station in Fermanagh was subjected to a mortar attack. On 13 January, an RUC mobile patrol passing along Kennedy Way, in west Belfast, was subjected to a rocket attack. On 18 January, another patrol came under mortar fire in Downpatrick, County Down. Two days later, two bombs were thrown at the Mountpottinger police station in Short Strand, Belfast. Seven days later, the Provisionals carried out a rocket attack on an RUC patrol in Toomebridge, County Antrim. On the following day, two rockets were fired at a patrol on the Springfield Road in Belfast.

The middle of February saw the last British Army soldier to be killed in Northern Ireland at the time of writing. On the evening of 12 February, Lance Bombardier Stephen Restorick was on duty at a vehicle checkpoint (VCP) in Bessbrook, County Armagh. Unknown to him and his comrades of 3rd Regiment Royal Horse Artillery, a three-man Provisional IRA sniper team had parked its car, a Mazda 626 hatchback, just over 100 yards away, hidden by a concrete bus shelter. In the rear of the vehicle was a Barrett 90 .50 calibre sniper rifle mounted so that it fired through a 12-inch square aperture in an armoured steel shield fitted in the rear of the vehicle. Crouched behind it was the sniper. In front were his two accomplices: the driver and another man who, armed with an AK-47, was responsible for providing protection.

As the terrorists watched, a car drew up at the VCP and Lance Bombardier Restorick bent down to talk to the driver and inspect her driving licence. As he finished doing so the sniper fired, the bullet hitting Restorick's SA80 Individual Weapon and fragmenting into three pieces, the largest of which passed through his body and exited from his right side. The driver of the car, a woman, was hit in the forehead by part of the SA80's smashed SUSAT sight unit which was sent hurtling into the car. Lance Bombardier Restorick fell to the ground mortally wounded; by the time he arrived at a hospital in Newry, he was dead.

The sniper and his two accomplices had by then made good their escape, driving to a quarry where other Provisionals relieved them of the car and weapons. At a nearby safe house, they washed off all traces of firearms residue and burned their clothing before dispersing to their respective homes. As described in Chapter 14, however, it was not long before four terrorists were brought to book for the murders of Lance Bombardier Restorick and others.

The following month saw further bombings in the province. On Friday 7 March, near Dungannon, in County Tyrone, the Provisionals planted a bomb which was defused by the Army. Next day, the Loyalist Volunteer Force (LVF) attacked the offices of the Northern Ireland Tourist Board in Newcastle and Banbridge, causing considerable damage. Five days later, the Provisional IRA carried out a bomb attack in East Belfast, wounding a soldier and a police officer. On 29 March, a bomb with an estimated eight of 1,000 pounds was found close to the Army base at Ballykinlar, in County Down, and was defused.

The latter part of March and the month of April saw the return of Provisional IRA bombers to the British mainland as part of a plan to cause maximum disruption during the run-up to the general election. On 26 March two bombs were planted at Wilmslow railway station in the north-west of England, resulting in widespread disruption to the rail networks. On 3 April, the Provisionals gave warnings of bombs on the M1, M5 and M6 motorways, again causing considerable disruption, and a number were found on the M6.

In the early afternoon of 5 April, the Provisionals earned themselves universal condemnation by telephoning a hoax bomb warning to Aintree, the scene of the Grand National which was being attended that year by the Princess Royal. She and all the 70,000 racegoers at Aintree that day had to be evacuated. Two days later, however, the race was run in defiance of the terrorist threat, being won by Lord Gyllene whose jockey, Tony Dobbin, was from Northern Ireland.

Two bombs were planted and further hoax warnings about devices on various motorways and parts of the rail network were given on 18 April, once again causing widespread disruption. Three days later, London was also the target for a number of hoax warnings.

On 1 May the general election took place and a Labour government under Tony Blair came to power. Five weeks later, a general election in the Irish Republic saw victory for a coalition of Fianna Fáil and Progressive Democrats under Bertie Ahern. Meanwhile, Provisional IRA attacks against the security forces continued: on 10 June, terrorists fired at an Army patrol in Londonderry, but no casualties were caused; on 16 June, two police officers, Constables Roland Graham and David Johnston, were shot dead by gunmen; they were the first police officers to be killed since the ending of the Provisionals' ceasefire on 9 February 1996.

Sunday 20 July saw another ceasefire declared by the Provisional IRA. The province was, however, still plagued by sectarian murders, internecine feuds and punishment attacks on an almost daily basis, while a threat was still posed by IRA splinter groups who soon made their presence felt. On 31 July, a large bomb was planted by the Continuity IRA at the Carrybridge Hotel in County Fermanagh, subsequently being defused by an Army EOD team. On 16 September, a 400-pound bomb exploded outside a police station in Markethill, County Armagh, the Continuity IRA subsequently admitting responsibility. The area was evacuated as a result of a warning beforehand and the only casualties were cattle at a market nearby. On 30 October, the Continuity IRA unsuccessfully attempted to carry out a bomb attack on government offices in Londonderry and a month later, on 30 November, planted a small device in Belfast City Hall. During the same period another group, the Revolutionary Republican Strike Force (RRSF), despatched parcel bombs to Robert McCartney, leader of the United Kingdom Unionist Party, and to Jeffery Donaldson and David Trimble of the Ulster Unionist Party (UUP), the latter being the party leader. All the bombs were defused by the Army.

The end of 1997 saw a major incident take place between nationalist and loyalist prisoners which led to further sectarian killings. At 10 a.m. on 27 December three prisoners, members of the INLA, climbed over the roofs of one of the prison's blocks and shot Billy Wright, a loyalist prisoner, who was sitting in a van awaiting transportation to another part of the prison. Wright was leader of the LVF, a group comprising former members of the UVF, but was under a death threat from former associates because of his opposition to the loyalist ceasefire also in force at the time. Reprisal killings were not long in coming: a Catholic, Seamus Dillon, was shot dead by the LVF in Dungannon, County Tyrone, outside a hotel where he worked as a security guard. Two other security guards and a barman were shot and wounded in the same incident. During the following weeks, ten more Catholics were killed in retaliation for Wright's death. One of these, Eddie Traynor, was shot dead on 31 December at the Clifton Tavern pub in North Belfast; five other Catholics were wounded during the same attack by the LVF.

The period from January to March of the following year, 1998, saw further attacks by republican splinter groups as part of a campaign against Sinn Fein's involvement in the talks being held between all political parties over the future of Northern Ireland. In January a 500-pound bomb was planted in Banbridge, County Down, but was defused. Other attacks were also carried out in the towns of Enniskillen, Moira and Portadown which were severely damaged by them.

On 10 March, in the early hours of the morning, a police station in Armagh City came under attack when five mortar bombs were fired at it from a range of 400 yards. Only two of the bombs exploded, one inside the station area; a sixth bomb was found at the launch site where it had apparently misfired. They had been fired by an electric timer from a battery of tubes fixed to a frame weighed down with breeze-blocks. Fortunately, a soldier had spotted the firing frame some fifteen minutes before the timer activated the electrical firing system and people were evacuated from their homes nearby. No responsibility for the attack was admitted by any group but the finger of suspicion pointed to members of the Provisional IRA in North Armagh.

Twelve days later, on 22 March, Irish security forces discovered a large bomb, weighing 1,300 pounds, concealed in a vehicle parked in a garage on the outskirts of Dundalk, in County Louth, and clearly intended for an attack on a target north of the border. The vehicle had been stolen and fitted with false number plates. Two days later, two men were charged in Dublin with illegal possession of home-made explosives and bomb-making equipment. The composition of the bomb was similar to that of a 600-pound device found at Ballybinaby earlier in the month and suspected as having been planted by the Continuity IRA.

On 2 April, the Gardai Siochana scored another success when they intercepted a large bomb concealed in a BMW car about to board a ferry for Anglesey at the port of Dun Laoghaire. Apparently it was a sophisticated device, comprising 980 pounds of home-made explosive fitted with a booster charge. The driver of the car, a man from County Kildare, was arrested and held for questioning.

On 11 April 1998, seventeen hours after a previously established deadline, the long-running negotiations over the future of Northern Ireland came to an end when the British and Irish governments, together with all the political parties in the province, finally reached a deal. Thereafter known as the Good Friday Agreement, it provided for an assembly at Stormont, a joint Northern Ireland/Irish Republic council of ministers and other bodies which would be responsible for decision-making on a joint basis. However, despite previous assurances to loyalists from Prime Minister Tony Blair that Sinn Fein would not be permitted to take part in the new assembly until the IRA had surrendered its weapons, this condition was not included in the agreement document. Furthermore, the handing in of IRA weapons over a two-year period was declared an aim rather than a mandatory requirement. Equally controversially, the agreement also provided for the release of convicted IRA and loyalist terrorists during the following two years.

During the early part of the following month, as the date for the referendum on the Good Friday Agreement approached, a republican splinter group calling itself the Real IRA declared that it would mount a new campaign of terror against the United Kingdom. Hitherto little had been divulged about this organisation. Allegedly led by Michael McKevitt, previously alleged to be the quartermaster-general of the Provisional IRA, it was one of a small number of groups strongly opposed to Sinn Fein's involvement in the Good Friday Agreement. McKevitt was also alleged to be one of the founder members of the 32 Counties Sovereignty Committee, a political pressure group similarly opposed to the agreement.

McKevitt, who in his previous appointment had allegedly been responsible for all IRA arms caches and the supply of weapons and explosives to Provisional IRA cells in Northern Ireland, had allegedly resigned from the Provisionals in October 1997. He was alleged to have undertaken not to make use of Provisional arms, but it would seem that he allegedly reneged on that agreement. The 500-pound bomb planted in Banbridge in January had been the work of the Real IRA and was found to be fitted with two detonators, one of which was from a batch purchased in the United States by the Provisionals in 1989; the other was an improvised type well known to forensic investigators as a 'Provisional IRA Mk.3'. Furthermore, McKevitt was alleged to have recruited several of the Provisionals' most experienced bomb-makers. The bombings in Moira, Portadown, Newtownhamilton were reportedly all the work of the Real IRA.

On 24 May, the people of Northern Ireland voted by an overwhelming majority (71.12 per cent) to accept the proposals laid down in the Stormont Good Friday Agreement despite the efforts of those opposed to it. This was more than matched in the Irish republic by a 94 per cent vote also in favour of the agreement.

Nevertheless, the terrorists continued to demonstrate that they believed in the bomb and bullet rather than the ballot box. On 23 June, a 200-pound bomb exploded at Drumintree, on the main road between Newry and Forkhill. Next day, a bomb devastated the centre of the village of Newtownhamilton in South Armagh. On 2 August, a car bomb exploded in Banbridge, County Down, badly damaging the town centre. Despite the fact that hundreds of people were in the town's main street at the time, there were only six casualties and these suffered minor injuries.

It was on 15 August, however, that terrorists carried out an attack so appalling that it inspired revulsion and outrage around the world. At 3.10 p.m. on Saturday 15 August a car bomb, later estimated to have comprised approximately 500 pounds of explosive, exploded in the market town of Omagh, County Tyrone which was crowded with people doing their weekly shopping and awaiting a carnival shortly due to pass through the town centre. Forty minutes earlier, three telephone warnings had been given that a bomb had been planted outside the courthouse at the top of the high street and the police were thus evacuating a large number of people several hundred yards away to the area of Dublin Road and Market Street. The warning had been incorrect as the car containing the bomb was in fact parked at the junction of the two streets, within the safe area cordoned off by the RUC. The result of the blast was devastating: twenty-nine people died and 330, including many children, were injured. Buildings in the area of the explosion were wrecked and people inside were trapped. In the streets, the dead and injured lay in a scene of carnage while panic-stricken people searched for the families and friends with whom they had been only seconds earlier.

Three days later, the Real IRA admitted responsibility for the bombing. Its spokesman denied, however, that the warning had been erroneous or misleading, claiming that the three warnings, two made to Ulster Television and the third to the Samaritans, had clearly stated that the bomb's location was 300 to 400 yards from the courthouse. By this time, however, the RUC had determined that the warning had come from one of two telephone boxes near the village of Silverbridge and had removed both for forensic examination. By the night of 18 August, five men were being held for questioning. Next day, the Real IRA announced a 'complete cessation' of its activities. On 21 September, six men were arrested in Northern Ireland in connection with the Omagh bombing and three more were apprehended in the Irish Republic for their suspected involvement in the theft of the car used to carry the bomb.

In the days following the devastation of Omagh, further reports revealed that the Israeli intelligence service, Mossad, had passed information to the British authorities that members of the Real IRA had attended meetings with Libyan officials. The first apparently took place in Athens at the end of July, followed by another in Tripoli shortly before the signing of the Good Friday Agreement. A third meeting was reported to have been held in Amsterdam forty-eight hours before the bomb attack in Omagh. According to the Israeli reports, the Real IRA representatives approached the Libyans with a request for the latter to sell them arms.

The funds to purchase the weapons were supposed to have come from the proceeds of the armed robbery on 1 May of a Securicor armoured cash-in-transit van carrying a consignment of £300,000. Unknown to the Real IRA, however, the Gardai Siochana had become aware of the plan beforehand and mounted a surveillance operation. On the day of the raid, its Emergency Response Unit (ERU) was lying in wait for the terrorists who were heavily armed with AK-47 assault rifles, a pump action shotgun, two handguns, a replica RPG-7 rocket-launcher designed to terrorise the Securicor crew, and cutting equipment for attacking the van's body.

At 5.15 p.m. on 1 May the terrorists, dressed as local authority workers, set up roadworks diversion signs some two and a half miles outside Ashford where the Securicor van had been collecting cash from shops throughout the area. As the vehicle approached, the terrorists deployed from a van parked at the side of the road, but at that point members of the ERU appeared and ordered them to lay down their arms. The terrorists, however, opened fire and a battle ensued, during which one of them, Ronan McLoughlin, was shot dead. Some of his accomplices meanwhile hijacked a passing car and attempted to make their escape; in so doing they rammed a school bus full of children and were arrested. The remainder of the gang fled over nearby fields but were apprehended soon afterwards.

Despite the Real IRA's declaration of a ceasefire, it soon became apparent that, together with the Continuity IRA, elements within the organisation had every intention of continuing the war against the security forces in Northern Ireland. During October, it was reported they were planning an attack and in early December the Gardai Siochana raided a house in Dundalk where they arrested a man and discovered bomb-making equipment and weapons believed to belong to the Real IRA. Four days later, both the British and Irish media reported republican sources quoting statements made at a meeting of a newly elected IRA Army Council which had apparently ruled out any possibility of arms being handed over in accordance with the Good Friday Agreement. The same sources continued by saying that the Council had ruled unequivocally that no arms would be surrendered until the organisation's objectives had been achieved: the disbanding of the RUC and the Irish Army, and the establishment of a united Ireland comprising all thirty-two counties. Despite ensuing denials from the Continuity IRA and

Real IRA that any such meeting had taken place, or that any such statement had been made, this announcement no doubt caused dismay within the newly elected Labour government in Britain which had released more than 200 republican prisoners while the IRA had not surrendered one single weapon.

Just over two weeks into the new year of 1999, an IRA arms cache was discovered by Irish security forces. On Thursday 14 January, two .50 Browning heavy machine-guns and a .30 GPMG were found, together with 200 rounds of ammunition, near a derelict house at the end of a track off the main road between Carrickmacross and Crossmaglen. The find was significant because IRA terrorists had previously used machine-guns on a number of occasions to engage British helicopters operating in the areas north of the border.

During the following month, evidence that the Provisional IRA was using the ceasefire to acquire new weapons came to light with the discovery of an arms cache containing an AR-15 rifle, a large quantity of ammunition and explosives in a house in West Belfast. Forensic examination revealed that some detonators found among the explosives had been manufactured during 1998 and that the items had only recently been concealed in the cache.

The following month saw loyalists carry out the murder of a lawyer well known for representing nationalists charged with terrorist offences. On 15 March Rosemary Nelson, a solicitor who was also a leading human rights campaigner, was blown up in her car near her home in Lurgan, County Armagh. A prominent figure, her support for the nationalist cause had led to her visiting Downing Street for a discussion with Prime Minister Tony Blair, and her abilities as a lawyer were such that she was respected within her profession as well as throughout the nationalist community.

During the summer of 1999, sectarian murders and punishment attacks were carried out by loyalists and republicans alike. On the evening of 5 May, a number of Catholics were watching a football match in a bookmaker's shop in Belfast when two loyalists drew up in a car outside. One of them, armed with a pistol, opened fire but the weapon jammed after firing four rounds and the men were forced to drive off. RUC sources were later quoted as stating that they believed members of the UDA to be responsible. That same evening, the Emergall Gallery, situated in the Donegall Pass area of Belfast, was burned down by members of the UVF, the owner having previously refused to pay protection money. During the first week of June, a Protestant woman married to a Catholic died when she picked up a bomb thrown through the window of her home in the loyalist area of Portadown; five men were subsequently arrested and suspicion centred on a splinter group called the Red Hand Defenders.

In August, the Provisional IRA kidnapped and murdered a man suspected of being an informer; he was subsequently shot in the head at close range with a shotgun and his body dumped behind some buildings in the area of the Falls Road. RUC reports for that month state that the IRA carried out three further shootings with another eight being carried out by loyalists.

Meanwhile, the security forces in the province and in the Irish Republic were becoming increasingly concerned that IRA splinter groups such as the Real IRA would obtain weapons from Provisional IRA arms dumps whose locations were allegedly known to its alleged leader Michael McKevitt. According to estimates made public at the time, it was believed that the Provisionals were in possession of some six tons of Semtex supplied by Libya, six SAM missiles, six general-purpose machine-guns, about 600 AK-47 assault rifles, some 200 pistols and an unspecified quantity of M-16 or AR-15 rifles and 12-gauge shotguns. It was reported that the Security Service knew of at least one consignment of weapons supplied by Libya, including AK-47 rifles, which had been smuggled into the Irish Republic in 1996 following the bombing in London's Docklands in February of that year. It was also reported that five large arms caches were concealed in underground bunkers in County Kerry, in the south-west of the Irish Republic, and a number of smaller ones were located south of the border with Northern Ireland. Small quantities of weapons were also believed to be held in up to fifty safe houses and other buildings situated just over the border as well as in Belfast and Londonderry.

Proof that the Provisional IRA was actively seeking to increase its arsenal of weapons came when eight small shipments of pistols and revolvers, concealed in packages of toys and baby clothes, were intercepted at Coventry Airport on 6 July. The weapons came to light when an x-ray machine detected a Ruger .357 Magnum revolver in a package bound for the Irish Republic. A search of seven other packages, also destined for Ireland, revealed more weapons. Meanwhile in Florida the FBI was already investigating the activities of two Irishmen, Anthony Smyth and Conor Claxton, and an Irishwoman, Siobhan Browne. The Bureau's interest in them had been aroused by Browne's purchase of five handguns from a Fort Lauderdale arms dealer which had initially alerted the Bureau of Alcohol Tobacco and Firearms (BATF) whose agents had placed the trio under surveillance. This led to the uncovering of the smuggling operation and according to reports at the time, the FBI believed that the trio had acquired about 200 weapons, predominantly handguns. On 26 July, the FBI agents arrested Smyth and Browne at an apartment in a suburb of Fort Lauderdale. Conor Claxton was meanwhile apprehended at a motel in nearby Boca Raton where other agents were reported as having found ten handguns, three packaged and ready for despatch to Ireland. All were subsequently charged with exporting weapons without a licence, sending concealable weapons through the US Mail and conspiracy.

On 27 July, the Gardai Siochana arrested a man and two women at a house in Galway where a search uncovered six handguns. Two days later another consignment of weapons, comprising two handguns packed in boxes labelled as containing karaoke equipment, and thirty rounds of .50 calibre ammunition suitable for use with Barrett sniper rifles, was discovered at a mail sorting office in Dublin. It had been posted in Philadelphia where another Irishman, Martin Mullen, was arrested a few days later.

October brought further evidence of activity on the part of the Real IRA when the Gardai Siochana raided a derelict farm near Herbertstown in County Dublin. Eight men and two youths, both of whom were later identified as being members of Fianna, the radical youth wing of Republican Sinn Fein, were arrested when police stormed an underground bunker in a cellar under some derelict buildings where they found a firing range. A machine-gun, an AK-47 assault rifle, a Beretta pistol and 150 rounds of ammunition were discovered and seized. Four days later, on 25 October, the Gardai Siochana scored another success when an arms cache containing bomb-making equipment, a nearly finished bomb comprising three pounds of Semtex, ammunition and a brand-new Russian-manufactured RPG-18 light anti-armour weapon was discovered near Gormanston, in County Meath. Subsequent reports indicated that the cache belonged to the Real IRA.

Meanwhile the presence of an ASU, comprising members of the Real IRA/Continuity IRA, had been detected on the mainland. Its members were reported to be in London and Manchester, and in November it was revealed that they were planning a campaign to disrupt the peace deal based on the Good Friday Agreement. As 1999 drew to a close, the peace in Northern Ireland appeared to be as fragile as ever.

In France, meanwhile, 1994 had seen the capture of its most wanted terrorist enemy, Ilich Ramírez Sánchez, alias 'Carlos'. As described in Chapter 2, by the late 1980s he was living in virtual retirement in Damascus where his movements had been closely monitored by the French. By 1991, the regime of President Hafez al-Assad had decided that it no longer wished to be seen as an obstacle to peace in the Middle East and was seeking a *rapprochement* with the West, particularly the United States. In September Ramírez, his wife Magdalena Kopp, five-year old daughter, mother and right-hand man, Johannes Weinrich, were expelled from Syria. They sought sanctuary in Libya but were refused entry and were forced to return to Damascus. Syria then sent them to the Yemen, but once again they were turned away and returned to Damascus. Shortly afterwards Ramírez and Magdalena Kopp separated; she and their daughter, accompanied by his mother, flew to Venezuela. Ramírez was not alone for long, however, having already established a relationship with a young Jordanian dental student named Jarrar Lana whom he married shortly afterwards.

Seeking a new home, Ramírez turned to the Iranians. Instead of refuge, however, they gave him a sum of money and suggested he approach the Sudanese. In the latter part of 1993, accompanied by his wife, Weinrich and his long-standing Syrian intelligence aide, Ali al-Issawe, he flew to Khartoum where he was made welcome by the Muslim fundamentalist regime of Sheikh Hassan al-Turabi which, as covered later in this chapter, was supporting Islamic extremist groups throughout North Africa and Asia.

It was not long before news of Ramírez's arrival in Khartoum was known to the CIA which despatched a team to track him down. This was not a difficult task because Ramírez, who had always enjoyed a penchant for the good life, was soon enjoying the night life of Khartoum where he and his wife posed as a Jordanian couple. His location was passed to the French who gave the task of securing his capture Carlos to General Philippe Rondot, a former army and SDECE officer serving with the DST, the French security service. While Rondot made contact with the chief of the Sudanese intelligence service, General Hachim Abou Zeid, requesting his assistance, the French government approached Iran, which enjoyed close relations with the al-Turabi regime, and whose help was obtained by returning to Tehran two Iranians previously arrested and imprisoned in France for the murder in 1990 of a leading Iranian dissident.

After lengthy negotiations with the French, al-Turabi agreed that Ramírez would be handed over. In August 1994, the latter entered hospital for a minor operation; on the pretext that they had discovered a plot to kill him, the Sudanese insisted that he recuperate in a government-owned villa on the outskirts of Khartoum. Three days later, while asleep in bed, he was overpowered by a group of Sudanese, tranquillised and taken to Khartoum airport where he was handed over to a team of DST officers led by Rondot who bundled him aboard a French government executive jet. On arrival in France, he was taken to Paris and, having been charged with the murders of two of the three DST officers he had shot in June 1975, was incarcerated in La Santé prison in Paris. On 12 December 1997 Ramírez stood trial on charges of murder and terrorism, subsequently being found guilty on all counts and sentenced to life imprisonment.

Meanwhile France was being threatened by terrorism from a different quarter, that of Islamic extremism. On 26 July 1995, a bomb exploded in Paris at St-Michel–Notre-Dame station, which is on the RER suburban rail network linked to the Metro, killing eight people and injuring eighty-four. No organisation claimed responsibility, but the finger of suspicion was pointed at Algerian Islamic extremists. Moreover, an off-duty gendarme had spotted a group of North African men leaving the train at Châtelet, the station before St-Michel–Notre Dame. In addition, a report in the Algerian press had previously stated that five men, all of whom had fought as Mujahideen during the war in Afghanistan, had travelled to France to carry out a punitive operation against the French government.

On the afternoon of 17 August a bomb, consisting of a gas cylinder filled with explosives and nuts and bolts, exploded in a rubbish bin at the entrance to the Charles de Gaulle metro station near the Arc de Triomphe, injuring seventeen people. Shortly afterwards, two suspects were arrested by police. Twenty-four hours later, the RTL radio station received a telephone call from the Armed Islamic Group–General Command (GIA–CG), claiming responsibility. Investigations revealed that the bomb was similar to that planted at St-Michel–Notre-Dame. It was later reported that RTL had also received telephones from the same caller, claiming responsibility for the St Michel bomb and for the murder on 10 July of Sheikh Abdel Sahraoui, the imam of a mosque in Paris. Sahraoui, one of the founders of the Islamic Salvation Front (FIS) in Algeria, was a moderate and had been threatened previously by the GIA for favouring dialogue with the Algerian government.

There were several possible motives for attacks by Algerian extremists. Since 1993 the French government had been supporting the Algerian government in its war against Islamic fundamentalist groups, supplying financial and military aid.

Furthermore, as described in Chapter 12, a French counter-terrorist unit had stormed a hijacked Air France airliner at Marseilles in December 1994, killing the four terrorists who were holding the passengers and crew hostage and threatening to blow up the aircraft. The French authorities thus believed that revenge for their deaths could also be a motive for the bombings.

On 21 August, an Algerian named Abdelkarim Deneche was arrested in Stockholm. A leading member of the GIA, operating under the pseudonym of Abdessabour, he was subsequently identified, from photographs supplied by the Algerian security service, as having been one of the North Africans observed leaving the RER train at Châtelet on 26 July. Eight days later, a 50-pound bomb was found planted beside the high-speed railway line, next to one of the electricity pylons providing power for TGV trains travelling between Paris and Lyon. A number of trains had passed by that day, but fortunately the device's detonator had failed to explode. The bomb was of similar construction to the device planted at St-Michel–Notre-Dame, comprising a gas bottle filled with explosives; fingerprints on adhesive tape holding the detonator in place were subsequently found to belong to a 24-year-old Algerian named Khaled Kelkal, who was living with his family in Vauxen-Velin, a suburb of Lyon heavily populated by North Africans. When police arrived at the family's apartment, however, he had disappeared.

Meanwhile, the French authorities had revealed that they were investigating an Islamic fundamentalist network operating throughout Europe, a number of its members having been trained in guerrilla camps in Afghanistan and in the *département* of Ardèche, in southern France. According to French newspaper reports at the time, this network had been established following an Islamic fundamentalist conference in 1992, in the Albanian capital of Tirana, held in the wake of the Algerian government's decision to scrap elections which the FIS was expected to win. During the conference, the decision was taken to use France as a base for European operations against Algeria. In November 1993 an Algerian living in France, Moussa Kraouche, was arrested and charged with terrorist offences; it transpired that he had attended the Tirana conference. During the following year, three North Africans had been arrested for an attack on a hotel in Marrakesh: subsequently convicted and sentenced to death, they had given details of their training which had taken place in Ardèche and of their subsequent involvement in fighting in Bosnia where they had fought against the Serbs.

On 11 September, police and gendarmerie units carried out raids in the Muslim ghettos of Paris and Grenoble, arresting forty people and discovering quantities of weapons and forged documents. Their principal quarry, however, was Khaled Kelkal and a few days later a report of a group of men seen sleeping rough led police to his lair. A large operation, involving 700 gendarmes supported by helicopters and dogs, was mounted in the hills surrounding Lyon. On 20 September, four men were discovered in a camp in woods; one opened fire and was wounded when gendarmes responded; two others were captured. The fourth man, Kelkal, made good his escape. A search of the camp revealed a submachine-gun, two rifles and ammunition. On 30 September, telephone surveillance of Kelkal's contacts picked up two calls which were traced to the Lyon area and on the same day he was spotted in the village of Vaugneray. Shortly afterwards he was confronted by gendarmes and opened fire with a pistol, being killed in the ensuing firefight despite orders that he should be taken alive to avoid his becoming a martyr among Muslim extremists in France, and so that he could subsequently be questioned.

The bombings continued despite Kelkal's death and the demise of his group. A few hours after his funeral on 6 October, a nail bomb exploded outside a Metro station in Paris, injuring thirteen people. Next day the GIA published a communiqué in Cairo signed by Abou Abdelrahmane Amine, the alias of Djamel Zitouni, who was the leader of a unit within the organisation. Claiming responsibility for the bombings, it announced that they had been carried out as reprisals for the deaths of the four members of the GIA killed at Marseilles in December 1994.

Algerian extremists were not alone in posing a terrorist threat to France during this period. The end of 1995 saw a recurrence of bomb attacks by the separatists of the Corsican National Liberation Front (FLNC). In 1990, the FLNC had split into two organisations: the moderate faction became the FLNC–Canal Habituel, publicly represented by the Movement for Self-Determination (MPA), while the militants formed the FLNC–Canal Historique with the Cuncolta Naziunalista as its political front. The latter still persisted in its demands for independence for Corsica, an aim no longer maintained by the MPA.

During the night of Sunday 24 December and the early hours next day, bombs exploded on Corsica in tax offices in Bastia and Ajaccio, causing considerable damage to buildings and vehicles parked nearby, but no casualties. Early in the New Year, six more bombs exploded on the island. A 55-pound bomb wrecked part of a government office block in Ajaccio, and eight armed terrorists attacked a holiday camp at Macinaggio, on the north coast, and blew up the main building. New Year's Day saw evidence of inter-factional feuding between the two elements of the FLNC with the shooting of a member of the FLNC–Canal Habituel by the FLNC–Canal Historique which shortly afterwards declared a six-month truce in order to allow the French government to produce proposals to solve the question of autonomy for Corsica. In April, the organisation announced that it was extending the truce by a further six months

On 13 May, however, the FLNC–Canal Historique threatened to terminate the truce unless the French government acted within two weeks. Next day, following the arrests in the northern town of Balagna of twelve members of the Cuncolta Naziunalista alleged to be involved in narcotics and arms trafficking, the organisation's head, François Santoni, suspended all further contacts with the government. On the same day, gunmen attacked government buildings with bombs and automatic weapons, their targets including the law courts in Ajaccio, a police barracks on the southern coast at Porto Vecchio and a police station at Peri. At the end of the month, a threat was issued by the secretary of the Cuncolta Naziunalista, Charles Pieri, who stated that the FLNC–Canal Historique might carry out attacks in Paris if its demands were not met.

In June and September, bombs were planted in Bordeaux, but were defused; although it was suspected that they were the work of the FLNC–Canal Historique, this was never confirmed as there was a suspicion that Basque separatists might have been responsible. On 5 October, a bomb exploded at the city's Palais Rohan which was badly damaged although no casualties were caused.

The end of 1996 saw further attacks. On 28 November, two bombings took place on the French mainland at the Marseilles headquarters of the shipping line SNCM and a tribunal building in Limoges. The day before, a mess building at the French Air Force base at Solenzara in Corsica, had also been attacked. On the night of 29 November, bombs exploded outside tax offices in Bastia, Ville de Pietrabugno, Corte and Migliacciaro. In the early hours of 3 December, a bomb exploded outside a bank in Ghisonaccia; a second device planted outside another bank in the city failed to explode and was defused. On the French mainland, meanwhile, a bomb exploded outside a tax office in the city of Perpignan, in southern France, causing considerable damage to the building; another large device was found outside a post office in Marseilles and was defused.

Three weeks later in Corsica, two gunmen on a motorcycle hurled a bomb at the gendarmerie barracks in Ghisonaccia and opened fire with automatic weapons. Three days later, on 23 December, a bomb exploded at the offices of the French national statistics institute in Paris, causing damage but no casualties. On the following day on Corsica, a bomb attack was carried out on the law courts in Corte and on 26 December attacks were launched in the southern Corsican town of Figari on the offices of Renault and a police barracks. On the following night four bombs exploded, one badly damaging a government building in Pietrabugno, and an anti-tank rocket was fired at the law courts building in Bastia, in northern Corsica. Two days later, a bomb exploded in a residential district of Ajaccio, badly damaging an apartment block.

December 1996 also saw further bombings by Algerian extremists. On 3 December, a bomb exploded in Paris aboard a commuter train during the evening rush-hour at the Port Royal station, situated in a residential area on the edge of the city's Latin quarter. Two people died and forty-seven were injured in the blast which blew out the windows of the carriage in which the device had been planted. Although the GIA did not claim responsibility, forensic examination revealed that the bomb, a gas cylinder filled with explosives and nails, was identical to devices planted previously by the organisation.

The bombing was followed by a massive security clampdown by the French authorities who during the previous months had been attempting to break up the Islamic fundamentalist networks established throughout France. They had achieved a certain amount of success in Paris, Lyon and Lille where extremists had been arrested. At the beginning of April in the northern industrial town of Roubaix, police cornered four members of a cell, two Algerians and two Moroccans, who died when the house in which they took refuge was set ablaze. Two others, however, escaped and fled across the border into Belgium where one was shot dead by police; the other surrendered later in the town of Courtrai after taking two women hostage. It transpired that this cell specialised in robbing vehicles carrying cash and valuables in northern France and Belgium, using grenades and automatic weapons to force the vehicles to halt.

Until now, however, the authorities had failed to catch the extremists' ringleaders among whom was an Algerian, Ali Touchent, who used a number of aliases and passports. Suspected of being the mastermind who had orchestrated the bomb attacks during the previous twelve months, he was known to travel throughout Europe and in early December was reported to be in London. In early 1997, the authorities in Morocco had intercepted a car en route to England from Algeria. Three of its four occupants were found to have connections with a GIA newspaper, *Al-Ansar*, published at a secret address in London, and a search of the vehicle revealed bomb-making equipment. A major surveillance operation was subsequently mounted in London by the Security Service and the

Metropolitan Police Special Branch against suspected Islamic extremists, and in June a number of raids were carried out on houses in south London. Nine men, including three Algerians and a French national, were arrested on suspicion of being members of the GIA. Searches of the houses uncovered manuals on bomb-making and quantities of chemicals for the manufacture of explosives, including lead nitrate which is used in detonators. Also found were false French and Italian passports and a large quantity of Islamic fundamentalist literature calling for a holy war against 'unbelievers' and the establishment of a world-wide Islamic state.

Two of those seized in London were among the alleged ring-leaders of the Algerian group responsible for the bombings in France. In December, Mohamad Kerouche and Mohamad Chalabi were extradited to France where they subsequently stood trial on terrorism charges. During 1997 a number of other extremists were also tried, among them Djamel Lounici, a senior member of the Algerian FIS, who was convicted of heading a terrorist network and sentenced to five years' imprisonment.

During 1998, police throughout Europe cracked down on Islamic extremist networks established by the GIA, the FIS and its military wing, the Islamic Salvation Army (AIS). In Brussels, seven GIA suspects were arrested after a gun battle with police; among them was an Algerian, Farid Melouk, who had been wanted by the French authorities since 1995. In Italy, police arrested fourteen North Africans, all members of an Islamic extremist cell in Bologna.

Meanwhile in Corsica, the end of 1997 saw the FLNC–Canal Historique continuing its campaign of violence with some 200 bomb attacks and shootings. Of some seventy-five incidents which took place in the first quarter of the year, sixty were attributed to the organisation. These attacks were primarily aimed at symbolic targets such as banks, government buildings and police barracks or stations, the majority taking place in Corsica, but some being mounted in France. In January 1998, however, the head of the Cuncolta Naziunalista, François Santoni, being hunted by the police in connection with a bomb attack on 13 December 1997 on the security building of a holiday resort and golf club at Sperone in southern Corsica, surrendered himself to the authorities as the net closed in on him. The resort's owner had earlier refused a demand for $800,000 protection money from an intermediary allegedly representing Santoni and after the attack had reported the attempted extortion to the police, an action unheard of in Corsica where *omerta*, the law of silence, had ruled for centuries.

Forty-eight hours earlier Santoni's girlfriend, a lawyer named Marie-Helene Mattei, also wanted for questioning in relation to the same incident, had been arrested by police at Bastia airport. Both were subsequently charged with attempted extortion. On 9 January 1998, fifteen more members of the Cuncolta Naziunalista were arrested and another of the organisation's leaders, Jean-Michel Rossi, surrendered shortly afterwards. A third leader, Charles Pieri, remained at large, but had been rendered largely ineffective after being severely injured in a car bomb attack in the summer of the previous year.

The loss of its leaders and a number of rank-and-file members effectively beheaded the Cuncolta Naziunalista organisation, but the FLNC–Canal Historique was obviously determined to show that it was still a force to be reckoned with. On 26 January it announced that it was terminating the truce which had been in force for seven months. On 6 February in Ajaccio, two gunmen on a motorcycle murdered Prefect Claude Erignac, the French government's senior administrator in Corsica. He had parked his car and was walking, unescorted by bodyguards, along a crowded street towards the capital's Le Kallyste theatre when the gunmen struck, shooting him in the back of the head three times. As they fled, however, they dropped one of the two 9mm pistols with which they were armed. Three days later, responsibility for the attack was claimed by a FLNC–Canal Historique splinter group calling itself Sampieru; in a written communiqué sent to the police, the group gave the serial number of the 9mm Beretta pistol used in the attack and dropped as the assassins fled. Examination of the weapon revealed that it was one stolen during an attack on a gendarmerie post in Pietrosella during the previous September for which Sampieru had claimed responsibility.

The French government responded by sending its top counter-terrorist investigators and gendarmerie reinforcements to the island. A dragnet operation was launched and a number of people, mainly in Ajaccio, were arrested. Among them was one of Sampieru's founders, a known separatist named Lorenzoni. The motive for Erignac's murder was not clear, but it was known that he had opposed certain tourist industry development projects because he had suspected that the finance backing them came from organised crime. Despite the arrests of some 340 people and the questioning of more than 600 others, however, by the end of 1998 the investigation into Erignac's murder had not resulted in the identification of those responsible for his death. This was apparently due largely to the mutual suspicion and dislike that existed between Corsica's different law enforcement agencies which comprised the judicial police, the counter-terrorist unit, the gendarmerie and the Renseignements Généraux, the island's intelligence service. Such was the deep enmity between them that none of these organisations would co-operate with any of the others, to the extent of being almost farcical.

At the end of April 1999, a major scandal broke in Corsica when three members of a specialist gendarmerie unit, the GPS, were arrested and charged with setting fire to a beachside restaurant at Coti Chiavari. On 20 April the building had been found burned to the ground and a search of the surrounding area had unearthed two petrol cans, a gendarmerie radio, a military combat knife and a blood-stained balaclava. Further investigation revealed that a GPS officer had been admitted to hospital with burns on his face and hands. The trail led to two other GPS officers who, when questioned, claimed that they had been on a surveillance mission and had discovered the restaurant ablaze. Eventually, however, they confessed and the senior of the three, Captain Norbert Ambrose, admitted responsibility, but revealed that he had been acting on the orders of the senior gendarmerie officer in Corsica, Colonel Henri Mazères. On being questioned, the latter and his chief of staff, Lieutenant Colonel

Bertrand Cavalier, told the investigators that the attack on the restaurant had been ordered by Bernard Bonnet, who had replaced Claude Erignac as Prefect of Corsica, and that it was to be blamed on the FLNC–Canal Historique. Further investigations revealed that two weeks prior to the burning of the restaurant, Mazères and Bonnet's chief of staff, Gerard Pardini, had set another restaurant ablaze.

Bonnet denied all knowledge of the affair, but it was well known that he was strongly opposed to the island's beach restaurants, most of which were unauthorised and did not possess planning permission. The restaurant concerned, Chez Francis, situated on the popular Aqua Dori beach, was one of those that had provoked his ire. Furthermore, he distrusted Corsica's police, whom he claimed were riddled with separatist informants, and preferred to put his trust in the para-military gendarmerie. The formation of the GPS, a 95-strong unit, had been his idea. On 5 May, Bonnet was relieved of his post and together with Mazères, Cavalier and the three GPS officers, was placed under arrest.

May, however, also saw results in the hunt for Claude Erignac's killers with the arrests of five men. A sixth man, Yvan Colonna, a goatherd from the small village of Cargese, was subsequently named as having shot Erignac. It was reported that he had succeeded in avoiding arrest after being tipped off by a contact in the Renseignments Généraux, and had fled to the mountains where he had gone into hiding.

Meanwhile the terrorist attacks continued. On 25 November, two large bombs caused serious damage to two government buildings in Ajaccio, a telephone warning barely giving time for them to be evacuated before the explosions occurred. Thirteen people were injured in the blasts, responsibility for which was claimed by a hitherto unknown group calling itself Clandestinu. By now, however, the local population was sick of the constant violence plaguing the island and there was little sympathy for the separatists' cause. In early December, Prime Minister Lionel Jospin and five of his ministers attended a meeting with Corsican officials. This apparently proved to be fruitful because on 23 December a news conference was held by the FLNC–Canal Historique, Clandestinu and two other groups, at which an unconditional truce was declared.

No sooner had the problem of violence in Corsica apparently subsided then another appeared to plague the French government. During the first week of December, the Spanish Basque separatist group ETA announced that it was terminating its fourteen-month-old ceasefire. That same week saw two bombs planted by the Breton separatist group, the Breton Revolutionary Army (ARB). The French security authorities had long been aware of the connections between ETA and the ARB and had been co-operating closely with their Spanish counterparts in tracking down members of ETA seeking refuge in France. During 1997, the French arrested more than 140 ETA suspects, tried more than sixty of them and extradited twenty-three to Spain, including two of the organisation's leaders.

The Basque region of France had long provided refuges for ETA and it was for this reason that it had always discouraged its French counterpart, Iparretarrak, from indulging in terrorist activity. In May 1997, however, the latter had bombed a restaurant in St-Jean-de-Luz, causing extensive damage, but no casualties. ETA had meanwhile sought assistance from elsewhere in France and in particular Brittany. This came to light in late 1997 when eight members of ETA and a number of Bretons were arrested. By the end of 1999 it was apparent that ETA and the ARB were in collaboration, the latter posing a new separatist problem for France.

The mid-1990s found Spain facing a resurgence in terrorism. In 1994 ETA's political wing, Herri Batasuna, resurfaced after having been virtually moribund since a limited degree of home rule had been granted by the Spanish government to the Basque region in 1982. The militant element of ETA had remained active and in the first four years of the 1990s carried out a number of attacks and bombings in Madrid and elsewhere. However, 1994 saw the apprehending in France of one of its most prominent members: on 25 August Maria Idoia Lopez Raino, known as The Tigress, was arrested in Aix-en-Provence. Alleged to be responsible for the deaths of seventeen Civil Guards and a number of soldiers during the period

1980 to 1986, she was a member of ETA's Madrid Commando cell. In November, ETA suffered a further blow when the Basque Autonomous Police mounted an operation against the organisation's Vascaya Command, attacking and virtually destroying it.

In January 1995 ETA struck back when it assassinated Gregorio Ordonez, the regional leader in the Basque country of the opposition Popular Party and a favourite to win the election in May for mayor of the city of San Sebastian, who was shot dead in a restaurant by an ETA gunman. Three months later in Madrid, an attempt was made on the life of the leader of the Popular Party, José Maria Aznar, when on 19 April his three-car convoy was ambushed by a remote-controlled bomb positioned at a road junction. The 55-pound charge, concealed in a stolen car, exploded as the convoy passed by, Aznar's armoured Audi 200 saloon taking the full blast. Miraculously, he escaped with just a small cut on his head, but sixteen other people, including four of his police escort, were injured in the blast. The three ETA terrorists responsible for the attack made good their escape in another stolen vehicle which was later found blown up near Madrid's railway station.

In July, allegations surfaced of involvement by senior government ministers in the murders of members of ETA during the 1980s. Contained in a file passed to the Supreme Court, these stated that the individuals concerned had been involved in the establishment of an organisation of hit-squads called the Grupo Anti-Terrorista Liberación (GAL). Comprising members of the French underworld, some of them former members of the Organisation de l'Armée Sécrète (OAS) of Algerian War fame, these groups had been paid from Spanish Interior Ministry secret funds to hunt down and kill members of ETA in south-west France, ultimately accounting for twenty-eight of them. The aim of these attacks was to force the French government to take action against Basque separatists. Those members of the government and Socialist Party named as being involved with the establishment of GAL were: the Prime Minister and party leader, Felipe Gonzalez; the former Deputy Prime Minister, Narcis Serra; the third most senior member of the Popular

Party, Txiki Benegas; and the former Interior Minister, José Barrionuevo. Another individual, former Security Minister Rafael Vera, had been arrested in February on suspicion of involvement.

Gonzalez strenuously denied the allegations, which were potentially extremely damaging politically, and stressed that such measures would have been illogical and unnecessary as the French government had already agreed to co-operate in combating the separatists. Nevertheless, two months later, the Spanish Senate announced the convening of a special inquiry into the allegations.

ETA meanwhile escalated its bombing campaign, turning its attention to Spain's holiday resorts in an effort to disrupt the country's tourist industry. Bombs exploded at Denia in the southeast and at Alicante, while at Tarragona, on the east coast, a small device was defused after being found in a hotel accommodating 300 British holidaymakers.

During the summer, ETA mounted an operation to assassinate His Majesty King Juan Carlos while he was on holiday with the rest of the royal family on the island of Majorca. First to learn of the threat were the French who immediately passed a warning to the Spanish authorities. On 17 July, a three-man ETA hit-team arrived in Majorca aboard a French-registered yacht, *La Belle Poule*, in which it had sailed from Nice. After mooring offshore at Alcudia, a resort on Majorca's northern coast, the terrorists made their way to Palma where they rented an apartment near the Marivent Palace, the royal family's summer residence, overlooking a nearby naval base and the jetty where the king's personal yacht, *Fortuna*, was moored. The ETA team was led by Juan José Rego, one of the organisation's most experienced terrorists, who had previously been arrested and imprisoned in 1978 for plotting to assassinate the king on the island of Ibiza. On his release he had moved to France where he had been arrested and imprisoned for terrorist offences, being released in 1988.

During the next three weeks, Rego and his accomplices watched the royal family's movements closely, unaware that they themselves were under surveillance by police. On Wednesday 10 August, the latter stormed the apartment, capturing all three terrorists and seizing pistols, submachine-guns, a sniper rifle, a bomb and a quantity of documents. At the same time, a police team boarded and searched *La Belle Poule* where she lay off Alcudia. Meanwhile, eight other suspects were arrested in France and another in San Sebastian. It was later discovered that ETA had also gathered a considerable amount of detailed information about a skiing holiday in the Pyrenees being planned by the royal family.

A week later, ETA struck back with a wave of bombings in northern Spain, some of which took place on the railways where they caused major disruption. On 17 August a 100-pound bomb exploded outside a Civil Guard barracks in the town of Arnedo, injuring forty people.

Attacks continued throughout the following months. On the afternoon of 11 December, a 130-pound remote-controlled car bomb exploded near a motorway in Madrid as a minibus carrying naval personnel was passing by; six sailors died and twenty other people were injured in the blast which caused considerable damage to the surrounding area.

Early 1996 saw further attacks. On 9 January, ETA terrorists shot dead an Army colonel outside his home in Madrid. On 6 February a prominent Basque politician, Fernando Mugica, was killed in San Sebastian, his murder one of a number intended to disrupt Spain's forthcoming general election. Eight days later, one of the country's most senior judges, Francisco Tomas y Valiente, was murdered by a gunman in his office at the Autonomous University in Madrid; on this occasion the attacker was identified by witnesses as an individual named Bienzobas, a member of ETA's Madrid Commando, which had been responsible for a number of attacks, including the bombing in Madrid on 11 December.

On 4 March the results of the general election held the day before saw the conservative Popular Party of José Maria Aznar win a narrow victory over the Socialist Party of Felipe Gonzales. However, Aznar's fifteen-seat majority was such that it did not give him an overall mandate and he was forced to indulge in horse-trading with the Catalan and Basque nationalist parties before he was able to announce the formation of a government with a working majority.

The summer of 1996 saw ETA turning its attention once again to Spain's tourist industry. In June, a number of bombs exploded at resorts on the Costa del Sol, but no casualties were caused because telephone warnings were given beforehand. On 21 July, however, a bomb exploded at the airport at Reus on the Costa Dorada, the coast of eastern Spain, injuring thirty-three people. Two others blew up outside hotels in the resorts of Salou and Cambrills, but there were no casualties, in both instances the areas having been cleared before the devices exploded.

Two days later, on 23 July, the terrorist responsible for orchestrating these attacks was arrested in south-west France. Julian Atxurra Egurola, ETA's quartermaster-general and a member of the three-man council controlling the organisation, was arrested in a dawn assault by gendarmerie troops on an isolated farmhouse at Lasseube, near Pau. A search of the building uncovered two portable computers, a number of electronic databanks, weapons, explosives, forged identity cards and a quantity of documents. This was a major victory for French and Spanish security forces in the long-running battle against Basque separatists on both sides of the border. Egurola himself had long been sought by the Spanish for the murders of a number of police officers and other terrorist offences.

In north-west Spain on the day following Egurola's arrest, Spanish security forces scored another coup against ETA when members of the Guardia Civil stormed an apartment in Pontevedra which had been under surveillance for four days. Inside they found three members of the organisation, two men and a woman, three weapons and, most important of all, 300 computer disks which were subsequently handed over to technical experts to decipher the encoded data stored on them.

Towards the end of 1996, yet another success was scored against ETA when on 19 November French police in Bordeaux arrested Juan Maria Insausti who was responsible for training throughout the organisation. His arrest led to the discovery of documents which showed that ETA was planning to assassinate the French Interior Minister Jean Louis Debré and his predecessor, Charles

Pasqua, to express its anger at the imprisonment in France of some fifty of its members. Similar documents, giving details of plans for other operations in France, had also been found among those seized during the arrest in July of Julian Atxurra Egurola. These suggested additional targets in France which included two senior officials involved in the war against terrorism: Laurence Le Vert, an investigating magistrate; and a senior police officer, Roger Marion.

In February 1997, details of a further plot by ETA against the Spanish royal family came to light after the arrest of another member of the organisation in France. José-Luis Urrusolo Sistiaga was apprehended near Bordeaux and documents found in his possession revealed that he had been carrying out surveillance on Princess Elena, the elder daughter of King Juan Carlos and Queen Sophia, who lived in Paris with her husband. During the period leading up to Sistiaga's arrest, the Princess had been staying in the south-west of France where he had been monitoring her movements.

Despite the setbacks caused by these arrests, ETA continued its campaign of violence in Spain. On 10 February, a supreme court judge was shot dead by two masked members of the organisation outside his home in Madrid. In Granada on the same day, the driver of a military vehicle and seven men were injured when a car bomb exploded.

In July, however, ETA carried out an act which shocked the Spanish nation by its senseless brutality and unleashed a tide of revulsion against the terrorists. On Thursday 10 July Miguel Angel Blanco, a young Popular Party councillor in the Basque town of Ermua, was kidnapped by ETA which threatened to kill him unless 450 of its members, held in jails in Spain, were transferred immediately to jails in the Basque region, a demand rejected by the government. His kidnappers set a deadline of 4 p.m. on Saturday 12 July. Demonstrations in protest against the kidnapping took place throughout Spain and in Bilbao the Prime Minister himself led a march of several hundred thousand people pleading with ETA to release its hostage unharmed.

Tragically, all this was to no avail. An hour after the deadline had expired, Blanco was found lying beside a railway line near the town of Lasarte; he had been shot in the head but was still alive. Despite undergoing emergency treatment in San Sebastian, however, he died. The shock and outrage at this senseless killing spread throughout Spain and Blanco's funeral, attended by the Crown Prince, Prime Minister José Maria Aznar, senior politicians and military officers, became a centrepoint for a national protest against ETA and its campaign of violence. Mass demonstrations against the terrorists also took place elsewhere in the country and there were attacks in several towns on the offices of ETA's political front organisation, Herri Batasuna, while in Ermua its headquarters was set on fire. Any sympathy for ETA among the Basque people had been dramatically reduced, if not killed off, by the brutal murder of Blanco.

Despite the dramatic fall in support for its cause, ETA continued its campaign of terror. In October another plot to assassinate King Juan Carlos, at the opening of the Guggenheim Museum in Bilbao on 18 October, was uncovered a few days beforehand. Basque police officers stopped a vehicle carrying two men who opened fire, killing one of the policemen, before fleeing on foot. A search of the vehicle revealed automatic weapons and grenades. During November, French police discovered an ETA arms cache near St-Pée-sur-Nivelle in south-west France; it contained two submachine-guns, a number of grenades and a large quantity of explosives. On 17 November, a man was arrested near Bilbao and found to be in possession of explosives and detonators concealed in his car.

The government had meanwhile taken action against ETA's political front, Herri Batasuna, by charging its entire 23-strong executive with the offence of collaborating with terrorists. On 2 December, all were found guilty and sentenced to seven years' imprisonment. ETA responded by changing tactics and concentrating its attacks on members of the ruling Popular Party. One of these took place on 12 December when José Luis Caso, a councillor in Renteria, a suburb of the city of San Sebastian near the border with France, was shot dead. A month later, on 10 January 1998, another councillor, José Iruretagoyena, was killed by a car bomb in the town of Zarauz, near San Sebastian. Attacks also took place outside the Basque region: in the early hours of 30 January Alberto Jimenez Becerril, a leading local politician, and his wife were shot dead outside their home in the southern city of Seville.

ETA's new tactics caused major problems for the Spanish security forces which were faced with the impossible task of providing protection for some 25,000 local Popular Party politicians throughout Spain. The situation was not helped by lack of co-ordination between the Basque Autonomous Police, which answered to the regional government, the Guardia Civil and the Policia Nacional which were both controlled by the national government in Madrid. This inevitably led to disagreements and discord between the three forces, not only at operational levels, but also among the political bodies responsible for co-ordinating policy in the war against ETA.

In early May, yet another plot to murder King Juan Carlos was uncovered. On this occasion the attempt was to take place in July, in San Sebastian, a remote-controlled car bomb being used to ambush his motorcade as it drove through the city where the king was due to perform an opening ceremony.

Attacks against Popular Party politicians continued during the summer. On 6 May Tomas Caballero, a councillor in the city of Pamplona, was shot dead by two gunmen outside his home. On 26 June another councillor was killed in Renteria. During the previous month one of his colleagues had resigned after receiving death threats against herself and her family.

Early June had, however, seen another success on the part of the Basque Autonomous Police. On the 6th they stormed a second-floor apartment in Guernica occupied by members of ETA's Vizcaya Commando. A woman, Ignacia Ceberio, was killed when she opened fire and a man was injured when he attempted to escape by jumping out of the window. A search of the apartment uncovered a large cache of weapons. A number of raids took place elsewhere throughout the region and thirteen people were arrested in an operation which foiled a number of operations about to be launched by ETA.

The latter part of July and early August 1998 witnessed the conviction and imprisonment of twelve individuals for involvement in the operations by GAL death squads against ETA during the 1980s. Among them were José Barrionuevo, who had served for most of the 1980s as Interior Minister in the Socialist Party government of Felipe Gonzales, and Rafael Vera, who had been Minister for Security; the remainder were senior police officers or Interior Ministry officials. Barrionuevo and his accomplices had been arrested in January 1996, following an investigation headed by Baltazar Garzon, a leading investigating judge, which had heard evidence from two former senior police officers imprisoned in the late 1980s for recruiting gunmen for the GAL death squads which had been paid by them. All twelve had subsequently been charged with kidnapping, misuse of Interior Ministry funds and association with an armed organisation.

In September 1996 there had been further revelations about the alleged use of GAL hit-squads. Articles in the Spanish press maintained that in 1988 the Spanish military intelligence service, CESID, had been involved in a plan to kidnap a leading member of ETA, José Antonio Urretikoetxea, living in France. The intention had been to inject him with a drug to render him unconscious before spiriting him away over the border into Spain. The operation took place in December 1983, but the wrong man was kidnapped; he was released unharmed but somewhat shaken several days later.

Despite a chorus of demands for explanations, however, Prime Minister José Maria Aznar had refused to allow any information concerning CESID's involvement with GAL operations to be disclosed, heightening suspicions of a major cover-up of the involvement of government departments. Such suspicions had already been strengthened nine months earlier with the arrests of José Barrionuevo and Rafael Vera.

In mid-September, ETA announced a ceasefire and a cessation to its campaign of terror. While it was undoubtedly recognised that the terrorists had been under pressure from the security forces, which had carried out a series of arrests in recent months, and from the public outcry against terrorist violence, there was considerable cynicism on the part of those who recalled that the previous cease-fire had lasted no more than a week and pointed out that regional elections were due to take place during October. Others speculated whether the IRA ceasefire in Northern Ireland and the signing of the Good Friday Agreement had influenced ETA in its latest move. Meanwhile, the government reacted cautiously in the face of the communiqué broadcast by ETA which, while announcing the ceasefire, declared that the organisation would not disarm and would defend itself if attacked. At the same time, it reiterated demands for an independent Basque state.

Two months later the government established a dialogue with ETA via one of the latter's front organisations, the Basque National Liberation Movement, and in January 1999 the terrorists agreed to peace talks. In July, the executive of Herri Batasuna was released from prison after its seven-year' prison sentence was quashed by the Constitutional Court in Madrid. Meanwhile, the government agreed to the transfer of a number of prisoners to the Basque region and released some 200 others. In August, however, the hitherto improving situation deteriorated sharply when ETA cut off all contact with the government, accusing it of duplicity.

On 30 September, evidence that the terrorists were rearming came to light when French police arrested three ETA suspects on the outskirts of Pau. The latter were found to be in possession of two and a half tons of explosives and 5,000 detonators which had been stolen in Brittany two days earlier. This reinforced earlier reports that ETA had moved its French base from south-west France to Brittany where it had established an alliance with the ARB. On 29 November, ETA issued a communiqué announcing that it was terminating its ceasefire which had by then lasted fourteen months, blaming continuing acts of repression on the part of the Spanish and French governments. The population of the Basque region reacted by taking to the streets and holding silent protests demonstrating against the terrorists' announcement. Throughout Spain, the government and people braced themselves for further bombings and murders.

During the 1990s, the most significant terrorist threats throughout the world emanated from Islamic fundamentalist groups. All through the decade, countries in North Africa, the Middle East, Asia, Africa, Europe and the Americas were subjected to acts of terrorism perpetrated by Islamic extremists carrying out a jihad (holy war) in their pursuit of their goal of a world-wide Islamic empire.

In Algeria, Islamic extremism had first gained a toehold in 1989 after the Islamic Salvation Front (FIS), a coalition of ten fundamentalist groups, had been granted legal status by President Chadli Benjedid in a move designed to co-opt the Islamists. In December 1991, however, the FIS won the legislative elections. Fearful of an Islamic government coming to power, the Army staged a coup in January 1992 and deposed Benjedid, replacing him with Liamine Zeroual. At the same time it declared the result of the election to be null and void and cancelled the forthcoming general election which the FIS was expected to win.

These measures were followed by a crackdown during which a number of the FIS leadership were imprisoned or forced to flee abroad. The movement subsequently splintered into several groups, among which the most militant and violent was the Armed Islamic Group (GIA) which embarked on a long-running campaign of violence and terror. Large numbers of refugees fled to France, the former colonial power in Algeria, and to other countries in southern Europe. It was not long before it became apparent that should the extremists gain control in Algeria, France alone would see an influx of more than a million Algerian immigrants which would reduce its already overburdened social welfare system to a state of chaos. Moreover, an Islamist victory would undoubtedly cause unrest in neighbouring countries such as Morocco and Tunisia which already had problems with extremists; any collapse on their part would have potentially destabilising ramifications for the rest of North Africa, the Middle East and southern Europe.

It was principally for these reasons, therefore, that in 1993 France secretly commenced supplying military and economic aid to Algeria. The GIA responded by exporting the war to France, establishing a network of its members throughout the country and, as described earlier, training camps in the Ardèche. This became a major concern to the French who, already worried about the effects of extremism on the country's large Muslim population, cracked down on extremists, arresting them in large numbers and deporting suspected ringleaders to Algeria. In November 1994, the French uncovered a plan by extremists to attack Israeli and other Jewish targets inside France and traced links between the network in France and others in Britain, Germany, Italy, The Netherlands and Canada.

On 24 December 1994, four members of the GIA hijacked an Air France Airbus A-300, Flight 8969, due to fly from Algiers to Paris with 227 passengers aboard, in an operation designed to punish France for its support of the Algerian government in its war against the fundamentalists. The hijackers murdered three of their hostages before the aircraft was permitted to fly to France where it landed at Marseilles. An account of the hijack and the ensuing hostage rescue operation mounted by the French is given in Chapter 12.

The next five years saw a reign of terror in Algeria by the GIA which targeted foreigners living in the country. Among those assassinated were foreign industrialists, who were considered to be supporting the government, and Roman Catholic priests and nuns who were condemned as 'defilers of Islam'. Journalists, both Algerian and foreign, were also considered to be legitimate targets on the grounds that they were generally anti-Islamic in their views.

Wholesale slaughter was perpetrated by the GIA and other small splinter groups: on 11 December 1995 Algiers was subjected to fifteen car bombings which killed fifteen people and injured hundreds more. In January 1996 a massive bomb exploded in a crowded area of the city, killing forty people and injuring more than 300 others. The following four years would see many such bombings in the capital, resulting in very large numbers of dead and injured. In the rural areas, villages were attacked at night by extremists who cut the throats of their victims before beheading them; 155 villagers died in such attacks during January 1997 while in April 225 were butchered with chain saws, axes, shovels and knives. On 22 September 1997, 200 people were massacred in a suburb of Algiers during an attack with knives and axes. During the rest of the decade, the numbers of those murdered by the GIA rose until by 1997 they totalled almost 100,000.

Egypt has suffered problems with fundamentalists since the early part of the 20th century when the Moslem Brotherhood, formed in 1928 by Sheikh Hasan al-Bana, figured prominently in efforts to expel the British from the country. Successive governments had thereafter maintained an uneasy relationship with the Islamists, at times granting them concessions and limited power in order to retain their co-operation and at others subjecting them to crack-downs and proscription. During the 1970s, President Anwar Sadat encouraged the Islamists to counterbalance the communists. Towards the end of the decade, however, when the country was wracked by internal problems caused by a collapsing economy and endemic corruption, as well as political upheaval resulting from the peace treaty with Egypt, the Islamists turned on him. On 6 October 1981, he was assassinated by members of al-Jihad (also known as Islamic Jihad), a Moslem Brotherhood splinter group headed by an extremist named Ayman al-Zawahiri, which had infiltrated the ranks of the Egyptian army.

Following Sadat's death, the fundamentalists increased significantly as a force in impoverished southern Egypt and in the country's universities. Half a dozen Islamist groups actively sought to overthrow the government of his successor, President Hosni Mubarak, who proceeded to crack down on them. The largest and most militant of these was the Islamic Group (Al-Gama'at al-Islamiya) whose leadership comprised members of the professional classes but whose rank-and-file were recruited from the young and unemployed. Like their Algerian counterparts of the GIA, many of the Islamic Group's military wing were sent to Afghanistan to join the Mujahideen with whom they saw service during the war against the Soviet Union. Thereafter they spent further time training in Sudan and the Yemen before returning home to Egypt.

In 1992 the Islamic Group started to target Egypt's tourist industry, a major source of income for the government, killing seven foreign tourists during the next two years and causing tourism in Egypt to drop by a third. At the same time, it concentrated on infiltrating the Egyptian armed forces and assassinating senior officers and government officials. In 1990, the Speaker of the Egyptian parliament, Rifa'at el-Mahgoub, was murdered and attempts made to kill several ministers. This resulted in a major crack-down on Islamists by the security forces which drove some of the leadership abroad, among them Mustafa Hamza who sought sanctuary in Afghanistan from where he continued to orchestrate the Islamic Group's campaign of violence.

Another was the blind spiritual leader of the Islamic Group, Sheikh Omar Abdel-Rahman, who during the early 1980s was imprisoned on charges of issuing the fatwa which had resulted in the death of President Sadat. After three years in prison he was acquitted and in 1985 travelled to Pakistan and Afghanistan where he assisted in co-ordinating the activities of some of the groups of Mujahideen, coming into contact with the CIA and Pakistan's military intelligence agency, the Inter Service Intelligence (ISI), who considered him a valuable 'asset'. From Pakistan Sheikh Omar thereafter travelled to many parts of the world preaching his gospel of extremism and jihad, returning to Egypt and visiting Islamic people in Asia and Europe. He also travelled to Sudan where he met Hassan al-Turabi whom he met frequently thereafter. In 1990 he went to the United States, entering the country on a tourist visa, where he spent the next three years establishing a base for Islamic extremists.

In Egypt, meanwhile, at least two attempts were made on the life of President Hosni Mubarak during the first half of the 1990s, the first in 1993 during a visit by him to a town on the border between Egypt and Libya to meet the Libyan leader, Colonel Muammar Gadaffi. On 26 June 1995, another attempt was made during a visit by the president to the Ethiopian capital of Addis Ababa for a conference of African leaders. Members of the Islamic Group ambushed his motorcade as it drove from the airport to the city, but Mubarak escaped death or injury thanks to his armoured saloon car which received several hits. Two of the six terrorists were killed by the president's bodyguard and a subsequent search of a nearby house uncovered a cache of weapons comprising AK-47 assault rifles, RPG-7 rocket-propelled grenades and explosives.

Five months later, on 19 November, a massive car bomb exploded in the Egyptian embassy in Islamabad, Pakistan, killing seventeen people and seriously wounding more than sixty. The embassy was destroyed and the Indonesian and Swiss embassies nearby were badly damaged. Three groups claimed responsibility: an organisation calling itself the International Justice Group was the first to do so in a fax to a news agency; an agency in Cairo meanwhile received telephone calls from al-Jihad and the Islamic Group who stated that the attack had been a reprisal for extradition from Pakistan of five Islamic terrorists wanted in Egypt for their involvement in attempts to topple the regime of President Mubarak. Large numbers of Arab fundamentalists who had fought in Afghanistan had subsequently remained in Pakistan, taking sanctuary in the border areas of the North West Frontier Province which were ruled by the Pushtun tribes rather than the federal government.

In 1996 the extremists turned their attention once again to Egypt's tourist industry, this time with far more devastating results. On 19 April three terrorists opened fire on tourists outside the Europa Hotel near the pyramids in Giza and then entered the hotel where they sprayed a ground-floor restaurant. Eighteen people, mostly elderly Greek women, died in the attack. On 18 September 1997, nine German tourists were killed when Muslim extremists fire-bombed and machine-gunned a bus in central Cairo.

The most devastating of all the attacks on tourists, however, occurred two months later, on 17 November, at Queen Hatshepsut's temple at Luxor in southern Egypt on the west bank of the Nile. Six members of the Islamic Group opened fire on a busload of tourists who had just arrived from the nearby Valley of the Kings, where they had visited Tutankhamun's tomb, and were walking across the courtyard to the temple. Some of the tourists were killed immediately, others fled for cover among the colonnades or in the chapels on either side of the tomb, but four of the terrorists pursued them. Those they found were shot, their throats cut and, in some instances, beheaded. Within twenty minutes, the courtyard and chapels resembled a charnel-house as the terrorists massacred fifty-eight tourists who were mostly Swiss and Japanese but included some Britons, French and Germans. By then the alarm had been raised and the terrorists fled in a commandeered minibus. A few miles down the road, however, they were stopped by police and a crowd of villagers who, horrified and outraged at the atrocity, pursued them with sticks and stones. One terrorist was shot by the police, but the others escaped into the mountains. Hours later, they were tracked to a cave where, after a gun battle lasting three hours, they were all killed.

By 1997, after five years of repression, the Islamic Group was broken as an organisation. A ruthless campaign by the Egyptian authorities against the movement had seen 20,000 men arrested and held in prison without trial, more than ninety of them being sentenced to death by military courts since 1992. The organisation thereafter split into five groups, one being the Vanguards of Conquest, and many of its members fled abroad, some seeking political asylum in Britain where they established a support network.

Throughout the 1990s Israel continued to be subjected to attacks, primarily from three terrorist organisations: Hizbollah, HAMAS and Palestinian Islamic Jihad. The latter two groups concentrated their attacks within Israel, the Gaza Strip and the West Bank in a campaign to force the Israelis to withdraw from the occupied territories. Meanwhile Hizbollah, supported and funded by Iran, continued to be active against Israeli forces occupying the security zone in South Lebanon, stretching from the Lebanese coast south of Tyre to Mount Hermon and the northern end of the Israeli-occupied Golan Heights, which had been established three years after the Israeli invasion of the Lebanon in 1982 during which the Palestinians had been driven out of the south of the country. In late 1991, Hizbollah switched tactics. Dispensing with the suicide bombers which had been its trademark during the 1980s, it established a battalion-size guerrilla unit of some 700 men trained by Iranian Revolutionary Guards. Well armed and equipped, as well as highly trained, Hizbollah's guerrillas soon began to make their mark in operations against Israeli forces in the Lebanon.

HAMAS is the Arabic acronym of Harakat al-Muqawama al-Islamiya (Islamic Resistance Movement) which came into existence in the Gaza Strip in 1987 as a splinter group of the Moslem Brotherhood in Egypt. Like its parent organisation, HAMAS's ultimate aim is the establishment of an Islamic fundamentalist state throughout the Muslim world. Towards the end of the 1980s, it had established itself as the principal rival to the PLO. Unlike the latter, it favoured direct action against Israel in its campaign for the establishment of a Palestinian state, a policy which found favour among young and disgruntled Palestinians throughout the Gaza Strip, particularly when the Intifada began to spread throughout the Israeli-occupied territories in December 1987. Initially, HAMAS was happy to co-exist with the PLO, but in 1991, following a conference in Tehran at which HAMAS represented a number of other Palestinian organisations, the PLO refused to grant it a significant presence on the Palestine National Council. This resulted in a major split between the two organisations, subsequently leading to violence between them.

The Palestinian Islamic Jihad (PIJ) is a name used by a loose affiliation of groups, as opposed to a single organisation, which seek the establishment of a Palestinian state. Like HAMAS, it seeks the destruction of Israel which is regarded as the principal enemy of Islam. Similarly, it has carried out attacks against Israeli targets on the West Bank and the Gaza Strip, as well as inside Israel itself. One of the earlier attacks during the decade took place on 2 May 1992, when PIJ terrorists carried out an attack at the Red Sea resort of Eilat, killing a tourist. Two of them were killed and a third captured during a follow-up operation by Israeli security forces. A year later, in April 1993, a HAMAS suicide bomber killed eight Israelis.

October 1994 saw the kidnapping by HAMAS of an Israeli soldier, Corporal Nachson Waxman, on the West Bank. His kidnappers demanded the release of Sheikh Ahmad Yassin, the organisation's spiritual leader who had been imprisoned in 1989 for the kidnap and murder of two Israeli soldiers, plus the release of 200 other prisoners. Corporal Waxman was held for a total of ten days, during which the Israelis launched a massive intelligence-gathering effort. On 19 October, he and his captors were located in a house and a rescue operation was mounted. However, it proved unsuccessful and Waxman was killed by the kidnappers before the rescue force could reach him. That same day, a HAMAS suicide bomber killed twenty-two people and injured forty-seven on a bus in the centre of Tel Aviv.

Four months later, on 22 January 1995, the PIJ carried out a double suicide bombing outside an army base five miles north of Tel Aviv. Nineteen people, mostly soldiers, died and sixty-five people were injured when two terrorists detonated their bombs in the centre of a crowd waiting at a bus stop. On 10 April, in the Gaza Strip, the PIJ struck again when a terrorist rammed a car containing a bomb into a bus carrying troops and settlers travelling from the town of Ashkelon to the settlements at Gush Katif, killing seven people and wounding forty. Two hours later, a second car bomb exploded beside a military vehicle near a settlement at Netzarim, wounding nine people.

On 23 June, the Israelis appeared to be striking back when Mahmud al-Khawaja, one of the PIJ's military commanders, was shot dead as he was walking to his office at the United Nations World Refugee Agency (UNWRA). He was the second PIJ leader to be killed: in November 1994, Hani Abed had died when a bomb exploded in his car and the Israelis had been accused of being responsible for his murder too.

During the following month, HAMAS struck back with another suicide bomb. During the rush-hour on the morning of 24 July, a terrorist exploded a bomb aboard a bus in a suburb of Tel Aviv, killing five people and injuring thirty others. This and other bombings were timed to coincide with peace talks between Israel and the Palestinians on extending Palestinian self-rule from Gaza and Jericho to the remainder of the West Bank. In the aftermath of these attacks it became obvious that many Palestinians, by then enjoying the effects of limited autonomy and looking forward to an extension of it, no longer approved of the terror campaign being waged by HAMAS and the PIJ.

On 21 August, HAMAS carried out another suicide bomb attack during the rush-hour in Tel Aviv. A female terrorist exploded her bomb aboard a bus, killing five people and injuring 107. The attack was followed by violent anti-Arab demonstrations which lasted throughout the day and into the night, with police being forced to use water cannon and tear gas to break up mobs of demonstrators. This and the other bombings were believed to have been master-minded by HAMAS's master bomber, Yehiya Ayyash, a member of Izzedin al-Kassam, the organisation's military wing.

The end of September saw the signing of the pact formally trans-ferring further parts of the West Bank from Israeli to Palestinian control. While the rest of the world applauded, Palestinian and Jewish opponents of the pact demonstrated their displeasure. Ten days later, HAMAS reluctantly accepted the agreement, but stated that it would not halt its attacks on Israel.

A month later, on 26 October, the leader of the PIJ, Fathi Shiqaqi, was assassinated in Malta. Travelling as a Libyan busi-nessman under the alias of Ibrahim Ali Shawesh, he was shot five times in the head with a silenced pistol by a gunman riding pillion on a motorcycle as he walked out of his hotel in Sliema, near Valletta. The finger of suspicion was immediately pointed at Israel which, while admitting nothing, scarcely attempted to deny any involvement in the killing.

On 3 November, the PIJ retaliated with two suicide car bomb attacks. The first took place when the driver of a car detonated his bomb near a bus carrying Israelis travelling to work in settlements in the Gaza Strip, injuring eleven people. Shortly afterwards, a second vehicle exploded but caused no casualties.

In January of the following year, HAMAS also lost a key member of its organisation when its chief bomb-maker, Yehiya Ayyash, was assassinated. On 5 January, he received a telephone call from his father on a mobile telephone belonging to a man named Isama

Hammad, the owner of the house in which he was hiding at the time. As he identified himself, the device exploded, killing Ayyash immediately. It transpired that the telephone had been a gift to Hammad from a relative who subsequently disappeared and was duly reported to have fled to the United States. Later reports indicated that the telephone conversation had been monitored by the Israelis who had detonated the explosive charge by remote control. Ayyash, who had been on the run from the Israeli authorities for two years, was reported as having been responsible for the deaths of more than seventy Israelis during the suicide bomb campaign waged by HAMAS since the early part of the decade.

Retribution for his death was not long in coming. On 25 February, a HAMAS suicide bomber exploded his device aboard a bus in the centre of Jerusalem, killing twenty-two people and injuring some fifty more. Less than an hour later another exploded his car bomb after ramming a queue at a bus stop near the town of Ashkelon, killing two people and injuring about thirty. These were reportedly the work of Yehiyah Ayyash's successor as chief bomb-maker, a Palestinian electrician named Muhi a-Din Sherif, who had been on the run from the Israelis since August.

The Israeli and Palestinian authorities responded by cracking down on the extremists. Families of known bombers or suspected leaders of groups were evicted from their homes by Israeli troops and their houses demolished or sealed. Elsewhere, troops closed the border between Israel and the West Bank and the Gaza Strip, while others carried out raids on areas in the West Bank and arrested more than 100 suspects. This resulted at the beginning of March in HAMAS's military wing, Izzedin al-Kassam, declaring that it was willing to lay down its arms, but this was rejected by the Israelis who continued with their crackdown.

In March, it was reported that Britain had become the principal overseas headquarters and fund-raising base for HAMAS. According to one report, evidence of this had surfaced after an American had been arrested and imprisoned in Israel for supplying arms to the organisation. Under questioning, he had revealed he had been instructed to travel to London to receive his orders from a HAMAS leader, Abu Obeida, who was alleged to have been the mastermind behind a number of terrorist attacks in Israel. It would appear that there was some substance in the Israeli allegations, as Obeida fled immediately after the American's arrest and took refuge in Sudan. Another who did so was Ramadan Shallah, the successor to the assassinated PIJ leader, Fathi Shiqaqi, who flew to Damascus and was given refuge by the Syrians. Educated at Zaqazik University in Egypt and in America, Shallah had been a founder member of al-Jihad in Egypt. Entering the United Kingdom in 1986, he studied for a doctorate in economics at Durham University, qualifying in 1991. During this period he was believed to have headed PIJ fund-raising operations in Great Britain and to have been involved in Islamic extremist activities in the United States.

HAMAS meanwhile received financial support from Iran, notably from the Department of Islamic Liberation Movements which funded Islamic extremist groups world-wide as part of Iran's policy of exporting fundamentalism throughout the Muslim world. In addition to funds, Iran also provided training for large numbers of HAMAS terrorists, some of the instructors being members of Hizbollah.

In March 1997 the first bomb for almost a year exploded at a café in Tel Aviv, killing three Israeli women and injuring more than forty other people. This heralded a new wave of suicide bomb attacks prompted by Palestinian frustration at the lack of further progress in the peace process which had slowed since the election, in June of the previous year, of the centre-right coalition government of Benjamin Netanyahu who had promised during his campaign to halt the creation of a Palestinian state. On 1 April, two suicide bombers carried out attacks in the Gaza Strip, but no casualties were caused. On 31 July, however, two terrorists caused devastation when their bombs, each containing an estimated twenty-two pounds of explosive packed with nails, exploded within seconds of each other in a crowded market in Jerusalem. Fifteen people died and 170 were injured in the blast which took place at the Mahane Yehuda market in the west of the city. HAMAS subsequently claimed responsibility for the attack, stating that it had carried it out in revenge for a poster displayed in Hebron depicting the prophet Mohammed as a pig. A few weeks later, West Jerusalem was subjected to another atrocity when, during the early afternoon of 4 September, three terrorists exploded their bombs in a crowded mall, killing four people and injuring more than 170 and devastating the area. Once again, HAMAS claimed responsibility.

Later that month, the Israelis retaliated. On 25 September an attempt was made on the life of one of HAMAS's leaders, Khaled Meshal, as he was about to enter his office in the Jordanian capital of Amman. Two men walked past him and sprayed poison into his ear; pursued by one of his two bodyguards, they fled but were subsequently arrested by Jordanian police. His two assailants were subsequently found to be Mossad agents posing as Canadian tourists and the diplomatic embarrassment caused to Israel was considerable. In order to prevent Jordan breaking off diplomatic relations, Israel was forced to release HAMAS's founder and spiritual leader, Sheikh Ahmad Yassin, who was flown to Jordan on 1 October. He was subsequently allowed to return to Gaza in exchange for Jordan's release of the two Mossad agents who returned to Israel. Khaled Meshal recovered from the attack after Crown Prince Hassan of Jordan obtained the antidote for the poison.

A year of relative calm followed, during which there were no bombings by HAMAS. On 27 August 1998, however, a bomb exploded in central Tel Aviv, wounding twelve people. Two months later, on 29 October, Israeli troops in the Gaza Strip narrowly averted an attempt by a suicide bomber in a car to blow up a school bus full of children. In an effort to ensure that the next stage of the Israeli withdrawal from the West Bank, due to be put into effect on 2 November, still went ahead, the Palestinian authorities responded by arresting 100 members of HAMAS and placing Sheikh Ahmed Yassin under house arrest. This inevitably resulted in a backlash from HAMAS which condemned Palestinian Authority Chairman Yasser Arafat as a traitor and threatened to take action against him. On 6 November, a HAMAS suicide bomber killed himself and wounded twenty people with a car bomb which fortunately failed to explode fully outside the Mahane Yehuda market in West Jerusalem.

The year 1999 saw further efforts on the part of Iran to sabotage the Middle East peace process in the wake of the election of Israeli Prime Minister Ehud Barak who, unlike his predecessor, was committed to regenerating the peace process. Barak's moderate stance, advocating an agreement with all Arab states and a peace treaty with Syria, alarmed the fundamentalist ayatollahs in Iran who were implacably opposed to any form of deal with Israel. In August, it was reported that £3,000,000 had been given to HAMAS to fund further operations against Israel, the money being channelled at the end of July via bank accounts in Damascus. Within HAMAS itself, a split had developed between the leaders of the organisation in the West Bank and Gaza Strip, headed by Sheikh Ahmad Yassin, and the more extreme faction based in Jordan, Syria and the Lebanon. It was with the latter that Iran forged an alliance during a conference in Khartoum when the decision was taken to launch a series of attacks designed to derail the peace process.

On 5 September a car bomb exploded in Tiberias, a holiday resort on the Sea of Galilee, killing the two terrorists in the vehicle and injuring three people nearby; another blew up in the port of Haifa, killing the bomber. These attacks came in the wake of the Israeli government's approval of the next stage of the Israeli withdrawal from the West Bank, to be conducted concurrently with the release of 350 Palestinian prisoners. Four days later, the first 200 prisoners were freed. On 15 October, the remaining 150 prisoners were also released in accordance with the agreement signed during the previous month by Prime Minister Ehud Barak and the Chairman of the Palestinian Authority, Yasser Arafat.

Meanwhile, Iran increased funds and supplies of arms to HAMAS, the PIJ and Hizbollah in a further effort to derail the peace process. On 1 November terrorists opened fire on a bus near the village of Tarkumiya, wounding five Israelis. Six days later, three bombs exploded in the town of Netanya, injuring twenty-seven people; a fourth bomb was found and defused. On 31 December, a

Hizbollah suicide bomber detonated a car bomb near Marjayoun in the Israeli security zone in south Lebanon, killing himself and injuring four Israeli children in a car passing nearby.

As mentioned earlier, by the mid-1990s Britain was a major international centre for Islamic extremists with a large number of organisations based in London. There were a number of reasons for this, notably: the country's easily exploited asylum laws, its tradition of tolerance towards dissidents, a large Muslim population offering fertile ground for preachers of extremism, a large international student population and London's prominence as a centre for international finance. These made Britain an ideal choice for a base from which to control and support terrorist groups in Islamic countries.

Among those individuals based in London were Omar Bakri Mohammed, leader of an organisation of Islamic militants called al-Muhajiroun (the Emigrants). In 1996, he had allegedly attempted to organise an Islamic rally in London, but the authorities barred some of the principal speakers and the idea was abandoned. Another prominent figure was Sheikh Abu Hamza, a regular preacher at north London's Finsbury Park mosque, who allegedly called for a holy war in order to establish a world-wide Muslim state; he was suspected of having links with the Algerian GIA and its alleged mouthpiece, the *Al-Ansar* newspaper published in London. Such was Great Britain's prominence as a centre for Islamic militancy that it was attacked in November 1997 by President Mubarak for giving sanctuary to extremists and allowing them to mastermind operations throughout the Middle East and North Africa. He alleged that London was being used as a centre for money laundering and was reported as having provided documentary evidence of large sums being routed through the city by the Islamic Group.

Another extremist organisation funnelling money through London was that of Osama bin Laden, the wealthy Islamic extremist who during the 1990s replaced Ilich Ramírez Sánchez as the world's foremost terrorist. The son of a wealthy Saudi construction magnate, bin Laden first came to prominence in 1980, following the Soviet invasion of Afghanistan in November 1979 when he formed

Mekhtab Al-Khidemat Al-Mujahideen (MAK) (Service Office of the Mujahideen) which subsequently became the principal organisation for recruitment of guerrillas to fight in Afghanistan. His partner in forming the MAK was Sheikh Abdullah Azzam, a Palestinian who was a close friend of Sheikh Omar Abdel-Rahman, the blind Islamic cleric mentioned earlier in this chapter. Until heeding the call of the jihad, Azzam had previously been a professor of *shari'a* law at the University of Jordan. Thereafter, until his death in Peshawar on 24 November 1989, when he was killed by a remote-controlled car bomb, he devoted himself to heading the MAK.

The MAK established offices throughout the world as well as training camps in Afghanistan and neighbouring Pakistan where the guerrillas were trained by members of the Afghan Bureau of Pakistan's military intelligence agency, the Inter Service Intelligence (ISI). Many of the volunteers were initially sent to camps established by Osama bin Laden in the Sudan from where they were despatched via the Yemen to Pakistan. Bin Laden meanwhile became one of the principal fund raisers for the Mujahideen, eliciting money from Saudi Arabia and throughout the Middle East, and ultimately from the United States.

In the wake of the Soviet withdrawal from Afghanistan in February 1989, bin Laden was left with an army, numbering several hundred, of his own Mujahideen in Pakistan. He formed an organisation, called al-Qaida (Islamic Salvation Foundation), to provide support for his men and, in order to ensure their security, during the following year donated large sums of money in support of the Islamic Democratic Alliance, headed by Nawaz Sharif, who had publicly stated that he would bring in a hard-line Islamic state if elected.

He himself returned to Saudi Arabia where in 1991 he became prominent among those who were implacably opposed to the presence of Western non-Muslim troops on Saudi soil. His opposition to the West increased when it became clear that US forces would remain in Saudi Arabia and he turned his anger on the Saudi royal family whom he infuriated by suggesting that they should be ousted. By 1991 his activities in the Sudan, and the presence of his training camps there, were causing anxiety in Egypt, Algeria and the Yemen which put pressure on the Saudis to persuade him to desist.

Meanwhile, Pakistan no longer wished to accommodate bin Laden's army whose members, based in camps in the North West Frontier Province, had become unwelcome guests because of the extremist brand of Islam they espoused and preached. Eventually the Pakistanis lost patience and threatened to 'dump' bin Laden's men, and those of other factions, on the US embassy in Islamabad unless arrangements were made for them to transported out of Pakistan. According to journalist and Middle East specialist Adel Darwish, the US government, which had been instrumental in financing and arming the Mujahideen during the war in Afghanistan, pressurised Saudi Arabia and other countries in the Persian Gulf into issuing passports to the guerrillas who were flown to different locations from where they subsequently dispersed. Some 900 travelled to Algeria where they joined the GIA and took part in the bloody campaign of terror and violence throughout the rest of the 1990s. Others made their way to Egypt, where they fell in with extremist groups seeking to topple the government of President Hosni Mubarak, or to Bosnia where they joined Muslims fighting Bosnian Serb forces. Others appeared in Lebanon and in the Gaza Strip.

By the end of 1991, bin Laden had transferred his headquarters to Sudan where he was joined during the early 1990s by his army of Mujahideen who were settled in three large camps. He established other camps for Muslims from countries throughout North Africa, the Middle East, Asia and Europe. Al-Qaida, which had hitherto provided support for his men in Afghanistan and Pakistan, now became the umbrella organisation for an international army. Its military operations were placed under the overall command of one of bin Laden's most trusted aides, Sheikh Tassir Abdullah.

Bin Laden also transferred most of his substantial business empire to Sudan and established companies which generated funds for al-Qaida while also acting as fronts for the procurement of arms and equipment from China and Iran. Among these were two investment companies, Ladin International and Taba Investments, which were used to control his funds and channel them wheresoever they were required. He also established companies, Islamic banks and investment houses overseas in other countries including Kenya, the Yemen and Albania. In addition, he established offices in the capitals of various countries, London among them, to facilitate the movement of funds to different parts of the world.

Bin Laden had been enraged by the United States' role in expediting the ejection of the Mujahideen from Pakistan. At the same time, he had declared a crusade against the presence of US troops in Saudi Arabia, the home of Islam's two holiest shrines: Mecca and Medina. Indeed, the aim of the expulsion of the American 'infidels' from the Islamic holy land was used as the ultimate goal in the indoctrination of those who flocked to his training camps in Sudan.

The USA was and continues to be the principal target for Islamic extremists and in 1992 al-Qaida mounted its first attack against the 'Great Satan'. On 29 December, in the Yemeni capital of Aden, a bomb exploded in a hotel used by US military personnel travelling to and from Somalia where US forces were deployed as part of the United Nations peacekeeping forces there. Two Austrian tourists died in the blast. Meanwhile at Aden's airport, a group of terrorists were arrested as they were about to open fire on US aircraft.

Early 1993 saw a devastating attack launched by Islamic extremists in the United States. On 23 February, a massive bomb, concealed inside a rented van, exploded in a car park directly beneath the twin towers of the World Trade Center in New York. Six people died and more than a thousand were injured in the blast which severely damaged the building. Four Islamic extremists, Mahmoud Abouhalima, Mohammad Salameh, Ahmad Ajaj and Nidal Ayyad, were subsequently arrested and tried, being convicted on 24 May 1994 for their parts in the bombing and sentenced to life imprisonment. There is reportedly to date no concrete evidence of direct involvement by Osama bin Laden, but there are strong suspicions that he provided support for it, possibly through funding and the provision of other facilities. Links with bin Laden were uncovered by US investigators who, having found the safe house used by the bombers, checked telephone records and established that a large number of overseas calls had been made to numbers subsequently identified as belonging to him.

The investigations into the World Trade Center bombing led to another Islamic extremist group in New York after links were established between the bombers and the blind Muslim cleric Sheikh Omar Abdel-Rahman, who as mentioned earlier, had entered the United States in 1990. Use of an informant, a former Egyptian Army officer named Emad Salem who knew Abdel-Rahman well, revealed the existence of a group which was planning a series of bomb attacks in the area of New York, New Jersey and Manhattan. Salem succeeded in insinuating himself into the extremists' confidence and the FBI was able to establish surveillance which led it to the building where the bombs were due to be manufactured. On 23 June 1993, the Bureau struck and arrested twelve men in the process of manufacturing the explosives. On 2 July, Abdel-Rahman was also arrested and on 30 January 1995 he and eleven others were brought to trial. Eight months later, he and nine of his accomplices were found guilty of conspiring to bomb the United Nations building, the George Washington Bridge, the Lincoln and Holland tunnels and an FBI building in New York. Abdel-Rahman himself received a prison sentence of life plus sixty-five years.

Meanwhile, the individual responsible for the bombing of the World Trade Centre, Ramzi Ahmed Yousef, was still at large. Nothing was heard of him until March 1994 when he attempted to mount a bomb attack in Bangkok. A large bomb was concealed in a hired truck and on 14 March was being driven to its target, later thought to be either the Israeli or US embassy, when it was involved in a collision with two other vehicles. The terrorist driver panicked and fled, abandoning his vehicle. The bomb was not discovered until three days later when the vehicle's owner reclaimed it from the police, discovering in the back of the vehicle the body of his driver who had been strangled by one of Yousef's accomplices. Yousef's fingerprints were discovered on the bomb, but by that time he had fled Thailand

and returned to Pakistan. In August an Iranian national, Hossein Shahriarifar, was arrested and charged with murder, illegal possession of explosives and intent to carry out sabotage. Subsequently convicted and sentenced to death, he served four years in prison before being acquitted on appeal in February 1998 because of ambiguous and conflicting testimonies on the part of witnesses.

Although there is no firm proof, it is thought that Yousef's next attack took place three months later in Iran in co-operation with an Iranian dissident group, the Mujahideen-e-Khalq. On 20 June 1994 a bomb exploded at a Shi'ite shrine in the city of Masshad, in the province of Khorasan. Twenty-six pilgrims were killed and more than 200 were injured in the blast which also caused severe damage to the shrine itself.

Yousef's next assignment was reportedly carried out on behalf of Osama bin Laden. At some point in mid-1994 he flew to the Philippines to provide technical assistance and training for a Muslim separatist group, Abu Sayyaf, which was seeking to establish an independent Muslim republic in Mindanao, in the southern part of the country. Formed and led by an Afghan intellectual, Professor Abdul Rasul Sayyaf, the group comprised several hundred men who fought in Afghanistan, during which time it was based in Peshawar, the capital of Pakistan's North-West Frontier Province, being financed by Saudi Arabia and later by Osama bin Laden. By the mid-1980s a nucleus of the group, headed by Abdurajak Abubakar Janjalani, had left Pakistan and moved to the southern Philippines where, under the name of Abu Sayyaf, it commenced its campaign for a Muslim republic. It carried out a sustained campaign of kidnappings and bomb attacks aimed at preventing peace negotiations between the Filipino government and the Moro National Liberation Front (MNLF), the principal Muslim organisation in the country. By the 1990s, it had established a reputation as the most extreme and violent Islamist group in South-East Asia. Osama bin Laden was reportedly continuing to fund Abu Sayyaf and had asked Yousef to provide training in bomb-making for the group.

Yousef spent several weeks at the Abu Sayyaf base on the island of Basilan where he instructed a group in bomb-making. In September 1994, he travelled to the Filipino capital of Manila where he met two members of another Islamic extremist group, Hezbul Dawah Al-Islamiah, which had cells throughout the world including the Philippines. With their help, he recruited a group of some twenty Muslims as he made preparations for another mission given to him by Osama bin Laden: the assassination of President Bill Clinton during a forthcoming visit to Manila by the latter in mid-November. Yousef devoted a great deal of time to planning the operation, but ultimately abandoned it because of the extremely high level of security surrounding the President. He then turned his attention to an alternative but equally prominent target, His Holiness Pope John Paul II, who was due to visit Manila in January of the following year.

During the previous weeks, Yousef had designed and developed a highly sophisticated, small but very powerful bomb intended for use in attacks against airliners. His intention was that numbers of these bombs would be planted on aircraft around the world, causing large numbers of deaths when they exploded. On 11 December he carried out a trial of one of these devices: aboard a Philippines Air Lines Boeing 747, carrying 273 passengers and twenty crew from Manila to Tokyo via the Filipino city of Cebu, he planted the bomb in the life-vest under his seat and left the flight at Cebu. Two hours after the aircraft had departed from Cebu for Tokyo, the bomb exploded, killing a Japanese passenger in the seat previously occupied by Yousef and blowing a hole in the floor of the aircraft. Despite the extensive damage to the aircraft, the pilot succeeded in reaching Okinawa where he landed without any further loss of life.

A few days later, Yousef returned from Cebu to Manila before flying to Islamabad, in Pakistan. Accompanied by a long-standing friend, Abdul Haki Murad, he returned to Manila to continue the training of his group of extremists and the manufacture of more bombs. During the first week of January, a fire in the apartment where he was preparing the explosives forced him and his accomplices to flee as the local fire brigade arrived; when the blaze had been extinguished, police entered the apartment and were confronted by a bomb factory. A search uncovered a lap-top computer, bomb-making manuals, chemicals, electronic timing devices and a considerable amount of other equipment and documentation. Abdul Haki Murad was arrested after returning to the apartment to recover the computer.

Initial examination of its hard disk revealed Yousef's plan to attack airliners flying from South-East Asia to destinations elsewhere in the region and to the United States. Further investigation and analysis of the bomb-making equipment and the computer's contents by the FBI revealed a mass of other information which proved invaluable in revealing details of Yousef's murderous activities and in particular his connection with the bombing of the World Trade Center.

Yousef fled back to Pakistan, but at the end of January 1995 travelled with an accomplice to Thailand to mount a bomb attack against a US aircraft flying from Bangkok to the United States. This plan came to nought and both men returned to Islamabad. A few days later, however, Yousef's accomplice contacted the US embassy and gave details of his whereabouts to members of the Diplomatic Security Service (DSS). On 7 February a small force of FBI and DSS agents, reinforced by a team of ISI officers, arrested Yousef in a guest house later reported as belonging to a member of Osama bin Laden's family.

Yousef's immediate extradition to the Unites States was followed by reprisals carried out by extremists in Pakistan and elsewhere. On 8 March, three members of staff of the US consulate in Karachi were attacked by gunmen: two of them were killed, and the third was wounded. Three weeks later a force of 200 Abu Sayyaf guerrillas attacked Christians in the town of Ipil, in the southern Philippines, killing more than fifty people and wounding hundreds.

At the end of May 1996, Ramzi Ahmed Yousef was brought to trial on charges relating to the bombing of the Philippines Air Lines aircraft, the murder of the Japanese passenger on 11 December 1994 and conspiracy to carry out bomb attacks on aircraft, subsequently being convicted on all counts on 5 September 1996. He later stood trial for the bombing of the World Trade Center and on 12 February 1997 was convicted and eventually sentenced to 240 years' imprisonment.

A few weeks prior to the beginning of Yousef's trial, however, a major terrorist incident took place in the United States. On 19 April a massive bomb exploded at the Alfred P. Murray Federal Building in Oklahoma City, killing 168 people and injuring another 600. There was a considerable amount of circumstantial evidence pointing to the possibility of Yousef's involvement with the bombing. One of the two culprits responsible, an American named Terry L. Nichols, had been in the Philippines during the period from mid-November 1994 until an unspecified date in January of the following year. Furthermore, it was known that he was in the city of Cebu at the same time as Yousef during November-December 1994. In addition, a leading member of the Abu Sayyaf group had stated, while being interrogated by officers of the Philippines National Police and National Bureau of Investigation, that he had met Yousef and Nicholls together in the town of Davao on the island of Mindanao. As author Simon Reeves points out in his book *The New Jackels*, there were very few other terrorists who could have given Nicholls the sort of information he required to be able to blow up a building with a 5,600-pound bomb manufactured from ammonium nitrate and nitromethane.

Meanwhile, Osama bin Laden was continuing his war against the United States, Saudi Arabia and other regimes in North Africa and the Middle East whom he considered to be allies of the 'Great Satan'. He was reported as having been behind the attempted assassinations of Crown Prince Abdullah of Jordan in June 1993 and of President Hosni Mubarak of Egypt during his visit to Ethiopia in June 1995. By this time, however, his activities were causing serious concern in Washington, Riyadh and elsewhere. In April 1994 he had been stripped of his Saudi citizenship and in the following year Sudan, which was by then beginning to enjoy the initial stages of a *rapprochement* with the West and the United States in particular, came under pressure to ask him to leave.

On the morning of 13 November 1995, in the Saudi capital of Riyadh, a truck bomb exploded outside a Saudi Arabian National Guard communications centre. Five Americans and two Indians were killed and more than sixty, including thirty-four Americans, were injured in the blast which caused massive damage to the three-storey building. Responsibility was subsequently claimed by two organisations, the Islamic Movement for Change and the Tigers of the Gulf, the latter stating, 'If the Americans don't leave the Kingdom as soon as possible, we will continue our actions.' Four Saudi Muslim extremists, Abdul Aziz bin Fahd bin Nasser al-Mothem; Khalid bin Ahmed bin Ibbrahim al-Sa'eed; Riyadh bin Suleiman bin Is'haq al-Hajen; and Muslih bin Ayedh al-Shemrani, were subsequently arrested and after being interrogated were beheaded on 30 May 1996. Three were former members of the Mujahideen who had fought in Afghanistan, while the fourth had fought with Muslim forces in Bosnia. While it has been reported that the Saudis were well aware that Osama bin Laden was behind the attack, any confirmation of this was prevented by the speedy execution of the four men; indeed, it has been suggested that their swift demise was designed to effect just that.

The attack served to infuriate the Saudis who decided to give bin Laden a warning. Shortly after the bombing at Riyadh, his home in Khartoum was subjected to an attack by four gunmen who raked it with automatic fire. Three of them died in a firefight with his guards and the fourth was captured, subsequently being executed by the Sudanese.

Early in the following year, another unsuccessful attempt was made on bin Laden's life. This had also been orchestrated by the Saudis who had earlier offered to reinstate his Saudi citizenship and allow him to return to his home country if he abandoned his war. Bin Laden had rejected the offer out of hand and thus the Saudis, together with the United States and Egypt, proceeded to increase the pressure on Sudan which eventually acquiesced and asked bin Laden to leave. In May of that year, accompanied by his family and some 200 followers, he flew to Afghanistan where he established a new base.

During the night of 25 June 1996, a huge truck bomb exploded outside a US Air Force housing complex called Khobar Towers at the King Abdul Aziz Air Base near Dhahran in Saudi Arabia, killing nineteen US servicemen and injuring 385 others, women and children being among the dead and wounded. The building nearest the blast was completely destroyed and another nearby was badly damaged. It later transpired that a 5,000-gallon fuel tanker had been parked just outside the perimeter fence, close to a dormitory building accommodating US personnel. Two men had been seen leaving the area in a small white car three minutes before the explosion took place. Two organisations claimed responsibility: the 'Legions of the Martyr Abdallah al-Huzayfi' and the 'Hizbollah – the Gulf'. While there was no firm evidence of involvement by Osama bin Laden, who described the bombing as 'heroic', suspicions seemed to be confirmed after telephone intercepts by the US National Security Agency picked up conversations between him and Ayman al-Zawahiri, the leader of the Egyptian al-Jihad, during which the latter complimented him on the bombing.

Eighteen months later, however, there was firm evidence of bin Laden's involvement in terrorism. On 7 August 1998, a massive truck bomb exploded outside the US embassy in the Kenyan capital of Nairobi, killing more than 200 people and injuring more than 4,500. Five minutes earlier, another had exploded outside the US embassy in Dar-es-Salaam, the capital of Tanzania; eleven people died and eighty-five were injured.

Both attacks had been mounted by suicide bombers belonging to bin Laden's organisation, al-Qaida. Evidence of this was confirmed when Mohamed Saddiq Odeh, the Palestinian leader of the cell which had organised the attack in Nairobi and had flown to Pakistan on the evening before, was arrested and interrogated by the Pakistani authorities and then extradited to the USA. Meanwhile other members of the cell were arrested elsewhere, providing further information under interrogation. Among them was Mohamed Rashed Daoud al-Owhali (alias Khalid Salim) who was arrested in Nairobi. He had arrived the week before from Pakistan and had been aboard the vehicle carrying the bomb, jumping clear and running for his life before his accomplice, the suicide bomber driving the vehicle, detonated the bomb. Injured in the blast, he had been taken to hospital for treatment. Tracked down a few days later, he was also arrested and extradited to the United States. A fourth member of the cell, later identified as Fazul Abdullah Mohammed, succeeded in escaping from Kenya.

Meanwhile, one of those responsible for the Dar-es-Salaam attack was also arrested. Muhammad Sadiq Howaida, another Palestinian, had assembled the bomb and had flown to Pakistan prior to the attack, subsequently being arrested as he attempted to enter Afghanistan on a false passport. He was also extradited to the United States where under questioning he provided details of the bombing.

On 20 August, the Americans launched a retaliatory attack against bin Laden. Seventy-five RGM-109 Tomahawk cruise missiles were launched by US warships from a carrier group in the Arabian Sea at terrorist bases in Afghanistan. Among those hit was the Al Badr II camp belonging to al-Qaida and the Amir Muawiya belonging to the Harakat ul-Ansar (HUA), a Kashmiri terrorist group supported by bin Laden in its campaign for independence from India. Seven HUA guerrillas were killed and some twenty injured during the attack. The Amir Muawiya camp was one of three reported to be operated by Pakistan's ISI which assisted in the training of the HUA guerrillas.

At the same time, missiles were fired by warships in the Red Sea at the El-Shifa pharmaceuticals manufacturing plant situated in the industrial area of Bahri, a few miles to the north-east of the Sudanese capital of Khartoum, reducing it to smouldering rubble. Intelligence reports had indicated that it had been producing chemicals for use in the production of VX nerve gas, but it later transpired that it had been manufacturing veterinary products. In the event, however, the missile attacks achieved little. Bin Laden himself had been warned beforehand and had taken refuge in northern Afghanistan. The casualties incurred among his followers only served to increase their hatred of the United States and their devotion to their leader while promoting his standing among Muslim extremists elsewhere.

This became all the more apparent when on 25 August a bomb exploded in a Planet Hollywood restaurant in Cape Town, South Africa, killing two people and injuring twenty-seven. A telephone caller claiming to be a representative of Muslims Against Global Oppression claimed responsibility, stating that the attack had been in retaliation for the US missile attack. Cape Town has a large Muslim population and a number of extremist groups were formed during the 1990s, among them the Muslims Against Global Oppression, reported as having links with an extreme anti-apartheid organisation called Qibla, and another called People Against Gangsterism And Drugs (PAGAD) which had originally been formed as a vigilante group.

Following the US attack on his bases, Osama bin Laden established new ones in northern and eastern Afghanistan. Al-Qaida's headquarters was relocated to the province of Kunduz, close to the border with Tajikistan, and camps were established at Tora Bora, Derunta, Melawa and Farm Hadda near the city of Jalalabad in the east of the country, and Galrez which is situated some thirty miles west of the Afghan capital of Kabul. Two more were built at Khwaja Mastoon Ghundai and Sati Kundao near the border with Pakistan. Bin Laden's network extended into Pakistan itself via Peshawar, the capital of the North West Frontier Province, where a number of safe houses were established for use as transit centres for members of al-Qaida travelling to and from Afghanistan.

By the beginning of 1999, however, the Taliban government of Afghanistan was coming under increasing pressure from the US and British goverments to expel Osama bin Laden. The British authorities were becoming concerned about increasing evidence of the involvement of British Muslims with extremist groups after reports of training, allegedly organised by London-based organisations, being conducted at weekends in clandestine camps throughout the country. Young Muslims attending these camps were allegedly being encouraged to seek military training overseas in the Yemen and

Afghanistan and one report stated that large numbers, up to 2,000 each year, have done so. On 24 December 1998, a group of eight were arrested in the Yemen on charges of conspiring to carry out bomb attacks in Aden, the targets being the British consulate, an Anglican church and two hotels. According to reports at the time, at least one member of the group had undergone training in Shabwa, a province in eastern Yemen, at a camp run by a group which on 28 December had kidnapped sixteen Western hostages in an attempt to secure the release of the eight prisoners. Four of the hostages, three Britons and an Australian, died when the Yemeni Army carried out a rescue operation on the following day. On 9 August 1999, all eight were convicted; three, however, were released on the grounds of time served, while the remainder received prison sentences of between two and seven years.

In February 1999, meanwhile, Osama bin Laden had been reported as having disappeared, but in March Western intelligence services located him in eastern Afghanistan, moving between his network of camps south of Jalalabad. At the same time, there were further reports of his support for the Kashmiri HUA which was also alleged to be receiving assistance from Pakistan's ISI. The HUA comprises two groups: the Harikat ul-Mujahideen, led by Fazular Rehman Khan, and the even more radical Harakat ul-Jihad. Both were formed during the 1980s, with CIA and ISI support, to fight in Afghanistan. During early 1999, it was revealed that the HUA was recruiting not only from Kashmir but also Afghanistan, Pakistan and Britain.

Evidence of efforts to recruit British Muslims, not only for service in Kashmir but also in Pakistan, Kosovo and Chechnya, was revealed in October 1999 when *The Sunday Telegraph* revealed that Mohammed Sohail, an information technology security adviser working for the company Railtrack, had allegedly been using the company's computer and e-mail address to recruit volunteers. Working for the Global Jihad Fund, a London-based organisation headed by a Saudi dissident named Mohammed al-Massari, Sohail was also alleged to have assisted in raising funds for fundamentalist groups including the HUA. During a conversation with the journalists conducting the investigation, Sohail stated that he worked for al-Massari and Osama bin Laden.

The HUA first came to prominence during the mid-1990s when it kidnapped a number of Westerners in Kashmir. Two Britons were seized during the summer of 1994, but were released unharmed shortly afterwards. In October of that year, three Britons and an American were kidnapped in the Indian capital of New Delhi and held prisoner in Sharanpur, a small town 150 miles north of the city, while demands were made for the release of ten Kashmiri extremists in exchange for them. Two weeks later, however, the four men were rescued by Indian police. In July 1995 Harakat al-Mujahideen, then named al-Faran, kidnapped six Westerners, four Britons, one American and a German, and held them hostage while demanding the release of twenty-one Kashmiri militants jailed previously in Kashmir and India, including the leader of al-Faran, Malauna Masood Azghar (alias Wali Azam). One of the hostages subsequently escaped and another was found beheaded. The remains of one of the Britons, Paul Wells, were claimed to have been discovered in January 2000, having been identified by DNA tests carried out in India. Further tests in Britain, however, proved that the latter were incorrect. At the time of writing, the fate of the four hostages remains unknown.

In July 1999, the existence of a group even more extreme than al-Qaida was revealed when it was reported that it was hunting Osama bin Laden whom it had condemned as a 'false god'. Called Takfiris, this hitherto little-known group was formed in the 1970s in Egyptian prisons, following the arrests of large numbers of Muslim extremists. Many of its members fought alongside bin Laden and the Mujahideen in Afghanistan, but at the end of the war the group disappeared from sight. During the first half of 1999, however, it surfaced again amid reports that it had made at least three attempts on bin Laden's life and that there had been a number of shooting incidents between members of Takfiris and al-Qaida.

In October 1999, the Taliban government agreed to close down the terrorist training camps and despatch large numbers of Islamic extremists back to Pakistan. This came about after a visit of the ISI chief, General Khawaja Ziauddin, who attended a meeting with the Taliban leader, Mullah Omar, on behalf of the Pakistani Prime Minister, Nawaz Sharif. The Taliban refused, however, to hand over Osama bin Laden to the United Nations, to stand trial in the United States, and thus on 14 November the latter imposed sanctions on Afghanistan. These included the freezing of the Taliban government's bank accounts overseas and the £300 million assets of the Afghan state airline, Ariana, in the United States. This resulted in riots in Kabul and in three bomb and three rocket attacks in Islamabad against the US embassy, the offices of the UN Pakistan Mission and the headquarters of the UN World Food Programme.

While the Taliban government had rejected out of hand the demand to hand over bin Laden, the UN sanctions presented it with a dilemma. On the one hand, it was seeking international recognition and aid while on the other it was harbouring the world's most wanted terrorist suspect with a $3 million price on his head. The precariousness of his position was obviously not lost on bin Laden himself who was reported to be in fear of assassination and moving constantly, accompanied only by his family and a small bodyguard. Despite the problems facing him, however, he was believed by Western intelligence agencies still to be receiving substantial funds from a number of sources. Some of these were reported to be in Saudi Arabia, among them five wealthy businessmen allegedly paying protection money to him on a regular basis.

The end of 1999 and the eve of the millennium saw a number of countries on a high state of alert for possible attacks by terrorist organisations. In the United States, such fears appeared to be well founded when on 14 December, an Algerian named Ahmed Ressam was arrested at Port Angeles, in the north-west state of Washington, after arriving on a ferry from the Canadian city of Victoria, British Columbia. A search of his car revealed nitro-glycerine and other bomb-making components, including four timers of a type used previously in attacks attributed to Osama bin Laden's organisation. Ressam, who had fought in Afghanistan with the Mujahideen, had previously been living in Montreal under an alias and was known to have links with the GIA in Algeria. Police subsequently divulged that they believed he intended to attack a millennium celebration in Seattle before escaping to the United Kingdom. When arrested, he was found in possession of air tickets for flights from Seattle to London via New York.

Three days after Ressam's arrest, it was learned that an Algerian accomplice of Ressam's, Abdel Dajid Dahoumane, had entered the United States from Montreal. Four days later a third Algerian, Bouabide Chamchi, was arrested as he attempted to enter the country from Canada using a false French passport. A search of his vehicle revealed sufficient explosives to manufacture four large bombs. His travelling companion, a Canadian woman, was subsequently reported as being suspected of having links with an Algerian extremist organisation.

In Asia meanwhile, the final week of the 20th century saw the hijacking on 24 December of an Indian Airlines A-300 Airbus, Flight 814, with 174 passengers and eighteen crew aboard, flying from the Nepalese capital of Kathmandu to New Delhi. The six hijackers, four Pakistanis, an Afghan and a Nepali, armed with pistols, grenades and knives, took control of the aircraft immediately after its departure from Kathmandu and forced the pilot to fly to Amritsar where it landed at 1.35 p.m. local time and was refuelled. After leaving Amritsar, the aircraft flew to Lahore where, having landed without permission, it was permitted to refuel before taking off at 5.13 p.m. Having been refused permission to land at Kabul and then Muscat, in the Sultanate of Oman, the aircraft flew to Dubai where it landed at a military airbase at 8.05 p.m.

At just after half an hour past midnight, the hijackers released twenty-eight passengers. Twenty minutes later, the aircraft took off for an unknown destination; at 3.03 a.m. on Saturday 25 December it landed at Kandahar in Afghanistan and shortly afterwards was surrounded by Taliban troops. At this juncture the hijackers demanded the release of the leader of the Harakat ul-Mujahideen, Malauna Masood Azghar, from prison in Kashmir where he had been since February 1994.

The hijack lasted eight days, during which one hostage was stabbed to death on the first day when he disobeyed an order not to look at the hijackers' faces. On the fifth day, the terrorists threatened to start shooting some of the nine Westerners aboard the aircraft unless their demands were met, but backed down when Taliban troops approached the aircraft and threatened to storm it if the hostages were harmed. On the following day, new demands were made: a ransom of £120 million, the release of thirty-five HUA extremists from Indian jails and the return of the body of an extremist killed earlier in the year. Meanwhile, the passengers and crew remained aboard the Airbus in which conditions were deteriorating rapidly in the stifling heat.

Negotiations with the hijackers were conducted by a team of Indian government officials located in the airport control tower. On 30 December the situation had reached deadlock, but the Taliban interceded and persuaded the hijackers to drop their demands for the ransom and the dead body. At the same time, however, they told the Indian negotiators to produce a rapid solution or the aircraft would be forced to leave Kandahar. Shortly afterwards, the hijackers reduced their demands to the release of three members of the HUA: Malauna Masood Azghar, a British Muslim named Ahmad Omar Sayyed Sheikh, and Mushtaq Ahmad Zargar who was one of the founders of the HUA. The Indian government agreed to this reduced demand and on 1 January 2000 Masood and his two companions landed at Kandahar in the company of Indian officials. Shortly afterwards, the hijackers left the aircraft and were escorted away by Taliban troops.

No account of Islamic extremism during the 1990s would be complete without mention of the role played by Iran which established an extensive network of eleven training camps, staffed by members of the Revolutionary Guards and the Iranian intelligence service, the Ministry of Information Service (MOIS), to train some 5,000 terrorists from throughout the world each year. One of these camps, at Qasvim north-east of Tehran, was reported to train terrorists in the skills of assassination, the bodies of recently executed criminals being used as targets. Another, located at Mashhad in western Iran, specialised in bomb-making, and training in advanced explosives and booby-traps was given at a number of camps in the area of Isfahan. The airport at Mashhad was reported to be used for training in aircraft hijacking and other aspects of aviation-related terrorism.

Some camps trained terrorists of specific nationalities: that at Hamadan, south-west of Tehran, being for the exclusive use of Lebanon's Hizbollah while one at Qom, south of the capital, was used principally by Turkish extremists. Saudi terrorists of the Organisation of Islamic Revolution of Jezier al-Arab and the Hizbollah of the Hejaz were meanwhile trained in east Tehran at the Imam Ali camp, the largest of the eleven training facilities. The camp at Mashhad trained terrorists from Egypt, Algeria, Jordan and the Lebanon. At Bandar 'Abbās, on the coast of southern Iran, the Revolutionary Guards provided instruction for those being trained as combat swimmers and in the use of miniature two-man submarines supplied by North Korea.

The Revolutionary Guards also provided the major element of support given by Iran to fundamentalist groups in the Middle East. From 1991 onwards, they provided HAMAS with approximately $20 million per annum to finance its campaign against Israel. Following the signing of the Declaration of Principles by Israel and the PLO in September 1993, Iran pledged further support to the major rejectionist groups in their campaign against the peace process. In addition to providing funds to HAMAS and other groups in the West Bank and Gaza Strip, the Revolutionary Guards provided training for Palestinians in camps in southern Lebanon while at the same time promoting good relations between them and Hizbollah. This support was further boosted in 1999 as part of Iran's efforts to sabotage any further efforts on the part of Israel at achieving peace with the Palestinians. In July, it increased its funding of HAMAS to finance further attacks against Israel which had hinted at an all-embracing peace deal with the Arab world and a peace treaty with Syria, a prospect which alarmed hard-line elements in Tehran who were implacably opposed to any form of long-lasting agreement between Arab states and Israel.

Throughout the decade, the hand of Iran was detected behind a number of attacks carried out worldwide by Islamic extremists. On 17 March 1992 a bomb destroyed the Israeli embassy in the Argentinian capital of Buenos Aires, killing twenty-nine people and injuring scores more. Responsibility was claimed by Hizbollah which was thought to have carried out the attack in retaliation for an earlier Israeli attack which had killed the head of its military wing. However, US electronic intelligence intercepts and subsequent forensic investigation revealed that Iran had supplied the explosives.

On 18 July 1994, eighty-six people died and more than 200 were injured when a car bomb exploded in Buenos Aires outside a seven-storey building belonging to two Jewish social welfare groups: the Mutual Israeli/Argentine Association (AMAI) and the Delegation of Argentine/Iraeli Associations (DAIA). On the following day, a bomb exploded aboard a commuter aircraft in Panama, killing twenty-one people, mostly Jewish businessmen. A hitherto unknown group called Ansarallah (Partisans of God) claimed responsibility for both attacks, but the CIA subsequently stated that the group was a sub-unit within the Lebanese Hizbollah organisation and was headed by Sheikh Sobhi Tiufeili, the leader of its most extreme faction. Once again, subsequent investigations revealed possible Iranian involvement in the bombing.

During this period, Iranian agents were actively hunting down those who opposed the regime of Ayatollah Sayyed Ali Khomenei. In December 1994, two Iranians were convicted by a French court of the murder in 1991 of the former Iranian Prime Minister Shahpour Bakhtiar, who had subsequently become a leading dissident, being condemned by the late Ayatollah Ruhollah Khomeini who had earlier declared him to be 'an enemy of the Islamic Revolution'.

During the second half of the decade, the Iranians stepped-up their intelligence and terrorist activities in Europe. This was in response to diplomatic sanctions imposed against them following a decision by a German court in April 1997 that Iran's Special Affairs Committee, whose members included President Hashemi Rafsanjani and Ali Fallahian, head of the MOIS, had ordered the murder in September 1992 of a Kurdish opposition leader, Sadiq Sharafkindi, and three aides at a restaurant in Berlin. The murder had been carried out by a five-man team led by an Iranian belonging to the Revolutionary Guards; his four accomplices were Lebanese, all of them members of Hizbollah.

Fallahian despatched additional agents to Britain, Germany, France, Belgium, Italy and Cyprus while others were sent to the United States and Russia. Their brief included the activation of terrorist cells in each country. During 1997 alone, ten new cells were established by the MOIS in Europe; members of one were arrested in Antwerp while planning attacks on Israeli and other Jewish targets in France and Germany. The Iranians' presence in Europe was strongest in Germany, the embassy in Bonn being the hub of their European networks which were controlled by six senior MOIS officers accommodated on its third floor. In addition, Germany also had a large Turkish Islamic *gastarbeiter* community which provided a large reservoir of recruits as well as safe houses and other facilities.

Iran was among those Muslim nations which responded to a request in October 1992 from Bosnia's President Alija Izetbegovic for military assistance against Yugoslav-backed Bosnian Serb forces. Indeed, Iran had already been supplying arms for more than a year beforehand, sending them via Turkey and Croatia in contravention of a United Nations Security Council arms embargo imposed in September 1991. Mid-1994 saw the despatch of approximately 400 Revolutionary Guards and by the following year there were more than 2,000 Iranians accommodated in some fifteen camps. In addition, a significant number of Hizbollah guerrillas from Lebanon also found their way to Bosnia, including former members of the Mujahideen who had fought in Afghanistan.

During the latter part of 1996, the Iranians began to concentrate their attention on Turkey which in February had signed an agreement on military co-operation with Israel, predictably causing alarm in Tehran. Iran had for some time supported fundamentalists in Turkey where it had established an Islamic network throughout the country. It also provided support for the outlawed Turkish fundamentalist group Islamic Action, some of whose members had received training in Iran. Among these was the group's leader, Irfan Cagarici, who had been arrested in March 1990 after assassinating a Turkish journalist. Under interrogation, he admitted his involvement in other killings and revealed that the weapons had been supplied by Iran via four diplomats at its embassy in Ankara. Another fundamentalist group was Hizbollah which had close links with its Lebanese counterpart. In October 1994, a team of six Turkish Hizbollah terrorists was arrested while preparing to assassinate a well-known figure. When questioned, they also admitted to having undergone training in Iran and revealed that they had received their orders from Iranian diplomats orchestrating operations against Iranian dissidents in Turkey. Investigations by the Turkish security services subsequently led to the unmasking of a senior MOIS officer working under diplomatic cover in Istanbul.

As part of its efforts to destabilise Turkey, Iran also supported the Kurdish separatists of the PKK which by the early part of the 1990s was estimated to total some 10,000 militants and supporters with its military wing, the ARGK, claiming to number some 15,000. Located in camps in Turkey, Armenia, Azerbaijan, Syria, northern Iraq and Iran, the latter comprised well-trained and well-equipped uniformed guerrillas organised along military lines in units and sub-units of battalions, companies and platoons. Operations were conducted along classic guerrilla lines: raiding, ambushing, sabotage and assassinations.

By the early 1990s, the PKK's attacks on the Turkey's tourist industry, the security forces and diplomatic representatives abroad, had forced the government to take a tougher line against it. In March 1993, the organisation signed a collaborative agreement with the Turkish Hizbollah with which it had hitherto been engaged in a bloody feud; during the previous two years, the latter had assassinated a number of pro-PKK activists, including journalists and politicians. Meanwhile, the PKK continued its attacks on Turkey's tourist industry and kidnapped a number of foreign tourists. During the following year, however, it proposed a ceasefire and at the end of the year published a document which, while making high-minded declarations of the organisation's intent to adhere to humanitarian law and the Geneva Convention, also stated that all members of the Turkish security forces were legitimate targets to be attacked.

In addition to its ARGK units, the PKK also possessed its own intelligence and counter-intelligence service whose members were deployed in cities and rural areas throughout Turkey. Extortion was one of the organisation's principal methods of raising funds to finance its operations and purchase arms, with Kurdish and Turkish communities overseas proving to be fertile ground: in 1993 it was reported that the PKK raised £2.5 million in Britain alone during that year. In addition, it was also heavily involved in the narcotics trade and was reported as earning in 1993 alone some £19 million from trafficking operations in Europe. Furthermore, the organisation possessed a number of commercial 'front' companies which also produced revenue. The PKK's estimated average annual income from extortion, narcotics trafficking and other sources of revenue during the 1990s was £53.75 million.

The war between the Turkish government and the PKK escalated during the latter part of the 1990s. Commencing in 1996, much of the fighting took place on the borders with Syria and Iraq, and in northern Iraq. In May 1998, the Turkish army launched a major offensive using 15,000 troops and 2,000 Kurdish irregulars. This broke the back of the ARGK which had in fourteen years of war suffered an estimated total of over 22,000 killed. Meanwhile, the PKK was also suffering setbacks in Turkey and in September its leader, Abdullah Ocalan, announced a unilateral ceasefire from his base in the Syrian capital of Damascus. In Europe, the PKK's representatives also sued for peace, stating that the organisation wanted to establish a dialogue with the Turkish government in an effort to seek a peaceful solution.

In October 1998 Turkey pressurised Syria to expel Ocalan, close down the PKK training camps and cease all further support for the guerrillas. Forced to leave Damascus, Ocalan initially travelled to Moscow, seeking political asylum which was refused. From there he flew to Italy where he was arrested at Rome airport on arrival and held briefly before being freed. Turkey immediately demanded his extradition, but the Italians refused, on the grounds that their constitution barred the extradition of anyone to a country where he could possibly face a death sentence, and this resulted in a major diplomatic rift between the two countries.

On 16 January 1999, Ocalan left Italy and disappeared, flying to a number of countries in a desperate effort to seek asylum. His journey eventually ended on 2 February in Kenya where, with the assistance of officials from the Greek embassy, he took refuge in a villa on the outskirts of Nairobi. When the Kenyan government learned of his presence, however, he was ordered to leave immediately and arrangements were made for him to fly to Holland. On the afternoon of Monday 15 February, escorted by Greek officials, he was taken to Nairobi airport where he was met by Kenyan police officers who took him away and handed him over to a Turkish Army special forces team which had flown in to arrest him and escort him back to Turkey. Drugged, gagged and bound hand and foot, Ocalan was flown to Turkey where he was incarcerated in a prison on the heavily guarded island of Imrali, off the coast near Istanbul.

Meanwhile, hundreds of PKK suspects were rounded up in Turkey and the government launched an operation in northern Iraq to put further pressure on the PKK which shortly after Ocalan's arrest retaliated by resuming its campaign of violence with a number of bombings in Istanbul and elsewhere. At the same time, it turned its attention once more to Turkey's tourist industry, warning tourists to stay away. With the help of another terrorist group, a Maoist organisation called TIKKO, it also targeted provincial governors in central and southern Turkey, carrying out suicide bomb attacks on three of them.

On 20 June, Abdullah Ocalan was brought to trial on charges of treason and nine days later was convicted and sentenced to death. Immediately, however, an appeal was made to Turkey's supreme court. The announcement of the death sentence resulted in further attacks by the PKK which threatened to widen its terror campaign throughout the entire country. Meanwhile, some 10,000 Turkish troops attacked PKK enclaves in northern Iraq while police rounded up more suspects in south-western Turkey. In early August, however, responding to an order from Ocalan, the PKK ceased hostilities and towards the end of the month the ARGK commenced withdrawing its forces from Turkey into northern Iraq. At the beginning of September, the PKK announced that it was giving up its armed struggle and would thereafter seek its goals through political means. Towards the end of November, Turkey's appeals court announced that the death sentence on Ocalan would be upheld, but in mid-January 2000 the Turkish government suspended it pending an appeal by him to the European Court of Human Rights.

Five years earlier, in 1995, Iran had commenced extending its influence into Africa. At the beginning of the year, a plan for the spreading of Islamic fundamentalism throughout the continent was approved by the Supreme Council for National Security. It called for Iranian intelligence operations to be mounted in certain countries while at the same time terrorist cells were established for use at a later date against Western targets.

The Iranians were already active in North and South Africa. Training camps had been established in the Sudan and Iranian instructors were despatched to train and equip extremist groups in Algeria, Egypt and Tunisia. In September 1996 in South Africa, the Iranians had formed an alliance with the vigilante organisation People Against Gangsterism And Drugs (PAGAD) which agreed to gather intelligence in exchange for training in terrorist skills. The Iranians then turned their attention to West and East Africa. In the west, the Ivory Coast, with its large population of Shi'ite Muslims, offered an ideal base for covert operations; in the east, Tanzania, beset with political and economic problems, provided fertile ground for Iranian support of militant opposition groups and others in Zanzibar seeking independence from Dar-es-Salaam. In Uganda, the Iranians supported the political activities of militant Muslim activists.

During the early 1990s, some of the highest levels of terrorism were to be found in Latin America. As mentioned earlier, 1992 saw the bombings of the Israeli embassy and the AMAI/DAIA building in Buenos Aires in 1992 and 1994 respectively. In July 1993 the US embassy in Santiago was bombed, but a crackdown by the Chilean authorities saw a major reduction in the terrorist threat thereafter. That same year saw the discovery in Nicaragua of a major terrorist arms cache belonging to El Salvador's Farabundo Marti National Liberation Front (FMLN), the contents of which included shoulder-fired surface-to-air missiles and documents which linked the FMLN to ETA in Spain.

Colombia, meanwhile, was suffering from a very high level of violence perpetrated by the Revolutionary Armed Forces of Colombia (FARC) and the Army of National Liberation (ELN) which launched a large number of bomb attacks against government targets and foreign-owned concerns. They also carried out a number of cross-border operations into neighbouring countries: in March 1993, FARC kidnapped three US missionaries, Mark Rich, Richard Tenenoff and Charles Mankins, from their camp in Panama and abducted them across the border into Colombia, demanding US $5 million for their release.

In Peru the principal threat was from the Sendero Luminoso whose leader, Abimael Guzman, had been captured on 12 September 1992 and imprisoned. The group concentrated on civilian targets and the tourist industry in particular; in July 1993 it kidnapped and tortured two Swiss tourists.

By the mid-1990s terrorist activity had increased, principally in Colombia where FARC continued its campaign of kidnappings, bombings and murders, ignoring peace initiatives from the government which made little or no progress in dealing with the problem. In June 1995, during a chance encounter with Colombian security forces, the organisation murdered two US missionaries, Steven Welsh and Timothy van Dyke, whom it had kidnapped during the previous year. Two months later, it attacked a police base in Miraflores, killing six members of a special counter-narcotics unit and wounding twenty-nine others. Indeed, Colombian forces and US advisers deployed on counter-narcotics operations frequently encountered FARC guerrillas in coca-growing areas where they provided protection for drug traffickers and narcotics processing facilities.

In Peru the government continued to crack down on the Sendero Luminoso and the country's other terrorist organisation, the Tupac Amaru Revolutionary Movement (MRTA). A number of arrests were made in April 1995: among twenty members of the Sendero Luminoso apprehended was a member of the organisation's leadership, Margi Clavo Peralta. In December the deputy leader of the MRTA, Miguel Rincon, surrendered after a gun battle with police who raided one of the group's safe houses.

The situation in 1996 remained much the same in Colombia with FARC and the ELN ignoring government peace initiatives and continuing to target the security forces and foreign-owned interests. The oil industry in particular suffered; the national oil company, EcoPetrol, was forced to close down production and foreign-owned oil companies' employees were kidnapped and held to ransom. This was a major source of income for the two organisations which received ransoms totalling millions of dollars on an annual basis. In 1996 alone, more than thirty foreigners were kidnapped.

The major terrorist incident during this period took place on 17 December 1996 when fourteen members of the MRTA seized the Japanese Ambassador's residence in the Peruvian capital of Lima during a celebration attended by more than 1,000 guests comprising members of the diplomatic community, members of the government, senior military and police officers, and members of the business community. Many of them were held hostage during the ensuing siege which lasted 126 days before a successful rescue operation was carried out, a full account of which is given in Chapter 13.

The year 1997 saw increasing US involvement in Colombia. The Americans were becoming ever more concerned by the continuous terrorism linked to narcotic trafficking and during that year US $50 million of military equipment was supplied to the Colombian armed forces to assist them in operations against FARC and the ELN who meanwhile had stepped up their activities which frequently spilled over into neighbouring Venezuela and Panama. Both organisations continued to carry out kidnappings, the ELN abducting a US geologist in February. During that same month, the body of another American, geologist and mining consultant Frank Pescatore, who had been kidnapped in February 1996 by FARC, was found; he had been killed by his captors who were still holding hostage the three American missionaries abducted from Panama in March 1993.

In Peru, meanwhile, the Sendero Luminoso was still active in Lima and elsewhere in the country. In May, it carried out a car bomb attack on a police station, injuring twenty people, and later in the year planted a number of bombs in Lima which caused little damage. In August, it kidnapped thirty employees of a French oil company, but released them after two days in exchange for food, clothing and other items.

In Colombia, May 1998 saw FARC and the ELN, who already controlled 40 per cent of the rural areas, moving into the cities and towns to establish terrorist cells which were estimated to number 300 in Bogotá alone. Both organisations were reported as establishing training centres, arms caches and safe houses as part of their plans to extend their control over the whole of the country. Two months earlier, FARC had scored a major success against government forces when it ambushed a company of an élite Army unit, killing sixty-two soldiers and capturing forty-three. In addition to inflicting a major blow on the government, the attack illustrated the calibre of the guerrillas who were proving to be more than a match for the Army.

A large number of bombings took place in Colombia during 1998, totalling seventy-seven in all. In October, the ELN attacked the main pipeline in the country, blowing it up with a massive explosion that resulted in the deaths of seventy-one people. A total of 1,726 terrorist acts were committed, an increase of 12 per cent over the total for the previous year. 1998 was also notable for the number of kidnappings that took place throughout its duration: a total of 2,000, of which FARC was reported as being responsible for 60 per cent. A report stated that by the end of 1998, an estimated combined total of US $5.3 billion was raised by FARC and the ELN during the period from 1991 to 1998: $2.3 billion from the narcotics trade; $1.2 from kidnappings and $1.8 billion from extortion.

In December 1998, it was reported that the US government was to finance the formation of a special 1,000-strong counter-narcotics unit in an attempt to fight the growing threat from Colombian drug-trafficking; in addition, it would establish an intelligence centre and electronic monitoring posts in the country. During that year US aid had risen to a figure of $289 million, a considerable increase over the figure of $50 million for the previous year. According to US spokesmen, this dramatic increase in aid reflected the growing concern at the increasing threat from Colombian drugs traffickers who were supplying 80 per cent of the cocaine and 60 per cent of the heroin imported into the United States. Some observers, however, believed that the Americans' primary concern was the increasing threat from FARC and the ELN, and that it was using the narcotics threat as a way of legitimising its military intervention in Colombia.

In Peru, 1999 saw the capture of the last remaining leader of the Sendero Luminoso. At the beginning of July, a major operation was launched by large numbers of troops, supported by helicopters and ground-attack aircraft, in the remote highlands east of Lima. Its aim was to hunt down and capture Oscar Ramirez Durand who had been reported as being in the area. During the previous month, there had been an increase in activity by the guerrillas and on 3 June they had attacked a village, killing three people. Next day they had ambushed a truck, killing six more.

During the operation, troops encountered and overpowered two groups of guerrillas, killing two and capturing the remainder. Durand and a small group narrowly escaped capture on a number of occasions, but on 14 July he was finally run to ground and arrested, his capture being a major blow to the remnant of the

Sendero Luminoso which was a shadow of what had once been the most feared guerrilla organisation in Latin America.

Meanwhile, the high level of violence in Colombia had continued into 1999. In February three American aid workers, Terence Freitas, Lahe'ena'e Gay and Ingrid Washinawatok, were kidnapped. Early in March their hooded and bound bodies were found over the border in Venezuela; each had been tortured before being shot in the head and chest. Subsequent reports, based on radio transmissions intercepted by government forces, stated that FARC was responsible for the murders. On 12 April, forty-six people were kidnapped after their aircraft, flying from Bucaramanga to Bogotá, was forced to land at an airstrip seventy-five miles from Bucaramanga. The crew of a search and rescue aircraft later reported observing guerrillas herding the passengers into canoes on the nearby River Magdalena.

Mid-1999 saw growing opposition in Colombia to the tactics of the rebels and in June, a week after 143 people had been abducted by the ELN while attending a church service, a huge demonstration by 400,000 people demanding an end to kidnappings and the guerrilla war took place in Cali. The terrorists' response was to kidnap another eleven people and demand payment for their release. Despite this, further demonstrations against the war were held throughout the country in October.

Meanwhile, the government resumed negotiations with FARC at a town in an area in the south of Colombia from which all government forces had been withdrawn as a measure to encourage the guerrillas back to the negotiating table. FARC, however, had proceeded to take control of the entire area, measuring some 16,000 square miles. By the end of 1999, the organisation had consolidated the bulk of its forces and logistical structure there, building up stockpiles of weapons and launching attacks on government forces from the area. There were reports that it was also holding up to 600 hostages in the area, keeping them beyond the reach of government forces.

In late November 1999, it was reported that Iran had offered to construct a cold storage plant in the area. This caused considerable alarm in Colombia and the United States where fears arose that the Iranians would supply arms and training to the guerrillas and gain a foothold in the country. During the previous year Argentina, Brazil and Paraguay had been taking measures to counter activity in their respective border regions by individuals linked to Islamic extremist groups among the large Shi'ite Muslim communities living there. In early 1998, Argentina had asked Iran to remove a number of diplomats from its diplomatic mission in Buenos Aires as a result of increasing controversy over growing evidence of Iran's involvement in the 1992 and 1994 bombings of the Israeli embassy and the AMIA/DAIA building.

In South Asia, meanwhile, the beginning of the 1990s found the war between the Sri Lankan government of President Ranasinghe Premadasa and the Tamil Tigers of the LTTE continuing unabated. On 21 May 1991, events took a dramatic turn when a female suicide bomber assassinated Indian Prime Minister Rajiv Gandhi as he was about to address a political rally at Sriperumbudur near Madras, the capital of Tamil Nadu. Seventeen other people also died in the attack which was reportedly carried out because the LTTE leader Velupillai Prabhakaran believed that Gandhi was opposed to the Tamil liberation struggle and feared that Indian forces might return to Sri Lanka.

Until the death of Gandhi, the LTTE had continued to maintain a substantial presence in India, mainly concentrated in Tamil Nadu. It was well organised and comprised twelve branches in different districts, each with its own area of responsibility. These covered intelligence, communications, arms production, explosives, propaganda, political work, food and essential supplies, medical supplies, fuel, clothing, transport and finance. Supplies were despatched to Sri Lanka from the district of Vedaraniym while those from LTTE ocean-going vessels were unloaded in Nagapattnam; wounded LTTE terrorists were treated in Tiruchi. Each centre was in radio communication with the others, the LTTE communications centre being located in Thanjavur.

In order to maintain such a presence, it was obviously necessary for the LTTE to enjoy the support and goodwill of Tamil Nadu politicians and indeed some were known to have visited LTTE bases in the jungles of Sri Lanka to express their support. In addition, the LTTE achieved high-level penetration of government agencies within the state; on one occasion, information concerning a decision taken by intelligence agencies at a very high level about anti-LTTE operations reached the terrorists within twenty-four hours. It has been alleged that it was due to such influence that the organisation was able to mount the operation to assassinate Rajiv Gandhi within Tamil Nadu. A few months earlier, an LTTE team had assassinated the leader of another Sri Lankan Tamil terrorist group, the EPRLF, but no action was taken as a result of the alleged intervention of the state's chief minister.

Following the murder of Gandhi, however, there was a crackdown on the LTTE which was forced to dismantle its infrastructure in Tamil Nadu. The political and propaganda elements were moved to western Europe, principally Britain and France, while the military and logistics components were relocated in South-East Asia. A residual infrastructure was kept in India, however, and this enabled the Research & Analysis Wing to infiltrate the organisation. The latter then engineered a rift between the LTTE leader, Velupillai Prabhakaran, and his deputy, Gopalasamy Mahendrarajah (alias Mahattaya), who was subsequently assassinated.

Two years later, President Ranasinghe Premadasa himself was assassinated by a suicide bomber while attending a May Day rally. The finger of suspicion was pointed at the LTTE, but no clear motive for his murder has emerged since; it can only be surmised that he had outlived his usefulness to the terrorists. His death came eight days after the murder of an opposition politician, Lalith Athulathmudali, who was shot dead while addressing a rally during provincial elections.

In November 1994 the leader of the People's Alliance and incumbent prime minister, Mrs Chandrika Kumaratunga, was elected as president; in a situation perhaps unique in the history of politics, her mother, Sirimavo Bandaranaike, who had served as the world's first elected woman prime minister in the 1970s, was appointed to the post again. Chandrika Kumaratunga was elected on a platform of alleviating the poverty which was widespread throughout Sri Lanka and ending the long-running war with the LTTE. Shortly after being elected, determined to force the LTTE to the negotiating table, she launched a peace initiative in which the organisation was offered devolution for a Tamil homeland state. The initial response was positive and a truce was signed in January 1995.

In April, however, the LTTE claimed that the government was not meeting its demands and in the early hours of the 20th a team of four suicide bombers carried out a sabotage attack on the naval base at Trincomalee, blowing up two patrol craft and shattering the truce. On the same day, fighting broke out when terrorists attacked a military base at Elephants Pass, 180 miles north of Colombo. During the following month the LTTE shot down two Sri Lankan Air Force (SLAF) Avro HS-748 transport aircraft, killing ninety-seven men, with *Strela* SAM-7 shoulder-fired surface-to-air missiles; this was the first time that the Russian-manufactured weapons had been used by the terrorists who had acquired them from Cambodia earlier in the year. The missiles, reportedly supplied by corrupt generals, had been transported in three shipments from Koh Kong, in the south-west of Cambodia, through Thailand to the town of Chumporn. From there, they were sent across the Kra Isthmus to the LTTE base at Phuket from where they were shipped to the Jaffna Peninsula.

In June, the terrorists turned their attention to Sri Lanka's tourist industry. An attempt was made to carry out a bomb attack on Colombo's international airport, a warning being received beforehand from the 'Ellalan Force', a group suspected as being a front for the LTTE. Fortunately the 77-pound bomb, packed in a van parked at the airport, failed to explode when the detonator went off. The end of the month saw severe fighting break out when, on 28 June, the LTTE launched a major assault with a force of more than 1,000 on an Army base at Madativu, seventy-four soldiers and at least fifty terrorists being killed during the ensuing battle. Elsewhere, the LTTE carried out four other attacks on police and troops in the north and east of the country.

The latter part of July saw the government massing 40,000 troops in the northern region of the island in preparation for a major offensive designed to drive the terrorists out of their stronghold in the Jaffna Peninsula and cripple them militarily. The LTTE meanwhile continued its attacks elsewhere. On 7 August a suicide bomber blew himself up in a government office in Colombo, killing twenty people and injuring scores of others. On 30 August, a ferry bound for Jaffna was hijacked after leaving the port of Trincomalee. Two naval patrol craft who went to its aid were attacked and destroyed as the ferry was escorted away by two LTTE Sea Tiger craft. Two weeks later, on 13 September, an SLAF Antonov An-32 transport aircraft, carrying seventy passengers and five crew from Colombo to Pallalai, was blown up in mid-air by a bomb concealed in its cargo. During the following month, the LTTE brought the war to Colombo again. On the night of 22 October, forty or so terrorists attacked Sri Lanka's two main oil storage depots with rocket-propelled grenades, mortars and explosives, setting the installations ablaze and causing some £20 million worth of damage.

On 17 October, meanwhile, the government had launched Operation 'Sun Ray', its major offensive in the Jaffna Peninsula. Fierce fighting ensued, but after five days Sri Lankan Army units had advanced to within five miles of Jaffna itself. During November, some 400,000 refugees fled from the city, heading for Vavuniya which was occupied by government forces. By the end of the first week of December, most of the peninsula was in government hands and the LTTE had lost not only its main stronghold, but also its principal source of revenue within Sri Lanka, taxes raised from the local population, forcing it to rely largely on funds raised by its overseas networks. LTTE casualties were estimated at 2,000; the Sri Lankan Army suffered losses of 500.

Retribution was not long in coming. On 31 January 1996, a massive truck bomb exploded outside the Central Bank building in the main business district of Colombo, killing ninety-one people and injuring 1,400. The bomb, later estimated as containing some 450 pounds of high explosive, devastated the entire area. It subsequently transpired that the explosives used in this attack were from a large consignment, comprising fifty tons of TNT and ten tons of RDX, acquired from a chemical plant in the Ukraine.

Earlier in the month an LTTE vessel, the MV *Yahata*, carrying a large shipment of weapons, ammunition and explosives, had been intercepted. The consignment had been kept under surveillance by Indian aircraft and naval vessels during its voyage from Phuket in Thailand across the Bay of Bengal; she was intercepted on 13 January, but was blown up and scuttled before she could be boarded. During the following month another vessel, the *Comex Joux 3*, carrying a consignment of arms reportedly supplied by Cambodia, was also intercepted; she was attacked and sunk by gunboats and SLAF aircraft while transferring the cargo to Sea Tiger craft alongside.

On the night of 17 July the LTTE launched a major assault on the Sri Lankan Army base at Mullaitivu, situated on the north-east coast, 175 miles north of Colombo, which was held by a garrison of two understrength battalions and the headquarters of the 25th Infantry Brigade. Some 3,000–4,000 terrorists, including members of the LTTE's Charles Anthony Infantry Brigade, Leopard commando units, a Sea Tiger unit, the 'Sujolan' underwater operations unit and other units, were involved in the operation. Government forces, primarily special forces and commando units, attempted unsuccessfully to break through to the beleaguered garrison of 25th Infantry Brigade, but were unable to do so despite the support of artillery, SLAF aircraft and helicopter gunships.

Reinforcements were despatched by sea, but these encountered units of Sea Tigers which attacked and sank a gunboat escorting the two landing craft, ramming it with a speedboat packed with explosives. The landing subsequently took place under fire and it took the relieving troops two days to reach the base. By that time, however, it had been overrun and the garrison wiped out, only some forty soldiers surviving the massacre. Government casualties totalled 1,240 troops killed; those of the LTTE were estimated at some 400.

The loss of the base at Mullaitivu was a major victory for the LTTE and a blow to the government and its armed forces. In September, however, the LTTE suffered a major reverse when its headquarters in the town of Kilinochchi was captured and a large number of terrorists killed. Fighting continued through into 1997 and in March the Sri Lankan Navy scored a success when it sank ten enemy boats and killed eighty terrorists during an action off the islet of Iranativu when a large number of Sea Tiger craft, armed with mortars and machine-guns, attacked a flotilla of gunboats transporting troops and supplies from Trincomalee to the Jaffna Peninsula.

Despite a fresh peace initiative in April, fighting continued throughout the following months as government forces launched 20,000 troops in another offensive, optimistically named Operation 'Sure Victory', to secure the main northern highway leading to the Jaffna Peninsula. On 15 October, the LTTE staged another major attack in Colombo when a team of terrorists drove an 800-pound truck bomb into the city's main business area and left it in the car park of the Galadari Hotel situated next to the newly completed World Trade Centre. Nine people died and 150 were injured in the blast; twelve terrorists were killed in a battle with troops and police immediately afterwards while five others escaped. Four days later, 100 terrorists were killed during a four-hour long action between Sri Lankan Navy vessels and four Sea Tiger craft off the north-east coast; nine naval personnel died when a naval gunboat was rammed and sunk by a speedboat packed with explosives. In December, however, 144 members of the Sri Lankan Army's special forces died during fighting in the Jaffna Peninsula.

The year 1998 followed a depressingly similar pattern with heavy casualties being incurred on both sides. On 5 March, thirty-two people died and more than 250 were injured when an empty bus, carrying explosives packed with ball-bearings and driven by a suicide bomber, exploded in a street in Colombo. On 17 May the mayor of Jaffna, Mrs. Sarojini Yogeswaran, was shot dead by two LTTE gunmen at her home in the city. The following month found govern-ment forces still attempting to secure the northern highway to

Jaffna, having by then suffered some 1,300 casualties. Morale in the Army was low, evidence of such being the 19,000 desertions from its ranks during the previous twelve months. In September Jaffna lost another mayor when a bomb killed Ponnuthurai Sivapalan, Sarojini Yogeswaran's successor, during a meeting on 11 September between local authorities and senior military and police officers.

September 1998 saw another major defeat inflicted on the Sri Lankan Army. On the morning of 27 September some 2,500 terrorists, supported by 81mm medium mortars, attacked military bases at Paranthan and Kilinochchi in an operation intended to prevent the Army from continuing with its offensive to secure the northern main highway to Jaffna. Heavy casualties were sustained by the Army which admitted that more than 600 troops had been killed; other reports quoted a considerably higher figure of 1,500 killed and 1,500 wounded. In addition, the Army suffered considerable losses of weapons and equipment.

Throughout 1999 the situation in Sri Lanka remained largely unchanged, with no end to the fighting in sight. On 18 December an attempt was made to assassinate President Kumaratunga, a bomb exploding as she was addressing a rally in Colombo, wounding her slightly in the face and eye with shrapnel. A few weeks earlier in India, on 5 November, four of the twenty-six LTTE terrorists originally convicted on 29 January 1998 of the assassination of Prime Minister Rajiv Gandhi were due to be hanged, but in the event the sentence was in abeyance because of a large number of protests in South India and pressure from human rights organisations, some of whom had been infiltrated by the LTTE; the sentence has still not been carried out at the time of writing this book. A further three had also been condemned to death, but their sentences were subsequently commuted to life imprisonment. The other nineteen, who had also originally been convicted and sentenced to death, were acquitted on appeal in May 1998.

By the end of the 1990s, the LTTE had developed into a pan-Tamil movement reportedly funded to the tune of some US $2 million per month, two-thirds of that figure being contributed by its overseas network based on the sixty million Tamils who live over-seas. Those who resisted the approaches of its fund raisers soon found to their cost that the LTTE had no scruples about the use of coercion or violence against those who opposed it.

In 1998 it was reported that the organisation was deriving further income from the narcotics trade, having established connections with traffickers throughout western Europe, Asia and North America. During the late 1980s and early 1990s, a number of its members were arrested and charged with drugs trafficking. Since then, however, there has been no further hard evidence of the organisation's involvement in drugs trafficking, but there have been reports from within the international security and intelligence community that the LTTE has since concentrated on the 'whole-sale' side of the business, shipping only large quantities of narcotics to different parts of the world. Given its sophisticated infrastructure world-wide, it is well placed and equipped for this illicit activity.

In Japan, meanwhile, the mid-1990s saw the manifestation of one of the nightmare scenarios envisaged by those responsible for conducting the long-running war against terrorism: the use of chemical and biological weapons by a terrorist group against a major centre of population. In June 1994, members of an extremist religious sect, the Aum Shinrikyo, carried out an attack with the chemical nerve agent sarin in the northern Japanese town of Matsumoto. The gas was sprayed from tanks mounted in a van which drove through the town; seven people died and 150 were injured.

On 20 March 1995, the sect struck again when its members placed containers of sarin on crowded commuter trains on the Tokyo subway. One, however, was observed doing so at the station at Kodenmacho and, as the container was kicked out of the carriage by a passenger, other commuters pursued and arrested him, handing him over to police shortly afterwards. Ten commuters died and some 5,000 were injured by the gas which affected much of the subway network, requiring decontamination of trains and stations throughout the system by Army chemical warfare specialists.

Subsequent analysis of the sarin revealed that it had been diluted to decrease its lethality, allowing the terrorists to make good their escape after planting the containers. A few days later, police raided the quarters of the sect's 800-strong commune at Kamikuishiki, a village near Mount Fuji, and discovered a fully equipped chemical laboratory in a three-storey building. In warehouses elsewhere they found 150 tons of chemicals, including large quantities of fluorine and organophosphate compounds used in the manufacture of sarin. They also discovered quantities of small arms, including automatic weapons, and explosives. Even more deadly, however, were the large amounts of clostridium botulinium, a bacterium which attacks the central nervous system, and peptone, a chemical for cultivating bacteria, which were found in another laboratory belonging to the sect.

It was later revealed that the sect had tested the sarin at a remote cattle station in Western Australia, at Banjawarn 450 miles north-east of Perth, which it had purchased in 1993. Traces of the chemical were later found in the soil and in the bodies of dead sheep discovered by police carrying out investigations into the cult's activities in Australia. A subsequent unconfirmed report stated that in 1992 members of the cult had travelled to Zaire where there was an outbreak of Ebola Fever for which there is no cure; 90 per cent of victims normally haemorrhage to death. They were apparently investigating the possibility of developing a biological weapon from the virus.

On 16 May 1995, the leader of the sect, Shoko Asahara, a half-blind acupuncturist whose real name is Chizuo Matsumoto, was arrested in a secret bunker in a building at Kamikuishiki after a lengthy hunt for him. Since the subway attack, warrants had been issued for the arrest of forty-one other members of the sect, twenty-seven of whom had already been apprehended by police. Meanwhile, the organisation's chief chemist, Masami Tsuchiya, had confessed to manufacturing the sarin and further questioning of him and others revealed that the sect intended to attack other Japanese cities as well as ultimately carrying out similar operations in the United States where it planned to release a total of twenty tons of sarin in New York and Washington.

During June 1995 Asahara and six of his followers were indicted on charges of terrorism and murder; nine others were charged with conspiracy to murder. A further twenty were charged with offences relating to the gas attack on the Tokyo subway. The following month, however, saw another attack when a container of sulphuric acid and sodium cyanide crystals, fitted with a timer and a fan unit, was discovered at the subway station at Kayabacho. A few hours later, a similar device was found at Shinjuku railway station. Although there was no firm evidence, the finger of suspicion pointed once more at the Aum Shinrikyo.

In October, Asahara confessed to masterminding the attack on the Tokyo subway; by then, all but a few of those also arrested had admitted fully their involvement. Shortly afterwards, the trials commenced of all those indicted and during the following three years sentences ranging from ten years to life imprisonment were handed down to those convicted. Asahara was charged with seventeen counts of murder and at the time of writing his trial was still in progress.

Thus the 20th century drew to a close, its last three decades having seen international terrorism leave few parts of the world untouched. In most instances, terrorist organisations have so far failed to achieve their long-term objectives and this has been due largely to the considerable resources devoted to combating them by governments world-wide. Together with law enforcement agencies and security services in their respective countries, military and para-military special forces have formed the cutting edge in the fight against terrorism which continues today.

4

GLOBAL RESPONSE

The massacre by Black September of the Israeli athletes in September 1972 was the catalyst which resulted in nations throughout the world adopting measures to combat international terrorism.

The response from Israel had been typically swift and ruthless. A secret government committee, known as Committee X and headed by Prime Minister Golda Meir and Moshe Dayan, took the decision to retaliate by assassinating any members of Black September known to have been directly or indirectly involved in the Olympics massacre. Special teams, called 'Wrath of God' and headed by a senior operative named Mike Harari, were despatched by Mossad to hunt down those responsible. The first to suffer retribution was Wael Zwaiter, Al-Fatah's representative in Rome, who was shot dead in October 1972 in the elevator in the apartment block where he lived. Next was Mahmoud Hamshari, the PLO's representative in Paris, who was killed by a remote-controlled telephone bomb. His death was followed by that of Dr. Bassel Rauf Kubeisy, a leading member of the PFLP, who was also killed in Paris, being shot at close range.

Most important of all the Wrath of God teams' targets in Europe was the Algerian Mohamed Boudia, who was Wadi Haddad's's chief operative in France. On the morning of 28 June 1973, he was killed by a bomb placed under the driver's seat in his car which had been parked in the Rue des Fosses St-Bernard in Paris.

In July a Wrath of God team located Ali Hassan Salameh who, being responsible for overseeing Black September's operations in western Europe, had planned the attack at Munich. In addition, he was the commander of Force 17, the personal bodyguard of PLO chairman Yasser Arafat. The Israelis tracked him down in Norway, in the town of Lillehammer. During the evening of 21 July a man was shot dead, but next day the Israelis discovered that they had killed the wrong man: a Moroccan named Ahmad Bouchiki who was married to a Norwegian woman who had witnessed his murder. The hit-team had already left the country, but to Mossad's great embarrassment six of its agents, members of a support team, were arrested. All six were tried and convicted of involvement in Bouchiki's murder, each being sentenced to between two and five and a half years' imprisonment although none served more than twenty-two months.

It was five and a half years before Mossad finally caught up with Salameh whom it tracked down in the Lebanon. On 22 January 1979, as he was driving along a road in Beirut, a massive bomb, packed into a car parked at the roadside, exploded as he passed. He and his car were literally blown to pieces.

Governments in the West and elsewhere had meanwhile soon realised that their security forces were ill-trained and equipped to deal with heavily armed and well-trained terrorists conducting well-planned operations. In West Germany, on 13 December 1972, decisions were taken to form special counter-terrorist units. At federal level, the role was given to the Bundesgrenzschutz (BGS), the federal border guard, which subsequently formed Grenzschutzgruppe–9 (Border Guard Group 9), popularly known by its acronym GSG–9, which would earn its operational laurels some four years later.

The task of forming this new unit was given to Lieutenant Colonel Ulrich Wegener who had been a member of the BGS since 1958, prior to which he had served in the police in Baden–Württemberg. He had an extensive knowledge of terrorism, having trained with the FBI in the United States and the Israeli Border Police. From 1970 to 1972, prior to being selected to command GSG-9, he had served as BGS liaison officer at the federal Ministry of the Interior, during which time he had attended the NATO Defence College in Rome.

Wegener lost no time in tackling the job. He trawled the BGS for suitable volunteers who had served a minimum of two and a half years and had a good service record. Officers and other ranks were interviewed, medically examined, and underwent a three-day selection procedure which tested for psychological aptitude, intelligence, general knowledge, physical fitness and marksmanship. The failure rate was high, some 60 per cent; those who passed underwent five months' basic and three months' advanced training.

The basic phase included unarmed combat and martial arts, police tactical operations, marksmanship, legal studies (covering federal, state and criminal law) and elementary psychology. The advanced phase concentrated on the skills required by members of a special action team (SET) which included aircraft and building assault, close-quarter combat (on foot and in vehicles) and high-speed driving. Once a volunteer had completed the advanced phase, he qualified as a member of the unit and took his place in an SET. Those members of the unit selected as communications or intelligence specialists, explosives experts, divers or technical support personnel, received further specialist training

GSG–9 was operationally ready by the latter part of 1973. Based at St. Augustin, near Bonn, and numbering some 200 all ranks, it was organised into a headquarters with three platoon-sized combat teams, each numbering thirty men organised in turn into a command element and five five-man special action teams. In addition, the unit was given its own communications, intelligence, engineer and training sections, and logistical support element. Air support was provided by a BGS helicopter unit, also based at St. Augustin. Ten years later, a fourth combat team was added to the establishment of the unit and the strength of each team increased to forty-two men.

Members of the special action teams were, and still are, cross-trained so that they could be deployed as either assault groups or sniper teams. They also received training in the requisite body-guard skills for VIP protection tasks. The standard sidearm for each man was originally the Heckler & Koch (H&K) P9S 9mm pistol or the Smith & Wesson Model 66 .357 Magnum revolver. These were subsequently replaced by the Smith & Wesson Model 19 and H&K P7. Each man was also issued with the H&K MP5-A2 9mm subma-chine-gun; the short H&K MP5K and suppressed MP-5SD2 vari-ants were also available for special tasks. For sniping, four 7.62mm calibre rifles were adopted by the unit: the bolt-action Mauser 66, the H&K G3SG-1 and PSG-1, and the Walther WA2000. Other weapons in GSG–9's armoury included the H&K Model 502 semi-automatic 12-gauge shotgun, MZP-1 40mm grenade-launcher and G8 7.62mm assault rifle/light machine gun.

GSG–9 also enjoyed a generous scale of other equipment which was evidence of the federal government's decision to spare no effort in establishing an effective counter-terrorist response. This included night vision equipment, radio communications systems, bomb-disposal equipment, diving equipment and boats, specially equipped high-performance Mercedes 280 SE saloon cars, Thyssen TM170 armoured personnel carriers and a fleet of specialist support vehicles.

Facilities at the St. Augustin base became extremely comprehensive, including a highly sophisticated training complex boasting buildings and airliner interior simulators for practising hostage rescue operations and other operational scenarios, and an underground firing range system.

Four years after its formation, GSG–9 won its operational spurs when in October 1977 one of its sub-units carried out a hostage rescue operation at Mogadishu, in Somalia, a detailed account of which is given in Chapter 7. Prior to that, the unit had led a low-profile existence, but thereafter it found its services much in demand to provide assistance to units being established in other countries. GSG–9 training teams were later despatched as far afield as Saudi Arabia and Singapore.

GSG–9 was subsequently reorganised into three combat units and a support element, the latter comprising its administrative and technical sections. GSG–9/1, comprising approximately 100 men, was tasked with the original role. GSG–9/2, also numbering some 100 men, became a combat swimmer unit tasked with the maritime countermeasures role, protecting German shipping and offshore installations. GSG–9/3 became an airborne unit trained in HAHO and HALO free-fall parachuting.

Unlike West Germany, Britain allocated the responsibility for forming a counter-terrorist capability to the Army which gave the role to its Regular special forces unit, 22nd Special Air Service Regiment (22 SAS), which since the end of its deployments in the Middle East in 1967 had been tinkering with the concept of forming a counter-terrorist team. In early 1972 the Commanding Officer of 22 SAS, Lieutenant Colonel Peter de la Billière, had commissioned a study on how the regiment could be involved in combating terrorism within the United Kingdom. This had conceived the idea of a specialist team or sub-unit trained in hostage rescue and operations of similar ilk. A paper was submitted via Headquarters SAS Group, 22 SAS's parent formation, to the Ministry of Defence which at that time took the matter no further. Within days of the Munich massacre, however, Prime Minister Edward Heath had asked the Director of Operations how the Army could assist in countering terrorism. The request had been passed to de la Billière who had produced a copy of the 22 SAS paper. Events moved swiftly and soon afterwards the regiment was directed to establish its counter-terrorist team.

Responsibility for this was given to a department specially created within the regiment for the task, the Counter Revolutionary Warfare (CRW) Wing whose staff proceeded apace to develop techniques and tactics. Some of these were based on those already in use by the Bodyguard Cell which trained members of the regiment deployed on VIP protection duties in the United Kingdom and overseas. Methods of entry into a variety of different types of target areas, including buildings, aircraft, vehicles and ships, and close-quarter battle (CQB) skills were among those which were developed and practised constantly in an indoor range facility dubbed the 'Killing House'. The proposed organisation of 22 SAS's counter-terrorist teams called for an assault team supported by sniper and command and communication groups and thus the necessary skills required for the two latter elements were also developed and perfected by the CRW Wing.

Considerable attention was paid by CRW Wing to the procurement of suitable weapons and equipment for the new role. Initially the Ingram MAC-10 9mm submachine-gun, a weapon with a very high rate of fire, was adopted but was subsequently replaced by the infinitely more reliable and accurate Heckler & Koch MP-5 with its closed roller-bolt action. The Browning Hi-Power 9mm pistol, which had been in service with the British Army for some years and was popular with members of 22 SAS, was retained. Remington 870 pump-action 12 gauge shotguns were acquired for shooting off door locks and hinges, with special 'Hatton Round' ammunition being developed for the task.

Stun grenades, christened 'flashbangs', were also developed for use by assault teams. Producing a dazzling flash and a deafening explosion, they were designed to disorient and incapacitate personnel within a target area without harming them, thus providing assault team members with an advantage as they entered and engaged their targets. Later versions of the grenade were equipped with up to six charges which produced a series of rapid flashes and explosions.

Other items incorporated into CRW Wing's rapidly expanding inventory were explosive charges for use in blowing holes in walls, or blowing in windows, for entry into buildings. Known as Charges Linear Cutting (CLC), they comprised lengths of explosive encased in a flexible lead sheath which enabled them to be bent and fashioned into a frame-charge measuring the exact dimensions of the aperture to be blown.

Protective clothing was initially somewhat rudimentary, comprising one-piece black coveralls worn with the hood of a nuclear biological chemical (NBC) warfare suit. Custom-designed flame-retardant assault suits were subsequently developed because of the high risk of injury from flash and fire within a target area. If CS or CR gas was to be used, the standard issue Avon S6 respirator (later replaced by the S10) was also worn, as was black Bristol body armour fitted with plates of ceramic hard armour to provide protection against high-velocity weapons if necessary. Also worn was a belt fitted with a holster for the Browning 9mm pistol and a carrier for three submachine-gun magazines. Over the body armour was worn an assault vest fitted with pockets and pouches for a radio, stun grenades, torch, small axe and other items.

The teams' sniper groups were similarly equipped, but were also issued with camouflaged 'ghillie suits' for use when they were deployed in rural surroundings. Each sniper was issued with two rifles, one fitted with a telescopic sight and the other with an image intensifier for use at night. Initially, these were the Army's standard issue L42A1 7.62mm calibre sniper rifle which was based on the Lee Enfield No. 4. In addition, a smaller calibre weapon, the Tikka Finlander M55 .22/.250, was adopted for use at ranges of up to 300 metres. These two weapons were subsequently replaced by the Heckler & Koch G3/SG-1 and the Accuracy International L96A1 PM.

The acquisition of all the new weapons and equipment was costly in financial terms, but the aftermath of the Munich massacre also resulted in the allocation of further funds for the new role, enabling the regiment to acquire special transport for the team in the form of specially modified Range Rovers, radio communications equipment, surveillance systems, entry equipment and a wide range of other items.

The counter-terrorist role, code-named Operation Pagoda, was initially allocated to a hand-picked team which was assembled for the task within five weeks of the decision to establish it, being separately accommodated with its vehicles and equipment and on twenty-four hours' standby. Subsequently, however, it was allocated to individual sabre squadrons on an approximately five-month rotating basis and the same system has been in use since then. For the entire period, one squadron was exclusively employed in the role, being located at the regiment's base at Hereford and organised in two identical Special Projects teams designated Red and Blue respectively. Both teams were on standby, one being restricted in the distance it was permitted to travel from the regimental base so that it could be on-site and ready to move within fifteen minutes. The second team had to be capable of being ready to move within one hour.

The principal advantage of this system was that the regiment's other three squadrons could be fully deployed on other training or operations elsewhere. Furthermore, the five-month tour was of sufficient duration that the in-role squadron could reach a peak of efficiency and maintain it, but short enough that the two teams would not become stale with the continual highly intensive training required, a problem experienced by units dedicated solely to the counter-terrorist role.

The first operational deployment of the counter-terrorist team occurred in January 1975 when an aircraft was hijacked at Manchester by an Iranian armed with a pistol who demanded that the pilot fly to Paris. The aircraft took off and flew southwards for two hours. As it did so, the Special Projects team was deployed to Stansted Airport in Essex while a major deception operation swung into action: a French-speaking air traffic controller guided the aircraft down to the airport where it was met by police dressed in what appeared to be French Gendarmerie uniforms. As the hijacker negotiated with the 'gendarmes', the team stormed the aircraft and overpowered him. He was fortunate not to be killed; his weapon turned out to be a harmless replica.

The end of 1975 saw the team deployed again, this time to London. On 6 December, a four-man Provisional IRA ASU was trapped by police in a flat in Balcombe Street, in north-west London. As described in Chapter 1, a siege developed and the Special Projects team was deployed, but its services were not required because, following a BBC announcement on the eighth day that the SAS were on the scene and preparing to mount an assault, the four terrorists surrendered and the siege ended without loss of life.

In October 1977, two members of 22 SAS were involved in Operation 'Fire Magic', the hostage rescue operation carried out by West Germany's GSG–9 at Mogadishu, in Somalia. A full account of this operation is given in Chapter 7.

It was just over two and a half years later, on 5 May 1980, that an event took place which, in front of the electrified gaze of the world, revealed the existence of 22 SAS's counter-terrorist role. A few days earlier, a group of six terrorists demanding autonomy for the Iranian province of Khuzestan occupied the Iranian embassy in Princes Gate in west London. A siege lasting six days ensued before a hostage rescue operation, code-named 'Nimrod', was carried out by Special Projects teams of B Squadron 22 SAS, a detailed account of which appears in Chapter 8.

In 1982, a Special Projects team returned to Stansted on standby to deal with another hijack. On this occasion, an Air Tanzania Boeing 737 had been hijacked on an internal flight and the pilot was forced to fly to England where it landed at Stansted. It transpired, however, that the hijackers were not terrorists, but Tanzanians seeking political asylum in Britain. They surrendered peaceably and the operation ended without bloodshed, the hijackers themselves subsequently being tried and convicted for air piracy.

Meanwhile, in 1975, the United Kingdom's counter-terrorist capability had been enhanced with the allocation of a new maritime countermeasures (MCM) role to the Royal Marines which was to provide a rapid response to terrorist threats to shipping and off-shore oil installations. The unit initially consisted of three sub-units comprising a rifle troop, a section of the Special Boat Squadron (SBS) and a company which were respectively on two, four and twenty-four hours' standby respectively.

The SBS section, 1 SBS, was dedicated to the new MCM role for which new tactics and techniques had to be evolved and perfected. These included the capability of insertions into target areas from the air or sea with men, weapons and equipment either being dropped by parachute or helicopter, or delivered by submarine or surface craft. Methods of entry on to oil rigs and ships also had to be developed together with equipment and systems designed to facilitate such.

Five years later, in 1980, a new independent unit was formed for the task of providing a rapid response MCM force. Designated Commacchio Group, it numbered some 300 all ranks and was based at Royal Marines Condor, a shore base in the town of Arbroath on the east coast of Scotland. The unit was also assigned the role of escorting convoys transporting nuclear warheads, between the nuclear submarine base at Faslane and maintenance facilities elsewhere, and for guarding them at high-security storage sites. 5 SBS was deployed in the MCM role on permanent attachment to Commacchio Group while 1 SBS returned to the squadron's base at Poole, in Dorset, where it provided an MCM response to any terrorist threat to shipping.

In 1987, the Special Boat Squadron was redesignated the Special Boat Service and thereafter was organised into three squadrons. C Squadron comprised the swimmer-canoeists, while S Squadron incorporated those specialising in the operation of swimmer delivery vehicles and high-speed surface craft for long-range insertions. M Squadron, comprising 1 SBS and 5 SBS which were amalgamated with two rifle troops, was assigned the MCM role. It was organised into three troops, designated Black, Gold and Purple respectively, Gold and Purple having an underwater capability and Black specialising in aerial delivery by helicopter.

In 1987, British special forces underwent a degree of rationalisation with all units coming under the Director SAS and HQ SAS Group redesignated Director Special Forces (DSF) and Headquarters Special Forces (HQSF) respectively. These included the Army's specialist intelligence and surveillance units deployed in Northern Ireland which are covered in Chapters 5 and 14.

Despite the fact that during the early 1970s it was harbouring elements of several of the world's most hard-line terrorist organisations, it was not until March 1974 that France established its counter-terrorist capability in the form of the Groupe d'Intervention Gendarmerie Nationale (GIGN), based at Maisons-Alfort outside Paris. The Gendarmerie Nationale is the country's para-military police force which comes under the authority of the Ministry of Defence and is responsible for law enforcement outside the towns and cities of France. Initially, two such units, GIGN 1 and GIGN 4, were formed, with responsibility for covering the north and south of France respectively, but three years later these were amalgamated into one unit. Commanded by Lieutenant Christian Prouteau, it was initially small, numbering only two officers and forty other ranks organised into a small command element and three twelve-man combat teams, the latter subsequently being increased to four. Later, the unit was increased in size to four fifteen-man detachments and a logistical support element.

Volunteers for the unit were, and continue to be, drawn solely from the Gendarmerie Nationale, being required to attend a preliminary interview before undergoing a week-long tough selection course which tests physical fitness, strength, stamina and standards of marksmanship. Those who passed progressed to eight months of training in skills in which all members of the unit were required to qualify: marksmanship with pistol, submachine-gun, shotgun and rifle form a major part of GIGN training, together with tactics and close-quarter combat skills, the latter including the use of vehicles. All members of the unit were required to qualify as parachutists and combat swimmers, and to be expert in abseiling or fast-roping down from helicopters, as well as in the high-speed driving of vehicles, in order to be capable of being inserted into target areas via a variety of means.

Initially, GIGN was equipped with the French MAT-49 9mm submachine-gun, but, like its counterparts in GSG-9 and 22 SAS, soon adopted the ubiquitous H&K MP-5 in its different configurations. Other weapons included the Manurhin MR-73 .357 Magnum revolver, the MAB PAP F1 9mm pistol and FR-F2 7.62mm sniper rifle. Over a period of time, GIGN established extensive training facilities, including a specially designed training complex and ranges which enabled it to practise a variety of operational scenarios, including aircraft and building assault.

With its area of operations also covering former colonies where France has retained interests, GIGN did not have to wait long to receive its operational baptism of fire. On 3 February 1976 in Djibouti, six terrorists of the Front de Libération de la Côte de Somalie (FLCS) hijacked a school bus near the border with Somalia. It was carrying thirty French children, the sons and daughters of French Air Force personnel serving in Djibouti.

The French reacted swiftly, immediately flying Lieutenant Prouteau and nine of his men to Djibouti. There they were reinforced by paratroops of the Foreign Legion's 2e Régiment Etranger de Parachutistes (2e REP) who took up positions covering those of Somali border guards at a post close by with whom the terrorists appeared to be in close touch. The post was equipped with two general-purpose machine-guns (GPMGs) and Prouteau assigned two of his snipers to deal with their crews if so required.

The flat and featureless terrain surrounding the bus made a hostage rescue difficult, but an embankment of sand and large rocks some 200 metres from the vehicle provided cover for the small GIGN group. Having reconnoitred the area, Prouteau decided that the only viable plan was to neutralise all six terrorists simultaneously by sniper fire; this in itself would be difficult to achieve depending as it did on all targets being in the snipers' sights at precisely the same moment.

Prouteau and his men lay in the searing heat waiting for their chance while negotiators attempted to persuade the hijackers to allow food to be brought in for the children. Eventually the terrorists agreed and a meal arrived, heavily laced with a sedative to cause the children to fall asleep and, it was to be hoped, slump down in their seats, their heads below the windows of the bus. The plan worked and about an hour and a half later the heads of the four terrorists still on board the bus were all in the snipers' sights. Prouteau gave the command to fire and all were killed instantly while a fifth terrorist died standing outside the bus.

Meanwhile the Somali border guards opened fire with their two GPMGs, initially preventing Prouteau and his men from approaching the bus. Under covering fire from one of his snipers and some of the 2e REP detachment, however, Prouteau and the rest of his men dashed for the vehicle, followed by legionnaires in jeeps. As they reached the bus, a member of GIGN spotted the sixth terrorist entering the vehicle by a rear door which faced the Somali border post. Launching himself through the front door, the gendarme came under fire from the terrorist who was armed with a submachine-gun; some of the children and the teacher were hit, one little girl being mortally wounded, as the gendarme took cover behind the driver's seat. At this point, a legionnaire entered the bus and attempted to shoot the terrorist but missed; this gave the gendarme the opportunity to open fire with his revolver, hitting the terrorist in the head and killing him outright.

Meanwhile, a battle was raging outside the bus between the Somali border guards and the legionnaires who attacked the post with an armoured vehicle in support. Nevertheless, the GIGN team and the legionnaires lost little time in removing the children, the teacher and the bus driver from the vehicle and evacuating them rapidly from the area in the 2e REP detachment's jeeps.

The Somali troops withdrew at this point, having lost twenty-eight killed. As Prouteau and the legionnaires inspected the abandoned post, they came upon the body of a blond Caucasian dressed in a camouflage uniform which they recognised instantly as being Russian. Documents found in the pockets identified the man as a major in the Soviet Army; Prouteau was of the opinion that he was in all likelihood an officer in the Spetsnaz (Soviet Special Forces) and had been directing the hijack operation.

Like its counterparts in GSG–9 and 22 SAS, GIGN was also called upon to provide training and assistance to other countries. The best-known example of this was the occasion in 1979 when armed Muslim extremists occupied the Great Mosque at Mecca during the annual Haj pilgrimage. The attack began on 20 November when the mosque was crowded with some 40,000 pilgrims. A large group of some 200 heavily armed men entered and shot dead one of the imams before taking up positions around the building. They were members of a fanatical Sunni sect and followers of a former member of the Saudi Arabian National Guard (SANG), Juhaiman Saif al-Otaiba, an Islamic fundamentalist who believed that the Saudi regime was corrupt and consisted of 'unbelievers' who had to be purged. Their aim in occupying the mosque was to 'purify Islam' prior to the end of the world.

A Moroccan pilgrim at his devotions heard the shots and gave the alarm. Police and units of the SANG arrived shortly afterwards and surrounded the mosque. Attempts at negotiations soon proved unsuccessful and the Saudi authorities, having first obtained permission from the Ulama, the council of religious judges, ordered the SANG to storm the mosque. The attack was repulsed and the latter suffered heavy casualties. At this point the Saudis turned to France for assistance and a five-man team from GIGN, headed by Captain Philippe Legorjus, was despatched to Jeddah. There the team provided training and advice for members of the SANG's Special Security Force (SSF), and assisted in the planning of an operation to end the siege.

On 25 November, the operation began and lasted four days during which fierce fighting took place throughout the labyrinthine corridors and crypts of the mosque. The fundamentalists were well equipped, possessing a large quantity of weapons, ammunition, respirators and food, all of which had been smuggled into the mosque beforehand on stretchers ostensibly bearing the bodies of dead pilgrims which had been carried round the Kaaba, the sacred black stone veiled with the Kiswa, the black cloth bearing gold-embroidered verses from the Koran, around which pilgrims must pass seven times as part of their devotions. On 29 November, the SSF succeeded in overcoming the last pockets of resistance and the remaining fundamentalists, comprising forty-one Saudis, ten Egyptians, six South Yemenis, a North Yemeni, three Kuwaitis, a Sudanese and an Iraqi, were arrested. During the operation, more than 250 people had been killed and some 600 wounded.

In January 1980 all sixty-three fundamentalists were brought to trial and were convicted and sentenced to death. On 9 January all were executed in eight different locations throughout Saudi Arabia.

The 1980s saw GIGN deployed on a number of occasions on tasks which ranged from hostage rescue operations, at Orly and Marseilles in 1983 and 1984 respectively, to dealing with serious rioting in prisons where the authorities had lost control.

In 1985, a team of the unit was deployed to the French island colony of New Caledonia, in the Pacific, which had been racked by trouble caused by Kanak nationalists who had attacked the local gendarmerie barracks and had taken some hostages before returning to their bases deep in the jungle which covered most of the island. The French government decided to take action to prevent further trouble and the fourteen-man GIGN team was despatched under the unit commander, Captain Philippe Legorjus, together with a detachment of legionnaire paratroops of the 2e REP who were dressed as gendarmes.

Legorjus and his force tracked the Kanak guerrillas to a base deep in the jungle, the trail leading to a clearing in the middle of which was a small house; nearby was a cave in which the kidnappers were holding their hostages. Four GIGN snipers moved into positions to cover the building in front of which were three men sitting on the ground; two armed guerrillas meanwhile patrolled nearby. One of the three men was soon identified as Machoro, the leader of the Kanak movement. As soon as the snipers had all confirmed that they had their respective targets in their sights, Legorjus gave the order to fire. Within a few seconds all five guerrillas were dead and shortly afterwards Legorjus himself freed the hostages from the cave.

Almost ten years after the formation of GIGN, the Gendarmerie Nationale formed a second special forces unit: the Escadron Parachutiste d'Intervention Gendarmerie Nationale (EPIGN). Numbering 160 all ranks and organised into a head-quarters element and four platoons, the new unit's role was that of quick response, possibly in support of GIGN, to a threat in France or to French nationals overseas. During 1985, the squadron found itself deployed in support of other Gendarmerie Nationale units in the French Basque country, stretching along the frontier with Spain, where ETA terrorists were active.

In 1985 another specialist French unit was established to counter the rising tide of terrorism and violence which was plaguing France during the 1980s. Based near Paris at Bièvres and known by the acronym RAID (Réaction, Assistance, Intervention, Dissuader), this new unit was formed by the Police Nationale. Totalling some eighty in strength, it was organised into a command element, four fifteen-man assault groups and a ten-man team of specialists who included negotiators, dog-handlers and EOD personnel. Members of the unit were, and continue to be, drawn from police officers throughout France. In December 1985, almost twelve months after RAID's formation, members of the unit took part in an operation in Nantes to rescue hostages being held in a courthouse by four leaders of the terrorist group Action Directe.

In 1973 Austria formed a specialist counter-terrorist unit, the Gendarmerie Kommando (GK), but the inadequacies of the unit were revealed two years later during the raid in December 1975 on the Vienna headquarters of OPEC by Ilich Ramírez Sánchez and his accomplices of the Red Army Faction and PFLP–SOG. As described in Chapter 2, an attempt to storm the floor of the building on which the terrorists were holding their hostages failed abysmally and it soon became apparent that the GK lacked the expertise to mount an effective hostage rescue operation. This view was reinforced by the successful operation at Mogadishu by GSG–9 in October 1977 which undoubtedly influenced the Austrian government into enhancing its counter-terrorist capability.

Three months later, in January 1978, a new unit was formed to replace GK. Designated Gendarmerieeinsatzkommando (GEK) and commanded by Colonel Johannes Pechter, it numbered some 200 all ranks and was apparently modelled on the lines of GSG–9. Volunteers were drawn from throughout the Gendarmerie and had to have served three years before being eligible. Selection was rigorous and failure rates high with only some 20 per cent qualifying.

As was the case with GSG–9, the Austrian government spared little expense in forming and equipping the GEK. An extensive armoury and an impressive fleet of transport, including Mercedes SE 300 saloon cars and other specialist vehicles, featured in the unit's inventory. Self-contained underwater breathing apparatus (SCUBA) and parachutes were later added when the unit formed special combat swimmer and airborne sections to its order of battle.

In The Netherlands, the counter-terrorist role was allocated to a specialist unit formed in early 1973. Called the Bijzondere Bijstandseenheden (BBE – Special Support Unit), it comprises three elements: BBE/P, a police sniper unit; BBE/K, a military sniper unit; and BBE MARNS, an assault unit comprised of members of the Royal Netherlands Marine Corps (RNLMC). The organisation of the BBE remains unchanged to this day.

The BBE MARNS was, and continues to be, organised into two operational 33-man platoons, each comprising four assault teams, and a training section responsible for running the selection course for the unit. The latter also provided instruction for new members undergoing forty-eight weeks of training before joining one of the operational platoons. In addition to counter-terrorist skills, some members of the unit were and still are trained as parachutists and combat swimmers. Weapons used by the BBE's assault teams included Glock 17 and SIG-Sauer P226 9mm pistols as well as the H&K MP-5 9mm submachine-gun in its various confgurations, while its snipers were equipped with the H&K G3 PSG-1 and Steyr SSG 7.62mm x 51 sniper rifles.

In the event of being deployed on a maritime countermeasures operation, the BBE MARNS was tasked with working in close co-operation with 7 Netherlands Special Boat Section (7 NL SBS) which was given the role of protecting Dutch offshore oil installations. The section was organised into four six-man assault teams which trained regularly with the BBE.

BBE MARNS also received training in riot control and it was in that role that it was first deployed operationally in October 1974, being used to storm a cell block in the prison in Scheveningen which had been taken over by rioting inmates led by four Palestinians, jailed for terrorist offences, who were holding twenty-two people hostage. After four days, BBE MARNS was tasked with resolving the crisis; the marines gained entry to the block and used stun grenades to overpower the rioters, some of whom were armed; the hostages were rescued without loss of life.

During the 1970s The Netherlands suffered a number of terrorist incidents. On 13 September 1974, three members of the Japanese Red Army seized the French embassy in The Hague and took hostage the Ambassador, Jacques Senard, while demanding the release of a member of their organisation, Yutaka Buraya, who was in prison in France. The BBE was deployed during this incident, but its services were not required as consultations between the French and Dutch governments led to Buraya's being released and flown to Holland. Shortly afterwards, all four terrorists were allowed to depart in an aircraft provided for them.

The 1970s also saw a number of incidents involving members of the South Moluccan community who were campaigning for independence for their homeland, the islands of the South Moluccas in the Indonesian archipelago. Formerly known as the Spice Islands, they had been a Dutch colony until after the Second World War when they became part of Indonesia. In the late 1960s a number of extremists living in Holland, primarily the Dutch-born descendants of South Moluccans, had formed a movement to pressurise the government into supporting their demands for independence from Indonesia.

On 2 December 1975, a train was hijacked at Wijster by seven Moluccans. Fifty-seven passengers were taken hostage, two being killed by the terrorists during the hijack itself. The train was surrounded by Dutch security forces and the BBE was deployed to carry out a hostage rescue operation if so required. Lengthy negotiations took place and eventually the terrorists surrendered.

Meanwhile, in Amsterdam on 4 December another group of Moluccan terrorists had seized the Indonesian consulate, demanding Dutch government support for South Moluccan independence from Indonesia. This incident complicated matters for the BBE which had to deploy sniper and assault teams to both Wijster and Amsterdam. The crisis lasted until 19 December when the Dutch government promised to start a dialogue with Moluccan leaders in Holland. All the hostages in the consulate survived with the exception of one who died after attempting to escape by jumping out of a window.

Nearly two and a half years later, on 23 May 1977, a group of nine armed South Moluccans hijacked a train between the towns of Assen and Groningen in northern Holland, while another four occupied a nearby school at Bovensmilde. Fifty-one people were held hostage on the train and 110 inside the school, by the terrorists who, as police and troops surrounded the train, once again reiterated demands for independence from Indonesia for their homeland. They also demanded that several South Moluccans held in Dutch jails should be released and that an aircraft should be made available at Amsterdam's Schipol airport to fly them and the hijackers to a destination of their choice. Any doubts that the terrorists were serious in their demands were quickly dispelled when the train driver was shot and his body thrown from the train.

The siege lasted almost three weeks, during which negotiations were conducted between the terrorists, who released all but four of their hostages in the school as well as some of those on the train, and the Dutch authorities who were reluctant to use force to end the affair. During this time, the BBE deployed to a nearby Royal Netherlands Air Force base at Gilze Rijn where it rehearsed assaults on a train of the same type, and on the school. Meanwhile, members of the unit swam across a canal near the train's location and placed surveillance devices on and around the train which pinpointed the terrorists' positions and enabled the latter's conversations to be monitored. Further intelligence was gained by policemen who delivered food to the train. Forced to strip naked so that the terrorists could see they were unarmed, they nevertheless used their powers of observation to good effect. Additional information about the hijackers and their dispositions on the train was also obtained from hostages who were released, one of them a pregnant woman.

By 10 June, however, the situation aboard the train had deteriorated and it became apparent that the hostages were in growing danger from the terrorists who were becoming increasingly frustrated at the lack of response to their demands. The decision was taken to launch simultaneous assaults on the train and school and so, in the early hours of 11 June, the BBE assault teams moved to their start lines. At 4.35 a.m., as RNAF F-104 Starfighters swooped overhead, using their afterburners to distract and confuse the terrorists, BBE snipers opened fire as the assault teams placed frame-charges against the train doors and blew them open. In the ensuing assault, seven terrorists were killed and two surrendered.

Two hostages, who disobeyed the marines' shouted commands to lie down, were killed accidentally after standing up; a third was wounded by one of the terrorists. At the school at Bovensmilde, meanwhile, a BBE assault team stormed the building in armoured personnel carriers and captured all four terrorists, rescuing the four hostages unharmed.

On 13 March 1978, the South Moluccans once again made an appearance when three terrorists occupied a provincial government building in Assen and took sixty-nine people hostage in yet another attempt to gain independence for their homeland. At the same time, they demanded the release of a number of south Moluccans being held in prison in Holland. Shortly after seizing the building, the terrorists showed that they meant business by murdering one of the hostages and threatened to kill more. The BBE was deployed and shortly after its arrival, with negotiations having broken down, the decision was taken to carry out a hostage rescue operation. On 14 March, the marines of BBE MARNS stormed the building and killed all three terrorists; six hostages were hit by terrorist gunfire during the assault, one dying later in hospital.

As described in Chapter 1, Italy was one of those countries that suffered badly from terrorism during the 1970s, but it was not until 1978, in the aftermath of the kidnapping of Aldo Moro, that it formed specialist counter-terrorist units within its security forces. The first was the Nucleo Operativo Centrale di Sicurezza (NOCS), its members being nicknamed the 'Leatherheads' because of the leather helmets worn by them. Based on the island of Sardinia and trained and equipped along similar lines to units such as GSG–9 and GIGN, this police unit came to public attention in January 1982 when it took part in a combined US–Italian operation to locate and rescue Brigadier General James Dozier, the senior US Army officer kidnapped by terrorists of the Red Brigades in Verona in December 1981. A full account of the operation appears in Chapter 9.

The other counter-terrorist unit formed in 1978 by Italy was the Gruppo di Intervento Speciale (GIS). Recruited from personnel of the Carabinieri's parachute battalion and numbering some 100 men in total, the new unit established itself at a base outside the town of Lavarno, north of Rome. As with all specialist units, selection standards and failure rates were high among those who volunteered for service with the GIS. In addition to the normal range of counterterrorist tactics and techniques, members of the GIS also underwent training as combat swimmers and mountaineers, ensuring that they were capable of conducting operations in those parts of Italy covered by mountain ranges or anywhere along the country's extensive coastlines. In October 1985, GIS combat swimmers were on standby to mount a hostage rescue operation on the *Achille Lauro*, the cruise liner hijacked by terrorists of Abu Abbas's Palestine Liberation Front, as described in Chapters 2 and 9. In the event, however, they were not deployed.

Italy is a major manufacturer of small arms and this was reflected in the choice of weaponry in both Italian counter-terrorist units. The standard 9mm submachine-gun was the Beretta M-12S, although variants of the H&K MP-5 were adopted later. Other weapons in the GIS armoury included the Beretta M-92 SB 9mm pistol and SC70/90 5.56mm assault rifle, Smith & Wesson .357 Magnum revolvers, H&K PSG1 and Mauser SP86 7.62mm x 51 sniper rifles, and Franchi SPAS 12 gauge shotguns.

Like Germany, France and Italy, Belgium established its counterterrorist unit from its national para-military police force, in this instance the Gendarmerie Royale. Formed in December 1972 under the command of Major Arsène Pint, the unit was originally designated 'Le Groupe Diane' and initially comprised only a small number of men, of whom some were former members of the Belgian Para-Commando Regiment, organised into six small mobile teams. In 1974, the unit was redesignated the Escadron Spécial d'Intervention (ESI) and by 1980 had expanded to a total of some 200 at which point it underwent re-organisation. Thereafter, commanded by a lieutenant colonel, it comprised a headquarters/ command element, an intervention platoon, a surveillance platoon and a logistics platoon. Volunteers for ESI, drawn from throughout the Gendarmerie Royale, were required to undergo a two-week selection course; those who passed received three months' training in requisite skills before joining their respective platoons.

In addition to counter-terrorist operations, however, ESI was also tasked with countering organised crime, drugs trafficking, kidnapping and other specialist duties such as providing escorts for dangerous prisoners. This inevitably resulted in the unit becoming overstretched and subsequently it was reorganised yet again into five units based at regional Gendarmerie Royale headquarters throughout Belgium.

European countries were not alone in forming counter-terrorist units; the Scandinavians followed suit, alarmed by the prospect of terrorist outrages within their respective territories. Finland was the first to do so, forming a small specialist police marksman unit designated ETY and comprising twelve officers who were on-call from their normal police duties. In 1975, a new 40-man unit was formed and trained fully in counter-terrorist and hostage rescue skills.

Denmark meanwhile established a 100-man counter-terrorist unit within its national police force. Formed in 1975 and designated Politiets Efterretningstjeneste (PET), it provided a police tactical response to terrorist threats. The counter-terrorist capability was subsequently enhanced by the formation of a specialist sub-unit within the Jagerkorpset, the Army's special forces unit. The MCM role was meanwhile allocated to the Frømandskorpsets, the Danish Navy's combat swimmer unit based at Kongsore.

In 1975 Norway formed the Beredskapstroppen, a specialist unit of the National Police. Unlike its counterparts in other countries, it was not a permanently formed entity; its members continued to perform their normal police duties while also carrying out training in the skills required of them as members of a counter-terrorist unit. Nevertheless, volunteers for the unit were required to undergo a rigorous selection course and, if successful, receive three months' training before joining it. Like Denmark, Norway allocated the MCM role to its naval special forces unit, the Marinejägerlag (MJL).

Despite the high level of terrorist activity on the part of the Basque separatists of ETA from the early 1970s onwards, it was not until

1978 that specialist counter-terrorist units were established in Spain. The Grupo Especial de Operaciones (GEO) of the Policia Nacional was formed with the assistance of GSG–9, its initial strength totalling some sixty men, but subsequently being increased to approximately 120. Organisation was similar to that of GSG–9, whose strong influence could be seen in the training and equipping of the unit, being based on the five-man assault team of which there were twenty-four in the unit. Weapons adopted by the GEO included: the H&K P9S 9mm pistol; different variants of the MP-5 submachine-gun; the G3SG/1, Mauser 66 and SIG-Sauer 2000 7.62mm sniper rifles; H&K HK33 5.56mm assault rifle; and both the Franchi SPAS 12 and Remington 870 gauge shotguns. The unit also acquired a large number of vehicles, including armoured personnel carriers, and could call on helicopters of the Policia Nacional.

From the very start, training in the GEO was rigorous and continues to be so today. After passing a tough selection course, during which they were tested for mental as well as physical aptitude, volunteers underwent training in a wide range of skills, including: marksmanship, swimming, climbing, abseiling, demolition, close-quarter battle skills, helicopter insertion techniques and high-speed driving. A considerable percentage of the members of the unit were, and continue to be, trained combat swimmers who form a section responsible for the conduct of MCM operations, and parachutists who are qualified in both static-line and HALO skills.

As has been described earlier in Chapter 2, Spain was suffering from a high level of terrorism during the early 1980s and the terrorist groups on both sides of the political spectrum resorted to robbery to fill their coffers. In some areas, their tactics were copied by other criminal elements. In May 1981, in Barcelona, a 27-man armed gang occupied the Banco Central de Barcelona and took 200 hostages. A siege developed and the GEO was called in to prepare for a hostage rescue operation, surrounding the building and reconnoitring possible routes and methods of entry, including explosive entry via the sewers under the building, while negotiators attempted to persuade the gunmen to surrender.

When all efforts to produce a peaceful solution failed, the unit was given the order to storm the building. During the assault, only one hostage was wounded while one member of the gang was killed and ten captured; the remainder succeeded in slipping away among the hostages as the latter were evacuated from the building. It was initially suspected that the terrorist group GRAPO was responsible for the raid, but it later transpired that the gang were criminals and the entire affair had been masterminded by a well-known local villain, J. J. Martínez Gómez, known as 'El Rubio'.

Kidnapping and extortion were also practised by ETA and one of its earlier victims was Dr. Julio Iglesias Puga, the father of the singer Julio Iglesias, who was kidnapped in 1982. He was incarcerated in a house in Trasmoz, a village in the Basque region of Spain, while a ransom was demanded for his release. Intelligence eventually reached the police that ETA was holding an unidentified hostage in Trasmoz, guarded by two or three terrorists. Further information pinpointed the building which, surrounded by a stone wall, lay on the outskirts of the village. Shortly afterwards, a close reconnaissance was carried out by the commander of the GEO, Major Carlos Holgado, accompanied by a female police officer. In plain clothes and posing as a courting couple, Holgado and his companion succeeded in examining the locked heavy wooden doors in the wall and in observing the surrounding area.

In the early hours of the following morning, a 30-strong GEO detachment arrived at Trasmoz and a twelve-man assault team took up its position by the doors in the wall as snipers and cut-off groups did likewise around the building. A frame charge of linear cutting explosive was placed in position and a few seconds later the doors were blown. The assault group stormed into the house and succeeded in capturing all three terrorists, two men and a woman, still in their beds. Dr. Iglesias was found locked in a bedroom, but unharmed.

The 1980s saw the GEO deployed on a large number of operations against left- and right-wing terrorist groups in Spain. 1982 also saw another hostage rescue operation carried out by the unit, this time at the Banco de Vizcaya in Bilbao in 1982. Five years later, in 1987, it conducted another in Barcelona, at the Banco de Sabadell. Like its French and Dutch counterparts, the GEO was also called upon to help with riots in prisons. On two occasions, during 1983 and 1985, the unit rescued staff at Carabnachel Prison under threat from rioting inmates and carried out a similar operation in 1986 at Basauri prison.

The Spanish also formed two other counter-terrorist units, both within the Guardia Civil, the para-military force which, like the Gendarmerie Nationale in France, comes under the Ministry of Defence and is responsible for law enforcement in rural areas. The first of these, the Unidad Especial de Intervencion (UEI), was formed in 1978 with assistance from GIGN, being organised into a headquarters/command element with eight assault teams and intelligence, communications and logistics sections.

The UEI's role was, and continues to be, the conduct of counter-terrorist operations in the more remote areas throughout Spain. This was reflected in the training of UEI personnel which, in addition to the full range of skills required in a counter-terrorist unit, also featured a curriculum more associated with military special forces than para-military police, instruction being provided by the special forces units of the Spanish Army and Navy. Volunteers for the UEI had to have served for a minimum period of five years with the Guardia Civil before applying for selection. The failure rate was and still is high, with only a very small percentage of volunteers succeeding in joining the unit.

The unit's role included provision of support for the Guardia Civil's other counter-terrorist unit, the Grupos Antiterroristas Rurales (GAR). Commanded by a lieutenant colonel and of approximately battalion size, totalling some 600 in strength, the GAR was tasked with patrolling the remote areas of Spain, calling on the UEI for tactical support when dealing with major terrorist incidents.

Neighbouring Portugal meanwhile had established the Grupo de Operaçoes Especials (GOE) in December 1979 as part of the Policia de Seguranca Publica, although it did not come into existence until 1982. The nucleus was provided by former members of the Marine Corps' special warfare unit, the Special Missions Detachment, recruited into the police. April 1982 saw the first selection course conducted for the new unit; the failure rate was high, with only 10 per cent passing the rigorous physical and psychological tests to which volunteers were selected and the twelve months of gruelling training which followed thereafter.

By 1983 the unit comprised some 150 personnel, a number of whom had undergone training in the United Kingdom with 22 SAS, and that year saw the GOE deployed for the first time. On 27 July six members of the Armenian terrorist group ASALA attacked the Turkish embassy in Lisbon. Having failed to gain entrance to the embassy's chancery building after coming under fire from armed security personnel, who killed one of their number, they retreated to the ambassador's residence where they took a number of hostages. The GOE arrived at the scene shortly afterwards and, having surrounded the building, took up its positions while negotiators tried to persuade the terrorists to surrender. When it became apparent that a peaceful outcome to the siege was unlikely, the unit prepared to carry out an assault. At this point, however, a massive explosion rocked the building, apparently caused by one of the terrorists accidentally initiating an explosive charge while setting up a booby-trap switch on the doors at the residence's main entrance. All five terrorists were killed, together with a Turkish diplomat and his wife.

Like Great Britain, Israel gave the counter-terrorist role to its premier Army special forces unit, in this case the Sayeret Matkal (General Staff Reconnaissance Unit) which was formed in 1957 by Major Avraham Arnan. Modelled on Britain's SAS and commanded initially by Lieutenant Meir Har-Zion, its role was long-range deep penetration reconnaissance and intelligence-gathering. Among those recruited for the new unit were former members of Unit 101, a short-lived commando unit formed in the early 1950s.

Reporting directly to the Army's Chief of Staff and known familiarly as 'the Unit', Sayeret Matkal consists of both regular soldiers and reservists, the latter completing a minimum of sixty days' service per annum. It recruits from volunteers from other units of the Israeli Army, notably the parachute units. During the selection and basic training course, which lasts for more than a year, recruits have to master a wide range of small arms and support weapons, both Israeli and foreign, as well as becoming expert in close-quarter battle skills, explosives, radio communications equipment and surveillance systems of different types. They also become expert in navigation, map-reading, the interpretation of aerial photographs, and in camouflage and concealment. The final phase of training is a navigation exercise during which recruits march more than 100 miles, followed by a night-firing exercise.

The first hostage rescue operation known to have been carried out by Sayeret Matkal took place on 9 May 1972 when an aircraft of the Belgian airline Sabena, Flight No. 517, carrying ninety passengers from Brussels to Tel Aviv, was hijacked by four armed terrorists of Black September, two men and two women. The aircraft was forced to fly to Lod airport where it landed, the terrorists subsequently demanding the release of 371 Arab prisoners being held in Israeli jails or the aircraft would be blown up. Negotiations were conducted by officials of the Red Cross and lasted for twenty hours. These were brought to an abrupt halt when a Sayeret Matkal team, led by the unit's commanding officer, Lieutenant Colonel Ehud Barak, and disguised as airline maintenance personnel, stormed the plane, killing the two male terrorists and capturing their two female accomplices. An officer named Lieutenant Benjamin Netanyahu, later to become the leader of the Likud party and prime minister of Israel, was wounded during the assault. Interestingly, Ehud Barak would later become Army Chief of Staff, leader of the Labour party and successor to Netanyahu as Prime Minister.

As described in Chapter 1, on 5 September 1972 Black September terrorists kidnapped eleven Israeli athletes during the Olympic Games in Munich. The Sayeret Matkal was put on standby to fly to West Germany, but the Israeli offer of assistance was turned down. The incompetence of the West German security forces in mishandling the affair and its tragic consequence has already been described. There is no doubt that the outcome would have been very different if it had been the Unit which had carried out the operation to rescue the athletes.

In February 1973 approval was given for a raid, code-named Operation Spring of Youth, on senior elements of Black September living in Beirut, to be carried out as part of the reprisals for the massacre of the Israeli athletes at Munich. Specific targets were identified as: Black September leader Mohammed Najar, alias Abu Yusuf; Kamal Adouan, the Palestine Liberation Organisation's (PLO) chief of operations; and Kamal Nasser, the PLO's spokesman in Beirut. Detailed information on all three men had been made available to the Unit, including full details of the apartments where they lived in the Rue Verdun, in the A-Sir neighbourhood of Beirut.

On the night of 9 April 1973 a small team of the Unit, commanded by Lieutenant Colonel Barak, was transported in Israeli Navy patrol craft to a point off the Lebanese coast from where it was taken inshore in inflatable assault craft of the Israeli Navy's special forces unit, Shayetet 13. On landing, it made its rendezvous with Mossad agents who were waiting with cars. Dividing into three groups, the team drove into Beirut.

On reaching the Rue Verdun the team, some of whom were disguised as women, spotted a team of three bodyguards, members of the PLO's Force 17 unit, sitting in parked cars. Once these had been swiftly despatched with silenced .22 pistols, Lieutenant Colonel Barak and two other members of his group remained in the street while the remainder made their way to the apartment blocks where the three terrorists lived. One group, commanded by Captain Muki Betser and accompanied by the Unit's second-in-command, Major Yonathan Netanyahu, stormed the apartment of Mohammed Najar, and shot him dead. Across the street, the rest of the team dealt with the second- and third-floor apartments of Kamal Adouan and Kamal Nasser, killing them both.

Meanwhile a force of paratroops, commanded by Lieutenant Colonel Amnon Shahak, attacked the six-storey headquarters of George Habash's PFLP in the southern part of the city; this did not prove to be such an easy task because the building was heavily guarded. A fierce battle ensued, in which two Israelis were killed and two wounded, but after some thirty minutes the building was blown up, incurring heavy casualties among its defenders. A third force, consisting of paratroops and members of Shayetet 13, meanwhile attacked and blew up PLO weapons factories and fuel dumps in the area of Tyre and Sidon. Their tasks completed, all three groups withdrew by road and returned to the coast where the evacuation beach had been secured by Shayetet 13. All were extracted safely to the patrol craft waiting for them offshore.

Another Sayeret Matkal counter-terrorist operation took place on the morning of Sunday 15 May 1974, Israel's Independence Day and a national holiday, after a group of three terrorists of the Democratic Front for the Liberation of Palestine (DFLP) had occupied a school at the town of Ma'alot which lies about ten kilometres from Israel's northern border with Lebanon. The terrorists had crossed into Israel two days earlier and had ambushed a van carrying Arab workers to work, killing two women and wounding the driver. They then headed for Ma'alot which they reached that night, shooting a man they met in the otherwise deserted streets before entering an apartment block. Forcing their way into an apartment, they killed a couple and their three-year-old child. The terrorists then went on to the school which was closed for the holiday, but unfortunately was occupied by some 100 children from the town of Safed who were staying overnight in Ma'alot. Some of the accompanying adults, together with fifteen of the children, succeeded in escaping by jumping from second-floor windows as the terrorists forced their way into the building.

By dawn on 15 May the school was surrounded by Israeli police and troops. The terrorists were demanding the release of twenty Arabs held in Israeli jails and that the ambassadors of France and Romania act as intermediaries on their behalf. Captain Muki Betser was the first member of Sayeret Matkal to reach the scene, followed almost immediately by an advance element of the Unit which arrived by helicopter. Using a loudspeaker, the negotiators were trying to buy time by telling the terrorists that their demands were being considered by the Israeli government. Meanwhile Lieutenant

Colonel Giora Zorea, who had assumed command of Sayaret Matkal from Lieutenant Colonel Ehud Barak in June of the previous year, and his officers were using the time to plan a hostage rescue while a decision was awaited from Prime Minister Golda Meir as to whether the government would agree to one or give in to the terrorists' demands.

There were differing opinions at senior level over whether or not a rescue operation should be mounted. Defence Minister Moshe Dayan, who was present at Ma'alot, objected strongly to any negotiations with the terrorists and advocated the mounting of a rescue; General Mordechai Gur, the recently appointed Army Chief of Staff, who was also on the scene, opposed any such operation as being too risky. Meanwhile, the negotiations continued, disrupted only by the killing of a soldier, home on leave in Ma'alot, who foolishly climbed a nearby water tower to get a better view and was shot dead by one of the terrorists.

Lieutenant Colonel Zorea and his men were ready. The Unit's snipers were in their positions, covering the school building from all sides, while the two assault teams waited on their start-lines. Just before 5 p.m. the government gave the order for the operation to proceed. Zorea issued the command over his radio and the snipers opened fire on the single terrorist visible on the porch of the entrance to the school. Although wounded, he managed to crawl back inside and warn his two accomplices. The two assault teams flung their ladders against the walls of the school and raced up them, one team climbing towards a window on the first floor while the other headed for another on the floor above. Firing and explosions broke out inside the building and panic-stricken children, some wounded by shrapnel, leaped from the windows of the building.

The leading man of the first assault team had reached the top of his ladder when one of the terrorists threw a grenade out of the window. The team was forced to jump clear to avoid the blast which wounded an elderly man who had appeared from some nearby woods to help the injured children. The troops headed immediately for the main entrance to the building and made for the second floor.

The second assault team, led by the Unit's second-in-command, Major Amiram Levine, had meanwhile unfortunately missed the second floor and reached the third before realising its error. While descending to the floor below, a member of the team ill-advisedly threw a smoke grenade to provide cover, filling the corridor with smoke and rendering visibility almost nil. Shortly afterwards, however, one of the terrorists appeared and was swiftly shot dead. A second suffered a similar fate almost immediately afterwards while attempting to detonate explosives which the terrorists had planted in the building.

When the first assault team reached the second floor, a scene of carnage confronted them. The terrorists had crowded all eighty-five children into one room and opened fire on them with their AK-47 assault rifles and grenades. Eighteen children had been killed immediately, three died later in hospital; fifty suffered wounds of varying severity while a few escaped without injury.

At this juncture Moshe Dayan, General Mordechai Gur and Lieutenant General Rafael Eitan, the commander of the Israeli Army's Northern Command in whose area Ma'alot lay, arrived on the scene as medical personnel moved in to evacuate the dead and wounded children. As they did so, a Sayeret Matkal officer spotted the third terrorist who, dressed in Israeli Army uniform, had taken cover among the bodies of the dead children. As the terrorist stood up, he aimed his AK-47 at Moshe Dayan and General Eitan, but was immediately shot dead by Captain Muki Betser.

The aftermath of the Ma'alot massacre saw Golda Meir and Moshe Dayan exonerated of any blame, but such was the level of public anger and political backlash that both left office shortly afterwards. Criticism was, however, levelled at the Sayeret Matkal which was ordered to devote more effort and resources to the conduct of counter-terrorist rescue operations in particular, its establishment being increased by a further forty men to enable it to do so. Together with the Navy's commando unit Shayetet 13, it was also directed to form a special team for the conduct of counter-terrorist and hostage rescue operations outside Israel; this was subsequently designated Unit 269. Its naval counterpart, called D4, would be responsible for MCM operations outside Israel's territorial waters.

The decision was also taken to develop additional military counter-terrorist capabilities within other Israeli special forces Sayeret units within the Northern, Central and Southern Commands into which Israel was divided. In addition, the National Police Border Guard intervention unit, the Yechida Mishtartit Meyuchedet, more familiarly known by the abbreviation Ya'ma'am, was to assume the role of conducting counter-terrorist and hostage rescue operations inside Israel.

A few weeks after the Ma'alot incident, Sayeret Matkal, which was then still the only unit with any form of counter-terrorist or hostage rescue capability, was called upon again to carry out a hostage rescue operation. Two terrorists had forced their way into an apartment in the town of Bet Shean, in the north of Israel, only some eight kilometres from the border with Jordan, and were believed to be holding an elderly couple hostage.

By the time the leading elements of the Unit arrived, Lieutenant General Rafael Eitan had established his tactical headquarters behind some buildings across the street from the apartment occupied by the terrorists. Lieutenant Colonel Giora Zorea and Captain Muki Betser carried out a close target reconnaissance, using a ladder to enter the apartment next to that occupied by the terrorists and listen to them talking.

The main body of the Unit arrived under the second-in-command, Major Nehemia Tamari, and shortly afterwards he, Captain Betser and six soldiers attacked the apartment, blasting in the front door with a burst of fire and killing one of the terrorists before he could move. The other dashed into an adjoining room but was killed by a grenade tossed after him. As they entered the room, however, the assault team discovered the bodies of the two elderly hostages who had apparently been killed by the terrorists shortly after they had occupied the apartment.

The next two years saw much further development in Israel counter-terrorist capabilities with considerable resources being allocated to them. The first opportunity for Unit 269 to carry out its new role came in 1976 during an operation which would signal to terrorists that they could no longer operate with impunity and that Israel would go to any lengths to protect its nationals throughout the world. On Sunday 27 June, an Air France A-300B Airbus, bound for Paris from Tel Aviv, was hijacked by four terrorists: two were members of the Red Army Faction, their two accomplices belonged to Wadi Haddad's PFLP–SOG. The pilot of the aircraft, which was carrying 256 passengers and twelve crew, was forced to fly to Uganda where it landed at Entebbe airport. During the next two days, 152 passengers were released and were flown to Paris; the remaining eighty-three, of whom the majority were Jews, were held hostage at the airport by the terrorists, who were joined there by six accomplices, and troops of the Ugandan Army. Israel subsequently mounted a rescue operation, code-named Operation Thunderball, a detailed account of which is given in Chapter 6.

By 1980, those elements of Israeli units tasked with the counter-terrorist and hostage rescue role were fully operational. On 6 April of that year Unit 269, reinforced by elements of the Golani Brigade's reconnaissance unit, carried out a hostage rescue operation at a kibbutz in northern Israel after it had been attacked by terrorists of the Arab Liberation Front who took twenty school children hostage and barricaded themselves inside the kibbutz's nursery building. All the terrorists died in the assault, but not before they had killed two of the hostages, a member of the kibbutz and a two-year old girl, and a soldier in the Golani Brigade unit.

Despite the fact that its role was the conduct of counter-terrorist operations inside Israel, 1982 found Ya'ma'am deployed in southern Lebanon where it acted in support of National Police Border Guard units and operated alongside elements of Shin Bet, the Israeli military intelligence service. Among its operations were the capture of a large number of notorious Palestinian terrorists.

Four years later, on 12 April 1984, a bus en route from Tel Aviv to Ashdod was hijacked by three terrorists, but was stopped by police just short of the Gaza Strip and a siege developed. Ya'ma'am arrived on the scene, but for some unexplained reason the decision to use Sayeret Matkal instead was taken by the commander of Southern Command. The Unit stormed the vehicle in the early hours of 13 April, killing one terrorist and capturing the other two. One hostage, an off-duty female soldier, also died in the assault.

In 1985, a specialist training establishment, designated Unit 707, was formed at the Army's Mitkan Adam base and thereafter counter-terrorist training of Army units was carried out on a centralised basis, all tactics and techniques being standardised throughout.

In 1988 Ya'ma'am was in action again after three heavily armed members of the PLO's Force 17 crossed the border from Egypt into Israel during the early morning of 7 March and hijacked a car carrying four Israeli Army officers through the Negev desert in the south of Israel. The alarm was raised after the four Israelis succeeded in escaping and local police and Army units in the area set off in pursuit of the terrorists speeding through the desert. After successfully avoiding a roadblock, and with Israeli police still hot on their heels, the terrorists hijacked a bus, taking eight women and a man hostage. Police and troops arrived almost immediately afterwards and took up positions surrounding the vehicle at a distance.

Unit 269 arrived first, followed by Ya'ma'am and a score of senior Israeli officers. Efforts by negotiators to establish a dialogue with the terrorists proved fruitless, the latter constantly firing bursts from automatic weapons at the surrounding troops while shouting demands for the release of Palestinians held in Israeli prisons and a safe conduct out of Israel. Frustrated at the lack of response, the three Arabs turned their guns on the hostages, shooting one of them dead. The Ya'ma'am assault team took up its assault positions and fifteen minutes later, after more firing had been heard from inside the bus, stormed the vehicle, killing all three terrorists, but not before the latter had killed two more hostages.

A month later, Sayeret Matkal avenged these deaths. On 16 April 1988, it took part in a joint operation with Mossad in the assassination of Khalil Wazzir (alias Abu Jihad), who had replaced Abu Yusef as second-in command of the PLO and commander of its military wing, at his home in Tunisia.

A year earlier, the Israeli Army had formed another specialist counter-terrorist unit, the Mista'arvim, with the role of operating undercover and gathering intelligence within the West Bank area, recruits being sought from volunteers from the Parachute Brigade. This first Mista'arvim unit was code-named 'Cherry'; a second, formed a year later, was designated 'Samson'. The emphasis on training for members of the Mista'arvim was on close target reconnaissance, covert intelligence gathering and the ability to pass themselves off as Arabs. Recruits were required to become Palestinian in every aspect, immersing themselves in the Arabic language and culture. The lengthy training course also included marksmanship, CQB (close quarter battle) skills, unarmed combat, radio communications and combat medicine.

During the 1980s, operational deployment of Israeli counter-terrorist units was somewhat haphazard, being based on which was the nearest or on the degree of influence individual commanders had with senior officers at formation headquarters levels. In 1990 this problem was resolved with the introduction of a formalised system known as the T'zahavach Plan, which laid down individual unit roles and responsibilities inside Israel and on foreign soil.

The late 1970s saw Egypt form a specialist counter-terrorist unit in response to an increasing threat from extremists within the country as well as from Libyan-backed Middle Eastern terrorist groups. In 1977 a small unit was formed from volunteers from within the Egyptian Army's As-Saiqa special forces. Numbering no more than fifty all ranks in total, its early deployments were initially against terrorist training camps across the border with Libya.

The new unit did not, however, have long to wait before being required to carry out its first hostage rescue operation, despite the fact that it was not properly trained for such a task. On 18 February 1978 two PFLP terrorists in Nicosia, Cyprus, shot dead Yusuf Sebai, the editor of a leading Egyptian newspaper and close confidant of Egyptian president Anwar Sadat, in protest at the latter's recent peace mission to Jerusalem. They then took refuge in a hotel where they barricaded themselves in with thirty hostages. A siege developed with police surrounding the hotel and the two terrorists demanding transport to the airport and safe conduct out of Cyprus.

The Cypriot authorities eventually gave in to the terrorists' demands and provided a bus which took them and fifteen hostages to Nicosia airport where a Cyprus Airways DC-8 was waiting to fly them to a destination of their choice. The aircraft, carrying the terrorists and their hostages, took off but soon found that all airports in the Middle East were closed to it. Eventually, it was forced to return to Cyprus where it landed, remaining parked on the runway surrounded by police and units of the Cypriot National Guard.

President Sadat had meanwhile ordered As-Saiqa to despatch its counter-terrorist unit to carry out a hostage rescue operation. When informing the Cypriot government, the Egyptians stated, however, that a team of negotiators was en route and made no mention of a counter-terrorist unit. As-Saiqa flew from Cairo to Nicosia in an Antonov transport of the Egyptian Air Force and during the hour-long flight, a plan was cobbled together for storming the hijacked aircraft.

At Nicosia the Antonov taxied to a halt and the entire force, dressed in civilian clothes, deployed and began running towards the DC-8. The Cypriot National Guardsmen and police, assuming that these were more terrorists arriving to reinforce those aboard the hijacked aircraft, opened fire. The resulting battle lasted over an hour during which fifteen Egyptians were killed.

In November 1985 another, equally disastrous, hostage rescue was attempted by the Egyptians, this time carried out by a unit designated Force 777 which had been formed in 1978 as the successor to the original As-Saiqa unit and is reportedly still operational today.

On the evening of 23 November an Egyptair Boeing 737, flying from Athens to Cairo, was hijacked by four members of the Egyptian Liberation Organisation, a group believed to have the support of Abu Nidal, in retaliation for the imprisonment in Italy of four members of the Palestine Liberation Front who during the previous month had hijacked the Italian cruise liner *Achille Lauro*;

a full account of the hijacking appears in Chapter 9. Egypt was subsequently blamed for not having done more to protect them and the hijack of the aircraft was carried out as a reprisal.

As the terrorists tried to take over the aircraft, a brief firefight took place between them and two Egyptian skymarshals, both of whom were killed, during which the aircraft's fuselage was punctured. The pilot was forced to make an emergency landing at Luqa airport on the island of Malta where the aircraft was quickly surrounded by troops. Having released eleven women passengers and two female members of the crew, the terrorists demanded the release of the *Achille Lauro* hijackers and threatened to kill hostages every hour until the Maltese refuelled the aircraft.

When news reached Cairo of the hijacking, eighty members of Force 777 were despatched with the reluctant agreement of the Maltese government. Travelling in an Egyptian Air Force C-130 transport, they arrived at Luqa by which time the terrorists had shot five of their hostages, two Israelis and three Americans, and tipped their bodies out on to the tarmac. One of them, 23-year-old Israeli Nitzan Mendelson, died, but the others survived.

While Maltese negotiators attempted to reach a peaceful compromise with the hijackers, the Force 777 troops made little effort to use the time to carry out surveillance or to question the released hostages about the number of hijackers, their locations in the aircraft and their weapons. Eventually, when it became clear that the terrorists were not prepared to surrender and that there was a grave risk of more hostages being killed, the Maltese handed over to the commander of the unit who ordered his men to deploy.

At just before 9.15 p.m. on 24 November, the assault teams made their way to their start-lines and the unit's snipers moved into position. A six-man team took position under the belly of the aircraft while others climbed onto the wings. The team under the aircraft opened the cargo hatch and positioned an explosive charge to blow a hole through the floor. Unfortunately, however, the charge proved too powerful and blew six rows of seats off their mountings, killing nearly twenty passengers. At the same time, assault teams entered the aircraft from both wings and for some unknown reason started throwing smoke-grenades and firing at any visible target. The terrorists, who had been alerted by the sound of the cargo hatch opening, returned their fire and also threw grenades. While the battle raged, the rear of the aircraft was set ablaze and in the pandemonium fifty-seven hostages died: eight from grenade fragments, seven from gunshot wounds and the remainder from the effects of the fire. Three terrorists were killed, but the fourth, 22-year-old Omar Mohammed Ali Rezaq, survived.

Following the débâcle at Luqa, little was heard thereafter of Force 777 which was based near Cairo at the main Egyptian Army special forces base, together with a dedicated helicopter unit. Numbering some 250 all ranks, it was reported as having received training from a number of units, including GSG-9 and GIGN. Further reports also stated that it was involved in counter-terrorist operations against Islamic extremist groups inside Egypt.

Another country in the Middle East which had cause to form a counter-terrorist unit was Jordan which in 1970, as described in Chapter 1, found itself involved in a war against the PFLP which resulted in the Palestinians being driven out of the country. The Palestinians swore revenge and during the following year began reprisals against the Hashemite kingdom: on 28 November assassinating Prime Minister Wasfi al-Tal, subsequently attacking and wounding Ambassador Zeid Rifai in London during the following month.

The Jordanian Army's response was to form in the mid-1970s a special unit within its 101st Special Forces Battalion. On 26 March 1976 it was deployed for the first time in Amman when, on the morning of 26 March, four heavily armed members of the PFLP stormed the Intercontinental Hotel. They sprayed the hotel lobby with automatic fire and threw grenades, killing two members of the hotel staff and five guests, and wounding a large number of others. The counter-terrorist unit was rapidly deployed and a fierce battle took place which resulted in three of the terrorists being killed and the fourth captured, while the unit suffered two of its members killed.

As a result of this operation, the unit was reorganised and placed on a permanent footing. Numbering approximately 100 all ranks, it was divided into three assault teams, each comprising three assault groups and a sniper group. Volunteers were, and still are, recruited from within the Special Forces, being required to undergo a selection course, comprising physical and psychological tests, for entry into the unit. Training was initially provided by 22 SAS and followed the normal syllabus of subjects, including: marksmanship; CQB; hostage rescue operations in differing types of scenarios; and helicopter-borne operations to mention just a few. Weapons and equipment mirrored those found in the majority of other counter-terrorist units. During the early 1990s, the counter-terrorist unit was detached from the Special Forces and came under the direct command of the Ministry of Defence.

The late 1970s also saw the formation of a specialist counter-terrorist capability by India which faced a primarily internal threat of terrorism from separatist groups and extremist sects. Initially, the role was allocated to the Special Frontier Force (SFF), which was formed in November 1962 and based at Chakrata, 100 kilometres from the city of Dehra Dun in northern India. Numbering 12,000 men, the SFF was organised into six battalions recruited entirely from Tibetans exiled from their homeland by the Chinese. Raised by India's intelligence service, the Research & Analysis Wing (RAW), with help from the CIA, the SFF's original role was the conduct of unconventional warfare operations against China in the regions bordering both countries. In the early 1970s, however, after several unauthorised incursions into China had taken place, the SFF was prohibited from operating within ten kilometres of the Indo–Chinese border.

In the late 1970s, by which time relations between India and China had improved, the SFF's role was changed to that of counter-terrorism. In 1977 a specialist unit, known simply as the Special Group, was formed within the SFF, being comprised of 500 Indian Army troops and members of the SFF and coming under the direct command of the SFF Inspector-General. Shortly afterwards, however, the Tibetans were removed and returned to their previous units. With the exception of the Special Group, the SFF reverted to its former unconventional warfare role with three of its units being re-roled as special forces battalions, one being stationed with Indian Army units on the Siachen Glacier in the Karakoram Range in Kashmir, near the Indo-Pakistani border. The other three were reorganised and retrained as unconventional warfare units for operations inside China.

On 25 May 1984, 100,000 Indian troops were deployed to the Punjab which had seen weeks of violence caused by militant Sikh separatists, led by Jarnail Singh Bindranwale, demanding independence for their homeland of Khalistan. A number of murders had been committed, including that of Deputy Inspector General of Police A. S. Atwal. During this period, Bindranwale and his followers had increased their grip on the Punjab to such an extent that Prime Minister Indira Gandhi was forced to impose federal rule on the Punjab. When this failed, she was forced to adopt more drastic measures, sending in troops to impose martial law and clear the Golden Temple, in the city of Amritsar, where Bindranwale and his followers had established their headquarters. The temple itself had been heavily fortified and its defence organised by two retired Indian Army officers, Major General Shahbeg Singh and Narinder Singh Buller, who were among the leading advocates for the establishment of Khalistan, an independent Sikh homeland. Moreover, many of the separatists were former soldiers.

Fighting in Amritsar began on 1 June when police marksmen opened fire on Bindranwale who was observed sitting on the roof of part of the temple; they missed and some of his followers returned their fire. Fighting continued throughout the night, leaving eleven dead and twenty-five wounded.

The SFF Special Group was despatched to Amritsar for the attack on the Golden Temple, code-named Operation Blue Star, which began on 4 June when troops opened fire on the temple complex with machine-guns and mortars, engaging the separatists who returned fire. Fighting lasted five hours and at least 100 men were killed on both sides.

Next morning, tanks of the 16th Cavalry Regiment advanced on the temple while artillery blasted the tops off its two 18th-century towers. Meanwhile the Special Group was forcing an entry from the rear via a narrow alleyway; some of its teams succeeded in reaching the roof of the temple, but were driven back by heavy fire. Later in the morning, troops of the 1st Para Commando Battalion also launched an attack, but these too were driven back after suffering heavy casualties. Two companies of the 7th Battalion Garwhal Rifles then joined the battle and after heavy fighting succeeded in establishing themselves on the roof of the temple's library where they were subsequently joined by two companies of the 15th Battalion The Kumaon Regiment.

At midnight on 5/6 June, armour was used to smash a way into the main area of the temple complex, an armoured personnel carrier being knocked out by an anti-tank rocket in the process. Two troops of tanks then entered the temple, blasting the main building with their armament, their 105mm HESH (high explosive squash head) shells causing devastating damage. Meanwhile the temple's magnificent golden dome was being badly damaged by light artillery fire. By 1 a.m. on 6 June all resistance had been crushed, apart from sporadic sniper fire from the wreckage of buildings, and by 1 p.m. the Army was firmly in control.

The heavy fortifications of the temple and the defenders' well-sited positions had been principal factors in the attacking forces incurring heavy casualties and forcing them to resort to the use of armour and artillery. During the battle, Major Generals Shahbeg Singh and Narinder Singh Buller had directed the defence of the temple by radio; their bodies, and that of Bindranwale, were among those found in the temple afterwards.

As a counter-terrorist operation, Operation Blue Star was an unmitigated disaster. Official figures for casualties stated that eighty-three troops had been killed and 249 wounded, 493 separatists and civilians killed, and 592 separatists and eighty-six civilians wounded.

Other estimates state that these figures were grossly underestimated and that the actual numbers of those killed was in the region of 1,500 with thousands wounded.

Five months later, on 31 October, Prime Minister Indira Gandhi was assassinated by two of her Sikh bodyguards, Sub-Inspector Beant Singh and another police officer, Satwant Singh, in revenge for the attack on the Golden Temple for which she personally had given the order. Beant Singh was shot dead almost immediately afterwards by members of the Indian Border Police; Satwant Singh was wounded, but recovered to stand trial, subsequently being convicted and sentenced to death.

The SFF Special Group was discredited for its poor performance during Operation Blue Star. During the following year the counter-terrorist role was given to a new group specially formed for the purpose, the National Security Guard (NSG), popularly known as the 'Black Cats' because of the black assault suits worn by unit personnel. Numbering approximately 700 all ranks, the NSG was organised into two units: the Special Action Group (SAG), recruited primarily from the Army's airborne and special forces; and the Special Ranger Group (SRG), the latter being a 2,000-strong para-military unit whose members are drawn from Indian police and para-military forces. Training for the SAG was reportedly provided by 22 SAS and GSG–9.

On 30 April 1986 members of the NSG stormed the Golden Temple at Amritsar in an operation, code-named Black Thunder I, aimed at capturing Sikh separatists and their weapons, but nothing was found.

Two years later, on 12 May 1988, the unit was deployed once again on another operation in Amritsar, code-named Black Thunder II. On this occasion, in a repeat of events four years earlier, the Golden Temple had been occupied by Sikh separatists, once again demanding independence for their homeland, following several days of terrorism and violence in the Punjab which had resulted in the killing of a senior police officer. A total of 1,000 members of the NSG were involved in the operation. Members of the SRG surrounded the area of the temple while SAG snipers took up their positions.

On 15 May, the assault teams of the SAG began their assault, using machine-guns and rocket launchers to blow holes in the temple's towers and minarets from which the separatists were bringing fire to bear, following up with CS gas canisters which were fired through them. Once the towers had been cleared, the SAG used explosives to blow holes in the walls of the basement and gained entry to the temple. Fighting continued until 18 May by which time all resistance had been overcome. A large number of separatists were killed and wounded during the battle while NSG casualties totalled two wounded.

During the late 1980s, India also established an MCM capability. The role was given to the Indian Navy which in February 1987 formed its first special forces unit, the Indian Marine Special Force (IMSF) which first saw action only a few months later when it provided a detachment for beach reconnaissance tasks during the deployment of Indian peacekeeping forces in Sri Lanka in 1987.

In November 1988, members of the People's Liberation Organisation of Tamil Eelam (PLOTE) attempted a *coup d'état* in the Maldives. An operation was mounted by India to restore the former government and Indian troops were flown into the islands on 4 November. However, one group of the PLOTE rebels avoided capture and succeeded in escaping by ship with twenty-seven hostages, including the Maldivian minister of education. On the following day, Indian aircraft located the vessel and Indian Navy warships steamed to intercept it. On the morning of 6 May, a detachment of the IMSF boarded the vessel and took control without encountering any resistance.

At the end of the 1980s, the IMSF was renamed the Marine Commando Force (MCF) and reorganised into three groups stationed within the Indian Navy's Western, Southern and Eastern commands at Bombay, Cochin and Vizag respectively. Each group formed a Quick Reaction Section which was tasked with the MCM role, protecting India's offshore oil and gas installations. Aviation support was provided by Indian Navy Sea King helicopters.

All volunteers for the MCF were required to undergo a strict selection course of one month. Those who passed went on to complete nine months' training in weaponry, all aspects of naval special warfare and intelligence gathering. This was followed by operational reconnaissance training at the Combined Commando School at Sirsawa, followed by parachute and diving training. On completion of their nine months' training, the newly qualified MCF personnel joined one of the unit's three groups.

India's neighbour, Pakistan, established its counter-terrorist capability in the early 1970s by giving the role to the Army's special forces, the Special Service Group (SSG), which in turn converted its combat-swimmer company into a counter-terrorist unit. Training was provided by 22 SAS and other foreign units.

In 1981, the new unit received its baptism of fire when on 30 September five Sikh terrorists hijacked an Indian Airlines aircraft flying to Lahore. After the aircraft had landed, they threatened to blow it up unless the Indian government met their demands. The counter-terrorist company was deployed by helicopter from the SSG base at Cherat, in the mountains of the North West Frontier Province, and flown to Lahore. Hours later, when all attempts to negotiate a peaceful outcome had failed, an assault team dressed as airline employees approached the aircraft. Producing pistols from their overalls, they stormed the aircraft and, after a brief firefight, overpowered the hijackers and freed the hostages.

Three years later, the SSG counter-terrorist company was in action again. On 5 September 1986 four members of Abu Nidal, posing as Pakistani security officials, succeeded in bluffing their way on to a Pan Am Boeing 747, Flight 73 from Bombay to New York, on the ground at Karachi airport just after 358 passengers had boarded. Led by a terrorist using the alias of 'Abbas' and armed with assault rifles and grenades, they took control of the aircraft and shortly afterwards shot dead an Indian naturalised American named Kumar Jajish, pushing his body out on to the tarmac below.

As they did so, however, the flight crew succeeded in escaping from the cockpit via a rope, thus immobilising the aircraft

Troops surrounded the 747 and the Pakistani authorities established communication by radio with the hijackers who issued a series of demands, including the release of three terrorists imprisoned in Cyprus for the murder of three Israelis in 1985. Meanwhile, the SSG had been alerted and the counter-terrorist company was flown in immediately from Cherat, establishing its command post and communications links in a hangar where it rehearsed for an assault on a Pakistan International Airlines 747. Fifteen hours passed, during which the terrorists constantly reiterated their demands while threatening that hostages would be killed if they were not met.

Suddenly, the generator supplying power to the 747 failed and darkness filled the interior of the aircraft. Believing this heralded an assault, the terrorists panicked and started firing down the cabin. In the pandemonium, however, a stewardess, Neerja Bhanot, succeeded in opening the emergency doors and deploying the escape chutes, being shot dead almost immediately afterwards while shielding some children. Nineteen passengers died while the remainder, panic-stricken, threw themselves out in frantic efforts to escape the gunfire. Meanwhile, hearing the firing, the SSG troops sped in their vehicles from the hangar to the aircraft and immediately stormed it. Abbas, who was wounded, and his three accomplices were all arrested.

Recruitment for the counter-terrorist company is from throughout the SSG which comprises a brigade of three battalions plus specialist wings and a logistical support element. The base at Cherat is located in a barracks, originally constructed by the British during the days of the Raj, sited on a mountain top. Carved in the rock face above the SSG headquarters building are the cap badges of British regiments which served there until the creation of Pakistan in August 1947. The base is surrounded by extremely harsh terrain ideal for training in mountain warfare, one of the SSG's specialisations. Volunteers for the counter-terrorist company must have served a minimum of six months in the SSG before applying. Training and equipment mirrors that of other counter-terrorist units, weaponry including the H&K MP-5 9mm submachine-gun, PSG-1 7.62mm sniper rifle and Glock 9mm pistol. Training with units from other countries, including 22 SAS, is conducted on a relatively regular basis.

Given its isolated location surrounded by three oceans, Australia could perhaps be forgiven for believing that it would avoid the attentions of terrorist groups. In February 1978, however, any such misconceptions were shattered when a bomb exploded at Sydney's Hilton Hotel. This resulted in a six-month federal government study of counter-terrorist capabilities in other countries and in May 1979 the decision was taken to form a counter-terrorist unit. The Australians followed the British example and allocated the responsibility to the Army which gave the role to its Regular special forces unit, the Special Air Service Regiment (SASR).

Within the SASR, the task of training for the new role was given to Guerrilla Warfare Wing. Construction of special training facilities at the regiment's base at Campbell Barracks at Swanbourne, West Australia, was commenced later in the year and completed by March 1980. The counter-terrorist unit was designated the Tactical Assault Group (TAG) and consisted of a small headquarters, comprising the regiment's commanding officer, the operations officer, and two signallers; and an assault force consisting of a command element, three assault teams (each of three men) and a ten-man sniper team. The TAG was drawn from 1 Squadron which was reorganised, with B Troop becoming the TAG and commencing its training in March 1980, its commander and a senior NCO having undergone training with 22 SAS during the previous year. On becoming fully operational in May, it was designated Gauntlet 1. A Troop began its counter-terrorist training in September and was fully operational by November, being designated Gauntlet 2 and relieving Gauntlet 1.

In July, however, the SASR was given the additional commitment of providing a sub-unit for MCM operations to protect offshore oil and gas installations in Australia's Bass Strait. This resulted in the formation of the Offshore Assault Group (OAG), with assistance from the Royal Marines SBS who provided instructors. Also drawn from 1 Squadron and designated Nullah 1, it was operational by the end of October 1980. A second OAG, Nullah 2, subsequently commenced training and relieved Nullah 1 during 1981, by which time the OAG designation had been changed to Offshore Assault Team (OAT).

The counter-terrorist commitment was by now a major drain on manpower for the SASR which at that time only had two sabre squadrons, 1 and 3, as 2 Squadron had been disbanded in 1971 at the end of the SASR's involvement in operations in South Vietnam. Due to the pressure of being at a constant high state of readiness, TAG and OAT personnel had to be relieved after approximately one year, the point at which it was felt their effectiveness would deteriorate. This meant that for the TAG requirement alone during 1980, 1 Squadron had one troop operational with two others in training for the role. The added OAT manpower commitment caused further problems for the SASR and as an initial measure seventeen clearance divers of the Royal Australian Navy were seconded to the regiment, all having passed a selection course beforehand. Further measures were also taken to alleviate the manpower problem, including the introduction of non-SAS personnel to take over administrative and support posts within the regiment, thus freeing trained SAS soldiers for operational employment. The long-term solution, however, was the reformation of 2 Squadron which took place at the end of January 1981, but it was not until 1984 that it was fully up to strength.

During early 1983, further rationalisation took place. The entire SASR counter-terrorist force, comprising 1 Squadron, the Commanding Officer's command group and a signal troop, became the TAG. Gauntlet and Nullah were redesignated A and B troops respectively and the term OAT was discarded.

By 1987 there was sufficient counter-terrorist experience in the SASR for it to adopt the system whereby each sabre squadron was tasked in rotation with the counter-terrorist role for a period of one year, leaving the other two squadrons to concentrate on the regiment's war role. At the end of that year, 2 Squadron took over the counter-terrorist role from 1 Squadron. The late 1980s also saw a major enhancement of training facilities for the SASR, including an extensive CQB training complex and sniper range at Swanbourne, a special counter-terrorist CQB complex and sniper range at Bindoon, and an aircraft mock-up at Gin Gin airfield.

Training and equipment was initially along the same lines as that of 22 SAS which provided much assistance during the adoption of the counter-terrorist role by the SASR. The H&K MP-5 featured largely, together with the SIG-Sauer P228 9mm pistol and Beretta RS202 M1-M2 12 gauge shotgun. Sniper rifles used by the TAG included the H&K PSG-1 7.62mm and Tikka Finlander M55 .22/.250.

During the 1980s the TAG was placed on alert on at least three known occasions: in December 1982, after the bombing of the Israeli consulate in Sydney; in January 1983, after a threat to bomb aircraft of Trans Australia Airlines; and in August 1983, after intelligence reports indicated that Armenian extremists were planning terrorist operations in Australia.

Another SAS unit tasked with the counter-terrorist role is New Zealand's 1st NZSAS Group. Located at Papakura Military Base, it comprises a headquarters, two sabre squadrons, a training wing and logistical support element. Each of the sabre squadrons, comprising a headquarters and four sixteen-man troops, provides a counter-terrorist team on a rotational basis.

Hong Kong was also among those countries that recognised the need for an effective counter-terrorist capability and in 1974 formed a small team designated the Special Duties Unit (SDU). In 1978, assistance was provided by 22 SAS which sent a training team to the colony. Two teams were subsequently trained and the unit thereafter expanded to an eventual strength of more than 100 personnel. In 1982 an MCM capability was added, with the assistance of the Royal Marines SBS, through the addition of a team of combat swimmers.

SDU equipment reflected that used by 22 SAS, its choice of weapons including the ubiquitous MP-5 family of 9mm submachine-guns and the Browning Hi-Power 9mm pistol. Throughout the rest of the 1970s and 1980s, training was conducted with a number of overseas units, including the Australian SASR, GSG-9 and 22 SAS. In addition to its counter-terrorist role, the SDU was also deployed in operations against gangs of heavily armed criminals. Aviation support was provided by the Hong Kong Government Flying Service which was equipped with two Blackhawk helicopters. For MCM operations, the SDU's combat swimmer team could call on a special boat team equipped with six high-speed craft which also formed part of the unit.

The SDU was organised into a headquarters element, which also performed the role of intelligence cell, and the tactical group which comprised three teams: the assault team for operations on land; the sniper team and the combat swimmer team. In addition, there were specialist support elements: a medical section, comprising highly trained para-medics; a training section, responsible for the conduct of induction courses, continuation training and the operation of the unit's specialist training facilities; and the special boat team.

Indonesia's first experience of a major terrorist incident came during the early 1980s when it did not possess a specialist counter-terrorist unit. On 28 March 1981, a DC-9 airliner belonging to Garuda, the Indonesian national airline, was hijacked during a flight from the capital of Jakarta to the city of Medan, on the island of Sumatra, via Palembang. The hijackers had struck after the aircraft had left Palembang: while one made his way to the cockpit, the other stood in the aisle where he was joined by three others. All five were armed and were members of the Jihad Commando, a group of Muslim extremists who had been responsible for a number of attacks on police station and military bases, as well as acts of sabotage, during the previous four years.

The hijackers forced the pilot to fly the aircraft to Malaysia where it landed and refuelled; shortly afterwards, an elderly woman passenger having been released, it flew on to Don Muang airport in Thailand where it landed again. At this juncture the terrorists issued their demands: the release of fellow members of the Jihad Commando previously imprisoned by the Indonesian authorities, an aircraft to fly them to an undisclosed destination and US $1.5 million in cash. Failure to meet these demands would result in the aircraft being blown up.

In Indonesia, meanwhile, planning for a rescue operation, code-named Woyla, was under way. The task of carrying it out was given to KOPASSANDA, the acronym for Kommando Pasukan Sandi Yudha, a newly formed special forces unit which had undergone limited counter-terrorist training during the previous year. News of the hijack had reached Jakarta at midday on 28 March and that evening KOPASSANDA borrowed another DC-9 to plan and rehearse a hostage rescue assault.

Time was not on the Indonesians' side; there was concern that the hijacked aircraft would leave Thailand and fly on to the Middle East. Furthermore, because of the presence of American nationals aboard, the US Ambassador in Jakarta was pressurising the Indonesian authorities to take effective action as soon as possible. The Indonesian government thus approached their Thai counterparts, requesting that it be allowed to send a military force to Don Muang to carry out a hostage rescue operation if so required. The Thais were reluctant, preferring to negotiate a peaceful solution as they had previously in 1972 when Palestinian terrorists had occupied the Israeli embassy in Bangkok. Finally, however, they were persuaded on the basis that the hijacked aircraft was Indonesian, as were the majority of passengers and the terrorists themselves, and thus it was Indonesia's responsibility to resolve the crisis.

On 29 March a 35-strong detachment of KOPASSANDA, led by the unit's commanding officer, Lieutenant Colonel Sintong Panjaitan, flew to Don Muang in a C-130 transport of the Indonesian Air Force where they were met by the CIA's station chief of station in Thailand who handed over specialist equipment for use in an assault. By the early hours of 30 March it appeared that negotiations with the hijackers were not proving successful and at 2.30 a.m. the assault group silently approached the aircraft. Minutes later, Thai air force commandos moved into stop positions to prevent any of the terrorists from escaping during or after the assault.

The KOPASSANDA group was divided into four teams, each of which moved to its allocated positions: two teams climbed on to the aircraft's wings while two others positioned themselves by the front and rear doors respectively. At a pre-determined signal, all four teams would break into the aircraft and begin the assault.

At 2.43 a.m. the signal was given. The team at the rear door entered first, but encountered an alert terrorist who immediately opened fire, mortally wounding the leading soldier, Lieutenant Achmad Kirang, in the groin before turning his own weapon on himself and committing suicide. The teams on the wings entered through the emergency exits, killing two other terrorists as the passengers threw themselves flat. The fourth team, entering the aircraft by the forward door, shot a fourth terrorist in the head as they opened the door. The soldiers then shouted to the passengers to leave the aircraft; as they did so, one of the terrorists joined them and, having exited the aircraft, attempted to throw a grenade but was shot dead.

The entire action lasted three minutes during which three more terrorists were killed; according to one report, one was killed outside the aircraft. Unfortunately, the pilot was shot by a terrorist during the assault and died despite the best efforts of paramedics to save his life. All fifty-five hostages were rescued unharmed.

In the aftermath of Operation Woyla, a specialist counter-terrorist unit was formed. Designated Detachment 81, its first commanding officer was Lieutenant Colonel Prabowo Subianto who had undergone training with GSG–9. Under the direct command of the Special Forces, whose name was subsequently changed from KOPASSANDA to KOPASSUS (Kommando Pasukan Khusus – Special Forces Commando), Detachment 81 numbered 300 all ranks and was modelled on the lines of GSG–9 and other such units. Weapons and equipment, purchased from the United Kingdom, were identical to those used by 22 SAS who provided training, as did GSG–9. As far as is known, Detachment

81 was not deployed on any counter-terrorist operations during the 1980s, but was deployed on intelligence gathering and counter-insurgency operations in East Timor and elsewhere in the Indonesian archipelago.

In 1985, KOPASSUS formed a combat swimmer unit within Detachment 81 and tasked it with the MCM role. At the same time, the Indonesian Navy formed Detachment Jala Mangkra, a unit comprising members of the Navy's combat swimmer unit and others from the Indonesian Marine Corps. Its primary role was, and continues to be, MCM, but during the 1980s it did not see operational deployment in that role. Like Detachment 81, it was deployed on intelligence gathering and counter-insurgency operations.

5

THE UNDERCOVER WAR – PART I

By the early 1970s, the conflict in Northern Ireland had become what has been described aptly as a 'dirty war'. The violent activities of the plethora of republican and loyalist factions and terrorist groups was such that in certain parts of the province the RUC was hard pressed to maintain a semblance of law and order. Moreover, the war against the terrorists was being fought by a number of different forces. In addition to the RUC and its Special Branch, the Secret Intelligence Service (SIS), the Security Service, popularly known as MI5, and the Army's military intelligence organisation were also active. Each jealously guarded its own 'turf' and on occasions indulged in underhand tactics to ensure that others did not encroach on to it. It can truly be said that the early 1970s were the dark years of the conflict in Northern Ireland: in 1971 more than 5,000 Catholics and 2,000 Protestants were burned out of their homes, and in 1972 alone there were more than 10,000 shooting incidents.

During that period, the Army generally held the RUC in low regard as a discredited force and was thus reluctant to share intelligence with it. This view was reinforced in 1971 with the arrival of the policy of internment without trial, and the wholesale incarceration of 1,571 suspects. These arrests were, however, based on poor intelligence from the RUC and of the 342 individuals arrested within the first twenty-four hours, 115 were released after two days. Furthermore, in the wake of the 1969 riots and following the Hunt Report published in 1970, the RUC had been restructured and its role changed to one of non-retaliation. Primacy for law and order in the nationalist areas had been handed over to the Army and it would be another five years before the RUC regained it.

The Army, deciding that it could only rely on its own resources, set about creating its own intelligence-gathering apparatus in the province. One of the first elements put in place was the Mobile

Reconnaissance Force (MRF) which was created at the beginning of 1971 by Brigadier Frank Kitson, the commander of 39 Infantry Brigade and a veteran of operations against the Mau Mau in Kenya, Communist terrorists in Malaya during the Emergency and EOKA in Cyprus. Kitson, whose brigade was responsible for the city of Belfast and the eastern part of the province, was an old hand at playing terrorists at their own game and he formed a unit which would operate undercover to locate and identify them.

Members of the MRF were recruited from units throughout the British Army and included members of the Royal Marines Special Boat Squadron (SBS). Training in surveillance techniques, weapons and tactics was provided by a team from 22 SAS which was flown in from Hereford to the MRF base at Palace Barracks, Holywood. Operating in four-man groups, normally comprising an officer, a senior NCO and two soldiers, the members of the unit wore plain clothes and used unmarked cars. Their principal role was surveillance and intelligence gathering, including the photographing of known terrorists and suspects, and the establishment of clandestine observation posts in deserted buildings. An MRF team would move into a house or shop at night and set up its surveillance equipment which included night observation devices and audio surveillance equipment; it would remain there for the required length of time, subsequently leaving under cover of darkness with no trace of its presence left behind.

The MRF copied a technique used by Brigadier Kitson during his service as a district intelligence officer in Kenya and by the Special Branch in Malaya during the Emergency: the use of former terrorists as informers. The unit ran about a dozen of them. Known as 'Freds', they were former members of nationalist and loyalist terrorist groups who had been 'turned'. In many instances, they were coerced into co-operating, being told that unless they did so there was sufficient information for them to be prosecuted and convicted of terrorist offences for which they would receive lengthy prison sentences. Handled by a special section within the unit, the 'Freds' were used to identify members of the IRA and the locations of safe houses and other areas of interest to their handlers with whom they toured the streets in cars or armoured personnel carriers; those whom they pointed out were photographed and files were opened on them.

One MRF operation which proved highly successful involved the running of the Gemini Health Studio massage parlour at 397 Antrim Road in Belfast, close to the Catholic and nationalist areas of the city. Providing a full range of services for clients, its rooms were wired up for bugging and linked to audio surveillance equipment installed in the flat above and operated by a retired Army major and an officer in the Women's Royal Army Corps (WRAC). The venture was apparently highly successful in that a considerable amount of useful information was elicited from some of the parlour's clients. One of them, Paddy Wilson, a leading figure in the nationalist community, was in the habit of visiting the parlour after his visits to a nearby bar and on one occasion felt sufficiently relaxed to divulge the names of three members of the Provisional IRA, all from the Ardoyne area, who on the night of 11 March 1971 had murdered three members of the 1st Battalion Royal Highland Fusiliers based at Girdwood Barracks on the Antrim Road. The three soldiers had been lured from a bar in the Cornmarket area of the city after being invited to a party by three men and two women, all of whom were Provisionals: the men were members of the 3rd Battalion PIRA while the women belonged to Cumann na mBann, the female branch of the Provisional IRA. After being driven out of the city, the three soldiers had been shot dead on the Hightown Road. In October 1972, however, the massage parlour operation was 'blown' as the result of another of the MRF's operations, hitherto highly successful, being uncovered by the Provisional IRA.

During the early 1970s, laundry vans were a familiar sight on the housing estates in the nationalist stronghold of Andersonstown in West Belfast. One of these belonged to the Four Square Laundry and was crewed by a young Belfast couple known to the local people as Ted and Sarah. In fact, both were members of the MRF: 'Ted' was Sapper Ted Stuart of the Royal Engineers and 'Sarah' Lance

Corporal Sarah Warke, a member of the WRAC who prior to joining the MRF had been serving with a Royal Military Police unit.

On 2 October, at 11.20 a.m., the Four Square Laundry van appeared in Juniper Park on the Twinbrook housing estate in Andersonstown. As Lance Corporal Warke collected a bag of washing from a mother of two at No. 8, Sapper Stuart watched her from his position in the driver's seat of the vehicle which was parked only a few yards away. As she was filling in the necessary forms, two gunmen suddenly appeared on the driver's side of the vehicle and opened fire at close range with automatic weapons. The vehicle was hit by sixteen bullets and Stuart was mortally wounded. Lance Corporal Warke reacted swiftly, diving through the front door of No. 8 and dragging the mother and her two children with her. Fortunately, the two gunmen ignored her and fled in haste. Having waited in the house for a few minutes, she left by the back door and eventually made her way to the MRF base at Holywood. Meanwhile, some of the local inhabitants had arrived on the scene and two of them, accompanied by a local priest, on seeing that Sapper Stuart was still alive, drove the van to Lisburn police station. Unfortunately, he died before they reached it.

At about the same time as the attack on the van was in progress, two others were being carried out elsewhere. Three Provisionals approached 397 Antrim Road, but mistakenly entered the building next door and made their way to the first floor. It later transpired that they were unaware of MRF's massage parlour operation next door and were looking for the offices of the Four Square Laundry. As they went upstairs, they respectively produced a Thompson submachine-gun, an M-1 .30 carbine and a Colt .45 pistol. However, the man with the Thompson tripped and accidentally fired his weapon, wounding himself, whereupon the three panicked and fled, all thoughts of their mission forgotten. Shortly afterwards, at 15 College Square East near the centre of Belfast, gunmen opened fire on offices which the Provisionals had reason to believe were being used by the MRF.

Forty-eight hours later, the Provisional IRA claimed responsibility for all three attacks, stating that it had killed five British agents belonging to a special Army intelligence unit which had used offices in Belfast and had operated the laundry service. The statement about MRF casualties was of course totally untrue and was based on exaggerated claims made by the Provisionals' 3rd Battalion, reportedly commanded by Brendan 'Darkie' Hughes, which had carried out the attack on the van and the aborted one on the Gemini Health Studio, and by the 2nd Battalion which had attacked the office at 15 College Square East. The terrorists' error at 397 Antrim Road had provided a warning to the two members of the MRF in the flat above the parlour which was vacated in haste and subsequently stripped of its contents after the area had been cordoned off by troops almost immediately afterwards. Furthermore, the offices at 15 College Square had been deserted at the time of the attack on them.

Unfortunately, however, the MRF and two of its most successful intelligence-gathering operations had been 'blown' and it subsequently transpired that one of its 'Freds' was responsible. During the summer of 1972, the intelligence officer of D Company of the 2nd Battalion PIRA, which operated in the Lower Falls area in Belfast, became suspicious of one of its members, Seamus Wright, and had reported his suspicions to his unit commander who ordered that a watch be kept on him.

During the first week of February, Wright had been arrested and taken to the MRF base at Palace Barracks, Holywood, where, threatened with evidence of his involvement in a bombing, he had been coerced into becoming a 'Fred'. Thereafter he had travelled in the company of an MRF 'minder' to the British mainland from where he contacted his wife, telling her that he had escaped and was in hiding. Shortly afterwards, his wife travelled to Birmingham where she met him in the company of his 'minder'; he told her that he would be returning to Belfast and would be released within a few days. In fact, he did not return home until the end of March; during that time he was at Palace Barracks being taught the skills required of a 'Fred'.

On returning home Wright notified the commander of his Provisional unit, explaining that he had been arrested and detained. He also told him that he had been interrogated and had eventually been forced to reveal details of other members of his unit. The intelligence officer of his unit had not been convinced, however, and it had been decided to keep him under surveillance.

A few weeks later, however, Wright disappeared again and this time the Provisionals decided to question him further. When he returned to Belfast, he was taken to a house near his home and was subjected to forty-eight hours of interrogation. Realising that he was likely to be executed, he quickly cracked and confessed to being an informer. He also revealed the circumstances of his arrest, being accused of involvement in a bombing which had resulted in the death of a member of the security forces, and subsequent questioning at an interrogation centre at Castlereagh, where an offer had been made to drop all charges against him in exchange for his agreeing to co-operate with the security forces. His revelations about MRF and the existence of the other 'Freds', whose identities were unknown to him, were of the utmost importance to his interrogators; they realised that this was the most serious threat they had yet faced from the security forces.

Under normal circumstances, Wright would have been summarily executed. He was fully aware of this and thus offered to become a double agent, knowing that the Provisionals needed to learn more about MRF and its 'Freds' operation before they could take effective countermeasures. The latter also realised this and agreed to his proposal while also making clear what would befall him if he betrayed them again.

During August and the first half of September, the Provisionals fed information to Wright who passed it on to his MRF handlers. This helped to maintain his credibility with them and thus facilitated his task of learning more about the unit and its operations. It was during this period that he acquired details of the Four Square Laundry operation and discovered the identity of another 'Fred', a fellow Provisional named Kevin McKee, who was abducted by the Provisionals a few days later. McKee broke after two days of interrogation, eventually giving full details of the Four Square Laundry operation after being confronted with Wright who was also being held by then. He revealed that the collected washing was tested forensically for evidence of contact with firearms and explosives, while the van which toured the housing estates was a special vehicle equipped with a secret compartment in the roof designed to accommodate two MRF personnel equipped with cameras and a radio.

Four days later, the whole affair was referred to the commander of the 2nd Battalion PIRA who in turn passed it to the command of the Provisionals' Belfast Brigade. The decision was taken to establish the truth about the Four Square Laundry operation; if the information given by Wright and McKee could not be corroborated, the two men were to be tried and executed immediately. Meanwhile, they were both to be released but kept under surveillance.

By the latter part of September the Provisionals had apparently pinpointed the offices next door to the Gemini Health Studio at 397 Antrim Road and those at 15 College Square East where the Four Square Laundry van was seen parked on a number of occasions. At the end of the month, they decided to act and on 2 October mounted their attacks on both offices and the van as described earlier. Shortly afterwards, Seamus Wright and Kevin McKee underwent Provisional IRA 'court martials', were found guilty and taken to different locations in South Armagh where they were imprisoned under guard, executed and buried in secret locations.

Wright was not the only 'Fred' who became a double agent. Another, a member of a Provisional IRA unit in Andersonstown, informed the Provisionals that he had been recruited and proceeded to feed information to them, including details about members of the MRF and vehicles used by it. In this instance, however, his duplicity was soon discovered and his MRF handlers were able to intercept and alter the information which was communicated to the Provisionals via a dead-letter box in the wall of a house. Eventually, however, the Provisionals realised that the information was false and exacted retribution by shooting him dead not far from the Royal Victoria Hospital in Belfast.

In February 1973, the existence of the Army's undercover operations in Northern Ireland was revealed in some detail as the result of the trial of a member of the MRF who was charged with attempted murder and malicious wounding. On the morning of 22 June 1972, four men standing at the Bunbeg bus terminus on the Glen Road in Belfast came under fire from an automatic weapon fired from a passing car. Two of them were wounded, as was another man lying in bed in a nearby house who was hit by a stray bullet.

At the time, such an episode might have been put down to a sectarian attack by loyalists or internecine feuding between the Official IRA and the Provisionals, but unfortunately for those in the car an RUC vehicle was nearby and was soon in pursuit. After forcing it to pull over, the police arrested its occupants, one of whom was subsequently identified as a senior NCO named Sergeant Clive Williams. The RUC, who had long been unhappy about Army undercover operations, proceeded to charge both men with unlawful possession of a Thompson submachine-gun found in the car and Williams with attempted murder and malicious wounding.

On 27 February 1973, the case came to trial in the High Court in Belfast. It transpired that the Thompson had been fired from the car by Sergeant Williams who claimed that he had come under fire from two gunmen in the terminus and had returned it. Under cross-examination, Williams revealed the existence of the MRF and its operations. He stated that it numbered some forty men in total and operated in civilian vehicles, also divulging that he had fifteen men in his own team. On the day in question, he had given a briefing to some new arrivals in the MRF, followed by familiarisation training on the range at the MRF base at Palace Barracks with weapons in use by terrorist groups, including the Thompson submachine-gun. Subsequently, accompanied by one of the trainees, he had travelled to the Army headquarters at Lisburn before returning to Holywood via West Belfast. For some unexplained reason, instead of being armed with the normal MRF team armament of a Sterling 9mm submachine-gun and Browning Hi-Power 9mm pistol, he had been carrying one of the unit's two Thompsons which were normally used for familiarisation training only. The weapon had been concealed in a holdall hidden under one of the seats.

Williams stated that he had decided to drive through the Andersonstown area of the city to show it to his trainee. Shortly afterwards, however, he had received a radio message from one of his patrols that a man armed with a pistol had been sighted at the Bunberg bus terminus. He had then headed for the terminus and had spotted two gunmen who had opened fire on his vehicle, shattering the rear window. He had returned their fire with the Thompson as his vehicle sped away.

On 2 May, the charge of unlawful possession of the submachinegun was dropped against Sergeant Williams and his companion. In October 1973, despite the fact that forensic investigation revealed that none of the four men at the terminus had fired a weapon and that the Army vehicle showed no sign of having been hit by a bullet, the judge directed the jury to find Williams not guilty on the charges of attempted murder and malicious wounding on the grounds of insufficient evidence.

As a result of the Four Square Laundry débâcle, an assessment of the MRF and the whole question of undercover operations in Northern Ireland was carried out almost immediately. Its conclusions were that the unit had served its purpose, but, having been blown, should be disbanded forthwith. However, it was recognised that the concept of undercover surveillance and reconnaissance was sound and decided that a new, properly trained and equipped unit should be formed for the role.

The decision to replace the MRF was taken towards the end of 1972. Its successor was formed in 1973, but did not become operational until the following year when it emerged in the form of a specialist surveillance unit which has over the years used a variety of cover names, including Northern Ireland Training Advisory Team and 14 Intelligence & Security Company, the latter adopted later, during the 1980s. It became known as '14 Int' or '14 Company' and for convenience the latter will be used from hereon.

Such was the importance attached to the new unit and the determination that there would be no repetition of the errors made with the MRF, that from the very start all members were required to pass a strict selection and highly specialised training process before being admitted to the unit. Initially, instructors were provided by 22 SAS, but as time went by these were replaced by qualified personnel from within the unit itself.

Selection and training comprised three stages, the first consisting of three weeks of rigorous physical fitness and basic training during which candidates were subjected to lack of sleep and an unpredictable routine designed to test their ability to carry out lengthy operations under periods of considerable stress and fatigue. Trainees could fail at any point during this phase, and there was generally a high failure rate. The few who completed selection successfully progressed to the second phase of basic training which lasted four weeks and included: advanced driving skills; photography; mobile surveillance techniques; physical training, including unarmed combat; CQB training with the Browning Hi-Power pistol; radio communications; map reading and navigation; reconnaissance skills, including close target reconnaissance, covert observation posts (OPs) and airborne photographic reconnaissance.

Basic training would also see a number of trainees failing tests or being weeded out as unsuitable, with the remainder graduating to advanced training. During this stage much emphasis was placed on further CQB training with different weapons, including the Walther PPK 7.65mm pistol, Heckler & Koch MP5K 9mm submachine-gun, HK53 5.56mm and G3K 7.62mm assault rifles, and the Remington 870 pump-action 12-gauge shotgun. Trainees also received in-depth training in CQB tactics such as vehicle, anti-ambush and hostage rescue drills. Other subjects included: advanced first-aid; operations in urban areas, including methods of covert entry into buildings and establishment of OPs; voice training, in which trainees were taught to imitate the accents from different regions of the province; and resistance to interrogation. Throughout this period of advanced training, trainees were continually practised and tested in all the skills in which they had been trained.

On completion of their training, the newly qualified 'operators', as they were called, were flown to Northern Ireland where they joined

14 Company. Initially, in the early days after its formation, almost half the strength of the new unit consisted of members of B Squadron 22 SAS, who on paper were returned to their parent units before being posted to 14 Company. As time went on, however, volunteers, including women, were drawn from all three armed services.

14 Company was initially organised into a headquarters element and three detachments or 'dets', each numbering approximately twenty operators and commanded by a captain, giving rise to its nickname among those who have served in the unit or know of its existence as the 'Det'. Each detachment was entirely self-contained with its own intelligence and logistic support elements. One of only two published descriptions of a detachment base is given by a former member of 14 Company, James Rennie, in his book, *The Operators – On the Streets with 14 Company*, published in 1996. In it he describes the base of South Detachment in which he served:

If we had driven on to the set of a James Bond movie we wouldn't have been more surprised than we were at the sight that greeted us when at last we clambered out of the van at our destination. We had driven into the heart of a large warehouse-like structure on an industrial estate which housed a self-contained village of Portakabins, set out in neat rows. Along one side were two parallel sets of two-storey blocks, with some low brick buildings behind them. Ranged along the other side were rows of ordinary civilian vehicles – motorbikes, vans, saloons, hatchbacks, estates and trucks. As we unloaded our kit I saw that the place was alive with activity. Brightly lit workshops set back against the walls on each side echoed to the sound of pop music as scruffy technicians and mechanics worked under cars held aloft on hydraulic ramps. A thirty-metre pipe range (thirty metres of two-foot-diameter concrete drainage pipe set horizontally, abutting brick and sand embrasures, used to test-fire rifles in a restricted space) was reverberating to the thump of 7.62mm rounds as someone test-fired their weapon. Operators in various states of dress moved purposefully to and fro between the blocks, some carrying grips and holdalls which obviously contained weapons. High above, the roof was strung with rows of strip-lights, alternating with long horizontal windows, which between them provided an unchanging artificial environment, pretty well sealed from the outside world. Soon we would learn that exit from the camp involved a complex ritual of passing through a series of gates, barriers and compounds, until at last one emerged into a network of isolated side roads.

Besides accommodation for all its operators and support personnel, each detachment base also contained briefing and operations rooms run by a section of Intelligence Corps NCOs, an armoury and a 'killing room' range equipped with a cine-target system.

The cars used by 14 Company's operators were modified for the role although outwardly appearing entirely normal, albeit well-used. In addition to carrying concealed lightweight armour fitted according to each operator's preference, each was equipped with a sophisticated encrypted radio communications system, brake light cut-out switches and concealed remote-controlled cameras covering the front, back and sides of the vehicle. During later years further modifications included a launcher, fitted to the chassis, which at the press of a button would eject four stun grenades to the front, rear and both sides of the car.

14 Company's three detachments were deployed on attachment to brigades whose headquarters were in Londonderry, Belfast and Newry respectively. Like their parent unit, they also used cover names: the one attached to 3 Infantry Brigade was at one time designated 4 Field Survey Troop RE and was based with a Royal Engineers unit at Castledillon, in County Armagh. During the period from 1974 to 1976, 14 Company was the only special forces unit operating in Northern Ireland and thus a large number of incidents in which the Provisional IRA in particular claimed the SAS was involved could in fact be put down to 14 Company.

In addition to close target reconnaissance and surveillance tasks, 14 Company detachments also provided support for Security Service technicians flown over from England to carry out bugging operations. On these occasions operators would escort the technicians to the target area, effect the entry and provide protective surveillance while listening devices or miniature cameras were being planted, and then spirit the technicians away while ensuring no signs of their presence had been left behind.

One of the earliest operations carried out by 14 Company was targeted on the staff of the Provisional IRA's Belfast Brigade. Information was received that a meeting of senior members of its staff would be held at a house in the city and the decision was taken to arrest them. A surveillance operation was mounted and as soon as all the senior Provisionals, including the republican leader Gerry Adams and Brendan Hughes, had entered the building, it was surrounded by troops and those inside arrested shortly afterwards.

Brendan Hughes escaped from prison shortly afterwards but it was not long before 14 Company played a principal role in his being caught again. In early 1974 Special Branch received intelligence from an informer in the Belfast Brigade quartermaster's department that the Provisional IRA was bugging the telephones in the Army headquarters at Lisburn. This had apparently been achieved with the assistance of a telephone engineer installing telecommunications equipment in one of the headquarters buildings; he had tapped the lines being used by military intelligence personnel and was taping conversations on them. The operation was being masterminded by Hughes, using the alias of Arthur McAllister, from a flat in a house in Malone Road in the Myrtlefield Park area of Belfast which was also used as a cache for weapons and explosives. On receiving the first batch of tapes, however, the Provisionals had discovered that the conversations had been scrambled. This problem was overcome by the engineer who stole an anti-scrambling device from the headquarters, thus enabling Hughes and his accomplices to listen to the tapes.

Following the informer's tip-off, a surveillance operation was mounted on the house by 14 Company with one operator positioned in the garden nearby. Special Branch officers eventually carried out a raid and apprehended Hughes and another Provisional, Denis Loughlin. The telephone engineer, who was en route to the house at the time, narrowly escaped arrest. A search of the flat uncovered four rifles, a submachine-gun, two pistols, over 3,000 rounds of ammunition and command cable for use with remote-controlled bombs. Also discovered were a quantity of documents revealing the Provisionals' detailed plans for a 'doomsday defence' of nationalist parts of Belfast and the occupation of Protestant areas in the west of the city.

Suspecting an informer in their midst, the Provisionals launched a hunt but it took them some time to pinpoint him. Two years later, the individual concerned was flagged down at a roadblock by men dressed in British Army uniforms. Dragged from his vehicle, he was told by his captors, whom he believed to be members of the SAS, that they knew that he was a Provisional and were going to shoot him. Terrified, he gave the codeword given to him by his Special Branch handler but that was his undoing. Subsequently 'court-martialled', he was murdered and buried in a secret location.

The Myrtlefield Park and and other operations carried out by 14 Company and the RUC Special Branch during the rest of 1974 and the following year proved highly successful and resulted in a large number of Provisional IRA leaders being arrested and the organisation placed under great pressure.

The beginning of 1976 saw the official arrival of 22 SAS to Northern Ireland when on 7 January it was announced that a squadron would be deployed on patrolling and surveillance. Prior to that date elements of the regiment had been active in the province in the intelligence-gathering role, but this had been a closely guarded secret. Only on two occasions had any of its squadrons been committed there. In August 1969 D Squadron was deployed for two months to search for suspected loyalist arms caches and to search vessels suspected of bringing in weapons; based at Newtownards, its members wore uniform and made no attempt to conceal their unit identity. In 1974, members of B Squadron were sent to the province to help in initial operations by 14 Company which was still in its infancy and thus under strength. As mentioned earlier, they had officially been returned to their parent units before being posted to 14 Company; once their assistance was no longer needed, they were withdrawn and returned to 22 SAS.

The principal reason for the government's decision to deploy elements of the regiment in the province was the very high level of sectarian violence which had been plaguing Northern Ireland throughout 1975, culminating in the massacre by the Provisional IRA of eleven Protestant workmen near Whitecross, in South Armagh, in January of the following year. Under pressure from loyalists to provide an effective response, Prime Minister Harold Wilson announced the deployment of the SAS, officials informing the press that up to 150 SAS troops were being sent to the province. This announcement, broadcast on television and radio, took the Ministry of Defence (MoD) by surprise and there was a furious reaction: the Director SAS was summoned by the Chief of General Staff, General Sir Michael Carver, who demanded an explanation. The Director in turn contacted 22 SAS at Hereford and, in the absence of the commanding officer who was in Oman, spoke to the second-in-command who was equally mystified.

Inevitably, those at senior levels in the Army and MoD who were not enthusiastic supporters of the SAS, and thus seldom wished it well, took the view that the regiment had been plotting to insinuate itself into Northern Ireland and had been pulling strings at high level. In fact, nothing could have been farther from the truth for, quite apart from the fact that it had been as astonished as everyone else at the Prime Minister's announcement, 22 SAS did not have 150 men to send to the province. Of its four sabre squadrons, one was on exercise in Norway, another was on operations in the Sultanate of Oman and a third was committed to the counter-terrorist role. The fourth, D Squadron, had only just returned from operations in Oman and the majority of its members were already committed on various tasks.

In the event, 22 SAS could only initially deploy a group of eleven men, comprising members of D Squadron and instructors from its Training Wing led by the regiment's second-in-command, as this was the only manpower available at the time. Of those, five were still recovering from wounds received on operations in Oman. Furthermore, such was the short degree of notice that there was no opportunity to carry out any of the training and thorough preparation normally conducted prior to an operational tour. Nevertheless, the group was flown to the province where, after an initial period spent in Belfast, it was transferred to a base at Bessbrook, in South Armagh, where it was subsequently joined by the rest of D Squadron.

Initially, the squadron came under command of the unit responsible for South Armagh, the 1st Battalion The Royal Scots. This was highly unusual because the SAS normally operates under direct command of a theatre headquarters and, furthermore, received its intelligence from a very high level. The second-in-command of 22 SAS paid a visit to the intelligence branch at the Army headquarters at Lisburn, where he himself had worked in 1974 as GSO 2 Intelligence Liaison, but encountered a hostile response from the Colonel GS (Intelligence). The latter refused him entry and informed him that the squadron was to operate under command of the Royal Scots who would also provide it with intelligence. In the event, this arrangement proved far from satisfactory and so the squadron turned to the RUC and Special Branch for assistance.

The squadron's link with the RUC and Special Branch was Captain Robert Nairac, a Grenadier Guards officer who had previously served as one of three liaison officers attached to 14 Company, each working with one of its three detachments. Nairac had been attached to the 'det' located at Castledillon. Working under the cover name of 4 Field Survey Troop RE and commanded by a former SAS officer, Captain Tony Ball, it operated in South Armagh under the auspices of 3 Infantry Brigade. Nairac had served with the detachment for nine months, returning to his regiment in the summer of 1975. At the beginning of the following year, however, at the request of the second-in-command of 22 SAS who had met him previously and knew of his work with the 14 Company detachment, he returned to Northern Ireland and 3 Infantry Brigade where he took up the post of liaison officer for D Squadron just after its arrival in January.

As described by John Parker in his book, *Death of a Hero*, Nairac's role was to act as the interface between D Squadron and the RUC, including Special Branch, on whom it would rely for intelligence. He was the ideal choice for the job because he was already known to the head of Special Branch and other senior RUC offices in South Armagh from his previous tour, and was on good terms with them; indeed, it was for that reason that the second-in-command of 22 SAS had asked for him. Nairac's excellent relations with the RUC were of considerable benefit to D Squadron which lacked good intelligence and received little if anything in the way of assistance from the Army headquarters at Lisburn where, as mentioned earlier, it had received a cold reception.

It was not long before the squadron made its presence felt in the area. On 12 March Sean McKenna, a leading local Provisional, high on the wanted lists in Northern Ireland, was apprehended by an Army patrol, reportedly drunk. McKenna maintained that he had been abducted during the night at gunpoint by two men from his home in the Irish Republic and taken north over the border where he was handed over to the patrol.

On 15 April, a patrol of the squadron took part in the arrest of Peter Cleary, a staff officer in the Provisional IRA's 1st Battalion of its South Armagh Brigade. Intelligence had been received that Cleary would be visiting his fiancée at her sister's home at Tieve-crum, the house being situated only fifty metres or so north of the border with the Irish Republic. The building had subsequently been placed under surveillance three days earlier by a five-man patrol, some of whom were in a hide position only some 100 metres away while the remainder were located to the rear of the house. During the evening Cleary was seen driving away, but he returned at 9.30 p.m. Shortly afterwards, dogs outside the building detected the presence of the patrol and a number of men came out of the building and began to search the surrounding area with torches. Two of them stumbled across the hide and the soldiers in it had no option but to deploy from it, firing a warning shot as they did so.

The house was swiftly surrounded and all the occupants lined up outside. Cleary was identified and taken to a nearby spot selected as a landing zone for a helicopter which would take the patrol and its prisoner back to the squadron base. One man guarded him as the other four members of the patrol held lights to guide in the aircraft. With the border only a short distance away, Cleary suddenly made a bolt for freedom and, grabbing the soldier's weapon by the barrel, attempted to wrest it from him. The latter fired three rounds, hitting Cleary in the chest and killing him instantly. Inevitably, there was considerable controversy over his death and the IRA claimed that he had been murdered out of hand.

An operation during the following month ended in disaster. On the night of 5 May two members of D Squadron were deployed to carry out a reconnaissance on foot of a possible location for an OP. Dressed in combat kit, they were taken to the area in an unmarked car, manned by two other members of the squadron in civilian clothes, and dropped off. The plan was for the vehicle to return to Bessbrook and await a call by radio to pick up the two men. At 10.50 p.m., however, the vehicle accidentally drove over the unmarked border at Cornamucklagh, after taking a wrong turning in the area of Carlingford Lough, and 550 yards south of it encountered a roadblock manned by members of the Gardai Siochana and the Irish Army. The two soldiers were arrested and a search of them and their vehicle revealed that they were armed with a Sterling submachine-gun and Browning pistols.

Shortly after midnight, the squadron's operations officer despatched four men in two cars to search for the missing vehicle and its crew. Before doing so, however, he briefed them carefully on the route and the possible problems which they might encounter in the area. Having picked up the two-man reconnaissance patrol, the second party went in search of the missing vehicle. Unfortunately, however, they committed the same map-reading error and consequently suffered a similar fate, arriving at the roadblock where they found the missing pair and their vehicle and where they were also disarmed and arrested.

All eight men were subsequently taken to Dublin and charged with possession of firearms with intent to endanger life before being released on a total of £40,000 bail and returned to Northern Ireland. A year later, all eight stood trial in Dublin but were acquitted. Each man was, however, fined £100 for being in possession of unlicensed weapons.

Inevitably, the incident was of great propaganda value to the Provisional IRA, which accused the SAS of deploying 'hit squads' south of the border, and no doubt caused smirks of satisfaction among those in the British military establishment in the province who had not welcomed the arrival of the SAS. The fact was, however, that a genuine error had been made as the result of an ambiguity in the maps. Lieutenant Colonel (later Brigadier) Peter Morton, the Commanding Officer of the 3rd Battalion The Parachute Regiment which had taken over in South Armagh from the 1st Battalion The Royal Scots on 15 April, subsequently checked the maps of the area thoroughly and discovered a discrepancy between the 1:20,000 and one-inch scale versions. As he later recounted in his book, *Emergency Tour – 3 PARA in South Armagh*, he found that the one-inch scale map showed a T-junction located 200–300 metres west of the border whereas no such feature was shown on the 1:20,000 map which showed the road crossing a stream and continuing over the border. The D Squadron patrols were using the one-inch scale map and thus were anticipating a T-junction which was in fact non-existent.

At the beginning of the following year, however, the SAS scored another victory against the Provisionals in South Armagh. On 2 January, a junior NCO in the 1st Battalion Royal Highland Fusiliers was killed in Crossmaglen by a mortar bomb. No sign of the IRA mortar team had been found, but there had been a report of a car in the vicinity at the time. Two weeks later, on the evening of Sunday 16 January, a vehicle matching the description given was reported as being parked on a roadside near the border. An SAS patrol was deployed and staked out the vehicle. After some time a man wearing a black balaclava, and carrying a sawn-off shotgun and cartridge belt of ammunition, approached the car in the dark and a member of the patrol rose from his position to challenge him. On seeing him, the gunman raised his weapon and the soldier opened fire, hitting him several times. At that moment, other terrorists concealed in a hedgerow nearby opened fire and this was returned by the other members of the patrol. The dead man was identified as 20-year-old Seamus Harvey, who lived in the nearby village of Drummakaval; a blood trail found later in a ditch at the scene of the action indicated that at least one other terrorist had been wounded.

The success of this and subsequent operations reduced considerably Provisional IRA activities in South Armagh while elsewhere in the province, meanwhile, other successes were also scored against the terrorists. During the first six months of 1977, seventy-five members of the organisation were arrested and charged with offences as a result of combined SAS, 14 Company and Special Branch operations. By that time, the SAS squadron in the province was no longer concentrated at Bessbrook, but had been split up: one troop was allocated to 3 Infantry Brigade and remained with the squadron headquarters at Bessbrook; the second was with 8 Infantry Brigade in Londonderry; the third was with 39 Infantry brigade in Belfast; and the fourth was held in reserve under the direct orders of the Commander Land Forces in the province.

The year 1977 was also notable, however, for the death of Captain Robert Nairac, 3 Infantry Brigade's SAS liaison officer. The controversy and circumstances surrounding Nairac's death have been covered already in detail by a number of authors, most notably by John Parker, and thus only an outline will be given here.

On the evening of Saturday 14 May, Nairac booked out with the operations room of Λ Squadron, at that time the resident SAS unit in the province. The duty officer pointed out that he should have a back-up team in support, but Nairac declined, saying that he did not need one and that he would return by 11.30 p.m. This proved to be a fateful decision. Leaving the base at 9.25 p.m., he headed south from Bessbrook towards the small village of Drumintree and its pub, the Three Steps Inn, which he had visited on a number of occasions during the previous two weeks. At 9.58 p.m. he reported over the radio in his car that he had reached the pub.

By midnight nothing further had been heard from him and he was by then thirty minutes overdue. Following the laid-down procedure, A Squadron's duty officer reported the matter to his squadron commander who decided to wait a further forty-five minutes before raising the alarm. By 12.15 a.m. on 15 May, however, there was still no sign of Nairac and the squadron commander contacted the GSO 2 Intelligence at the headquarters at Lisburn to report him missing.

At dawn, a helicopter took off to carry out an aerial search and almost immediately Nairac's car, a red Triumph Toledo, was spotted in the car park of the Three Steps Inn. Some twenty more helicopters, more than 300 troops and 100 extra police were drafted into the area to join the search. Although they scoured Drumintree and the surrounding countryside, they found no sign of him. Examination of Nairac's car and bloodstains on the ground beside it, however, revealed signs of a violent struggle.

It later transpired that Nairac had been abducted by a gang of five local men who had been drinking in the pub and suspected him of being a member of the SAS working undercover. A popular place, the Three Steps Inn featured a local band and he had unfortunately been unwise enough to draw attention to himself by climbing up on stage and performing a number of songs. He remained in the pub until after the band finishing performing and shortly afterwards was seen in the car park making his way towards his car, followed by three men. It appears that he was attacked at that point and, despite putting up a very stout resistance, was overpowered.

On 16 May, the Provisional IRA issued a statement, announcing that it had captured and executed Nairac. Meanwhile, Irish security forces were searching the area south of the border and on 18 May a Gardai Siochana mobile patrol was stopped by two men who had been fishing. They showed the police officers two pistol cartridges which they had found by a bridge over the River Flurry in Ravensdale Forest. A search of the area revealed bloodstains beside the parapet of the bridge and by the river in the corner of a field.

Ten days later the Gardai Siochana arrested a 24-year-old unemployed joiner, Liam Patrick Townson, at a roadblock near the border. Listed as a suspected member of the Provisional IRA, Townson lived north of the border at Meigh, just outside Newry. Four days later, he admitted under questioning that he had personally shot Nairac dead after being called south of the border by the gang which had abducted him. In his statement, he related how Nairac had revealed nothing despite being beaten up very badly before being murdered.

Meanwhile, the RUC was also active in hunting down the gang and before long had arrested five men from South Armagh. Gerard Fearon, Thomas Morgan and Daniel O'Rourke were subsequently charged with murder while Michael McCoy was charged with kidnapping. The fifth man, Owen Rocks, was charged with withholding information. Two other men also wanted for questioning, Kevin Crilly and Pat Maguire, had by then already fled to the United States.

In November 1978, Liam Townson and his accomplices were brought to trial in Dublin. On 15 December, all were found guilty as charged. Townson and Fearon both received life sentences and the latter a further twenty-two years for causing grievous bodily harm. O'Rourke received ten years for manslaughter while McCoy was sentenced to five years. Rocks received two sentences of three years each to run concurrently. In the event, however, all six only served the minimum terms before being released: Townson was released after twelve years while Fearon and Morgan were freed in 1985 and 1986 respectively. McCoy and Rocks only served one and two months respectively after their time spent in prison on remand was taken into account.

In 1979, Captain Robert Nairac was awarded a posthumous George Cross. His body has never been found and to this day the Provisional IRA continues to remain silent as to its whereabouts.

Above: The blowing up of four airliners at Dawson's Field in Jordan, in September 1970, sent shockwaves throughout the West which had hitherto ignored warning signals emanating from the Middle East. Photo: Popperfoto

Right: In August 1975, one of a group of five members of the Japanese Red Army herds hostages aboard a bus in Kuala Lumpur, Malaysia, where he and his accomplices had earlier attacked the US consulate and Swedish embassy. Subsequently joined by a further five terrorists released from prisons in Japan, they were flown to Libya. Photo: Associated Press

Above: The aftermath of the bombing by Hizbollah of the US embassy in Beirut on 18 April 1983. Key members of the CIA, including its most senior officer in the Middle East and its Beirut station chief, died in the blast. Photo: AP/Wide World Photos

Below: The scene at Frankfurt Airport on 19 June 1985 after a bomb planted by members of the Red Army Faction exploded in a crowded departure lounge, killing three people and injuring twenty eight. Photo: Popperfoto

Right: Members of the Provisional IRA's Derry Brigade during the mid-1980s. The terrorist in the centre is armed with an FNC 5.56mm assault rifle, the two others with Heckler & Koch 7.62mm G3s. Photo: Pacemaker Press International

Below: An interior view of a special forces covert observation post in South Armagh. Photo: Defence Picture Library

Above: The wreckage of the car in which the governor of Spain's Guipuzcoa province, General Rafaël Garido, and his family died on 25 October 1986. ETA terrorists placed an explosive charge on the roof of the vehicle as it was being driven through the streets of San Sebastian in northern Spain. Photo: Associated Press

Below: An aerial view of the police station at Loughgall, in County Armagh, which was badly damaged during the Provisional IRA attack on 8 May 1987. Eight terrorists, whose van can be seen centre foreground, were killed in the ensuing ambush by the SAS. Photo: Pacemaker Press International

Above: Members of GIGN storm the hijacked Air France Airbus at Marseilles Airport on 26 December 1994. All four terrorists were killed and nine gendarmes were wounded in the gun battle inside the aircraft which lasted for some twenty minutes. Photo: Rex Features

Below: Colombian police with the body of one of their number killed in an attack by FARC terrorists in eastern Meta province on 4 October 1997. The attack followed less than twenty-four hours after another in which eleven policemen, soldiers and judicial officials died. Photo: Popperfoto

Above: Smoke billows over the Japanese ambassador's residence in Lima, Peru, on 22 April 1997 as special forces carry out a hostage rescue operation, ending a 126-day-long siege which began on 17 December 1996 when fourteen members of the MRTA stormed and occupied the building. Photo: Agence France Presse

Left: Special forces troops move past hostages on the second floor of the Japanese ambassador's residence during their assault on the building. Photo: Reuters

Above: The Barrett .50 calibre sniper rifle used by Provisional IRA terrorist Michael Caraher, shown in its firing position in the back of the Mazda 626 in which it was used in attacks on members of the security forces in South Armagh. Photo: Kelvin Boyes

Below: Members of GSG 9 ordering a car to pull over and stop. The trooper in the rear of the BMW is training his MP-5 submachine-gun on the driver of the target vehicle, ready to open fire if he attempts to escape. Photo: Grenzschutzgruppe 9

Left: Two members of Spain's Grupo Especial Operaciones at the unit's base at Guadalajara. Both are equipped with ballistic helmet and body armour, while one is armed with a Heckler & Koch MP-5 SD2 9mm silenced submachine-gun and the other with a pump-action shotgun. Photo: TRH Pictures

Below: Members of a 22 SAS Special Projects team fast-roping from a Chinook helicopter of one of the Special Forces flights of No.7 Squadron RAF prior to assaulting a 'hijacked' bus during training. Photo: Barry Davies

The undercover war continued. On 26 February 1978, an SAS patrol was staking out a cache of home-made mortar bombs concealed in a farmyard near Ardboe, located in the staunchly republican area south-west of Lough Neagh. Two days earlier an informer had revealed the existence of the cache and the patrol had deployed to its ambush position shortly afterwards. At just after 5 p.m. a white Volkswagen pulled into the farmyard and two men, both members of the Provisional IRA, walked over to the cache. As one of them, Paul Duffy, extracted one of the mortar bombs, the SAS patrol opened fire, killing him. His accomplice ran back to the car which was hit several times as he drove away. Several hours later he surrendered in order to receive medical attention for three wounds he had received while escaping.

In March 1978, 14 Company suffered two casualties when Lance Corporal David Jones was shot dead and another NCO wounded after challenging three armed men. Both men had, however, succeeded in returning the terrorists' fire and wounded one of them, Francis Hughes, who despite wounds to his legs managed to escape and remained at large for several hours until found by tracker dogs. Hughes was a known terrorist bomber responsible for a number of deaths and was thus high on the wanted lists. Subsequently tried and convicted, he later died on hunger strike.

On the night of 21 June 1978 a four-man Provisional IRA ASU drove in a hijacked car into the loyalist area of Ballysillan in West Belfast. Equipped with incendiary bombs, they planned to attack the postal depot there. The ASU was led by William Mailey who was accompanied by Denis Brown, James Mulvenna and a fourth, unidentified man. Having parked their vehicle nearby in Wheatfield Drive, Mailey, Brown and Mulvenna headed towards their target carrying their bombs, each of which comprised a plastic container of petrol to which an explosive charge and a timer were attached. They entered an alleyway which led to a compound, surrounded by a high wire fence, housing vehicles and equipment.

Unknown to the terrorists, information about their plan had reached the ears of the security forces and an operation was mounted to thwart it. A team from G Squadron, together with some members of Special Branch and a section of the RUC's Special Patrol Group, was inserted several days before. This force comprised a covert OP concealed in a nearby house, a reaction group hidden in some undergrowth near to the entrance to the alleyway and cut-off groups positioned around the compound.

As the three Provisionals entered the alleyway, one of them threw a bomb over the fence and two others prepared to follow his example. At that point, the reaction group opened fire, killing two instantly and a third as he attempted escape down the alley. These were subsequently identified as Mailey, Mulvenna and Brown. The fourth man, who had remained with the vehicle, fled the area on foot and succeeded in escaping. Unfortunately, at that moment two men appeared on the scene. When challenged, one remained still and put up his hands. The other, later identified as a Protestant named William Hanna, turned and ran, but was immediately shot dead. Tragically, it transpired that the two men were both innocent of any involvement in the attack and had been returning home from a nearby pub.

Three weeks later, another operation ended in tragedy when a sixteen-year-old boy named John Boyle stumbled across a Provisional IRA arms cache hidden on his family's farm at Dunloy in County Antrim, and told his father. The RUC were informed immediately and the task of staking out the cache passed to G Squadron which immediately deployed a team to lay an ambush at the site of the cache. Unfortunately, however, the RUC failed to warn the family that an operation was being mounted and thus to stay away from the area, an oversight which had tragic consequences. As the ambush team lay in wait, it spotted a figure approaching the cache. Kneeling down, it pulled out an Armalite rifle and stood up. In so doing, however, it apparently pointed the weapon in the direction of two members of the team who opened fire. As the latter went forward, however, they discovered that their victim was none other than young John Boyle whose curiosity over his earlier discovery had obviously proved irresistible.

A great deal of controversy surrounded the killing, which had taken place at 10 a.m. in broad daylight, and the question was asked as to why the soldiers had not challenged Boyle as he approached the cache, rather than waiting until he had taken hold of a weapon. Both soldiers were subsequently tried for murder, but were acquitted, although the judge, Sir Robert Lowry, the Lord Chief Justice of Northern Ireland, had harsh words for the SAS.

Further controversy arose in September when a Protestant, James Taylor, was killed by the SAS while shooting game with friends near Lough Neagh. Entering a field, legitimately armed with a shotgun, he was shot dead by a patrol which had earlier come across the shooting-party's car.

Two months later, the SAS deployed a team inside a house at 2 Maureen Avenue, in Londonderry, in which an arms cache had been discovered. On 24 November Patrick Duffy, a 50-year-old known member of the Provisionals, arrived in a car and parked outside the house. Entering the building, he made his way to the first floor where the weapons were concealed in a wardrobe and proceeded to clean and oil them. At that point, the SAS team opened fire and killed him. During the subsequent trial, one of its members maintained that he had shouted a warning beforehand. The somewhat confused and conflicting evidence did little to shed light on what had happened.

By the end of 1978, the SAS had shot dead ten people, three of whom had died in controversial circumstances, having no connection whatsoever with any terrorist organisation. This led to a change in policy and for the next five years the SAS role was switched from ambushing to covert observation and surveillance. Moreover, by this time the RUC had regained its primacy in policing and had extended its operations once again into rural areas which until then had been policed primarily by the Army.

The late 1970s saw the creation of Tasking & Coordination Groups (TCGs), a system of integrated intelligence centres designed to enhance co-operation between the RUC and the Army. Commanded by a Special Branch officer, each was staffed by representatives from the Army, Special Branch, the Criminal Investigation Department (CID) and on occasions the Security Service. The first TCG was established at Castlereagh to cover Belfast, with others located in Armagh and Londonderry to cover the southern and northern regions of the province respectively. Each TCG had a TCG Liaison Officer (TCGLO), either a member of the SAS or 14 Company, whose role was to advise the RUC on the Army's capabilities.

At the same time, Special Branch also underwent an extensive reorganisation, being divided into five divisions, each of which carried the prefix 'E'. Of these, E3 handled intelligence and was divided into three sub-divisions, designated E3A, E3B and E3C, which were responsible for operations against republican, loyalist and subversive left-wing organisations respectively. E4 was responsible for surveillance with E4A supplying the 'watchers', whose role was similar to that of the operators of 14 Company, with E4B carrying out technical electronic surveillance and both E4C and E4D conducting photographic surveillance.

A unit was also formed to provide an armed response force for the Special Branch. Called the Special Support Unit, its members received training at the Army's base at Ballykinlar and in England, some of it from 22 SAS. In addition, two further special squads were formed to provide armed support for the rural areas, with E4A and 14 Company being able to call on them for back-up when so required. Designated Headquarters Mobile Support Units (HMSUs) and each numbering some twenty-five to thirty police officers, they were heavily armed with automatic weapons and travelled in unmarked armoured saloon cars.

Three Special Branch regional headquarters were established, each headed by a chief superintendent with officers deployed at RUC stations throughout the province. Also based at headquarters and divisional levels were military intelligence officers (MIOs), military intelligence liaison officers (MILOs) and field intelligence NCOs (FINCOs) of the Special Military Intelligence Unit (SMIU). Numbering some fifty officers and NCOs, the SMIU's principal role was to maintain liaison between the Army and Special Branch and to act as the main conduit for intelligence between the two. It was, however, also involved in the collection of intelligence and ran its own small force of agents.

There was close cooperation between Special Branch and the Security Service which had become heavily involved in Northern Ireland from 1973 onwards. Two years earlier, however, the Secret Intelligence Service had established a presence in the province. From the mid-1970s onwards there was intense rivalry between these two services and the other intelligence-gathering bodies in the province. This reportedly led on occasions to attempts by some units or organisations to interfere with the operations of others as they competed within the same areas for the limited number of potential agents among the republican and loyalist factions. The internecine strife eventually became so serious that the post of Director & Coordinator of Intelligence was established in October 1979 by Prime Minister Margaret Thatcher in an attempt to resolve the problem. The first to hold the appointment, the former SIS chief Maurice Oldfield, found it to be a poisoned chalice and experienced great difficulty in resolving the sometimes bitter disputes between the various intelligence agencies and units involved.

Special Branch also operated hand-in-glove with 14 Company whose effectiveness by the end of the 1970s was such that demands for its services had inevitably increased, resulting in a constant heavy workload. This led in 1979 to the number of its detachments being increased from three to nine. In 1980 a rationalisation of special forces serving in Northern Ireland took place. A new formation, designated the Intelligence & Security Group but frequently referred to merely as 'the Group', was established, comprising 14 Company, the SAS, whose presence was reduced from a squadron to a reinforced troop, an intelligence collation team and technical and administrative support elements. Tasking of the assets of the Intelligence & Security Group was thereafter carried out centrally by the TCGs.

Also incorporated into the Intelligence & Security Group was the Force Research Unit (FRU) whose role was the recruiting and handling of agents, a task which, since the demise of the 'Freds' section of the MRF, had been handled by other elements of the Army intelligence-gathering apparatus in Northern Ireland, including the intelligence sections of infantry units. In 1977 each infantry brigade took over responsibility for agent handling, establishing specialist cells for the task, until 1980 when it was handed over to the newly formed FRU.

The FRU was formed in 1979 by Major General James Glover, the Commander Land Forces in Northern Ireland at the time and an infantry officer with experience in military intelligence; he would later serve as Assistant Chief of Defence Staff (Intelligence). Commanded by a lieutenant colonel, the new unit was based in Lisburn at Headquarters Northern Ireland, and numbered some 180 including administrative and support personnel. Like 14 Company it was organised in detachments or 'dets' deployed in different parts of the province and was recruited from members of the Intelligence Corps and volunteers from throughout the Army and Royal Marines, all of whom had been screened thoroughly. After passing a series of interviews during which any unsuitable candidates were filtered out, volunteers underwent seven weeks of intensive training under the auspices of 14 Company and 22 SAS. This took place at a highly secure establishment in England and included a considerable amount of physical fitness and CQB training. The latter was carried out with a similar range of weapons to those used by 14 Company because FRU handlers were required to meet terrorists face-to-face and thus would be frequently operating in situations of very high risk to themselves. Like their counterparts in 14 Company, trainee handlers also underwent training in advanced driving skills as well as CQB vehicle and anti-ambush drills, being taught how to drive or fight their way out of tight corners.

Agent handling techniques were taught by instructors from the Intelligence Corps and other arms of the military intelligence apparatus. Trainees were taught how to handle informers, usually referred to as 'touts', and to school them in 'tradecraft', the techniques they would need to use to carry out their work without arousing suspicion within their own communities.

The task of recruiting informers was a difficult one, given the tightly-knit nature of the nationalist and loyalist communities in Northern Ireland, and the success rate was approximately 10 per cent. Opportunities mainly arose when individuals were arrested and held for questioning, a process which usually resulted in much being learned about them. Physical coercion was never used, being considered totally counter-productive, and an approach to a potential informer was frequently a lengthy process with a handler only broaching the subject of providing information when he was sure of his man.

In some instances money was used to ensnare potential informers, generally individuals who were out of work or short of money. A man would find himself suddenly receiving sums of money from an anonymous source for a period of several weeks. This would be followed by visits from a handler who, having established a friendly relationship, would eventually broach the subject of how his friend could continue to receive sums of money on a regular basis. This method was reasonably effective, achieving a success rate of about 20 per cent.

Like that of their counterparts in 14 Company, the work of the FRU handlers was very dangerous. Indeed, the degree of risk facing all members of units within the Intelligence & Security Group had been highlighted three years earlier. On 12 December 1977, during a surveillance operation in the Bogside and Brandywell areas of Londonderry, a member of 14 Company was sitting in his unmarked car when he was approached by two members of the INLA, Colm McNutt and Patrick Phelan, who had spotted the vehicle and decide to hijack it. McNutt, who was armed with an unloaded Webley .38 revolver, forced the operator, a junior NCO, out of the car. As Phelan got into the driver's seat, McNutt walked round to the passenger's side. At this point, the operator drew his Browning pistol and shot McNutt dead; Phelan meanwhile dived out of the car and escaped but was arrested later.

Two days later, however, another member of 14 Company, Corporal Paul Harman, was approached and overpowered by terrorists as he stopped his vehicle at the junction of Monagh Avenue and Monagh Road in the Turf Lodge area of Belfast. Next day he was found dead, having been shot in the head and back; his car had been set on fire and his pistol stolen.

By the end of the 1970s the British security forces in Northern Ireland had developed a formidable counter-terrorist capability. During the following twenty years, however, they would find that some of the terrorist groups opposing them, notably the Provisional IRA, had become increasingly sophisticated in their organisation and modus operandi and thus presented even greater threats.

6

OPERATION THUNDERBALL

By 1976, such had been the scale of terrorism in Europe and the countermeasures adopted by governments, as described in Chapter 4, that Wadi Haddad's PFLP–SOG was finding it increasingly dangerous to operate there. In West Germany, his allies of the Red Army Faction, although still a potent threat, had been largely dispersed into splinter groups and their leaders imprisoned. The Japanese Red Army had seen its strength reduced to some thirty trained terrorists and his chief assassin, Ilich Ramírez Sánchez, was now wanted throughout the western hemisphere. Furthermore, the civil war in Lebanon had forced Haddad to move his headquarters from Beirut to Aden, in the South Yemen. He was thus forced to look for fresh areas in which to operate and Africa offered opportunities.

In January 1976 three Palestinians visited the British consulate in Beirut, which represented Kenya in Lebanon, and obtained visas to visit Kenya. All three were members of the PFLP–SOG and were under surveillance by the Israeli intelligence service, Mossad. Later that month, travelling on false passports, they arrived in the Kenyan capital, Nairobi, and on the 18th were arrested on the perimeter of Nairobi's Embakasi airport in possession of two Soviet-manufactured *Strela* SAM-7 shoulder-fired surface-to-air missiles. Under interrogation by the Kenyan security service, the General Service Unit (GSU), they admitted to being members of a PFLP–SOG team planning to shoot down an El-Al aircraft, with 110 passengers aboard, which was due to land at Nairobi an hour after they had been arrested. The missiles had been smuggled previously into Kenya from Uganda whose unpredictable and dangerous ruler, Idi Amin, had supplied them together with a quantity of pistols, submachine-guns and grenades, all of which were found in a car hired by the three men. It transpired that two of the terrorists had taken part in the unsuccessful attacks carried out by Ilich Ramírez

Sánchez on the El-Al aircraft at Orly airport in January of the previous year.

Mossad discovered that none other than Colonel Muammar Gadaffi of Libya was behind the plot in an attempt to avenge the shooting down by the Israelis of a Libyan airliner in the Sinai in February 1973. The aircraft, a Boeing 727, had become lost during a severe sandstorm while en route from Benghazi to Cairo; having overshot the latter, it had flown over the Israeli-occupied Sinai in the direction of Tel Aviv. Fearing it had been hijacked and was being used in a kamikaze attack on their capital, the Israelis shot it down with the loss of 106 lives.

The arrest of the three men was kept secret. Concerned as to their fate, Wadi Haddad despatched a West German couple, Thomas Reuter and Brigitte Schulz, who were both members of the Red Army Faction, to investigate their whereabouts. On arrival at Nairobi on 21 January, they too were arrested and interrogated; Brigitte Schulz was found to be carrying instructions for a further attack on an El-Al aircraft. On 3 February, all five terrorists were handed over to the Israelis who spirited them away to Israel where they were subsequently tried, convicted and imprisoned.

Five months later, at Athens airport on Sunday 27 June, a couple travelling under the names of Mrs Ortega and Mr Garcia boarded an Air France A-300B Airbus, Flight 139 bound for Paris via Athens from Tel Aviv. They were in fact members of the Red Army Faction: Wilfried Böse, the associate of Ilich Ramírez Sánchez, and his girlfriend, Brigitte Kuhlmann. Also aboard the aircraft were two Arabs using the aliases Fahim al-Satti and Hosni Albou Waiki; they were senior members of Wadi Haddad's organisation: Fayez Abdul-Rahim Jaber and Jayel Naji al-Arjam. Security was lax at Athens and the four terrorists had succeeded in avoiding walking through the metal-detector systems and submitting their hand baggage for inspection.

Not long after the aircraft had taken off from Athens, passengers in the economy class cabin heard a scream from the forward part of the aircraft. At the same time, they saw two men run up the aisle and disappear into the first-class cabin. Shortly afterwards, members of the cabin crew appeared, visibly shaken, and proceeded to reassure the by now thoroughly alarmed passengers in the rest of the aircraft. A minute later, a female voice came over the loudspeaker system, announcing that the aircraft was under the command of the 'Ché Guevara Group and Gaza Unit of the Popular Front for the Liberation of Palestine'.

Shortly afterwards Brigitte Kuhlmann appeared in the economy cabin. With a pistol in her hand, she ordered the passengers in harsh strident tones to raise their arms above their heads and remain still. One of them, a Frenchman, was brave enough to try and resist, but was knocked to the floor by Kuhlmann and her accomplices who proceeded to beat him severely. During the next two and a half hours, the passengers were called forward individually and searched before being permitted to return to their seats. Meanwhile, the two Arab terrorists patrolled the aisles of the aircraft, ensuring that Kuhlmann's orders were obeyed.

At about 3 p.m. Athens time, the Airbus landed at Benghazi in Libya. There it remained for two hours, during which one woman passenger, an Englishwoman with Israeli dual nationality, was allowed to leave the aircraft after managing to convince her captors that she was pregnant and feeling unwell. Meanwhile the terrorists collected the passengers' passports and other identification documents, threatening death to anyone who did not hand them over. After six and a half hours on the ground and having been refuelled, Flight 139 took off from Benghazi and headed south.

The absence of any radio communication from the Air France aircraft, which had ceased shortly after its take-off from Athens, had caused concern among Greek air traffic controllers. Their transmissions had been monitored by Israeli electronic intelligence listening posts which had immediately flashed a message to the government in Tel Aviv, advising it that Air France Flight 139, flying from Tel Aviv to Paris via Athens with twelve crew and 251 passengers aboard, including eighty-three Israelis, had disappeared. This was followed by further information including a report that two Arabs had transferred to the flight at Athens from Singapore Airlines Flight 763 which had arrived from Bahrain. There was, however, no clue as to the aircraft's fate nor its whereabouts.

Two hours later, the Israeli government's crisis management team was convened. In addition to Prime Minister Yitzhak Rabin and five members of his cabinet, it included Lieutenant General Mordechai Gur, the Chief of Staff of the Israeli Defence Forces (IDF). Two to three hours later came a report that the aircraft was about to land at Benghazi, thus confirming the team's worst apprehensions that it had a hijack on its hands. Remembering the Sabena hijacking four years earlier, in which the Sayeret Matkal had carried out its first hostage rescue operation, it initially appeared that history was about to repeat itself. The Sayeret Matkal base was alerted and Unit 269 deployed to Lod airport.

The first definite information concerning the identity of the hijackers came from London where the British authorities had questioned the Englishwoman released by the terrorists after feigning pregnancy and feeling unwell. Having flown to London that evening, she had been questioned by police and others who had elicited as much information from her as possible. The Israelis were informed that two of the terrorists were German and their accomplices Arabs, that they were armed and apparently equipped with explosives which had been placed at the aircraft's doors. The British concluded by stating that the hijackers' destination appeared to be Africa.

The flight from Benghazi to the terrorists' next destination lasted five hours, during which Brigitte Kuhlmann had patrolled the aisles of the aircraft, venting her spleen on those passengers who incurred her displeasure. In the early hours of Monday 28 June, Wilfried Böse announced over the loudspeaker system that the aircraft would soon be landing in Uganda, at Entebbe airport near the capital of Kampala. As it did so, passengers were ordered to pull down the blinds on the windows; when the Airbus taxied to a halt, powerful searchlights were trained on it. As dawn broke, however, some of the passengers were able to open the blinds slightly and observe armed Ugandan troops surrounding the aircraft. Nine hours after landing, they were disembarked and taken to an abandoned airport terminal where they were confined to its lounge, guarded by Ugandan paratroops who ringed the building. The terrorists meanwhile disappeared.

On arrival, Böse and the other three hijackers were met by three accomplices, among whom was none other than Ilich Ramírez Sánchez's Lebanese associate, Fouad Awad alias Antonio Dagues-Bouvier. He was accompanied by two more members of the PFLP–SOG: Abdel al-Latif and another known simply as Abu Ali who was later thought to be the member of the PFLP–SOG who had established initial contact with the Japanese Red Army in 1970. They brought additional arms, including automatic weapons and grenades, to supplement the hijackers' pistols and explosives. On his arrival, Awad appeared to take command of the entire operation.

During the afternoon, a helicopter arrived and shortly afterwards the imposing figure of President Idi Amin filled the doorway of the terminal lounge. Accompanied by Fouad Awad and the other terrorists, he addressed the hostages, the passengers' being such by then, and announced himself as 'Field Marshal Dr Idi Amin', declaring that he had been 'appointed by God Almighty to be your saviour'.

Idi Amin was no doubt revelling in his role that afternoon. During the 1960s, Uganda had enjoyed close relations with Israel which, shortly after the former gained independence in 1962, had begun providing military assistance. In 1965, however, Amin had been infuriated by the Israelis' refusal to assist him in an invasion of neighbouring Tanzania. Thereafter the relationship had deteriorated, being further poisoned by Colonel Muammar Gadaffi who, as part of a plan to win over Africa from Israel, had promised Amin large sums of money and extensive Libyan military aid. The Ugandan dictator was easily seduced by Gadaffi's promises of massive financial aid and expressions of fraternity for a fellow Muslim, and in February 1972 joined the Libyan ruler in a declaration supporting the Arabs against Zionism and imperialism and calling for the withdrawal of Israel from all Arab territories and the restoration of the rights of Palestinians to their own lands. During the following month, Amin expelled his Israeli military advisers and broke off diplomatic relations with Israel.

Thereafter, except in South Africa, Israeli fortunes had suffered a major reversal throughout the African continent with the exception of South Africa where relations remained close. The PLO was quick to take advantage, establishing itself in several countries in the wake of Israeli departures. In Uganda, no sooner had the Israeli Ambassador departed than his residence, at 17 McKinnon Road in Kampala, was handed over to the PLO's representative, Haled al-Sid. In addition, Amin permitted the PLO to establish training camps in Uganda and thereafter the latter used it increasingly as its centre of operations in Africa, forming links with black guerrilla movements fighting the Portuguese in Mozambique and the Smith regime in Rhodesia, while also establishing a network of offices throughout the continent. At the same time, more than 300 Palestinians took over Ugandan civil service posts previously held by Asians who had been expelled from the country. Meanwhile, Libya lived up to its promises, supplying Amin with a Palestinian 300-man bodyguard, MiG fighter aircraft and Soviet-manufactured armoured vehicles.

This was the background setting for Wadi Haddad's Operation Uganda which was intended to be a terrorist spectacular designed to strike a major blow at Israel while improving Palestinian credibility which was suffering from internal disputes within the various movements operating under the umbrella of the PLO.

To assist him with his planning Haddad called on Ilich Ramírez Sánchez, their choice of target being an aircraft carrying a large number of Israelis. Athens airport was selected as the launching point of the operation because of its poor security which was known to be particularly lax during the summer months when large numbers of tourists were passing through. It was agreed that two Europeans and two Arabs would carry out the initial phase of the operation. Ramírez selected Böse and Kuhlmann while Wadi Haddad chose two of his most trusted officers: Fayez Abdul-Rahim Jaber, one of the founders of the PFLP and a close friend of George

Habash, and Jayel Naji al-Arjam, deputy chief of the PFLP–SOG's foreign relations department.

The following months were spent in extensive planning and training for the operation with at least one dry run being carried out. The security measures and procedures at Athens airport were studied and the lay-out of an Airbus airliner learned and memorised. The drills and procedures for the hijack itself, the subsequent control of the passengers, the collection of passports and the separation of Jews from non-Jews – all were rehearsed to perfection. In order to ensure that he knew that the pilot would be following his instructions, Wilfried Böse learned the skills of aircraft navigation, familiarising himself with charts and the instrument panel of an A-300B Airbus.

The operation could not, however, be carried out without the co-operation of others, including the assistance of Palestinian sympathisers at Bahrain airport who allowed Fouad Awad and his two accomplices to board the Singapore Airlines flight with their weapons. The aircraft had to be refuelled en route to Uganda and that facility was provided by Libya. The agreement of Idi Amin had to be sought for the aircraft to land at Entebbe, where the principal drama would be played out, and for facilities to be supplied for incarceration of the hostages. Finally, Wadi Haddad approached the government of Somalia with a request to establish a forward headquarters in its capital, Mogadishu, from where he would control the operation. All of those approached had agreed without exception to provide assistance.

At Entebbe, the morning of Tuesday 29 June saw the return of the terrorists who had obviously been resting after the flight. That afternoon, Fouad Awad announced their demands in the form of a communiqué, transmitted over Uganda Radio, claiming responsibility for the hijack and stating: 'Flight 139 was taken in order to remind the world of our intention to expel Zionists so that we may replace Israel with a social democracy ...' The communiqué demanded the release, by 2 p.m. Thursday 1 July, of fifty-three terrorists imprisoned in five countries – forty in

Israel, six in West Germany, five in Kenya, and one each in Switzerland and France. It also demanded US $5 million in cash.

The list of terrorists held in Israeli prisons included: Archbishop Hilarion Capucci, primate of the Greek Orthodox community in Jerusalem, convicted of gun-running on behalf of Al-Fatah; Kozo Okamoto, the surviving member of the Japanese Red Army group responsible for the Lod Airport massacre on 31 May 1972; Fatma Barnawi, an African member of Al-Fatah convicted of planting a bomb in a cinema in Jerusalem in 1968; William George Nasser, a member of Al-Fatah, convicting of carrying out sabotage and murdering a Druze watchman in Jerusalem; Muzna Kamel Nikola, a member of Al-Fatah, convicted of spying and recruitment operations in Israel; Kamel Namri, a member of Al-Fatah, convicted of acts of sabotage; and Samir Darwish, a member of PFLP–GC, convicted of planning the escape of two prisoners from Ramleh Prison. As mentioned in Chapter 1, those listed in West Germany were members of the Red Army Faction or an affiliated splinter group, the 2nd June Movement: Jan-Carl Raspe, Fritz Teufel, Ralf Reinders, Inge Viett, Ingrid Schubert and Werner Hoppe. Those in Kenya were the PFLP–SOG three-man missile team and two West Germans arrested in Kenya in January.

At the end of their communiqué, the terrorists stated that the hostages would be executed if the demands were not met by the deadline. That evening, the situation in the terminal building became more sinister when the terrorists separated all Israelis and Jews of other nationalities, numbering 103 in all, from the rest of the hostages and confined them in an adjoining room.

Next day, Wednesday 30 June, following another visit by Idi Amin, events took an unexpected turn when the terrorists announced that forty-seven passengers, mainly French nationals, would be released. Later in the day, all forty-seven were taken to the French consulate in Kampala before being driven to the new terminal at Entebbe, some two kilometres from the building where the hostages were imprisoned, and flown to Paris on an Air France flight that evening. On the afternoon of the following day, Thursday

1 July, a further 101 hostages were released and flown to Paris, leaving the eighty-three Israelis, twenty French nationals of Jewish origin and Flight 139's crew of twelve, headed by the pilot Captain Michel Bacos, still in captivity.

By this time three more terrorists, all of them high-ranking members of the PFLP, had arrived at Kampala from Somalia, bringing the terrorists' total strength to ten. Two of them were later identified as Abdul Razag (alias Abu Dardai), one of Wadi Haddad's most experienced operational commanders who had previously carried out several missions in Europe, and Abdul Khaled al-Khalil.

During the afternoon of Thursday 1 July, news arrived which lifted the hostages' spirits: the Israeli government had agreed to the terrorists' demands. Furthermore, the latter had agreed to an extension of their deadline to noon on Sunday 4 July.

In Israel, meanwhile, the first reports of Flight 139's arrival at Entebbe had come from the Voice of Israel radio service. Thereafter, further reports came from other news networks which had correspondents in Kampala, including the BBC. Once it became apparent that Flight 139 was no longer heading for Tel Aviv, the Unit 269 team at Lod airport stood down and returned to its base.

A major information-gathering operation was put into full swing with an Israeli Navy warship, equipped with electronic monitoring equipment, being despatched on 28 June to a location off the East African coast to listen to all transmissions to and from Uganda.

During the following five days of the crisis, the Israeli government deliberated over the two courses open to it: either surrender to the terrorists' demands or mount a rescue operation. For Prime Minister Yitzhak Rabin, the decision on which course to pursue was an agonising one. At this juncture, possessing nothing in the way of a viable military option, he and his cabinet were forced to conclude that negotiation with the terrorists appeared to be the only solution. On Wednesday 30 June, the cabinet convened to hear reports from the various government departments and ministries involved in trying to resolve the crisis. The foreign ministry had been urging the governments of other countries to persuade Idi Amin to withdraw his support of the terrorists; France had complied, attempting to use its influence with other African states. Israel's ambassador to the United Nations had meanwhile been seeking the support of the UN Secretary General, Kurt Waldheim.

Meanwhile, direct communication with Idi Amin had been established through a retired Israeli Army officer, Colonel Baruch Bar-Lev, who had known the dictator well during the 1960s while chief of the Israeli military mission in Uganda. Bar-Lev initiated a series of telephone calls from Tel Aviv to Amin in Kampala, during which he emphasised to him the importance of his role in the crisis and pointing out how, by rescuing the hostages, he could take the opportunity to prove that he was a great man. He urged Amin to intervene, pointing out that he was the ruler of Uganda and that he, and not the Palestinians, should be making the decisions. Despite Bar-Lev's best efforts, including a suggestion that he might win the Nobel peace prize, Amin remained obdurate, insisting that the fate of the hostages was not in his hands and that Israel had to meet the terrorists' demands.

On Wednesday night, two Israeli government ministers attended a meeting with relatives of the hostages who demanded that action be taken to secure their release without any risk. The latter were obviously dissatisfied with the response they received and early next morning they invaded the government compound where the prime minister's office is located. Once again, they reiterated demands for action to be taken to secure the release of the hostages, insisting that those listed in the terrorists' demands should be freed without further delay.

At 7.45 a.m. on Thursday 1 July, Rabin and his cabinet met to review the situation and it was agreed that diplomatic efforts should continue. At 8.30 a.m., with the terrorists' deadline only three and a half hours away, the unanimous decision was taken to negotiate. During the morning, Colonel Bar-Lev received a telephone call from Idi Amin, advising him to listen to a broadcast on Uganda Radio. At 1 p.m., the announcement was made that the terrorists had extended their deadline to midday on Sunday 4 July.

In the meantime, Mossad had been busy inserting its agents into Uganda. Some drove from Kenya via the Rift Valley; others flew in light aircraft from Nairobi's airport, flying high above Lake Victoria and photographing Entebbe airport. Another group of six agents, four Israelis and two Kenyans, crossed Lake Victoria in a Kenya police launch and was landed on the Ugandan shore. A proposal to plant listening devices in the residence of PLO representative Haled al-Sid was dropped after it was discovered that the house was heavily guarded by Palestinians. Meanwhile, Mossad officers met the two flights bringing in the released hostages to Orly airport at Paris. Each individual was questioned closely about the terrorists, their weapons, locations of the hostages, dispositions of the Ugandan troops and any other relevant information. In London Pat Heyman, the English/Israeli woman who had been released at Benghazi, provided further information on the hijackers.

Another Mossad team flew into Nairobi on Wednesday 30 June, arriving on El-Al Flight 535 in the guise of businessmen. Contact was made with a number of powerful figures in the Kenyan government establishment, among them the Kenyan police chief, Bryn Davies, and the chief of the GSU, Geoffrey Karithii. In addition, Mossad agents also contacted Bruce McKenzie, a former wartime officer in the SAS who had settled in Kenya after the end of the Second World War. A close adviser to President Jomo Kenyatta, McKenzie also had connections with Britain's SIS whom he kept well informed about events and developments throughout Africa. McKenzie approached President Kenyatta and secured his permission for Mossad to use Kenya as an operating base for a rescue operation.

The Mossad team used Kenyan agents to reconnoitre Entebbe, confirming the airport's defences and the dispositions of Ugandan troops. Meanwhile, El-Al pilots and staff casually questioned pilots from other airlines about the location of the refuelling point at Entebbe and the condition of the runways, essential information for the pilots of the rescue force aircraft.

One crucial point raised with the Kenyans was whether they would permit the rescue force aircraft to refuel at Nairobi on the return trip. The answer was given by the GSU chief, Geoffrey Karithii, who intimated that Kenya would cooperate and that his department and the police would cordon off the rescue aircraft while refuelling was in progress. The Kenyan attorney-general, Charles Njojo, stated that facilities could not be withheld as long as the Nairobi airport authority considered no international civil aviation laws had been broken.

Mossad also mounted a deception operation in order to buy time. Among the measures employed were the use of open telephone lines on which conversations took place giving the impression that the Israeli government intended to accede to the terrorists' demands. Information was let slip to a diplomat of another country to the effect that the only obstacle in the way of negotiation with the terrorists was the drafting of a statement that would be politically acceptable to Israel.

While the prime minister and his cabinet agonised over the course of action to be taken, the IDF was busy producing plans for the second option – a rescue operation. On the orders of the Chief of Staff, Lieutenant General Mordechai Gur, a seven-man planning team, comprising officers of the intelligence branch and the Sayeret Matkal, was hard at work producing four different plans. The airport terminal at Entebbe had been constructed by an Israeli company so the planners were able to obtain plans of the building. Other information about the airport was obtained from a variety of sources. At the same time, up-to-date information on the dispositions of Ugandan forces in the area of Entebbe also arrived. It appeared that half of the Ugandan Army's 21,000 troops were based between Entebbe and Kampala some twenty miles away while the airport was guarded by troops equipped with Soviet weapons and armour. Thirty MiG-17 and MiG-21 aircraft were based at the airport, their airfield being near the old terminal. A mass of data was gradually accumulated and by Wednesday the planning team had produced the four options.

The first proposed a combined Unit 269 and Israeli Navy Shayetet 13 operation involving a parachute drop on Lake Victoria followed by a hostage rescue operation at the airport, the rescuers and hostages thereafter surrendering to the Ugandans. This proposal relied on the assumption that Idi Amin would want to help the Israelis and thus clear himself of any involvement in Wadi Haddad's operation. The second option, counting on assistance from Kenya, proposed a rescue force crossing Lake Victoria in a large vessel; again, however, it also assumed Amin would be willing to cooperate.

The third option was more sophisticated and called for a rescue force, some disguised as prisoners, being flown to Entebbe in an Israeli Air Force (IAF) Boeing 707 painted in El-Al livery. On landing, the entire force would disembark, attack the terminal and free the hostages. Once again, however, a successful withdrawal would depend on the co-operation of the Ugandans. The fourth and final option was for a rescue force to be flown in IAF C-130 transports to Entebbe, carry out the rescue operation and withdraw. The principal problems facing such an operation would be the round-trip of 2,200 miles and the threat of radar detection by Egypt, Saudi Arabia and the Sudan. The IAF was, however, confident that it could carry out such a task successfully.

On Wednesday 30 June, Mossad produced information which indicated that Idi Amin was heavily involved in aiding the terrorists. This meant that the first three options were no longer viable, leaving only the fourth. The Chief of Staff nevertheless required four options to be proposed and all four were submitted by the planning team. Within a very short time, the team was told to concentrate on producing a plan based on the fourth option, code-named Operation Thunderball.

On the following day, Thursday 1 July, the team worked on the plan and at 4 p.m. were visited by Brigadier General Dan Shomron, the Israeli Army's chief of infantry and airborne forces, who was briefed on the proposed operation which called for a force of picked troops to be transported to Entebbe in four IAF C-130 Hercules transports. The aircraft would land under cover of darkness and taxi to the old terminal where the assault force would disembark and storm the building, killing the terrorists and any

Ugandan troops offering any opposition. The hostages would be freed and embarked on the C-130 transports which would then fly back to Israel. The planners envisaged that the entire operation would require the aircraft and rescue force to be on the ground at Entebbe for no more than an hour.

No sooner had he been briefed by the planning team, then Brigadier General Shomron was called by the IDF's Chief of Staff and Chief of Operations, Major General Yekutiel Adam, to present the plan to the Defence Minister, Shimon Peres, and the Chief of Staff, Lieutenant General Mordechai Gur. Shortly afterwards the team was advised that approval for the operation would be subject to a Cabinet decision but that planning should proceed with all haste.

That night, the final details of the plan were put in place by Brigadier General Shomron, the planning team, and representatives of the units which would take part in the operation. In outline, the plan was as follows. As the first C-130 landed and taxied down the runway, a team from the Sayeret Tzanhanim, the reconnaissance unit of 35th Parachute Brigade, would disembark via the rear ramp and lay beacons to guide in the other three aircraft in the event that the runway lights were switched off by the Ugandans. On halting near the old terminal, the leading aircraft would disembark a fifteen-man detachment of Unit 269, disguised as Ugandan troops and travelling in a black Mercedes staff car and two Land Rovers, who would approach the building and eliminate the terrorists.

The second C-130 would touch down seven minutes after the first, bringing in nineteen more members of Unit 269, equipped with two Soviet-manufactured armoured personnel carriers (APC), who would establish a defensive perimeter around the terminal building. This would be followed closely by the third aircraft bringing in more members of Sayeret Matkal and troops of the Sayeret Tzanhanim and the Sayeret Golani, the reconnaissance unit of the Golani Infantry Brigade, also equipped with two APCs. The Sayeret Tzanhanim would secure the new terminal building and the airport refuelling area while the Sayeret Golani would secure the area between the two terminals and be ready to assist the hostages aboard the first aircraft. Meanwhile, one of their two APCs would cover the Ugandan MiGs, which were parked nearby, while the other would join the other two already patrolling the area of the old terminal. The fourth C-130, equipped as an airborne field hospital, would also have landed by then and take on board any casualties. A second field hospital would be deployed in an IAF Boeing 727 to Nairobi airport where the Kenyan government would be advised of the operation as it took place and be asked for landing clearance for the four C-130s withdrawing from Uganda. Throughout the entire operation, an airborne command and communications centre, located in an IAF Boeing 707 carrying Major General Yekutiel Adam and the commander of the IAF, Major General Benny Peled, would orbit overhead while maintaining communications with Tel Aviv.

In giving his initial qualified approval to the concept of the plan on Thursday afternoon, Prime Minister Yitzhak Rabin had emphasised, however, that given the situation at that point, his cabinet's decision to negotiate with the terrorists still remained in force. He stipulated that he would not countenance an operation that would not guarantee the return of the rescue force, nor could he justify risking the lives of even one of the hostages. The leader of the Likud opposition, Menachem Begin, who had been made privy to the decision, had agreed that negotiation was the only option under the circumstances.

Despite the fact that no final approval had been given for the operation to proceed, Thursday night saw the rescue force beginning to rehearse it at the Sayeret Matkal base under the watchful eye of the Unit's commanding officer, Lieutenant Colonel Yonathan Netanyahu. A model of the terminal building had been constructed from timber covered in hessian and canvas and the fifteen-man Unit 269 assault group practised repeatedly the storming of the building and the clearing of its rooms. At dawn on Friday 2 July, an IAF C-130 landed at the base and was used to practise the disembarkation and embarkation phases of the operation. Also present were the Ugandan Army 'staff car', in reality a white Mercedes taxi resprayed black for the occasion, and the two Land Rovers in which the assault group would disembark and approach the terminal building. Throughout the rest of that day, the force continued its rehearsals until every man knew his own individual tasks to perfection. It was joined by Lieutenant General Mordechai Gur who, with Brigadier General Dan Shomron, watched the training and continually quizzed Lieutenant Colonel Netanyahu and his officers over different aspects of the operation.

On Friday night, while the force continued its rehearsals, the pilots who would fly the leading C-130 flew the Chief of Staff to the southern end of the Sinai Peninsula where they demonstrated to his satisfaction that they could land the aircraft in darkness without the use of its lights or those on the runway. They returned later that night and in the early hours of Saturday 3 July Lieutenant General Gur informed Lieutenant Colonel Netanyahu and his officers that he would be advising the Prime Minister and the cabinet, which was meeting at 9 a.m., that the operation could be carried out.

At 11 a.m. on Saturday 3 July the rescue force, led by Brigadier General Dan Shomron, left the Sayeret Matkal base and moved to an IAF airbase where it emplaned with its vehicles aboard the four C-130s. Shortly afterwards, the aircraft took off and headed for Sharm el Sheikh, on the southern tip of the Sinai peninsula where they refuelled. At just after 1 p.m., the force was in the air once again and heading for Entebbe while awaiting the final signal which would order them either to proceed or turn back. Twenty minutes later a radio message was received by Brigadier General Dan Shomron, who was travelling in the lead aircraft, from Major General Yekutiel Adam: the Israeli cabinet had given clearance for Operation Thunderball to proceed.

The four C-130s headed south down the Red Sea, flying low to avoid detection by Egyptian radar. Meanwhile the two IAF Boeing 707s, one equipped as an airborne command and communications centre and the other containing a fully equipped field hospital, were also in the air. Both painted in El-Al livery and bearing civil registration numbers, they followed the normal route used by civil aircraft passing down the Red Sea, swinging south-west across Ethiopia before crossing into Kenya and landing at Nairobi's Embakasi airport. Both aircraft refuelled, the command and communications aircraft preparing to take off as soon as the rescue force aircraft began their approach to Entebbe.

Meanwhile the Hercules transports, in loose formation and following the same route flown earlier by the two 707s, were flying at wavetop level to avoid detection by Russian electronic monitoring stations in the southern part of the Red Sea. Turning south-west, they flew nap-of-the-earth, at one point encountering a ferocious storm which caused considerable turbulence and discomfort for those crammed in the hot and noisy hold of each aircraft. Twenty minutes prior to H-hour, the troops carried out final checks on their weapons and equipment and prepared for the landing.

The four Hercules made their final approaches in two pairs. The leading pair would land on the old runway, approaching Entebbe from the north-west, while the second approached from the south to land on the new runway. In the distance, the crews of the leading pair could see the lights on the new runway. At one minute past midnight local time on the morning of 4 July, the leading C-130 floated down almost noiselessly, its wheels touching down gently on the end of the runway. The pilot, Major Yehoshua Shani, allowed the aircraft's momentum to fall away on its own, refraining from using his brakes or his engines in reverse thrust, the noise of which would have drawn attention to the landing. At the same time, his co-pilot, Major Ram Levi, commenced lowering the aircraft's ramp.

As the aircraft slowed to a walking pace, the Sayaret Tzanhanim team jumped down from the ramp and began placing beacons beside the runway to guide in the second aircraft, due to land seven minutes later. Seconds later the aircraft halted gently and the assault group deployed in the Mercedes 'staff car' and the two Land Rovers which drove steadily towards the old terminal building.

As the vehicles approached, a Ugandan sentry spotted them and prepared to issue a formal challenge prior to saluting. As the Mercedes approached him, Lieutenant Colonel Netanyahu and another member of the assault group opened fire with silenced .22 pistols; the soldier fell, but was only wounded. Staggering to his feet, he aimed his weapon at the Mercedes, but was killed by a burst of fire from a soldier in the Land Rover following behind.

The element of surprise was lost and the Ugandan troops were quick to react, opening fire on the three vehicles whose occupants were forced to abandon them and run for the cover of the terminal building, led by Major Muki Betser, the second-in-command of the rescue force and the commander of the assault group. Heading for the entrance assigned to him and his group, Betser spotted one of the terrorists coming out of another door. Firing twice, he missed and the terrorist ran back inside the building.

The assault plan was coming adrift and Ugandan troops were bringing heavy fire to bear from the old airport control tower near the terminal housing the hostages. Betser and his men found their assigned entrance into the old terminal blocked and were forced to run to the next door. Bursting into the building, two of them led the way and spotted one of the Palestinian terrorists who was immediately shot and killed. A split second later Wilfried Böse and Brigitte Kuhlmann suffered a similar fate as they raised their weapons. A second Palestinian terrorist then appeared from behind a column and opened fire, mortally wounding one of the hostages, Ida Bobovitz, but was immediately shot and killed by Major Betser and a member of his group. Another hostage, 52-year-old Pesko Cohen, was fatally wounded by a stray bullet as the troops returned the terrorist's fire. In the hall, the hostages lay screaming with terror; one of them, a young French Jew named Jean Jacques Maimon, jumped to his feet and was immediately shot dead by the troops who mistook him for a terrorist. At that point, one of the assault group began using a megaphone, ordering the hostages in English and Hebrew to remain lying down and telling them that the IDF had arrived to rescue them.

Elsewhere in the old terminal, other elements of the assault group were clearing the rest of the rooms in the building. As they moved down a corridor, they encountered two men in a corridor and challenged them; one produced a grenade and the troops opened fire, killing them both. Shortly afterwards, another man was spotted and shot dead, bringing to a total of seven the number of terrorists accounted for so far. Some Ugandan troops were encountered by another assault group team on the upper floor and were also summarily despatched. In addition to Wilfried Böse and Brigitte Kuhlmann, five of the Palestinian terrorists died during the assault: Fayez Abdul-Rahim Jaber, Jayel Naji al-Arjam, Abdul Khaled al-Khalil, Abdul Razag and Abu Ali. Of Fouad Awad, Abdel al-Latif and the other Palestinian in their group there was no sign; it was later discovered that they were away from the airport at the time and thus escaped with their lives.

The battle inside the terminal lasted only a few minutes, by which time the other three C-130s had landed. The second Sayeret Matkal group disembarked from the second aircraft with its two APCs and established a defensive perimeter around the terminal. The third C-130, which had landed on the new airport runway, meanwhile disgorged the Sayeret Tzanhanim and Sayeret Golani troops, supported by the other two Sayeret Matkal APCs, who secured the new terminal, the refuelling point and the runway for the withdrawal phase of the operation. As planned, both APCs then headed across to the old terminal to reinforce the troops protecting it. The fourth C-130, carrying medical personnel and guarded by a detachment of the Sayeret Golani, positioned itself to receive casualties ferried over from the old terminal in the two Land Rovers. All four aircraft remained at their assigned stations with engines turning, ready for the embarkation and withdrawal phase of the operation to begin.

The Ugandan troops continued to engage the rescue force in and around the old terminal. At this juncture, Major Muki Betser received a radio message from the command group's signaller that Lieutenant Colonel Netanyahu had been wounded. He left the building and found his commanding officer lying badly wounded and unconscious on the ground outside, having been shot by a sniper firing from the old control tower. After contacting Brigadier General

Dan Shomron, who was directing the securing of the new terminal and the runway on the other side of the airport, Betser assumed command. Meanwhile a medical officer, who had accompanied the assault group, performed emergency treatment on Netanyahu.

All resistance from the Ugandan troops had ceased and three of the aircraft now approached the old terminal to embark the hostages and the rescue force. The exhausted and terrified hostages, shielded by troops, made their way across the tarmac to the waiting C-130s while the Land Rovers ferried Lieutenant Colonel Netanyahu, three members of the assault group who had also been wounded and the three dead hostages across to the hospital aircraft. Meanwhile, IAF technicians were positioned at the refuelling point, ready to refill the C-130s' tanks. At this juncture, however, a radio message was received from the command and communications aircraft, circling overhead, that the Kenyan government had given clearance for the rescue force aircraft to land and refuel at Nairobi, thus dispensing with the need to do so at Entebbe and reducing the time the force would have to remain there.

As the troops began to escort the hostages from the terminal to the aircraft, Ugandan troops opened fire with a machine-gun from the old control tower. This was met with heavy fire and rocket-propelled grenades from one of the APCs which, after two attempts, succeeded in silencing the machine-gun. As the embarkation continued, one of the APCs drove over to eleven MiGs parked some 100 metres away and proceeded to destroy them with machine-gun fire and rocket-propelled grenades. Shortly afterwards, all the hostages and the entire rescue force had been embarked and the aircraft began to taxi towards the new runway. In the last C-130, troops standing on the still-lowered ramp tossed out explosive charges fitted with delay fuses to discourage any follow-up by the Ugandan troops and to provide a smoke-screen to shield the withdrawing aircraft.

At 1 a.m., fifty-nine minutes after the first aircraft had landed, the four C-130s took off and headed for Nairobi. Their departure was watched by a Mossad team on the north shore of Lake Victoria which had observed the entire operation through night observation devices. Packing up its radios and equipment, it headed for the shore of the lake from which it was extracted shortly afterwards.

Thirty minutes later, the rescue force landed at Embakasi airport at Nairobi where it was joined by the command and communications Boeing 707 which had already signalled news of the success of the operation to Tel Aviv. While the five aircraft were being refuelled, the wounded were transferred to the field hospital in the second Boeing. Shortly afterwards, however, Major Muki Betser and his men were told of the death of Lieutenant Colonel Yonathan Netanyahu, the only member of the rescue force to be killed. Before dawn, the four C-130s and the Boeing 707 hospital aircraft took off from Nairobi, followed later by the second Boeing. Heading south over the Kenyan coast, they swung northeast, flying parallel to the coast of Somalia before rounding the Horn of Africa and entering the Gulf of Aden. After passing through the straits of Bab el Mandeb, they headed northwards up the Red Sea towards Israel and home.

A brutal postscript to Operation Thunderball took place on the following day. Unknown to the rescue force, one of the hostages, an elderly woman named Dora Bloch, had been taken to hospital in Kampala after choking on some food and was thus missing from the airport when the rescue took place. On the day after the operation, she was hauled from her bed by Ugandan thugs, taken away and murdered.

Two years later, Idi Amin exacted further revenge for Operation Thunderball. Former SAS officer and farmer Bruce McKenzie died when a bomb, planted in his private aircraft by Libyan agents on behalf of the Ugandan dictator, blew up. Israel did not forget him, however, and a forest of 10,000 trees in the hills of Lower Galilee was planted in his memory – paid for with funds raised by the Association of Israeli Intelligence Veterans.

The presence at Entebbe of such senior members of the PFLP–SOG as Fayez Abdul Rahmin Jaber, Jayel Naji al-Arjam and Abdul Razag, demonstrated the importance that Wadi Haddad had attached to Operation Uganda. In the event, however, it proved to be a disaster for the organisation, causing it immense damage politically. There had already been major differences of doctrine and policy between George Habash and Wadi Haddad, resulting in the split between them in 1972, and the débâcle at Entebbe only served to increase these. The PLO was also adversely affected by the political fall-out and great harm was done to the Arab cause as a whole. All the more so when it later transpired that Egyptian president Anwar Sadat had known from intelligence reports that Wadi Haddad was planning a major hijack; he had been in a position to prevent it, but had not done so because he had not wished to be seen as having abandoned the Palestinian cause. Furthermore, he was apparently frustrated at the lack of diplomatic efforts in the Middle East by the United States, where the administration of President Gerald Ford was in the middle of an election year and was unwilling to upset its Jewish supporters. He thus saw the PFLP–SOG operation as being a terrorist spectacular which would shake the Americans out of their diplomatic slumber.

Operation Thunderball was an outstanding success and a warning to terrorists worldwide that, wherever they were, they were not beyond the reach of Israel. For the rest of the world, it served as a model as to what could be achieved by a well trained force, using skill, daring and determination to carry out a viable, thoroughly planned and exhaustively rehearsed operation. Indeed, it was not long before such a combination was required again when, fifteen months after Thunderball, West Germany was faced with a similar crisis.

7

OPERATION FIRE MAGIC

As recounted in Chapter 1, by the late 1970s international terrorism was rife and a number of major terrorist outrages had taken place, one of these being the kidnap on 5 September 1977 of the West German industrialist Hanns Martin Schleyer by the Red Army Faction. After five and a half weeks of negotiations with the West German government, which was playing for time, the terrorists decided to step up the pressure. On 13 October, Lufthansa Flight LH 181 was hijacked by four members of Wadi Haddad's PFLP–SOG on behalf of the Red Army Faction.

The Boeing 737 aircraft took off at 11 a.m. from Palma, on the island of Majorca, en route for Frankfurt. About thirty minutes later, as it was passing over Marseilles, the terrorists struck. The first move was made by two men, Zohair Yousif Akache (alias Ali Hyderi) and Wabil Harb (alias Riza Abbas), who made their way to the aircraft's flight deck. Forcing their way in and screaming hysterically at the top of their voices, they pulled the co-pilot, Jürgen Vietor, from his seat and forced him out. Meanwhile two female accomplices, Suhailah Saych (alias Soraya Ansari) and Hind Alameh (alias Shanaz Gholoun), both of whom were armed with pistols and grenades, were hustling the aircraft's three stewardesses, Gaby Dillmann, Hannelore Piegler and Anna-Maria Staringer, to the rear of the economy section where Vietor joined them. There was pandemonium as hysterical passengers cowered under a constant torrent of screamed threats.

While Harb stood with a pistol pointed at the pilot, Captain Jürgen Schumann, a highly nervous Akache left the flight deck and made his way to the rear of the aircraft where he announced that it was now under the command of 'Captain Martyr Mahmoud of the Martyr Halimeh Commando' and that anyone disobeying his instructions would be shot.

All male passengers were ordered out of their seats and searched for weapons. The terrorists then went through both sections of the cabin, removing all items of hand baggage and inspecting their contents before depositing them in the first-class section. All four were highly nervous and Akache occasionally lost his temper, striking passengers and terrifying them with his violent outbursts. Meanwhile occupants of the first-class cabin were moved into the economy section.

By this time, the aircraft was over the Mediterranean. At 2.38 p.m. precisely the West German Chancellor, Helmut Schmidt, received a telephone call from his Interior Minister, Werner Maihofer, who told him that Flight LH 181 had apparently been hijacked.

At 3.45 p.m. local time, the aircraft landed at Rome's Leonardo da Vinci airport. Akache, who had occupied the co-pilot's seat, ordered Schumann to stop some 1,000 yards from the airport's buildings and shortly afterwards Italian troops and armoured vehicles surrounded the aircraft. He then broadcast a tirade which included a list of demands. In addition to the release of the eleven members of the Red Army Faction already listed in the communiqué published by Hanns Martin Schleyer's kidnappers six weeks earlier on 6 September, these included the release of two Palestinians jailed in Turkey for terrorist offences, a ransom of US $15 million and the insistence that all the released terrorists should be flown to South Yemen, Somalia or Vietnam. All demands had to be met by a deadline of 8 a.m. GMT on Sunday 16 October or the aircraft, with everyone in it, would be blown up.

The West German Interior Minister, Werner Maihofer, meanwhile had contacted his opposite number, Francesco Cossiga, and requested that his troops shoot out the aircraft's tyres out to prevent it leaving. The Italians, however, did not wish to become embroiled in the affair, and declined to acquiesce with Maihofer's demands which had been made without consulting his own experts who were horrified when they learned of them. Meanwhile, Akache had demanded that the aircraft be refuelled and the Italians obliged with alacrity.

At 5.45 p.m., two hours after landing, despite not having received air traffic control clearance to do so, the aircraft took off and headed for Cyprus where it landed at Larnaca at 8.28 p.m. local time and taxied to a position at the far end of the runway. A demand by Akache for refuelling was met and at 10.50 p.m. Flight LH 181 took off once more. Akache instructed Schumann and Vietor to fly to Beirut, but was shortly afterwards informed that the Lebanese had blocked the airport. Requests to land at Baghdad and Damascus were similarly turned down by the Iraqi and Syrian governments so the aircraft was flown to Kuwait but was again met by a refusal. By now fuel was running low and in desperation Akache told Schumann to land at Bahrain. Despite an initial refusal by the Bahraini air traffic control, the aircraft landed at 1.52 a.m. local time on Friday 14 October with only three minutes of fuel left in its tanks.

As soon as the aircraft had come to a stop, Akache established radio communication with the airport control tower, announcing himself as 'Captain Mahmoud of the Kaffre Gadum Operation of the Martyr Halimeh Commando' and demanded that the aircraft be refuelled. Bahraini troops surrounded the Boeing, causing the terrorist leader to panic and threaten to shoot the co-pilot. Initially, they refused to withdraw and it was only after a plea from Schumann and Vietor over the radio that they did so. The Boeing was refuelled and took off into the night, this time bound for the Emirate of Dubai.

Meanwhile in West Germany, news of the hijack had reached the headquarters of the GSG-9 which had been put on standby. During the afternoon of Friday 13 October, Chancellor Schmidt told Maihofer to contact Lieutenant Colonel Ulrich Wegener and order a team to be prepared for a hostage rescue operation code-named Fire Magic. At 7.42 p.m. Maihofer called Wegener again and confirmed that the decision had been taken to proceed with the operation. The latter lost no time in calling in the commanders of his three combat teams, Captains Schmidt, Weigolt and Tutter. Only one would be required so the three drew lots, Weigolt being the winner. Wegener would be in command of the 30-strong team which would also include his adjutant, Captain Baum, two explosives experts, a communications specialist and Captain Weigolt with twenty-four of his men.

By 9.45 p.m. the team was at Cologne airport with all its weapons and equipment and by 10.13 was aboard a Lufthansa Boeing 737 bound for Cyprus where Flight LH 181 was still sitting on the runway at Larnaca. A few hours later, at around 10.30 p.m., Cypriot local time, GSG-9's aircraft reached its destination. Twenty minutes later, however, Flight LH 181 took off and headed for Bahrain.

In Bonn next morning, Friday 14 October, the headquarters of the Bundeskriminalamt (Federal Criminal Bureau) received copies of two messages from the hijackers which not only stated their demands, but also provided confirmation of their links with the Red Army Faction. The first, signed by 'The Struggle Against World Imperialist Organisations' stated that 'the lives of the passengers and crew and the life of Hanns Martin Schleyer depend on the fulfilment of the following demands', which were a reiteration of the demands made by Akache at Rome. The second message had been relayed from the 'Kaffre Gadum Operation of the Martyr Halimeh Commando', the phrase used by Akache whenever he was issuing demands over Flight LH 181's radio. It declared unity with the 'Siegfried Hausner Commando', a name frequently used by the Red Army Faction, in its struggle against neo-Nazism, Zionism and imperialism.

In London, meanwhile, a request for assistance and advice from 22 SAS had been received from the West German government. This had been swiftly granted and two members of the regiment, its second-in-command Major Alastair Morrison, and an NCO from G Squadron, Staff Sergeant Barry Davies, were despatched in haste. On Saturday 15 October, after flying from RAF Brize Norton to Bonn, they were driven to the GSG-9 base at St. Augustin where they were briefed by Major Klaus Blätte, the unit's second-in-command. Shortly afterwards, the two men left on a Kuwaiti Airways flight from Frankfurt to Kuwait from where they flew to

Dubai to rendezvous with the GSG–9 team. They carried with them a case of stun grenades, a weapon unknown to GSG–9 at that time, and, should it prove imperative to pay the ransom demanded, a very large aluminium suitcase containing $15 million.

Meanwhile, Flight LH 181 had initially met with a refusal to its request to land at Dubai where the authorities had blocked the runway with fire engines. Akache, however, refused to accept this and ordered Captain Jürgen Schumann to land. The latter radioed the control tower that he was running out of fuel and as he made a single pass over the airport, the runway was cleared. The aircraft landed a few minutes later and taxied to a halt on the runway. It was 5.40 a.m. local time on Friday 14 October.

In the meantime, GSG–9's aircraft had remained on the ground at Cyprus for just over five hours, taking off again at 4 a.m. local time on 14 October. Initially, Lieutenant Colonel Wegener and his team were ordered to return to West Germany, but shortly afterwards were instructed to fly instead to Ankara, in Turkey. After landing, he and a small reconnaissance group flew on to Dubai while the remainder of the team remained at Ankara. Arriving there on the night of Saturday 15 October, he met the West German Minister of State, Jürgen Wischnewski, and a psychologist named Wolfgang Salewski who was an adviser to Chancellor Helmut Schmidt.

Wegener learned that negotiations with the hijackers were being conducted by Sheikh Mohammed bin Rashid, the Minister of Defence of the United Arab Emirates, who had successfully negotiated peaceful outcomes to four previous hijacks. Wischnewski had asked for permission for the GSG–9 team to mount a rescue operation, but this request had been politely refused by Sheikh Mohammed who insisted that any operation would be carried out by his own men. At 2 a.m. on Sunday 16 October, Major Alastair Morrison and Staff Sergeant Barry Davies arrived in Dubai and shortly afterwards linked up with Lieutenant Colonel Wegener and his group.

In view of Sheikh Mohammed's refusal to allow a GSG–9 operation, the only solution was for Bahraini troops to be trained to storm the aircraft in co-operation with Wegener's group in the event of the hijackers starting to kill the hostages once the 8 a.m. GMT (11 a.m. local time) deadline had passed. Sheikh Mohammed agreed to this and training commenced on a Gulf Air Boeing 737, commandeered for the purpose, which was brought into a hangar out of sight of curious eyes. The *ad hoc* team consisted of three members of the GSG–9 group, Morrison and Davies, three British officers of the Dubai Defence Force and four Arab soldiers of the Emir of Dubai's Palace Guard. One of the British officers, Captain David Bullied, had served as a troop commander in 22 SAS and was thus known to Morrison and Davies; on leaving the British Army he had joined the Dubai Defence Force as a contract officer and was serving in the Palace Guard. Using his contacts, he was able to assemble rapidly much of the equipment required to storm the aircraft.

Throughout that day, 16 October, the hastily formed assault team was drilled in the plan produced by Lieutenant Colonel Wegener and his group. The team would approach the aircraft from the rear under cover of darkness. Using ladders, two men would climb on to each wing and prepare to enter the aircraft through the emergency exits, with two more on the ladders waiting to follow them. At the same time, two more groups with ladders would position themselves below the doors at the front and rear of the port side of the aircraft. On the signal to commence the assault, those on the wings would push in the emergency doors on the wings; the pair on the starboard side would clear the aircraft towards the rear while the pair entering on the port side would do likewise forward towards the cockpit. Meanwhile, the second pair on each wing would enter the aircraft immediately afterwards, controlling the centre area of the aircraft cabin and providing support for the leading pairs if required.

Meanwhile, aboard Flight LH 181, the situation for the passengers and crew had become increasingly uncomfortable since the aircraft had landed on the morning of 14 October. Having been unable to leave their seats for nearly seventeen hours, the passengers were at last permitted to use the aircraft's lavatories. The atmosphere aboard the aircraft was claustrophobic, exacerbated by all the window blinds on the aircraft being pulled down at the insistence of the hijackers. A catering truck arrived with food and drink ordered by Akache who also demanded newspapers; at Vietor's whispered suggestion Schumann ordered four copies, thereby signalling the number of hijackers to those listening in the airport control tower. He also wrapped four cigarettes together and, unnoticed by Akache, threw them into the refuse which was taken away by the catering truck crew.

The terrorists, and Akache in particular, veered between periods of calm and hysteria. During one ferocious outburst over the loudspeaker system, he announced that he would execute three Jewish women at 8 o'clock on the following morning. Thereafter he relapsed into calm and, sitting in Schumann's seat in the cockpit, proceeded to give an hour-long lecture on the history of Palestine and the oppression of the Palestinians. Once again, he worked himself up into a state of hysteria and in his agitation accidentally fired his pistol, sending a bullet into the co-pilot's seat.

The aircraft's systems were being powered by its own generator and that evening Schumann warned Akache that the fuel would soon run out, causing the temperature inside to reach unbearable levels. Two hours later, the generator fell silent and all power failed, the aircraft interior filling with an impenetrable darkness. Schumann switched to the back-up battery which gave a further thirty minutes of electricity and switched off all non-essential electrical equipment in order to conserve power. Meanwhile, chaos reigned in the passenger cabin as the interior temperature reached over 120°F. Some female passengers fainted and the terrorists were forced to open the doors to allow fresh air into the aircraft. Such was their discomfort that some of the passengers stripped to their underwear.

Akache meanwhile was demanding that the aircraft be refuelled, but it was only after he had explained the passengers' extreme state of distress that Sheikh Mohammed gave permission for a bowser to be sent across the runway to the aircraft to provide 800 litres of fuel. Unfortunately, however, this was pumped into the starboard wing tanks whereas the generator took its supply from the port wing. As the situation aboard the aircraft deteriorated further, Schumann radioed the control tower for an emergency power unit vehicle. Sheikh Mohammed agreed and one was sent over to the aircraft, accompanied by two Lufthansa captains, who had arrived earlier from Ankara to provide technical assistance, and a technician.

As the vehicle approached, Akache called out for it to halt and told the three men to bring the power unit up to the port side of the aircraft. As one of the Lufthansa captains explained that the unit had to be positioned by the connection point on the starboard side, Schumann recognised him and, for some inexplicable reason, told Akache that the man was German. This only served to reduce the terrorist leader to another bout of hysteria; leaning out of the door he fired the complete magazine of his pistol down below at the three Germans who took cover behind the power unit before fleeing into the darkness.

At this juncture, Jürgen Vietor persuaded Akache to allow him to connect the power unit to the aircraft. After lowering himself to the ground, using a blanket as a rope, Vietor connected the power unit, but despite his best efforts was unsuccessful because the aircraft's 24 volt battery, which was needed to provide the necessary connection, was by now too weak. The radio was now dead, so Vietor contacted the control tower using a torch to flash a message by Morse Code. Just before dawn on Saturday 15 October, a vehicle carrying a replacement battery arrived and shortly afterwards power was restored to the aircraft.

The situation aboard improved thereafter and the appearance of a catering truck with breakfast restored the atmosphere to a state of relative calm. At this juncture, Akache discovered that it was the birthday of one of the stewardesses, Anna-Maria Staringer, and requested that a birthday cake be sent to the aircraft. Not long afterwards, however, he flew into yet another of his rages after becoming convinced that Vietor was Jewish and threatened to shoot him. Shortly afterwards, a birthday cake, complete with candles, and six bottles of champagne arrived with the compliments of Sheikh Mohammed and an impromptu birthday party was soon in full swing.

The rest of that day and the following night passed without further incident. Just after dawn on Sunday 16 October, however, Akache radioed the control tower again and demanded that the aircraft be refuelled by 9 a.m. or he would start executing some of the passengers. At 8.50 a.m. a fuel bowser approached the aircraft and shortly afterwards a catering vehicle appeared with breakfast.

Sheikh Mohammed meanwhile pleaded with Akache to release the hostages, or at very least the women and children. Unmoved, the latter rejected the request, repeating demands for the release of terrorists in West German prisons. At this juncture, Sheikh Mohammed received a telephone call from his father, Sheikh Rashid, who instructed him to let the hijackers' aircraft depart. Shortly afterwards, Akache ordered Vietor to start the Boeing 737's engines and at 12.19 p.m. the aircraft took off. Initially Akache told him to fly to Oman, but as the aircraft reached Omani airspace, permission to land was refused and he then gave the next destination as Aden.

Some three or four hours later Flight LH 181 reached Khormaksar airport on the outskirts of Aden, the capital of South Yemen. Initially permission to land was refused and both runways were blocked with armoured vehicles, but Akache insisted that Victor land the aircraft. As dusk was falling and with only a few minutes' fuel left in his tanks, the latter carried out an emergency landing on an area of soft sand between the airport's two runways. Captain Schumann feared that the aircraft might have suffered damage, but an inspection by him of its undercarriage revealed that it had survived unscathed. Yemeni troops and armoured vehicles had by now surrounded the aircraft and any expectations that the hijackers might have had of being welcomed with open arms were soon dispelled. The Yemenis made it clear that they would provide fuel and any technical assistance required, but after that the aircraft had to leave immediately. This came as an unwelcome surprise to Akache who argued with them but to no avail.

At this juncture Captain Schumann, after inspecting the undercarriage, asked Akache if he could walk over to the airport control tower and request fuel. The latter agreed, but after a while became agitated at the length of time the pilot had been absent. Flying into another of his violent rages, he contacted the control tower and threatened to shoot some of the passengers unless Schumann returned to the aircraft immediately. Some time later, having been escorted back by Yemeni soldiers, the Lufthansa captain appeared out of the darkness and climbed aboard. Beside himself with rage, Akache screamed and ranted at him while hitting him in the face and accusing him of treachery. Suddenly, without any warning and despite Schumann's protestations of innocence, Akache pointed his pistol at the pilot's face and shot him dead. Not long afterwards the aircraft's fuel was exhausted and the generator died, plunging the interior into darkness,

The Yemenis partially refuelled the aircraft during the night and brought up an auxiliary power unit which enabled Vietor to start the engines and eventually, with difficulty, to taxi the aircraft out of the sand on to the end of one of the runways where refuelling was completed. With only one of the aircraft's headlights still operational, visibility was very poor and he requested permission to take off at dawn, which was some two hours away, but was told by the airport control tower to do so immediately. Fearing that the Yemenis would open fire on the aircraft if he did not comply, and despite anxiety that the engines had been damaged by sand, he launched his aircraft down the runway into the darkness. Climbing steadily, he cleared the mountains ringing the South Yemen capital and headed out over the Gulf of Aden, whereupon Akache ordered him to fly to Mogadishu, the capital of Somalia.

By a remarkable feat of navigation, given the absence of radar covering the region and a paucity of radio beacons, some of which were either weak or switched off, Jürgen Vietor succeeded in doing so. A few hours later, having first flown west to Djibouti and then south over Eritrea and Ethiopia to Somalia, he saw Mogadishu's runway on the coastline ahead of him. Nearing his destination, he did not announce his approach for fear of finding the runway being blocked. At 6.22 a.m. local time on Monday 17 October, Flight LH 181 landed at Mogadishu.

The departure of the aircraft had taken everyone at Dubai by surprise, not least the GSG–9 group which had still been hard at work polishing its aircraft assault drills. A few hours later, however, a Lufthansa Boeing 707 took off from Dubai, carrying Minister of State Jürgen Wischnewski, the GSG–9 group and its two SAS companions who had readily agreed to a request from Wischnewski to accompany them. By now news of Flight LH 181's arrival at Aden had been received and the pilot of the 707 was instructed to fly there. On radioing Aden, however, he was told that permission to land would be refused and he was obliged to fly to Jeddah, in Saudi Arabia.

Leaving his companions on the aircraft, Wischnewski disembarked for discussions with the Saudi authorities who contacted the South Yemen government. Negotiations continued for a few hours and at one point it appeared that the Yemenis and the hijackers had agreed to release the hostages in return for a ransom of $15 million. The Yemenis would permit Wischnewski's aircraft to land at Aden, but on one condition: there were to be no military personnel aboard. While the GSG–9 group, together with Major Morrison and Staff Sergeant Davies, were preparing to transfer to another aircraft which would fly them back to West Germany, news arrived of the murder of Captain Jürgen Schumann. This resulted in an immediate hardening of the West German government's line: negotiations were broken off immediately and Wischnewski announced that he and his group would now storm the aircraft and rescue the hostages in Aden. As Lieutenant Colonel Wegener and his companions began their planning, news arrived of Flight LH 181's arrival at Mogadishu. A few hours later, their aircraft took off from Jeddah and headed for Somalia.

During the flight, the Somali government granted permission for the 707 to overfly its territory and land at Mogadishu and in a few hours the airport came into sight. Skilfully carrying out a short landing on the single runway, the Lufthansa pilot managed to bring his aircraft to a halt short of the hijacked 737. Turning it around, he headed away from it towards the airport buildings without the hijackers being alerted to the presence of another aircraft. Shortly afterwards, President Siad Barre himself arrived to meet Minister of State Wischnewski and it transpired that he had earlier been speaking to Chancellor Helmut Schmidt on the telephone for an hour.

While Wischnewski left with the president, Lieutenant Colonel Wegener and his group were taken to a hotel. Meanwhile a team of German negotiators, including the West German chargé d'affaires in Mogadishu, Dr. Michael Libal, and the psychologist and government adviser Wolfgang Salewski, remained at the airport where negotiations with Akache were being conducted by the Somali chief of police, Abulahi Mahmud Hassan. An hour or so later news came that the terrorists had given a deadline of 4 p.m. that day for their demands to be met or the aircraft would be blown up. Wegener and his group returned immediately to the airport where they met Wischnewski and the negotiators.

By this time, the Somali government had agreed that a hostage rescue operation could be mounted. The remainder of Lieutenant Colonel Wegener's team, which had earlier flown back to West Germany from Ankara and returned to its base at St. Augustin, had remained on standby and on Sunday 16 October had been ordered to fly to Mogadishu to rejoin him. On Monday morning the team of twenty-eight men, under the command of Major Klaus Blätte, took off from Cologne airport in a Lufthansa Boeing 707 which refuelled in Crete before flying on via Djibouti to Mogadishu where it arrived at approximately 8 p.m. local time on Monday 17 October.

The GSG–9 team lost no time and by 10 p.m. its snipers were in their reconnoitred and predesignated positions covering the hijacked aircraft. Meanwhile the assault groups carried out a full rehearsal, using the Lufthansa 707.

Prior to the team's arrival, the assault plan had been revised and checked thoroughly by Major Alastair Morrison and Staff Sergeant Barry Davies. Under cover of the team's snipers, the assault groups would approach the aircraft from the rear, taking up their respective positions by the wing emergency exits and the doors at the front and rear. Meanwhile, the negotiators in the control tower would maintain a constant dialogue with Akache to keep him in the cockpit, advising him that his demands had been met: the release of the Red Army Faction and PFLP terrorists from West German and Turkish prisons and a $15 million ransom. Once the assault teams were in position, a fire would be lit as a diversion by Somali troops some 300 yards in front of the aircraft. Almost immediately afterwards, as the assault was launched, Major Morrison and Staff Sergeant Davies would throw stun grenades over the wings and cockpit to distract and confuse the terrorists further. Once the assault was over, the hostages would be evacuated from the aircraft and guided away to the rear where they would remain in the care of the sniper group which would come forward as soon as the assault was over.

Meanwhile, the situation in the aircraft during the day had become dire as the terrorists' deadline of 4 p.m. approached. Despite the best efforts of the Somali police chief to persuade him otherwise, Akache had refused to extend the deadline and at 3.50 p.m., radioed the control tower to ask the Somalis to withdraw their troops as he was about to blow up the aircraft. At this point the Somali Minister of Transport stepped in, playing for time and requesting an extension to enable the troops to be withdrawn to a safe distance. After some discussion with his accomplices, Akache granted a further thirty minutes.

Meanwhile Wischnewski, in collusion with Wolfgang Salewski, had come up with a plan to try to stall the terrorists and persuade them to extend the deadline until the following morning. The chargé d'affaires, Dr. Michael Libal, radioed Akache, advising him that the terrorists' demands had been met: the Red Army Faction and PFLP terrorists had been released from their respective prisons in West Germany and Turkey; they would be flown to Mogadishu but the distance from Cologne to Mogadishu, via Turkey, was such that the aircraft would not reach Mogadishu until the early hours of the following day, Tuesday 18 October. Akache was also told that the ransom of $15 million was already in Mogadishu, on board the negotiators' aircraft.

Akache greeted this news with suspicion, but having consulted Jürgen Vietor, who confirmed that the flight time and distance figures were correct, agreed to an extension of the deadline to 2.30 a.m. local time next day. The news of the apparent agreement by the West German government to the terrorists' demands, and the latter's agreement to an extension of the deadline, was greeted with joy and relief by the hostages who by now were in the depths of despair, some of them having resigned themselves to dying.

At midnight, a reconnaissance group under Major Blätte moved to a position a short distance from the 737 from which, using image intensifiers, it was able to confirm by radio that Akache and another terrorist were in the cockpit.

At 1 a.m., the assault groups formed up in a column in their holding area and at 1.30 moved forward to an assembly point on the edge of the runway to the rear of the hijacked 737. As they advanced to within 150 metres of the aircraft, they realised that they were illuminated by lights from the airport buildings which were causing the team to cast long shadows which might have been seen by the terrorists, but they succeeded in reaching the aircraft unobserved. Ladders were set against the wings and fuselage and the groups moved silently to their respective positions, those on the wings crawling into position by the emergency hatches. A problem occurred with the rear door ladder which had been adjusted for use on the Boeing 707 on which the rehearsal had been carried out: being higher off the ground than the 737, the 707 required a longer ladder. There was no way that it could be shortened so its base had to be placed further away and this caused the top to slip on the curved fuselage. Two members of Wegener's medical team were called forward to hold the ladder in place while the first pair of the assault group stood on it.

Meanwhile, the negotiators were keeping up a constant stream of dialogue with Akache in the cockpit, advising him that the aircraft carrying the released terrorists had just taken off from Cairo and he would soon be able to speak by radio with them in their aircraft. Akache responded with a list of demands, including that no press should be present and that no one was to approach his aircraft without permission, while at the same time dictating the procedure for the exchange of hostages and released terrorists.

At 2.07 a.m., Lieutenant Colonel Wegener initiated the assault. On his command over the radio, the Somali troops set a huge fire ablaze 300 yards forward of the aircraft. This apparently had the desired effect, drawing the attention of Akache and Wabil Harb, both of whom were in the cockpit at the time. Simultaneously, Major Morrison and Staff Sergeant Davies both lobbed their stun grenades which exploded with deafening detonations and blinding flashes over the cockpit and wings. As they did so, the assault groups opened the escape hatches and doors, those entering via the rear door shooting dead Hind Alameh as they entered the aircraft.

Wabil Harb staggered out of the cockpit, disoriented by the blast from the stun grenades, but was blocked by Suhailah Sayeh running into the lavatory from the first-class compartment, fleeing from an assault group advancing forward through the aircraft. Harb was cut down by a burst of automatic fire as the door to his right opened and another assault group entered the aircraft. A split second later, Akache also fell in a hail of bullets. As he did so, however, he dropped two grenades whose pins he had quickly pulled; both rolled into the first-class compartment and exploded. At this point, Suhaileh Sayeh opened fire with her pistol from inside the lavatory but was met with an instant response which wounded her.

The entire assault was over in some four or five minutes, the code-word for success, 'Springtime', being radioed by the assault groups at 2.12 a.m. Success had been complete: one terrorist, Hind Alameh, had been killed instantly; Akache had been mortally wounded, dying hours later in hospital, as had Wabil Harb who died shortly after being taken off the aircraft; Suhailah Sayeh was wounded and later recovered. All eighty-six passengers and the remaining four crew had been released, only four suffering wounds which were not serious, and the only casualty among the assault groups being one man slightly wounded.

At approximately 3.15 a.m. on Tuesday 18 October, the West German government negotiators' Boeing 707 took off, carrying all eighty-six passengers, a small escort group from GSG–9 and the negotiators themselves on the flight back to West Germany. Following close behind was the second Lufthansa 707 carrying Lieutenant Colonel Ulrich Wegener, the rest of his men and the two members of 22 SAS. During the early afternoon on the same day, both aircraft arrived at Frankfurt where the passengers disembarked to a massive reception. Shortly afterwards, the GSG–9 group and their two SAS companions continued their journey to the federal capital of Bonn. While Lieutenant Colonel Wegener and his men were receiving an official welcome, Major Alastair Morrison and Staff Sergeant Davies were spirited away on a British Airways flight to the United Kingdom.

Like the operation at Entebbe, Operation Fire Magic demonstrated to terrorists that they could not operate with impunity and that some Western countries had rapidly developed the capability to operate beyond their own borders in order to rescue their nationals if so required.

8

OPERATION NIMROD

In London, on 30 April 1980 at about 11.30 a.m., the weather was cold and the sky overcast as six young men made their way along Princes Gate in the Knightsbridge area of the city. All six were Arabs and had arrived in London at the end of March from the Iraqi capital of Baghdad. Since then, they had been living in nearby Earl's Court, an area frequented by large numbers of foreigners of different nationalities occupying its small down-at-heel hotels, flats and boarding-houses. Thrown out of one flat after a week because of their rowdy behaviour, five of them had moved to another where they were subsequently joined by the sixth member of the group.

All six men were from Khuzestan, a province of south-western Iran which lies at the head of the Persian Gulf with Iraq on its western border. More than half of the population are Arabs who live on the desert plains of the region, the remainder being Persians who live in the cities. To the north and east of the province's deserts are the Zagros Mountains which divide it from the rest of Iran; to the south is the coastal province of Bushehr and the Persian Gulf.

Until the 1920s, Arabistan had existed as a small, independent enclave governed by its own ruler, Khaz'al Khan, the Sheikh of Mohammerah (now called Khorramshar). Although nominally owing allegiance to the Iranian central government in Iran, the sheikhdom of Mohammerah, which differed ethnically and culturally from the rest of Iran, was permitted virtual autonomy in the management of its internal affairs.

Khaz'al Khan believed that Iran would ultimately disintegrate, breaking up into a number of self-governing states among which would be the independent nation of Arabistan. In 1898 he approached the British, who already possessed important strategic and commercial interests in the area, with the proposal that he would ensure stability within the region in return for British support for an autonomous Arabistan and agreement that he should become an independent ruler if Iran disintegrated.

Oil had been discovered in 1908 by the Anglo–Persian Oil Company (now called British Petroleum) of which the British government became a 51 per cent shareholder in 1914. The company employed some 20,000 local people and paid Khaz'al Khan for the exploration rights as well as royalties for the oil extracted. This had strengthened the ties between Britain and the Sheikh who was knighted in 1910 and subsequently provided active support for the British during the First World War despite the neutrality of the Iranian central government.

In the post-war years, however, Khaz'al Khan's position was undermined when Britain failed to make Iran a protectorate. In February 1921, it was further weakened when the ruling government of the Shah of Iran, Ahmad Shah, a young and weak monarch who preferred the pursuit of pleasure to the responsibilities of ruling his country, was overthrown by a *coup d'état* led by a colonel in the Iranian Army, Reza Khan, who appointed himself Minister of War and commander-in-chief of all Iranian forces. The new government pursued a policy of centralisation and soon turned its attention to Arabistan and Khaz'al Khan with whom war broke out. In October 1924, Khaz'al Khan's forces were defeated and in early 1925 he was arrested and sent into exile in Tehran, dying there under house arrest in 1936.

The year 1925 saw Ahmad Shah deposed as monarch while absent in Europe undergoing medical treatment; despite the entreaties of Reza Khan and the Majlis (the Iranian parliament) to return to Iran, he had refused to do so. The Majlis had subsequently voted to depose him and Reza Khan was elected Shah in his place, being crowned in April of the following year and adopting the name of Reza Shah Pahlavi. Meanwhile, Arabistan's status had been reduced to that of a province and its name changed to Khuzestan. Large numbers of Persians were transported to settle in the province and the official language changed from Arabic to Farsi.

In 1958, by which time Mohammed Reza Pahlavi had succeeded to the Peacock Throne on the abdication of his father in 1941, resistance to the rule of the central government began to flare up again in Khuzestan. A number of Arab movements were formed, among them the Arabistan Liberation Front and the Front for the Liberation of Ahvaz. All of them were supported by Iraq where King Faisal II had just been deposed and killed in a *coup d'état* led by two senior Army officers, Abd al-Salam Arif and Abd al-Karim Qasim. As relations between Iran and Iraq deteriorated, so the latter increased its support for the Arabistan liberation movements.

One such group was a Marxist–Leninist organisation calling itself the Democratic Revolutionary Movement for the Liberation of Arabistan (DRMLA). With its headquarters in Baghdad and recruiting its membership among middle-class Arabs educated in universities throughout the Middle East, by 1970 it proved to be the most effective in campaigning for autonomy for Khuzestan. This was recognised by the Iranian authorities, and in particular the much-dreaded SAVAK, the Shah's secret police, who cracked down ruthlessly on the DRMLA in an effort to stamp it out completely.

In 1975, however, Iran and Iraq made up their differences and signed a pact, the Rabat Agreement. One of its clauses called for Iraq to terminate its support for the Arabistan liberation movements in general and the DRMLA in particular. Expelled from Iraq, the organisation was forced to look elsewhere for sanctuary, first in Syria and then Libya, with its guerrillas undergoing training in camps elsewhere in the Middle East alongside Palestinians and terrorists of other nationalities.

During the late 1970s, however, contact was made with the followers of Ayatollah Ruhollah Khomeini who were by then plotting the downfall of the Shah. In December 1978, some of the DRMLA leadership returned clandestinely to Iran, thereafter lending active support to the ayatollahs as they prepared for the Islamic Revolution which took place in January 1979.

By June of that year, however, the DRMLA realised that it had little in common with Khomeini and his regime which had no interest in granting autonomy to Khuzestan. Meanwhile Iraq, where Saddam Hussein seized power as president in July, became seriously worried by the threat of Iranian-inspired Islamic fundamentalism and thus once again offered support, in the form of funds, arms and training facilities, to the DRMLA and other Arabistan movements. Two camps were established at Basra and Baghdad, by the Iraqi Army and the Mukhabarat (the Iraqi intelligence service) respectively, and in late 1979 attacks were mounted against Iranian oil installations in Khuzestan. These resulted in savage reprisals by the Iranians who imprisoned and executed large numbers of Arabs suspected of sabotage.

It was at this juncture that the DRMLA decided, with the apparent encouragement of Iraq, that it would bring its struggle for autonomy to the attention of the world while at the same time striking a humiliating blow at Iran. In the DRMLA headquarters, at that time still located in the Libyan capital of Tripoli, a plan was drawn up for the hijacking of the Iranian embassy in London and the taking hostage of its twenty-five staff. The operation would be used to draw world attention to Khuzestan's struggle for autonomy and the price for the release of the hostages would be the freeing of ninety-one members of the DRMLA being held in captivity in Iran.

A team of six was selected for the task, each having undergone training in one of the guerrilla camps in Iraq. The leader was Awn Ali Mohammed (alias Salim), a 27-year-old member of a middle-class Khuzestan family. Educated at university in Tehran and fluent in Farsi, Arabic, English and German, he had fallen foul of the authorities during the Shah's reign and had apparently been imprisoned and tortured. The other members of the group were: Shakir Abdullah Fadhil (alias Feisal); Thamir Mohamed Husein (alias Abbas); Shakir Sultan Said (alias Shai); Makki Hounoun Ali (alias Makki); and Fowzi Bedavi Nejad (alias Ali). It is known that they were fully briefed in Baghdad on the details of the operation: they were shown plans of the embassy and given details of the twenty or so individuals who made up the embassy's staff. They were also instructed on the demands to be made and on a strict timetable to be adhered to: if no demands had been met after twenty-four hours, the first hostage was to be shot and thereafter others were to be killed at the rate of one every hour.

On 30 March Salim, accompanied by Feisal, Abbas, Makki and Shai, arrived in London. Travelling with them was a senior member of the DRMLA named Sami Mohammed Ali. Next day, Salim and two of the team rented a flat at 20 Nevern Place, in Earls Court, where they stayed for a week before being thrown out for rowdy behaviour. On the same day, they succeeded in renting another flat nearby, No. 3 at 105 Lexham Gardens, where they were subsequently joined by Ali and his brother Foad, the latter a senior member of the DRMLA. Others also joined them there, among them Sami Mohammed Ali who took part in numerous lengthy late-night planning sessions during the next three weeks. Other meetings took place at two addresses in Kensington: 24 and 55 Queens Gate, both only a few steps from the office of the Iraqi Military Attaché.

The Iranian embassy in London is situated at 16 Princes Gate, part of an imposing Victorian terrace in the Knightsbridge area of London. During the reign of the Shah it had been the scene, as had a magnificent country house in Surrey, of lavish entertainment dispensed on a major scale to those of influence whom Iran wished to cultivate. It also acted as the headquarters in Britain of SAVAK whose agents constantly monitored the activities of those opposing the Shah's regime. With the arrival of Ayatollah Khomeini and his regime of Islamic fundamentalism, however, the embassy became a very different place. All evidence of luxurious living vanished, being replaced by a regime of austerity; the country house was sold off and the SAVAK agents disappeared. Those members of the embassy staff considered to be irrevocably tainted were despatched back to Iran, being replaced by dedicated followers of Khomeini.

At 9.40 a.m. on 30 April, Salim and his team left their flat in Lexham Gardens and disappeared, telling other residents in the block that they were going to France. Behind them in the flat, they left their suitcases which were subsequently collected by Sami

Mohammed Ali who returned to Baghdad later that day. Just over an hour and three-quarters later, at just before 11.30 a.m., Salim and his team walked along Princes Gate towards the embassy; just before reaching the building, they pulled keffiyehs, the patterned cotton head scarves worn by Arabs throughout the world, over their heads and faces. Under their jackets two of them carried compact Skorpion machine-pistols while the others were armed with three Browning 9mm pistols, an Astra revolver and Russian RGD-5 fragmentation grenades. Without further ado they walked rapidly towards the embassy's main entrance.

On duty at the embassy that day was Police Constable (PC) Trevor Lock, a member of the Metropolitan Police Diplomatic Protection Group which was responsible for providing protection for all embassies and diplomatic residences in the London area. Some warranted higher levels of protection than others and the Iranian embassy was obviously not deemed to be under a high level of threat: it was provided with a single police officer armed with a .38 Special calibre revolver in a holster under his tunic.

PC Lock would normally have been standing outside the main entrance, but on this chilly morning the embassy doorman, Abbas Fallahi, had offered him a cup of coffee which he drank in the small lobby between the outer main entrance door and the security doors giving access to the building's main hall. It was fortunate for Lock that he was not outside as he would have been forced to confront six terrorists armed with machine-pistols, handguns and grenades, against whom he would have stood little chance.

The first Lock knew of the terrorists' arrival was as he opened the outer door to return to his post. As he did so, he bumped into a masked figure attempting to draw a pistol. Slamming the door shut, he succeeded in transmitting an alarm call on his personal radio. As he did so, one of the terrorists opened fire on the outer door, shattering a glass panel and blinding Lock with flying splinters and cutting his face. Forcing the door open, the terrorists charged through the security doors into the embassy's hall, one of them firing a burst from his machine-pistol into the ceiling. Meanwhile, Lock was relieved of his radio; sensibly, he refrained from reaching for his revolver and put up his hands as he was pushed into the embassy reception area where he joined a number of people who had been waiting for appointments with various members of the embassy staff.

Among these were BBC newsman Chris Cramer and a colleague, sound-recordist Sim Harris, who were visiting the embassy to apply for visas to visit Iran, while Ali Tabatabai, an employee of the Bank Marzai in Iran attending a course in England with the Midland Bank, had called in to collect a film and map for use as aids in a presentation on Iran that he was due to give. Mojtaba Mehrnavard, an Iranian carpet dealer living in London, was waiting for his appointment with the embassy's medical adviser, Ahmed Dadgar. Also waiting were Vahid Khabbaz, an Iranian biology student and correspondent for a Tehran newspaper, *Keyhan*, and Ali-Gholi Ghazanfar, a Pakistani educationist due to visit Iran later in the year. All stood transfixed as PC Lock was pushed into the room at gunpoint, followed by two female members of the embassy staff.

On the third floor Mustafa Karkouti, a Syrian journalist and European correspondent for the Lebanese newspaper *As-Afir*, was interviewing Dr. Abul Fazl Ezzatti, the embassy's cultural attaché. At the sound of firing from below, they joined members of the embassy staff dashing upstairs to the embassy's top floor where they all locked themselves in an office. A few minutes later, however, the door was kicked open and a shot was fired into the ceiling by two of the terrorists who appeared, holding pistols and grenades. Karkouti, Ezzatti and the others were then escorted to Room 9 on the second floor where they joined Cramer, Harris and the others from the reception area.

On the fourth floor the embassy's British caretaker, Ron Morris, had run downstairs when he had heard the firing. On seeing a man armed with a machine-pistol herding Lock and Abbas Fallahi into the reception area, he ran back to his office and was dialling 999 when he heard the sound of footsteps running up the stairs accompanied by shouting. Replacing the receiver, he remained sitting at his desk as one of the terrorists entered the room and told him to follow.

Meanwhile, three members of the embassy staff had managed to escape. The female head of the embassy's medical section, Zari Afkhami, working in her office on the ground floor, heard the firing and, opening the door, saw the terrorists grab PC Lock. Accompanied by another female member of the medical section, she climbed out of her office window; spotting two workmen, she quickly told them what was taking place inside the embassy. Counsellor Fahy Gity, working on the first floor, climbed out of a window on to a balcony and across to a window of the adjoining building which housed the Ethiopian embassy.

On the first floor Mohammad Farughi, an Indian journalist and editor of *Impact International*, a Muslim magazine, had been interviewing the Chargé d'Affaires, Dr. Ali Afrouz, in the latter's first-floor office which overlooked Princes Gate when they heard the firing from the ground floor. As they went to the door, Farughi was tackled by one of the terrorists; in the confusion, Dr. Afrouz succeeded in jumping out of the window but landed badly, bruising his face and spraining his wrist. Half-senseless, he was quickly recaptured and pulled back into the embassy where he joined the other hostages.

Salim and his team searched the rest of the building and rounded up the remainder of the embassy staff who were also taken to Room 9 on the second floor, bringing the total number of hostages to twenty-six. These latter arrivals comprised: Issa Naghizadeh, the First Secretary; Ahmed Dadgar, the medical adviser; Mohammad Moheb, accountant; Mohammad-Taghi Kojouri, assistant accountant; Ali-Akbar Samadzadeh, press attaché; Abbas Lavasani, press attaché; Roya Kaghazchi, secretary; Haideh Kanji, secretary to the accountants; Nooshim Hashemian, secretary in the press section; Zahra Zomorrodian, a member of the press office staff; Frieda Mozaffarian, secretary to the press attachés; Shirazeh Boroumand, telephonist; and Aboutaleb Moghaddam, telex operator.

By this time, the alarm had been sounded. At 11.30 a.m. PC Lock's message was received at New Scotland Yard which soon received a report that embassy staff were jumping out of windows at the back of the building. Shortly afterwards, police officers arrived outside the embassy; one armed officer venturing round the back of the building was threatened with being shot if he approached any nearer. By 11.42 a.m., the Metropolitan Police had confirmed that one of its officers was being held inside the embassy at gunpoint and that a shot had been heard.

The police presence in the area grew as the police put contingency plans into action. The entire area was sealed off and a forward command post, code-named Alpha Control, was established in the attic of the Montessori Nursery School at 24 Princes Gate. A senior officer, Deputy Assistant Commissioner John Dellow, took charge of the operation and positioned himself at Alpha Control with a team of highly trained negotiators. These included an Iranian who was a Farsi interpreter, and a psychologist who would monitor telephone conversations between the negotiators and the terrorists, and advise on the terrorists' state of mind. A field telephone, providing a direct and secure link with the terrorists, was subsequently passed through the front door of the embassy and communication was established.

That day also saw the convening of the crisis committee established to oversee and control any major emergencies within the United Kingdom. Based in the Cabinet Office Briefing Room and known by the acronym COBRA, it is chaired by the Home Secretary and comprises representatives of the Foreign Office, Home Office, Ministry of Defence, the security and intelligence services and other public bodies as required. On this occasion the Right Honourable William Whitelaw, the Home Secretary, was presiding over a group which also included representatives of London's gas and water boards as well as the British Airports Authority. The Ministry of Defence was represented by the Director of Military Operations, Major General Derek Boorman, and the Director SAS, Brigadier Peter de la Billière.

Meanwhile at the embassy, at about 2 p.m., Salim entered Room 9 and announced to the hostages that he and his men belonged to 'the Democratic Revolutionary Front for the Liberation of Arabistan', and that he was going to read a statement to the hostages. This was read first in English, then in Farsi, and included the terrorists' demands for the granting of autonomy for Arabistan and the release of ninety-one prisoners held in Iranian jails.

The terrorists first made contact with the outside world via Mustafa Karkouti, the Syrian journalist, who was permitted by Salim to telephone the BBC. At 2.45 p.m. Karkouti spoke to Michael Brown, the senior duty editor of BBC External Services, to whom he explained that he was a hostage passing on one of the terrorists' demands, namely the release of ninety-one members of the DRMLA held in Iranian prisons. He also said that he had been instructed to point out that the gunmen occupying the embassy were from Iran, not Iraq.

Shortly afterwards, one of the female hostages, Frieda Mozaffarian, became ill with a series of fits followed by vomiting. After persistent requests from the other hostages, Salim dialled 999 and requested that a doctor be sent to the embassy to treat Mrs Mozaffarian; an hour later, the police responded by refusing and insisting that she be released. At 4.30 p.m. she was pushed out of the front doors of the embassy and was taken to hospital.

At 5.45 p.m., Salim ordered Mustafa Karkouti to telephone the BBC External Services again. Taking the receiver himself, he repeated his previous demand for the release of the ninety-one prisoners in Iran, this time threatening that unless they were freed by twelve o'clock midday on the following day, the embassy would be blown up and the hostages killed.

At about 11.30 p.m., Dr. Afrouz was permitted to telephone the Iranian Foreign Ministry in Tehran and repeat the terrorists' demands for autonomy for Khuzestan. Shortly afterwards, he received a telephone call from the Foreign Minister, Sadegh Ghotzbadeh, who launched into a diatribe accusing Salim and his accomplices of being in the employ of the United States; infuriated, Salim grabbed the telephone and hurled a stream of insults at Ghotzbadeh before cutting him off.

Almost twelve hours earlier and some 200 miles away, a telephone call had been received at 11.44 a.m. by Lieutenant Colonel Michael Rose, the Commanding Officer of 22 SAS. The caller was a former corporal in D Squadron, now a dog-handler with the Metropolitan Police counter-terrorist 'hard dog' section based at Heathrow airport, and on his way to Princes Gate. Taking it upon himself to alert his old unit, he had called Rose to let him know that the Iranian embassy had been occupied by a group of armed men who were holding a police officer at gunpoint and that firing had been heard in the building.

Rose immediately telephoned the Director SAS, Brigadier Peter de la Billière, and asked him to obtain confirmation from the Ministry of Defence. At 11.48 a.m., Rose sent out the alert signal to the 25-man Special Projects team which was on immediate standby; within a matter of minutes, they was being briefed and shortly afterwards were in their Range Rovers on their way to London. Rose meanwhile flew by helicopter to London; making his way to the area of Princes Gate, he reported to the senior police officer in charge, Deputy Assistant Commissioner John Dellow, before carrying out an initial reconnaissance of the area of the building. The Special Projects team, comprising members of 6 Troop of B Squadron, which had just taken over the counter-terrorist role from D Squadron, was by now halted at an Army base at Beaconsfield and waiting to be called forward as soon as the Ministry of Defence received a request for military assistance from the Home Office.

The team was called forward to London that night and at 3.30 a.m. on Thursday 1 May arrived at a forward holding area in the premises of the Royal College of General Practitioners at 14–15 Princes Gate, next door to the embassy. This had been reconnoitred earlier by Lieutenant Colonel Rose who had discovered a concealed approach to the building which led through a block of apartments at the rear of Princes Gate, accessible through a garden and along a passage running along the back of the terrace. The initial task of the team, designated Red Team, was to produce a plan for immediate action if the terrorists started killing hostages. Meanwhile B Squadron's other Special Projects team, designated Blue Team, was on standby at Hereford ready to travel to London if required.

During the next hour, the plan was assembled by the team with assistance from Lieutenant Colonel Rose and B Squadron's commander. It would involve an entry from the roof and upper floors, the team having to clear the building from the top downwards in the hope that it could reach the hostages before they were massacred by the terrorists. It could only be hoped that the negotiators could buy more time which would be used for the essential intelligence-gathering and detailed planning required for a deliberate assault.

Fortunately, details of the embassy's lay-out were available on architectural plans which were quickly procured. Furthermore, 22 SAS had been asked to carry out a survey of the building during the years of the Shah's reign and had made a number of recommendations concerning improvement of security, including the installation of bullet-resistant glass to the ground- and first-floor windows. All this information and more was fed into the plan. Meanwhile, carpenters produced a scale model of the embassy for use in planning while a full-sized mock-up was erected in a hangar at Regent's Park Barracks in north London for rehearsals.

Early on Thursday morning all the hostages were assembled in Room 9 once more, the women having been moved to an adjoining one, 9A, during the previous night. By now the mood was one of sombre apprehension, the initial excitement of the previous day having worn off. Dr Afrouz was suffering considerable pain from his injuries and Chris Cramer, the BBC newsman, was suffering increasingly from severe dysentery contracted during a recent trip to Zimbabwe; he was lying on the floor, writhing in pain. Sim Harris begged Salim to call for a doctor but the latter replied that the police had refused. Eventually, however, he allowed Harris to contact the police negotiation team.

Harris pleaded for a doctor, but the negotiators insisted that Salim release Cramer. After more negotiations, Salim eventually agreed, but threatened to shoot three hostages if the police tried any tricks. At 11.15 a.m., forty-five minutes before the terrorists' deadline for their demands to be met was due to expire, the front door of the embassy was opened and Chris Cramer staggered out, making his way across the road to a waiting ambulance. Once he had received medical attention, police officers debriefed him, extracting every possible item of information.

Meanwhile, the negotiators were trying to persuade Salim to extend his deadline which was approaching rapidly. Chief Superintendent Fred Luff, the senior negotiator, followed by the female Farsi interpreter wearing body armour, approached the embassy. Showing himself to be unarmed, he established a conversation with Salim and eventually succeeded in persuading him to extend the deadline. At 12.40 p.m., Salim telephoned the negotiators and dictated a statement in which he declared that the deadline was extended until 2 p.m. and thereafter all responsibility for subsequent events was that of the Iranian government. He also demanded that the latter agree to negotiate with the British government in order for the deadline to be extended further. An hour and twenty minutes later, the deadline came and went without any further occurrence inside the embassy or any demands from the terrorists.

Inside the embassy, Salim and his accomplices were becoming worried by sounds that they were convinced they could hear coming from the walls. Despite assurances from PC Trevor Lock that they were probably caused by mice, the terrorists became increasingly anxious. During Thursday evening, Salim pinpointed one sound as coming from an electric point in the wall on the second floor. In a further effort to reassure him, Lock removed the point from the wall and listened but professed to hear nothing. He then lifted the carpet and discovered a hole which disappeared under the skirting board. Salim appeared convinced by Lock's explanation that it was a mouse hole and the terrorists relaxed.

In fact, Salim had good cause to be suspicious because the faint sounds emanating from the walls were being caused by specialists of the technical surveillance branch of the Metropolitan Police who were busy installing surveillance equipment via the Ethiopian embassy at 17 Princes Gate. This involved the partial dismantling of the adjoining walls of the two buildings, which were of considerable thickness, a slow and painstaking process requiring removal of individual bricks with the minimum amount of noise. Minute holes then had to be drilled as silently as possible in the remaining masonry to allow the insertion of fibre-optic probes fitted with pinhole lenses through which surveillance of the embassy interior could be carried out. A similar process was used to introduce microphones to monitor conversations within the building.

In order to provide noise to cover any sounds being made, a gas maintenance crew was brought in to start drilling in the road outside, but this only served to irritate the terrorists and the workmen had to be withdrawn. Lieutenant Colonel Rose then had the brainwave of rerouting aircraft arriving at Heathrow so that they passed overhead, the noise of their jets drowning any sounds. Although this proved effective, Salim and his men were still convinced that they could hear noises coming from the walls of the building.

The morning of Friday 2 May found the terrorists in an agitated state. Despite frequent contact with the police negotiation team, their demands were not being met and Salim told Mustafa Karkouti and PC Lock that he would have to start killing hostages to increase the pressure. Karkouti and Lock begged Salim not to take such measures and suggested that they talk to the negotiators again. Salim agreed, but, seizing Dr. Abdul Fazl Ezzatti, the cultural attaché, and holding a pistol to his head, pulled him to the first-floor window where Lock was leaning out and talking to police negotiators below. A demand that Salim be allowed to talk to the media met with a flat refusal; for a moment it appeared that he would carry out his threat but he suddenly let go of the unfortunate Ezzatti who slumped to the floor, vomiting in sheer terror.

Salim then returned to the window and demanded that he be allowed to talk to someone from the BBC who was known to Sim Harris, the BBC sound recordist. The negotiators accepted this demand and Salim agreed to extend his deadline, but without specifying a time. Late that afternoon Tony Crabb, the managing editor of BBC television news services, appeared in front of the embassy to talk to Sim Harris who stood at the same first-floor window with Salim behind, pointing a gun at his back. It was at this point that it became clear that the latter had modified his demands which now concentrated on his group being allowed to leave the country. Repeating Salim's words, Harris dictated them to Crabb who wrote them down: first, a coach to take the terrorists, hostages and the ambassador of an unidentified Arab country to Heathrow where the non-Iranian hostages would be released; secondly, an aircraft to take the terrorists, the remaining hostages and the ambassador to an unspecified Middle East country.

Salim continued by stating that the demands should be negotiated with the British government on his behalf by the ambassadors of Iraq, Jordan and Algeria, and ended by saying that he required a statement concerning these and his group's grievances to be broadcast over the British media that night. By 11 p.m., however, no such broadcast had been made and at 11.30 p.m. an abbreviated and incorrect version of his statement was broadcast on the BBC news. This infuriated Salim, heightening the fear of the hostages. Unknown to him, the COBRA committee had earlier dismissed his demands and ruled out any possibility of the terrorists being allowed to go free, a view firmly supported by the Prime Minister, Margaret Thatcher.

Meanwhile, the SAS presence had been reinforced at 3.30 a.m. on Friday when B Squadron's Blue Team arrived at the forward holding area at 14–15 Princes Gate. There it relieved Red Team which had been on standby for nearly twenty-four hours, and which now moved to Regent's Park Barracks for some well-earned rest before commencing rehearsals on the embassy mock-up.

The fourth day of the siege, Saturday 3 May, continued with further communication between the police negotiators and Salim who demanded to talk again to Tony Crabb of the BBC and, becoming agitated, threatened that a hostage would die unless his demands were met. Once again, however, he was eventually calmed down by PC Lock, Sim Harris and Mustafa Karkouti, agreeing to do nothing until he had spoken to Crabb.

During the late afternoon Crabb, accompanied by one of the police negotiators, appeared again in front of the embassy and Harris made it plain that the BBC had to broadcast Salim's statement accurately and in its entirety if the terrorists were to be prevented from carrying out their threats. Ensuring that it was word perfect, the negotiator wrote down Salim's statement which was dictated from the first-floor window by Mustafa Karkouti. Salim then demanded a guarantee that it would be broadcast on the 9 p.m. news, his new deadline. Sensing an opportunity, the negotiators demanded the release of some hostages in return. After some haggling, Salim agreed to free two, but subsequently insisted that they be held until after the broadcast had been made. The negotiators insisted otherwise and he flew into one of his increasingly frequent rages, only calming down after Mustafa Karkouti begged him on his knees not to carry out his threat of killing a hostage.

Salim then compromised, allowing Mrs Haideh Kanji, the secretary in the embassy accounts section, to walk free before the broadcast was made. The other hostage to be freed would be released after the broadcast. At 9 p.m., the terrorists heard the voice of Deputy Assistant Commissioner Peter Neivens of the Metropolitan Police read Salim's statement out in full. The terrorists and hostages were jubilant and shortly afterwards Ali-Gholi Ghazanfar, the Pakistani educationist, walked out of the embassy's front door. Later a meal, ordered by the police negotiators, arrived from a Persian restaurant nearby and the fourth day of the siege drew to a close with those inside the embassy optimistic of a peaceful outcome to the crisis.

Outside in the darkness, however, shadowy figures were moving stealthily over the roof of 14–15 Princes Gate, making their way across to that of the embassy. Covered by snipers, a reconnaissance group of Red Team made its way to a skylight shown on the plans of the building. Finding it locked, one of the group removed a pane of glass and unfastened the skylight before closing it again without leaving any trace of its having been disturbed. The group then withdrew without a sound.

The fifth day of the siege, Sunday 4 May, dawned with terrorists and hostages alike in cheerful mood after the developments of the previous evening. As the day wore on, however, the sombre mood returned and some of the terrorists, seeking to relieve their boredom, scrawled anti-Khomeini slogans over the walls of the embassy, provoking an argument between two of the hostages, Dr. Ali Afrouz and Abbas Lavasani, and the terrorists. One of the latter, Feisal, drew his pistol and the situation became extremely ugly until Mohammad Farughi, the Indian journalist, stepped in and calmed both sides down.

By this time, approaches by the British government to the Ambassadors of Jordan and Kuwait to act as mediators, as demanded earlier by Salim, had fallen on stony ground. At 3.30 p.m. on Sunday, a meeting was held at the Foreign & Commonwealth Office, but proved fruitless as did another with the Syrian Ambassador later in the afternoon. By that evening, Salim had reduced the number of stipulated ambassadors to one and his demands to a guarantee of safe passage for his group out of the country.

During the evening Mustafa Karkouti suddenly became ill, suffering from bouts of fever and diarrhoea which became increasingly severe. At 8 p.m., Salim suddenly announced that he would release him and shortly afterwards the Syrian emerged from the embassy.

Before dawn on the sixth day of the siege, Monday 5 May, Salim and one of his group woke PC Lock, saying that they had heard noises during the night and were convinced that strangers were in the building. Lock accordingly set off on a tour of the rooms of the building, subsequently reporting to Salim that he had found nothing.

The jittery mood of the terrorists was not improved when later that morning a telegram addressed to the hostages arrived from the Iranian Foreign Minister, Sadegh Ghotzbadeh. In it he stated that Iran was proud of their 'steadfastness and forbearance in the face of the criminal actions of Ba'athist Iraq, the forces of imperialism and international Zionism'. He declared that Iran would spare no effort in obtaining their release and that 'tens of thousands of Iranians are just ready to enter the premises of the Embassy, not with weapons but with cries of "Allahu Akhbar" and thus bring punishment to these mercenaries of Ba'athist Iraq in the manner they deserve'.

About an hour later, a highly agitated Salim ordered PC Lock downstairs to the first-floor landing where he pointed at a large bulge in the wall separating the embassy from the Ethiopian embassy next door. Pointing at it, he demanded to know if the police were trying to break in. By now Lock had a pretty shrewd idea that something was afoot on the other side of the wall and that the noises had not been a figment of the terrorists' imaginations. He could no longer dismiss them with light-hearted suggestions of mice at work and he concentrating on calming Salim by saying that the police would never try to break into the building in daylight.

This seemed to have the right effect, but shortly afterwards the terrorists moved all the male hostages out of Room 9 and into Room 10, also on the second floor, which housed the embassy's telex machines and overlooked Princes Gate. The women remained in Room 9A which overlooked the rear of the building. There was an air of heightened tension and it became apparent that the terrorists were becoming even more apprehensive as they donned their keffiyehs and jackets. In an effort to improve the situation, PC Lock and Sim Harris asked if they could talk to the negotiators and after an initial refusal Salim agreed, limiting them to ten minutes. At 12.02 p.m., Lock and Harris stepped out on to the first-floor balcony and shouted to police officers on the other side of Princes Gate, asking them to call a negotiator.

Shortly afterwards Chief Superintendent Fred Luff, accompanied by another officer, appeared and Lock and Harris left him in no doubt as to the perilous situation inside the embassy: the terrorists' patience was exhausted and time was running out. The complaint that the Foreign Office appeared to be dragging its feet met with the response that everything possible was being done and that discussions with the Arab ambassadors were still taking place.

Confirmation of this was given on the BBC news at 1.00 p.m., but only served to infuriate Salim when he realised that no final decision over mediation had been made. Immediately telephoning the negotiators, he demanded that an ambassador be brought to the telephone or he would shoot a hostage in forty-five minutes' time.

This was reinforced by PC Lock being brought to the telephone and confirming that a hostage had been selected and would be shot unless Salim's demand were met. This message was passed to COBRA but by 1.40 p.m. there had been no response.

Inside the embassy meanwhile Abbas Lavasani, one of the embassy's two press attachés, had been taken to the ground floor and, his hands bound behind his back, tied to the banisters at the foot of the stairs. At 1.45 p.m., Salim telephoned the negotiators and held the receiver next to Lavasani who identified himself as one of the hostages. No sooner had the negotiators heard him say his name than they heard another voice cut in, shouting 'No names! No names!' Immediately afterwards came the sound of two or three shots followed by a long choking groan. Salim then came on the line again and announced that he had killed a hostage.

This news was passed immediately to COBRA which in turn called the Home Secretary at his residence at Dorneywood, near Slough in Berkshire. William Whitelaw returned immediately to London where he held discussions with the Director of Military Operations, Major General Derek Boorman, and the Director SAS, Brigadier Peter de la Billière, during which the latter outlined the military option and the plan developed and rehearsed by Lieutenant Colonel Rose and B Squadron. Whitelaw instructed de la Billière to place his troops on standby, the order being passed to Rose via Deputy Assistant Commissioner John Dellow at Alpha Control. Rose advised Dellow that he would need two hours to bring his men to a state of immediate readiness; at 3.50 p.m., the latter asked him to proceed with his preparations for an assault on the embassy,

In the embassy, meanwhile, contact had been made with the negotiators again. PC Lock telephoned to confirm that a hostage had been killed and passed on a message from Salim stating that another would be shot in half an hour's time. At this point the embassy's British caretaker, Ron Morris, approached Salim and persuaded him to extend the deadline for the appearance of an ambassador to 5 p.m.

The police meanwhile took the initiative in trying to find a mediator. At 3 p.m. a senior officer in the Anti-Terrorist Squad, Superintendent Bernard Hodgets, spoke on the telephone to the senior imam at the Central Mosque in Regent's Park, Dr. Sayyed Darsh, whom he had met a few weeks previously. Explaining the situation, Hodgets asked Dr. Darsh to intercede in an effort to save the lives of the hostages. The imam's position required him to distance himself from politics so he was initially reluctant to become involved, but when Hodgets emphasised the desperate state of the situation at the embassy, he finally agreed. At 3.30 p.m. he was collected from the mosque and driven to Hyde Park police station.

At 4.45 p.m., the field telephone in the embassy buzzed. To Salim's fury, the call was merely to tell him that a letter from the Commissioner of the Metropolitan Police, Sir David McNee, was being sent to him but could not be delivered by the 5 p.m. deadline. Salim was unwilling to wait for the letter, but was persuaded to do so by PC Lock who suggested that the letter might contain conditions as to how the crisis could be ended peacefully. He eventually agreed and extended the deadline to 6.30 p.m.

Meanwhile at the Foreign Office, junior minister Douglas Hurd had been making further efforts with Arab ambassadors, informing them of the shooting in the hope that one of the more amenable might volunteer to mediate. At 5 p.m., a meeting of all Arab ambassadors in London, with the exception of that of the Sultanate of Oman, was held at the Arab League. They were all of the same view: that they would only act as mediators on the basis made clear earlier by the Jordanian Ambassador. All had been irritated by what they saw as a misleading impression, in their eyes promoted by the Foreign Office, that the initiative for mediation in the crisis had come from Arab countries rather than from Britain. They decided to draft a press release which, while emphasising their commitment to saving lives, would correct this.

At 5 p.m., Lieutenant Colonel Rose informed Deputy Assistant Commissioner Dellow that his force was ready and on ten minutes' standby to carry out an assault.

In the embassy the situation had become very grave as tension heightened. The letter from Sir David McNee had arrived, being posted through the letterbox by a policeman. It did nothing to improve matters: written in English and Farsi, it merely stated that the police were being reasonable and exhorted the terrorists to remain calm. It also gave an undertaking that the police would only use violence if the terrorists did so first. The latter had already done so, however, a point not lost on Salim who told the hostages that the letter was meaningless.

At 6.20 p.m., Dr. Sayyed Darsh was brought to Alpha Control where he was briefed as to how he could assist and on what the police wished him to say to the terrorists. It soon became clear to him that he was being asked to tell them to surrender rather than being asked to negotiate. Shortly after he entered the negotiators' cell on the second floor of the building, the telephone rang and Darsh found himself talking to Salim. The conversation, conducted in Arabic, was brief: Darsh's attempt at reminding Salim that Islam did not allow bloodshed and that there could be no justification for the killing of the hostages was cut short by the latter who declared that he had already executed one hostage and would do so again in five minutes unless he was permitted to talk to the Arab ambassadors. With that, he rang off.

On relating the gist of the conversation to the negotiators, Darsh was told that the ambassadors were at a meeting and could not be disturbed. Darsh called Salim immediately and begged him to extend his deadline until after the meeting was over. This ploy worked; he agreed to extend the deadline by a further thirty minutes. Once again, Darsh reminded him that murder was against Islamic law but the latter terminated the conversation abruptly, replying that he was not interested. As Darsh was giving the negotiators the gist of this second conversation and advising them of his concern at the terrorist's tone of voice, the telephone rang again. It was Salim, telling him that he had changed his mind and would kill a hostage in two minutes' time. Darsh once again begged him not to do so, but Salim rang off. Darsh called him back, quoting from the Koran and imploring him to wait while efforts were made to contact the Arab ambassadors. Shortly afterwards the telephone rang again; as Darsh picked it up, the sound of three shots could be clearly heard by those listening. A few seconds later, the front door of the embassy opened and a body was dumped unceremoniously outside. Shortly afterwards policemen ran across to the embassy and carried the body away on a stretcher.

News of the second shooting and the appearance of the body, identified as that of Abbas Lavasani, was flashed to COBRA where William Whitelaw immediately telephoned the Prime Minister in her car, requesting permission for the SAS to carry out an immediate assault. Having obtained it, he passed it on to the Commissioner of the Metropolitan Police who in turn relayed it to Deputy Assistant Commissioner John Dellow. At 7 p.m., the latter handed over control of the assault phase of the operation to Lieutenant Colonel Rose.

B Squadron's Red and Blue Teams needed ten minutes to take position on their start-lines. As they did so, the negotiators kept up a dialogue with Salim, telling him that a coach was being made available to take his group and the hostages to Heathrow, and that one of the Arab ambassadors was en route to the embassy to oversee the evacuation. Salim was suspicious and cut them off more than once, but PC Trevor Lock played a major part in restoring communication and allowing the deception to be prolonged, thus buying Red and Blue Teams precious time.

At 7 p.m., as Salim was still talking to the negotiators, two large explosions reverberated through the embassy building and the assault began.

The plan, drawn up by Lieutenant Colonel Rose and B Squadron's commander, called for all floors of the embassy to be attacked simultaneously by Red and Blue Teams. Red was responsible for clearing the top half of the building, with two groups of four men abseiling in two waves from the roof to the second-floor balcony at the rear of the building where they would force an entry via three windows. Meanwhile, another group would assault the third floor using a ladder to descend from the top of the building to a lower roof. The top floor would be cleared by another group entering via the skylight on the roof reconnoitred three nights earlier. Blue Team was tasked with clearing the lower half of the building comprising the basement, ground- and first-floors. Explosives would be used to blast through the bullet-resistant glass of the French windows at the rear of the building and the windows on the first-floor balcony at the front. Members of Blue Team would also be responsible for firing CS gas canisters through the second-floor windows. The two teams would begin their assaults simultaneously on receipt of the code-word 'London Bridge'.

As the police negotiation team was discussing the arrangements for the coach with Salim, Red Team's groups were moving into their respective positions on the roof, covered by snipers, located in an apartment block behind the embassy, as they laid out their ropes and awaited the order to begin. Dressed in a black assault suit and wearing body armour and respirator, each man in both teams was armed with an H&K MP-5 submachine-gun and a Browning 9mm pistol. In addition, one group in each team was equipped with a frame charge manufactured from linear cutting charge explosive mounted on a lightweight wooden frame. As the teams took up their positions, an explosive charge was lowered and suspended just above a glass roof covering the building's stairwell.

On receiving the code-word 'Road Accident', Red Team moved to its start-lines. This was followed shortly afterwards by 'Hyde Park', signalling the abseil groups to clip themselves on to their ropes and prepare to drop. Seconds later came 'London Bridge' and the assault began.

The abseilers dropped off the roof, but the team leader, Staff Sergeant 'M', encountered a problem. Having dropped some fifteen feet or so, his rope became jammed on his abseil device, leaving him swinging above the second-floor balcony several feet below. Other members of his group, sliding down beside him, tried to free him, but while doing so inadvertently broke a window. The noise was such that the squadron commander, who was controlling the operation, gave the order to attack.

The charge above the stairwell's glass roof detonated with a huge explosion, blowing it in and sending a shockwave through the building. At the same time, members of Blue Team began firing CS gas canisters through the second-floor windows while the rear assault group, unable to use its frame charge to blow in the French window doors because of the risk of injury to Staff Sergeant 'M' still swinging on the end of his rope, attacked them with sledge hammers instead.

At the front of the building, meanwhile, the other Blue Team assault group had clambered across from the next door building on to the embassy's first-floor balcony. As oné of them placed a frame charge in position against the window, he spotted Sim Harris looking at him. Fortunately, the latter quickly obeyed the frantic gestures to get out of the way. Seconds later the frame charge exploded, blowing in the window, and was followed by a stun grenade. The four-man group piled into the room and, having shoved Sim Harris out on to the balcony with strict orders to remain there, cleared the room. As the leading pair, Lance Corporal 'A' and Trooper 'B', moved through the door on to the landing, they heard sounds of a struggle coming from a room to their right. On entering it, they found Salim locked in a struggle with PC Trevor Lock who had drawn his weapon, but was unable to use it. Shouting at Lock and wrenching him out of the way, Lance Corporal 'A' fired a burst into Salim, Trooper 'B' doing the same. Hit in the head and chest, Salim died instantly.

Meanwhile the other pair, Lance Corporal 'C' and Trooper 'D', who had moved towards the rear of the building, approached the door of the ambassador's office. As they tried the handle, it was wrenched open and one of the terrorists, Abbas, appeared. Trooper 'D' opened fire, wounding the terrorist who staggered back and disappeared into the room which was full of smoke. Joined by another member of Blue Team who had come up from the ground floor, the two soldiers probed their way through the smoke and eventually spotted Abbas slumped on a sofa near the window. He raised his weapon but died in a hail of bullets.

At the rear of the building, meanwhile, four members of Red Team had gained the second-floor balcony where they smashed two of the windows of Room 9 in which the hostages had been confirmed earlier, and threw in stun grenades. Unfortunately, these ignited newspapers lying all over the floor which had been soaked with cigarette lighter fuel. Within a few seconds these were ablaze, but the four soldiers leaped in through the windows and attempted to open the door leading to the landing. Outside, still suspended on his rope above the balcony, Staff Sergeant 'M' was attempting to avoid the flames licking up out of the windows and burning his legs. Eventually, one of the Red Team group still on the roof cut him free and he dropped on to the balcony, fighting his way through the flames into the room to join his men who were attempting unsuccessfully to blast open the door which had been barricaded on the other side.

One member of the team, Trooper 'P', climbed back out of the window on to the balcony and leaned across to the window of the next room. Inside was another of the terrorists, Shai, busy attempting to set fire to newspapers scattered on the floor. Smashing the window, 'P' lobbed a stun grenade into the room; looking up, Shai dashed from the room, heading for Room 10 where the hostages had been herded and where he was joined by Feisal, Ali and Makki. Without further ado, Feisal opened fire on the hostages with his machine-pistol while one of the others did likewise with his pistol. Ali-Akbar Samadzadeh, one of the embassy's two press attachés, was killed and Ahmed Dadgar, the medical adviser, seriously wounded in the chest. Dr. Ali Afrouz was hit twice in the legs while Abbas Fallahi was hit, but escaped injury when a coin in his pocket stopped a bullet. A split second later Trooper 'P' entered Room 10 and, seeing Shai, shot him dead with a single bullet to the head from his Browning pistol. As he did so, he was joined by Staff Sergeant 'M' and the other members of his assault group.

By the time Trooper 'P' had entered Room 10, however, Feisal, Makki and Ali had dropped their weapons and jumped in among the hostages screaming in terror on the floor. As the hostages were shoved out of the room towards the stairs, a member of Red Team spotted Makki and forced him on to the floor. As the soldier started to search him, Makki made a sudden movement and was immediately shot in the back, dying instantly. On being turned over, he was found to be holding a grenade.

Meanwhile, the hostages were being hustled down the stairs which were lined by members of both Red and Blue Teams. Feisal was among them and as he was shoved towards the stairs he was identified as a terrorist. As he was almost thrown downstairs, a grenade was spotted in one of his hands. Trooper 'I', positioned half-way down and unable to fire for fear of hitting other members of Blue Team, struck Feisal on the back of his neck with his submachine-gun, sending him rolling to the bottom of the stairs where he was shot dead immediately. Fortunately the grenade's safety pin had not been extracted and thus those on the stairs and in the basement area escaped death or serious injury.

As the hostages emerged from the embassy basement into the garden at the rear, they were immediately seized and their hands bound by other members of Blue Team who positioned them lying face-down on the grass. Among them, however, was the last remaining terrorist, Ali, but soon afterwards he was identified by the other hostages. Having been searched, he was arrested and taken away. At just after 8 p.m., having checked the building for any further terrorists, Red and Blue Teams withdrew and made their way back to the forward holding area next door. Staff Sergeant 'M', who was suffering from severe burns to his legs, was meanwhile taken away to hospital. Shortly afterwards, both teams left the area unobtrusively in unmarked vans and headed for Regent's Park Barracks where they were later joined by the Prime Minister, Mrs. Margaret Thatcher, who was unstinting in her congratulations and praise.

Operation Nimrod sent a clear signal throughout the world that the authorities would deal firmly with any terrorist threat within Britain's own borders. It also revealed some of the capabilities of 22 SAS in the counter-terrorist role and there were subsequently requests from other countries for assistance in forming and training specialist units to combat the threat of terrorism.

9

ENTER UNCLE SAM

Despite the major threat posed by terrorism in the Middle East and the West from the late 1960s onwards, the United States was slow to establish a specialist counter-terrorist capability within its armed forces. The US military establishment was by tradition highly conservative and had long viewed the field of unconventional warfare with considerable suspicion: the formation of the US Army's 1st Special Forces in 1952 had met with opposition and, despite the considerable part played by 5th Special Forces Group (Airborne), Military Assistance Command Vietnam – Studies & Observation Group, Project DELTA, Long Range Reconnaissance Patrol (LRRP) units, US Navy SEALs and others during the Vietnam War, US unconventional warfare capability was cut to the bone in the aftermath of the United States' withdrawal from South Vietnam in 1974.

During the mid 1970s, however, an unofficial study on the formation of a specialist counter-terrorist unit was carried out by Major General Bob Kingston, Commander of the John F. Kennedy Center for Military Assistance (JFKCMA) at Fort Bragg, North Carolina, and Colonel Charles Beckwith, Commandant of the Special Forces School. Beckwith had served a year-long exchange tour with 22 SAS in the early 1960s and had been convinced that the US Army needed a similar unit in its order of battle. On taking up his appointment at the Special Forces School, he had submitted a paper, proposing the formation of a unit along the lines of the SAS, to General Kingston. The proposal was submitted to higher levels in August 1976 and Kingston was ordered to develop it further.

During the following months, Beckwith's proposals subsequently underwent scrutiny at progressively higher levels until, in September 1977, initial approval was given by the Chief of Staff of

the US Army, General Bernard Rogers, for the formation of 1st
Special Forces Operational Detachment – DELTA, which would
become more familiarly known as Delta Force or just Delta.
Authority to activate the new unit was finally granted on 19
November and Colonel Beckwith appointed as its commander.

Beckwith threw himself into forming Delta which was based in
Fort Bragg's Stockade, a military prison facility whose buildings
provided ample accommodation for the new unit. One of his principal
problems, however, was recruiting volunteers from within the 5th, 7th
and 10th Special Forces Groups and his initial request for permission
to do so was met with reluctance as it was feared that Delta would
strip these units of their best men. Nevertheless, during late 1977
thirty volunteers took part in the first selection course, much of which
was based on that of 22 SAS, and seven passed. Thereafter, a Delta
recruiting team visited US Army units throughout the United States
and Europe, seeking suitable volunteers for the second selection
course which took place in January 1978.

Beckwith also found himself facing a problem with the US
Army's Readiness Command whose commander had decided that
an interim counter-terrorist capability was required because it
would be two years before Delta would be fully operational. This
was established without official authority by forming another unit,
code-named Blue Light, from forty members of the 5th Special
Forces Group whose commander was of the opinion that a counter-
terrorist unit could be raised from existing Special Forces assets
and thus considered Delta to be unnecessary. This caused difficul-
ties for Beckwith, not least because Blue Light, with support from
JFKCMA, lost little time in competing for resources intended
solely for Delta. Furthermore, the existence of the two units soon
began to cause confusion within other US government agencies as
to which had officially been allocated the counter-terrorist role.

Eventually, the situation over these and other problems came to a
head in March 1978. The upshot was that Delta, while formally
subordinated to JFKCMA, was given a direct line of communication
to both the Deputy Chief of Staff for Operations & Plans and the

Department of the Army which would exercise operational control of the unit. At the same time, JFKCMA was ordered to lift all restrictions on Special Forces personnel volunteering for selection for Delta. By now, it was apparent that the unit was there to stay and shortly afterwards, with Beckwith having pointed out that it was superfluous, Blue Light was disbanded.

Freed from any further major hindrance, Delta proceeded apace and by the end of April 1978 had conducted five selection courses during which a total of seventy-three men, sufficient to form one squadron, had qualified to undergo five months of counter-terrorist training to join the unit. This covered a wide range of subjects which included marksmanship, close quarter battle (CQB) skills, tactics, climbing and abseiling, radio communications, surveillance, combat medicine, driving (wheeled and tracked vehicles), navigation, hostage rescue and protection, and the conduct of airborne, airmobile and maritime operations.

Much emphasis was placed on marksmanship, with anything up to five hours every day being spent on the ranges. A special indoor CQB training facility, christened the 'House of Horrors' was constructed and this enabled Delta personnel to carry out different levels of training under a variety of conditions. One of its four rooms was designed for shooting in darkness, with troops using night vision goggles, while another was designed as the interior of an airliner cabin for training in aircraft assault.

In addition to training, Delta devoted a considerable amount of effort and time in other directions. Specialist wings, concerned with intelligence, communications and other aspects of the unit's role, were formed and much attention was paid to the acquisition and evaluation of weapons and equipment; in many instances, items were designed and produced to Delta's specifications. Visits were paid to overseas units, including 22 SAS, GIGN, GSG–9 and Sayeret Matkal's Unit 269, as part of the process of learning as much as possible in the shortest time.

Colonel Beckwith had been given two years to have his unit formed, fully trained and ready for operations. During the first three days of November 1979, with two fully formed squadrons, Delta underwent a full evaluation and exercise to test it in all aspects of its new role, after which it was declared operationally ready. This proved to be just in time because on the morning of Sunday 4 November, the US Embassy in the Iranian capital of Tehran was invaded and occupied by 500 Revolutionary Guards and Islamic revolutionaries, and its staff of sixty-three Americans taken hostage.

Dubbed 'the 'Great Satan', the United States was perceived by the extremist Islamic regime of Ayatollah Ruhollah Khomeini as its principal enemy. Khomeini had come to power in January 1979, following the downfall of the Shah, Mohammed Reza Pahlavi, who had ruled Iran for thirty-eight years before fleeing to the United States; ultimately, he was given sanctuary in Egypt where he spent the remainder of his life until his death from cancer in 1980. The Shah, who had been backed by the West, had been an absolute ruler and his reign had at times been tyrannical, any opposition being rapidly snuffed out by SAVAK, his dreaded secret police. The Islamic revolution which saw his overthrow was a popular one, even enjoying the support of the wealthy middle classes, but it was not long before the people of Iran realised that they had merely swapped one tyrant for another.

During the revolution there had been vociferous displays of anti-Western sentiment by large mobs led and controlled by Khomeini's shock troops, the Revolutionary Guards or Pasdaran. The US embassy, located in Tehran's Taleghani Avenue, had in particular become the scene of such demonstrations, but there had been no indication that it was under any real threat. Thus it was that the occupation of it, and the taking of its staff as hostages, caught the United States off-guard. It soon became apparent that Khomeini and his fellow ayatollahs were in no mood for any form of negotiations for a diplomatic solution and on Tuesday 6 November the White House instructed the Pentagon to prepare for a rescue mission.

At Delta's base at Fort Bragg, meanwhile, Colonel Charles Beck-with despatched three liaison officers to work with planners in the

Joint Chiefs of Staff (JCS) department at the Pentagon on Operation Rice Bowl, the code-name given to the planning stage of what would be a major hostage rescue operation. On Sunday 11 November, he received orders for Delta to move to a secure training facility, called Camp Peary, where it was to prepare and train.

Belonging to the CIA, Camp Peary is familiarly known as 'The Farm' and is the Agency's principal base for training the members of its Directorate of Operations and others in the skills of covert operations and unconventional warfare. Comprising an area of some 25 square miles, it is located a short distance north-east of Williamsburg in Virginia. During the next few weeks, a Joint Task Force (JTF) was formed under the command of Major General James Vaught, an officer who had served with the US Army's airborne forces and Rangers, to carry out the rescue operation, code-named Eagle Claw.

Delta and the JCS planners worked night and day to produce a feasible plan. The principal problems facing them were fourfold: first, the distances over which the rescue force would have to be transported; secondly, the lack of accurate intelligence – incredibly, the CIA did not possess a single 'asset' within Iran; thirdly, the locations of the hostages within the embassy compound which comprised some fourteen buildings in an area of more than twenty-five acres – this problem was exacerbated by the fact that three of the hostages were being held in the headquarters of the Iranian Foreign Ministry; fourth and last, the operation would be conducted in a hostile country without the support that would normally be expected from a government permitting such an operation to be carried out on its own soil.

During this early stage of planning the flow of information being fed to Delta was slow and much of the data was irrelevant. The unit's own intelligence specialists meanwhile extracted information from a variety of sources, including television news coverage of the events taking place in Tehran. Footage of the embassy compound, the surrounding areas and the Revolutionary Guards was taped and linked together. A highly detailed large-scale model of the embassy compound, measuring eight feet by twelve, was constructed and delivered to Delta. This showed that the compound comprised fourteen buildings situated in twenty-seven acres of heavily wooded land surrounded by high walls. There was little or no information as to where within the compound the hostages were located. In late November, however, matters improved dramatically with the return to the United States of thirteen of the hostages released by the Iranians: these provided the much needed information, including the unfortunate fact that three of the hostages were imprisoned in the headquarters of the Iranian Foreign Ministry.

Meanwhile, Delta's assault teams concentrated on training for their respective parts in the operation. Using the scale model, they worked out methods of gaining entry to the compound and specified buildings, neutralising guards, evacuating the hostages and extracting them. Tactics and techniques were developed, revised and practised repeatedly, while endless hours were spent on the ranges, shooting with a variety of weapons by day and night.

Much consideration was given to the method of insertion into the target area: by parachute, helicopter or truck being among the options considered. Eventually the helicopter was selected as being the most practical. However, the size of the assault force and the distances to be covered was such that only one type of aircraft could be considered: the Sikorsky RH-53D Sea Stallion which was in service with the US Navy in the mine-sweeping role. At that time, this aircraft was the only one in the US armed forces' inventory possessing sufficient range and payload capacity for the operation.

Soon afterwards, seven Sea Stallions were flown to Delta's base at Camp Peary where they were joined by US Navy aircrews. It soon became apparent that the latter were unsuited to the low-level flying, using night vision goggles, that would be required for the operation and they were subsequently replaced by US Marine Corps aircrew who were despatched with their aircraft to the desert areas of Yuma, Arizona, where they practised flying without lights. Shortly afterwards, Delta followed them for joint training, most of which was conducted at night.

By the middle of December, a plan had evolved which was considered feasible. A force of 119, comprising ninety-two members of Delta and a number of attached personnel, including a detachment of US Air Force (USAF) ground crew, would be flown in two C-141 Starlifter transport aircraft of the USAF Military Air Command from the United States to Frankfurt, West Germany. It would be joined there by a thirteen-man Special Forces team which had trained to carry out the rescue of the three hostages being held in the headquarters of the Iranian Foreign Ministry. From Frankfurt the entire force would fly to Egypt where it would land at an airbase at Wadi Qena, near Cairo. Thereafter, it would continue its journey in the two C-141s to the island of Masirah, off the coast of the Sultanate of Oman, from where the operation would be launched.

During the first phase of the operation, the force would be flown in three MC-130 Combat Talons of 8th Special Operations Squadron USAF to a location code-named 'Desert One', situated 265 miles south-east of Tehran, in the Dasht-e-Kavir Salt Desert. Three EC-130 aircraft, borrowed from a tactical airborne command and control squadron, would follow the three MC-130s, each carrying two 3,000 gallon bladders of aviation fuel.

Shortly after arrival at Desert One, the force would be joined by the eight Sea Stallion helicopters which would fly in from the aircraft carrier USS *Nimitz*, stationed in the Gulf of Oman. After refuelling, six of them would fly Delta to a location, code-named 'Fig Bar', some three hours' flying time from Desert One in an area of abandoned salt mines some fifty miles south-east of Tehran. The helicopters would then fly on and lie up in another location, about fifteen miles further to the north-east, ready for the extraction phase of the operation. The MC-130s and EC-130s would in the meantime return to Masirah, taking with them all the personnel left at Desert One.

Meanwhile, a four-man reconnaissance team would already be in Tehran. Its leader was a former Special Forces officer, Dick Meadows, who had seen extensive service in Vietnam and, like

Beckwith, had served an exchange tour with 22 SAS. Meadows had been hired by Beckwith as a civilian consultant to assist with the formation of Delta and was one of his three liaison officers despatched to the Pentagon to work with the JCS staff. The three other members of Meadows' team comprised two Special Forces sergeants, 'Scotty' and 'Clem', and a USAF sergeant, 'Fred', who had been born in Iran. The team's tasks would include reconnoitring both landing sites and all planned routes, pre-positioning transport, planning alternative routes to be used if necessary, keeping the embassy and Foreign Ministry headquarters building under surveillance and maintaining listening watch on its radio.

Meadows' reconnaissance team would rendezvous with Beckwith's force at Fig Bar and lead it five miles to a pre-reconnoitred lying-up place (LUP) in a wadi. There Beckwith and his men would remain until after dark when they would be collected in a bus and another vehicle. While Beckwith carried out a reconnaissance of the route to the embassy in the pick-up, his men would be driven in the bus to a warehouse on the outskirts of Tehran where they would transfer to six trucks. Thereafter, Delta would split into three groups designated Red, Blue and White: Red would be responsible for attacking the western part of the embassy compound, and releasing any of the hostages it found, while Blue did likewise in the eastern part – Red and Blue would be preceded by a four-man team which would be responsible for neutralising the guards on the east wall of the embassy compound, overlooking a main thoroughfare called Roosevelt Avenue. White would meanwhile secure the withdrawal route for Red and Blue sections and cover them as they and the released hostages withdrew to a large sports stadium, located nearby on the other side of Roosevelt Avenue, from which they would be extracted by helicopter.

During the assault on the embassy the thirteen-man Special Forces team, guided by Scotty and Clem, would attack the Foreign Ministry headquarters, release the three hostages held there and move to an adjacent car park to await extraction by helicopter. During this phase of the operation, two AC-130 Spectre gunships would orbit overhead, suppressing any opposition from Iranian units. Air cover against attack by the Iranian Air Force would be provided by fighters from USS *Nimitz* and another carrier, USS *Coral Sea*.

On a signal from the forward air controller accompanying the Delta assault force, five of the six Sea Stallion helicopters would deploy from their LUP south-east of Tehran and carry out a series of extractions from twelve predetermined locations, including the sports stadium. The sixth aircraft would meanwhile fly to the Foreign Ministry headquarters and extract the Delta team and three hostages from the Foreign Ministry car park. All six helicopters would then head for a disused airstrip at Manzariyeh, some thirty-five miles south of Tehran, which would have been secured by a company of Rangers flown in earlier in C-141 Starlifters. Once the entire force, including the hostages and the reconnaissance team, was complete at Manzariyeh, it would be flown out in the C-141s.

By April 1980, all elements of the task force were fully trained. Colonel Beckwith was concerned that the constant delays in launching the operation were having a detrimental effect on Delta, some of whose members were becoming jaded with the constant and repetitive training. It was with great relief, therefore, that on 16 April the decision was taken to deploy the unit to Egypt pending a final decision to launch the operation.

On the morning of Sunday 20 April, Delta and its accompanying attached personnel emplaned aboard two C-141 Starlifters at Pope Air Force Base, North Carolina, and flew to Frankfurt, West Germany, where it was joined by the Special Forces team tasked with attacking the Iranian Foreign Ministry building. The entire force was now assembled and totalled 132 in number: ninety-two members of Delta; the thirteen-man Special Forces team; a twelve-man team of Delta support personnel and Rangers, responsible for securing Desert One and maintaining a watch on a nearby road; twelve Farsi-speaking drivers; and two Iranian former generals, one of whom would remain with Beckwith and his men while the other, a former Iranian Air Force officer, would be attached to the commanding officer of the helicopter squadron after his arrival at Desert One.

The two Starlifters touched down at Wadi Qena airbase in Egypt on the morning of 21 April. The next three days were spent in testing and checking of weapons and equipment and in final rehearsals. During this time information was received that all fifty–three hostages within the embassy compound were being held in the chancery building. This would make matters simpler for Delta, so Beckwith and his group commanders hurriedly revised the plan for the assault on the compound.

At the same time as Delta landed in Egypt, Dick Meadows arrived in Tehran, the other three members of his team arriving separately on the same day. Already in the city were two other agents, a retired CIA operative named Bob Plan and an Iranian, 'Franco', who had worked for the Agency in the days of the Shah, collecting information about the Soviets in Iran. Plan, who was Franco's control, was operating under deep cover as a German businessman and travelled to and from Iran in order to maintain contact with his own controllers. Both men had been in Iran for four months, during which time Franco had collected six trucks and two vans which were concealed in a warehouse.

During the next two days, Meadows and his team carried out their final preparations. Meadows himself reconnoitred the LUP where Delta would lie up before driving into the city under cover of darkness, and moved it to an area where it would be less likely to be discovered. He also carried out a maintenance check on all the vehicles to ensure that they were fully fuelled, and reconnoitred the area of the embassy and the nearby sports stadium from which the rescue force and the hostages would be extracted.

At 2 p.m. on 24 April, the force landed on the island of Masirah where the MC-130 transports and EC-130 tanker aircraft were waiting for it. Early that evening, the force emplaned and at 6 p.m. the first aircraft took off from Masirah. During the flight, confirmation was received by radio that all eight helicopters had taken off from *Nimitz* and were en route to Desert One. The landing area had been secretly reconnoitred at the end of March by a three-man USAF reconnaissance team, flown in by a STOL aircraft, which had determined that it was suitable for use by transport aircraft, particularly the heavily laden EC-130s. The team had also positioned three remote-controlled beacons which could be activated from a distance of three miles. At 10 p.m., the pilot of the leading aircraft switched them on, pinpointing the landing strip in the distance.

Shortly afterwards, the first MC-130 landed. As Beckwith and his Blue group deplaned, the twelve-man team responsible for securing Desert One and maintaining a watch on the nearby road deployed to its positions. At this juncture, however, a bus appeared unexpectedly and was forced to stop after its tyres had been shot out by the road watch team. Ordered off the vehicle, the driver and his forty-five passengers were moved to an area where they were placed under guard. Further misfortune struck soon afterwards when a petrol bowser drove into view and was immediately fired upon by one of the road watch team with an M72 light anti-armour weapon (LAW) which hit the vehicle and set it ablaze, lighting up the night sky. A small van, which appeared immediately afterwards, stopped to pick up the bowser's crew and disappeared into the darkness.

In the meantime a USAF combat control team, responsible for controlling air traffic during this phase of the operation, had also deployed from the MC-130. Shortly afterwards, the aircraft took off and headed back for Masirah. Minutes later the other two MC-130s, bringing in the remainder of the force, also landed and were followed by the three EC-130 tanker aircraft. The second MC-130 took off for Masirah soon afterwards, leaving the remaining four aircraft parked near the landing strip with their engines idling. As Colonel Beckwith awaited the arrival of the eight helicopters, a signal was received from the two members of Dick Meadows's reconnaissance team waiting at Fig Bar, the landing zone (LZ) to which Delta would be flown during the next phase of the operation.

Only six helicopters arrived at Desert One and they landed at 8.45 p.m., an hour and a half late. Mechanical breakdown and instrument failure had claimed the two missing aircraft, forcing one to land and be abandoned by its crew which was picked up by one of the other helicopters, and the other to turn back to USS *Nimitz*. The remaining six encountered bad weather, including severe sandstorms, which reduced visibility to zero. By the time they landed, the operation was running forty-five minutes behind schedule.

More problems arose when, as Delta was emplaning one of the helicopters was found to have sprung a leak in its hydraulic system, rendering it unserviceable and reducing the number of aircraft available for the rest of the operation to five. Six was the absolute minimum number required and Colonel Beckwith, who had not planned for the eventuality of having to proceed with less than that number, decided that the operation must be aborted. He insisted on that course of action despite apparently receiving, via Colonel James Kyle, the USAF officer in command at Desert One, a request from Major General James Vaught, the JTF commander whose command post was located in Cairo, to consider proceeding with five aircraft. Vaught in turn contacted the White House where he spoke to President Jimmy Carter who agreed that the operation should be cancelled. On receiving confirmation that the operation was to be aborted, Beckwith gave the order for the entire force to embark on the MC-130 and three EC-130s; the six helicopters were to be destroyed.

It was now that the misfortune dogging the operation turned to outright disaster. As one of the helicopters was manoeuvring to refuel from one of the EC-130s at the northern end of Desert One, its rotors struck the port side of the tanker which exploded in a fireball. Members of the Blue group, essentially B Squadron under its commander Major Logan Fitch, were already aboard the EC-130 and were forced to leap for their lives as fire engulfed both aircraft, killing the EC-130's five crew and three of those aboard the helicopter. Total confusion now reigned throughout Desert One as the flames turned night into day and exploding ammunition and

Redeye missiles provided an impromptu fireworks display. Without further delay, all personnel boarded the three remaining aircraft which took off for Masirah; in the haste to depart, however, the destruction of the five remaining, now abandoned, helicopters appeared to have been forgotten.

Dick Meadows, accompanied by Fred and Clem, had meanwhile been waiting at Fig Bar ready to receive Delta. He had established radio communications with Desert One and had been informed that the helicopters had been delayed. At 2.40 a.m. on 25 April, he received a message telling him that the operation had been aborted. Cacheing their radio, the three men returned to Tehran. During the afternoon, Meadows heard a BBC report of the crash at Desert One on the radio in his hotel room. Realising that it was only a matter of time before the Iranians started checking on foreigners in the capital, he decided that he and his team must leave the country as quickly as possible. The problem was that all the airline offices were closed, it being Friday, the Muslim weekend, and he and his team would have to wait until the morrow.

It was not until Saturday evening that the Lufthansa office in his hotel opened and he was able to buy a ticket on the Sunday morning flight to Frankfurt. On arrival at the airport he spotted the other members of the team who had already passed through customs and immigration and were waiting to board the aircraft. After being briefly apprehended for inadvertently omitting to obtain one of a number of necessary stamps on his passport, and being questioned as to the amount of currency he had in his possession, Meadows was allowed to proceed, but he had no doubt that his description was being compared to those of Westerners wanted for questioning. Shortly afterwards, he and his team left Iran on Lufthansa Flight 601 bound for Frankfurt.

Operation Eagle Claw ended in disaster, tragically with the loss of eight lives. Inevitably, in its aftermath there was much in-depth investigation and analysis into the reasons for its failure; much of it has already been published in detail and it would serve little purpose to repeat it here. There was also a degree of recrimination among the different elements involved in the operation, although none was directed at Delta. There was considerable acrimony between the US Marine Corps and the USAF, the latter eventually being provoked into revealing that the Marine aircrews had abandoned their helicopters without destroying them. According to two reports, however, Major General Vaught had requested that an airstrike by US Navy aircraft be carried out on the abandoned helicopters but this had been vetoed by President Carter and the JCS because of the problems of locating the targets on the ground and the risk of encountering Iranian aircraft. Nevertheless, the revelation concerning the helicopters being left intact became all the more serious when it was revealed that the Iranians had discovered inside them secure communications equipment and documents giving details of the operation, including the warehouse in which the vehicles were hidden, and of American agents within Iran. This was an appalling and inexcusable violation of operational security.

The Carter administration suffered from the political fallout and the Secretary of State, Cyrus Vance, resigned although he had not been involved in any way with the planning of the operation. A scapegoat was needed, however, and the luckless Colonel Charles Beckwith was singled out. He was forced to give a press conference at which he had to explain his decision to abort the operation, while concealing the fact that President Carter had concurred with it.

Beckwith later gave evidence before Congress which conducted an inquiry into Operation Eagle Claw. In reply to questions from Senator Sam Nunn, asking him what he had learned from the operation and what could be done to prevent a similar disaster in the future, Beckwith stated that the JTF assembled for the operation had been an *ad hoc* affair which had not operated as a team nor possessed the same motivation as Delta. He recommended the formation of a special command encompassing the special operations forces of all three US armed services.

Meanwhile, undeterred by the disaster of Eagle Claw, the Pentagon lost little time in starting to plan another rescue mission, code-named Operation Snow Bird. Once again, command was vested in Major General James Vaught, his deputy being Major General Richard Secord, a USAF officer with extensive experience in the world of special operations. This operation, however, would be very much more difficult because it was known that the Iranians had dispersed the hostages in anticipation of a second rescue mission being mounted. Moreover, there had been indications of an increase in Soviet electronic and satellite surveillance of the United States and thus any training or movement of troops and aircraft inside the country and through the Middle East would have to be carefully concealed. Massive security measures were put in place as planning and training for the new operation proceeded.

Several lessons had been learned, not least the fact that the new operation would require a properly assembled task force equipped with aviation assets capable of carrying Delta to and from its target areas. This aspect of Snow Bird was code-named Project Honey Badger and a new Army helicopter unit was formed for the task. Designated Task Force 158, it comprised forty pilots and 160 support personnel, all volunteers from the 158th, 159th and 229th Aviation Battalions of the 101st Airborne Division (Air Assault). Commencing in June, the unit underwent a period of intensive training during which crews were required to fly at night at very low levels using night vision goggles. Within a relatively short time, it established a level of expertise unequalled among other US Army aviation units. On its formation, the unit was initially equipped with standard aircraft: twenty-eight OH-6 Cayuse light observation helicopters, thirty UH-60A Blackhawk utility helicopters and sixteen CH-47 Chinook medium lift helicopters; all underwent extensive modifications for the special operations role, being fitted with special radio communications, forward-looking infra-red (FLIR), night vision, refuelling and navigation systems.

Intelligence was of prime importance for the new mission and, in view of the CIA's inability to assist, the decision was taken to form a new Army unit to provide it. Formed in July 1980 and designated the Foreign Operating Group (FOG), it comprised fifty personnel carefully selected from the Special Forces and military intelligence units. During the summer of 1980, members of the FOG travelled undercover to Iran where they reconnoitred areas of Tehran, including the locality of the US embassy complex. Unfortunately, however, they were unable to pinpoint the locations of the hostages.

Meanwhile, training and preparation for Operation Snow Bird continued throughout the summer into the autumn and by September the task force was ready to go. In October, the CIA reported that the majority of the hostages had been returned to the embassy while the remainder, some fifteen, were being held in two large houses in the northern part of Tehran. The task force's intelligence officers, headed by the deputy commander, Major General Richard Secord, and President Carter's advisers were dubious about the reliability of this information. Because of this and a projected risk of thirty per cent casualties among the hostages and the rescue force, the President eventually took the decision not to launch the operation. A few weeks later, on 20 January 1981, as Ronald Reagan was being inaugurated as the fortieth president of the United States, Iran released the American hostages and the Snow Bird task force was stood down.

In the aftermath of the failure of Operation Eagle Claw, an official review of the operation had been ordered by the Pentagon. A commission under Admiral James Holloway produced a report highlighting the *ad hoc* nature of the force formed to carry out the operation and recommending the formation of a Counter-Terrorist Joint Task Force (CTJTF) directly responsible to the JCS for the planning and conduct of counter-terrorist operations. In addition, the report recommended the establishment of a Special Operations Advisory Panel with the task of reviewing and assessing special operations planning.

On 22 October 1980, the Joint Special Operations Command (JSOC) was formed at Fort Bragg, North Carolina. Overseeing its activities was the Special Operations Division which had been formed on 26 February 1981; headed by Lieutenant Colonel James Longhofer, it formed part of the Pentagon's Directorate of

Operations and was tasked with co-ordinating all US Army counter-terrorist operations.

Delta was placed under command of JSOC, together with another military counter-terrorist unit formed in 1980, the US Navy's SEAL (Sea Air Land) Team 6. During the aftermath of Operation Eagle Claw, SEAL units had begun training for maritime countermeasures (MCM) operations. SEAL Team 2, based on the east coast of the United States, had subsequently formed a dedicated MCM force of two platoons designated Mobility Six (MOB 6). This was disbanded in October 1980 and SEAL Team 6 was formed in its place, becoming fully operational six months later. Totalling some 175 all ranks, the unit was based at a US Navy base in Norfolk, Virginia and underwent training in the United States and abroad with units such as the Royal Marines SBS, the French Navy's Commando Hubert and West Germany's GSG–9.

During the 1980s, specialist aviation support for Delta and SEAL Team 6 counter-terrorist operations was provided by the helicopter unit originally assembled for Operation Snow Bird, but since redesignated as Task Force 160. On 1 April 1982 it was officially formed as the 160th Aviation Battalion. In 1986, having been increased in size, it was redesignated yet again as 160th Special Operations Aviation Group (Airborne), but continued to be popularly known as Task Force 160 or the 'Night Stalkers'.

The unit adopted two highly specialised light helicopters, initially based on the OH-6A Cayuse and designated AH-6 and MH-6 respectively. The AH-6 attack variant was designed to carry a wide array of weapons, including 7.62mm miniguns, two seven-shot 2.75 rocket pods on a purpose-designed mounting system, .50 calibre heavy machine-guns, Mk.19 40mm grenade launcher, Hellfire missiles and ATAS, the air-to-air version of the Stinger missile. Some of the AH-6s were equipped with nose or rotor mast-mounted weapon sight systems. The MH-6 variant was designed to carry six personnel on platforms mounted outside the doors for rapid insertion or extraction, later aircraft being fitted with a fold-away system. Other items of equipment developed for use with the

MH-6 included lightweight wire ladders, for delivery or extraction of personnel, and a hoist. Both the AH-6 and MH-6 were designed to be fitted with a nose-mounted FLIR system which, combined with a sophisticated navigation system and a night vision goggle (NVG) compatible cockpit, enabled the aircraft to be flown in pitch darkness. Other features included an advanced communications suite, radar warning receiver and infra-red suppression equipment if required.

Task Force 160 also adopted the MH-60A, the first special operations variant of the Blackhawk utility helicopter. This was a standard UH-60 fitted with auxiliary fuel tanks, infra-red suppressed exhaust system, 7.62mm miniguns, radar warning receiver, an infra-red transmission jammer, FLIR and a satellite communications system. During the late 1980s a further variant, the MH-60L, appeared. This was fitted with upgraded electronics, lightweight armour for crew protection, a folding tail to facilitate shipborne use and the capability to be armed with Hellfire missiles. An attack variant, designated AH-60L DAP (Defensive Armed Penetration), was also produced. The MH-60L would later be replaced by the MH-60K which featured an NVG-compatible cockpit, electronic sensors, electronic countermeasures and a mission management system.

For operations requiring a heavy-lift capability, Task Force 160 was equipped with a special operations variant of the CH-47 Chinook. Like the MH-60, the early versions of the MH-47 were standard CH-47s specially equipped for the special operations role. Subsequent variants have been increasingly upgraded; the latest, the MH-47E, being equipped with weather-mapping radar, an integrated avionics system allowing mission management as well as global communications and navigation, FLIR and multi-mode radar for nap-of-the earth and low-level flight operations, fuel tanks with twice the capacity of those of the CH-47D and an in-flight refuelling system.

Co-existing with Task Force 160 was another aviation asset, jointly operated by the Army and the CIA, which also provided support for Delta and SEAL Team 6. Formed on 2 March 1981 and designated Seaspray, it was a highly secret 'black' covert unit operating under the cover-name of First Rotary Wing Test Activity and based at Fort Eustis in Virginia. It was equipped with a variety of aircraft including the McDonnell Douglas MD-500 which, like Task Force 160's AH-6s and MH-6s, had been extensively modified for special operations. The troop-carrying variant could carry nine Delta operators and long-range fuel tanks on collapsible skids fitted on each side of the aircraft. Both variants were fitted with sophisticated electronic and navigational systems including FLIR.

For clandestine long-range heavy-lift transportation of personnel and equipment, a commercial organisation was established in late 1982 to avoid the use of USAF C-130 Hercules and C-141 Starlifter transports which were too easily recognisable as military aircraft. A recently retired USAF officer, Lieutenant Colonel Richard Gadd, formed a company, Sumairco, which leased aircrews and aircraft from Southern Air Transport, a company which operated L-100 Hercules transports (the commercial version of the C-130) from its base in Florida and which had for some years provided air transport for the CIA. Sumairco was subsequently contracted by the Special Operations Division to provide a twenty-four-hour service, 365 days a year.

In addition to these covert aviation support assets, a highly secret intelligence unit was formed to support counter-terrorist operations world-wide. Designated the Intelligence Support Activity (ISA), it was created from the FOG and commanded by Colonel Jerry King who had formed the latter. The role of the ISA was, in the event of a terrorist outrage or crisis involving US nationals or interests, immediately to infiltrate its agents into the theatre involved and provide intelligence and support for other US counter-terrorist forces during any subsequent operations. Operating under a variety of different code-names, including 'Granite Rock' and 'Powder Keg', the ISA was a totally 'deniable' asset and no trace of its existence would ever be found in any Pentagon records.

Based in Arlington, Virginia, the ISA numbered approximately 100 all ranks. Two-thirds of its number were former members of the Special Forces, the remainder being intelligence personnel specialising in both human intelligence (humint) and signals intelligence (sigint), the latter's role being the interception, monitoring of electronic transmissions and the pinpointing of their sources; this was frequently carried out from specially equipped aircraft. The ISA also possessed its own assault and sniper unit whose members were trained along similar lines to those of Delta.

As in the majority of specialist counter-terrorist units, ISA personnel were required to undergo a rigorous physical and psychological selection procedure before being considered eligible. Those who were successful underwent intensive training in a variety of military and intelligence skills. The latter included the techniques of establishing covers, acquiring false passports, establishing false credentials, setting up of front companies in overseas countries, recruitment of agents and the full gamut of 'tradecraft' as practised in the hidden world of intelligence operations. The majority of ISA personnel were deployed in sections and sub-units based at locations around Washington and the neighbouring states of Virginia and Maryland. For maximum security, members only knew the identity of personnel within their own section.

Logistical support for the newly formed counter-terrorist units and support assets was provided by an equally clandestine organisation called the DARCOM Receipt, Issue, Storage & Support Activity, but generally known by its acronym DARISSA. Formed in late 1981 and operational by July 1983, it was commanded by a former Special Forces officer, Colonel Robert Redmund, and based at the Lakehurst Naval Air Engineering Center in New Jersey. DARISSA supplied Delta and SEAL Team 6 with all their specialist weapons and equipment. Those items not already in existence, such as specialist ammunition, miniaturised explosive devices or laser guidance systems, were designed in co-operation with the John F. Kennedy Special Warfare Center at Fort Bragg and manufactured by DARISSA which also serviced Seaspray's aircraft and installed specialist equipment and systems in them. A considerable amount of technical development interchange reportedly took place with 22

SAS and GSG–9. DARISSA also provided isolation and concealed storage facilities. Its New Jersey base included a former airship hangar, 200 feet in height and sufficiently large to accommodate a multi-storey building up to which C-130 or C-141 transports could taxi for loading and unloading unseen by unauthorised eyes.

The 1980s saw a number of operational deployments overseas by US military counter-terrorist units, only a few of which have become public knowledge.

On the afternoon of 17 December 1981, Brigadier General James Dozier, a senior US Army officer serving as the Deputy Chief of Staff (Logistics & Administration) at the NATO headquarters in Verona, in northern Italy, answered the door bell of his apartment in the city. Outside were two workmen who said they were plumbers investigating an apparent leakage of water from the general's apartment into one on the floor below. Unthinkingly, Dozier allowed them to enter; as he did so, two more 'workmen' appeared and attacked him, beating him badly and knocking him unconscious. While they were doing this the first pair of thugs bound and gagged his wife. The four men then produced a trunk into which they unceremoniously bundled the senseless officer, subsequently loading it into a small van and disappearing into the streets of Verona. A few hours later, the Red Brigades announced that they had kidnapped Dozier.

This kidnapping served to highlight problems and internal conflicts which existed within the US command structure. By now JSOC was in command of all US counter-terrorist units and operations world-wide, reporting directly to the Chairman of the JCS. This was designed to reduce the chain of command to the minimum, permitting decisions to be made with the least possible delay. However, in instances where US troops were deployed on foreign soil, they came under command of the US ambassador in the country concerned until such time as they actually went into action, at which point JSOC would take over. A further complication arose with the US system of geographical commands under which forces in each area of the world come under command of the respective commander-in-chief. In certain instances some commanders-in-chief were 'double-hatted', as was the case with General Bernard Rogers, Dozier's chief, who was not only commander-in-chief of the US European Command (EUCOM), but also, in his appointment as Supreme Allied Commander Europe (SACEUR), of NATO. Dozier himself also wore two hats, being on the staffs of both NATO and EUCOM.

When the news of Dozier's kidnapping reached the Pentagon in Washington, the JCS ordered JSOC to despatch a six-man team from Delta, under the command of Colonel Jesse Johnson, the unit's second-in-command, to Italy to act in support of the Italian authorities who by this time were conducting a full-scale manhunt for Dozier and his kidnappers. They neglected, however, to inform the US Ambassador and Headquarters EUCOM which by then had decided to send its own task force of operations and intelligence personnel to Italy to assist the Italians. Thus, when the Delta team arrived at Headquarters EUCOM, Colonel Johnson was greeted with a hostile reception from the deputy commander of EUCOM who informed him that the Delta team would come under his command, dismissing Johnson's insistence that he and his men were under JSOC.

Johnson and his five men departed for Rome. In the meantime, a dispute had arisen between Washington and the US Ambassador, Maxwell Rabb, who was angered by the fact that the Pentagon had not requested clearance to send the Delta team beforehand, but had merely announced that it was doing so. Fortunately, the dispute had been resolved by the time the team arrived in Rome and headed for the embassy. After briefing the Ambassador and leaving two of his communications specialists at the embassy, Johnson and the rest of his team went to the US Army base at Vicenza, some fifty kilometres east of Verona, arriving there on the evening of 20 December. There they encountered their EUCOM counterparts, a three-man team commanded by Colonel Norman Moffett, the commander of Special Forces Task Force Europe.

Confusion reigned as a major dispute arose between EUCOM, the JCS, JSOC and the US embassy in Rome. Ambassador Rabb despatched a senior official to Vicenza to act as his personal representative while Colonel Moffett contacted his immediate superior, Admiral Thomas Kinnebrew, in an effort to clarify the situation. The latter contacted Ambassador Rabb, insisting that the Delta team and any other JSOC assistance to the Italians would have to be passed through EUCOM. Rabb dismissed this demand, stating that he was the senior US government representative in Italy and thus was in command of all US counter-terrorist forces deployed in Italy on Winter Harvest, the code-name for the operation to locate and recover Dozier.

Meanwhile the Italian authorities, somewhat bemused at the behaviour of the Americans, continued with the search for Dozier, but without success. The Pentagon offered to send a 25-man ISA surveillance team but this was met with a flat refusal from EUCOM which appeared to be more concerned with protecting its territory than recovering the luckless Dozier.

On 27 December the Red Brigades, who had maintained silence since issuing their single communiqué claiming responsibility for the kidnapping, released a photograph of Dozier, showing him seated in front of the Red Brigades emblem, a five-pointed star, together with a statement which announced that he was to be put on trial.

The Italian authorities, convinced that the terrorists were holding Dozier in the north of Italy, were meanwhile concentrating their search around the cities of Verona and Padua. The Carabinieri, who were leading the hunt, were putting their main effort into the acquisition of information by attempting to track down and arrest as many members of Red Brigades as possible, but this was easier said than done because the terrorists were organised in small independent cells. It was discovered, however, that they were using radio communications and this gave the Americans an opportunity to provide valuable technical support in locating transmitters which were based in the terrorists' safe houses. An ISA sigint detachment with its specially equipped helicopters was despatched and a massive electronic monitoring programme ensued. In addition to their airborne monitoring apparatus, the ISA also fielded ground-based systems. Further support was provided by the National Security Agency (NSA), which tasked its satellites to orbit over Italy, and by US Army sigint stations.

By the middle of January 1982, by which time Dozier had been in the hands of the terrorists for nearly a month, these intercept operations had pinpointed the locations of several Red Brigades safe houses. By the end of the third week of January, the Carabinieri had arrested more than twenty suspected members of the organisation in different parts of Italy and had uncovered several caches of arms. The massive dragnet had an additional side effect in that it inadvertently uncovered Mafia operations throughout the country. This caused considerable discomfiture to a large number of Mafiosi whose godfathers ordered their respective 'families' to co-operate with the Italian authorities in the hunt for Dozier's kidnappers in order to bring it to a satisfactory conclusion as soon as possible.

By the fourth week of January, a combination of sigint and information from an informer had pinpointed an apartment block in Padua. The building was placed under surveillance, with US technicians monitoring the telephone lines and electricity consumption of each apartment within the building. A comparison of previous records showed differentials relating to a second-floor apartment. On the morning of 28 January, a ten-man team of the NOCS 'Leatherheads' was briefed for an assault on the apartment and at midday carried it out. Under cover of noise from a nearby construction site, the team battered down the front door, bursting in and overpowering Dozier's captors, one of whom was in the process of aiming a weapon at the American as he was seized.

In the aftermath of the Dozier affair, there was considerable recrimination over the infighting that had taken place between the different factions attempting to exercise overall command of the US units involved in the operation. After further disagreement between the Pentagon and the State Department over who should exercise control in future, the National Security Council (NSC) took the decision to establish a proper crisis management team designated the Terrorist Incident Working Group.

The following year, 1983, saw a terrorist bomb attack in April against the US embassy in Beirut, followed by another on the headquarters of the 24th Marine Amphibious Unit USMC which was then providing the US element of the multi-national peace-keeping force in the Lebanon. These resulted in the deployment of two successive ISA teams in the Lebanon. Following the kidnappings in 1984 of American civilians and the CIA station chief, William Buckley, a hostage rescue force comprising JSOC, Delta, ISA and SEAL Team 6 was deployed to the Mediterranean area. A full account of these deployments and operations is given in Chapter 12.

In October, Delta, Task Force 160 and SEAL Team 6 were deployed among a number of US special operations units during the invasion of the island of Grenada in the Caribbean. A British colony until 1974, the island had a troubled history and since independence had been governed by a chief minister, Sir Eric Gairy, who was head of the Grenada United Labour Party. His rule was little short of dictatorship, any opposition being swiftly crushed by the police and the Grenada Defence Force who were backed up by a gang of thugs known as the Mongoose Gang. In March 1979 Gairy was deposed in a coup covertly supported by Cuba and led by Maurice Bishop, the Marxist leader of the New Jewel Movement (NJM) opposition party who immediately formed the People's Revolutionary Government (PRG). Any optimism on the part of the island's population that the coup would bring welcome change was soon shattered as it soon became apparent that the new regime was as equally repressive as its predecessor albeit in a more subtle fashion.

During the next four years, with the help of Cuba and Guyana, Grenada became a militarised state under the People's Revolutionary Armed Forces (PRAF), the military wing of the PRG.

During the period of 1980 to 1982, Cuba supplied large quantities of Soviet-manufactured arms and equipment, including armoured vehicles, under the terms of three agreements signed with the Soviet Union. The third of these agreements also provided for the supply of Cuban and Soviet advisers to train the PRAF; a 27-man Cuban military mission, comprising infantry, engineer, signals and logistics specialists, arrived in 1982.

On 19 October 1983, Bishop was deposed in a coup mounted by members of the Central Committee of the NJM headed by the party's deputy leader and PRG Finance Minister, Bernard Coard. Power was placed in the hands of the Revolutionary Military Council (RMC), a group comprising sixteen officers of the PRAF headed by General Hudson Austin, the PRG Secretary of Defence and PRAF commander. Coard meanwhile adopted the role of *éminence grise* to the RMC.

In the United States, Britain and Canada, meanwhile, there was serious concern for the nationals of all three countries living in Grenada; among the US community of approximately 1,000 were some 600 students attending the St. George's University School of Medicine. Elsewhere in the Caribbean there was grave anxiety among the islands forming the Organisation of East Caribbean States (OECS) who were concerned at the potentially destabilising effect of the latest coup in Grenada. After some deliberation and having agreed to participate in a combined military operation to invade Grenada, the OECS formally asked the United States for military assistance. President Ronald Reagan gave his approval and on 23 October signed the necessary National Security Decision Directive ordering US armed forces to carry out an invasion of Grenada with all due haste. While the safety of the 1,000 or so Americans and other Westerners was the stated reason for the United States agreeing to intervene, in reality it was the opportunity to wrest Grenada away from Soviet and Cuban influence and thus prevent its becoming a base from which a programme of destabilisation and revolution could be launched throughout the rest of the Caribbean.

Urgent Fury, as the operation was named, was a large under-taking of which only those elements conducted by Delta, Task Force 160 and SEAL Team 6 are within the context of this book.

Responsibility for planning and executing the operation was given to the Commander-in-Chief Atlantic, Admiral Wesley L. McDonald. An *ad hoc* formation, designated Joint Task Force 120, was assembled under the command of Vice Admiral Joseph Metcalf, the commander of the US Navy's Second Fleet, comprising a carrier battle group and Task Force 124, the latter comprising the US Navy's Amphibious Squadron Four and the 22nd Marine Amphibious Unit.

The special operations element of the invasion force comprised Task Force 123, under JSOC commander Major General Richard Scholtes, and included Delta, SEAL Team 6, elements of 1st and 2nd Battalions 75th Ranger Regiment, a USAF combat control team and Task Force 160. Further air support for JSOC would be forthcoming from the USAF's 1st Special Operations Wing with its MC-130E Combat Talons and AC-130 Spectre gunships.

Task Force 123 was responsible for securing the southern half of the island while the 22nd Marine Amphibious Unit of Task Force 124 was allocated the north. During the initial phase of the operation on the night of 23/24 October, elements of SEAL Team 6 and the USAF combat control team would infiltrate Port Salines airfield on the south-west tip of the island. Throughout that night until dawn on 24 October they would carry out a reconnaissance of the area to determine enemy strength and dispositions before planting radar beacons to guide in the MC-130E Combat Talons bringing in the Ranger force which would be dropped on to the airfield at 2 a.m. on 25 October. Meanwhile, another detachment of SEAL Team 6 would be inserted by helicopter and seize the Radio Free Grenada radio station at Beausejour on the west coast of the island. A short distance to the south, a third detachment of SEAL Team 6 would carry out an attack on the Governor-General's residence at St. George's and rescue Sir Paul Scoon who was being held under house arrest. Meanwhile Delta and a company of Rangers, flown in by helicopters of Task Force 160, would attack Fort Rupert which housed the headquarters of General Hudson Austin and his RMC, and Richmond Hill Prison where large numbers of Grenadan opponents of Bernard Coard's regime were incarcerated.

At just after last light on the evening of Sunday 23 October, twelve members of SEAL Team 6 and the four-man USAF combat control team were dropped in two eight-man sticks, each accompanied by an inflatable craft, from two MC-130E Combat Talons approximately thirty kilometres off the south-west tip of Grenada. Waiting for them below were two Boston whaler boats deployed by the destroyer USS *Clifton Sprague* which would land them on the coast. The 25-knot wind and rough sea resulted in the boat crews experiencing great difficulty in locating the parachutists in the water. In the first stick, three SEALs were lost and drowned and the parachute release mechanism on the inflatable failed to release, the high winds causing the parachute to remain inflated and overturn the craft. Meanwhile, the second stick was dropped wide of the intended drop zone and another SEAL was also lost.

Despite these serious setbacks, the remainder of the team continued with their mission in one of the Boston whalers, but as they approached the coastline they spotted a Grenadan patrol boat and were forced to cut the boat's engine and let it drift to avoid detection. The situation deteriorated further when the engine, soaked by the choppy sea, refused to start; when it finally did so, there was no alternative but to abort the mission and rendezvous with the USS *Clifton Sprague* which had been searching for the missing SEALs without success. A second attempt to carry out the mission was made on the following night, but was aborted after the boats became swamped by heavy surf and the combat control team lost much of its equipment. The mission was aborted once again and the team withdrew. The failure of the initial path-finding mission resulted in a postponement of the scheduled 2 a.m. assault on Point Salines airfield until 5 a.m. on Tuesday 25 October. This meant that all missions would take place in daylight and the loss of surprise would considerably shorten the odds of success.

During the night of 24/25 October, two of Task Force 160's MH-6 Little Birds and nine of its MH-60 Black Hawks were flown in USAF C-5A Galaxy transports to Barbados where they were to be re-assembled at Grantley Adams airport. Two of the Black Hawks would carry one of the SEAL Team 6 assault groups to seize the Radio Free Grenada radio station at Beausejour while two more would fly the other team to the Governor-General's residence. The remaining five would transport members of Delta and Company C 1st Battalion 75th Ranger Regiment for the assaults on Fort Rupert and Richmond Hill Prison. Due to the late arrival of the transports and subsequent problems which occurred as the helicopters were assembled, the SEALs and Rangers did not take off until 5.30 a.m., an hour and a half after their scheduled departure time of 4 a.m.

As they did so, the combined force of the 1st and 2nd Battalions 75th Ranger Regiment was commencing its drop on Point Salines airfield. Jumping from a height of 500 feet, the leading element of the 1st Battalion encountered heavy fire from anti-aircraft artillery which forced the remaining aircraft to abort its approach while an AC-130 Spectre gunship was called in to suppress the anti-aircraft fire. At 5.52 a.m. the drop recommenced, but further problems, principally due to the large number of aircraft in the area, meant that the last element of the battalion did not drop until 7.05 a.m. The 2nd Battalion, however, experienced no problems and its drop was completed in thirty seconds, the entire unit being on the ground by 7.10 a.m. Heavy fighting took place on and around the airfield, but by approximately 10.30 a.m. the Rangers had seized all their objectives.

The first of the two SEAL Team 6 missions had begun, one hour behind schedule at 6 a.m., with the two Black Hawk helicopters landing the SEAL detachment in the area of the Radio Free Grenada radio station. A quick assault was mounted and the small detachment of PRAF personnel guarding it were swiftly overcome and tied up. The detachment commander then deployed his men in ambush positions by the main road near the station and before long a member of the PRAF driving a van was captured. Shortly afterwards a truck carrying members of the Peoples Revolutionary Militia (PRM) was attacked; five militiamen died and a number of others were wounded. Minutes later a number of vehicles, including an armoured personnel carrier, appeared and a battle started with PRAF troops bringing heavy fire to bear on the lightly armed SEALs. After an hour or so, the latter withdrew to the beach where they lay up until dark. After another brief engagement with the PRAF they took to the water and swam out to sea, eventually making a rendezvous with the destroyer USS *Caron*.

Meanwhile, the other seven Black Hawk helicopters had arrived over the Governor-General's residence at approximately 6.15 a.m. and encountered heavy fire from four anti-aircraft guns at Fort Rupert and two more at Fort Frederick and D'Arbeau respectively. The two aircraft carrying the 23-man SEAL detachment experienced difficulty in locating the designated landing point in the grounds of the building. Accounts differ as to the exact sequence of the ensuing events, but eventually the SEALs succeeded in fast-roping down on to their objective and securing the residence in which they took up defensive positions around and inside the building, having shepherded Sir Paul Scoon and his staff into the dining-room which offered the most cover.

Not long afterwards, the PRAF counter-attacked with the support of an armoured personnel carrier. This was beaten off at about 10.15 a.m. by a Spectre gunship which subsequently had to withdraw after running out of ammunition. By midday the SEALs were once again finding themselves hard-pressed as PRAF troops kept up heavy though inaccurate fire on the residence, but once again a Spectre gunship appeared and beat off the attackers. Despite this, however, it was considered too dangerous to try and extract the Governor-General by helicopter and it was decided to wait until the arrival of reinforcements next day. Fighting continued throughout the night until 7.30 a.m. on 26 October when marines of G Company 2nd/8th Battalion Landing Team arrived to relieve the SEAL detachment.

The assault on Richmond Hill Prison proved an unmitigated disaster. As the five Black Hawks carrying the members of Delta and the Ranger company approached their objective, it became apparent that it was very different from what they had been briefed to expect. The prison was situated on a high razor-backed ridgeline whose steep slopes were covered in dense jungle. The prison itself was virtually impregnable, being surrounded by high walls topped with barbed wire, and watch towers. More seriously, it was dominated by Fort Frederick situated 300 metres away on a higher ridge and manned by a large garrison equipped with anti-aircraft guns.

As the aircraft appeared, flying low up the valley between the prison and the fort, they came under heavy fire. Without any escorting gunships, the Black Hawks were vulnerable and were soon taking hits. Casualties began to mount among their passengers and the aircraft swung away out of range to regroup. A second attempt met with the same response and the pilot of one aircraft was killed. Fighting to keep his aircraft airborne, the co-pilot succeeded in clearing the area and, escorted by another Black Hawk, flew south with the aim of reaching Port Salines airfield and friendly forces. Unfortunately, the aircraft was hit again by ground fire as it flew over a PRAF base and crashed shortly afterwards, breaking in two. The remaining four crew survived, as did all but three of the Rangers in the back of the aircraft. Not long afterwards, another Black Hawk appeared and hovered over the crash site as nine members of Delta fast-roped to assist the wounded. PRAF troops subsequently approached from the north, but were driven off by a Spectre gunship after a brief engagement. The wounded were then moved to a small beach nearby and at just after 10 a.m. the whole group was evacuated by a US Navy rescue helicopter.

The assault on Fort Rupert, meanwhile, had encountered no problems. Members of Delta attacked the RMC headquarters complex and swiftly rounded-up its occupants. Shortly afterwards they and their prisoners were extracted by Task Force 160 aircraft and flown out to the helicopter carrier USS *Guam*.

Operation Urgent Fury was loudly proclaimed by the Reagan administration and the senior elements of the US military as a resounding success. The special operations aspects of it, however, proved to be less so, with some missions not achieving success through no fault of those on the ground. Lack of detailed planning and an absence of sound up-to-date intelligence had resulted in SEALs, helicopter crews and troops being badly briefed. This was particularly so in the case of the Richmond Hill Prison mission which had proved costly in terms of casualties among highly trained troops as well as the loss of an aircraft and damage to others.

In June 1984, elements of Delta and Task Force 160 were reportedly deployed to Chad in North Africa, although there has never been any official confirmation of this. However, in his book, *Twilight Warriors*, journalist Martin Arostegui includes an account given to him by an Englishman, a former member of The Parachute Regiment, serving with the Foreign Legion's parachute unit, the 2e Régiment Etranger de Parachutistes (2e REP) on Operation Manta, the covert French operation to support the Chadian forces of President Hissène Habré which French and US special forces, including members of Delta, were training.

It was known that Libyan instructors were providing training for terrorists from Palestinian and European groups in camps located north of the 16th Parallel, an area separating Chad from Libya. The camps had been identified by satellite photography and the task of close target reconnaissance was carried out by six four-man patrols from the 2e REP's own long-range reconnaissance patrol company, the Commando de Recherches et d'Action dans la Profondeur (CRAP). These had been inserted on the Libyan border at night and made their way to their individual objectives where they had established covert OPs from which to carry out surveillance of the camps. During the following day, they had observed and filmed groups undergoing weapon training and carrying out live firing with small arms and anti-armour weapons under Libyan instructors. The CRAP patrols also filmed and recorded the lay-out of the camps and, after night had fallen, planted remote-controlled sensors around the perimeters of the camps to monitor further activity. Under cover of darkness, they then withdrew and marched to a pre-arranged rendezvous where they were extracted by MH-60 Blackhawk helicopters, reportedly belonging to Task Force 160.

Six weeks later an attack was mounted on one of the terrorist camps. According to Arostegui's account, three MH-60 Blackhawks arrived at midnight, approaching the camp at a height of little more than twenty feet. The camp's guard post was neutralised by machine-gun fire from two of the aircraft before they landed to disgorge two assault teams. One team attacked the camp's headquarters and radio communications centre, taking files and radio communications equipment before destroying both buildings and setting ablaze six vehicles parked nearby. Meanwhile the other team attacked the accommodation housing the trainee terrorists and their instructors, riddling it with automatic fire and grenades before entering the buildings and ensuring that no one had survived. Thereafter, bodies were apparently filmed for subsequent identification. Demolition charges were placed on the armoury and magazine which exploded with a huge detonation as the teams embarked in the two MH-60s. The third aircraft was meanwhile extracting a reconnaissance patrol from a position near the camp. Although there has never been any confirmation, the member of 2e REP CRAP interviewed by Arostegui clearly believed that elements of Delta took part in the operation.

On 5 December of that year, Delta deployed to the island of Masirah in response to the hijacking two days earlier, by members of the Lebanese group Hizbollah, of a Kuwaiti airliner en route from Dubai to Karachi. The crew were forced to fly instead to Tehran from where the terrorists issued demands for the release of the seventeen members of the extremist Shi'ite Al Dawa movement, imprisoned in Kuwait for a series of bomb attacks carried out in December 1983. The Iranians made little effort to resolve the situation and the Kuwaiti government maintained its hard line of refusing to release the prisoners. In a crude effort to force the United States to put pressure on the Kuwaitis, the hijackers turned their attentions to the American passengers aboard the aircraft, killing two, Charles Hegna and William Stanford, and torturing two others. Eventually, however, the Iranians were forced to intercede: security forces boarded the aircraft disguised as a medical team and succeeded in disarming the terrorists. During this crisis, Delta was on standby to carry out a rescue operation if the aircraft left Iran and flew to one of the Gulf states.

In June 1985 elements of JSOC, Delta, ISA and SEAL Team 6 deployed to the NATO base at Sigonella, in Sicily, and to the British base at Akrotiri, Cyprus, after TWA Flight 847 was hijacked by Shi'ite Muslim terrorists and flown to Beirut, subsequently flying on to Algiers. Thereafter the hijackers, once again demanding the release of the eighteen members of Al Dawa imprisoned in Kuwait, forced the aircraft to shuttle back and forth between Beirut and Algiers in a ploy to prevent US forces mounting a rescue operation. The full story of the hijacking and its aftermath is told in Chapter 10.

Five months later, JSOC units were deployed again. On Monday 7 October, the 24,000-ton Italian cruise liner *Achille Lauro* was hijacked by four members of the Palestine Liberation Front (PLF) headed by Abu Abbas (alias Abu Khaled). The vessel had sailed from her home port of Genoa on 3 October, and subsequently anchored off the coast of Egypt. On the morning of the 7th she had disembarked most of her 750 passengers at Alexandria for a day's tour of the Pyramids before sailing for Port Said where they were to rejoin her that evening. Ninety-seven predominantly elderly passengers, of whom twelve were Americans, had remained aboard and were at lunch when two terrorists ran into the dining-room aiming bursts of automatic fire into the ceiling. The American hostages, together with two Austrians and six British female dancers, were separated from the rest and confined in the lounge. Two other terrorists had meanwhile stormed the bridge, taking control and demanding that the vessel steam northwards for the Syrian port of Tartus.

Despite the speed of the attack, *Achille Lauro*'s radio operator had managed to transmit an SOS which was picked up by a radio ham in Gothenburg, Sweden. News of the hijacking was flashed to the United States where the Terrorist Incident Working Group was immediately convened in Washington. An Emergency Support Team was assembled and departed that night from Andrews Air Force Base for the NATO base at Sigonella. JSOC, under Brigadier General Carl Stiner, and Delta flew direct from Fort Bragg, North Carolina, to the British base at Akrotiri. SEAL Team 6, delayed by the breakdown of its C-141 transport, followed as soon as another aircraft had been found.

Meanwhile, the hunt was on for the *Achille Lauro* which, due to maintaining radio silence, had disappeared into the Mediterranean during the night. Aircraft from the carrier USS *Saratoga*, part of the Sixth Fleet, joined the search as did USAF electronic intelligence (elint) aircraft. It was not until Tuesday morning, when the terrorists began radioing for permission to enter Tartus, that the liner was located off the Syrian coast.

The terrorists' request to enter the port had met with a refusal from the Syrians and they had to look elsewhere for a refuge. In fact, the Syrian government had told the Italian Ambassador in Damascus that it was prepared to allow the vessel to dock so that negotiations could be conducted, but only on condition that both the Italian and US governments agreed. The Italians had agreed, but the Americans, who were already planning a rescue operation, refused.

Meanwhile, the terrorists issued their demand for the release of fifty Palestinians imprisoned in Israel. At the same time, aware that they were vulnerable to attack, they moved the twelve American hostages, two Austrians and six British dancers on to the top deck where they could easily be seen. Increasingly angered and frustrated by the Syrians' refusal to allow the ship to dock, the terrorists' leader, Majed Molqi, seized one of the American hostages, a 70-year-old, wheelchair-bound man named Leon Klinghoffer, and pushed him to the starboard side of the ship. Killing him with a single pistol shot to the head, Molqi ordered two members of the ship's crew to throw his body overboard. He then selected his second victim, an American woman named

Mildred Hodes, and threatened over the radio to kill her also unless the Syrians allowed the ship to enter Tartus. The latter, however, remained adamant.

Before Molqi was able to carry out his threat a radio message was received, via an Arabic-language radio station in Cyprus, from an individual identifying himself only as 'Abu Khaled'. He was in fact Abu Abbas, leader of the PLF and mastermind behind the hijacking. He instructed Molqi to treat his hostages well and head back to Port Said. He also instructed him to apologise to the passengers and crew and to explain the reason for the hijack. The transmission was monitored by the Israelis who immediately made its contents public as proof of the involvement of Abu Abbas himself.

As darkness fell on Tuesday night, the liner turned south and headed for Egypt. As she entered the busy shipping lanes of the Mediterranean, she disappeared again among hundreds of other vessels and at one point it was suspected that the terrorists might be making for Cyprus. On Wednesday morning, however, the vessel was spotted by an Israeli warship which reported her location and course which indicated that she was indeed en route for Port Said. A few hours later, the *Achille Lauro* anchored outside the port and early that afternoon Abu Abbas, who had arrived from Cairo at the orders of PLO chairman Yasser Arafat, went out in a tug and boarded the vessel accompanied by a group of Egyptian officials.

By this time, SEAL Team 6 had deployed aboard the amphibious assault ship USS *Iwo Jima* which was positioned within striking distance of the *Achille Lauro* just over the horizon. The plan was for the SEALs to be deployed after dark by helicopter, dropping into the sea with fast rubber assault craft which would be used to make the final approach to the vessel. They would then climb the stern of the ship and carry out an assault.

In Cairo meanwhile, the Egyptian government had been trying to bring the crisis to a peaceful conclusion. The Foreign Minister, Abdel Meguid, was attempting to persuade the ambassadors of the countries whose nationals were among the hostages, namely the United States, Britain, Italy and West Germany, not to press for extradition of the terrorists if they agreed to surrender because this would place the Egyptian government in an invidious position vis-à-vis the governments of other Arab countries. At this point, there was no knowledge of the murder of Leon Klinghofer; during a radio broadcast, made earlier under duress, appealing for no rescue attempt to be made, the *Achille Lauro*'s captain had stated that all on board were safe and well. At just after 5 p.m., however, Meguid received a telephone call informing him that the four terrorists had surrendered.

It rapidly became apparent that the Egyptians, who had been notified of the impending rescue operation, had warned Molqi and his men that the Americans were preparing to carry out an attack on the liner. On being told of this, the terrorists had needed little further encouragement to surrender and had immediately left the vessel in the company of Abu Abbas and the Egyptian officials. The already infuriated Americans were further enraged when they learned that the Egyptians had given the terrorists safe passage out of the country.

Shortly after Abu Abbas and his men left the *Achille Lauro*, the captain broke the news of her husband's death to Mrs. Marilyn Klinghofer who had hitherto been unaware of it. The information did not reach the US Ambassador, however, until he arrived aboard the vessel at midnight to see the American hostages. On learning of the murder, he radioed the news to members of his staff ashore in Port Said and instructed them to call Meguid and insist that the terrorists be put on trial.

The Egyptians claimed that it was too late, the terrorists had already left the country. President Hosni Mubarak himself confirmed that they had done so, maintaining that Molqi and his accomplices had possibly travelled to Tunis. In fact, the Egyptians were lying. The terrorists, accompanied by Abu Abbas and a minor official from the PLO's office in Cairo, were at that moment at an airbase at Al Maza, north-east of Cairo. Moreover, the Americans were well aware of the terrorists' presence in Egypt and knew their exact location. Israeli humint sources at air bases and airports within Egypt, combined with aerial reconnaissance, confirmed that they had not left the country, while monitoring by the NSA of Mubarak's telephone conversations pinpointed their location. Further surveillance identified the Boeing 737 airliner at Al Maza waiting to fly them out of the country.

Refusing to accept defeat, members of the NSC staff put forward a proposal that the terrorists' aircraft be intercepted as soon as it had left Egyptian airspace and forced to fly to the NATO airbase at Sigonella where they could be arrested. This proposal was put to the Deputy National Security Adviser, Vice Admiral John Poindexter, who was standing in for Robert McFarlane, the National Security Advisor, who was away from Washington with the President. Poindexter obtained initial approval from the Chairman of the Joint Chiefs of Staff, Admiral William Crowe, before contacting McFarlane who put the outline proposal to the President who gave his approval.

Orders were flashed to the Sixth Fleet and the USS *Saratoga* launched two E-2C Hawkeye early-warning aircraft and six F-14 Tomcat fighters. On the ground, meanwhile, Israeli humint and sigint sources gave warning of the Egyptian aircraft's departure from Al Maza. Its interception proved difficult and it took three attempts before it was located. Thereafter, the Hawkeyes and Tomcats shadowed it as it flew to Tunisia where it was refused permission to land. The pilot then radioed Cairo for instructions and, having been told to return, began to turn back. At this point he was intercepted and found himself flying in close formation with four F-14s while being ordered to accompany them to Sigonella.

Also en route from Cyprus to Sigonella were JSOC and Delta in two C-141 transports which would land at the base immediately after the terrorists' aircraft. Once the Boeing had landed, the terrorists would be transferred immediately to one of the C-141s and flown with JSOC and Delta to the United States.

In Washington, meanwhile, agreement for the Egyptian aircraft and the two C-141s to land at Sigonella had been obtained from the Italian prime minister, Bettino Craxi. Unfortunately, however, this authority was not conveyed to the Italian commander of the base. When the Boeing 737 landed, followed closely by the two C-141s, it was surrounded by a group of SEALs who were quickly joined by Delta which deployed rapidly from its aircraft. Almost immediately afterwards, however, a force of Carabinieri troops appeared and surrounded the Americans and a ludicrous stand-off developed with the Italians refusing to allow Brigadier General Stiner and his men to remove the terrorists from their aircraft. Even without the presence of the Italians, however, Delta and the SEALs would still possibly have had a fight on their hands because a ten-man detachment of Egyptian special forces troops had accompanied the terrorists during their flight.

After hours of frantic communications between Rome and Washington, during which the stand-off between Stiner's force and the Carabinieri continued, neither side being prepared to give way, the Italians announced that they were claiming jurisdiction over Abu Abbas and his men on the grounds that the latter had committed the crime of hijacking aboard an Italian ship. On the morning of Friday 11 October, the Americans were forced to back down and swallow the bitter pill of seeing the four hijackers led off the aircraft and into custody by the Italians. Before they left the base, however, they were identified by four of the hostages from the *Achille Lauro*, including Mrs. Marilyn Klinghofer, who were among seventeen flown in on a C-141.

Meanwhile, their principal target, Abu Abbas, and the PLO official from Cairo remained on the aircraft. During the evening, it was announced that they were to be flown to Rome for questioning by Italian federal prosecutors and that night the Boeing 737 took off from Sigonella with an Italian Air Force escort of four fighters. On Brigadier General Stiner's orders, a US Navy executive jet followed it to Rome, landing beside it at Ciampino airport.

Two days later, despite a formal request from the US government for his extradition, which was accompanied by a mass of irrefutable evidence of his involvement in the hijacking, Abu Abbas and the PLO official were permitted to leave Italy on a flight to Yugoslavia. The government of Bettino Craxi, it appeared, was more concerned with preserving the *status quo* with the PLO and other groups in the Middle East than in bringing the terrorists to justice.

The *Achille Lauro* hijacking was not the only occasion on which an operation would end unsatisfactorily. On several occasions during the 1980s, US counter-terrorist units found themselves either powerless to act or frustrated by the very nature of the enemy they faced. This was never more so than in Lebanon.

10

TERROR IN THE LEVANT

As described in Chapter 1, September 1970 saw the expulsion of several thousand PLO guerrillas and Palestinian refugees from Jordan by King Hussein's Arab Legion and their flight to Lebanon where they established themselves in the south of the country. By 1975, the Palestinian population in the country had increased to some 350,000. During that year civil war broke out in Lebanon as the deep-seated and centuries-old enmity between Christian and Muslim exploded into violence, aggravated by Christian efforts to expel the Palestinians.

By 1976, Lebanon was divided into areas ruled by different factions: West Beirut was in the hands of the PLO, the eastern sector was controlled by Christian militias. To the south-east of the capital lay the Chouf Mountains where Christians and Druze Muslim forces were engaged in a long-running struggle for control. Beyond them was the Bekaa Valley, dominated to the east by the mountainous border region with Syria. To the south of Beirut were the battlefields of southern Lebanon where the PLO also established itself and from which it launched operations into Israel, provoking retaliatory air raids and artillery bombardments.

In March 1978 PLO guerrillas launched a seaborne raid from Lebanon into Israel which resulted in a bus being hijacked. During an ensuing confrontation with Israeli security forces, thirty-six people were killed and a number of others wounded. Israeli retaliation was massive, taking the form of an invasion of southern Lebanon with some 25,000 troops. Thousands of Lebanese and Palestinian refugees fled towards Beirut as the Israeli forces advanced northwards, being halted along the Litani River. During that month, United Nations forces arrived to take up positions along the river which thereafter became the forward demarcation line of Israeli-occupied territory in southern Lebanon.

The Israelis provided support for the right-wing Christian Phalangists and the South Lebanese Army, a Christian militia commanded by Major Saad Haddad, which controlled an enclave just north of Lebanon's border with Israel. Despite the presence of UN forces, the Israelis continued their operations against the PLO.

In April 1981, however, fighting in Lebanon escalated when Israeli aircraft supporting Christian Phalangist forces shot down two Syrian helicopters over the Bekaa Valley; Syria responded by deploying SA-6 surface-to-air missile (SAM) batteries in the valley. Israeli aircraft meanwhile also carried out attacks on the PLO in West Beirut, the latter responding with rocket attacks into northern Israel. The fighting was brought to a halt in late July after a cease-fire negotiated by the US Special Middle East Envoy, Philip Habib. Thereafter, an uneasy peace reigned for nine months.

On 4 September, the French Ambassador in Beirut, Louis Delamère, was murdered as he was being driven in his unarmoured car, through the Museum area of West Beirut. A white BMW swerved in front of the vehicle, screeching to a halt and blocking the road. Four gunmen leaped out and one, running up to Delamère's car, fired six bullets into him at point-blank range, killing him instantly. Leaping back into their car, the gunmen drove through one of two nearby Syrian army checkpoints from where Syrian troops had watched the entire episode without attempting to intervene.

The motives for Delamère's murder have never been fully explained. A week beforehand, however, the Lebanese magazine, *Al Watan al Arabi*, had published an article stating that the Syrian intelligence service was plotting to kill him in an effort to stop French efforts to secure the withdrawal of all foreign troops, including those of Syria, from Lebanon. It has been suggested that there were other reasons for the killing, notably that the Syrians had been upset by French activity elsewhere in the Middle East and in particular by a meeting in Beirut, between PLO chairman Yasser Arafat and the French Foreign Minister Claude Cheysson, which had been set up by Delamère.

Deciding that it would take reprisals against those it found to be responsible, the French government handed the task to its foreign intelligence service, the DGSE, whose chief, Pierre Marion, delegated it to his 200-strong Action Service. As recounted in Martin Arostegui's book, *Twilight Warriors*, within the latter was the newly formed 29e Service d'Action (29 SA), a highly secret unit responsible for special operations. Commanded by Colonel Georges Grillot, who had previously commanded the Foreign Legion's famous parachute unit, the 2e Régiment Etranger de Parachutistes (2e REP), it comprised officers and soldiers recruited from 2e REP and other French Army airborne units as well as combat swimmers from the French Navy's Commando Hubert.

In late 1981, a detachment of twenty members of 29 SA travelled individually from different locations in Europe and the Middle East to Beirut. On arrival they were formed into three teams and began the search for those responsible for Ambassador Delamère's murder. It was not long before they discovered that the hand of Syria was involved. Informants were recruited among young Arabs disenchanted with the Syrian-backed terrorist organisations operating in Beirut, and a series of OPs was established to carry out surveillance on the headquarters and training camps of two groups known to have close links with Syria: Abu Nidal and PFLP–GC. Unfortunately, however, one two-man OP was detected and came under fire from automatic weapons, both men being wounded.

The operation lasted eight months and finally led the 29 SA detachment to a town in the Bekaa Valley where further information was obtained about Ambassador Delamère's killers: five men belonging to the Red Knights, an organisation formed in Syria by Rifaat al-Assad, the brother of President Hafez al-Assad, and trained by his special forces. Two of these were identified as Sadek Mousawi and Muhammad Yacine, both known assassins in the pay of the Syrians; the other three men had provided support for the operation to kill the Ambassador. All five were kept under surveillance by a 29 SA team of eight men, a close watch being maintained on their daily routine and any meetings with other individuals.

Two weeks later Mousawi, Yacine and a third man were ambushed as their Mercedes was passing along the street from Mousawi's home. As the driver slowed at a cross-roads, a car carrying three members of the 29 SA team cut across the Mercedes' path and slewed to a halt. Two soldiers jumped out and opened fire with silenced submachine-guns at close range, killing the driver almost instantly. Meanwhile, a second car with three men had halted behind and two more soldiers emerged: one opened fire from the rear of the Mercedes, spraying the occupants, while the other kept watch. Two soldiers then opened fire from either side of the Mercedes, ensuring that Mousawi, Yacine and the third terrorist had all received multiple hits by the time they ceased firing. Seconds later the hit-team made a swift getaway, leaving the three terrorists for dead.

The 29 SA team had not achieved total success, however. Despite being seriously wounded, Mousawi had survived and was taken to a hospital in Beirut. A week later two members of the 29 SA team gained entry to the intensive care unit where he was undergoing treatment. While one stood guard outside the door to Mousawi's room, the other walked up to the unconscious terrorist and shot him in the head with a single bullet.

It was not long before 29 SA's teams were in action again, this time hunting down a terrorist, Hassan Attich, who had murdered a DGSE agent and his wife in April on the orders of the Syrian intelligence service's chief in Beirut, Major Nouredine. 29 SA's pursuit of Attich and other operations in Beirut uncovered further extensive Syrian involvement in the support of terrorist attacks against French targets not only in Lebanon but also in France. Syrian embassies were playing a principal role, not only by using the diplomatic bag for movement of weapons, but also by providing money, forged passports and safe houses for terrorists travelling to Europe from the Middle East. Such was the quantity of evidence accumulated that eventually the DGSE chief, Pierre Marion, advised President François Mitterand that either the Syrian intelligence headquarters in Beirut should be attacked or a warning should be given to Rifaat Assad, brother of the Syrian president, Hafez Assad, and head of the Syrian intelligence service.

Mitterand chose the latter course and Marion was instructed to contact the Syrian intelligence chief. The meeting took place in France, at a château some fifty kilometres from Paris. On the day before, however, 29 SA was ordered to give Rifaat Assad a warning by shooting at Hassan Dayoub, a senior member of a Syrian-backed terrorist network, working under diplomatic cover as a cultural attaché at the Syrian embassy in Madrid. The 29 SA sniper was ordered to 'fire to miss', but to leave Dayoub in no doubt that he was being targeted. On the morning of 17 April 1983, as Dayoub approached the limousine waiting for him outside his home in Paris, a bullet whistled past his head and slammed into the wall behind him.

Despite Rifaat Assad's demand that he attend the meeting unarmed and unaccompanied, Pierre Marion took the wise precaution of deploying members of 29 SA in the grounds of the château, which belonged to a member of the Saudi Arabian royal family. During the meeting, Marion made it abundantly clear to Assad that the DGSE had detailed knowledge of the Syrian-backed terrorist network in France and that all its members, and Assad himself, would be assassinated unless all terrorist activity by Syria in France ceased immediately. Very wisely, Assad complied with the French demand.

In June 1982 the truce in Lebanon had broken down after the attempted murder, by gunmen belonging to Abu Nidal's Black June movement, of the Israeli Ambassador in London, Shlomo Argov. Israel responded by mounting a major offensive, code-named Operation Snowball, crossing the truce demarcation line on the Litani River on 6 June and striking farther north into Lebanon. This was virtually an all-out invasion of the country, although at the time the Israelis claimed that they merely wished to push the PLO further north, out of range of the border and northern Israel. Five divisions and two reinforced brigade groups, totalling some 90,000 troops, took part in a three-pronged attack. On the western flank, two divisions advanced along the coast road, taking the cities of Tyre and Sidon where they linked up with a commando force which had already landed and secured a beachhead north of Sidon. In the centre, another division attacked the PLO stronghold of Beaufort Castle, subsequently handing it over to the South Lebanese Army of Major Saad Haddad, before advancing and taking the town of Nabatiyeh and then swinging westwards towards Sidon.

Two days later, two more divisions advanced northwards into Syrian-controlled eastern Lebanon with the task of cutting the strategically valuable Beirut–Damascus highway. Having driven the Syrians out of Jazzin, the Israelis continued their advance northwards, but five miles short of the highway encountered a brigade of Syrian paratroops in mountainous terrain around Ayn Zhalto who were well dug-in and put up a fierce resistance. The Israelis were unable to advance and needed air support, but the area was well covered by Syrian air defences comprising a total of twenty-one batteries of SA-6 surface-to-air missiles (SAM). These were initially neutralised on 9 June by a high-flying Israeli Air Force Boeing 707 electronic warfare aircraft which jammed all the SAM radars. Air strikes were then carried out on the batteries, knocking out nineteen of them. That same day saw the Syrian Air Force take to the skies and lose twenty-nine aircraft without a single loss to the Israelis. During the next two days, a further fifty Syrian aircraft were shot down.

The fighting continued for three more days during which, despite inflicting heavy casualties on a Syrian armoured division, the Israelis were unable to break through to the Beirut–Damascus highway. On 11 June, however, Israel and Syria agreed to a truce negotiated by the US Special Envoy to the Middle East, Philip Habib.

The Israelis did not include the PLO as being a party to the truce and proceeded to turn their attention on them. From 14 June onwards they subjected the western area of the city, where the PLO and the bulk of its forces were by now concentrated, to constant bombardment by artillery and airstrikes while Israeli Navy gunboats shelled them from offshore. Meanwhile, the UN forces in Lebanon (UNIFIL) stood powerless.

The siege of West Beirut lasted for seventy days during which the Israelis not only kept it under constant bombardment, but also conducted airstrikes against those areas in which they believed PLO leader Yasser Arafat and his senior commanders were hiding. Arafat was meanwhile under pressure from Lebanese leaders who had hitherto supported the PLO but now wished it to leave to avoid prolonging the suffering of the local population. Communicating and negotiating with Habib through intermediaries, Arafat eventually agreed that the PLO would withdraw from Beirut, but on the condition that a multi-national peacekeeping force be present to oversee the withdrawal and protect the Palestinian civilians who would remain in the city. The situation was further improved by agreement from Syria and Tunisia that they would provide refuge for the PLO guerrillas.

On 21 August a force of 350 French paratroops, the leading element of troops provided by the United States and France, arrived by sea. The first PLO guerrillas embarked by sea for Cyprus, and overland to Damascus, on the same day. On the morning of 25 August the remainder of the multi-national force, led by 800 men of the US Marine Corps' 32nd Marine Amphibious Unit (32nd MAU), commanded by Colonel James Mead, landed in Beirut. By 1 September, 8,000 PLO guerrillas, 2,600 PLA regulars and 3,600 Syrian troops had left Lebanon.

On 23 August Bashir Gemayel, head of the Phalange Party, was elected President of Lebanon. In August of the previous year, he had made a secret 48-hour visit to the United States for a series of meetings with President Ronald Reagan and senior US government officials, having been smuggled out of Beirut by the CIA to a US Navy aircraft carrier from which he had been flown to Washington. The organisation of his return trip had been handled by the Pentagon's Special Operations Division. Three Seaspray MD-500 helicopters, painted in civilian livery, were flown in a C-141 transport to Cairo and a day later Gemayel arrived in a US Army executive jet. Communications support was provided by the ISA which deployed personnel, equipped with a portable satellite communications system, to monitor the progress of the operation from the US embassy in Cairo. Gemayel was then flown at night by Seaspray to the port and Christian enclave of Junieh, north of Beirut, the three helicopters flying at wavetop height to avoid detection by Syrian radar. At Junieh, he was met by a CIA agent who accompanied him back to Beirut.

Israel had supported Gemayel's coming to power in the hope of signing a peace treaty with Lebanon which would result in the withdrawal of Syrian forces and prevent the return of the PLO. Gemayel, however, soon dispelled any such hopes by announcing that no treaty would be signed as long as Israeli forces remained in Lebanon. Three weeks later, on 14 September, he was assassinated by a bomb. The bomber was soon arrested and investigations quickly established the possibility of Syrian involvement. He was succeeded by his brother, Amin, who also opposed a continuing Israeli presence in Lebanon.

Two days after Gemayel's death, the Phalangists exacted their revenge, vowing to wipe out those Palestinians remaining in Beirut. On 16 September, Israeli troops surrounding the two camps at Sabra and Shatila allowed some 400 Christian militiamen to enter the camps ostensibly to check whether any guerrillas were hiding among the refugees. During the next two days, as Israeli troops stood outside the camps or watched from the tops of buildings that overlooked them, the militiamen slaughtered 2,750 Palestinians: men, women and children.

The massacres resulted in the Lebanese government's request for the re-deployment of the multi-national force which returned to Beirut on 29 September, this time also including troops from Britain and Italy. The Americans, once again represented by the 32nd MAU, occupied an area adjacent to the airport while the French took over responsibility for the western area of the city and the port. The Italian contingent deployed into the area between West Beirut and the airport.

As with the French, it was a terrorist attack on diplomatic personnel in 1983 that resulted in the first deployment of a US unit on counter-terrorist operations in Lebanon.

At 1 p.m. on Monday 18 April 1983, a van packed with explosives was driven at high speed past the Marine guard at the gate to the

US embassy compound in Beirut and crashed into the embassy building itself, exploding in a huge fireball. Sixty-three people died and more than 100 were injured in the blast which destroyed the main part of the seven-storey building and caused devastation in the surrounding area. Ambassador Robert Dillon survived despite being trapped under masonry for a while. Among the dead, however, was Robert Ames: the CIA's former station chief in the Lebanon and the Agency's senior officer in the Middle East, he was also unofficial Middle East adviser to Secretary of State George Schultz. Eight other CIA officers attending a meeting with Ames also died: the station chief, Kenneth Haas, his deputy and six others. Also killed was Sergeant Terry Gilden, a member of Delta who was the Ambassador's bodyguard.

Responsibility for the attack was claimed by a group calling itself Islamic Jihad, but NSA sigint soon intercepted radio traffic which pointed to the involvement of Iran. Shortly after the attack, the Lebanese intelligence service arrested four suspects, one of whom, a Palestinian, had been employed in the embassy. Under interrogation and torture, all four confessed to their involvement and provided details of a fifth member of the group. When interrogated, the latter gave details of a Syrian intelligence officer who had carried out the final installation of the bomb in the truck.

The attack had in fact been carried out by a unit of Hizbollah, the Iranian-backed Muslim extremist group, as part of a campaign by Iran and Syria to drive the United States out of Lebanon. Established with the role of conducting missions against Western targets in the Middle East, it was headed by an individual named Imad Mugniyeh who would thereafter become notorious during the 1980s for the kidnapping of foreigners working in Beirut.

Hizbollah, which translates as 'Party of God', was formed in the aftermath of the Israeli invasion in June 1982. Until then, Syria had blocked attempts by Iran to send forces and arms overland via an unmetalled road, running from the town of Zebdani in Western Syria through the mountains along the Lebanese–Syrian border into eastern Lebanon's Bekaa Valley. With the arrival of the

Israelis in southern Lebanon, however, the Syrians stood aside and in July allowed Iran to send 600 Revolutionary Guards to help their Shi'ite brothers throw out the invaders. The Iranians initially established a base at Zebdani which, manned by a further 400 men, acted as a logistical support centre for the Revolutionary Guards operating in Lebanon. Subsequently, they made their way to the city of Baalbek where they took up residence in a former Lebanese Army base, the Sheikh Abdullah Barracks,. They also established themselves in the city's al-Khayyam Hotel which thereafter became the headquarters of Iranian-backed operations in Lebanon, controlled from the headquarters of the Iranian Foreign Ministry in Tehran by none other than Hussein Sheikh-oleslam who had orchestrated and led the storming of the US embassy in Tehran in November 1979.

Shortly after their arrival, the Iranians formed an alliance with Hussein Musawi, the former commander of Amal, the largest of the Shi'ite movements in Lebanon headed by a French-educated lawyer named Nabih Berri. Musawi had become disenchanted with Berri's moderate stance and had formed his own extremist breakaway faction, the Islamic Amal. Not long afterwards, another Shi'ite movement, Hizbollah, was formed by Shia clergy, being modelled on the Iranian movement of the same name. Loosely organised and possessing little structure of any sort, Hizbollah's membership was recruited among the poor Shia of the Bekaa Valley who were subjected to constant and relentless indoctrination which extolled the Iranian revolution and the virtues of martyrdom.

Hizbollah leader Imad Mugniyeh, however, came from a middle-class Shi'ite family in southern Lebanon. Although not a particu-larly devout Muslim, he had been inspired by the Iranian revolution and, like many in his country, angered by the Israeli invasion. Having joined Amal, he had subsequently transferred to Hizbollah where he soon proved himself, eventually being appointed to head the bodyguard of Sheikh Hussein Fadlallah, the spiritual head of Hizbollah, and effectively becoming the movement's military commander. There had been several warnings of the threat posed by terrorist groups in Lebanon, but the Pentagon apparently had not taken any of them sufficiently seriously. There had also been indications based on NSA intercepts of coded transmissions from the Iranian foreign ministry in Tehran to the Iranian embassies in Beirut and the Syrian capital of Damascus. The decoded messages clearly indicated that operations against Americans in Beirut were being planned, one revealing that a payment of $25,000 had been approved for an unspecified operation. Unfortunately, there was no hint of the date or target.

Following the attack on the embassy, a five-man team of the ISA, commanded by Lieutenant Colonel William Cowan USMC, was despatched to Beirut. Its mission was to examine the procedures by which intelligence on terrorist threats was being collected, processed and disseminated, and subsequently used in threat analyses and assessments conducted as part of the decision-making process governing security measures for American military and civil personnel in Beirut.

When Cowan and his team arrived in Beirut on 26 May, they encountered a hostile reaction from embassy staff, the CIA station and US military personnel based there who regarded them as interlopers trespassing on their territory. Despite the lack of support afforded to it, the team set about its task and soon discovered that there was little, if any, security co-ordination among the various US elements in Lebanon which, in addition to the embassy and CIA station, included US Army Special Forces training teams and the US Marine contingent which formed part of the multi-national force based in Lebanon. Cowan and his men noted that, despite the recent attack on the embassy, security at the headquarters of the US Marine contingent, located at Beirut's international airport, was somewhat lacking.

On completion of their task, the ISA team returned to Washington and submitted a report criticising the lack of co-ordination in the collection, processing and dissemination of intelligence and suggesting that a special 'fusion cell' be established in Beirut for that specific purpose. It also clearly stated that there was a major threat to US forces from terrorist groups, and to the US Marine headquarters in Beirut in particular.

Tragically, their warnings proved all too accurate. On 17 October, members of the Lebanese Army being trained by US Army Special Forces advised their instructors that a large quantity of explosives had been smuggled into Beirut for use in an attack on the headquarters of the US Marine contingent. This information was given to two Marine warrant officers, but it either never reached their headquarters or was not heeded.

At 6.20 a.m. on Sunday 23 October, a large yellow Mercedes truck, loaded with at least 12,000 pounds of high-explosives, drove into the parking area outside the compound of the 24th Marine Amphibious Unit (24th MAU), which had earlier relieved the 32nd MAU, and circled before suddenly accelerating and heading at full speed for the headquarters of the 1st/8th Battalion Landing Team. Hurtling into the reinforced-concrete four-storey building, it blew up in a massive explosion which was heard and felt for several miles around. The building was reduced to a huge pile of rubble and 241 Marines and US Navy personnel died in the blast, while hundreds of others were injured.

Twenty seconds after the bomb demolished the US Marine headquarters, a similar attack was carried out on an element of the French contingent of the multi-national peacekeeping force. A red van containing 1,100 pounds of explosives was driven into the eight-storey building, known as the Drakkar, housing the headquarters of the French element of the multi-national peacekeeping force, killing fifty-eight paratroopers and injuring fifteen.

Once again, a group calling itself Islamic Jihad claimed responsibility for both attacks and demanded the withdrawal of all US forces in Lebanon. In reality, however, it was once again the Hizbollah unit led by Imad Mugniyeh which had perpetrated both outrages.

Ten days later, on 4 November in the city of Tyre, a truck crammed with explosives was driven into the headquarters of Israeli forces occupying southern Lebanon. Twenty-nine Israeli soldiers and thirty Lebanese and Palestinians, being held prisoner in the building, died in the blast.

Israel reacted by bombing Palestinian strongholds in eastern Lebanon and Shi'ite Muslim areas. The French did likewise after the DGSE's 29 SA obtained irrefutable information as to who was responsible: French Navy aircraft from the aircraft carrier *Foch* carried out a strike on the Sheikh Abdullah Barracks in Baalbek, but reconnaissance photographs taken afterwards showed that it had been unsuccessful. Meanwhile in Washington, the JCS could not agree on whether or not a retaliatory airstrike should be carried out. Despite President Reagan's enthusiastic support for the idea, the proposal was opposed by the Secretary of Defense, Caspar Weinberger, and was dropped.

In the Pentagon, meanwhile, investigations were being conducted into the inadequate security in force at the US Marine headquarters. It transpired that the sentries on the gate to the headquarters compound were not permitted to carry loaded weapons and that obstacles, in the form of large steel pipes, previously installed to prevent vehicle access to the compound, had been removed to facilitate entry by Marine supply trucks and not replaced afterwards.

At the same time, efforts were being made to identify those responsible for the attacks and before long there were indications that Iran and Syria had both played principal roles. Sigint interceptions of Iranian radio communications pointed to Hizbollah whose members had infiltrated into southern Beirut close to where the US Marine headquarters had been located. The purpose of the attack had been to inspire a wave of anti-American acts by Islamic fundamentalists throughout the Middle East. The Syrians' involvement was confirmed by other sources which stated that the movement of explosives through Syrian-held areas could only have been carried out with their knowledge.

Not long afterwards, the Israeli intelligence service Mossad passed information to the CIA tracing the connections between the perpetrators of the bombings of the US Marine and French headquarters with Iran and Syria. This information identified thirteen individuals as being principally involved, among them a lieutenant colonel in Syrian intelligence who had been involved in the planning of the attack, and Sheikh Fadlallah who had been present at a meeting in Damascus where the attacks were discussed three days before they were carried out.

The reasons for the attack on the US Marine headquarters and French multi-national peacekeeping force barracks lay in events which had begun some two months earlier.

On 28 August Shi'ite youths, putting up posters of Imam Musa al-Sadr who had disappeared mysteriously in Libya five years previously, had come under fire from gunmen who were subsequently alleged to be Christian Phalangists. Shi'ite gunmen belonging to Amal went in search of the culprits as Shia militiamen appeared with weapons and engaged their Christian counterparts. The fighting spread quickly and soon the Christian minority-led American-trained Lebanese Army became involved. Sunni and Druze Muslim militias joined the fray on the side of the Shia and it took a massive amount of force, including the use of armour and artillery, on the part of the Army before it managed to regain control of West Beirut, leaving the Shia in control of the southern area of the city which surrounded the area of the airport and the US Marine headquarters.

On 4 September Israeli forces withdrew south from the Chouf Mountains, which surround Beirut and dominate the airport, to a defensive line along the Awali River. This resulted in a break-out in fighting between Christian and Druze Muslim militias in the mountains, with the Druze eventually pushing the Christians back until they controlled 85 per cent of the Chouf and were besieging the resort of Souk al Gharb which was the Lebanese Army's final stronghold. Its capture would leave the way open for an advance into the Christian area of East Beirut.

In desperation, the Lebanese Army turned to the United States for immediate support in holding Souk al Gharb. On 19 September US forces received orders to provide the Christians with supporting fire. This order provoked vehement objections from Colonel

Timothy Geraghty, the commander of the 24th MAU, who was rightly concerned that the neutral peacekeeping status of his force would be compromised. He was overruled, however, and the cruiser USS *Virginia* fired more than seventy shells at the Druze militia forces; US Navy aircraft meanwhile took off to carry out ground strikes but their mission was aborted at the last minute.

The victory by Shi'ite forces in occupying southern Beirut and the intervention by the United States resulted in the latter losing its neutral status and remaining credibility. The US Marines' role as peace-keepers lay in tatters and the marines themselves became legitimate targets in the eyes of the Muslim factions, with gunmen carrying out sniping and harassing attacks on the 24th MAU compound. On 17 April, the Hizbollah bomber struck.

During the second week of November, the JCS decided that the protection of US forces and personnel in Lebanon was a priority task for which efficiently processed and rapidly disseminated intelligence was essential. The decision was taken to despatch a second ISA team to Beirut with the task of re-establishing the collection, collation and dissemination of intelligence, reviewing US counter-intelligence capabilities in Lebanon and assessing the terrorist threat. In addition, the team was to research the most effective ways in which the United States could carry out reprisals against Hizbollah and the Syrians.

On 1 December a five-strong team, with Lieutenant Colonel William Cowan again in command, left the United States and flew to Cyprus and thence to the helicopter carrier USS *Guam* lying off the Lebanese coast. Cowan and his team were brought in to Beirut by night and quietly slipped away on their mission.

It did not take long for the ISA team to discover that little had changed since Cowan's previous visit: it soon became apparent that there was little in the way of effective processing of intelligence by US forces in Lebanon. Another similarity to the previous mission was the initially hostile reception from the CIA station chief, William Buckley, who was concerned that Cowan and his team would trespass on his territory and possibly compromise his assets.

Reassured by the team's performance, however, Buckley was soon won over as Cowan provided him with briefings and gave him access to the team's satellite communications system; the US embassy was at this time temporarily accommodated within the British embassy and there were suspicions that the British were monitoring American communications.

The ISA team also lost little time in assessing targets for reprisals. Aircraft had already flown reconnaissance missions over Beirut, the Bekaa Valley and the Chouf Mountains to locate suspected terrorist camps. They had been engaged by Syrian SAMs and US Navy aircraft from the aircraft carriers USS *Independence* and *John F. Kennedy* were tasked with attacking the SAM sites on 4 December. One aircraft from the *Independence* was hit by an SA-7 SAM, but its pilot, Commander Ed Andrews, succeeded in turning back and clearing the coastline before ejecting; he was rescued by a fisherman and eventually returned to the *Independence*. Another, an A-6 from the *John F. Kennedy*, was shot down; its pilot, Lieutenant Mark Lange, was killed and the navigator, Lieutenant Robert Goodman, captured by Syrian troops. It was thus decided that the SAM sites would be attacked by a variety of methods, including naval gunfire or Marine artillery, but laser target designators would have to be positioned beforehand to illuminate them.

A retaliatory strike against Hizbollah would consist of airstrikes or attacks by Delta on a number of targets. The ISA team had identified some of them, including the ten-storey apartment block in the southern Beirut suburb of Bir al Abed where Sheikh Fadlallah lived, and the garage nearby where the explosives had been packed into the truck. A member of the team had a lucky break when he fortuitously met an American working for a US telecommunications company carrying out a contract to maintain Beirut's telephone system. On hearing that the latter's responsibilities included the southern area of the city, the team member enlisted his help by agreeing to allow a French-speaking US Army Special Forces communications specialist to accompany a repair crew at any future date. This would permit the monitoring of terrorist telephones or the cutting of all telephone communications in the area, thereby preventing the alarm being sounded in the event of an attack.

Cowan and one other member of his team meanwhile undertook the highly dangerous task of reconnoitring Syrian positions in northern and eastern Lebanon, on two occasions narrowly avoiding being stopped at Syrian roadblocks. The team also carried out a number of other tasks which included reconnoitring possible landing beaches and drop zones for use by Delta, locating safe houses, transport and storage.

The ISA team travelled far and wide within Lebanon and by the time they left the country at the end of December 1983, they had developed a number of options for reprisals on which they briefed CIA station chief William Buckley prior to their departure. On their return to the United States, Lieutenant Colonel Cowan submitted a detailed report on his team's assessments of the intelligence situation in Lebanon and recommendations concerning reprisals to be taken against Syria and Hizbollah. In the event, none of the latter were taken up by the JCS, apparently on the grounds that too many innocent civilians might be killed or injured. This was somewhat surprising, particularly in view of the fact that on 3 December the battleship *USS New Jersey* had fired 700 rounds with its 16-inch guns against Druze Muslim militia positions in the Chouf Mountains. Lacking the assistance of forward observers or laser target designators, the majority of the shells had missed their targets and instead hit civilian areas.

Despite the tough rhetoric of President Ronald Reagan, who had declared on 27 January 1981, 'Let terrorists beware that when the rules of international behaviour are violated, our policy will be one of swift and effective retribution', the attacks on the embassy and Marine headquarters and the deaths of 304 Americans went unavenged. During February 1984, the US Marine contingent was withdrawn under covering fire from USS *New Jersey* and another warship which engaged Syrian artillery positions, the last Marines leaving the Lebanese shore on 26 February. The *New Jersey* had by then fired 288 rounds, but, once again, lacking forward observers to report the fall of shot and provide the necessary corrections, all the shells had missed their targets.

The Pentagon had meanwhile decided to adopt Lieutenant Colonel Cowan's earlier recommendations, submitted after his first deployment to Beirut in May 1983, for a fusion cell to be established in Beirut to centralise all processing of intelligence and threat information. In early 1984 Lieutenant Colonel Dale Dorman was despatched to Beirut to establish such a cell, but on 5 March he was shot and wounded by a gunman in West Beirut.

On the morning of 16 March 1984, Hizbollah kidnapped CIA station chief William Buckley outside his apartment block in the area of Raouche. The terrorists could not have struck a more telling blow against the United States: not only did Buckley have with him a large quantity of highly secret documents, but he also possessed an extensive knowledge of CIA personnel serving undercover throughout the Middle East; prior to arriving in Beirut, he had been closely involved in selecting them for their respective posts. His own previous assignments had included CIA liaison officer to Delta and the Agency's representative on the Interagency Group on Terrorism, the body which was responsible for co-ordinating policy on counter-terrorism. He thus possessed not only a detailed knowledge of US intelligence operations throughout the Middle East, but also of US policies and strategy on counter-terrorism.

Lieutenant Colonel William Cowan offered the assistance of his team, which still possessed intelligence assets within Lebanon and was thus in the best position to assist in locating Buckley. His offer met with a refusal, apparently largely due to the resentment and jealousy with which the ISA was regarded elsewhere in the Pentagon. Once again, internal disputes and politics within the US military establishment had prevailed at a time of crisis.

Such was the importance of Buckley that the CIA mobilised all available assets in its efforts to locate him and his kidnappers who were soon identified as the Hizbollah unit led by Imad Mugniyeh. The Director of Central Intelligence, William Casey, instructed the Agency's covert operations arms, the Directorate of Operations, to take whatever measures were necessary to track down and rescue Buckley, including the establishment of a special rescue task force. Meanwhile, NSA communications intercepts were increased and satellites were tasked to photograph every inch of likely areas within Lebanon. A team of FBI agents who were experts in locating kidnap victims was despatched to Beirut, but returned after a month having achieved nothing.

In September 1984, Hizbollah struck once again at the United States, employing exactly the same method of attack it had used against the US embassy and Marine headquarters during the previous year and achieving an equal degree of success. On 20 September, a Chevrolet van drove through the eastern Beirut residential suburb of Aukar and approached the entrance to a cordoned-off area in which the US embassy annex was situated; two months earlier, the majority of staff from the embassy itself had been relocated there. The driver halted his vehicle at the gate and, according to eye-witnesses, there was a brief argument between him and the guard before a shot was fired at the latter and the vehicle accelerated towards the embassy annex. As it approached the building a member of the Royal Military Police close-protection team, escorting British Ambassador David Miers during a courtesy visit to his US counterpart, Reginald Bartholomew, opened fire on the van. The driver was hit and slumped over the wheel, his vehicle veered to the right and hit another parked nearby whereupon its load of 3,000 pounds of explosives detonated with a massive blast. Fourteen people, only two of whom were American officers, died and dozens were injured in the explosion. Both ambassadors were dug out of the demolished building, having suffered only minor injuries.

Ironically, the new annex had been dubbed 'Fortress America', but security measures had not been completed by the time of the attack. Three concrete obstacles had been positioned in front of the building and a massive steel gate had been delivered, but not installed; it was lying by the side of the gateway at the time. Closed-circuit television had been installed, but not switched on. The building had been inspected while the new security measures were being implemented and a recommendation was made that it should not be occupied until they were completed. Ironically, the officer conducting the inspection, Colonel William Corbett, a security expert from the headquarters of the US Army's EUCOM, warned that in his opinion the terrorists would attempt to attack the building with a truck bomb. His advice was ignored and the diplomats moved in, with tragic consequences, before the security measures were complete.

Within two days, the CIA had obtained firm evidence of the involvement of Hizbollah and its Iranian masters in the bombing. Aerial photographs of the Sheikh Abdullah Barracks revealed a mock-up of the concrete obstacles in front of the embassy annex and tyre marks showing that the driver of the van had practised driving through them at speed. Once again, however, the United States refrained from carrying out reprisals against the terrorists; yet again, it was Defense Secretary Caspar Weinberger's view, counselling against such action, which prevailed, much to the frustration and anger of others in the Reagan administration. A few weeks later all US military and diplomatic personnel, with the exception of a small group of six embassy staff, were withdrawn from Lebanon.

The CIA, meanwhile, had been planning its revenge for the kidnapping of William Buckley. In his book, *VEIL: The Secret Wars of the CIA 1981–1987*, journalist Bob Woodward describes how in the autumn of 1984 the Director of Central Intelligence, William Casey, submitted a plan to President Reagan for the training and insertion of three five-man teams of foreign nationals into Lebanon. When intelligence indicated an impending attack on a US facility, such as the embassy or a military installation, the task of these groups would be to intercept the terrorists and neutralise the threat. The entire operation would be totally deniable and thus not traceable to the CIA or the United States.

Casey encountered considerable opposition to his scheme from his deputy, John McMahon, but disregarded it and, with support from Secretary of State George Schultz, succeeding in winning over President Reagan who signed a covert action finding authorising the first phase of the operation: the recruitment and training of the teams. In the event, however, the CIA encountered problems in training the Lebanese who proved to be unsuitable: while happy to kill people, they were difficult to control. Moreover, some of the CIA personnel involved in the project appeared to have little stomach for it.

Frustrated, Casey decided to abandon his original plan and turned to the Saudi Arabian intelligence service who immediately offered assistance and financial support to the tune of US $3 million. In early 1985 he attended a meeting with Prince Bandar, the Saudi Ambassador in Washington, during which the latter was given the number of an account in a bank in Geneva, Switzerland, into which the money for the operation was to be paid. As Prince Bandar pointed out, the payment would be totally deniable with no record of it kept at the Saudi end. During the meeting, Casey and Bandar agreed that a major blow against Hizbollah would be to the benefit of both the United States and Saudi Arabia and that the target should be Sheikh Hussein Fadlallah.

As a result of the increasing reluctance within the CIA to become involved in counter-terrorism and in any form of 'termination with extreme prejudice', the Saudis assumed control of the operation and subsequently delegated responsibility to an Englishman, a former SAS officer, who had extensive experience of the Middle East and frequently travelled to and from Lebanon. This new arrangement suited both Casey and the Saudis, being completely deniable: even the money in the Swiss bank account was untraceable, having been laundered via several transfers from other accounts in different countries.

The former SAS officer was equally thorough in his precautions when setting up the operation. He used one source for obtaining explosives and another to supply a suitable vehicle. He hired informants to keep him apprised of Fadlallah's whereabouts and paid another group to mount a deception operation in the wake of the operation to ensure deniability on the part of the CIA and the Saudis. The men who would actually carry out the operation were hired by the Lebanese intelligence service.

The attack on Sheikh Fadlallah took place on 8 March 1985. A car packed with explosives was driven into the suburb of Bir al Abed and parked near the block in which his apartment was located on the fifth floor. Shortly afterwards it exploded, causing devastation to the surrounding area. Eighty people died and 200 were injured in the blast. The Sheikh, however, escaped unhurt and it did not take him long to point the finger of blame: a large banner was hung in front of a wrecked building emblazoned with the words 'MADE IN THE USA'. There was consternation in the Saudi camp and measures were taken to deceive Fadlallah and Hizbollah into believing that it was in fact Israel which was responsible. As a further measure, the Lebanese who had carried out the attack were betrayed to Hizbollah.

The Saudis then changed tack and offered Fadlallah the sum of US $2 million in exchange for warnings of terrorist attacks against Saudi or US targets. The Sheikh agreed, but was shrewd enough to insist on payment in kind: food, medical supplies and payment of educational fees for his followers, thus enhancing his own standing among them. The Saudis were happy to accept the deal and thereafter Fadlallah desisted from expressing support for any further attacks against the United States.

William Buckley was not the only victim of Hizbollah kidnap operations. A number of Westerners, notably American, British and French, were abducted from February 1984 onwards. The motive for the first four kidnappings lies in the bombings which took place in Kuwait on 12 December 1983 when attacks had been made against a number of targets, including the US and French embassies, which had left five people dead and eighty-six injured. The Kuwaitis had subsequently arrested eighteen suspects, fifteen of whom were members of the Shi'ite Al Dawa movement. The other three were Lebanese members of Hizbollah; one of them was Imad Mugniyeh's brother-in-law .

Mugniyeh set out to force the Kuwaitis to free his brother-in-law and his two companions by taking three Americans hostage. The first of his victims was Frank Regier, a lecturer at the American University of Beirut, who was abducted on 10 February 1984. He was followed on 7 March by CNN Beirut bureau chief Jeremy Levin and on 16 March by William Buckley. On 15 April, however, Regier was located and freed by Amal militiamen and so, on 8 May, Mugniyeh's group kidnapped the Reverend Benjamin Weir, a Presbyterian priest who had worked as a missionary in Lebanon for more than thirty years.

William Buckley, the Reverend Weir and Jeremy Levin were imprisoned in Baalbek, in a villa adjacent to the Sheikh Abdullah Barracks. Despite the best efforts of the United States to locate them, there had been no evidence of the location in which they were being held. On 14 February 1985, however, just under a year after he was kidnapped, Jeremy Levin succeeding in escaping from his prison. Courageously shinning down a makeshift rope of knotted blankets, he succeeded in avoiding the guards and made his way to a Syrian Army checkpoint about a mile away. After being taken to Damascus, he was handed over to the US embassy and was subsequently flown to West Germany where he was questioned closely. He was able to tell his questioners that he had seen William Buckley, who was in poor health, and to provide a complete description of the building which was subsequently identified from satellite photographs.

Inevitably, there were calls for a rescue mission to be mounted, but wisdom prevailed. Further satellite photographs showed signs that the building had probably been abandoned and it was assumed the hostages had been relocated elsewhere. This subsequently proved to be the case: William Buckley, the Reverend Weir and another hostage, the Reverend Lawrence Jenco, who had been kidnapped six days before Levin's escape, were moved on the evening of the day of Levin's escape. Initially, all three were held in the same location, but in March Buckley and the Reverend Jenco were moved to Beirut. After being moved again in April, they joined another American, Associated Press bureau chief Terry Anderson, who had been kidnapped by Hizbollah in the Ein Mreisse district of Beirut on 16 March.

On 28 May Hizbollah kidnapped another American. This time the victim was David Jacobsen, the administrator of the American University Hospital in Beirut, who joined the other hostages. A few days later, on 3 June, William Buckley died; although his health had deteriorated sharply during the previous months, his kidnappers had not made the slightest effort to alleviate his suffering and allowed him to die a lingering death. On 9 June, six days after his death, Hizbollah abducted Thomas Sutherland, the Dean of Agriculture at the American University.

By this time Imad Mugniyeh had obviously realised that kidnapping Westerners was not proving sufficient to force Kuwait to free the eighteen members of Al Dawa imprisoned in Kuwait, and he decided on more drastic measures. On 3 December 1984, as described in Chapter 11, members of his group hijacked a Kuwaiti airliner flying from Dubai to Karachi, in Pakistan.

Six months later, Mugniyeh tried again. On the morning of Friday 14 June, a TWA Boeing 727, Flight No. 847 from Athens to Rome, was hijacked by two members of his group: Mohammed Ali Hamadi, a member of a prominent Shi'ite family associated with Hizbollah, and Hasan 'Izz-al-Din. There had in fact been a third member of the team, Ali Atwa, but at the last minute he had been prevented from boarding the aircraft by airline staff because there was no seat available. Having stormed the flight deck, armed with pistols and fragmentation grenades, the two terrorists initially demanded that the aircraft be flown to Algiers. On being told, however, that there was insufficient fuel to reach Algeria, they instructed the pilot to fly to Beirut instead.

Before the hijackers gained entry to the flight deck, the co-pilot, First Officer Philip Maresca, had managed to radio Athens air traffic control that the aircraft had been hijacked and the pilot, Captain John Testrake, had activated the aircraft's transponder to transmit the international hijack code. News of the hijacking was flashed to Washington where it was first received by the Federal Aviation Authority which in turn informed the US State Department and the Department of Defense.

At the Pentagon, the newly created Joint Special Operations Agency (JSOA) established a crisis management centre and opened up lines of communications to JSOC and Delta. The latter, alerted by a news flash on CNN, was already assembling an assault force and equipment in preparation for immediate deployment. Similarly SEAL Team 6, Task Force 160 and elements of the 75th Ranger Regiment were also alerted and placed on standby to move. At JSOC, meanwhile, all relevant data, including information on Beirut airport and others throughout the Middle East, was being extracted from its computer databases.

Initially there was no information as to the identity of the group which had hijacked the plane, but within hours news came from Athens that Greek police had arrested Ali Atwa. Under interrogation, he revealed the identities of his two accomplices and gave details of the weapons they had smuggled aboard the aircraft.

Meanwhile, Flight 847 had landed at Beirut, despite the initial refusal by the Lebanese authorities to allow it to do so. During the flight, the two hijackers had terrorised the 153 passengers, beating some of them badly. On landing, they demanded fuel for the aircraft, but the Lebanese authorities refused. This resulted in an American named Robert Stetham, one of six US Navy divers returning from a task in Italy, being tied up and subjected to a particularly savage beating which broke all his ribs. After being told that the hijackers were going to shoot him, the Lebanese relented and the aircraft was refuelled.

At this juncture Captain John Testrake persuaded the hijackers to release seventeen women and two children by telling them that the aircraft, now that it had a full load of fuel, was overweight. Shortly afterwards, the hijackers issued their demands: the 'Al Dawa Eighteen' to be released by Kuwait; 700 Shi'ites to be freed by Israel and a further four set free from prisons in Spain and Cyprus. They also demanded that Israel withdraw from Lebanon and the United States admit responsibility for the unsuccessful bomb attack on Sheikh Fadlallah in Beirut which had killed eighty people and injured 200. Shortly afterwards, Flight 847 took off from Beirut and headed for Algiers.

The seventeen freed hostages were meanwhile flown to Larnaca in Cyprus where they were questioned closely by embassy officials about the hijackers. All details were transmitted immediately to the United States where they were fed to the JSOA and then JSOC where they were found to corroborate much of the information already supplied by the Greek authorities.

Shortly after Flight 847 landed at Algiers, the hijackers repeated their demands for the release of Shi'ite prisoners. Acting on a hint from the Americans, the Greek authorities released Ali Atwa who was flown to Algiers to join his two accomplices. This led to the release of a further twenty-one hostages who gave the US embassy officials further information about the terrorists.

Having demanded that the aircraft be refuelled, the hijackers became increasingly agitated when it appeared that the Algerians were in no hurry to oblige. It was only when Mohammed Ali Hamadi started to beat one of the American passengers, and then dragged him to the open door threatening to shoot him, that a fuel bowser appeared. Shortly afterwards, in the early hours of Saturday 15 June, the aircraft took off from Algiers and headed back to Beirut. Requests for clearance to land were again met with refusals from the control tower at Beirut and it was only at the last minute, with the aircraft making its final approach with very little fuel remaining in its tanks, that the Lebanese relented and switched on the runway lights. At 2.20 a.m. local time, Flight 847 landed at Beirut for the second time.

Meanwhile a twenty-strong Emergency Support Team, comprising personnel from the State Department, CIA, Defense Intelligence Agency (DIA) and Delta, was deployed from the United States, taking off from Andrews Air Force Base nine hours after Flight 847 had been hijacked. Led by a member of the State Department's Office for Combating Terrorism, its task was to provide advice, support and secure communications with Washington for the US Ambassador in Algiers, Michael Newlin. Its initial destination had been Cyprus and the Royal Air Force base at Akrotiri which the British government had placed at the disposal of the US rescue forces. When news arrived of Flight 847's arrival in Algiers, however, the Emergency Support Team diverted to the NATO base at Sigonella on the island of Sicily.

Delta's assault force of two squadrons totalling 200 men was also despatched to Sigonella. Its deployment had initially been delayed by disagreement between the Reagan administration's Terrorist Incident Working Group, which had wanted to send it immediately, and the Pentagon which had recommended waiting until Flight 847 had ceased flying around the Mediterranean and appeared to be remaining in one location. On its arrival in Sicily, Delta was joined by fifty members of SEAL Team 6, a large detachment from JSOC headed by its commander, Brigadier General Carl Stiner, and personnel from the ISA, CIA, USAF and US Navy. Helicopters from Task Force 160 and Seaspray also arrived at Sigonella.

In Beirut, the hijackers had once again repeated their demands and this time demonstrated their deadly intentions. Seizing Robert Stetham, one of the six US Navy divers who had earlier been bound hand and foot, Mohammed Ali Hamadi dragged him to the open door of the aircraft, which was parked in the middle of the runway, and shot him in the head before dropping his body out on to the tarmac below. Hamadi then ordered the pilot to taxi the aircraft over to the airport refuelling point.

Now events took an even more dramatic turn. Shortly after the aircraft halted at the refuelling point, twelve Muslim militiamen arrived and boarded the aircraft, bringing with them large quantities of weapons including assault rifles and heavy machine-guns. They were led by none other than Imad Mugniyeh, the architect of the entire operation. Shortly afterwards, four of the Navy divers, a US Army reservist named Kurt Carlson, the Greek singer Demis Roussos and his personal assistant, were taken off the aircraft and driven off into Beirut. Another group of five comprising three Americans, Richard Herzberg, Robert Trautmann and the remaining US Navy diver, together with two other passengers, were also taken away. Shortly afterwards, as dawn was breaking, the aircraft took off once again, heading for Algiers.

News of the arrival of Mugniyeh's heavily armed group reached the US counter-terrorist force which had by now moved to Cyprus where it was located in an aircraft hangar on the RAF base at

Akrotiri, hidden from Soviet spy satellites which the NSA and National Reconnaissance Office (NRO) knew were keeping the island under almost constant surveillance during daylight hours. The force was busy planning and rehearsing a rescue operation, but the situation was complicated by the refusal of the Algerian government, which was attempting to negotiate with the terrorists, to permit such an operation to be carried out. Furthermore the US Ambassador in Algiers, Michael Newlin, and the Commander-in-Chief of EUCOM, General Lawson, were also opposed to the idea. A request from the US State Department to prevent the aircraft from leaving Algiers also met with a refusal from the Algerians.

Despite these setbacks, planning for rescue operations in Algiers or Beirut continued. These involved covert insertions of ISA operatives into both airports beforehand to prepare landing zones for the helicopters bringing in the Delta and SEAL Team 6 assault teams. At this juncture, however, news arrived that the aircraft had taken off from Algiers and was yet again heading back to Beirut. Two ISA teams were briefed and subsequently flew from Washington to Frankfurt in West Germany. While one team remained there in case Flight 847 returned to Algiers, the other flew to Cyprus where it joined the rescue force.

Imad Mugniyeh and his group were well aware that the United States would attempt to mount a rescue operation and it was undoubtedly for that reason that Flight 847 had been kept shuttling backwards and forwards between Beirut and Algiers.

Flight 847 arrived back at Beirut for the final time, landing at 2.25 p.m. on Sunday 17 June. No sooner had it done so than the flight engineer faked an emergency with one of the engines, announcing that he was having to close it down. Captain John Testrake told the hijackers that the aircraft was thus unserviceable and could no longer fly. By this time, only some thirty passengers remained aboard the aircraft with the hijackers.

In the United States it had been recognised by this time that a rescue operation at Beirut airport, which was heavily guarded by well armed Amal militia, would need forces additional to Delta and SEAL Team 6 which did not possess sufficient firepower. The JCS estimated that a force of Rangers would be needed to engage the militia forces and establish a perimeter around the aircraft while Delta and the SEALs rescued the passengers. With the arrival of the information that some of the passengers had been taken off the aircraft and were being kept hostage somewhere in Beirut, however, it soon became apparent that a rescue operation was no longer feasible and that the best hopes for the release of the hostages lay in negotiation with the hijackers via a suitable intermediary. In this the leader of Amal, Nabih Berri, would have a key role to play and thus in the early hours of Monday 17 June, at about 2 a.m. Washington time, the US National Security Adviser, Robert McFarlane, contacted him to state the United States' position and commence negotiations for the release of the hostages. In Lebanon, meanwhile, at about 4 a.m. local time, the remaining passengers were disembarked and taken away into Beirut where they were incarcerated under guard in the basement of a building.

Elsewhere in Beirut an ISA operative, infiltrated into the city without the knowledge of the State Department or the US embassy, was already searching for the Flight 847 hostages. Before long, with the aid of local intelligence sources, he had located the building holding them; next door to it was another occupied by Imad Mugniyeh's terrorist group. This information was communicated by the operative on a secure radio link to the JSOC team in Cyprus. Plans were immediately commenced by JSOC for a rescue operation by Delta and SEAL Team 6 teams which would be inserted on the coast by MH-6 Little Bird helicopters of Task Force 160 and then make their way into Beirut. Once the hostages had been freed, the troops and the hostages would make their way to a nearby sports stadium where they would be extracted by Task Force 160 MH-60 Blackhawks while other helicopters would be on standby to evacuate anyone from the airport if so required. Covering fire would be provided by AC-130 Spectre gunships which would orbit the city and suppress any opposition.

The plan, which called for the precision bombing by US Navy aircraft of the building housing the terrorists, ran into trouble when it was realised that the Navy did not possess laser-guided bombs of the type required for such a mission. It had to be scrapped when it was discovered that the terrorists had dispersed the hostages and hidden them in different locations in southern Beirut. A further obstacle had by now arisen in the form of opposition from the US Ambassador, Reginald Bartholomew, who refused to allow an ISA team to be deployed in Beirut for intelligence-gathering, insisting that CIA or Delta personnel, the latter being stationed in Beirut on diplomatic protection tasks, be used instead. This subsequently proved to have been at the instigation of the CIA station chief who did not want ISA operatives trespassing on his 'patch' and possibly compromising his sources. Bartholomew was in any case justifiably concerned that any attempt at a rescue operation would endanger the negotiations being conducted with Nabih Berri and Hizbollah.

Despite these problems, and in defiance of Ambassador Bartholomew's veto, the Cyprus-based rescue force continued to produce contingency plans which called for ISA operatives to be infiltrated into Beirut to locate the hostages and make preparations for their exfiltration from Lebanon. Delta and SEAL Team 6 teams would then infiltrate into Beirut, rendezvous at safe houses established by the ISA operatives, and then, supported by Christian militia forces, attack the buildings where the hostages were being held. Task Force 160 MH-60 Blackhawks would then extract the troops and the hostages, subsequently flying them to the aircraft carrier USS *Nimitz* stationed off the Lebanese coast. Once again, however, the plan had to be scrapped; this time due to lack of accurate intelligence on the hostages' locations. Nevertheless the rescue force remained in Cyprus, poised to carry out such an operation.

While the State Department continued its efforts in negotiating with Nabih Berri, others tried alternative channels. Syria was approached by the US Ambassador in Damascus with a request to use its influence, while Israel, which had until then refused to accede to the hijackers' demands to free its Shi'ite prisoners, was asked for a secret assurance that it would do so if the hostages were released. It was also requested to use its contacts to approach the Iranians and this latter course proved to be the most fruitful: two days after the Israelis approached Iran, four of the Flight 847 hostages were released and handed over to the Syrians.

On 20 June, the US authorities informed Nabih Berri, via Swiss intermediaries, that Israel had agreed to release its prisoners and three days later, the Israelis freed thirty-one Shi'ites from their prisons. Ten days later, all the Flight 847 hostages were released by Hizbollah and taken to Damascus by the International Red Cross.

The hijacking of TWA Flight 847 and the subsequent negotiations for their release had served to highlight the plight of the other American hostages being held by Hizbollah. Their cause became a major priority for President Reagan and thus when, in the summer of 1985, the Israeli government informed Robert McFarlane that it was in contact with elements inside Iran who might be persuaded to use their influence to gain the hostages' release, the Reagan administration was happy to explore this possible avenue.

Iran was at that time embroiled in a long-running war with Iraq and was in desperate need of certain weapons, including US-manufactured TOW anti-tank and Hawk surface-to-air missiles, with which the Iranian Army had been equipped by the United States during the reign of the Shah and which were required to counter the Iraqi superiority in armour and air power. Furthermore, Israel was keen to promote its long-standing relationship with Iran and to supply the TOW and Hawk missiles from its own stocks. It could only do so, however, if the United States approved the transfer and agreed to replace the weapons.

In January 1985, a series of meetings took place between Manucher Ghorbanifar, an Iranian businessman living in France, and two Israeli arms dealers, Adolph Schwimmer and Yacov Nimrodi, Schwimmer also being a consultant to Israeli Prime Minister Shimon Peres. Also present at some of these meetings were Amiram Nir, an adviser to Shimon Peres on counter-terrorism since September 1984, and Adnan Khashoggi, a well-known Saudi arms dealer. At these meetings, the possibility of supplying arms to Iran had been discussed as a possible way of obtaining the release of the American hostages and of establishing a dialogue with the Iranians. On 4 May 1985 an NSC consultant, Michael Ledeen, travelled to Israel for a meeting with the Israeli prime minister.

In July, the United States received two requests from Israel for its agreement for the latter to supply arms to Iran. On 30 August, Israel delivered 100 TOW missiles to Iran and on 14 September a further consignment of 408 missiles. On 15 September the Reverend Benjamin Weir was released.

On 20 November Lieutenant Colonel Oliver North USMC, an officer on the staff of the NSC and a figure who would play a central role in the supply of arms to Iran, advised the Deputy National Security Adviser, Vice Admiral John Poindexter, that Israel would deliver eighty Hawk surface-to-air missiles to a staging area in Portugal on 22 November. The weapons would then be loaded aboard three chartered aircraft which would fly them to Tabriz, in Iran. Once the departure of the aircraft had been confirmed by Manucher Ghorbanifar, acting on behalf of the Iranians, the remaining American hostages would be released. None of the aircraft would land in Iran until the hostages had arrived at the US embassy in Beirut. North also advised that Israel planned to deliver a further forty missiles, in return for which Iran would undertake to ensure that there would be no further kidnappings.

In the event, the delivery of the Hawks did not go to plan. On 19 November, retired USAF Major General Richard Secord flew to Portugal to supervise the trans-shipment of the missiles. Two days later, however, problems arose when the Portuguese government for unknown reasons refused landing permission for the aircraft that would be bringing in the missiles from Israel. On 21 November Lieutenant Colonel North approached the CIA for assistance in overcoming the problem, but the latter's efforts failed. The CIA then arranged for aircraft from one of its own companies to take over the task, but on 22 November further problems arose when one of the Israeli arms dealers, Adolph Schwimmer, allowed the lease to expire on the three aircraft chartered to fly the missiles to Iran. Major General Secord, however, solved this problem by a replacement aircraft; in the meantime, the CIA found another country which would grant permission for overflight.

Meanwhile, the Iranians were hiking up their side of the deal: instead of five American hostages costing eighty Hawk missiles, the price had been increased to 120 Hawks, 200 Sidewinder air-to-air missiles and 1,900 TOW missiles. When he learned of this, Lieutenant Colonel North decided to keep this knowledge to himself for fear that the Iranians' demands might prove too outrageous even to those in the Reagan administration which so far had been prepared to accommodate them.

On 25 November the aircraft took off for Iran, carrying eighteen Hawk missiles which, contrary to the original plan, were delivered to Iran before the release of the hostages. Further problems arose when the Iranians discovered that the weapons were not the latest model, thus not meeting their requirements, and bore Israeli markings. One Hawk was fired at an Iraqi aircraft flying over Kharg Island, but the remainder were to be returned to Israel. In the meantime, no further hostages were released.

In October, meanwhile, US intelligence agencies had identified Imad Mugniyeh as being the individual exercising control over the hostages. Moreover, it was discovered that his brother-in-law was one of the eighteen members of the extremist Shi'ite group Al Dawa imprisoned in Kuwait for involvement in attacks on the US and French embassies in the emirate during 1983. During the negotiations for the release of the hostages, one of the Iranians' principal demands, in addition to arms, was the release of these seventeen terrorists.

By the end of October, the locations of the hostages had been pinpointed by a variety of means, including NSA satellite photography, sigint and humint. These had identified the building, known as 'Building 18', situated alongside the Sheikh Abdullah Barracks in Baalbek, which was known to be housing five of the American hostages. A highly detailed scale model of the barracks and surrounding area, based on enhanced satellite photographs showing an immense amount of detail, had been constructed by the CIA for use in planning any rescue operation.

Meanwhile, all avenues were being explored in efforts to obtain the release of the hostages. These resulted in approaches by, or contacts with, various factions in the labyrinthine world of Middle Eastern politics. In late October, Lieutenant Colonel Oliver North was approached by an intermediary acting on behalf of the Christian Phalange Party in Lebanon which offered, for an appropriate sum of money, to hand over 120 Shi'ite prisoners to Hizbollah in exchange for the hostages. Nothing came of this proposal.

In January 1986, North proposed a similar arrangement with a Christian Lebanese militia, the Israeli-supported South Lebanese Army commanded by Major General Antoine Lahad who had replaced Major Saad Haddad after the latter's death from cancer in January 1984. The Syrians were approached to use their influence with Hizbollah while the United States and Israel did likewise with Lahad. Meetings were held with the Syrians in Damascus in September, but any involvement by them was terminated suddenly in late October by the trial and imprisonment of Nezar Narwas Mansur Hindawi, the Jordanian terrorist convicted of attempting to carry out the Syrian-planned attack on an El-Al airliner, as described in Chapter 2. This was followed by the United States and Britain imposing economic and diplomatic sanctions on Syria.

On 6 January 1986 President Reagan signed a draft covert action finding and on the following day approved a plan whereby Israel would free twenty Hizbollah prisoners and supply TOW missiles to Iran in exchange for the remaining American hostages held by Hizbollah. Furthermore, Iran would ensure that all kidnappings ceased forthwith. On 17 January a further draft finding was signed by the President: this was virtually identical to the one signed by him on 6 January; however, its cover memorandum proposed that the CIA would purchase 4,000 TOW missiles from the Department of Defense and, after receiving payment, transfer them directly to Iran. Although Israel would still be responsible for making the arrangements for the transaction, the United States would now formally become a direct supplier of arms to Iran in contravention of the arms embargo placed by the Carter administration on sales of arms to either Iran or Iraq. Furthermore, sales of the Hawk and TOW missiles would also contravene the 1978 Missile Technology Control Regime, of which the United States was a signatory, which controlled the spread of missile technology and covered a wide range of military hardware, computer software and programmes for guidance systems. In addition, the agreement to supply arms to Iran contradicted the US government's publicly stated policy of refusing to deal with regimes supporting terrorism.

Planning now began for a hostage release operation code-named Recovery. This called for the United States to supply Iran with intelligence information, including satellite photographs of the areas covered by the Iran–Iraq conflict, and 4,000 missiles to be supplied in four shipments of 1,000 each. The hostages would be released immediately on commencement of the operation. Funds for the purchase of the first 1,000 missiles would be transferred by Manucher Ghorbanifar to an Israeli-owned bank account at the Crédit Suisse in Geneva. These would then be transferred to another account, controlled by Major General Secord, in the same bank. The sum of $6 million would then be transferred to a CIA-owned account, again in the same bank, and the CIA would wire that amount to the Department of Defense which would then transfer the 1,000 missiles to the agency.

On 18 February, the first 500 TOW missiles were delivered by an Israeli Boeing 707 to Bandar 'Abbās in Iran; on its return flight the same aircraft brought back the seventeen Hawk missiles previously rejected by the Iranians. Approximately a week later, on 27 February, the second batch of 500 missiles was also delivered to Bandar 'Abbās. Despite the proviso in the plan that all the American hostages would be released when the operation began, this did not happen. Nevertheless, the operation continued and arrangements were made for another delivery to be effected two months later.

On 8 March Lieutenant Colonel Oliver North, accompanied by a CIA officer and a former member of the Agency, George Cave, who was an expert on Iran and a Farsi speaker, attended a meeting with Manucher Ghorbanifar at which he handed over intelligence information, supplied by the CIA, on the disposition of Iraqi forces and the Soviet threat to Iran. Ghorbanifar handed North a list of 240 spare parts required for its Hawk missile air defence units. In Washington, it was subsequently proposed and agreed that the CIA would purchase the spare parts, which had a total value of $3.641 million, and that these would be supplied to Iran in return for the hostages.

Even Libya figured in the attempts to free the hostages. Proposals were submitted on 1 April for two intermediaries, a Libyan and a Shi'ite Lebanese, to conduct negotiations with Hizbollah via Amal for the release of the hostages in exchange for the sum of $10 million. Two weeks later, however, this plan was effectively scotched when on Tuesday 15 April American aircraft bombed Libya in reprisal for its apparent involvement in the bombing of the La Belle discotheque in West Berlin on 5 April in which one American serviceman died and another was fatally injured. In fact, Syria had been behind the bombing, but the Americans used it as a pretext to launch an attack on Colonel Muammar Gadaffi. Libya allegedly retaliated in turn shortly afterwards. Its agents in Beirut were reported to have 'bought' three hostages from their Shi'ite kidnappers, paying for them to be executed and their bodies left in the foothills of the Chouf Mountains: they were an American named Peter Kilburn, who had been kidnapped some sixteen months earlier on 3 December 1984, and two British teachers, Leigh Douglas and Philip Padfield, who had been abducted on 28 March, two weeks before the bombing of Tripoli. It was subsequently reported that a Libyan intelligence officer based in Damascus, identified as one Major Khalifa, was involved in the murders of the three men.

On 15 May, President Reagan approved a plan for a delegation comprising Robert McFarlane (who had been succeeded by Vice Admiral Poindexter as National Security Adviser on 30 November 1985), Lieutenant Colonel Oliver North and George Cave to carry out a secret visit to Tehran to meet senior Iranian officials, including Ayatollah Ali Akbar Hashemi Rafsanjani, and effect the release of the hostages. Vice Admiral Poindexter, meanwhile, had already insisted that there should be no delivery of the missile spare parts until the hostages had been released and had pointed this out to McFarlane.

The delegation arrived in Tehran on 25 May. Apparently unknown to McFarlane, it was accompanied by a pallet of Hawk missile spare parts, the remainder of the spares being aboard an aircraft on standby to fly to Iran once the hostages had been released. No senior Iranian officials met the delegation on its arrival and two days of talks produced no results. McFarlane demanded the release of the hostages while the Iranians insisted on the immediate delivery of the missile spare parts. By 6.30 a.m. on 28 May, the deadline set by McFarlane, no hostages had been freed and the delegation departed for the United States. Before it did so, however, the pallet of missile spare parts was removed from the aircraft by the Iranians.

Frustrated and angry at the failure of the visit, Robert McFarlane was of the opinion that further attempts at negotiation with Iran would be a waste of time and that there should be no further supplies of arms. There was considerable recrimination on the delegation's return, with Manucher Ghorbanifar pointing out that he had suggested that he and Lieutenant Colonel North should travel to Tehran beforehand to pave the way for McFarlane's visit, an idea that had been turned down by Vice Admiral Poindexter. Furthermore, he explained that senior Iranian officials had not met the delegation at the airport because the aircraft had arrived three hours ahead of schedule. It later transpired that Lieutenant Colonel North and George Cave had been well aware from early April onwards that only one hostage would be released if all the missile spare parts did not accompany the delegation to Iran. It appears that McFarlane may not have been aware of that condition as he had insisted on the release of all the hostages before the remainder of the spare parts were delivered. Furthermore, this had resulted in his refusal of an improved offer from the Iranians: two hostages to be released immediately and the other two after delivery of the remainder of the spare parts.

Vice Admiral Poindexter concurred with McFarlane's view that no further negotiations with the Iranians should take place and expressed the view that the idea of a military hostage rescue mission by US counter-terrorist units should be considered once again. He broached the subject to North who still considered that negotiations with Iran was the best avenue to pursue and was thus reluctant to jeopardise them. North recommended that planning for any such operation should be put in the hands of the CIA rather than the Pentagon because of the reluctance of the Joint Chiefs of Staff to go beyond the stage of initial consideration without firm evidence of the hostages' exact locations in Lebanon.

On 6 June, President Reagan gave his approval for the planning of a hostage rescue operation by the CIA which turned to JSOC and the ISA. During the first week of July a member of the ISA infiltrated into Lebanon from Cyprus and carried out surveillance and intelligence-gathering tasks in Beirut with the assistance of a Christian militia force, the Lebanese Front, which agreed to continue supplying intelligence. On 7 July the ISA operative returned to the United States and the Lebanese Front lived up to the agreement, supplying accurate information on a daily basis.

In September, however, the CIA ordered the ISA to cut off any further contact with the Lebanese Front on the grounds that the latter could not be trusted. Four weeks later, the Agency countermanded its earlier order and directed the ISA to recommence planning an operation to rescue the hostages, at least three of whom had been located with the help of the Lebanese Front. The plan was for Delta to carry out the operation, reportedly with assistance from British and French special forces. Support would be provided by the Lebanese Front which would provide a reception committee for Delta on its arrival as well as supplying transport and safe houses. In the event, the operation never took place. Although no explanation was ever given, those ISA personnel involved in the planning were later quoted as saying that it had been cancelled because of the risk that any rescue attempt posed to Operation Recovery.

Credence to the report of British participation in such an operation is possibly lent by the account given by Andy McNab in his book, *Immediate Action*, in which he gives details of a deployment of members of B and G Squadrons 22 SAS to Cyprus in preparation for an operation in Beirut to rescue Western hostages.

Meanwhile, despite the failure of the McFarlane delegation's visit to Iran and a decision by President Reagan on 20 June that there should be no further meeting with the Iranians, Operation Recovery continued. On 21 July Lieutenant Colonel Oliver North attended a meeting in London with Manucher Ghorbanifar and Amiram Nir to discuss the question of delivery of the remaining Hawk missile spare parts in exchange for the hostages. Five days later another hostage, Father Lawrence Jenco, was released by Hizbollah. On 29 July, Lieutenant Colonel North recommended to Vice Admiral Poindexter that presidential approval be given for shipment of the parts to Iran and for a further meeting with the Iranians in Europe. North's proposal was approved by the President on 30 July and on 3 August the spare parts were delivered to Teheran.

During September, however, the apparently improving situation regarding the hostages suddenly took a turn for the worse when two more Americans, Frank Reed, the director of the International School in Beirut, and American University financial controller Joseph Cicippio, were kidnapped on 9 and 12 September respectively. These abductions had been carried out by Imad Mugniyeh in a further attempt to force the United States to put pressure on Kuwait to release its eighteen Al Dawa prisoners.

By this time, another conduit for communications with the Iranians had already been established, replacing Manucher Ghorbanifar who was being blamed by the Americans for many of the problems experienced so far. On 25 July the former CIA agent George Cave, accompanied by Albert Hakim, a business associate of Major General Secord's, had attended a meeting in London with a relative of a very high-ranking Iranian figure in Tehran, later identified as the nephew of Ayatollah Ali Akbar Hashemi Rafsanjani, the Speaker of the Iranian parliament. A second meeting with the same individual and other Iranians took place on 26 August and this was followed by further meetings from 19 to 21 September in Washington between Lieutenant Colonel North, George Cave and the same group of Iranians.

Between 5 and 7 October Lieutenant Colonel North, George Cave and Major General Secord met their new Iranian conduit, Ayatollah Rafsanjani's nephew, in Frankfurt, West Germany. North put forward a seven-point proposal for the supply of weapons in exchange for the hostages, the body of CIA station chief William Buckley who was known to have died on 3 June 1985 (although his death was not announced by Hizbollah until 4 October), a debrief by those who had held him prisoner, and the release of an American, John Pattis, who had been arrested several months earlier by the Iranians who had accused him of espionage. The Iranians countered with a six-point proposal that undertook in part to secure the release of a hostage following delivery of further Hawk missile spare parts and further intelligence information on Iraqi dispositions. Eventually, the Iranians agreed to release two hostages in return for 500 TOW missiles, a proposal to which North's group apparently agreed.

Once again, however, negotiations for the release of hostages were marred by yet another kidnapping. On 21 October Edward Tracy, an American living in Beirut, was abducted by Imad Mugniyeh's group in a further attempt to obtain the release of his brother-in-law and the other seventeen members of Al Dawa held prisoner in Kuwait.

Towards the end of the same month, 26–28 October, a second meeting was held in Frankfurt to finalise arrangements for payment and delivery of the missiles. This time the Iranians 'upped the ante'. In exchange for one hostage, possibly two, and for making efforts to secure the release of others, they demanded not only 500 TOW missiles, but also an unspecified quantity of Hawks, an additional 1,000 TOW missiles, intelligence information and the release of the seventeen members of the Al Dawa group held prisoner by Kuwait. During this meeting, the Iranians warned the Americans that the story of the McFarlane delegation's secret visit had been published in a Hizbollah newspaper in Baalbek.

On 29 October 1986, President Reagan authorised the shipment of 500 TOW missiles. Due to a delay in the transfer in funds, these were shipped from Israel to Iran, 500 replacements being supplied to Israel a little while later. On 2 November another American hostage, David Jacobsen, was released by Hizbollah. On 3 November, the Lebanese magazine, *Al-Shiraa,* also published the story of the McFarlane delegation's visit to Iran and revealed that the United States had been supplying arms to Iran. Two days later, the Speaker of the Iranian parliament, Ayatollah Ali Akbar Hashemi Rafsanjani, publicly announced details of the US arms supply operation.

Needless to say, the revelations concerning the supply of arms to Iran were extremely embarrassing to the United States and highly damaging to the Reagan administration which had always vociferously advocated a firm stand against terrorism. Iraq in particular was angered by what it saw as American duplicity: while supporting Baghdad in its war against Iran as a bulwark against the spread of Islamic fundamentalism throughout the Middle East, the United States had been providing crucial military aid to Tehran.

Americans were not the only targets for kidnappings in Lebanon from 1984 onwards. On 14 March 1985 Geoffrey Nash, a British metallurgist working in the Lebanese Industry Institute, was abducted near his home in Beirut's Makhoul Street; on the following day another Briton, Brian Levick, the general manager of the Coral Oil Company, was kidnapped by five gunmen and disappeared with them into the Beirut suburb of Sakiet-al-Janzir. Both Nash and Levick were subsequently released; they had been mistaken for Americans. On 22 March, two French diplomats, Marcel Fontaine and Marcel Carton, were kidnapped by Hizbollah and three days later Alec Collett, a British freelance writer working for the United Nations, was kidnapped near an Amal checkpoint in the area of Khalde. He was later murdered, but his body was never found. A videotape purporting to show him being hanged was sent to the newspaper, *An-Nahar*, by an organisation calling itself the Revolutionary Organisation of Socialist Moslems, a name previously used by Abu Nidal whose organisation was by then based in Syria.

Kidnappers in Beirut did not, however, always have everything their own way. On 1 October, three Russian diplomats were abducted and one of them, Arkady Katkov, was shot. His body was subsequently found on waste ground in West Beirut. On this occasion, the kidnappers were Sunni Muslims who were attempting to pressurise the Soviet Union into ordering Syria to cease its military operations against the Tawheed militia in the city of Tripoli, in the north of Lebanon. Unlike the Western nations whose nationals had been taken hostage in the Middle East, the Soviet Union decided to demonstrate that it would fight fire with fire and enlisted the aid of the Druze and the brother of one of the kidnappers was abducted. Shortly afterwards, his family received two of his fingers and a few days later the two surviving hostages were released.

This, however, did not discourage organisations such as Hizbollah which continued to pursue its vendetta against the West. Among those who also fell victim to being abducted were four members of a French TV crew who were kidnapped by a group calling itself the Revolutionary Justice Organisation; this was yet another of Hizbollah's cover names. On Friday 11 April 1986 Brian Keenan, a lecturer in English at the American University, was kidnapped; six days later, on 17 April, John McCarthy, a British TV journalist working for Worldwide Television, was intercepted and seized by gunmen while making for the airport to escape Beirut in the wake of the US bombing of Tripoli two days earlier.

The following year saw more Westerners taken hostage. On 17 January 1987 two West Germans were kidnapped: Rudolph Cordes, an executive of the pharmaceuticals company Hoechst, was seized in his car outside Beirut and Alfred Schmidt was abducted in the west of the city; it was reported that both kidnappings were in reprisal for the imprisonment in West Germany of Mohammed Ali Hamadi, one of the hijackers of TWA Flight 847, who had been arrested earlier in the month by customs officers at Frankfurt airport when explosives were found in his luggage. Three days later, on 20 January, the Archbishop of Canterbury's envoy, Terry Waite, was kidnapped as he sought to negotiate the release of some of those already in captivity. On the 24th three Americans, Alan Steen, Jesse Turner and Robert Polhill, were kidnapped together with Mithileshwar Singh, an Indian who had formerly lived in the United States for eighteen years before moving to Beirut.

Six months later Charles Glass, an ABC journalist who had interviewed the crew of TWA Flight 847, standing by the aircraft parked on the runway at Beirut and talking to Captain John Testrake in the cockpit, was abducted on 17 June; a few weeks later, on 18 August, he escaped and handed himself over to the Syrians who took him to Damascus from where he travelled to his home in London. August also saw the release of Alfred Schmidt, one of the two West Germans kidnapped in January; it was reported that he was freed after 'certain assurances' concerning Mohammed Ali Hamadi had been given by the West German government.

On 17 February 1988 Lieutenant Colonel William Higgins USMC, commander of a force of UN troops, was snatched from one of two UN vehicles driving south on a coastal road from the city of Tyre. He would never see freedom again; in July of the following year, his kidnappers announced that they had killed him.

May 1989 saw further abductions, including that of Jackie Mann, a 74-year-old retired British pilot who had lived in Beirut for many years. On 16 May two more West Germans, Heinrich Stuebig and Thomas Kemptner, an administrator and nurse working for the relief organisation ASME-Humanitas, were kidnapped. Although no group claimed responsibility, it was reported to be the work of the same group which had abducted Rudolph Cordes and Alfred Schmidt and that the kidnappers were demanding the release by West Germany of Mohammed Ali Hamadi and his brother, Abbas Ali Hamadi. In May 1987, Mohammed had been tried and convicted of the TWA Flight 847 hijacking, being sentenced to life imprisonment. Abbas had joined him in prison in West Germany, having also being arrested at Frankfurt airport at the end of January

1987 and subsequently charged with possession of explosives and complicity in the kidnappings of Rudolph Cordes and Alfred Schmidt. During the following year, he was convicted and sentenced to thirteen years' imprisonment.

The process of negotiations between the West and the kidnappers proved to be an agonisingly drawn-out affair but the beginning of the 1990s finally saw releases taking place. On Sunday 22 April 1990 Robert Polhill was released and eight days later fellow American Frank Reed was also set free. Four months later, on 23 August, lecturer Brian Keenan was freed.

Further releases followed during 1991. British journalist John McCarthy, with whom Brian Keenan had spent most of his time in captivity, was set free on 8 August. American Edward Tracy was released on 11 August while a few weeks later the oldest of all the hostages, Jackie Mann, was released on 23 September. Two days later Jesse Turner, professor of mathematics at Beirut University College, was also set free. On 18 November, Thomas Sutherland and Terry Waite were freed together; on 2 and 3 December two American hostages, Joseph Cicippio and Alan Steen, were released respectively. On 4 December the last American hostage, AP Bureau chief Terry Anderson, was also set free.

The following year, on 1 June 1992, the last two Westerners still in captivity, West Germans Thomas Kemptner and Heinrich Stuebig, were also released by their kidnappers. Their release brought to an end the whole sorry saga of the hostage crisis and the humiliation of the United States in Lebanon.

11

OPERATION ACID GAMBIT

At the end of the 1980s, a small element of Delta and aircraft of Task Force 160 were involved in an operation which, while not part of a counter-terrorist scenario as such, has been included in this book because it graphically illustrates the hostage rescue capabilities developed by US counter-terrorist units during the 1980s.

In December 1989, US forces invaded Panama which at that time was a major conduit for drugs traffickers who shipped huge amounts of cocaine through the small republic and laundered billions of dollars through its banks. Panama itself was an area of major strategic importance for the USA, not only because of the Panama Canal, but also because of its role as the base for the US Army's Southern Command (SOUTHCOM) and for US troops deploying on military assistance operations in Central and South America.

At that time Panama was ruled by a *de facto* head of state, General Manuel Antonio Noriega, who had come to power in 1981. Of Colombian extraction, but educated in Panama and Peru, where he attended the Military School de Chorrios in Lima, Noriega had begun his military career in Panama's National Guard. While stationed in Colón he met a fellow officer, Captain Omar Torrijos, who was a rising star. In October 1968 both men took part in a military *coup d'état*, led by Major Boris Martinez, which overthrew the government of President Arnulfo Arias. Torrijos, by then a colonel, subsequently ousted Martinez with the help of Noriega and, promoted to brigadier general in the following year, subsequently emerged as the leader of the military junta.

Noriega was rewarded for his loyalty by being promoted to lieutenant colonel and appointed chief of intelligence for the National Guard. He excelled in his new post and during this period established contact with US intelligence agencies with whom he collaborated. He also attended courses at various US military training establishments. He gained favour in American eyes by providing facilities for US operations in support of the Contra rebels in Nicaragua and US special operations elsewhere in Central America. In return the US government, which regarded him as a bastion against Communism in the region, turned a blind eye to persistent reports that he was involved in drugs trafficking and to his use of intimidation and harassment against political opponents of Torrijos's regime which made him the most feared man in Panama.

On 1 August 1981, Torrijos was killed in an air crash while carrying out a tour of National Guard units. Two years later, Noriega succeeded him as Commander-in-Chief of the National Guard which he unified with other elements of Panama's security apparatus into the Panamanian Defence Forces (PDF), and assumed the rank of general. A highly unattractive individual, both physically and in character, he thereafter ruled Panama by fear, his diktat reinforced by his secret police and anti-riot units, the latter known as 'Dobermans', who terrorised those who were in any way opposed to his regime.

During the mid-1980s, there was mounting evidence of Noriega's involvement in the laundering of drugs money and the sale of restricted US technology and information. Furthermore his policy of brutal repression had become an embarrassment to the US government which hitherto had tried to disregard it. In 1985, he and two soldiers were found guilty in court of the murder of Hugo Spadafora, a former guerrilla and leading political opponent of Noriega. In 1987, in a move to increase his control of the PDF, Noriega decided to dismiss its Chief of Staff, Lieutenant Colonel Roberto Diaz-Herrera, who promptly declared that Noriega had rigged the presidential elections held in 1984, which had been 'won' by his candidate Nicolas Ardito Barletta, and that he was indeed guilty of the murder of Hugo Spadafora. This resulted in an outbreak of rioting and civil unrest which Noriega put down with great brutality, using his 'Doberman' units. On his orders, President Eric Arturo Delvalle declared a state of emergency and suspended Panama's constitution.

This brought Noriega into conflict with the United States and relations with the latter deteriorated rapidly, being made worse when the commander of SOUTHCOM, General Frederick Woerner, raised doubts as to the legitimacy of Noriega's status as *de facto* ruler. This infuriated the latter who became determined to show Washington that he was indeed the ruling force in Panama. This manifested itself in riots outside the US embassy in Panama City, followed in July by the brutal suppression of demonstrations against his regime, culminating in the shooting of several demonstrators and arrests of thousands. This was followed in October by a campaign of harassment of members of US forces and their dependants based in Panama. At this juncture the United States severed diplomatic links with Panama, and Headquarters SOUTHCOM began to plan for operations against Noriega and his regime.

During 1988, increasingly serious attacks were perpetrated by the PDF on US personnel. In February, meanwhile, two US federal grand juries tried Noriega *in absentia* on charges of drugs trafficking and related offences, finding him guilty on all counts. May of that year also saw presidential elections held in Panama with Noriega's candidate, Manuel Solis Palma, being resoundingly defeated by the opposition's Guillermo Endara. Two days later, Endara and his two vice-presidential candidates, Guillermo Ford and Ricardo Arias Calderon, were attacked by members of the 'Dobermans' who killed Ford's bodyguard.

During the following year, the situation in Panama deteriorated further and eventually President George Bush, who had assumed office in January, ordered the deployment of a further 2,000 troops to Panama. Meanwhile, there was mounting discontent against Noriega within the PDF and this manifested itself on 2 October in a coup by troops led by Major Moises Giroldi which resulted in Noriega being imprisoned. Giroldi however made the mistake of not executing him and during the following day other elements of the PDF, including an armoured unit, staged a counter-coup and freed the dictator who was swift in exacting retribution, killing Giroldi and the other coup leaders and imprisoning the rest. A few weeks later Noriega dismissed his puppet, Francisco Rodriquez, and declared that Panama was at war with the United States

By now it had become apparent to the Bush administration that Noriega and his entire regime would have to be toppled and replaced by a democratically elected government. In addition to the attacks on US military personnel and their dependants, the drugs trafficking and money laundering charges, there was evidence that Noriega had sold restricted US technology and information. Furthermore, under the terms of the Panama Canal Treaty 1977 signed between the United States and Panama, control of the strategically important Canal was due to be handed over to Panama at the end of 1999 and it was inconceivable that it should be placed in the hands of Noriega.

The final straw came towards the end of December 1989. On the night of the 16th, a young US Marine Corps officer was shot dead. Shortly afterwards a US Navy officer and his wife were abducted by PDF personnel and taken to the PDF headquarters where the officer was beaten up severely and his wife molested. When advised of these incidents, President Bush ordered that plans for the invasion of Panama, prepared during the previous months, be put into immediate effect.

Despite the degree of repression in Panama, a number of opposition organisations and groups were in existence. Among these was a small cell comprising an American named Kurt Muse and a group of Panamanian friends. Muse had been born in Arizona, but when he was four years old, his parents had moved to Cuba and then to Panama where he grew up in Panama City. Educated initially in Panama and thereafter in the United States, he served for a short time in the US Army before returning to Panama where he joined the family business which sold printing and graphics equipment in Panama and throughout Central America.

During the 1980s, like many in Panama, Muse had become increasingly unhappy with Noriega's repressive regime. In 1987 he incurred the latter's wrath after it was found that his business had printed leaflets announcing a rally by the National Civic Crusade, an organisation whose members came from all elements of Panamanian society, including students, teachers, businessmen and trades unionists. Noriega gave orders for Muse's business to be burned down. Fortunately, it was located between the offices of the national lottery organisation and the local electricity company; no sooner had the fire been started than the local fire brigade arrived and put it out, damage being limited to the front office.

Despite this warning, Muse and some friends formed a four-man opposition group. A Radio Shack scanner smuggled in from Miami by one of their number who owned a company selling communications equipment enabled them to listen to military radio frequencies, and having broken the codes used by the PDF, they were able to monitor military operations and movements. Muse had contacts within the US military establishment and the CIA, and on occasions passed on information gleaned from monitoring and recording PDF radio transmissions.

After purchasing additional equipment during trips to Miami, the group progressed to broadcasting messages on the PDF nets, transmitting bogus orders and warnings which caused confusion and disruption. Other transmissions, addressed to individual PDF officers by name, were designed to appeal to their conscience while they were engaged in harassing or terrorising Panamanian citizens.

The next step was to broadcast on the FM frequencies used by Panama City radio stations playing music. The group discovered that these operated low-powered transmitters whose broadcasts were relayed by repeaters to transmission towers which amplified and broadcast the signals throughout the area of coverage. They deduced that if they had a transmitter with a power output higher than that of the radio stations, by directing its signal at the transmission towers, it could drown out the station in question with its own transmissions. Without further ado, portable transmission equipment, contained in a briefcase and using crystals specially cut to operate on the five frequencies used by the different radio stations in Panama, was purchased and smuggled in from Miami.

Trials proved highly successful, on each occasion the transmitter drowning out the radio station with its own message.

Muse and his friends decided to inaugurate their new system on the occasion of Noriega's annual address to the nation which was listened to by the majority of the population and thus would provide the largest possible audience for the broadcast. Noriega was to make his address in front of an audience of 20,000 supporters in a stadium in Panama City. The group positioned its equipment on the top of a condominium building near the stadium with the antenna aimed at a nearby transmission tower and, as Noriega mounted the podium, transmitted a pre-recorded two-minute message from the 'Free Democratic People of Panama'. Having done so, the four men dismantled their equipment and swiftly dispersed.

Noriega was predictably furious and the Panamanian media gave full coverage to the broadcast, condemning it as propaganda on the part of 'imperialist Yankees', the CIA and US military intelligence. Panamanian security forces were soon out hunting for Muse and his accomplices, but due to the group's tactic of limiting broadcasts to thirty seconds, which made it difficult for the transmitter to be located by radio direction-finding systems, they were unsuccessful.

Shortly afterwards, the group acquired an FM transmitter which could operate over a range of frequencies, unlike their suitcase radio which operated only on its five pre-set frequencies. This new set had been smuggled into Panama for use by another opposition group which decided not to use it and passed it on to Muse and his friends. From the summer of 1988 onwards, this went on air as the Voice of Liberty, broadcasting pre-recorded messages. By now, however, Noriega had become frustrated by the PDF's lack of success in tracking down the pirate radio station and turned for help to East Germany which despatched specialists to assist in the hunt for the dissident group. They were equally unsuccessful and were replaced by Cuban radio monitoring and direction-finding troops.

The situation became more dangerous for Muse and his friends as the PDF and the Cubans began gradually to close in on the locations of the pirate station despite transmissions being carried out from different locations and the duration of daily broadcasts being limited to fifteen minutes. On occasions, the group detected PDF personnel in plain clothes staking out the areas in which they were operating, buildings subsequently being stormed by troops searching for the radio transmitter. The risk of arrest was growing, and in one particular instance it was only luck that prevented the radio being discovered: its signal had been located by direction-finding which fortunately was in error, although by a factor of only a few metres. This resulted in the PDF raiding an apartment virtually next door to that from which the station was transmitting a recorded broadcast at the time. One of the group, acting with great courage, went to the apartment and switched off the transmitter which was programmed to carry out another broadcast at the same time on the following day. Shortly afterwards, the group dismantled the station and spirited it away to another location.

Unsuccessful in their efforts to locate the pirate radio transmitter, the PDF resorted to jamming it. Undismayed by this tactic, the group continued to come on air every day, switching to other frequencies as soon as the PDF jammers cut in.

Early in 1989, Kurt Muse's luck ran out. He was a regular visitor to Miami where he purchased items of radio equipment that were shipped in a container with other goods being despatched to Panama. On this occasion, however, he was arrested as he arrived back in the country.

Muse was apparently arrested on suspicion of being a spy. He was taken in a vehicle from the airport to a secret police base where he was interrogated, then forced to take his captors to his house which was searched. His wife was away visiting a relative in the United States, but his daughter was at home; fortunately, having been given permission to leave the house, she had the presence of mind to slip a list of telephone numbers into her pocket and, from a friend's house, she made a number of calls. Within a few minutes, the rest of the group had been alerted to Muse's arrest. Shortly afterwards, twenty-seven people, comprising all the members of the group and their families, arrived at the US military base in the Canal Zone, and sought asylum.

Muse had meanwhile been taken to the PDF secret police headquarters in San Felipe where he was interrogated and forced to watch other prisoners being badly beaten up. Then he was moved to another location where he was interrogated non-stop for three days. During this time, the PDF searched his Jeep Cherokee and found evidence that revealed him as a member of the group operating the Voice of Liberty pirate radio station rather than a CIA agent. Despite this, Muse was never charged with any offence or crime.

Meanwhile, efforts were being made to trace his whereabouts by the US State Department, but the Panamanian authorities would not allow any US officials access to him. The State Department retaliated by cancelling all visas and shortly afterwards the Panamanians acquiesced to its demands, permitting officials to visit Muse regularly.

By this time he had been moved to Carcel Modelo Prison, a notorious establishment built in the 1920s to accommodate 250 prisoners, but now holding more than 1,000 who were living in conditions of the most appalling squalor. Here Muse was to spend the next nine months in a cell measuring eight feet by twelve with a small bathroom leading off it. Initially, his sole item of furniture was a filthy two-inch-thick foam rubber mattress on the concrete floor; later he was issued with a lightweight folding cot.

Confined to his cell, Muse suffered physical debilitation and his weight dropped by more than fifty pounds. Added to this was the strain of watching other prisoners being tortured; on one occasion a man was hung from a basketball hoop and beaten with rubber hoses and clubs. Torture continued at night, the screams of prisoners in agony echoing throughout the prison, giving Muse no respite from the horror.

On 3 October 1989, Muse was awakened in his cell by the sound of firing coming from the direction of the PDF headquarters, known as La Commandancia, which was situated across the street from the Carcel Modelo. From his small window, he saw troops running around in the area of the headquarters and later heard armoured vehicles moving into the area and the sound of more firing. These were PDF troops loyal to Noriega moving in to crush the coup led by Major Moises Giroldi.

Following the failure of the coup, the Carcel Modelo was taken over by the PDF whose troops replaced the civilian guards and established defensive positions around the prison. All prisoners except Muse were evacuated from the cells which were filled instead with those who had taken part in the attempted coup. Night and day throughout the next two weeks, interrogators tortured soldiers in their efforts to extract information from them. Muse, however, had not been forgotten by Noriega who now regarded him as a hostage to be used as a bargaining chip with the United States, should the latter take military action against Panama: a soldier was stationed outside his cell with orders to shoot him in the event of any attempt being made to rescue him.

However, the United States had not forgotten Muse either and an operation, code-named Acid Gambit, was being planned to effect his rescue as part of the initial phase of the invasion of Panama, the task being given to Delta and elements of Task Force 160.

At Delta's base at Fort Bragg, North Carolina, a sixteen-man assault team was rehearsing a rescue operation on a full-size mock-up of the prison which was constantly updated from information supplied by those visiting Muse in Carcel Modelo. The initial phase called for the deployment of two teams of snipers: one positioned in the hills to cover the guards within the prison area proper, the other to neutralise any interference from outside. An AC-130 Spectre gunship would orbit overhead and deal with any major threat from Panamanian troops outside the prison.

The assault team would be flown to the prison and landed on the roof by four MH-6 Little Bird helicopters of Task Force 160. Having carried out an explosive entry through an unguarded but locked door, the team would fight its way to Muse's cell on the second floor of the prison, its priority being to neutralise the guard assigned to kill Muse before he was able to do so. Once Muse had been freed, he would be taken to the roof from which he and an escort of six would be extracted by one of the Little Birds. The remainder of the assault team would be extracted by a Task Force MH-60 Blackhawk.

On the morning of 19 December, the day prior to the US invasion, Delta snipers in plain clothes moved unobtrusively through the streets in the area of the prison, observing and recording details of recently constructed PDF defensive positions, the dispositions of the guards and the types of weapons with which they were armed. In the hills above the prison, the other sniper team did likewise.

In the prison's visiting area, meanwhile, Kurt Muse received his last visitor, a senior US Army officer who warned him that it had come to the notice of US officials that orders had been given for him to be killed in the event of any US military action against Panama. As Muse listened, the senior officer continued by saying, in tones clearly audible to everyone in the area, that if any harm came to Muse no one would be permitted to leave the prison alive.

At 12.40 a.m. on 20 December the Delta sniper team in the hills above the prison radioed the most up-to-date information to the assault group which was already airborne and en route to the prison. It then concentrated its attention on those guards who could be seen and killed them within a matter of a few seconds. The snipers then turned their rifles on the prison generator, located in a small tin shack next to the prison entrance, smashing it with some well-aimed .50 calibre bullets and plunging the prison into darkness. In the distance, meanwhile, the sound of firing could be heard as the initial phases of the US invasion began elsewhere.

Shortly afterwards, the AC-130 Spectre gunship orbiting overhead opened fire with pinpoint accuracy on a PDF defensive position outside the prison, destroying it with a single round from the 105mm howitzer located under its port wing. Thereafter, it turned its attention to La Commandancia, turning its full battery of 20mm and 40mm cannon, as well as its howitzer, on the thirteen buildings which comprised Noriega's headquarters.

At that moment the four Task Force 160 Little Birds landed on the prison roof, lifting off seconds later as the sixteen-man assault group raced to the door giving access to the floors below. An explosive charge blasted open the door and the Delta operators sprinted down to the second floor, killing a couple of soldiers whom they encountered on the way.

In his cell, Kurt Muse had heard the distant firing and, taking cover in his bathroom, lay on the floor and peered round the corner, observing the space under the cell door. Some time previously, he had fashioned a makeshift weapon from one of the aluminium crosspieces of his cot. He had decided that in the event of trouble, he would hide in his bathroom and if his guard came in to kill him he would try to attack and disarm him and use him as a shield until help arrived. Shortly afterwards, he heard the sound of footsteps running up the stairs towards his cell and feared the worst, but they continued past his door and seconds later he heard a Panamanian soldier calling to one of his officers.

At that moment the Spectre gunship opened fire from the sky above, the explosion of the 105mm shell rocking the entire prison. As it attacked Noriega's headquarters, the noise of its guns echoed through Muse's cell and fragments of concrete ricocheted through the window.

Shortly afterwards, Muse heard firing inside the prison, followed by explosions and smoke which filled the passage outside. From his position on the floor, peering out of his bathroom, he saw narrow beams of light approaching through the smoke; these came from the flashlights mounted on the MP-5 submachine-guns of members of the Delta team as they made their way towards his cell. Seconds later Muse heard an American voice calling out to him and telling him to keep clear of the door. He ducked back into the bathroom and seconds later a small explosion blew open the cell door, followed by a Delta operator who proceeded to hand him a helmet and a set of body armour.

Within seconds he was being escorted from his cell, passing the guard who had been assigned to kill him who was now lying dead on the floor and another trussed-up nearby.

One of the four Little Birds had already returned and was waiting on the roof as Muse and his escort emerged and joined the rest of the assault team. A fierce battle was raging in the street below and the area of La Commandancia was being criss-crossed by thousands of tracer rounds. Seconds later the aircraft lifted off, carrying Muse and six Delta operators; the remainder of the assault team stayed on the roof, awaiting extraction by a Task Force 160 Blackhawk.

As the aircraft cleared the roof, however, it was hit by a burst of fire from the ground and immediately lost altitude, only the skill of its two pilots preventing it from hitting the prison wall. Coaxing his aircraft over the top of it, the pilot touched down before taxiing off down the darkened street away from the prison with his skids only just off the ground. Turning at an intersection, he taxied the aircraft into an area between some apartment blocks where he attempted to take off once again. As he did so the Little Bird came under fire again and was hit by several bursts. Out of control, it struck a building and bounced off it before crashing into the street below.

Some of the Delta operators had been wounded, one or two severely, but Muse was unharmed. Together with the two crew, all seven jumped clear of the aircraft but as they did so the operator next to Muse was struck on the head by one of the rotor blades which were still turning slowly. Fortunately, he was saved from serious injury by his helmet and, despite being stunned, he recovered his senses; it was a mark of his professionalism and dedication to duty that his first thought was for Muse, checking to see that he was unharmed before shepherding him into a nearby building where they both took cover while the rest of the group took up a defensive position around an abandoned vehicle.

Despite their wounds and injuries, the Delta operators returned the enemy fire. As a former soldier, Muse was capable of handling a weapon and had been given a pistol; he now joined in the defence of the position. After some fifteen minutes a helicopter gunship appeared and the Delta team succeeded in attracting its attention. The aircraft proceeded to lay down fire support for the team and relayed their location to US forces nearby. A few minutes later armoured personnel carriers appeared and extracted Muse and his rescuers.

Kurt Muse and the six Delta operators were evacuated to a US Army field hospital. From there, having bid farewell to his rescuers, he was flown to a reunion with his family. Bar the loss of the MH-6 Little Bird, Operation Acid Gambit had been a triumph, and the first known successful rescue of an American hostage by a US counter-terrorist unit.

12

ASSAULT AT MARSEILLES

At approximately 11 a.m. on Saturday 24 December 1994, at Algiers' Houari-Boumedienne airport, 227 passengers, some forty of them French nationals, boarded an Air France Airbus, Flight 8969, which was due to take off for Paris. Just as the last passengers were boarding and the cabin crew were preparing to close the doors and get ready for take-off, a car with airport authority markings drew up beside the aircraft and four men wearing the uniforms and security badges of Air Algérie officials boarded the Airbus.

Announcing that they were carrying out a passport check, they began to collect the documents of all the passengers. As they did so, one of the latter identified himself as an Algerian police officer. This was to prove a fatal error on his part because the four men were not security officials, but members of the Armed Islamic Group (GIA), Algeria's most violent Islamic fundamentalist terrorist organisation. They had resorted to violence following the voiding of the victory of the Islamic Salvation Front (FIS) in legislative elections in Algeria in December 1991 and the calling off of the general election due to be held in 1992, which the FIS was poised to win. The group was led by a 25-year-old named Abdul Abdallah Yahia, alias 'Abou', who was known to the Algerian authorities as the leader of a GIA gang which operated mainly in Harrach, a suburb in the main fundamentalist district of Algiers. Another member of the group was later identified as Moh Bab El Oued who had joined the GIA after spending six months in a government internment camp.

In the same way that Iranian fundamentalists regarded the United States as the Great Satan, so their Algerian counterparts viewed France, the former colonial power in the country, in a similar light, blaming it for the civil war that had torn the country apart since 1992 and for supporting the regime of President

Liamine Zeroual. There was some truth in the latter part of this claim because, while claiming to be neutral, France had since 1993 been secretly supplying specialist equipment to the Algerian government for use in the war against the Islamic insurgent groups. The GIA had thus decided to strike at France directly by hijacking a French aircraft and flying to Paris, guessing correctly that such an operation would inevitably attract world-wide publicity to the fundamentalist cause in Algeria.

Having collected all the passports, the four men suddenly closed the doors of the aircraft and, producing three AK-47 assault rifles, an Uzi machine-pistol and hand-grenades, declared that they were members of the GIA and were taking control of the aircraft. Having forced the pilot to taxi the Airbus to a position away from the airport buildings, they contacted the airport control tower via the aircraft's radio, demanding the release of some of the GIA's leaders being held in French and Algerian prisons and insisting that the aircraft be permitted to take off and fly to Paris or they would kill some of their hostages. At the same time, they reduced the passengers and crew of twelve to a state of abject terror, threatening them with instant death if they did not obey orders. Shortly afterwards, Algerian police established a cordon at a distance around the aircraft.

News of the hijacking was flashed to France where the Interior Minister, Charles Pasqua, immediately rejected the terrorists' demands. He gave orders for GIGN to be placed on standby and the unit's headquarters at Maisons-Alfort was alerted. Its commander, Commandant (Major) Denis Favier, and his men were on Christmas leave with their families when they were recalled to their barracks. By early afternoon on 24 December, however, the unit was assembled and deployed to a French Air Force base at Neuilly from where at 8 p.m. it flew to the island of Mallorca, landing at Palma airport and moving to an area reserved for use by the Spanish Air Force. There the unit made its plans and prepara-tions for a hostage rescue operation, if the Algerian government would permit one to be carried out; full details of the lay-out of the airport at Algiers were meanwhile sent from France. The Air

France aircraft provided for the ninety minutes' flight to Palma was an A-300 Airbus, the same type as the hijacked aircraft and this enabled the GIGN assault team to study its lay-out before deciding and rehearsing its tactics. Time and again, the team practised storming the aircraft under the critical eye of Commandant Favier.

GIGN was receiving some of its intelligence from a former commander of the unit, Philippe Legorjus, who was Air France's head of security and a member of the company's special crisis management team which was convened on such occasions. He was feeding GIGN with information obtained by the company which was in touch with both the French government and the crew of the aircraft. He was also in telephone contact with the police at Houari-Boumedienne and with the commander of the Algerian Army's special forces which had deployed to the airport.

In this way Commandant Favier and his command group were receiving a constant up-date of developments in Algiers where the authorities at the airport, headed by Interior Minister Abderahmane Meziane-Cherif, were attempting to negotiate with the hijackers who appeared to be implacable in their demands. The latter did, however, free some of their hostages: initially, they released nineteen women and children after some four hours of negotiations and subsequently a further forty-nine.

During the late afternoon, however, events took a more sinister turn when the terrorists, angered by the lack of response to their demands by the Algerian and French governments, carried out their threat and killed two hostages. First to be shot was the Algerian policeman who had revealed himself to the terrorists as they took his passport: despite falling to his knees and begging for mercy, screaming that he was married and had a little daughter, they killed him with a single shot to the head. The second victim was Bui Giang To, a commercial counsellor at the Vietnamese embassy in Algiers. He was killed because he was a communist and thus, in the crazed minds of his Islamic fundamentalist captors, an atheist who had to be killed immediately as an example to all 'non-believers'. Like the Algerian policeman, he was hauled to the door, shot in the head and his body thrown out on to the tarmac below. Covered in his blood, the terrorists then walked through the cabin, distributing money taken from their victim's wallet to the passengers who were forced to accept it under threat of death.

In Paris meanwhile, the French government's crisis management team, headed by Prime Minister Edouard Balladur, had also been convened. There was general agreement that the aircraft could not be permitted to fly to Paris; this view was reinforced by a report that the French consulate in Oran had received an anonymous warning that the terrorists' ultimate aim was to blow it up in mid-air over the centre of Paris. It was agreed, however, that should the Algerian authorities not permit a rescue operation to be carried out by GIGN, they should be persuaded to allow the aircraft to take off. Rather than heading for Paris, the crew would be told to fly to Marseilles on the pretext that the aircraft needed to be refuelled there before flying to Paris. The Algerians, however, refused the French request to permit the Airbus to depart, insisting that the terrorists were bluffing.

The dawn of Christmas Day saw a constant stream of communications between the two governments, the Algerians continuing to refuse to allow the aircraft to take off or GIGN to carry out a rescue operation despite advice from two French military advisers. By now it was apparent that the Algerians, regardless of the murder of the two hostages, were still hoping for a peaceful outcome. Inside the Airbus, the terrorists, who had in the early hours released more women and children, were becoming increasingly angry at the absence of response to their demands and threatened that if the mobile stairway were not removed and the aircraft permitted to take off, they would start killing a hostage every thirty minutes.

At 9.30 p.m. they decided to show once more that they were serious. Seizing Yannick Beugnet, a young chef at the French embassy in Algiers, who was travelling to France to see his wife and children, they dragged him to the front of the aircraft where he could be heard over the radio screaming that the terrorists were going to kill him and pleading for his life. The French government immediately renewed its demands that the Airbus be allowed to take off. By this time, the Algerian government was ready to give in to the French demands, but the hard-line commander of the special forces deployed at the airport refused to remove the mobile stairway positioned against the aircraft and withdraw his troops which were surrounding it.

At 10 p.m. the terrorists' patience ran out and they shot Beugnet in the head, throwing his body out of the aircraft. This was the final straw and the Algerian government after further communication with senior Algerian Army officers, agreed to the French demands. Shortly afterwards, the commander of the special forces was given a direct order by his superiors to withdraw the mobile stairway and his men; with very ill grace, he complied. At 2 a.m. local time on 26 December, Flight 8969 took off for Marseilles with 161 passengers still aboard, the terrorists having agreed to a refuelling stop before flying on to Paris. Shortly afterwards, GIGN's Airbus also took off, heading for Marseilles where it would arrive before Flight 8969.

Meanwhile, the sixty-three released hostages were being questioned closely by French and Algerian officials. Information from some of them, who had overheard the four hijackers on more than one occasion referring to martyrdom, appeared to corroborate the report from the French consulate in Oran, and a similar one received from the French embassy in Algiers, that they were planning to blow up the aircraft over Paris. Furthermore, some of the passengers confirmed that the terrorists were in possession of explosives, one of them having been forced to hand a wristwatch over to the hijackers who had indicated that it would be used as a timing device.

Since the early stages of the crisis, preparations had been in train at Marignane airport, some twenty-five miles north of Marseilles, local hospitals being alerted to the possibility of having to treat large numbers of casualties. Meanwhile a team of negotiators had arrived, as had the Gendarmerie Nationale's other counter-terrorist unit, the Escadron Parachutiste d'Intervention Gendarmerie Nationale (EPIGN), which would provide support for GIGN in a rescue operation. An area of the airport was allocated for the parking of the hijacked aircraft and cordoned off by Gendarmerie units.

By the time that Flight 8969 arrived, all preparations were in place for its reception. GIGN, which had arrived twenty minutes earlier, was in position as was EPIGN whose snipers were covering the area where the aircraft would be directed to park on arrival.

The hijacked Airbus touched down at Marignane airport at 3.30 a.m. local time and, following instructions from the control tower, taxied to the area allocated to it. Radio silence was maintained by the terrorists until 6 a.m. when the captain of the aircraft, Bernard Delhemme, came on the air and established contact with the negotiation team located in the control tower and headed by Marseilles' prefect of police, Alain Gehin. Delhemme requested 27 tons of fuel and permission to fly to Paris. The flight from Marignane to Paris would normally only require ten tons and this served to heighten fears that the hijackers either intended to blow up the aircraft over the capital or fly to a friendly Islamic country, such as Sudan or the Yemen.

As the morning drew on, the hijackers were growing impatient, demanding that the aircraft be refuelled and allowed to take off for Paris. In view of the warnings and information received earlier, however, there was no question of the aircraft being allowed to leave Marseilles. At 8.30 a.m., Abdallah Yahia lost his temper and told the negotiators that he was setting a deadline of 10 a.m.: if his demands had not been met by then, the aircraft would be blown up.

Commandant Denis Favier was under pressure from the government crisis management team in Paris to carry out a rescue operation as soon possible, but he resisted this, explaining that he needed time for listening devices to be planted on the aircraft so that GIGN could acquire the vital information it needed before carrying out an assault.

The negotiators meanwhile succeeded in persuading Yahia to release more of the passengers, mainly women, and in return food was taken aboard the aircraft. The terrorists accepted the offer for the aircraft to be cleaned and this provided the opportunity for

GIGN surveillance specialists, disguised as airline service personnel, to board the Airbus where they succeeded in planting miniature radio link surveillance cameras and microphone transmitters which thereafter permitted them to monitor events inside the aircraft.

At 3.30 p.m. the terrorists released two more hostages, an elderly couple, but thereafter reverted to radio silence. Thirty minutes later the GIGN assault team, led by Commandant Favier, took up its positions. The EPIGN snipers placed the crosshairs of their telescope sights on two of the terrorists who were on the flight deck with the crew. Their rifles were loaded with steel-cored armour-piercing ammunition which would penetrate the toughened windows.

At 4.50 p.m., however, the Airbus's engines suddenly started up and shortly afterwards it started to move in the direction of the control tower. Over the radio came Yahia's voice demanding that the aircraft be refuelled within fifteen minutes or he would blow up the aircraft. As the GIGN assault team swiftly moved to new positions, the senior negotiator attempted to reassure him, saying that the fuel bowser was on its way. Thirty yards from the control tower, the aircraft halted and one of the flight deck windows opened. Aiming his AK-47 at the control tower, one of the terrorists fired a burst which shattered the large window on the front of the tower, forcing the negotiators and air traffic control staff to take cover. During the next few minutes Alain Gehin kept talking to Yahia, playing for time.

In the meantime, twenty-five members of the assault team had positioned themselves beneath the aircraft while a further fifteen climbed a mobile stairway unit near the front door on the starboard side. Some two minutes after the hijacker had opened fire, Commandant Favier radioed the order to begin the assault. The leading gendarme on the mobile stairway leaned forward to the aircraft fuselage, operated the handle and slid the door open, swinging his legs clear of the stairway and using his body weight to keep the door from closing. The two men behind him swiftly entered the aircraft, lobbing a stun grenade into the first-class cabin where it detonated with a blinding flash and deafening explosion. Almost immediately, they encountered two of the terrorists heading up the aisle towards them, the nearest of whom was immediately shot in the head.

At the same time, Yahia and one of his accomplices opened fire from the flight deck, where they were hiding with the crew, and a seven-round burst hit the second gendarme, severely wounding him in the right arm and injuring three fingers of his right hand which was on the pistol grip of his MP-5 submachine-gun. His life was saved by his body armour, which was fitted with ceramic plates giving protection against high-velocity weapons, and by his British-manufactured ballistic helmet which, while not designed to protect against high-velocity weapons, deflected an angled strike. The leading gendarme was also hit, but likewise his life was saved by the visor of his helmet deflecting a bullet which would otherwise have killed him; his Manurhin MR-73 .357 Magnum revolver was hit and knocked flying from his hand. A split second later, a grenade thrown by one of the terrorists sent splinters and fragments flying as it exploded. The third gendarme to enter the aircraft was also hit in the back by several rounds which impacted in his body armour and another hitting him in the hip. Commandant Favier, who led the leading group, received a glancing strike which tore the ballistic visor off his helmet as he aimed at Yahia who was peering round the flight-deck door to aim his AK-47. Meanwhile, the gendarme who had opened the door had dropped to the ground and, having run up the mobile stairway, followed the remainder of his group into the aircraft and opened fire at the flight deck door with his Glock Model 17 9mm pistol. He too was hit by return fire, a bullet smashing his pistol and breaking his trigger finger.

All members of the leading seven-man group, except Commandant Favier, had been wounded by the time the second assault group of eight gendarmes made its way into the aircraft via the front door on the port side. As they entered, they came under fire from the flight deck and the leading gendarme responded with his MP-5, spraying the bulkhead on the port side before he was wounded in the legs and had to be pulled back out of the line of fire.

Meanwhile other members of the assault team, one group using a mobile hydraulic scissors-lift, had boarded the aircraft through the rear doors and evacuated the passengers via the emergency chutes while the battle continued at the front of the aircraft. All the latter escaped without injury other than a few cuts and bruises.

On the flight deck, meanwhile, the three aircrew were lying on the floor under their seats, attempting to take cover from the stream of bullets as the three remaining terrorists continued to fire through the bulkhead separating the flight deck from the first-class cabin. The co-pilot, Jean-Paul Borderie, seeing one of the hijackers hit by a burst from GIGN, took the opportunity of moving unseen to the open window; having clambered through it, he dropped to the ground, but broke one of his legs on landing. His two companions, pilot Bernard Delhemme and the aircraft's flight engineer, remained on the floor of the flight deck, the body of one of the terrorists providing some protection against GIGN's bullets ricocheting around above them.

In the cabin, two more members of the second assault group had also been hit as the battle continued. Then suddenly there was silence and Bernard Delhemme could be heard shouting for GIGN to cease firing. On the flight deck, the assault team found all three terrorists dead and the two remaining crew unscathed. Under the pilot's seat they discovered explosives fitted with a detonator and prepared for initiation.

The battle with the terrorists had lasted for some twenty minutes during which all four had been killed and nine members of GIGN wounded. Despite the latter casualties, however, the operation had been entirely successful: the three aircrew and all the remaining passengers had been rescued with only thirteen of the latter being slightly injured. The French had once again demonstrated that they would deal firmly with any terrorist threat and would not be held to ransom.

13

OPERATION CHAVIN DE HUANTAR

The scene in the residential compound of the Japanese Ambassador's residence in the Peruvian capital of Lima on the night of 17
December 1996 was a glittering one. The Ambassador, Morihisa
Aoki, was well known for the magnificence of his receptions and
parties, and invitations to them were much sought after among
Lima's government, diplomatic and business communities. On this
occasion, more than 1,000 guests had been invited to celebrate the
sixty-third birthday of Emperor Akihito and by 8 p.m. over 600 of
them had assembled in the embassy garden. It was expected that
Peru's president, Alberto Fujimori, the son of Japanese immigrants,
would arrive in due course. His mother, brother and sister were
already there, mingling with the government officials, senior military and police officers, diplomats, among them ten ambassadors,
and businessmen who largely made up those thronging the buffet
tables heavily laden with sushi and other Japanese delicacies.

Suddenly, at about 8.35 p.m., the party came to an abrupt halt as
an explosion rent the air and grenades were thrown into the garden.
Seconds later, fourteen heavily armed men stormed the residence
compound and engaged in a running gun battle with guards who
comprised three officers of the Japanese National Police Agency,
four guards from a Japanese security company and four Peruvian
policemen, none of whom proved a match for the attackers. The
guests meanwhile threw themselves flat on the ground in frantic
efforts to avoid the bullets whistling over their heads and ricocheting off walls nearby. They needed little encouragement, on
being ordered by the intruders to remain still and keep their heads
down, while the battle raged around them for the next forty
minutes, only ceasing after the guards had been overwhelmed and
the police had withdrawn. Even then, they had to remain in the
open, choking on the CS gas which the police, without apparently

taking them into consideration, proceeded to fire into the compound; the well-equipped intruders merely donned respirators and continued their operation.

The gunmen were all members of the Tupac Amaru Revolutionary Movement (MRTA) which, as mentioned in Chapter 2, was closely allied with the Sendero Luminoso (Shining Path) terrorist organisation and operated in the northern areas of Peru: Cajamarca, Jaen, La Libertad, Lambayaque and Amazonas. A Cuban-backed group, its members were mainly recruited from the poorest elements of Peru's population. It had carried out its first acts of terrorism in 1982, most of them aimed at the United States: rocket-propelled grenades launched at the US embassy, mortar bombs fired at the US Ambassador's residence and bomb attacks on several Kentucky Fried Chicken restaurants in Lima. Similar attacks were mounted in 1984, including a small-arms attack on the US embassy. In 1985 the MRTA attempted a bomb attack on the US embassy and carried out repeated attacks on the residence of the US Ambassador. In 1987, it seized six local radio stations, using them to make anti-government broadcasts.

In 1990, the MRTA pulled off a spectacular coup when fifty of its members, including the group's leader Victor Polay, tunnelled their way out of the Canto Grande high-security prison near Lima. Two years later, however, Alberto Fujimori came to power as president and, having assumed sweeping powers, cracked down on the country's terrorist groups. His measures included the establishment of anonymous military courts, the imposition of martial law and the granting of draconian powers to the police and Peru's national intelligence service. These had produced dramatic results and during the following months the Peruvian security forces had scored several major successes against the terrorists. By 1993, the leader of Sendero Luminoso, Abimael Guzman, had been arrested and imprisoned, and Victor Polay recaptured together with the MRTA's deputy leader, Peter Cardenas. In 1995, police arrested twenty-three members of the MRTA in a raid during which they discovered small arms, mortars, rocket-launchers and large quantities of ammunition together with plans for an attack on the Peruvian Congress. The latter included detailed plans of the building and a considerable amount of other information including locations of guards and their duty rosters. Fujimori had, perhaps somewhat prematurely, let success go to his head at the time by proclaiming that the MRTA would be defeated by the end of that year. Indeed, only days before the attack, he had told guests at his presidential palace that fighting terrorism was easy.

Inside the residence, three hours passed before the terrorists made their first move which was to release 300 women, among them the president's mother and sister. Apparently well aware of the value of media coverage, they next telephoned local radio and television stations, announcing their demands which included a safe passage to a destination of their choice and the release of 450 members of their organisation being held in prisons throughout Peru. Communication was made via mobile telephones, the terrorists having cut all the telephone lines at the residence. The authorities responded by cutting off all electricity and water supplies to the building although the terrorists soon discovered that it possessed its own petrol-driven generator.

It was not long before the world media was alerted to the attack on the residence and foreign television crews and journalists flooded into Lima to cover what had rapidly become a full-blown siege with the compound surrounded by police and Army units. The terrorists took full advantage of this and pictures were broadcast showing hooded gunmen posing with some of their hostages who appeared unharmed and in good health. President Fujimori was infuriated when the MRTA leader, Néstor Cerpa Cartolini, referred to him as a terrorist while repeating demands for the release of the 450 members of his organisation. Fujimori responded by naming replacements for two senior police officers and the president of the Peruvian Supreme Court who were among the hostages. In doing so, he sent a signal to the terrorists that he would not be held to ransom, nor would his government be brought to a standstill.

The government of Japan, which was a close ally of Fujimori, was naturally extremely concerned by the situation and put pressure on the president to pursue a peaceful outcome to the crisis rather than a military option which might result in bloodshed. The US authorities, meanwhile, were advising him not to surrender to the terrorists and had despatched a Delta advisory team to Lima. Israel, Germany and Britain also offered support, the latter reportedly sending a six-man SAS team and two negotiators from Scotland Yard as 'observers'.

Negotiations were conducted by the Roman Catholic Archbishop Juan Luis Cipriani who acted as an intermediary. After seventeen days most of the hostages had been released, all saying that they had been well treated and speaking in favourable terms of Cerpa himself. This inevitably improved the terrorists' image in the eyes of the world media which by now were encamped *en masse* around the area of the residence compound with batteries of cameras trained on the building. There was also a practical aspect to the terrorists' willingness to release hostages in that the reduced number could be controlled and guarded more easily. The remaining seventy-two hostages were separated into different groups: military and police officers, government officials and politicians, diplomats, business and professional men. These were kept under guard in separate rooms. Among the hostages were Peru's Foreign Minister, Francisco Tudela van Bruegal-Douglas, President Fujimori's brother Pedro, and the Japanese Ambassador himself. Ironically, they also included the head of the Peruvian counter-terrorist police, Maximo Rivera, and his predecessor, Carlos Dominguez.

The publicity surrounding the siege inevitably focused attention on the harsh tactics employed by Fujimori in his war on terrorism, led by the head of Peru's national intelligence service, Vladimiro Montesinos. Thousands had reportedly been imprisoned merely for sympathising with left-wing groups and conditions of imprisonment in such prisons as Canto Grande were said to be appalling. This was confirmed when, during the siege, Fujimori led journalists on a conducted tour of the prison and they were able to see the squalor in which the prisoners were held.

Angered by the televised broadcasts of Cerpa from the ambassador's residence, Fujimori cut off all negotiations with the terrorists for a week. He was still under pressure from the Japanese government which continued to urge a negotiated solution rather than the use of force. Eventually he offered the terrorists safe passage to Cuba, but continued to reject their other demands.

In fact, unknown to the Japanese, Fujimori had no intention of letting Cerpa and his group escape retribution. While the negotiations dragged on for weeks, the Peruvian security forces had been unobtrusively preparing for the military option – a hostage rescue operation code-named Chavin de Huantar. Miners had been brought in to dig tunnels from beneath neighbouring buildings to the residence. Steel-lined and spacious enough for two men to walk abreast and upright, they were equipped with electric lighting and ventilation. Two tunnels passed beneath the residence, terminating below the floors of two of the main rooms used by the terrorists. Five others surfaced at various points just outside the walls on all four sides.

It was a considerable feat of engineering. However, despite the best efforts to maintain maximum possible silence, with the Army using loudspeakers to broadcast military music to drown noise from underground, some sounds of digging must have been heard because Cerpa, apparently suspicious, moved the hostages to the first floor of the building. Fujimori had originally set a deadline of 15 February for the assault, but the terrorists had moved some of the hostages about and it was postponed until early March. After the hostages were moved to the upper floor, he extended the deadline to 22 April.

Meanwhile intelligence officers, posing as doctors checking the hostages' state of health, brought in items such as thermos flasks and books. Some of these, given to certain of the senior military and police officers among the hostages, had reportedly been supplied by the CIA and contained miniaturised transmitter/receivers. Through this means, two-way communication was apparently established with these individuals who signalled by opening curtains when it was safe for them to talk.

Tuesday 22 April, the final deadline for the assault, arrived, by which time the siege had lasted for 126 days. By now, not only the hostages, but also the terrorists were feeling the strain, boredom and low morale taking their toll. On the upper floor, in the bedrooms where they were confined, those equipped with the miniature transmitter/receivers suddenly heard a voice whispering, asking them to try and open the reinforced steel inner door leading from the master bedroom to the balcony outside, to which there was access via a stairway from the ground below. This they succeeded in doing, but found the wooden outer door locked.

Downstairs, Cerpa and seven of his men were playing football in one of the main rooms, their weapons stacked in a corner; below them, hard against the underside of the floor, was an explosive charge. A few metres back down the tunnel a team of special forces troops, wearing helmets, body armour and respirators, waited for the signal to begin the assault. Elsewhere in the complex of tunnels, other teams were similarly positioned and ready to storm the building.

At just after 3 p.m. President Fujimori was told that everything was ready and he gave the order for the assault to commence. Minutes later, the charges positioned at each of the seven tunnels exploded simultaneously. Five of the terrorists playing football were killed instantly as the ground blew up beneath their feet; the remaining three grabbed their weapons and fled upstairs as troops appeared out of the tunnel, and from another under an adjoining room, and began clearing the ground floor of the building. Outside, watched by television cameras, photographers and journalists, more troops appeared from the five other tunnels outside the walls and others stormed through the compound's two gateways.

One team, led by Lieutenant Colonel Juan Valer Sandoval, the commander of the 140-strong assault force, mounted the stairs leading to the first-floor balcony outside the master bedroom, where hostages had succeeded in opening the steel inner door, but found the outer wooden door locked. At that point, a terrorist inside the room fired a burst with his AK-47 through the door, killing Lieutenant Colonel Valer. The rest of his team returned the terrorist's fire before blowing the door open with an explosive charge and entering the room. As they began to clear the second floor, the team met terrorists fleeing up the stairs and shot them dead; among these was their leader, Cerpa.

In one of the bedrooms, a terrorist turned his AK-47 on the President of the Supreme Court, Carlos Giusti Acuña, wounding him severely before being shot dead himself as troops entered the room. Foreign Minister Francisco Tudela van Bruegal-Douglas also came under fire as he escaped, being hit in one of his legs. Elsewhere in the building a fierce battle raged as terrorists fought back against the assaulting troops. A team commander, Captain Raúl Jiménez Salazar, was killed and several hostages, among them Agriculture Minister Rodolfo Muñante Sanguinetti, narrowly escaped death when a terrorist ran into the room where they were hiding; seeing them, he raised his weapon but then turned and quickly disappeared.

By the time the firing ceased, thick smoke had filled the building and it was with difficulty that the hostages, guided by troops, crawled on their hands and knees out of the master bedroom on to the first floor balcony and then down the stairway to the ground below. Troops carried the wounded out of the building, leaving the bodies of the terrorists where they lay, that of Néstor Cerpa Cartolini lying on the stairs where he had been shot. It was still lying there when shortly afterwards President Fujimori, wearing body armour, appeared to congratulate his troops and walk through the bullet-scarred rooms of the residence.

Thus the operation drew to a successful conclusion. All the fourteen terrorists had been killed and of the assault force, two officers had been killed and one soldier severely wounded; he died a few days later. There had been only one fatality among the seventy-two hostages: President of the Supreme Court Carlos

Giusti Acuña, who had been wounded during the assault, died of a heart attack on his way to hospital. For the members of the Army and naval special forces, for whom it was the first operation of this type, it was a remarkable feat to achieve success without incurring heavy losses. For President Fujimori it was a personal triumph which, for a while, did much to boost his previously flagging popularity, but it did not remove the threat of terrorism within Peru.

14

THE UNDERCOVER WAR – PART II

In Northern Ireland in May 1980 the 22 SAS troop, drawn from G Squadron, was tasked with capturing a four-man Provisional IRA ASU armed with an M-60 7.62mm GPMG, one of six which, as described in Chapter 1, had been stolen from a US National Guard armoury in Boston, Massachusetts, and supplied to the Provisionals in 1977 by the Irish-American arms dealer, George Harrison. As was the case with all the Provisional units equipped with the M-60, the four members of the ASU were some of the organisation's most hardened veterans: Angelo Fusco, of Italian descent, had been brought up in West Belfast; Paul Magee; Robert Campbell, the ASU's operations officer; and Joe Doherty. The latter was quartermaster of C Company of the 3rd Battalion PIRA and had been released in December of the previous year after serving five years of a ten-years' sentence for possession of explosives.

According to a report by journalists Ted Oliver and Alastair McQueen published in the *Sunday Telegraph*, intelligence had pinpointed the weapon's location to a cache in a house on Limestone Road in North Belfast. The SAS troop was tasked with mounting surveillance on the building and, when it was known to be empty, a team from 14 Company gained entry and fitted the weapon with a tracking device which would transmit a signal enabling those monitoring it to pinpoint its location – a process known as 'jarking'. It was also modified so as to prevent it firing more than one round before it malfunctioned and jammed. It was then returned to its hiding-place and the 14 Company team withdrew without leaving any traces.

Not long afterwards, intelligence was received that the weapon was to be used to mount an ambush on an RUC vehicle and the SAS troop placed a team on immediate standby. This was organised in two four-man teams of which one was under the troop commander, Captain Richard Westmacott of the Grenadier Guards. On Friday 2 May the transmitter in the M-60 indicated that the weapon had been moved to another North Belfast address, 369 Antrim Road. An operator equipped with a tracking receiver followed it to a newsagent's shop and discovered to his dismay that it showed (wrongly as it turned out) the weapon to be in the flat above the shop whereas it had previously been pinpointed as being in the house next door. He was able to make radio contact with Captain Westmacott's team, who were already en route to the location, to advise it of this, but was unable to raise the other team.

Meanwhile, the four Provisionals had taken up positions in the house next door to the newsagent's shop, overlooking a road junction with traffic lights. The M-60 was sited in an upstairs window on the second floor, which gave a good field of fire. Also in the same room, and reportedly armed with a Heckler & Koch assault rifle, was Joseph Doherty. Angelo Fusco was positioned on the second floor while Paul Magee was guarding the owners of the house who had been confined to a room on the ground floor at the rear of the building.

The car carrying Captain Westmacott's four-man team was the first to appear. As it approached the newsagent's shop, the driver was forced to stop by a woman stepping out in front of the vehicle, pushing a pram. At the same time, one of the team spotted a bald man rubbing his head: this was a 'dicker' or watcher signalling the team's presence to the ASU. Surprise had been lost and Captain Westmacott and his three men had no choice but to deploy immediately. At the same time, the other team arrived and headed for the rear of the house.

As Westmacott and his team headed, mistakenly, for the newsagent's door, the terrorists opened fire with the M-60, hitting Westmacott in the head and neck and killing him instantly. The remaining three members of the team meanwhile took cover in the shop doorway as the weapon was traversed to fire at them. For some reason the modification carried out on it by 14 Company had not worked and a total of seventy rounds were fired in two bursts.

Meanwhile, the second team had gained entry to the rear of the house by battering in the back door with a sledgehammer. As they did so Magee attempted to escape, but was felled with a well-aimed punch which knocked him senseless. By this time reinforcements had arrived in the form of Army units and the RUC who threw a cordon around the area. A siege developed and the terrorists, who were now well aware that there was no escape, demanded that a local priest be present. They eventually surrendered after waving a white sheet out of a window.

Captain Richard Westmacott was the first member of 22 SAS to die in Northern Ireland since the start of the troubles in 1969. In May 1981, Robert Campbell and his three accomplices were brought to trial. On 9 June, however, two days before the trial ended, they and three others escaped from the Crumlin Road Prison in Belfast. All four were convicted *in absentia* of Westmacott's murder and sentenced to life imprisonment, the judge recommending that Campbell, Doherty and Fusco serve a minimum of thirty years and Magee twenty-five.

Joe Doherty escaped to the United States, but was eventually arrested. After nine years of legal proceedings, he was extradited to Northern Ireland in 1992 to serve his sentence. He was released on licence in 1999 under the terms of the Good Friday Agreement.

Angelo Fusco was recaptured in the Irish Republic in January 1982 and was sentenced to ten years for firearms and other offences. In 1986 he attempted to break out of the high-security prison at Portlaoise, for which he received a further three years. After his release, he appeared before a court in Dublin which ordered his extradition to Northern Ireland during the following month. Fusco appealed, however, and was released on bail, thereafter living in the Irish Republic until January 2000 when he was arrested again pending extradition. On 4 January, members of the Gardai Siochana were in the process of transporting him to the border with Northern Ireland when his lawyers succeeded in winning a stay of execution in the Irish High Court. He was subsequently granted leave for a judicial appeal against the extradition order which had been outstanding for eight years.

Paul Magee fled to the Irish Republic where he stayed until 1991 when he fled to England to avoid being extradited to Northern

Ireland to serve his 25-year sentence for Captain Westmacott's murder. He took part in the Provisional IRA bombing campaign in 1992, but was arrested for the murder of a special constable and the attempted murders of three police officers in North Yorkshire, subsequently being convicted in 1993 and sentenced to life imprisonment. After being transferred to the Irish Republic in 1998 to serve his sentence, he was released in December 1999 under the terms of the Good Friday Agreement. On 9 March 2000, however, he was arrested with regard to the nine-year-old warrant outstanding with regard to his extradition to Northern Ireland. He was subsequently freed on bail pending a hearing.

Robert Campbell also fled to the Irish Republic after his escape from the Crumlin Road Prison and was not seen again until October 1999 when he emerged briefly from hiding to attend the funeral of his son who had been killed by a drugs dealer. He has not been seen again since then, but is thought to be living in Belfast.

The 1980s saw no let-up in the undercover war, with the various elements of the Intelligence & Security Group operating throughout the province. 14 Company's detachments were constantly engaged in surveillance and close-target reconnaissance tasks, with the SAS troop and RUC HMSUs providing back-up when required, their targets including the loyalist UDA and UVF as well as the Provisional IRA and INLA. September 1980 saw the arrest of two Provisionals, Francis Quinn and Thomas Hamill, who were apprehended while extracting a sniper rifle from an arms cache, concealed in a hen coop on a farm in County Tyrone which was under surveillance by an SAS team.

At the beginning of the following year, an attempt by loyalist terrorists was made on the life of former member of parliament and H-Block campaigner Bernadette McAliskey (formerly Devlin) and her husband, Michael. On the early morning of 16 January a three-man UDA hit-team drove in a car to her isolated home, near Coalisland. On their arrival, two men approached the house while the third, the driver of the vehicle, proceeded to cut the nearby telephone line. On kicking in the door and entering the building, they shot the couple several times, severely wounding both of them. Thinking their victims were dead, the gunmen left the house.

The building was, however, under surveillance by an SAS patrol which had established an OP in a nearby copse during the previous night, acting on information received by the Intelligence & Security Group from Special Branch. As the three terrorists moved towards their car the patrol challenged and arrested them. Shortly afterwards a quick-reaction force, comprising troops of the 3rd Battalion The Parachute Regiment, arrived by helicopter. First-aid was rendered to the McAliskeys who were then despatched by helicopter to Belfast for emergency surgery, both ultimately recovering from their wounds.

All three members of the UDA hit-team were tried and convicted of the attempted murders of the couple. The pair who had entered the house were sentenced to twenty years imprisonment; the third man, identified as Raymond Smallwood, received fifteen years. In the event, he served only half of his sentence before being released. Thirteen years later, on 11 July 1994, he was murdered by members of a Provisional IRA hit team, comprising four men and a woman, outside his home in Lisburn.

During the aftermath of the attack on the McAliskeys, in answer to questions as to why the patrol had not intercepted the terrorists on their arrival, it was reportedly stated that the SAS had been expecting a radio signal from the RUC, warning that the hit-team was on the way. For some unexplained reason, however, this had failed to materialise and the terrorists arrived unannounced. Inevitably, however, there were suspicions in nationalist circles that the SAS had allowed the terrorists to carry out their task before arresting them.

On 14 March 1981, an SAS patrol surrounded a farmhouse at a remote spot near Rosslea in County Fermanagh. It was occupied by members of a Provisional IRA ASU led by Seamus McElwaine, a notorious 20-year-old who in February of the previous year had shot dead a part-time member of the Ulster Defence Regiment and seven months later murdered an RUC reservist. Such was

McElwaine's reputation and standing in the Provisionals that despite his age he had been given command of his own ASU. The four terrorists were well armed with an Armalite, a Ruger Mini-14 rifle, a Heckler & Koch assault rifle, an M1 carbine and some 180 rounds of ammunition.

McElwaine and his accomplices had been under surveillance by 14 Company which had followed them to the farmhouse. Members of the SAS troop surrounded the building and the terrorists were called upon to surrender. Realising that the odds were stacked heavily against them, they did so. A fifth member of the ASU was arrested later at another location.

Although the Intelligence & Security Group continued to score successes, there were occasional further reminders of the risks faced by its members. On 28 May 1981, the officer commanding 14 Company's North Detachment was making a lone reconnaissance in Londonderry. Having parked his vehicle, he walked past the target area, mentally recording important details. While he was away from his car, however, its registration number was recorded by Provisional IRA 'dickers' who checked it against a list of vehicles recently seen using approach roads to military bases in the Londonderry area. Unfortunately, this vehicle was on the list and the information was soon passed to the Provisionals' local unit. Within a few minutes four Provisionals, armed with three Armalite rifles and a pistol, had hijacked a car and were preparing an ambush.

As the operator was returning to his base, the terrorists followed him until he slowed down at a road junction where they overtook his vehicle and forced it into the side of the road. Two of the terrorists, later identified as George McBrearty and Charles Maguire, leaped from their car, Maguire deploying to the rear of the operator's vehicle and covering him with his rifle, while McBrearty advanced from the front. As the latter reached his door, the operator shot him dead through the car door and dived out of his vehicle as Maguire opened fire from the rear. The operator then turned and shot him dead before jumping back into his car and opening fire on the two remaining terrorists, wounding one of them, Edward McCourt.

Returning the fire of the other, he expertly reversed away into a high-speed J-turn and sped away. He was fortunate to escape, particularly as he had broken the rule of entering a high risk area without back-up; he rightly received a reprimand from a member of his own detachment for doing so.

The early 1980s saw the RUC beginning to play an increasingly primary role in the undercover war and up until the end of 1983 it took over the conduct of aggressive operations against the terror-ists. In October 1982, however, a series of killings focused attention on operations carried out by the HMSUs and resulted in major political repercussions.

In early October information was received by the RUC that a large quantity of explosives was being brought into Northern Ireland from the Irish Republic by the Provisional IRA which intended to use them for a major operation, details of which were unknown. The truck in which the consignment was being transported had been identified and was kept under surveillance as it crossed over the border and headed towards Lurgan, eventually making its way to a farm outside the town near a large republican housing estate. There the explosives were unloaded and concealed in a barn by a group of Provisionals. No sooner had they left than the cache was examined and found to contain 1,000 pounds of explosive and a quantity of weapons comprising some elderly rifles of First World War vintage without ammunition. These were left undisturbed and an audio surveillance device was planted by Security Service technicians brought in for the task. This would transmit conversations and any indications of movements within the building to the Army base at Mahon Road in Portadown. At the same time, a tracking device was concealed inside the explosives to give warning of any movement of the consignment. Meanwhile 14 Company established an OP to keep the barn under observation.

On 27 October 1982 three RUC officers, Sergeant Sean Quinn and Constables Paul Hamilton and Alan McCloy, were investigating a report of a motorcycle apparently abandoned at a location called the Kinnego Embankment near Lurgan. As they approached in an unmarked car, a massive bomb concealed in a culvert under the road exploded, killing all three officers and destroying their vehicle.

The bomb had comprised explosives from the cache in the barn and it transpired that the 14 Company OP had for unexplained reasons been stood down for twenty-four hours, allowing the members of a Provisional ASU to remove the quantity required. Furthermore, the audio surveillance and tracking devices had failed to work. These were replaced and the 14 Company OP returned to its position.

During the following month, intelligence was received that two of those suspected as being responsible for the bombing were local men named Eugene Toman and Sean Burns. Both had until then been in hiding in the Irish Republic after being involved in a shooting attack on an RUC patrol a few weeks earlier. On 11 November, the two men were located near Lurgan at the home of a known republican sympathiser, Gervaise McKerr. They were kept under observation by E4A and a three-man HMSU patrol was deployed.

On the night of the 11th, the three men left McKerr's home in a green Ford Escort with him driving, tailed by two E4A operators in another vehicle who reported the direction in which they were heading. Acting on this information, the HMSU patrol established itself near a T-junction on the Tullyglass East Road near Lurgan. When McKerr's vehicle appeared the patrol gave chase, firing at the Escort which was by then moving at high speed. After travelling some 50 yards, however, McKerr came to a roundabout where he lost control, his car careering off the road and down an embankment. Leaving their vehicle, the three HMSU officers approached the Escort and opened fire. All three of its occupants died, their bodies and that of the car reportedly riddled with 108 bullets. Other RUC officers arrived on the scene shortly afterwards and conducted a search of the vehicle but found no weapons.

In the aftermath of this incident, the explosives were removed from the cache in the barn but the rifles were left in place and the building remained under constant surveillance. Meanwhile, there was uproar over the deaths of the three men and there were allegations that they had been murdered. Their families' claims that none of them had any connections with the Provisional IRA were, however, contradicted by the organisation's North Armagh Brigade. At their funerals, their coffins were draped with the Irish tricolour and shots were fired over their graves.

The shooting of Toman, Burns and McKerr was subsequently investigated by the BBC journalist Chris Moore who alleged in a programme broadcast in 1988 that McKerr's car had been fitted with audio surveillance and tracking devices which permitted monitoring of conversations inside the vehicle as well as its movements, suggesting that the men had been targeted.

On the afternoon of 24 November, the audio surveillance device in the barn picked up sounds of movement in the barn and an HMSU patrol was deployed. As they approached the building, the three officers opened fire on it, its corrugated tin and breezeblock walls offering little protection for anyone inside. Accounts differ as to what happened next. According to the officers, as they entered the barn one of them allegedly shouted for those inside to come out. Seeing a movement in the pile of hay bales where the arms cache was concealed, they opened fire again. Hidden in the hay were two young local men, seventeen-year-old Michael Tighe and nineteen-year-old Martin McCauley who had been examining the old rifles which the latter later claimed they had found lying on the hay. Both had been hit by three bullets, Tighe being killed instantly and McCauley wounded.

On recovering from his wounds, the latter was charged with unlawful possession of the three rifles. At his trial, however, the judge expressed misgivings about the evidence presented by the RUC and gave him a two-year suspended sentence. McCauley later disputed the RUC's account of the incident, denying firmly that any order had been shouted by the three officers before they opened fire.

Nearly three weeks later, a further incident took place which would result in an investigation into the operations of the HMSU and responsibility for the conduct of aggressive operations being returned to the Army. On 12 December two members of the INLA, Seamus Grew and Roddy Carroll, crossed into Northern Ireland from the

Irish Republic. Unknown to them they had been tailed by an inspector in E4A as part of an operation, coordinated by the Tasking & Coordination Group (TCG) at Armagh, to catch the notorious INLA leader Dominic 'Mad Dog' McGlinchey who was expected to be accompanying them with a small quantity of weapons.

The E4A officer, travelling in a white Peugeot, had watched as Grew and Carroll had earlier driven into the Republic, taking a relative home from a family funeral before picking up McGlinchey who was carrying a holdall suspected of containing the weapons. Instead of accompanying them across the border, however, the latter had been dropped off beforehand and had disappeared. The TCG at Armagh was advised of this unexpected turn of events as the E4A officer continued to follow Grew and Carroll over the border. Meanwhile, an HMSU patrol and two 14 Company operators in a car had been deployed and a roadblock established. Shortly afterwards, however, disaster struck when the HMSU vehicle came to a halt unexpectedly and the 14 Company car, travelling too close behind, crashed into it. Seconds later Grew and Carroll passed the scene of the accident, followed shortly afterwards by the E4A officer who stopped. A member of the HMSU patrol, Constable John Robinson, jumped into his vehicle and the two men set off in pursuit of Grew and Carroll.

As the two vehicles were nearing the Catholic area of Mullacreavie Park in Armagh, the E4A officer overtook Grew's car and pulled up in front of it. Constable Robinson leaped out and opened fire at Carroll who was in the passenger seat of the Allegro, killing him instantly. He then reloaded his weapon and fired further rounds at Grew, shooting him dead. A subsequent search of the vehicle revealed that both men were unarmed at the time.

Following this incident, an internal RUC inquiry took place, as a result of which the Director of Public Prosecutions (DPP) decided to bring charges of murder against Constable Robinson and the three officers involved in the killing of Eugene Toman, Sean Burns and Gervaise McKerr: Sergeant Montgomery and Constables Brannigan and Robinson (a different officer of the same name). All four officers stood trial in 1984 and were acquitted. In the case of the killing of

Toman, Burns and McKerr, the judge, Lord Justice Gibson, was critical of the DPP's decision to bring Montgomery, Brannigan and Robinson to trial and commended the three officers for 'bringing the deceased men to justice, in this case, the final court of justice'. Lord Gibson ultimately paid dearly for uttering those words; as described in Chapter 2, he and his wife were later killed in April 1987 by the Provisional IRA in an act of revenge.

There was serious public disquiet over the three shootings and allegations were made that the RUC was conducting a shoot-to-kill policy. On 24 May 1984 Deputy Chief Constable John Stalker was appointed to head an inquiry into the incidents. The full story of his investigation has been described in his book *Stalker* and by others investigating the affair. Suffice it to say here that he was obstructed in the pursuit of his inquiry, being refused access to vital evidence which included tape recordings of audio surveillance in the barn where Michael Tighe was killed. Two years later he was removed from the inquiry pending investigation into his connections with a Manchester businessman, subsequently being cleared of any impropriety whatsoever. His findings during his period in Northern Ireland led him to believe, however, that there had been a cover-up over the three shootings and that in the cases of Tighe, Burns, McKerr, Carroll and Grew, all five 'were unlawfully killed by members of the Royal Ulster Constabulary'.

In December 1983 the Intelligence & Security Group resumed the role of ambushing. On 2 December a six-man SAS patrol was inserted into an area of countryside near the village of Coalisland in County Tyrone as a result of information, received the day before from Special Branch, about an arms cache in the area of Magheramulkenny. A close reconnaissance was carried out before first light on 2 December and a search of a small field enclosed by embankments topped with a thick hedge revealed the cache which was found to contain an AR-15 5.56mm rifle, a 12-gauge shotgun and a bag containing balaclavas and clothing. Just before dawn, the patrol had taken up its positions: two pairs were sited behind embankments some thirty metres from the cache and the third was positioned fifty metres from the others and ten from the road.

At around 3 p.m. on Sunday 4 December, a brown Sunbeam Talbot car appeared and halted by the field. Two men, a 23-year-old named Colm McGirr and his 19-year-old friend Brian Campbell, walked over to the cache. Both were known members of the Provisional IRA from the Coalisland area. McGirr knelt down and extracted the shotgun and the Armalite, handing the latter to Campbell who began to return to the car. At that instance, one of the SAS soldiers shouted a challenge and McGirr swung to face him with the shotgun in his hands. The patrol opened fire immediately, killing McGirr who was hit by thirteen bullets. Campbell was meanwhile running towards the car, but was hit twice and mortally wounded. Despite the efforts of the patrol, which administered emergency medical treatment in an attempt to save his life, he died five minutes later. The driver of the car, meanwhile, leaped back into the vehicle and sped away, pursued by heavy fire from two other members of the patrol concealed in a ditch by the road. The car was later discovered abandoned with bloodstains in its interior, but of the driver there was no sign.

Two months later, the Intelligence & Security Group was in action again, but on this occasion an operation resulted in the deaths of two members of 14 Company. In February 1984, a team mounted surveillance on a house at 10 Carness Drive in the hamlet of Carness, just outside the village of Dunlow in the north of County Antrim. It was occupied by the Hogans, a family with strong republican sympathies who had been forced out of their previous home after being subjected to intimidation by loyalists. One of the family, 21-year-old Henry Hogan, was a member of the Provisional IRA who had previously come to the notice of the security forces.

The 14 Company operators established a covert OP behind two wooden sheds in a field close to the road near the Hogan's house, giving a good view of the front of the building which was some eighty yards away. The OP was manned by Sergeant Paul Oram and another man who were equipped with cameras and radios, each being armed with a Browning 9mm pistol and a Heckler & Koch MP5K 9mm submachine-gun. In case of trouble, a back-up team was positioned in two cars on the outskirts of Dunloy and a quick-reaction force was on immediate standby to deploy by helicopter from the nearest Army base.

Unfortunately, however, the OP was under surveillance by the Provisionals who had been expecting security forces in the area. The reason for this lay in the presence of an arms cache located in Carness, and in particular the presence of a submachine-gun hidden in it. This weapon had been transferred from a Provisional IRA cache in the Andersonstown area of Belfast to which it had been delivered on 7 January by a Provisional named James Young who had brought it from County Down. Unknown to his fellow terrorists, however, Young was a Special Branch informer, having been recruited in November 1981. When asked by his local commander to transport the weapon to Belfast, Young had informed his two Special Branch handlers to whom he gave the submachine-gun on the night before he was due to travel. Both travelled with him on the following day, ensuring that he was not stopped at any RUC or Army checkpoints, and the weapon was duly delivered.

During just over two years of being an informer, Young had given his handlers a considerable amount of information which had resulted in the compromising of a number of Provisional IRA operations. Suspicion had inevitably been aroused and in December 1983 the Provisionals had initiated secret internal investigations into the potential sources of the leaks. By the beginning of February suspicion was centred on Young who was lured to South Armagh where he was kidnapped and interrogated. He confessed all to his interrogators who, among other things, questioned him about the transfer of the submachine-gun from County Down to Belfast. Young admitted that his handlers had escorted him, and that they had been in possession of the weapon. The Provisionals' principal concern was that the weapon might have been 'jarked'. On contacting the Belfast Brigade, Young's interrogators were told that the weapon had subsequently been transferred to County Antrim and an arms cache in Carness.

The Provisionals were aware that if the weapon had been 'jarked', it was highly likely that the cache would be under surveillance by a covert OP. They decided to turn the situation to their own advantage and attack any OP detected. The task was given to the North Antrim Battalion PIRA who in turn detailed three of its members, Henry Hogan, Declan Martin and another unidentified individual, to carry it out.

Hogan and his two accomplices kept the area surrounding Carness, and the cache, under surreptitious surveillance and on 21 February detected the presence of the OP in a field which overlooked the Hogan family home. Passing this information to his superiors, he was told to mount an attack on it that night.

At 8 p.m. Hogan and Martin approached the OP position from the rear. Armed with an AR-15 rifle and a submachine-gun, they crawled to within point-blank range unobserved. On their feet, they ordered the OP's two occupants to stand up. The latter reacted swiftly, opening fire on both terrorists and hitting them. As they fell to the ground, however, the one armed with the submachine-gun fired a burst. Sergeant Paul Oram was hit in the chest and died instantly; his companion was seriously wounded, being hit in the back, knee and thigh. Nevertheless the latter, on hearing sounds from Hogan and Martin lying in the darkness nearby, fired two more rounds at each before radioing the back-up team which deployed immediately. On its arrival, the latter advanced cautiously into the field and on encountering the two terrorists shot them dead. Meanwhile, the third member of Hogan's team escaped. A subsequent search of the field uncovered the AR-15, the submachine-gun and a shotgun.

The following month of March 1964 saw members of the Intelligence & Security Group involved in an operation to thwart a loyalist attempt to murder Gerry Adams, newly elected as member of Parliament for West Belfast. The FRU had received information from an informer in the UDA that an Ulster Freedom Fighters (UFF) hit-team would be waiting to gun down Adams as he left the magistrates court in Belfast where he was due to appear on 14 March to answer a charge of obstruction. This information was passed by the FRU to the TCG and the decision was taken to frustrate the loyalists' plan. The FRU informer had given his handlers details of the weapons to be used in the attack and the location of the cache in which they were concealed at Ballysillan, a loyalist area on the outskirts of Belfast. Operators of 14 Company located it in an outhouse where they found pistols and ammunition. Removing the bullet from each round, they extracted some of the propellant in the cartridge, thus reducing the power and velocity to a level which would be non-lethal. Each round was then reassembled and the weapons and ammunition replaced in the cache which was left without any signs of disturbance.

On 15 March, Adams left the court when it adjourned for lunch and accompanied by three companions, Sean Keenan, Kevin Rooney and Joe Keenan, was driving off in a car down Howard Street when the UFF team struck. A brown Rover car overtook Adams's car and two gunmen opened fire at close range. Twelve rounds were fired before the doctored ammunition caused the gunmen's weapons to jam. Some bullets hit the passenger door and Adams himself was hit in the neck, shoulder and arm. Sean Keenan, sitting in the rear of the car, was also wounded. Adams's driver meanwhile had kept control of the vehicle and immediately drove to the Royal Victoria Hospital where Adams and Keenan were treated for their wounds. In the meantime, several members of the Intelligence & Security Group had appeared while the shooting was taking place and shortly afterwards the two UFF gunmen, Gerard Welsh and John Gregg, were arrested with their driver, Colin Gray.

In July 1984, the SAS troop carried out an ambush operation in County Tyrone after information was received that the Provisional IRA would be mounting an incendiary bomb attack on a factory in the village of Ardboe. An eight-man team was inserted on the night of 12 July while another member of the troop waited near the village with a quick-reaction force provided by the 1st Battalion The Queen's Regiment. Two members of the SAS team moved in first, taking up a position on the Mullanahoe road as a stop group, and thirty minutes later the remaining five moved in to the factory area in two groups. Heavily armed, they carried Colt M-16A2 and Heckler & Koch HK53 5.56mm assault rifles, and Browning Hi-Power 9mm pistols.

About an hour and a half later, two men were observed entering the area and were challenged from a distance of some thirty metres. Both ran off into the darkness and the SAS opened fire, wounding one of them, 28-year-old William Price. At the same time, two more Provisionals, Raymond O'Neill and Thomas McQuillan, heard the shooting and decided to make themselves scarce. On the Mullanahoe road, however, they encountered the SAS two-man stop group who challenged them. O'Neill wisely complied with their order to halt, but McQuillan attempted to make a run for it. One of the SAS soldiers opened fire and McQuillan fell, but was unwounded.

Meanwhile, the rest of the SAS team were searching for the first two men in the fields behind the factory. One soldier stumbled on one of them who made a sudden movement. The soldier opened fire, killing the man who was subsequently identified as William Price. A search of the area uncovered a revolver, a pistol and several incendiary bombs.

During this period, the Provisional IRA was targeting members of the RUC and the Ulster Defence Regiment (UDR) as part of a programme of intimidation against locally recruited members of the security forces. In October 1984, a few days after the IRA's bomb attack at the Grand Hotel in Brighton, information was received that the Provisionals were planning to murder a part-time officer of the UDR and accordingly the Intelligence & Security Group was tasked by the TCG with carrying out an operation to thwart the terrorists' plan and, it was hoped, catch them in the act. An SAS team was inserted into a position covering a road junction through which the UDR officer drove each day on the way to and from his place of employment in Dungannon. Nearby was a yard belonging to a firm of haulage contractors, Capper and Lambe. Two of the team were concealed in a position behind some bushes near the entrance to the yard while the remainder were in three unmarked cars parked nearby.

At 8 a.m. on 19 October, a group of Provisionals arrived in a van which they had stolen in Coalisland. The SAS immediately attempted to intercept it, but failed and opened fire. Unfortunately, at that moment, a manager of the haulage company, 48-year-old Frederick Lambe, drove out of the yard and was hit in the chest by a stray bullet fired by a member of the SAS team. Mortally wounded, he died later in hospital. Meanwhile, the Provisionals made good their escape. Abandoning their van, which was found later, they disappeared into a republican enclave. The operation had proved a disaster: not only had the terrorists escaped, but an innocent member of the public had been killed accidentally.

Six weeks later, members of the SAS troop were deployed in response to information received about an impending bomb attack by the Provisional IRA in Fermanagh. At 9 p.m. on 1 December, a blue van had been hijacked by a group of four terrorists in Pettigo, across the border in Donegal in the Irish Republic, and loaded with several milk churns containing approximately 1,000 pounds of explosives. It had then been driven north over the border, its destination the village of Drumrush. The four men, all known Provisionals, were: a former member of the Irish Army named Tony MacBride; Kieran Fleming and James Clark, both of whom had escaped from the Maze prison during the mass break-out on 25 September 1983; and Patrick Bramley.

By 11.30 p.m. a seven-man SAS team had arrived in the area in two cars, having been briefed to look out for a blue van of foreign manufacture. At 12.30 a.m. on 2 December, a telephone call was received by the RUC, warning of incendiary bombs having been placed at a well-known local restaurant called Drumrish Lodge. This was intended to lure the security forces into the area, and in particular to the restaurant where the explosive-filled milk churns had been concealed in a culvert under the drive.

The first vehicle to appear was an RUC vehicle. Early warning was provided by MacBride in the van which was parked on a track by the side of the road. He was in radio contact with his three accomplices, who were concealed in a firing position behind one of the hedges which lined both sides of the road, and transmitted the code-word 'One' as the police vehicle approached. As it turned into the drive of the restaurant, the terrorists initiated the firing button but the initiation system failed and the charges failed to explode.

The SAS team had monitored MacBride's transmission and they positioned their cars to block each end of the road. The car farthest from the van was manned by three soldiers, two of whom left their vehicle and approached the van on foot, leaving the third soldier with the car to maintain radio contact. Unknown to them, however, they had parked their vehicle only a short distance from the terrorists' firing position. As the two soldiers approached, MacBride left his van and came to meet them. As one of the soldiers, Lance Corporal Alastair Slater, began questioning him, the three terrorists in the hedge line opened fire at point-blank range of some ten feet, mortally wounding Slater who nevertheless returned their fire.

The remainder of the SAS team responded swiftly and a short firefight ensued, during which MacBride was killed, before the other three terrorists fled, heading in the direction of the border. One of them, Kieran Fleming, drowned as he attempted to swim across the River Bannagh which was in spate; his body was found three weeks later. Clark and Bramley succeeded in crossing the border, but were arrested a few hours later by the Gardai Siochana.

Five days later, members of the Londonderry detachment of 14 Company and Special Branch took part in a large operation to forestall a Provisional IRA attack on a part-time member of the UDR who worked at the Gransha psychiatric hospital on the outskirts of Londonderry. On the morning of 6 December the troops deployed in cars around the area of the hospital. Meanwhile, an SAS soldier rode in the same bus as the UDR reservist as he travelled to work.

The terrorist hit-team comprised two men, Daniel Doherty and William Fleming, the latter a cousin of Kieran Fleming mentioned earlier. Armed with a pistol and revolver, they travelled to the hospital on a stolen motorcycle driven by Doherty with Fleming riding pillion. As they entered the hospital grounds they were rammed by one of the troops' cars. Fleming, whose leg was shattered by the impact, was knocked off and shot four times as he struggled to stand up. Doherty attempted to escape on the motorcycle, but came under fire, being killed by nineteen rounds.

Inevitably there was much controversy over the killing of the two men, with questions being raised in Parliament as to whether they could have been arrested rather than killed and whether a 'shoot-to-kill' policy was in force, the latter being firmly denied by the government. During the subsequent inquest, the three soldiers who had opened fire claimed that they had shot Fleming because he had a pistol in his hand and had attempted to stand up, and had killed Doherty in the belief that their lives were in danger.

Even more controversy was generated by an operation which took place two months later in February 1985. Intelligence was received from an informer that an attack on an RUC mobile patrol in the predominantly Catholic area of the town of Strabane was being planned. The information indicated that a Provisional IRA ASU had been detailed for the task for which it would be well equipped with special anti-armour grenades and Belgian-manufactured FNC 5.56mm assault rifles. A surveillance operation was mounted throughout the area of Strabane by elements of the Intelligence & Security Group with an RUC divisional mobile support unit (DMSU) on-call as a quick-reaction force.

On the night of 23 February, five members of the ASU withdrew from their ambush position on an isolated road, after it became apparent that their intended target was not going to appear. Leaving the road, two of them handed over their weapons to their companions and made their way home. The remaining three, carrying all the small arms and a holdall containing the anti-armour grenades and launcher, headed towards the location of a cache, where they would conceal their weapons, which lay about half a mile away. Unknown to them, however, it was under surveillance by three members of a six-man team of 14 Company whose OP was in a hedge at the top of a steep bank, looking uphill across a field towards the location of the cache; the other members of the team were at a nearby security forces base with the DMSU quick-reaction force.

As the terrorists approached, the troops in the OP opened fire with their HK53 assault rifles at a range of only a few metres. At that point, one of them overbalanced and fell backwards down a steep bank behind the OP position into the back yard of a house below; from there he radioed a contact report, as did one of the two soldiers still in the OP position who continued firing at the terrorists who by now were prostrate on the ground. The quick-reaction force arrived shortly afterwards and the firing ceased. The two soldiers in the OP moved out cautiously to check the terrorists, all of whom were dead. The three were subsequently identified as local men: two brothers, Michael and David Devine, and Charles Breslin. Almost immediately after the shooting, the DMSU quick-reaction force stormed a house nearby and arrested a fourth member of the ASU, Declan Crossan. The fifth man was never caught.

Considerable controversy followed the shooting of the three men, further increased by claims that they had initially been wounded then killed with *coup de grâce* pistol shots fired into their heads. In fact, the autopsy report clearly stated that the head wounds had been caused by high velocity rifle fire.

The remainder of 1985 saw a relative slackening in the number of incidents involving special forces in Northern Ireland. In February 1986, however, a Provisional IRA arms cache was located at Toome-bridge, in County Londonderry, after a suspect named Francis Bradley, who was under Special Branch surveillance at the time, was observed visiting it. The task of catching Bradley red-handed at the cache was given to the SAS troop which deployed a five-man team. At about 9.30 p.m. on 18 February, it took up an ambush position behind a hedge some forty metres from the cache which was hidden under a pile of rubbish lying by a shed in a farmyard to the rear of a house on the Toome road. Some thirty minutes later a car pulled up in the yard and two men made their way to the cache. One of them was Bradley who pulled out a rifle whereupon he was challenged by one of the SAS team. According to a subsequent statement made by the soldier, Bradley swung round sharply and the soldier, together with another member of the team, opened fire. Bradley fell wounded, but was still moving. As one of the SAS team moved forward, he fired a burst into Bradley which killed him. The driver of the car, Barney McLarnon, was arrested, as was the owner of the house, Colm Walls, but neither man was subsequently convicted of any involvement in the affair. A search of the cache uncovered an AR-15 and an FN assault rifle which forensic ballistic tests revealed had been used in four murders of members of the security forces and twenty other attacks, including a number in which Bradley had been a prime suspect. Yet again, there was considerable controversy and searching questions were asked as to the manner of his death.

Two months later, members of the SAS troop were deployed in response to a report from a member of an Army patrol which had noticed what appeared to be a command wire near a road at Mullagh-glass, near the border in the south of County Fermanagh. This report was passed to the Intelligence & Security Group and a covert recon-naissance of the area was carried out. At the end of the wire 800 pounds of explosive were found in a culvert under the road, ready to blow up any security forces vehicle which happened to pass.

On the night of 25 April, a four-man SAS patrol took up an ambush position in bushes near the bomb's firing position in a field overlooking the road. There they waited until the early morning of 26 April when two men, one armed with a Ruger Mini-14 rifle and the other with a Belgian FNC, approached the firing point. As they reached it, the SAS team opened fire, killing one man and wounding the other who managed to crawl away into the darkness. The dead man was none other than Seamus McElwaine who had been arrested by the SAS at Rosslea in March 1981, but, having been convicted and imprisoned, had subsequently escaped in the break-out from the Maze prison in September 1983. His accomplice was Sean Lynch who was found after a lengthy search of the area by the RUC and troops.

After the operation at Mullaghglass there was a lull of some fourteen months, but in the spring of 1987 a Special Branch informer reported that the Provisional IRA was planning a major operation. Further intelligence revealed that it was to be an attack on an RUC station at Loughgall by two four-man ASUs of the Provisionals' East Tyrone Brigade, commanded by two well-known terrorists, Patrick Kelly and Jim Lynagh, the latter at that time being in charge of cross-border operations. This information came from the monitoring by an electronic bug covertly installed in the home of Gerard Harte, the commander of the East Tyrone

Brigade, by operators of 14 Company. Close surveillance was kept on Kelly and Lynagh, and the members of their combined ASU, by 14 Company and E4A teams.

The terrorists' plan was for an attack on a small RUC station in the village of Loughgall, in the north of County Armagh and some thirty miles from the city of Armagh itself. Located on the Bally-gasey road on the outskirts of the village, the station was surrounded by a perimeter fence and manned by a sergeant and three constables during daylight hours. The Provisionals' intention was to break through the fence using a stolen mechanical digger which would have in its bucket scoop a bomb sufficiently large to destroy the station building when detonated against it. This was a technique used previously in a similar assault in 1985 on a small RUC post at The Birches, some five miles away from Loughgall; it had been one of a series of attacks on RUC stations in rural areas of County Tyrone during that year. The largest of the attacks had been at Balleygawley in late 1985 when the RUC station was attacked by a large force of terrorists who succeeded in wrecking the building and absconding with weapons and documents taken from the station's filing cabinets. Two RUC officers, Reserve Constable William Clements and Constable George Gilliland, were killed; the remaining three officers succeeded in escaping.

At Loughgall a major ambush operation, code-named Judy, was planned and mounted by the Intelligence & Security Group, the SAS troop being reinforced by an additional troop of G Squadron flown over from the 22 SAS base at Hereford. By the afternoon of Friday 8 May, when the station had been closed for the weekend and was ostensibly deserted, some forty SAS soldiers were already in position, heavily armed with G3K 7.62mm and M-16A2 5.56mm assault rifles as well as two L7A1 M7.62mm general-purpose machine-guns. One team was positioned in and around the building while another was located in a tree line and undergrowth opposite the station. Early warning and cut-off groups were in positions in the village, covering the approaches and possible escape routes, and on the road on either side of the station.

The terrorists had stolen a blue Toyota van from a street in Dungannon and a mechanical digger from a farm nearby. As they drove towards Loughgall, they were shadowed by operators of 14 Company and members of E4A. At about 7.15 p.m. the van appeared and drove through the village, returning shortly afterwards accompanied by the digger driven by a Provisional named Declan Arthurs with two others, Tony Gormley and Gerard O'Callaghan, aboard. The van halted and three terrorists, dressed in blue overalls and armed with Heckler & Koch G3 7.62mm and FNC 5.56mm assault rifles, emerged from it and one of them, Patrick Kelly, opened fire on the station. As he did so, the digger crashed through the perimeter fence and lumbered up to the building. At this point, the SAS opened fire, killing Patrick Kelly, as he stood beside the van, and Jim Lynagh and Patrick McKearney as they took cover in the back of the vehicle. Seamus Donnelly, the driver of the vehicle, died at the wheel. Arthurs leaped from the digger as Gormley and O'Callaghan lit the 200-pound bomb's fuse with a cigarette lighter. He dashed for the van, but together with another man named Eugene Kelly, died taking cover behind it. The bomb exploded within a few seconds, demolishing the police station and injuring a number of the SAS team inside. Gormley and O'Callaghan had initially taken cover behind a wall and now attempted to escape. Gormley was cut down immediately as he emerged from cover while O'Callaghan succeeded in reaching the road, but was killed by one of the cut-off groups.

All eight terrorists had been accounted for but the success of the operation was marred by the tragic death and wounding of innocent passers-by who suddenly appeared on the scene during the firefight. Two local mechanics, Anthony and Oliver Hughes, drove into the village just as the ambush was initiated. Mistaking them for terrorists, as both men were dressed in blue overalls, and seeing their car attempting to reverse, the SAS opened fire on them, killing Anthony and seriously wounding his brother. This tragedy could have been greater still because other cars appeared on the scene. One vehicle, driven by a woman who was accompanied by her daughter, also came under fire, but fortunately the lives of both were saved by the prompt and gallant action of the commander of one of the cut-off groups who rescued them. An elderly couple in another car also appeared on the scene, but saved themselves by leaping into a nearby ditch. The driver of another car stopped as he watched the blue van come under fire in front of him; jumping out of his vehicle, he ran for cover but was promptly apprehended by a soldier and held until after the action was over.

Forensic ballistic tests carried out on the terrorists' weapons revealed that they had been used previously in a number of attacks on members of the security forces. The Heckler & Koch G3 rifle carried by Patrick Kelly had been used to kill two members of the UDR in Dungannon earlier in the month, while the two other G3s and the two FNCs had been used in the murder of two members of the UDR in County Tyrone and County Londonderry respectively in April 1987. Also found at the scene was a 12-gauge shotgun and an RUC issue Ruger Security Six .357 Magnum revolver which had been taken from an RUC reservist killed during an attack on the police station at Balleygawley in late 1985. The revolver had subsequently been used during the following year in the murders of a member of the UDR and a building contractor employed by the security forces.

The operation at Loughgall was a major coup for the Intelligence & Security Group and a disaster for the Provisional IRA, resulting in the deaths of some of its most noted hard-liners at a time when its political wing, Sinn Fein, was already suffering from a considerable drop in electoral support throughout the province. Furthermore, the Provisionals' fighting strength had been drastically reduced by security force successes and other factors from 1,000 in 1980 to less than 250, of whom only some fifty were active members of ASUs with the remainder providing logistical support.

It was not long, however, before hard-line elements within the Provisionals, in particular those of the Belfast Brigade, were clamouring for revenge for Loughgall. The organisation's ruling Army Council was soon under pressure to provide it while at the same time needing to boost flagging morale within the republican movement.

In the wake of the Loughgall débâcle, the Council carried out a searching inquiry into how the operation had been compromised, but ultimately was unable to pinpoint whether an informer or poor security was responsible. Thereafter, it lost little time in turning its attention to planning a reprisal operation and selecting a suitable target of sufficient importance. The idea of an attack on a soft target within Northern Ireland was quickly dismissed because of the high level of surveillance being maintained by the security forces within the province. Consideration was also given to potential targets on the British mainland but since the October 1984 bombing of the Grand Hotel in Brighton, security was tight and again the police and the Security Service were maintaining a high level of vigilance. It was decided that the target would have to be outside the United Kingdom in an area where security was not high and the risk of losing any more men was negligible.

After careful consideration, the British base of Gibraltar was selected. In addition to accommodating a garrison of some 1,500 British troops, it also housed an important Government Communications Headquarters (GCHQ) and NATO listening post monitoring radio traffic and the movement of Russian naval forces through the straits linking the Mediterranean and the Atlantic. It was thus an important strategic outpost and any attack on it would have a major impact on Britain while also making the headlines worldwide.

The Council decided that a special ASU would have to be formed for the task and careful consideration was given to personnel selection. Eventually three of its most experienced people were chosen: Mairead Farrell, Danny McCann and Sean Savage. Farrell was a member of a middle-class family from West Belfast. Educated at a Catholic grammar school, she had joined the IRA at the age of eighteen and was the first female terrorist to be imprisoned following withdrawal of political status in 1976, being convicted and sentenced to fourteen years for the bombing of a hotel in Dunmurry in April of that year. As a prisoner in the Maze, she had joined the H-Block campaign's 'dirty protest' and in December 1980 went on a nineteen-day hunger strike. In 1987 she was released and thereafter had begun studying politics and economics at Queen's University in Belfast; at the same time, however, she resumed her activities as a member of the Provisional IRA.

Danny McCann was from the Lower Falls Road in Belfast and joined the IRA at the age of fifteen. In 1973 he was arrested and charged with riotous behaviour, subsequently being sentenced to six months in prison. At the beginning of 1979, he was arrested and convicted of possession of a detonator, receiving a sentence of two years. Released in January 1981, he was arrested again in May and spent four months on remand for allegedly being in possession of a firearm. In November he was arrested again, but released in April 1982. Three months later he was arrested with six others and, on the basis of information supplied by an informer, charged with the murder of a police officer who was killed in September 1981 in a RPG-7 rocket-propelled grenade attack on an RUC vehicle driving through the Suffolk area of Belfast. The charges were dropped after the informer retracted his statement. Sean Savage was also one of those charged and released. From Andersonstown in Belfast, he had been imprisoned briefly in 1982 after being charged with being a member of the IRA and with causing an explosion, but the charges were subsequently dropped and he was released.

A fourth member also joined the ASU; she would travel to Gibraltar ahead of the others and would be responsible for target reconnaissance and intelligence-gathering prior to their arrival.

The Provisionals' plan was for an attack on the troops Changing the Guard outside the Governor's residence, a ceremony carried out every Tuesday at 10.55 a.m. by the resident British infantry battalion in Gibraltar, in this instance the 1st Battalion The Royal Anglian Regiment which had just completed a tour of duty in Northern Ireland. The ceremony took place in a small square off the main road which runs past the residence, and on its completion the band and old guard marched to another square nearby before being dismissed. It was this latter square which was selected as the location for a car bomb attack.

It was not long, however, before the British were alerted to the possibility of a terrorist threat to Gibraltar. Information from an informer indicated that two well-known Provisionals were in

Malaga, on Spain's Costa del Sol, and that weapons and explosives had already been cached there. On 15 November, Savage and McCann were spotted at Madrid airport en route for Dublin, using the aliases of Robert Reilly and Brendan Coyne. The Spanish authorities passed this information to London and the British quickly decided that the presence of the two men, one a well-known bomb-maker, in the vicinity could only mean that an attack in Gibraltar must be anticipated.

Additional intelligence indicated that the Provisionals were planning to use a radio-controlled bomb. In January 1988 Belgian police, hunting a gang of thieves responsible for a series of robberies, discovered 110 pounds of Semtex explosive and other bomb-making equipment concealed in a Dutch-registered Renault 5 in a garage in Brussels. This information was passed to police forces throughout Europe, including those of Britain where particular interest was aroused because the vehicle had also contained a VHF radio control system. Two months earlier, on 8 November 1987, Royal Signals personnel in Gibraltar had picked up an unidentified radio signal on a military frequency. Direction-finding equipment located the transmitter as being in Spain, but nothing more definite could be deduced at the time.

The first deployment by the British was a surveillance team from the Security Service. In February 1988 an Irish woman, travelling under the name of Mary Parkin with a passport stolen from the wife of a journalist, was spotted in Gibraltar on successive Tuesdays. The guard changing had, however, been temporarily suspended while the residence was being refurbished. When the ceremony was resumed on 23 February, she was observed in attendance and again the following Tuesday, 1 March. Although she has never been named publicly, the identity of the woman using the alias of Mary Parkin is known to the security forces in Northern Ireland. According to one report, she is a member of Sinn Fein's Central Committee.

By this time a detailed threat assessment had been carried out, pointing to the strong possibility of a bomb attack on the troops carrying out the guard-changing ceremony; the Secret Intelligence

Service stating its conviction that the attack would be carried out on 8 March. On 2 March the Joint Intelligence Committee in London alerted the Joint Operations Centre at the Ministry of Defence which in turn gave orders for the deployment of a 22 SAS team from the squadron then in the counter-terrorist role. Next day, led by the squadron commander and accompanied by an Explosive Ordnance Disposal (EOD) expert and two senior officers from 22 SAS and Headquarters Special Forces, the team flew to Gibraltar where it linked up with the Security Service and Gibraltar Police Special Branch personnel already there.

Sean Savage and Daniel McCann meanwhile were in Belfast, having travelled there earlier from Dublin. On 4 March the two men, again travelling under the aliases of Robert Reilly and Brendan Coyne, flew to Malaga where they arrived at 8.05 p.m. They were joined at the airport by Mairead Farrell who had flown from Dublin to Brussels under the alias of Katherine Harper.

The Spanish authorities had been briefed about the three Provisionals and given details of the aliases under which they were travelling. Farrell and her two companions were watched by officers of the Policia Nacional as they passed through the airport, but unfortunately the latter lost them when Savage and McCann departed in a taxi and Farrell disappeared among the airport crowds. Consternation ensued. The police were successful in tracing the driver of the taxi who told them that he had delivered Savage and McCann to the Hotel Florida in Fuengirola. Neither of them had checked in there and the police began the lengthy process of visiting all the hotels in the region.

The two men had covered their tracks by driving to Torremolinos where at midnight they checked into the Hotel Residencia Escandinavia for two nights under the names of Coyne and McArdle. The room had three beds and enjoyed direct access to a street at the rear of the hotel. It seems that Mairead Farrell joined her companions there because a subsequent search later revealed women's clothes and makeup, although she had not been seen by any of the hotel staff.

On Saturday 5 March, Savage rented a white Renault 5 from a local branch of Avis while Farrell made a similar booking for a second vehicle with Rent-A-Car Marbesol in Marbella. At some point during that twenty-four hours, 141 pounds of Semtex explosive were collected or delivered in a red Ford Fiesta, registration number MA 9317 AF. This vehicle had been hired from the Autoluis car hire company in Torremolinos at about midday on Thursday 3 March by an Irishman, using the name John Oakes, who had been accompanied by a woman later suspected as being Mary Parkin. On the morning of 6 March, Savage, McCann and Farrell drove to Marbella where the latter collected a white Ford Fiesta, registration number MA 2732 AJ, which she drove to a nearby multi-storey Sun car park at Edificio Marbeland where she parked in the basement alongside the red Ford Fiesta. The explosives were transferred to the white Fiesta and shortly afterwards Sean Savage set off for Gibraltar in the white Renault 5, followed by Farrell and McCann in the red Ford Fiesta.

At midnight 5/6 March a briefing had been held in Gibraltar for all the SAS, Security Service and Gibraltar Police personnel involved in the operation, code-named Flavius, to apprehend the three terrorists. This included a detailed analysis of the threat, including the strong possibility that one of the Provisionals would be carrying a radio-control device to initiate the bomb from a distance. The SAS team was also briefed on the rules of engagement which were addressed to its commander and laid down the degree of force to be used in apprehending the three terrorists and the conditions under which the troops could open fire with or without a warning. These also expressly forbade the troops from entering Spanish territory or firing on anyone in it.

By the time the three Provisionals reached Gibraltar the Security Service 'watchers' and Special Branch personnel were all in their respective positions awaiting the arrival of the three terrorists who, it was assumed, would be armed and equipped with a large car bomb. At this stage the Spanish police, who had been trailing the trio, lost track of them and all crossed the frontier undetected. Sean Savage was first spotted at 12.15 p.m. while parking his white Renault 5 in the square where the guard and regimental band formed up prior to the ceremony every Tuesday. At 2.30 p.m. a Security Service 'watcher' spotted him again in the square and shortly afterwards others reported the arrival of McCann and Farrell who had crossed on foot from La Linea, the Spanish town adjoining the frontier with the Rock. Savage was then observed walking over to the white Renault and, having unlocked the door, fiddling with something inside for several minutes.

At this juncture two pairs of SAS soldiers, armed with Browning Hi-Power 9mm pistols, were deployed. One pair, later identified in statements as Soldiers A and B, shadowed Savage while the other, Soldiers C and D, followed Farrell and McCann as they made their way to the square which they reached at 2.50 p.m. All three terrorists then walked towards the Alameda Gardens and at 3.25 p.m. returned to the square where they examined the Renault before leaving it and heading for the frontier. The EOD expert approached the car and, having examined it externally, advised that in his opinion it could contain a bomb: the car was new, but was fitted with a rusty aerial in the centre of the roof and this was of major concern to him because it indicated that the vehicle might have been modified. At 3.40 p.m. in the operation's command post, the Commissioner of the Gibraltar Police formally transferred command to the SAS team commander. The order to proceed with apprehending the three terrorists was then passed by radio to the troops on the ground.

By this time Savage, McCann and Farrell were walking towards the Spanish frontier, followed by the two pairs of SAS soldiers. Suddenly, Savage separated from the other two and began to retrace his steps towards the town, passing Soldiers A and B who continued to follow Farrell and McCann. At that moment a police car nearby switched on its siren while trying to move through the heavy traffic, causing McCann to turn his head and make eye contact with Soldier A behind him. It seems that he immediately realised that the two men were following him and, according to a statement made by one of the soldiers later, made a suspicious movement with his right arm. As he did so, fearing he might be reaching for a radio control device to initiate a bomb, both soldiers drew their pistols. Soldier A shouted a challenge before shooting McCann once in the back and then, seeing her making a grab for her handbag, shooting Farrell once in the back also. He then fired three more rounds into McCann while Soldier B fired two rounds at Farrell and five at McCann.

By this time, Savage was some 120 yards away from McCann and Farrell. Hearing the shots, he spun round and was immediately challenged by Soldier C who shouted at him to stop. According to a statement made later, Soldier C saw Savage reach for his pocket. Fearing that he was about to activate a radio control device, he drew his Browning and, pushing a woman (possibly a Security Service 'watcher') out his way, fired six rounds at Savage while Soldier D fired nine; all fifteen bullets hit their target. The entire action was over within some four seconds, by which time all three terrorists lay dead on the ground.

At 4.06 p.m., shortly after the action took place, the SAS team commander handed back control of the operation to the police commissioner. As the four SAS soldiers left the area in a police car, the bodies were searched and it was found that the three terrorists had been unarmed; later that afternoon it was discovered that the white Renault 5 did not contain a bomb.

In the early hours of the following morning, 7 March, acting on a message from the Gibraltar Police sent at 5 p.m. the previous afternoon, Spanish police in La Linea searched the town for the red Ford Fiesta. The vehicle was soon found and once again there was no sign of any explosives. Discovered in the vehicle's glove compartment, however, was a key for another car, registration number MA 2732 AJ, which was the white Ford Fiesta left in the Sun car park at Edificio Marbeland. The registration was quickly traced to Marbella where police soon located the car and the 141 pounds of Semtex concealed in its boot. The discovery of the explosives confirmed suspicions that the white Renault 5 had merely been a blocking vehicle to occupy the parking space in the square until the arrival of the car carrying the explosives.

Needless to say, the controversy surrounding the killings of Savage, McCann and Farrell totally eclipsed that previously generated by previous deaths of terrorists at the hands of the SAS in

Northern Ireland. Despite the fact that a car containing a large quantity of explosives had been found in Malaga, and that the Provisional IRA confirmed on the morning of 8 March that the three terrorists had been on a bombing mission, the fact was that they had been unarmed and the car in the square in Gibraltar had not contained a bomb. Elements of the British media took the government to task over the affair, as did the left-wing of the Labour opposition, while the Provisional IRA lost little time in portraying the three terrorists as martyrs. A highly controversial television documentary, *Death on The Rock*, was screened on 28 April and added further fuel to the flames by alleging that the four SAS soldiers had opened fire without warning and had killed the three terrorists as they lay on the ground. The programme was subsequently discredited when, during the inquest held in Gibraltar in the following September, so-called key witnesses, on whose evidence the programme had largely been based, admitted that they had lied when giving statements saying that they had observed the killings. On Friday 30 September, the inquest jury gave its majority (nine to two) verdict: lawful killing.

14 Company and the SAS troop were not the only elements of the Intelligence & Security Group contributing to successes by the security forces against the terrorists. Much of the intelligence on which successful operations were based came from the informers handled by the FRU which recruited both nationalists and loyalists.

FRU detachments reported to the TCGs responsible for their respective areas. These in turn came under the Joint Irish Section (JIS). Formed during the 1970s following the Security Service's takeover of the leading role in Northern Ireland from the Secret Intelligence Service (SIS), the JIS was responsible for all intelligence operations in the province, reporting to the Joint Intelligence Committee in London.

All information from the various intelligence units and organisations in the province ultimately arrived on the desks of the JIS which comprised a staff of senior civil servants and Security Service personnel who were based at the Army headquarters at Lisburn with ther staff being based at Stormont Castle. Security Service officers also worked closely with Special Branch, 14 Company and the FRU, liaison officers being located in the operations rooms of each.

The FRU had enjoyed a large measure of success since its formation in 1979 and had succeeded in recruiting a number of informers within some of the republican and loyalist paramilitary organisations. On many occasions, these passed information to their handlers which resulted in terrorist operations being thwarted and lives being saved. One example of this came to light on 26 January 1986 when three large Provisional IRA arms caches were uncovered by the Gardai Siochana and the Irish Army at Carrowreagh in Roscommon and two locations near Sligo. They contained a total of 120 AK-47 assault rifles and 18,000 rounds of ammunition, at that time the largest discovery of arms in the Irish Republic. The find had come about as a result of information supplied to the Irish authorities by their counterparts north of the border.

The source was an informer working for the FRU, an individual named Frank Hegarty who was a member of the quartermaster's department of the Provisional IRA's Derry Brigade. He had been recruited in 1980 after the FRU had been tipped-off about his passion for gambling, a weakness known to make potential informers susceptible to financial enticement. He was kept under surveillance for some weeks and eventually a meeting, to all appearances by chance, took place between him and a member of the unit who befriended the gregarious Hegarty. Further meetings took place and only when the FRU was sure of its man was an approach made. He accepted and thus became a paid informer.

Hegarty's handlers learned from him that his gambling addiction had cost him his position with the Provisionals as the latter were well aware of it and thus of the possibility of his being enticed into becoming an informer. In order to return to IRA service, he would have to convince his former superiors that he was cured of his affliction. During the following months, he succeeded in doing so, assisted by the fact that his FRU handlers maintained control over the money paid to him, and was eventually readmitted to the ranks of the Derry Brigade where he once again assumed his position in the quartermaster's department, being responsible for the storage of the brigade's arms.

During the following four years, Hegarty passed information on a regular basis to his handlers who met him at a variety of prearranged rendezvous points. In 1985, however, he and other informers supplied information which indicated that a huge consignment of arms had arrived from Libya, having been unloaded from a ship off the coast of south-west Ireland and subsequently stored in large underground bunkers in the Irish Republic. Large quantities from this consignment were intended for the Provisionals' Belfast and Derry Brigades and Hegarty was involved in the movement of weapons and explosives to three caches near the border.

Shortly after the signing of the Anglo-Irish Agreement in November 1985, the British took the decision to pass the information concerning the arms caches to the Irish authorities as a sign of their commitment to the accord. This caused consternation within the FRU as such a move could only place Hegarty in great danger. Without delay, he was spirited away and flown to England where he was accommodated in a safe house in the town of Sittingbourne, in Kent. During this period, he was debriefed by members of the various intelligence and security agencies.

Immediately following the discovery of the arms, the Provisionals had launched an internal investigation to track down the source of the leak. It was not long before the finger of suspicion was pointed at Hegarty who had disappeared on the day before the caches were uncovered. The Provisionals knew, however, that there was every likelihood that, like many people from Northern Ireland who leave the province, he would eventually be plagued by homesickness and that it was possible that he would return of his own volition. They thus decided to play a waiting game.

Hegarty was permitted to telephone members of his family, among them his common-law wife and his mother, maintaining that he was working in England. The latter had meanwhile been approached by Martin McGuinness, the senior republican leader in Londonderry and allegedly the former Chief of Staff of the IRA Army Council, who had known the Hegarty family for many years. He allegedly promised her that no harm would come to her son if the latter wished to return to Northern Ireland. By this time, Hegarty was indeed suffering badly from homesickness and possibly regretting what he had done. The alleged message was passed to him and, unlike other informers who had ignored similar promises allegedly made by McGuinness, he decided to return home to his family.

In early May 1986 Hegarty went back to Londonderry. As he found to his cost, his faith in Martin McGuinness was allegedly grievously misplaced. Two weeks after his arrival he was abducted by the Provisional IRA, subsequently being interrogated and 'court-martialled'. On 25 May, the RUC was informed of a body lying by a road near Castlederg in County Tyrone. It was that of Frank Hegarty; bound hand and foot with his eyes taped shut, he had been shot in the head. In a statement issued following the murder, the Provisional IRA alleged that he had been a member of an Official IRA ASU which in 1974 had been responsible for the deaths of two Catholics, John Dunn and Cecilia Byrne, who worked at Ebrington Barracks in Londonderry. They were killed by a 50-pound bomb, attached to Dunn's car, which blew up as they travelled through the Waterside district of the city. The Provisionals maintained that the security forces had known of Hegarty's part in the bombing and had used it to force him to work as an informer.

According to one report, the Provisionals subsequently admitted that Frank Hegarty had caused serious damage to their organisation. There is no doubt that the removal of the arms and explosives resulted in the saving of a large number of lives and prevented massive damage to property.

Controversy has surrounded much of the FRU's operations in Northern Ireland, in particular that involving Brian Nelson, a former member of The Black Watch who, after leaving the Army in 1969, had settled in Northern Ireland and joined the UVF. In 1975 he had been tried and convicted for unlawful imprisonment of a Catholic man and possession of a revolver, being sentenced to seven years imprisonment. Released after three years, he had joined the UDA and by 1980 had been appointed an intelligence officer in the organisation. In late 1985, however, he offered his services to the security forces as an informer. According to Nicholas Davies, author of *Ten-Thirty-Three*, an in-depth and highly revealing account of Nelson's work as an FRU agent, his motive apparently was one of revenge after the attempted rape of his wife by a member of the UVF and the subsequent refusal by the UDA to discipline the individual concerned.

The Army, which possessed few intelligence assets within the loyalist organisations at the time, accepted Nelson's offer and thereafter he had been handled by the FRU. In April 1986, however, he and his family left Northern Ireland and moved to Munich, in West Germany, where he had obtained a job. In 1986, he was approached by his FRU handlers who had need of his services due to the escalation of violence and sectarian killings on the part of the UDA and other loyalist factions following the signing of the Anglo-Irish Agreement in November 1985. Under pressure from the JIS to obtain information on UDA and UVF intentions and plans, the FRU contacted Nelson in Germany and a meeting subsequently took place in September, at a Security Service safe house in London, between him and his former handlers. He revealed that he was still in contact with the UDA and agreed to remain in touch, passing on any information.

At the beginning of October Nelson contacted the FRU, informing his handlers that he had been approached by the UDA which had asked him to travel to South Africa to arrange a deal for the supply of arms. He subsequently flew to London where he was briefed by his FRU handlers, accompanied by two members of the Security Service, who provided him with £500 in cash. As described in Chapter 2, Nelson spent three weeks in Johannesburg, arranging the deal, under the watchful eyes of the SIS which monitored his activities.

Following his trip to South Africa, Nelson returned to Germany. By now the Army intelligence apparatus in Northern Ireland was so keen to recruit him that they took the unprecedented step of sending two FRU personnel to Munich to persuade him to return to Northern Ireland and work for the unit. Nelson readily agreed and in January

1987 returned to Belfast with his family. The deal struck with the FRU included provision of a house, a car and a weekly payment of £300 cash. In addition, a job as a freelance driver was arranged for him with a loyalist-owned taxi firm in the city. In order not to arouse any suspicions among his relations and friends as to his new-found wealth and sudden return to Northern Ireland, it was decided that he should win a £20,000 prize on a German lottery. This was arranged by the West German intelligence service, the Bundesnachtrichtendienst (BND), at the request of the SIS.

On his return to the province, Nelson was welcomed back into the UDA which, in recognition of his successful arms deal in South Africa, promoted him to chief intelligence officer. At a single stroke, the FRU had an agent placed near the top of the principal loyalist organisation.

Shortly after his return to Belfast, he was given a series of conducted tours of republican areas by the FRU, with establishments frequented by the Provisionals being pointed out to him. His task would be to provide information on Provisional IRA activists, in particular gunmen, bombers and others directly involved with acts of terrorism. In addition he would be expected to provide similar information on the UDA and its paramilitary wings, the UVF and UFF. Thereafter he met his handlers frequently; on some occasions he would ask the FRU for information on a particular individual and this would be provided in the form of highly classified 'P-Cards', containing full details of suspects, and computer print-outs.

In addition Nelson was provided with a computer by the FRU and given help by military computer specialists in establishing a database. He would eventually have the details of almost 500 people stored on it, much of the information having been supplied by the FRU and, as Nicholas Davies points out, apparently having originated from Crucible and Vengeful, two of the top secret intelligence computer systems operated by the security forces in the province.

Nelson was also supplied with the order of battle of the Provisional IRA's Belfast Brigade, together with full details of individuals, their addresses, vehicles, families and friends, as well as known safe houses. These were accompanied by similar information on the IRA's

Army Council, including details of Gerry Adams and Martin McGuinness, as well as its Northern Command. Documentary information was accompanied by photographs of suspects, many taken covertly by 14 Company and the RUC's E4A surveillance unit. Such was the quality and quantity of information supplied to Nelson that his standing within the UDA was increasingly enhanced. In return, he supplied the FRU with a wealth of intelligence on republicans, all of which was of high quality. He was well equipped to do so as by the end of 1987 he was in possession of databases which were rivalled only by those of the RUC and the intelligence branch at the Army headquarters at Lisburn.

Within a few weeks of Nelson taking up his post as chief intelligence officer of the UDA, however, loyalist gunmen had shot dead a Catholic named Dermot Hackett who was killed on 23 May while driving his bread van along the road from Omagh to Drumquin in County Tyrone. During the following five months, four more Catholics were murdered, the first two being taxi drivers Edward Campbell and Mickey Power, who were killed at the wheels of their cabs on 3 July and 23 August respectively. Next was Patrick Hamill who lived in Forfar Street, off the Springfield Road in West Belfast. He was killed by two gunmen who burst into his home, shooting him in the head and chest. His death was followed by that of Jim Meighan, a twenty-two-year-old who was shot dead in front of his fiancée on 20 September. On 9 October in West Belfast, pensioner Francisco Notarantino, a long-standing member of the republican movement, was shot dead by four UDA gunmen as he lay in bed with his wife at their home in Whitecliff Parade in the Ballymurphy area of the city.

It did not take long for Nelson's handlers to realise that information provided by them had been used to target the individuals concerned and they challenged him on the matter. On each occasion, however, he denied having had any prior knowledge that they were to be killed and shrugged aside his handlers' warnings about the Provisional IRA retaliating with tit-for-tat murders.

A sixth loyalist shooting, in July 1987, was unsuccessful and had major repercussions. On that occasion the intended target was a Sinn

Fein Belfast City councillor named Alex Maskey who was a well-known, much respected figure living in the Andersonstown area of West Belfast. Maskey's details, in the form of a P-Card, were provided to Nelson by the FRU and some three weeks later he was shot three times in the stomach at the door of his home by a UDA gunman posing as the driver of a taxi calling to collect him. Fortunately, due to prompt emergency surgery at the Royal Victoria Hospital, he survived. According to Nicholas Davies, Nelson's handlers not only advised him on where to obtain a sign identical to that used by a republican-owned West Belfast taxi company but also imposed an exclusion zone on the area where Maskey lived, ensuring that no RUC or Army patrols would be in the area. The RUC Special Branch investigated the attack and loyalist informers reported suspicions that the attack had been planned by Nelson, hinting that he had connections with elements of Army intelligence. This had caused alarm within Special Branch as monitoring the UDA was its exclusive preserve. Senior FRU officers were asked to check whether any of their personnel were handling UDA informers but in the event made no effort to do so.

By mid-1987 it had become apparent to Nelson's handlers that while he was happy to provide them with information on Provisionals and republican activists, he was reluctant to supply details of the UDA. Requests for information on the organisation, its order of battle, names of commanders and cell leaders, details of weapons and explosives stocks, locations of weapons caches and addresses of safe houses all went unheeded. Moreover, he was not passing on details of loyalist attacks before they occurred. The FRU was well aware, however, as was the JIS, that he was their only asset at a high level inside the UDA and that the information he provided on the Provisionals was of high quality. Moreover, the information supplied to him by the FRU ultimately resulted in loyalist attacks which exerted considerable pressure on the Provisional IRA, reducing its capability to carry out killings and bomb attacks in the province and on the British mainland, a situation which the JIS and ultimately the British government were keen to maintain.

Eventually, however, the situation came to a head and Nelson was forced to agree to supply details of UDA attacks before they took place. At the same time, it was suggested that he should establish his own force of agents from within the loyalist community to provide further intelligence on known members of the Provisional IRA and suspected republican activists. Nelson agreed with alacrity to this idea and soon had a band of forty loyalists working for him.

In June 1987, Nelson informed his handlers that the UDA was going to mount an attack on Gerry Adams; as mentioned earlier in this chapter, it had previously done so three years earlier in March 1984. On this occasion it would be carried out as Adams arrived for a weekly meeting of the Northern Ireland Housing Executive which he was in the habit of attending. Nelson provided full details of the plan which involved a member of the UDA, equipped with a radio, being positioned in a car parked outside the Executive's offices, ready to signal Adams's arrival to two men on a motorcycle nearby. The latter would time their arrival to coincide with the republican leader and his bodyguard stepping out of his chauffeur-driven car which was known to be armoured. The pillion passenger would open fire on both of them with a submachine-gun before he and his accomplice made good their escape.

Plans were put into effect immediately to thwart the UDA attack which was due to take place two days later. On the day in question the square outside the Housing Executive offices was staked out by members of 14 Company and twelve officers of E4A while uniformed troops and police officers were deployed throughout the area. Frustrated, the UDA called off the attack. Two weeks later, Nelson reported that a further attempt would be carried out. A similar operation was mounted by the Army and RUC to prevent it and once again the UDA was forced to call it off. Several months later, further plans were laid by the UDA to murder Adams using a limpet mine to be attached to the roof of his car by a motorcycle team drawing up alongside at a traffic lights. Eventually, however, they were abandoned.

In January 1988, the UDA's long-awaited arms consignment from South Africa was landed on the coast of County Down. Prior to its arrival, Nelson had discussed it with one of his handlers. According to a journal which he later wrote and which was obtained by the BBC *Panorama* programme in 1992, the latter told him that in order to avoid any suspicion that would be caused by the arms being seized, the landing would be permitted to take place without interception. Approximately two-thirds of the weapons disappeared into loyalist arms caches. That same month, however, a senior member of the UDA, a former British Army paratrooper named Davy Payne, was arrested near Portadown while transporting sixty-one AK-47s, RPG-7 rockets with launchers, 150 grenades and 30 Browning pistols; it transpired that these comprised the major part of the quantity allocated to the organisation. On 16 March, at the Milltown Cemetery in Belfast, a loyalist named Michael Stone attacked republican mourners attending the funeral of the three Provisional IRA terrorists killed in Gibraltar by the SAS. He did so in retaliation for the IRA bombing at Enniskillen on 8 November 1987, using a Browning pistol and Russian RGD-5 grenades which were among those purchased by the UDA from South Africa. Six years later, AK-47 rifles from the same consignment were used in an attack on a shop in Belfast's Ormeau Road in which five people died, as described in Chapter 3.

January 1988 saw the start of more killings by the UDA of Catholics who had been targeted by Nelson with information provided by the FRU. The first was Billy Kane who was murdered on the 15th by two gunmen who burst into his family's home and shot him dead as he lay asleep in the sitting room. On the following day UDA gunmen killed a man walking along the Ormeau Road in Belfast with his fiancée in the belief he was a Catholic; he was in fact a Protestant and a captain in the UDR named Timothy Armstrong. In May, two more Catholics fell victim to UDA gunmen: Seamus Murray and Terry McDaid. In the case of the latter, it was once again a case of mistaken identity. The intended victim was McDaid's brother Declan whom the UDA had been keeping under surveillance for some months.

In July 1988 the UDA targeted Brendan Davidson, a senior officer of the Provisional IRA who a year earlier had survived an attack, being wounded four times in the arm, while visiting a betting shop in Belfast's Cromac Road. Five years earlier, he had been arrested and tried on the evidence of a supergrass but had been acquitted. According to Nicholas Davies, Nelson consulted his FRU handlers who suggested that the UDA hit-team impersonate RUC officers in order to persuade him to open the door of his highly secure home. The FRU would meanwhile ensure that no RUC or Army patrols were in the area by imposing an exclusion order on the area. On 25 July two UDA gunmen, dressed in RUC uniforms, called at Davidson's flat in Friendly Way. As the latter opened his front door, they opened fire with submachine-guns, wounding Davidson in the head and stomach. Rushed to Belfast City Hospital, he died shortly afterwards.

The next victim was Gerard Slane, a suspected member of the Provisional IRA who had been convicted and imprisoned dring the 1970s for possession of a rifle and ammunition. The UDA believed that he had been involved in the killing of Billy Quee, a Protestant and member of the UDA who had been shot on 7 September by gunmen of the Irish People's Liberation Organisation (IPLO), a left-wing splinter group of the Provisional IRA, who believed that he had been involved in the deaths of a number of Catholics. Like many activists, Slane moved frequently between different addresses and only visited his home infrequently in order to avoid being tracked down by loyalists or the security forces. He made the mistake, however, of regularly visiting a bar known to be one of his haunts where he was spotted. After four days of keeping him under surveillance, the UDA struck and in the early hours of 23 September three gunmen burst into his house and shot him dead in front of his wife.

In November, another case of mistaken identity resulted in the killing of the brother of an intended victim despite Nelson's handlers emphasising to him that careful checks had to be carried out beforehand. In this case, they themselves checked on the intended target, a Sinn Fein councillor named Francis McNally. While he was a known republican, there was no evidence to suggest that he was in any way connected with the Provisional IRA. On 24 November three gunmen arrived at his home in Coagh, County Tyrone, and opened fire through a window at a man sitting in the kitchen, killing him instantly. It was not long before they learned that they had killed McNally's brother, Phelim.

While the deaths of hard-line Provisionals such as Brendan Davidson were undoubtedly welcomed by the FRU, those of Catholics who had no connections with republican terrorist groups caused grave concern and Nelson's handlers remonstrated with him on more than one occasion but apparently to little avail. Moreover, their apparently increasing problems with him were compounded by his heavy drinking and drug-taking.

The killing of individuals targeted by Nelson continued into 1989. On 18 January a Catholic named Ian Catney was gunned down by the UVF at his mother's shop in the Smithfield market area of central Belfast. Two years earlier, he had survived an attack by INLA gunmen, being wounded in the face, hip and leg. A week later, on a building site on the Knockmore Road in Lisburn, a Protestant named David Dornan was killed by UDA gunmen in the mistaken belief that he was a Catholic. Once again, it was faulty intelligence which had resulted in the killing of a totally innocent man. On this occasion Nelson had not advised the FRU that an attack was to take place and thus no exclusion zone had been placed on the area. Troops and police, supported by helicopters, were swiftly on the scene. The two gunmen had been seen running towards a nearby loyalist housing estate which was quickly sealed off. Shortly afterwards, four men were arrested and taken away for questioning. Nine years later, in December 1987, a man was eventually tried and convicted for the murder of David Dornan and four others, receiving five life sentences.

The following month saw the murder by the UDA of a prominent lawyer, Patrick Finucane. Two years earlier, Nelson had asked his handlers for information on Finucane who was well known for representing Catholics and republicans. Among those whom he had defended were the convicted terrorist and hunger striker Bobby Sands and the widow of Gervaise McKerr who, as mentioned earlier in this chapter, was shot dead by members of the RUC HMSU in November 1982. Nelson's handlers had attempted to discourage him from targeting Finucane and insisted that they should be given warning of any planned attack on him. Four months later, in September 1987, Nelson had reported that the UDA had decided to proceed with an attack on Finucane as he left the court in the Crumlin Road and headed for North Belfast. The FRU immediately informed the TCG which decided that measures should be taken to protect Finucane. Police and troops were drafted into the area while members of 14 Company and E4A were deployed to keep him under close observation. The UDA was forced to abort its operation.

At the same time, however, more attention began to be paid to Finucane's contacts with known senior members of the Provisional IRA and Sinn Fein activists. He was kept under close surveillance and there were increasing suspicions that he was involved in some way with the Provisionals. In March 1988 Nelson reported that the UDA was preparing again to move against Finucane. Once again, the TCG took measures to frustrate the loyalists' plans by ensuring that a heavy RUC and Army presence prevented any attack being mounted. At the same time, Finucane was warned of the threat against him and thereafter was accompanied by armed bodyguards.

On the evening of 12 February 1989, however, the UDA finally succeeded. Three gunmen succeeded in approaching his house unseen and entered via the front door which was unlocked. Seconds later Patrick Finucane lay dead while his wife had been wounded in the leg. The three terrorists meanwhile escaped in a waiting vehicle. The repercussions from Finucane's murder were considerable and far-reaching, and the UDA's action was condemned throughout the whole of Ireland and Britain.

Further killings by the UDA took place during the following months. One of them, however, was ultimately to prove the undoing of Brian Nelson and the FRU. On the night of 25 August a Provisional IRA intelligence officer, Loughlin Maginn, was gunned down by two men who fired through the window of the sitting-room of his home in Rathfriland, County Down. Wounded, he fled upstairs but was pursued by the two gunmen who entered the house to finish him off. The FRU had given details of Maginn, including a P-Card and photographs, to Nelson who had subsequently targeted him. Jubilant at having scored such a successful blow against the Provisional IRA, the UDA published a statement saying that it was confident of eliminating only republican terrorists as its intelligence was of such high quality. This was met with considerable scepticism, in the face of which the organisation reacted by producing a copy of a classified Army file in which Maginn was identified as a Provisional IRA intelligence officer.

The immediate result was that the government announced an official inquiry into the ensuing allegations of collusion between members of the security forces and loyalist paramilitary groups for the purpose of murdering republicans. Subsequently, on 15 September, it was announced that the inquiry would be headed by Deputy Chief Constable John Stevens of the Cambridgeshire Police.

There was alarm within the military intelligence community in the province and in particular the Security Service which, through the JIS as well as its permanent presence in the FRU operations room, was aware of all that had occurred with Nelson. Its response was to cast itself adrift from the FRU. Meanwhile, the latter decided to scale down the amount of information it was still passing to Nelson.

The Stevens inquiry team concentrated on investigating any leakage of intelligence from the RUC, including the Special Branch, and the UDR. It was not long, however, before Brian Nelson was mentioned and the team decided that he should be questioned. This caused alarm within the FRU and those elements of Army intelligence which knew of Nelson's activities. At one point, consideration was given to the idea of removing him from Northern Ireland and indeed, when it was learned that he was to be arrested on 11 January 1990, he was despatched on the day before to the British mainland in the company of an FRU handler.

On the day of Nelson's departure, a fire broke out in the locked offices of the Stevens inquiry team at the heavily guarded RUC barracks at Carrickfergus. Four of its officers happened to arrive as the fire was blazing and attempted to activate the buidling's fire alarm but it failed to work. Attempts to telephone for assistance also proved fruitless as the line was dead. By the time the local fire brigade arrived, most of the team's files and documentation had been destroyed. Stevens and his officers were convinced that the fire had been deliberately set and was part of a conspiracy to prevent their carrying out their investigation. This belief was reinforced by the results of the RUC investigation into the blaze which failed to explain the failure of the fire alarm system, the intruder alarms and the telephone.

A week after the fire, Brian Nelson returned to Northern Ireland and was immediately arrested and brought in for questioning. Despite earlier warnings to say nothing, he soon began to provide full details of his relationship with the FRU, naming his handlers and providing the Stevens team with details of those who had been targeted and killed by the UDA.

Stevens then turned his attention to the FRU itself, questioning those who had been involved with Nelson and listening to the tapes of conversations between him and his handlers. When his officers subsequently requested that all files relating to Nelson be handed over, however, this caused alarm at very high levels and it was only after a lengthy dispute, which ended with Stevens's deputy threatening to arrest military officers, that the Army gave in and surrendered the files.

In May 1990, Stevens produced an initial report which stated that collusion between the security forces and loyalist paramilitary organisations had not been widespread but had comprised leaking of classified documents which had been concerned with republicans suspected of terrorist activities. As a result of this report a total of 59 individuals, thirty-four loyalists and twenty-five serving members of the UDR, were arrested. Subsequently, twenty-three of them faced charges ranging from unauthorised communication of documents to others, unlawful possession of them, and unauthorised collection and recording of classified information.

A few months later, Stevens produced a second, very damning report which stated that the FRU had colluded with the UDA by assisting it in targeting members of the Provisional IRA. It was submitted to the Director of Public Prosecutions in Northern Ireland before being passed to the Attorney General. Eventually, after due deliberation, the decision was taken to prosecute Brian Nelson. No members of the FRU, however, would face charges.

During 1991, lengthy discussions took place between the Director of Public Prosecutions, Deputy Chief Constable John Stevens, Army intelligence and others over the offences with which Nelson should be charged. He himself was consulted and after some months of legal negotiations agreed to plead guilty to five charges of conspiracy to murder, fourteen charges of accumulating information likely to assist acts of terrorism and one of possessing a submachine-gun. He was advised that he would face a sentence of ten years which, after taking into account remission and time spent on remand, would mean that he would be freed in 1994. In return, following his release, he would be relocated anywhere of his choice and be provided with a house and a lump sum of over £75,000.

Just over a year after Nelson's arrest another Army intelligence agent inside the UDA, Noel Walker, disappeared. It later transpired that he had been taken into 'protective custody'. A third, Martin McDowell, vanished in a similar fashion in September 1992. Shortly afterwards, the RUC uncovered a small arms cache near his home; among its contents were a number of weapons from the South African consignment of 1988.

Brian Nelson was brought to trial on 22 January 1992, the trial itself taking place over four days during a thirteen-day period. As agreed, he pleaded guilty to all charges. Fifteen, including two of murder, were immediately dropped, the second day of the trial being taken up by the Crown counsel in a lengthy defence of the decision to do so. Only one witness was called by the defence: an Army intelligence officer, identified as Colonel 'J', who gave evidence on Nelson's service as an FRU agent and provided a plea of mitigation on his behalf. On 3 February, judgment was given by Lord Justice Kelly who sentenced Nelson to a total of 101 years imprisonment, each sentence to run concurrently, in effect reducing it to ten years. Four and a half years later, in late 1996, Brian Nelson was released from prison.

The late 1980s meanwhile saw continuing activity on the part of the other elements of the Intelligence & Security Group. On 30 June 1988 elements of the SAS troop were waiting in ambush as a three-man Provisional IRA ASU attacked an RUC station in North Queen Street, Belfast, firing a Soviet-manufactured RPG-7 rocket-propelled grenade from the vehicle's open roof while at the same time opening fire with an M-16 rifle. The SAS team inside the building opened fire, but the terrorists escaped, abandoning their vehicle and leaving behind the rocket-launcher and more rockets. Tragically, a passing taxi-driver was hit in the neck by an SAS bullet, which had already passed through the terrorist vehicle, and died three days later from his wounds.

Two months later the Provisionals encountered the SAS again. On 30 August Gerard Harte, the commander of the East Tyrone Brigade, and his brother, were killed during an attempt to murder a lorry driver who was a part-time member of the UDR. The plan had been compromised and an SAS soldier had taken the place of the intended victim.

Almost twelve months later, members of 14 Company were involved in a shooting incident in the Ardoyne area of Belfast. Two members of the UVF, Brian Robinson and Davy McCullough, rode up on a motorcycle beside a Catholic man, James McKenna, who was standing outside a shop. Robinson, riding pillion, fired eleven shots from a 9mm pistol, killing McKenna outright. The two men rode away, but were pursued by four members of 14 Company in two unmarked cars. The leading vehicle managed to ram the motorcycle and one of its crew, a female operator, opened fire on Robinson at close range, hitting him four times: once in the back and wrist, and twice in the head. His empty pistol was found lying a short distance away. McCullough was captured and subsequently tried and convicted of James McKenna's murder, receiving a life sentence.

The beginning of the following year saw another shooting incident in which elements of 14 Company were involved. On 13 January, members of the unit were in the area of the Falls Road and Whiterock Road on a surveillance operation when a robbery took place at a bookmaker's, Sean Graham's, on the corner of the two roads. Two armed men wearing balaclavas, later identified as Peter Thompson and Edward Hale, ran out of the shop and headed for a getaway car parked nearby. As they did so, they came under fire from 14 Company operators, each being hit between six and twelve times; the driver of the car, John McNeill, was also shot and killed. When the bodies were searched, it was found that Thompson and Hale had been armed with replica weapons and that McNeill had been unarmed. All three were Catholics from West Belfast and were members of a group calling itself the 'Hole in the Wall Gang'. It was subsequently claimed that a fourth man escaped death by remaining inside the bookmaker's shop and mingling with punters.

Three months later, on 18 April, a member of the Irish People's Liberation Organisation was shot dead by an SAS patrol. Martin Corrigan had dedicated himself to killing off-duty RUC officers and part-time members of the UDR to avenge the murder of his father by a loyalist gunman, which he had witnessed eight years previously. He had already killed three and was in the process of entering the home of his intended fourth victim when he was ambushed by the SAS and shot dead.

On the night of 9 October 1990, the area of Loughgall in County Tyrone was once again the scene of an SAS action when two well-known Provisionals were intercepted and shot dead at a barn near the village. Acting on a tip-off, a five-man SAS team was dropped off and moved to an OP near a barn. Just before midnight, one of the team watched two men entering the barn, followed shortly afterwards by a third. A few minutes later, two men emerged, carrying weapons, and headed towards the team which opened fire, killing both men who were subsequently identified as Desmond Grew and Martin McCaughey. Drew, who was suspected of involvement in sixteen murders, had formed and trained the ASU responsible for attacks on British servicemen in Germany and the murders of two Australians just over four months earlier, as described in Chapter 3. He had also been wanted for questioning by German police in connection with the murder of RAF Corporal

Maheshkumar Islania and his six-month-old daughter in October of the previous year.

Just over a month later, on 12 November, a member of the INLA also met an untimely end at the hands of the SAS. Alexander Patterson, who had been suspected of involvement in the deaths of several people, including women and children, was killed during an attack with an automatic weapon on the home of a part-time member of the UDR in the village of Victoria Bridge. Prior warning of the attack had been received beforehand and teams from 14 Company's North Det and the SAS troop were deployed. At about midnight two cars drove past the reservist's home and shots were fired from the second one. The SAS team returned fire and the vehicle sped off, but crashed into a tree shortly afterwards. Its occupants fled, but one of them, Patterson, was shot and killed. An automatic weapon was reportedly found in the vehicle.

A lull of some eight months followed before the next action in which members of the Intelligence & Security Group were involved in a firefight with terrorists. On 3 June 1991, acting on information received about a plan to murder a part-time member of the UDR, an operation was mounted in the village of Coagh in County Tyrone, involving members of 14 Company and the SAS troop with support from the RUC HMSU. A covert reconnaissance of the area was carried out before dawn and an SAS ambush team inserted; meanwhile, an SAS soldier took the place of the intended victim. At just before 7 a.m. a car, which had been hijacked in Moneymore the previous evening, drew alongside the UDR reservist's car and three Provisionals took aim at it. Before they could open fire, however, the ambush was initiated and the three terrorists were subjected to a heavy volume of fire. As they tried to escape, their car exploded and all three perished. They were subsequently identified as three well-known members of an East Tyrone ASU: Tony Doris, Lawrence McNally and Peter Ryan, the latter having been responsible for the deaths of a number of off-duty members of the RUC. Forensic examination of rifles found in the car revealed that one had been used in the murders on 7 March 1989 of three Protestants at a garage in

Coagh, not far from the scene of the ambush. The same weapon had also been used in another killing in Coagh two months before the ambush, on 9 April, when a Protestant named Derek Ferguson had been gunned down in front of his two sons by two Provisional IRA gunmen who broke into his home.

Nine months later, four more Provisionals fell to the guns of the SAS troop. On 16 February 1992, an attack was carried out on the RUC station at Coalisland, in County Tyrone, by a four-man ASU armed with three Kalashnikov AK-47 assault rifles and a .50 calibre (12.7mm) heavy machine-gun mounted on the back of a hijacked truck. Shortly afterwards the four men, Patrick Vincent, Sean O'Farrell, Peter Clancy and Kevin O'Donnell, were ambushed and shot dead by an SAS patrol in the car park of a church in the village of Clonoe.

The second half of the 1990s saw further successes by the Intelligence & Security Group in apprehending terrorists. According to Toby Harnden in his book, *Bandit Country*, an in-depth study of the IRA in South Armagh, during the period from September 1994 to mid-1996, a number of robberies of post offices by the Provisional IRA took place in the county. 14 Company was tasked with mounting surveillance on those suspected as being the culprits and eventually pinpointed a barn where a search revealed a rifle hidden under bales of hay; forensic tests revealed that it had been used in an attack on security force helicopters in Crossmaglen. A camera was placed inside the barn to keep the weapon under surveillance.

In June, a four-man SAS patrol was tasked with laying an ambush at the barn and shortly afterwards three men appeared in a stolen van. When the troops moved in to arrest them the three men, subsequently identified as Patrick Murphy, Stephen Murphy and Brendan Lennon, attempted to reverse away, but the soldiers opened fire, shooting out the vehicle's tyres before seizing its occupants.

Nine months later, the security forces apparently received a tip-off, thought to have come from a Special Branch informer in the Provisional IRA's South Tyrone Brigade, that the RUC station at Coalisland was once again about to be the target of a major attack.

Troops of the Intelligence & Security Group were tasked with intercepting it, but in the event it proved to be somewhat smaller than anticipated. On the night of 26 March three men appeared near the station and a small bomb was allegedly thrown, blowing a hole in the perimeter fence. Immediately after the device exploded, the troops fired four shots and wounded two of the men. During the firing, however, Father Seamus Rice, a Catholic priest, narrowly escaped injury when his passing car was hit by bullets. All three men were apprehended by the troops, but as the arrests were being carried out, an angry crowd of some 200 local residents gathered at the scene; a confrontation developed and RUC officers were forced to fire baton rounds to disperse the crowd.

The two wounded men were taken to the hospital at Dungannon, County Tyrone. One was subsequently identified as Gareth Doris, whose cousin Tony Doris had been shot dead during the SAS troop ambush operation in Coagh in June 1991. He was subsequently transferred to a hospital in Belfast where he was charged with attempted murder and causing an explosion. It appears that the other man meanwhile had escaped from the hospital in Dungannon and succeeded in having himself driven across the border where he was admitted to hospital in Dundalk, County Louth. On Tuesday 1 April, although still in need of further treatment, he discharged himself, but was arrested by the Gardai Siochana at the request of the RUC. Two days later, however, he was released without charge and returned to hospital for further treatment.

Two days after the attack at Coalisland, the Provisional IRA sniper team which had killed Lance Bombardier Stephen Restorick some six weeks earlier with its .50 calibre Barrett sniper rifle, as described in Chapter 5, struck again. During the evening of 29 March, it occupied a house in Forkhill and at 11.40 p.m. fired on a patrol of the 1st Battalion Welsh Guards as it left the base on foot for a patrol of the area, wounding one of two RUC officers accompanying it. Within minutes the sniper, Michael Caraher, and his two accomplices, Seamus McArdle and Martin Mines, had disappeared in their car over the border into the Irish Republic.

There had been suspicions for some time as to the identities of the members of the sniper team and for some months 14 Company had been involved in carrying out surveillance on them. The operation covered a wide area of South Armagh and the unit was forced to deploy considerable resources and manpower in watching and recording the movements of all the suspects. Its efforts eventually bore fruit, however, and a farm on the Cregganduff Road was pinpointed as being the team's base.

As recounted by Toby Harnden, the decision was taken to set a trap for the sniper team and TCG (South) tasked 14 Company with mounting surveillance prior to the SAS troop carrying out an operation to arrest the terrorists. This proved successful and on Monday 7 April Caraher, McArdle, Mines and a fourth man, Bernard McGinn, who had also taken part in the attack in which Lance Bombardier Restorick had been killed, were followed to a farm on the Creggan-duff Road. There the four men remained for several hours as they waited for a call on a mobile telephone notifying them that an Army patrol had been deployed. No such call came and it was not until the evening of 9 April, when local supporters had reported the presence of Welsh Guards patrols in the area of Silverbridge, that Caraher was observed arriving at the farm in a vehicle towing a livestock trailer.

Next morning McArdle collected McGinn from nearby Castle-blaney and dropped him at a cross-roads from where he could watch for security force patrols. McArdle then disappeared, but returned thirty minutes later with Caraher in the same Mazda car from which the latter had shot Lance Bombardier Restorick; it had been resprayed blue since that occasion. After collecting the armoured steel shield and fitting it into the rear of the vehicle, the three men returned to the farm where they waited for a call from one of a number of scout teams notifying them of a suitable target.

Unknown to them, however, two eight-man teams of the SAS troop were already in position in two vans parked near Cashel Lough Upper. Other members of the troop, together with operators of 14 Company, were also deployed in the area and helicopters with a quick-reaction force aboard were on standby. Having received a message from the operation's command post at Besbrook Mill, the two vans moved off towards Crosmaglen and the Cregganduff Road. As they turned into the farm, however, they were spotted by Bernard McGinn who ran to warn the others. The SAS teams deployed swiftly from their vehicles and, charging into the barn, seized McArdle, Mines and McGinn as they attempted to flee. The three men attempted to put up a fight, but were soon overpowered and hand-cuffed. Caraher meanwhile had escaped and was sprinting along a hedgerow pursued by two SAS soldiers who shortly afterwards found him hiding in a gorse bush. Frogmarched back to the farm, he joined his three accomplices and the farm's owner who had also been arrested. All were handcuffed and covered in forensic shrouds. Shortly afterwards, members of the RUC HMSU landed in a heli-copter and took charge of the five men.

Next day a thorough search of the farm was carried out by the RUC. Inside a hidden compartment under the floor of the livestock trailer were found the Barrett 90 .50 sniper rifle, an AKM assault rifle, a pair of ear defenders, fifty four rounds of ammunition, a quantity of spent cartridge cases and other items. A check on the Mazda 626 parked in the farmyard revealed that it had been stolen in Castle-blaney four months previously and that its registration plates bore the number of an identical vehicle belonging to an individual named Declan McCann, living in Castleblaney, whose mobile telephone had previously been linked to individuals implicated in the Provisional IRA bombings in Manchester in June 1996. Subsequent forensic examination of Michael Caraher's boots showed that the soles matched perfectly footmarks on the roof of a dog kennel at the house in Forkhill; he had rested his feet on it while aiming his rifle during the attack on the Welsh Guards patrol on the night of 29 March. Seamus McArdle's fingerprints matched those found in the wake of the London Docklands bombing in February 1996.

Ultimately, however, it was the confessions of Bernard McGinn during the days following his arrest that provided full details of the sniper team's operations. He also supplied information on the South Armagh Brigade attacks in Northern Ireland and England, including its involvement in bombings on the mainland since the early 1990s. Later, however, he was to retract his statements.

In March 1999, all four members of the sniper team were brought to trial, being charged with a number of offences. McGinn was convicted and sentenced to life imprisonment for the murder of Lance Bombardier Stephen Restorick and two others of whom one, Lance Bombardier Paul Garrett, had also been shot by a Barrett .50 sniper rifle. Seamus McArdle, by now already serving twenty-five years in prison for his part in the London Docklands bombing, received a further twenty years for attempted murder, as did Martin Mines. Michael Caraher, who was named in court by McGinn as having been the sniper who murdered Lance Bombardiers Stephen Restorick and Paul Garrett, was sentenced to twenty-five years for the attempted murder of Constable Ronnie Galwey, the RUC officer wounded during the attack on the Welsh Guards patrol at Forkhill on the night of 29 March 1997.

The convictions and imprisonment of the four men did not, however, remove the threat to the security forces in South Armagh from long-range sniping. It was believed that the South Armagh Brigade of the Provisional IRA had formed two sniper teams who had been responsible for the deaths of up to eight soldiers and two RUC officers; furthermore, it possessed at least two other .50 calibre sniper rifles.

The beginning of the following year saw an unfortunate incident, involving a member of 14 Company, which further illustrated the perils facing those operating undercover in Northern Ireland. In the early hours of 14 January 1998, during a surveillance operation, a female operator was driving through the Ardoyne area of north Belfast, accompanied by another vehicle from the unit, when she was observed by RUC uniformed officers in an unmarked car who became suspicious and drove after her. Observing the vehicle behind her, she accelerated and realised that she was being followed when the car behind did likewise. She headed down the Crumlin Road and by the time she reached Carlisle Circus her vehicle was reported as travelling in excess of eighty miles per hour. On reaching the roundabout she lost control and the car crashed. In the dark, observing one of the two men from the other vehicle approaching the passenger door of her car, and believing him to be a terrorist, she drew her Browning 9mm pistol and opened fire through the closed window, the man falling to the ground seriously wounded in the chest. It was only during the ensuing moments that it became apparent he was no terrorist, but an RUC officer who had believed her to be a joyrider. Two weeks after the shooting, it was reported that it had already been accepted that no blame had been apportioned to the operator who had acted with bravery and professionalism, and that it was probable that the principal cause of the incident lay in the failure of the respective TCG to ensure that RUC patrols had been informed beforehand that a surveillance operation was being conducted in the area.

The end of the 1990s brought the Good Friday Agreement and an uneasy peace. However, the freeing of large numbers of convicted terrorists from prison, and the short-lived return of devolved rule to Northern Ireland with participation by Sinn Fein, saw no reciprocation on the part of the Provisional IRA with regard to decommissioning of weapons. Moreover, it was reported on more than one occasion that the Provisional IRA and republican splinter groups were taking every opportunity to regroup, rearm and retrain. At the time of writing, it appears that there is still no end in sight for the undercover war.

GLOSSARY

AC-130 Spectre gunship variant of C-130 Hercules transport

AG Autonomous Groups (Germany)

AH-6 Special operations variant of OH-6 light helicopter

AIS Islamic Salvation Army (Algeria)

AK-47 Russian 7.62mm calibre assault rifle

ALF Arab Liberation Front

ALN National Liberation Army (Colombia)

ALQ Army for the Liberation of Quebec (Canada)

AMAI Mutual Israeli/Argentine Association (Argentine)

APC Armoured personnel carrier

AR-15 Semi-automatic only version of M-16 assault rifle

ARB Breton Revolutionary Army (France)

ARGK Military wing of Kurdistan Workers' Party (Turkey)

ASALA Armenian Secret Army for the Liberation of Armenia

ASU IRA/PIRA active service unit

ATAS Air-to-Air Stinger

BBE Special Support Group (Dutch counter-terrorist unit)

BGS Federal Border Guard (Germany)

BKA Federal Criminal Bureau (Germany)

BOAC British Overseas Airways Corporation

BPP Black Panther Party (USA)

C-5 Lockheed Galaxy strategic heavy transport aircraft

C-130 Lockheed Hercules tactical transport aircraft

C-141 Lockheed Starlifter strategic heavy transport aircraft

CCC Communist Fighting Cells (Belgium)

CH-47 Chinook heavy-lift helicopter

CIA Central Intelligence Agency (USA)

CID Criminal Investigation Division

COBRA Cabinet Office Briefing Room (Britain)

COLP Communist Organisation for the Liberation of the Proletariat (Italy)

CQB Close Quarter Battle

CRW Counter-Revolutionary Warfare

CTJTF Counter-Terrorist Joint Task Force (USA)

D4 Israeli Navy Shayetet 13 maritime countermeasures unit

DAIA Delegation of Argentine/Israeli Associations (Argentine)

DFLP Democratic Front for the Liberation of Palestine

DGSE Direction Générale de la Sécurité Extérieure (French intelligence service, post 1981)

DIA Defense Intelligence Agency (USA)

DMSU RUC Divisional Mobile Support Unit

DRMLA Democratic Revolutionary Movement for the Liberation of Arabistan

DSF Director Special Forces (Britain)

DSS Diplomatic Security Service (USA)

DST Direction de la Surveillance du Territoire (French internal security service)

E3 RUC Special Branch Intelligence Division

E4 RUC Special Branch Surveillance Division

E4A RUC covert surveillance unit

EC-130 Command and communications variant of C-130 Lockheed Hercules

Elint Electronic intelligence

ELN National Liberation Army (Colombia)

EOD Explosive Ordnance Disposal

EPIGN Gendarmerie Nationale Parachute Intervention Squadron (French counter-terrorist unit)

EROS Eelam Revolutionary Organisers (Sri Lanka)

ERP People's Revolutionary Army (Argentina & El Salvador)

ESI Special Intervention Squadron (Belgian counter-terrorist unit)

ETA Freedom for the Basque Homeland (Spain)

EUCOM US European Command

F-14 Grumman Tomcat carrier-based air superiority fighter

FALN Armed Forces of National Liberation (Venezuela & Puerto Rico)

FAR Rebel Armed Forces (Guatemala)

FARC Revolutionary Armed Forces of Colombia

FARL Lebanese Revolutionary Armed Factions (France)

FBI Federal Bureau of Investigation (USA)

FINCO Field Intelligence Non-Commissioned Officer

FIS Islamic Salvation Front (Algeria)

FLB Breton Liberation Front (France)

FLCS Front for the Liberation of Somalia

FLIR Forward Looking Infra-Red

FLNC National Front for the Liberation of Corsica

FLQ Front for the Liberation of Quebec (Canada)

FNC Belgian 5.56mm calibre assault rifle

FOG Foreign Operating Group (USA)

FPL Popular Force of Liberation (El Salvador)

FRU Force Research Unit (Britain)

FSLN Sandinista National Liberation Front (Nicaragua)

G-3 Heckler & Koch 7.62mm calibre assault rifle

G-3K Shortened version of G-3 assault rifle

G-3/SG-1 Sniper version of G-3 assault rifle

GAL Anti-Terrorist Liberation Group (Spain)

GAR Rural Anti-Terrorist Group (Spanish counter-terrorist unit)

GARI International Revolutionary Action Groups (France)

GEK Gendarmerieeinsatzkommando (Austrian counter-terrorist unit)

GEO Special Operations Group (Spanish counter-terrorist unit)

GIA Islamic Armed Group (Algeria)

GIA-CG Islamic Armed Group - General Command

GIGN Gendarmerie Nationale Intervention Group (French counter-terrorist unit)

GIS Special Intervention Group (Italian counter-terrorist unit)

GOE Special Operations Group (Portuguese counter-terrorist unit)

GPMG General purpose machine-gun

GRAPO First of October Anti-Fascist Resistance Group (Spain)

GS General Staff (Britain)

GSG-9 Border Guard Group 9 (German counter-terrorist unit)

GSO2 General Staff Officer Grade 2 (Britain)

GSU General Service Unit (Kenyan intelligence and security service)

HAHO High Altitude High Opening

HALO High Altitude Low Opening

HAMAS Islamic Resistance Movement

HK53 Heckler & Koch 5.56mm calibre assault rifle

HMSU RUC Headquarters Mobile Support Unit

HQSF Headquarters Special Forces (Britain)

Humint Human intelligence

IAF Israeli Air Force

IDF Israeli Defence Forces

IMSF Indian Marine Special Force

INLA Irish Nationalist Liberation Army

IPKF Indian Peace-Keeping Force

IPLO Irish People's Liberation Organisation

IRA Irish Republican Army

ISA Intelligence Support Activity (USA)

ISI Inter-Services Intelligence (Pakistan)

JCS Joint Chiefs of Staff (USA)

JFKCMA John F. Kennedy Center for Military Assistance (USA)

JIS Joint Irish Section (Britain/Northern Ireland)

JRA Japanese Red Army

JSOA Joint Special Operations Agency (USA)

JSOC Joint Special Operations Command (USA)

JTF Joint Task Force (USA)

JVP Janatha Vimukthi Peramuna (Sri Lanka)

KGB Soviet Intelligence & Security Service

KOPASSANDA Komando Pasukan Sandi Yudha (Indonesia)

KOPASSUS Komando Pasukan Khusus (Indonesia)

L96A1PM Accuracy International 7.62mm sniper rifle

LTTE Liberation Tigers of Tamil Eelam (Sri Lanka)

LUP Lying-up position

LVF Loyalist Volunteer Force

M-1 Garand .30-06 calibre rifle

M-1 .30 calibre carbine

M-2 .50 calibre heavy machine-gun

M-3 .45 calibre submachine-gun

M-16 5.56mm calibre assault rifle

M-19 19 April Movement (Colombia)

M-55 Tikka Finlander .22/.250 sniper rifle

M-60 7.62mm calibre general purpose machine-gun

MAK Service Office of the Mujahideeen (Afghanistan)

MAN Movement of Arab Nationalists

MAU Marine Amphibious Unit (USA)

MC-130 Combat Talon special operations variant of C-130 Hercules transport

MCF Marine Commando Force (India)

MCM Maritime Countermeasures

MD-500 Civilian version of OH-6 light helicopter

MH-6 Little Bird special operations light helicopter

MH-47 Special operations variant of CH-47 Chinook helicopter

MH-60 Special operations variant of UH-60 Blackhawk helicopter

MILO Military Intelligence Liaison Officer

MIO Military Intelligence Officer

MJL Marinejägerlag (Norwegian special forces)

MLN National Liberation Movement (Uruguay)

MoD Ministry of Defence (Britain)

MOIS Iranian intelligence service (post-Islamic revolution)

MP-5 Heckler & Koch 9mm submachine-gun

MP-5K Shortened version of MP-5 submachine-gun

MP-5SD Silenced version of MP-5 submachine-gun

MRF Mobile Reconnaissance Force (Britain/Northern Ireland)

MRTA Tupac Amaru Revolutionary Movement (Peru)

NATO North Atlantic Treaty Organisation

NCO Non-Commissioned Officer

NICRA Northern Ireland Civil Rights Association

NJM New Jewel Movement (Grenada)

NOCS Central Security Operations Group (Italian counter-terrorist unit)

NORAID Irish Northern Aid Committee (USA)

NRO National Reconnaissance Office (USA)

NSA National Security Agency (USA)

NSC National Security Council (USA)

NSG National Security Guard (India)

NWLF National World Liberation Front (USA)

NZSAS New Zealand Special Air Service

OAG Offshore Assault Group (Australia)

OAS Secret Army Organisation (France/Algeria)

OECS Organisation of East Caribbean States

OH-6 Cayuse light helicopter (USA)

OP Observation Post

OPEC Organisation of Petroleum Exporting Countries

PAGAD People Against Gangsterism And Drugs (South Africa)

Pan-Am Pan American Airlines

PCI Italian Communist Party

PCV Venezuelan Communist Party

PDF Panamanian Defence Forces

PFLP Popular Front for the Liberation of Palestine

PFLP-GC Popular Front for the Liberation of Palestine – General Command

PFLP-SC Popular Front for the Liberation of Palestine – Special Command

PFLP-SOG Popular Front for the Liberation of Palestine – Special Operations Group

PIJ Palestinian Islamic Jihad

PIO Palestinian Islamic Organisation

PIRA Provisional Irish Republican Army

PKK Kurdistan Workers' Party (Turkey)

PLA Palestine Liberation Army

PLF Palestine Liberation Front

PLO Palestine Liberation Organisation

PLOTE People's Liberation Organisation of Tamil Eelam (Sri Lanka)

PPSF Palestinian Popular Struggle Front

PRAF People's Revolutionary Armed Forces (Grenada)

PRG Peoples' Revolutionary Government (Grenada)

RAF Royal Air Force

RAID Réaction, Assistance, Intervention, Dissuader (French counter-terrorist unit)

RAW Research & Analysis Wing (India)

RDX Cyclotrimethylenetrinitramine – high explosive (commonly referred to as RDX)

RE Royal Engineers

2e REP 2nd Foreign Parachute Regiment (France – Foreign Legion)

RGD-5 Russian high explosive fragmentation grenade

RM Royal Marines

RMC Revolutionary Military Council (Grenada)

RNAF Royal Netherlands Air Force

RNLMC Royal Netherlands Marine Corps

RPG-7 Russian rocket propelled grenade launcher

RPG-18 Russian shoulder-fired light anti-armour weapon

RUC Royal Ulster Constabulary

RZ Revolutionary Cells (Germany)

29 SA 29th Action Service (France)

SA-80 5.56mm assault rifle

SAG Special Action Group (India)

SAM Surface-to-air missile

SAM-7 Russian Strela shoulder-fired surface-to-air missile

SANG Saudi Arabian National Guard

SAS Special Air Service

22 SAS 22nd Special Air Service Regiment (Britain)

SASR Special Air Service Regiment (Australia)

SAVAK Iranian secret police (during reign of the Shah)

SBS RM Special Boat Squadron, subsequently Special Boat Service

1 SBS No.1 Special Boat Section RM (Britain)

5 SBS No.5 Special Boat Section RM (Britain)

7 NL SBS No.7 Netherlands Special Boat Section

SDA Shankill Defence Association

SDECE Service de Documentation et du Contre Espionnage (French intelligence service, pre-1981)

SDS Students for a Democratic Society (USA)

SDU Special Duties Unit (Hong Kong)

SEAL Sea Air Land (USA)

SFF Special Frontier Force (India)

Sigint Signals Intelligence

SIS Secret Intelligence Service (Britain)

SLA Symbionese Liberation Army (USA)

SLAF Sri Lankan Air Force

SLR Self-loading rifle

SMIU Special Military Intelligence Unit (Britain/Northern Ireland)

SOUTHCOM US Southern Command

SRG Special Ranger Group (India)

SSF Special Security Force (Saudi Arabia)

SSG Special Service Group (Pakistan)

STOL Short take-off and landing

SUSAT Sight Unit Small arms Trilux (fitted to SA-80 rifle)

TAG Tactical Assault Group (Australia)

TCG Tasking & Coordination Group (Britain)

TCGLO Tasking & Coordination Group Liaison Officer

TLF Tamil Liberation Front (Sri Lanka)

TNT Trinitrotoluene – high explosive

TOW Hughes BGM-71 TOW (Tube-launched, Optically-tracked, Wire-guided) heavy anti-tank missile

TULF Tamil United Liberation Front (Sri Lanka)

TWA Trans-World Airlines

UDA Ulster Defence Association

UDR Ulster Defence Regiment

UEI Special Intervention Unit (Spanish counter-terrorist unit)

UFF Ulster Freedom Fighters

UH-60 Blackhawk medium-lift helicopter

UN United Nations

Unit 269 Counter-terrorist unit of Sayeret Matkal (Israel)

URA United Red Army (Japan)

USAF United States Air Force

USMC United States Marine Corps

UVF Ulster Volunteer Force

VPR Revolutionary Popular Vanguard (Brazil)

WRAC Women's Royal Army Corps (Britain)

SELECT BIBLIOGRAPHY

Adams, James. *The Financing of Terror – Behind the PLO, IRA, Red Brigades & M19 Stand the Paymasters.* Simon & Schuster, New York, 1986

Adams, James; Morgan, Robin; Bambridge, Anthony. *Ambush – The War Between the SAS and the IRA.* Pan Books, London, 1988

Adkin, Mark. *Urgent Fury – The Battle for Grenada.* Leo Cooper, London, 1989

Andrew, Christopher, and Mitrokhin, Vasili. *The Mitrokhin Archive – The KGB in Europe and the West.* Penguin Press, London, 1999

Arostegui, Martin C. *Twilight Warriors – Inside the World's Special Forces.* Bloomsbury Publishing, London, 1995

Barzilay, David. *The British Army in Ulster,* vols. 1, 2, 3. Century Books, Belfast, 1973

Beck, Chris Aronson; Emilia, Reggie; Morris, Lee; Patterson, Ollie. *Strike One to Educate One Hundred. The Rise of the Red Brigades in Italy in the 1960s–1970s.* Seeds Beneath the Snow, Chicago, 1986

Becker, Jillian. *Hitler's Children – The Story of the Baader-Meinhof Terrorist Gang.* Pickwick Books, London, 1989

Betser, Colonel Muki, and Rosenberg, Robert. *Secret Soldier.* Simon & Schuster, London, 1996

Billière, General Sir Peter de la. *Looking for Trouble – SAS to Gulf Command.* HarperCollins, London, 1994

Chinnery, Philip D. *Any Time, Any Place – A History of USAF Air Commando and Special Operations Forces.* Airlife Publishing, Shrewsbury, 1994

Clutterbuck, Richard. *Living with Terrorism.* Arlington House Publishers, New York, 1975

— *Protest and the Urban Guerrilla*. Cassell, London, 1973

— *Terrorism, Drugs and Crime in Europe after 1992*. Routledge, New York, 1990

Connor, Ken. *Ghost Force – The Secret History of the SAS*. Weidenfeld & Nicolson, London, 1998

Coogan, Tim Pat. *The IRA: A History*. Roberts Rhinehart Publishers, Niwot, Colorado, 1993

Cooley, John K. *Unholy Wars – Afghanistan, America and International Terrorism*. Pluto Press, London 1999.

Crawford, Steve. *The SAS Encyclopaedia*. Simon & Schuster, London, 1996

Darman, Peter. *A–Z of The SAS*. Sidgwick & Jackson, London, 1992

Darwish, Adel, and Alexander, Gregory. *Unholy Babylon – The Secret History of Saddam's War*. Victor Gollancz, London, 1991

Davies, Barry. *Fire Magic – Hijack at Mogadishu*. Bloomsbury Publishing, London, 1994

— *SAS Rescue*. Sidgwick & Jackson, London, 1996

— *SAS – The Illustrated History*. Virgin Publishing, London, 1996

— *The Complete Encyclopaedia of the SAS*. Virgin Publishing, London, 1998

Davies, Nicholas. *Ten Thirty Three – The Inside Story of Britain's Secret Killing Machine in Northern Ireland*. Mainstream Publishing, Edinburgh, 1999

Demaris, Ovid. *Brothers in Blood*. Charles Scribner's Sons, New York, 1977

Dewar, Michael. *The British Army in Northern Ireland*. Arms & Armour Press, London, 1996

Dillon, Martin. *The Dirty War*. Arrow, London, 1991

Dobson, Christopher, and Payne, Ronald. *The Carlos Complex – A Pattern of Violence*. Hodder & Stoughton, London, 1977

— *The Never-Ending War – Terrorism in the 80s*. Facts on File Publications, New York, 1987

Fisk, Robert. *Pity the Nation – Lebanon at War*. André Deutsch, London, 1990

Follain, John. *Jackal – The Secret Wars of Carlos the Jackal*. Orion Books Ltd., London, 1999

Ford, Sarah. *One Up – A Woman in Action with the SAS*. Harper Collins Publishers, London, 1997

George, Jackie, and Ottaway, Susan. *She Who Dared – Covert Operations in Northern Ireland with the SAS*. Leo Cooper, Barnsley, 1999.

Geraghty, Tony. *Who Dares Wins – The Special Air Service 1950 to the Gulf War*. Little, Brown & Co., London, 1992

Harclerode, Peter. *The Elite & Their Support* – vol. 1. Defence Publications International, Eton, 1985

Harnden, Toby. *Bandit Country – The IRA and South Armagh*. Hodder & Stoughton, London, 1999

Heikal, Mohammed. *Secret Channels – The Inside Story of Arab-Israeli Peace Negotiations*. HarperCollins, London, 1996

Hirst, David. *The Gun and the Olive Branch – The Roots of Violence in the Middle East*. Futura Publications, London, 1978

Hoffmann, Bruce. *Inside Terrorism*. Victor Gollancz, London, 1998

Holland, Jack. *The American Connection – U.S. Guns, Money and Influence in Northern Ireland*. Roberts Rhinehart Publishers, Boulder, Colorado, 1999

Holland, Jack, and Phoenix, Susan. *Phoenix – Policing the Shadows*. Hodder & Stoughton, London, 1996

Horner, D. M. *SAS: Phantoms of the Jungle – A History of the Australian Special Air Service*. Allen & Unwin, Sydney, 1989

Hunter, Gaz. *The Shooting Gallery*. Victor Gollancz, London, 1998

Janke, Peter. *Guerrilla and Terrorist Organisations – A World Directory and Bibliography*. Macmillan, London, 1983

Katz, Samuel M. *The Illustrated Guide to the World's Top Counter-Terrorist Forces*. Concord Publications, Hong Kong, 1995

Kemp, Anthony. *The SAS – Savage Wars of Peace 1947 to the Present*. John Murray, London, 1994

Kennedy, Michael Paul. *Soldier I SAS*. Bloomsbury Publishing, London, 1990

Koch, Peter, and Hermann, Kai. *Assault at Mogadishu*. Corgi, London, 1977

Ladd, James. *SAS Operations*. Robert Hale, London, 1998

Lewis, Rob. *Fishers of Men*. Hodder & Stoughton, London, 2000.

Loftus, John, and McIntyre, Emily. *Valhalla's Wake – The IRA, MI6 and the Assassination of a Young American*. Atlantic Monthly Press, New York, 1989

Martin, David C, and Walcott, John. *Best Laid Plans – The Inside Story of America's War Against Terrorism*. Harper & Row, New York, 1988

McKittrick, David; Kelters, Seamus; Feeney, Brian; Thornton, Chris. *Lost Lives – The stories of the men, women and children who died as a result of the Northern Ireland troubles*. Mainstream Publishing, Edinburgh, 1999.

Murray, Raymond. *The SAS in Ireland*. Mercier Press, Dublin, 1990

Parker, John. *Death of a Hero – Captain Robert Nairac, GC and the Undercover War in Northern Ireland*. Metro Books, London, 1999

— *SBS – The Inside Story of the Special Boat Service*. Headline Book Publishing, London, 1997

Philip, Craig, and Taylor, Alex. *Inside the SAS*. Bloomsbury Publishing, London, 1992.

Raviv, Dan, and Melman, Yossi. *Every Spy a Prince – The Complete History of Israel's Intelligence Community*. Houghton Mifflin, Boston, 1991

Reeve, Simon. *The New Jackals – Ramzi Yousef, Osama bin Laden and the Future of Terrorism*. André Deutsch, London, 1999

Rennie, James. *The Operators – Inside 14 Intelligence Company, the Army's Top Secret Elite*. Century, London, 1996

Rosie, George. *Directory of International Terrorism*. Mainstream Publishing Co., Edinburgh, 1986

Seale, Patrick. *Abu Nidal: A Gun for Hire.* Random House, New York, 1992

Segaller, Stephen. *Invisible Armies – Terrorism into the 1990s.* Harcourt Brace & Jovanovich, New York, 1987

Seymour, William. *British Special Forces.* Sidgwick & Jackson, London, 1985.

Smith, Colin. *Carlos – Portrait of a Terrorist.* Holt, Rhinehart & Winston, New York, 1976

Smith, Michael. *New Cloak, Old Dagger – How Britain's Spies Came in from the Cold.* Victor Gollancz, London, 1996

Stalker, John. *Stalker.* Harrap, London, 1988

Sterling, Claire. *The Terror Network – The Secret War of International Terrorism.* Holt, Rhinehart & Winston, New York, 1981

Steven, Stewart. *The Spy-Masters of Israel.* Hodder & Stoughton, London, 1981

Stevenson, William. *90 Minutes at Entebbe.* Bantam Books, New York, 1976

Strawson, John. *A History of the SAS Regiment.* Secker & Warburg, London, 1984

Thompson, Leroy. *The Rescuers – The World's Top Anti-Terrorist Units.* Paladin Press, Boulder, Colorado, 1986

Tophoven, Rolf. *GSG–9 – German Response to Terrorism.* Bernard & Graefe Verlag, Koblenz, 1984

Urban, Mark. *Big Boys' Rules – The SAS and the Secret Struggle Against the IRA.* Faber & Faber, London, 1992

Vague, Tom. *The Red Army Faction.* AK Press, San Francisco, 1994

Wardlaw, Grant. *Political Terrorism – Theory, Tactics and Counter-Measures.* Cambridge University Press, New York, 1982

Weale, Adrian. *Secret Warfare – Special Operations Forces from the Great Game to the SAS.* Hodder & Stoughton, London, 1997

— *The Real SAS.* Sidgwick & Jackson, London, 1998

Westwood, J. N. *The History of the Middle East Wars.* Bison Books, London, 1984

Woodward, Bob. *VEIL: The Secret Wars of the CIA 1981–1987*. Simon & Schuster, London, 1987.

Wright, Robin. *Sacred Rage*. Linden Press, New York, 1985

Yousaf, Mohammad, and Adkin, Mark. *The Bear Trap – Afghanistan's Untold Story*. Leo Cooper, London, 1992

Report of the President's Special Review Board, 26 February 1987

Terrorist Group Profiles. US Department of Defense, Washington, DC, 1988

The Observer newspaper. *Siege – Six Days at the Iranian Embassy*. Macmillan, London, 1980

The Sunday Times newspaper. *Siege! Prince's Gate, London, April 30 – May 5*. Hamlyn, London, 1980

INDEX

National Liberation Action (ALN), 66

National Liberation Army (ELN), 131

National Liberation Movement (MLN), 69, 70, 81,

National Popular Alliance (ANAPO), 67

National Security Guard (SRG), 304, 305

'Ndrangheta, 52

Neave, Airey, *see* Assassinations

Nee, Patrick, 137–41

Neivens, Deputy Asst Commissioner Peter, 398

Nejad, Foad, 387

Nejad, Fowzi Bedavi (*aka* Ali), 386, 387, 407

Nelson, Brian, 151, 152, 559–71

Nelson, Rosemary, *see* Assassinations

Netanyahu, Lt Benjamin, 219, 289

Netanyahu, Lt Col. Yonathan, 290, 359–61, 363–5

New American Movement, 62

New Camorra, 52

New Jersey, USS, 465

New Jewel Movement (NJM), 433

New Order, 52

New World Liberation Front (NWLF), 63

New Year's Gang, 62

Newlin, Michael, 474, 476

Newton, Huey, 63

Nichols, Terry L., 230

Nidal, Abu, 24, 117–27, 298, 451, 453, 490

Nikola, Muzna Kamel, 352

Nimitz, USS, 415, 417, 419, 478

Nimrodi, Yacov, 479

Nir, Amiram, 479, 487

Nishikawa, Jun, 81, 82

Njojo, Charles, 356

Noel, Cleo, *see* Assassinations

Nordeen, Capt. William, *see* Assassinations

Noriega, Gen. Manuel Antonio, 493–8

Norris, Percy, *see* Assassinations

North, Lt Col. Oliver, 480–8

Northern Ireland Civil Rights Association (NICRA), 35

Northern Ireland Training Advisory Team (NITAT), 323

Notarantino, Francisco, 562

Nouredine, Major, 452

Nucleo Operativo Centrale di Sicurezza (NOCS), 282

Nunn, Sam, 422

NZSAS Group, 1st, 310

O'Bradaigh, Ruairi, 45, 56

O'Brien, Edward, 172

O'Callaghan, Gerard, 547

O'Callaghan, Sean, 141

O'Connell, Martin, 40, 43

O'Doherty, Hugh, 40, 42, 43

O'Donnell, Kevin, 575

O'Dowd, Brendan, 40

O'Farrell, Sean, 575

O'Neill, Diarmuid, 174

O'Neill, Raymond, 540

O'Reilly, John 'Big Man', 146

O'Rourke, Daniel, 336

Oakes, John, 553

Obeida, Abu, 219

Ocalan, Abdullah, 127, 128, 244–6

October League, 62

October XXII Circle, 52

Odeh, Mohamed Saddiq, 232

Official IRA, 37, 38, 43, 44, 322, 559

Offshore Assault Group (OAG), 308, 309

Offshore Assault Team (OAT), 309

Ognibene, Roberto, 54

Ohnesorg, Benno, 26, 32

Okamoto, Kozo, 72–4, 352

Oldfield, Maurice, 341